THE NAVY IN THE WAR OF WILLIAM III

1689–1697

To
A. and R.E.

PLATE I

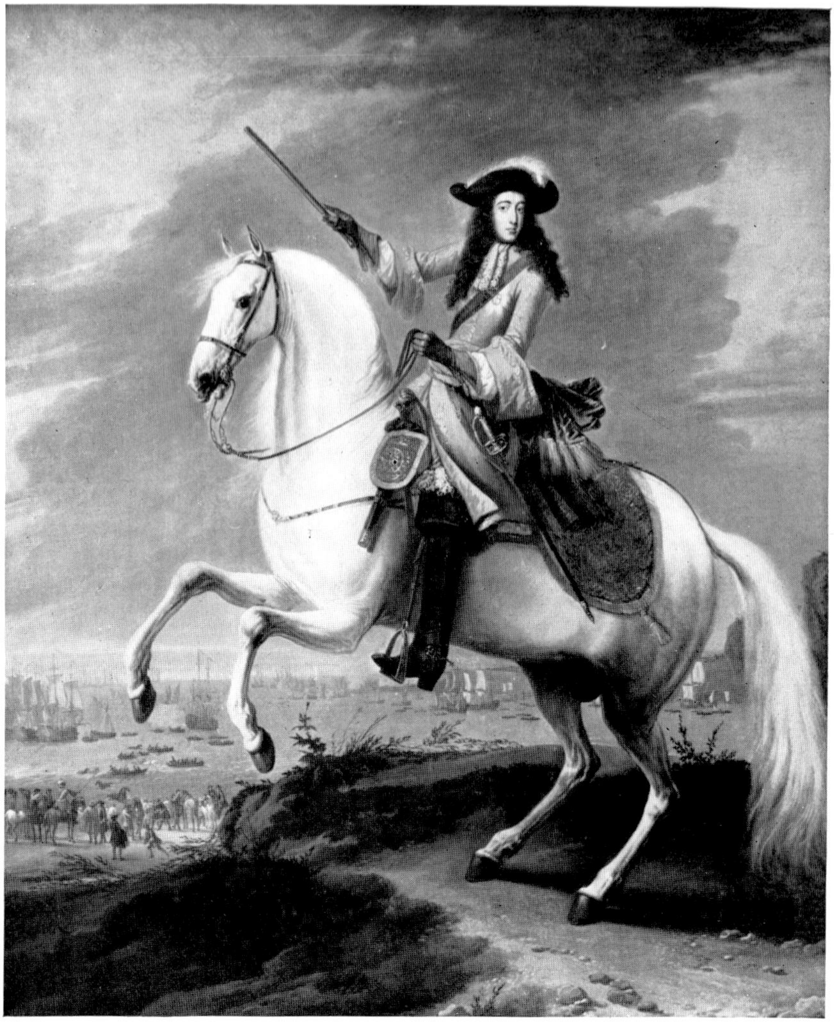

WILLIAM III

Ships in Torbay in background

[JAN WYK]

THE NAVY

IN THE WAR OF WILLIAM III
1689–1697
Its State and Direction

BY

JOHN EHRMAN, M.A.

SOMETIME FELLOW OF TRINITY COLLEGE
CAMBRIDGE

CAMBRIDGE
AT THE UNIVERSITY PRESS
1953

PUBLISHED BY
THE SYNDICS OF THE CAMBRIDGE UNIVERSITY PRESS

London Office: Bentley House, N.W.1
American Branch: New York

Agents for Canada, India and Pakistan: Macmillan

Printed in Great Britain at the University Press, Cambridge
(Brooke Crutchley, University Printer)

CONTENTS

Contents

ILLUSTRATIONS

PLATES

(Plates II–VII, and XI are from British Museum King's MS 43, and Plate IX from the print in the British Museum)

FIGURES

PREFACE

I must thank the Editors of *The Mariner's Mirror* and *The Cambridge Historical Journal* for permission to reproduce Chapter VIII, and parts of Chapters XI and XII, which have appeared respectively as articles in their journals.

The Plates have been reproduced by kind permission of the Trustees of the British Museum (Plates II–VII, IX, XI), the Trustees of the National Portrait Gallery (Plate X), the Trustees of the National Maritime Museum, Greenwich (Plates I, VIII) and the Westminster City Council (Plate XII). I must also acknowledge my gratitude to the following authorities and individuals for permission to quote from manuscripts or typescripts in their possession: to Major J. R. Hanbury and the Historical Manuscripts Commissioners, for the Finch manuscripts at present on loan to the Commission; to the Master and Fellows of Magdalene College, Cambridge, for papers in the Pepysian Library; the Librarian of the Admiralty, for the Corbett manuscripts; the Trustees of the National Maritime Museum, Greenwich, for the Sergison Papers and for the Admiralty papers recently acquired from the Bibliotheca Phillippica; the Trustees of the Beaulieu Manor Estate, for access to estate maps of the period; the late Mr W. H. L. Richmond, for permission to use my transcripts of some unpublished notes by the late Admiral Sir Herbert Richmond; Mr Norman McLeod, formerly Director of Labour at the Admiralty, for his unpublished paper on 'Shipwrights' Wages, 1496–1788'; and Mr G. F. James, of Melbourne University, for his unpublished chapters on 'The Lords Commissioners of the Admiralty, 1689–1714', and the Librarian of Birmingham University for sending them to me on loan. This last source has been of particular value, and I am much indebted to Mr James's generosity in allowing me to use his material and conclusions.

The following have kindly given me information on specific points. Miss Gladys Scott Thomson answered questions on Admiral Russell's correspondence in the possession of His Grace the Duke of Bedford; the late Librarian of the Admiralty, Mr D. Bonner Smith, gave me information on the history of the Admiralty building; the late Sir Geoffrey Callender drew my attention to the acquisitions from the Bibliotheca Phillippica now at Greenwich, and allowed me to consult them as soon as they arrived there, since otherwise I could not have used them; Professor M. A. Lewis first called my attention to the Sergison Papers, and Commander R. D. Merriman gave me the loan of his typed index to the Sergison Miscellany; the Hon. Clerk of the Worshipful Company of Shipwrights answered questions on the manuscripts in the possession of the Company; Dr J. H. Plumb suggested some of the authorities cited for information on the Admiralty Commissioners; the Provost of Oriel lent me a list of owners of privateers during the period; and the late Mrs Gerard Tharp gave me information on Chippenham Park, formerly the property of Admiral Russell. I must also thank the staffs of the Government and Literary Search Rooms at the Public Record Office, of the Manuscripts Room at the British Museum, and of the Bodleian Library for assisting me in my search for particular manuscripts which otherwise I should have missed. Mr Noel Blakiston very kindly had certain Admiralty papers brought back to the Public Record Office from their wartime storage, which I could not otherwise have consulted at the time.

Of those who helped me in the later stages of the book, I should like particularly to thank Commander Merriman, who corrected some of my remarks on technical detail, and Mr Lawrence Stone, who attended in detail, and at considerable expense to his time, to the style and treatment. The shortcomings which remain are my own. Mr G. V. Carey has undertaken the Index.

Lastly, I wish to record my gratitude to the Master and Fellows of Trinity College, Cambridge, who provided the opportunity and the reward for undertaking this work, and two of whom gave me assistance without which it could not have been completed in its present form. Dr G. M. Trevelyan, then Master, gave me the great benefit of his advice and support in conditions which were not always easy for research. Dr G. N. Clark, at that time at Cambridge, suggested the subject and supervised its treatment. Whatever I may have learned of historical method has been from him, and I am very glad that I can here record my debt.

This book was written to a time limit, and my subsequent work has been such as to prevent me from rechecking references as I should have liked, and from following the subject further in detail. I must therefore apologize for any errors that I may have committed in transcribing references, and for not mentioning certain articles and publications that have appeared since 1949.

J. E.

APRIL 1952

NOTE ON DATES

During this period two calendars were in use. In England and Ireland, the Julian or Old Style (O.S.) was used exclusively, while Scotland and all continental countries, except Russia, used the Gregorian or New Style (N.S.). The former was ten days behind the latter, so that 15 November abroad was 5 November in England. The Old Style also began the year on Lady Day, 25 March, whereas by New Style it began on 1 January. Thus 24 March 1688 in O.S. was 3 April 1689 in N.S. English envoys abroad, and English ships on foreign stations, sometimes used N.S., and sometimes gave both styles.

I have dated events throughout in Old Style, but have begun the year on 1 January. Thus 22 February 1688 (O.S.) would be given here as 22 February 1689. Where events were dated N.S. I have changed them into O.S., unless there has been any particular reason for giving both dates.

ABBREVIATIONS

Admty:Corbett	Admiralty Library, Corbett Manuscripts
B.M.Addnl.	British Museum, Additional Manuscripts
B.M.Harl.	British Museum, Harleian Manuscripts
Bodl. Rawl.	Bodleian Library, Rawlinson Manuscripts
Burchett	Josiah Burchett, *Memoirs of Transactions at Sea during the War with France* (1703)
Cal.S.P.Col., Am. & W.I.	*Calendar of State Papers, Colonial: America and West Indies*
Cal.S.P.Dom.	*Calendar of State Papers, Domestic*
Cal.Treas.Bks.	*Calendar of Treasury Books*
Cal.Treas.Papers	*Calendar of Treasury Papers*
Catal.	*A Descriptive Catalogue of the Naval Manuscripts in the Pepysian Library in Magdalene College, Cambridge*, ed. J. R. Tanner (4 vols., 1903–23)
Conduct	*The Conduct of the Earl of Nottingham*, ed. W. A. Aiken (1941)
D.N.B.	*Dictionary of National Biography*
E.H.R.	*English Historical Review*
Ec.H.R.	*Economic History Review*
Finch Transcr.	Transcript of the Finch Manuscripts at the Public Record Office
H. of L. N.S.	*Manuscripts of the House of Lords, New Series*
H.C.J.	*Journals of the House of Commons*
H.L.J.	*Journals of the House of Lords*
H.M.C.	Publications of the Historical Manuscripts Commission
M.M.	*Mariner's Mirror*
N.M.M., Bibl.Phill.	National Maritime Museum, acquisitions from the Bibliotheca Phillippica

N.M.M. MSS.	National Maritime Museum, unnumbered Manuscripts
N.R.S.	Publications of the Navy Records Society
Pep:Sea MSS.	Pepysian Library, Magdalene College, Cambridge, Sea Manuscripts (other than Admiralty Letters)
Pep:A.L.	Pepysian Library, Magdalene College, Cambridge, Admiralty Letters
P.R.O.Adm.	Public Record Office, Admiralty Papers
P.R.O. T.	Public Record Office, Treasury Papers
S.P.Dom.	Public Record Office, State Papers, Domestic
S.P.For.	Public Record Office, State Papers, Foreign
Serg.MS.	National Maritime Museum, numbered Sergison Manuscripts
Serg.Misc.	National Maritime Museum, Sergison Miscellanies
Serg:Mins.	National Maritime Museum, Sergison Manuscripts, Navy Board Minutes

INTRODUCTION

In the twenty-five years from 1689 to 1714, twenty-one of which—from 1689 to 1697 and again from 1702 to 1714—were occupied by wars with France, England became the dominating sea power of Europe. Throughout the half century that followed, as the classic authority on the subject has remarked, 'on the few occasions in which [the navy] is called on to fight its superiority is so marked that the affairs can scarcely be called battles'.[1] At the earlier date, the English fleet was second in size and quality to the French, and to contemporaries seemed not greatly superior to the Dutch. At the later date, the Dutch had fallen out of the race, while the French had been outstripped in numbers and had for nine years declined any serious challenge at sea. At the accession of William III, England was one of the three leading sea powers; at the accession of George I, she was the leading sea power, without a rival or even a companion.

The significance of the period lay not simply in the rise of the English navy in relation to its contemporaries, but in its establishment during that time upon foundations which endured for a further two centuries. For the fleet which expressed this growing power was itself only the reflection of other elements of maritime strength. These may be defined in various ways, according to the position from which the definition is made. The most recent classification, taking the material of naval power alone and made from the point of view of the statesman who must control it, has divided it into three elements: the fighting instruments themselves, the bases from which they operate, and the organization, particularly of transport, which supplies ships and bases alike.[2] If, however, with a different end in mind, we identify ourselves not with the statesman but with the fighting instrument, the factors may be grouped rather differently, and the latter may be seen as the product of the policy which employs it, the wealth which supports it, and the organization which supplies it. None of these three factors is independent of the others; and their combined result, which is naval power,

[1] A. T. Mahan, *The Influence of Sea Power upon History* (1889), p. 209.

[2] Sir Herbert Richmond, *Statesmen and Sea Power* (1946), p. x.

is to the fighting strength of the ships at sea as the iceberg is to the section which is visible on the surface.

At any time, however, the exact connexion between the three factors may be difficult to trace. They themselves are not always free from contradiction. It is seldom that policy at all its levels is clear, that the elements of national wealth complement and do not partly detract from each other, or that the state of administration reflects at all precisely the demands which will be made upon it; and their interaction is more or less complex according to the complexity of each factor. Such considerations affect all departments of national life in which administration is involved; but they are made more complex in naval affairs by the peculiar demands which the raw materials of sea warfare make upon the form of their organization. It is not only that many kinds of material are required, coming from different parts of the world, produced by different techniques and thus involving a variety of conditions for administration; nor that most of them are required in large quantities, so that it has to operate on a large as well as a varied scale; it is also that the rate at which administration develops bears a peculiar relation to the development of its object, the fleet. The fleet in turn depends upon the ships of which it is composed, for a large fleet is of little use unless it includes ships which can stand comparison with those of other fleets, while the type of ship in turn determines the size as well as the type of the fleet. The two seldom develop together, but changes in the size of the fleet, where they are not occasioned simply by changes in policy, usually follow changes in the performance of the ship. This was the case towards the end of the seventeenth century, when, after a sudden increase in the size of the man-of-war during its fourth decade, a more gradual increase was taking place in the size of the national fleet, affecting its character and the nature of sea warfare. Such a development reacts upon administration. At a certain point the material problem changes in kind as it increases in extent, and that point does not necessarily correspond with the point at which its organization changes. The rate at which naval administration develops, therefore, may not, and where the development is rapid usually does not, coincide with the rate of development of its object. It is quite possible for an administrative system to produce a fleet which it cannot satisfactorily administer.

This was the position in 1689. The type of ship around which grew the larger and more powerful fleet had been in existence for some decades; but the fleet itself had not yet reached the limits of the development made possible by the ship, and in consequence its organization, which lagged behind its own development, was still further behind the conditions which had been set for both. During the French war, which lasted for nine years and in which the fleet was used more strenuously than it had been in any of the Dutch wars, the balance was partly redressed, and while the material conditions of administration remained the same as they had been twenty years before, administration itself developed to meet them. The elements which combined to form the new type of navy were produced in the middle of the seventeenth century; but they were combined only in its last decade.

This development of administration in relation to its material was made more complicated in 1689 by the fact that it was being directed to an unfamiliar end. Its conditions had been formed during the three Dutch wars which took place between 1652 and 1673; but the new war was a French war, so that the strength which had been formed with one end in view had now to be concentrated upon another, and one moreover to which it was not altogether suited. For in the Dutch wars the chief protagonists had fought on the same terms. Each concentrated on the same area of campaign, in the Channel and North Sea, and the elements of naval power in each case were alike. Each relied for his prosperity principally upon overseas trade, and thus, provided that they were to be rivals, each required a more powerful navy than the other to protect his commerce. The struggle between the two was direct and unambiguous. French sea power, on the other hand, was not of the same kind as either Dutch or English. For whereas, in an age of national wars, the economy of Holland and England demanded a large fleet, that of France did not; and whereas their naval strategy was in each case based upon the necessity for superior strength, hers could be based successfully on a slight inferiority. Less dependent than England upon foreign trade, France could damage England by attacks upon English commerce more than she herself could be damaged by similar attacks; and thus, provided that her inferiority was not marked, she could, like all sea powers whose power does not come from the sea, largely dictate the course of sea warfare.

The new war, therefore, set new and difficult strategic problems.

They were obscured during its early years, owing to the French attempt to fight England on her own ground with the fleet which Colbert's organization had built up in recent years. But on the failure of this attempt, in the course of which the English navy was expanded to meet the familiar threat of superior strength, the change in strategic conditions was revealed. It was, moreover, given point by a strategic circumstance which had not hitherto existed. For the first time in the century, England found herself, in a war against a major Mediterranean power, a member of a European alliance which included other Mediterranean powers. There was therefore more than one possible area of campaign; and in the choice of areas the advantage lay with France. With her interior lines of communication, and her excellent ports in the south, she could develop a campaign there in which the English could rely only upon borrowed facilities. Under such circumstances, the weaker force could hope to dictate the conduct of the stronger. Material superiority did not, as in the recent past, automatically result in a strategic advantage, but was required rather to compensate for a strategic disadvantage; and the emphasis fell increasingly upon organization, which alone could ensure that the weight of material overcame the obstacles confronting policy. The virtues of administration were now required to offset strategic conditions, rather than directly to support them.

But at the end of the seventeenth century, all organization for purposes of war was difficult. Naval administration was more favourably placed than its military counterpart in one respect, for the service itself was popular, and a war at sea was always considered more natural than large-scale operations on the continent. There was never any hesitation to grant money for such a purpose, or to support it when necessary with legislation. But on the other hand, the material of naval administration was more complex than that of any other department. Stores for the fleet came largely from overseas, particularly from foreign powers, and many of them, owing to the technical demands made by the construction of the largest ships, were of unusual types; the men, or at least a fair proportion of them, had to be trained seamen, of whom there was only a limited number to share among the different seafaring activities of the country; victuals had to be provided in large quantities, often at unusual places and, with no reliable form of preservation possible, often at short notice; and the facilities for the construction and maintenance of the ships raised their own problems of labour, material and direction. The navy with its varied requirements presented an inherently difficult administrative problem. In the social conditions of the day it seemed at times almost impossible to administer, for it had so little control over the agents of supply. It was unable to commandeer its stores or its labour, to obtain accurate information on the numbers and whereabouts of the seafaring population, to buy its food and drink on its own terms, or to obtain priority for dockyard construction. It had instead to rely in war largely on the methods of peace; to bargain with domestic and foreign contractors for stores and with domestic contractors for victuals, and to attract as well as to impress seamen and workmen. It was at times given the power to deny to the enemy the resources at its command, by embargoes on native commodities and shipping and by forcibly restricting neutral trade; but it was not given the power to mobilize these resources in its own support. It remained throughout merely one, and not always the most favoured, of the national interests.

The only advantage, therefore, which the navy could hope to have over its rivals was financial; and here, on the contrary, it found itself at a disadvantage. For the financial sources of national wealth were as difficult to harness for war as the material sources. It was only quite recently that wartime expenditure had consistently outrun peacetime revenue; and while this was undeniably the case from 1689, the machinery of collecting and allocating the national income could not at that time meet the demands that were made upon it. The navy thus found itself chronically short of money, and with its contemporary methods of accounting was often unable to calculate its deficit or to estimate its future requirements. Under such circumstances, a reliable system of credit was needed; but while the cost of naval warfare meant that it could no longer be run on cash, the conception of running it on credit was accepted only within the strictest limits. Facilities for government credit existed, and were widely used; but they were intended purely as a temporary measure to meet a temporary deficit, and proved quite inadequate after a short time to deal with a perpetual and increasing debt. Thus the navy was unable to dictate its own terms, and unable to satisfy the terms of the agents through whom it had to work; and its administration suffered accordingly.

Many of these problems faced the department on a new scale, and others for the first time in 1689, and their combination was entirely unfamiliar. It was the answers provided to them that turned England from a small into a great naval power. In each case the solution was adumbrated in the first of the two French wars, although it was not in each case fully applied. The direct threat from the French fleet was defeated so as hardly to be raised again, and the consequences were demonstrated and partly met in the following years; while in the same years the answer was found to the difficulties of financing the war, although this was not fully developed to meet the peculiar difficulties of naval credit. In this new context of strategy and finance, administration itself was changing as the organization of the navy was developed to meet the physical expansion. When, therefore, the second French war began in 1702, the problems were already clarified and partly answered. Unlike its predecessor, which was faced largely with unfamiliar conditions, it resumed where the other had left off, and its task was to complete at sea a job already begun. The great material expansion had taken place: while the fleet had risen from 173 ships in 1688, with a tonnage of 101,892 tons and a gunpower of 6930 pieces, to one of 323 ships in 1697, of over 160,000 tons and 9912 guns, at the end of the second war in 1714 it consisted of 247 ships, of 167,219 tons and 10,603 guns; and the great increase in organization had accompanied it. But it was not only in their settings that the two wars differed, but also, and as a result, in the course of their events. The naval war of 1689–97 was a dramatic war, with a great defeat followed by a great victory. Its issue was in the balance at the beginning, and remained undecided for several years. Its successor was by comparison a placid war, in which the issue at sea was never in doubt from the start. Its monument is Gibraltar, the guarantee of a Mediterranean policy; but the monuments to William's war lie nearer home, in the naval dockyard at Devonport which guaranteed the Channel approaches, and in the hospital buildings at Greenwich which commemorate the defeat of an attempted French invasion of England.

As it was in the course of a war that the elements of sea power were developed, so they must be treated within its framework, and the naval organization seen in action under the external pressure of events. For while this organization operated within limits set by its material—of ships and men, of stores and provisions, and of shipyards and harbours—the men who had to run it were concerned principally with its results, and took the material itself very largely for granted in their daily business. The conduct of policy and finance, and of administration itself, cannot each be followed separately, out of their contemporary context; to do so would be to ignore what the makers of policy, the financial officials and the naval administrators were doing from day to day, and to elevate the three factors to a self-sufficiency and a logical development which was not perceived, intended or in most cases achieved at the time. While the material conditions of naval warfare remained the same throughout the war, their application varied according to its progress.

Once these conditions have been examined, therefore, the conduct of the war itself becomes a study in executive authority, wherein an executive process is followed, not by an analysis of the factors which compose it, but as it descends from one level of government to another, from the initial decision to its consequence in action. The pattern is chronological, and the story must be told as a story, recording the sequence of events. This applies to all executive processes in which different levels of authority are involved; but it applies particularly to a war, for of all human activities war most easily lends itself to narrative, in which the periods form naturally around the climax of an event. This study, therefore, falls into two parts, the first of which attempts to define the terms on which the war at sea was fought, and the second to describe its progress, within those terms, in chronological order. Such a treatment has three main disadvantages, and a word must be said about them before we proceed to the body of the work.

First, although a narrative is meant faithfully to record what happened, in fact it cannot do so. Each year, many of the same events recurred, and the same administrative processes were set in motion. Once these have been examined in detail, there is little point in examining them again until they change in some respect. Chronological treatment is necessarily selective, and thus a certain lack of proportion arises, and the interest in practice turns after a time from an investigation of the executive processes themselves to an investigation of the factors which affect them; from, for instance, an analysis of the annual mobilization of ships and men after a winter in harbour, to an analysis of the reasons for its failure on a particular occasion.

Secondly, the chronological treatment is not always even, for the relations between the different levels of authority are not always of the same kind and do not always develop at an even pace. At one time, they may need to be followed in equal detail, while at other times their significance may be best appreciated by examining each level in turn over a given, but not necessarily equal, period. This unevenness of treatment arises from the different types of material which have to be studied. For naval history is a microcosm of national history; it is not a subject with its own particular technique, but an application of different subjects, each with their own technique, to a particular field. It has its own economic and constitutional history, its own legal problems and its own relations with diplomacy and politics. If national history may be compared to a cake, the different layers of which are different aspects of national life, then naval history is not a layer but a slice of that cake. Thus, while the analysis of a war finds its best medium in chronological treatment, the chronological proportions are determined largely by the different types of analysis required.

Not all of these yield an equally valuable result, and a word must be said in particular about one technique which has frequently to be used, and whose limitations illustrate the limitations of the work in other respects. A study so largely concerned with material must be largely concerned with measurement. Not only must many of its conclusions be quantitative, but they in turn must form the basis for other conclusions which themselves are not quantitative. To determine, for instance, the reason for a certain act of policy, which cannot be assessed by measurement, it may be necessary to know the relative states of two fleets at a given time, not only numerically, but in stores of all kinds, in their condition and in men, all of which are discoverable by such means. At any time, such statistical investigations are subject to two limitations: first, that the techniques required in measuring different types of material are themselves different; and secondly, that figures are often compiled not on any absolute basis, but for specific purposes, and may not yield to measurement for other purposes. This second difficulty is a common experience when we come to examine the figures of another age. The authorities in the late seventeenth century often compiled their tables in a way which is useless to ourselves, because they were not asking the same questions of them; and in such cases, the interest of the figures lies in their illustration of an attitude of mind, or of the pertinence of the problem which they seek to answer at the time at which they attempt to answer it, rather than in the result of the calculations itself. Such an experience, however, is not uncommon in examining contemporary figures, drawn up for a specific purpose which is not our own. The great difference between the statistics of the late seventeenth century and those of the twentieth is that whereas in many cases the latter, although combined to suit a given end, have themselves been compiled on a statistical method which is not affected by that end, the former almost certainly have not. As a result, at times—particularly in investigating the figures of provisions, where quantitative measurement was peculiarly difficult—statistical inquiry ends merely in a vicious circle, in which the figures required are found to depend largely on the requirements. Thus, in a study which, from its nature, must often be concerned with measurement, measurement is often subjective and unsatisfactory; and whoever attempts to apply to the naval warfare of William III the objective criteria which, in this and other respects, may be applied more successfully to such warfare 250 years later, can only confess, as one such investigator confessed at the time, that he is 'well-knowing how far from infallible his best endeavours must be, that has to do with a subject so extensive, various, and complicate, as that of a Navy; and a Navy circumstanc'd as this happens to be within the limits of this Chapter'.[1]

[1] Samuel Pepys, *Memoires relating to the State of the Royal Navy of England* (1690), pp. 210–11.

PART ONE

THE BACKGROUND OF NAVAL ADMINISTRATION

CHAPTER I

THE SHIP AND THE LINE

Between the summer of 1688 and the winter of 1689, the three great sea powers of Europe, the English, the Dutch and the French, had occasion to survey their naval resources, and in particular the size of their fleets. The occasions were not all of the same type. In France the survey was made by the revision of the *Ordonnances du Roi* in the edition of 1689, which had been maturing for a considerable time. In Holland, it arose from the conflicting necessities of foreign commitments, leading before William's expedition to England in November 1688 to a comparison with the English, and after the French declaration of war at the end of that month to a comparison with the French. In England, it was undertaken during 1689 by the outgoing Secretary of the Admiralty, to record for his own satisfaction the results of his term of office.[1] At the end of 1688, the fleets and their auxiliaries upon which this attention centred, stood in each case as shown in the table on p. 4.[2]

To ourselves, whose training in such figures has been provided by our contemporary wars, lists of this type are merely a starting point for an analysis of their contents in other terms, such as those of total and individual fire-power and the performance and age of the ships. It is axiomatic to us that in naval warfare numbers in themselves mean little. But we must be careful not to read into the figures of another age more than in fact is in them. In the late seventeenth century, it was precisely and almost exclusively numbers that did matter. The quality and amount of equipment and the nature of the ships' performance were taken for granted as more or less equal within their rates; and, provided that they were in a state of repair, the date of construction was of minor importance. An examination of the lists, therefore, leads us to the same simple process of addition that was practised by their original compilers.

[1] Samuel Pepys, *Memoires relating to the State of the Royal Navy of England* (1690).

[2] In each case, the figures given are those of the ships as rated in 1688; occasionally, they were built under different rates or gun-power.

English*		Dutch†		French‡	
1st rates	9	*Over 90 guns*	4	*1st rates*	13
2nd rates	11	*80–90 guns*	4	*2nd rates*	20
3rd rates	39	*70–80 guns*	9	*3rd rates*	40
4th rates	41	*60–70 guns*	20	*4th rates*	20
		50–60 guns	16		
		40–50 guns	16		
	100		69		93
5th rates	2	30–40 guns	12	5th rates	21
6th rates	6	20–30 guns	7	Light frigates	17
Fireships	26	12–18 guns	4	Fireships	11
Bombvessels	3	Fireships	6	Bombvessels	10
Yachts	14	Yachts	3	Storeships	23
Auxiliaries	22	Snows	1	Sloops	10
				Galleys (Mediterranean only)	36
Total	173		102		221

* See Appendix I (A), p. 625. The italics represent the line of battle.

† *Society for Nautical Research, Occasional Publications*, no. 5, pt IV ('List of Men-of-War 1650–1700, United Netherlands'; compiled by A. Vreugdenhil), *passim*. The numbers given above exclude those which appear as 'not afterwards mentioned' after the date of their original construction; cf. list in John Charnock, *History of Marine Architecture* (1802), II, pp. 352–5.

‡ *Soc. Naut. Research*, op. cit., pt II ('French Ships', compiled by Pierre le Conte), *passim*; cf. list in Charnock, loc. cit. p. 310, for 1681, which excludes galleys.

To understand what we are adding up, we must approach the lists historically rather than directly by analysis. For since the latter is not an absolute process, in this way its factors may fall into place, and be given their proper emphasis within their appropriate conditions. These conditions will necessarily be material, for it is material that must be examined; and such an examination is of strictly limited importance. For in the last resort, the material out of which a process is formed is not its effective but its contingent cause. However direct the influence which it exerts, there must at some stage be the intention to use it in a certain way. It was because the sea powers of Europe wished to develop their maritime resources that the characteristics of these resources will be investigated; and while national ambition and the general conditions of national expansion alone were not directly responsible for the greater fleets and the more complex naval organization of the later over the earlier seventeenth century, neither did these develop inevitably and exclusively from the qualities of the material which built and maintained them. Throughout the account which follows, the foundations of national consolidation and rivalry must be taken as supporting the technical developments with which we are particularly concerned.

In turn, it is not for its own sake that the fleet is examined, but for its effects upon the different levels of naval organization. For in all affairs of state, policy and administration meet at one point, where the conditions for the operation of the former are provided by the latter's efforts, and to which the ramifying activities of the lower levels may be reduced and the intentions of policy related. In naval affairs, that point is represented by the ship, and in particular by the class of ship which forms the nucleus of the fleet. At once the climax and the foundation of naval achievement—the climax of the system of naval supply and distribution, the foundation for the direction of naval policy—she is the pivot of naval endeavour. In the later seventeenth century, the unit which occupied this position was the largest ship of the line.

'It will always be said of us with unabated reverence, THEY BUILT SHIPS OF THE LINE. Take it all in all, a Ship of the Line is the most honourable thing that man, as a gregarious animal, has ever produced.'[1] The ship of which Ruskin was writing had for over 150 years evoked in the national consciousness the same image and the same response, for the essentials of naval architecture had not changed since the beginning of the eighteenth century, and the admiration of his generation was anchored in a familiarity which gave to it a particular clarity and warmth. That admiration was not given to the great ship for her beauty alone, but because she was the embodiment, throughout the first and longest phase of its long period, of English maritime supremacy. She became largely a symbol; and it was to her symbolic rather than to her actual qualities that the poets and pamphleteers of the eighteenth century alluded. The properties of the ship herself, her size, her complexity, the mechanics of her construction and her management, could by then be taken for granted as conventional knowledge. But in the first decade of the century, and for forty years beforehand, it was precisely on these facts that contemporaries liked to dwell; and the well-worn phrases which had been used since the Renaissance to describe sea affairs, were used during these decades in a new setting and became imbued with a new sense of technical achievement, seldom expressed in technical language, but running through verses and pamphlets

[1] John Ruskin, *The Harbours of England* (1895), ed. T. J. Wise, pp. 24–5.

alike[1] and even, in James II's reign, finding its way into the usually laconic pages of the directory of government offices.[2] The dimensions of the great ship, and the demands which they made upon men and material, were still worthy of remark, for she was still a recent development. There were men alive in 1688 who could remember the launching of the first of the leviathans in 1637; it was still possible to recommend, as did one elderly official a few years later, that they should be abolished, and that the top-heavy organization and new-fangled tactics which they brought in their wake should be replaced by the more modest establishments and manœuvres of an earlier day.[3]

How recent this development was, could be seen in the nomenclature of the period. The very term 'ship of the line' appeared only during the reign of William III, as an alternative to the prevalent 'capital ship', itself a product of the Dutch wars;[4] and although older and miscellaneous phrases were falling into disuse, they had not entirely disappeared. Even in the next reign, Rooke employed on separate occasions the terms 'ship of war', 'ship of force', and 'great ship' to convey the same information.[5] Terminology lags behind practice. Rooke was a veteran of the Dutch wars, and his language reflects the persistence of earlier and less precise tactical conceptions. Ten years later, when the young men of the Dutch wars were replaced in command by the young men of William's war, the older terms disappeared. For in fact, although the secondary process, by which the line imposed itself as a generic term on the great ship, had not taken place by the beginning of the French wars, the first and most important stage had already been reached. By the end of the Dutch wars the great ship had evolved the line, which set the type and virtually became the arbiter of the major action at sea.

[1] For a good example of this combination, see the unlikely instance of the first chapter of Edward Ward's tract *The Wooden World Dissected* (1707).

[2] See the description of a first rate in Edward Chamberlayne, *Angliae Notitia* (13th ed. 1687), pt II, p. 162.

[3] Richard Gibson's 'Reflections', in B.M.Addnl. 11602, ff. 37–41, 57–61.

[4] L. G. Carr Laughton, 'Capital Ship', in *M.M.* XII, pp. 396–405, summing up previous articles in that journal. His earliest example of the term is from the year 1694. Its immediate predecessor was 'ships fit to lie in the line', which was used several times in 1690 (e.g. *H.M.C. Finch*, II, p. 315).

[5] *The Journal of Sir George Rooke*, ed. O. Browning (*N.R.S.* 1897), pp. 180, 251. He also referred to 'ships of the line of battle' on occasion (ibid. pp. 231, 256).

Her tactical contribution had been made, and it awaited only the sanction of use and time to be confirmed in the language of the fleet.

As the line was the product of the great ship, so the great ship was the product of the gun.[1] If the naval ordnance of the second half of the seventeenth century is examined, three main characteristics may be observed. First, that to develop the most considerable gun-power available, a heavy weight of metal had to be carried aboard ship; secondly, that within the limits of the heavier pieces, the greater their power the shorter their range; and thirdly, arising from the technical reasons for these characteristics, that both in appearance and performance the weapons had hardly changed since the end of the sixteenth century.

For the nature of the pieces themselves, as of their powder and shot, was limited by technological processes which were not modified appreciably between the reign of Elizabeth and the reign of Victoria.[2] The balance of development lay between the chemist and the metallurgist, and was normally tilted in favour of the former. Improvements in the refining of gunpowder since the later years of the sixteenth century had made it possible, thanks to a higher rate of combustion, to envisage a heavier shot.[3] But this process had its limitations, for the greater the explosion, the greater the recoil; the greater the recoil, the greater the mass required to take the stress; and, under the metallurgical conditions of the time, the greater the mass the greater the weight of metal. Certain improvements in the casting of brass and then of iron enabled the cannon of a given weight to take a stronger charge, but after a varying process in which its weight alternately increased and decreased, the heaviest piece, the Cannon of Seven, settled in the middle of the seventeenth century at between 7000 and 8000 lb.—much what it had weighed seventy years before, but with a greater strength of

---

[1] See the excellent statement of this argument in *Samuel Pepys's Naval Minutes*, ed. J. R. Tanner (*N.R.S.* 1926), pp. 425–6.

[2] See F. L. Robertson, *The Evolution of Naval Armament* (1921), pp. 69–82; C. Ffoulkes, *The Gun-Founders of England* (1937), pp. 1–37; Ernest Straker, *Wealden Iron* (1931), pp. 1–60.

[3] For details of the process in the later seventeenth century, see Thomas Sprat, *The History of the Royal Society of London* (1667), pp. 273–83; see also Nathaniel Nye, *The Art of Gunnery* (1674); Sir Jonas Moore, *A General Treatise of Artillery* (1683); and Gaya's *Traité des Armes* of 1678 (ed. C. Ffoulkes, 1911).

explosive. At this stage the gunfounder had exhausted the resources of his technique. He had also produced a gun with a performance on which it was inadvisable to proceed further. For since weight was the determining factor in increasing power, the shorter the gunbarrel the greater must be its calibre, and this in turn led to a decrease in range. With an effective range for the heavy cannon of perhaps about 400 yards,[1] the stage had clearly been reached beyond which it was pointless to go until penetrative power could be reconciled with distance of shot. As it was, the principles of English gunnery in the seventeenth century, unlike those of earlier[2] and later days, directly opposed to each other the two complementary qualities of the weapon and, where destruction and not damage was the object, sought incessantly to narrow the distance.

Although its performance had improved in the interval, the characteristics of the gun had thus not changed between the late sixteenth and the late seventeenth centuries, and the various types of ordnance in William's war were all known at the time of the Armada. They were divided into three main classes: the heavy cannon, 'of Battery' as it was sometimes called,[3] with its great weight of shot, its short barrel, and its short range; the culverin, throwing a shot of between a half and two-thirds the weight, with its long barrel and medium range; and the minor pieces—saker, minion, falcon and robinet—designed at short range to damage the decks and upperworks. The great difference between the two wars lay not in the design of the gun, but in the emphasis placed upon the different available pieces, which was made possible only by a revolution in ship design. It was through this medium that the principles of gunnery, and of the sea fight, changed even though the pieces themselves did not. The figures best illustrate the tale. At the beginning of the seventeenth century, the heaviest ship afloat, the *Prince Royal*, carried two cannon, and of her 55 pieces 35 consisted of demi-culverin, sakers and port pieces.[4] Twenty years later,

---

[1] It is difficult to ascertain exact ranges, for, with an eye to security, they were seldom tabulated. The conventional unit of measurement was the geometrical pace of five feet (cf. Sir Jonas Moore, *General Treatise of Artillery*, p. 91).

[2] See M. A. Lewis, 'Armada Guns', sections I and II, *M.M.* XXVIII, nos. 1 and 2.

[3] Moore, *General Treatise of Artillery*, p. 18.

[4] M. Oppenheim, *A History of the Administration of the Royal Navy, 1509–1660* (1896), p. 212.

the *Sovereign of the Seas* carried 20 cannon, and of her 104 guns only 44 were demi-culverin or below.[1] The figures of weight emphasize the nature of the change even more clearly:[2]

Prince Royal: total weight of guns	83	tons	8	cwt.
Sovereign of the Seas: total weight of guns	153	,,	10	,,
Weight on lower tier	64	,,	16	,,
Weight on middle tier	45	,,	4	,,
Weight on upper tier	27	,,	12	,,
Weight above deck	15	,,	18	,,

The *Sovereign* carried all her cannon and demi-cannon on the lower tier, which held no other type of gun. They alone therefore represented between a half and two-thirds of her total weight of ordnance, and three-quarters of the total weight of the armament carried in her greatest predecessor; and although she herself was over-gunned, and had soon to be reduced to 91 pieces, the marked and sudden change which had been inaugurated was a permanent one. The typical great ship of the Commonwealth had 91 guns, distributed in much the same way as those of the *Sovereign*,[3] and the establishment of 1677, which was still in force in 1689, laid down an armament for the first rate of 98 guns, of which 26 were cannon, 28 culverin and 44 sakers.[4]

The first and greatest requirement of the contemporary ordnance—that its most powerful pieces could be taken to sea—had thus been satisfied. This did not mean, however, that the lighter pieces disappeared to a proportionate extent. Indeed, their variety remained bewildering. The reason in this case lay not in any technological process, but in an attitude of mind; not in the nature, but in the popularity of the gun. The Elizabethan successes, in which it played a major part, had increased the reliance which seamen were already placing upon it, while the steady improvement in the techniques of casting in brass and iron and

---

[1] Ibid. p. 262. Both Oppenheim and W. Laird Clowes (*The Royal Navy, A History* (1898), I, p. 12) state that the *Sovereign* carried 102 guns; but both give the same details, which add up to 104. R. C. Anderson ('The *Royal Sovereign* of 1637' (III), in *M.M.* III, no. 6, pp. 168–9) compares Oppenheim's figures with other lists.

[2] Oppenheim, loc. cit. pp. 212, 262.

[3] Ibid. p. 341.

[4] *Catal.* I, p. 236. The 'sakers', as defined in this case, weighed between 16 and 22 cwt.

in corning powder spread the fame of English products abroad, particularly as the advance of English technique was paralleled by the stability of its European competitors after the earlier decades of the seventeenth century.[1] Working upon this conscious superiority of manufacture, English gunners became as renowned as their weapons. Throughout the seventeenth century the name of gunner was, where possible, synonymous with that of Englishman, in foreign warship, foreign merchantman and Barbary corsair alike.[2] With all the limitations and inaccuracies which to a later age seem overwhelming, to contemporaries English gunnery was the finest in the world.

With a conscious superiority in gunnery and at the same time an inadequate appreciation of its principles, it was not unnatural that the fashion under the Stuarts should have been to emphasize the number and variety of the weapons. Some of the earlier types, it is true, were already disappearing; the cannon pedro had gone, and basilisk and bastard cannon, bastard culverin and serpentine were going. But the habit of overgunning continued, in the belief that the superiority originally gained by quality would automatically be increased according to the increase in the quantity of the superior pieces. In terms of naval architecture, this meant decks. In James I's reign, an attempt had been made to build a three-decker in the *Prince Royal*, but although she was able to mount three tiers of guns above each other she did so not on the three flush decks of the later three-decker, but on two decks with a half deck above.[3] With the *Sovereign*, however, the impossible was achieved, and the first and typical reaction of the age was displayed by Charles I, when with a stroke of the pen he altered her projected establishment of 90 guns to an establishment of 102.[4] It was a tendency which defeated

---

[1] Oppenheim, loc. cit. pp. 159–213; J. U. Nef, 'The Progress of Technology and the Growth of Large-Scale Industry in Great Britain, 1540–1640', in *Ec.H.R.* v, pp. 11–12, 23.

[2] E.g. *Adventures by Sea of Edward Coxere*, ed. E. W. H. Meyerstein (1946), p. 43; *Samuel Pepys's Naval Minutes*, pp. 203–4.

[3] R. C. Anderson, 'The *Prince Royal* and Other Ships of James I' (I) in *M.M.* III, no. 9, pp. 272–5, and further articles loc. cit. (V), no. 1, pp. 10–15, and (VI) no. 11, pp. 329–32, forming part of a controversy on decks in that journal; and (VII) no. 12, pp. 362–7.

[4] Oppenheim, loc. cit. p. 262.

its own object, for rival powers with larger hulls for the same number of guns continually forced the English ships to fight a class larger than themselves; and under William III a process which had begun as an attempt to gain a superiority in armament ended in a building programme designed to reverse the inferiority which had arisen in general performance.

But if, in this respect, the *Sovereign* satisfied an exaggerated rather than a justifiable demand, in a third respect she met a genuine requirement of her armament. With her stout timbers and rigid construction, she was well able to endure the disorder of its discharge and the short-range battering of her opponents. The great ship of the seventeenth century was a forest of pillars and beams, of knees and stringers, designed specifically to support the shock of her own salvoes and of the enemy's balls. The former, indeed, might be as serious as the latter, for, relying largely on their truck carriages to take the stress of their recoil, and attached only by ropes and pulleys to the adjoining timbers, the great guns in action were liable to career haphazardly and with considerable violence about the decks. The loss of Balchen's *Victory* with all hands in 1744 was thought to have been due to her cannon breaking loose in a gale, and casualties in action frequently included guns' crews damaged by their weapons. But as striking as the rigidity of her structure was the thickness of the great ship's sides. To penetrate the midships timbers of the *Sovereign* just above the water-line, a shot had to pass through over two feet of oak, and every twenty odd feet along the sides of her gun-deck, oak knees two to three feet deep buttressed the planks.[1] The point-blank fire which was now favoured by English gunnery led the English shipwrights to concentrate the more closely on a toughness of construction which their material in any case induced them to adopt; and they could rely on ships of this type to stand the bludgeoning of a 60-lb. ball fired at a distance of under half a mile.

In describing the relations between the naval ordnance and the man-of-war, the *Sovereign of the Seas*, which was launched in 1637, has been taken as the example of conditions which obtained fifty years later. This, however, is no anachronism, for while the *Sovereign* was the first

[1] Pep:Sea MS. 2902.

she also remained the most famous example of the three-decked man-of-war.[1] Her launching in October 1637 was an event which, in its immediate effect, can be compared only with the launching of the *Dreadnought* in 1906. Like the *Dreadnought*, she reconciled different processes which until then had been following separate courses, and in so doing led to a revised conception of tactics. But, unlike the *Dreadnought*, she not only completed but broke with the past and, having superseded its efforts, set the type which endured for the future. If her tonnage is compared on the one hand with that of the largest ship which fought the Armada, and on the other with that of the *Victory* at Trafalgar, the position may be clearly seen. By the measurement of their own day, the Armada ship weighed 760 tons and the *Sovereign* 1637; by the measurement of a later day, the *Sovereign* weighed between 1141 and 1522 tons and the *Victory* 2162.[2] She was, in fact, over double the displacement of her predecessor of fifty years before, and approximately two-thirds that of her successor of almost 150 years later. Her dimensions set a pattern which changed even less than her tonnage. A naval constructor of the nineteenth century remarked on the similarity, both in size and proportions, between her and the larger men-of-war building in 1800;[3] and if we take the largest of these, the difference indeed is small:[4]

	Length of keel	Beam	Tonnage
Sovereign of the Seas	127 ft.	43 ft. 6 in.	1141–1522
Caledonia of 1800	170 ft. 11 in.	53 ft. 6 in.	2602

The equipment of the two ships changed almost as little as their dimensions. From her smooth-bore guns and wheeled, wooden gun-carriages to her hemp mooring-cables and wooden water-casks, the *Caledonia* was remarkably like her prototype. The crew of the *Sovereign*, once they had mastered the intricacies of the rigging and sail plan, and

[1] As the *Royal Sovereign*, she was finally burnt by accident at her moorings off Chatham in 1696, after being rebuilt twice in the middle of the century and suffering four changes of name.

[2] G. Callender, *The Portrait of Peter Pett and the Sovereign of the Seas* (1930), p. 5; *Soc. Naut. Research, Occas. Publns*, no. 5, pt 1 ('Lists of Men-of-War, 1650–1700, English Ships', compiled by R. C. Anderson), no. 1; Charnock, *History of Marine Architecture*, III, p. 245.

[3] Sir Nathaniel Barnaby, in his *Naval Development in the Century* (1904), pp. 17–18.

[4] *Soc. Naut. Research*, loc. cit. no. 1; Charnock, loc. cit. p. 245.

had found out how to work the pumps, would have had little difficulty in taking her to sea and handling her in action. In a single stride the *Sovereign* had carried the sailing ship towards the limits of her development, and there was less change in the appearance and performance of the larger ships of the line between 1637 and 1837 than there was in their counterparts either in the fifty years before the earlier or in any two decades since the later date.

With their superiority in gunnery, the advent of the three-decker was particularly welcome to the English; but the development was not a specifically English achievement. Five years before the *Sovereign* was launched in England, the *Couronne* of much the same size had been launched in France, and the characteristics of the three-decker were not confined to any one country. The subsequent stability of naval architecture was, indeed, a European and not a national phenomenon throughout two centuries of national rivalry, when its development along national lines might, on general premises, have been expected. National types, it is true, were recognizable in the later seventeenth century. The English concentrated primarily on strength and, compared with the Dutch, on a deep draught which enabled them to hold the wind rather better; the Dutch on beaminess and on a shallow draught suitable to the nature of their coastline; the French on capacity and draught, in both of which they exceeded their rivals.[1] To the men of the day in each country, moreover, these differences seemed important and their implications upon their own construction considerable. But although it was possible to modify the accepted standard, it was not possible to alter it. To the age of the steel ship and mechanical propulsion the differences between wooden sailing-ships seem trivial indeed, and their similarity, resting as it did upon the compelling limitations of both material and technique, overwhelming. Trees could grow only to a certain size and strength, and scarp and join as they might, marine architects and shipbuilders could not produce a wooden ship of more than about 2500 tons, nor, over about 1600 tons, could they do much to vary her lines or proportions. The relative stresses between different types of wood, the inherent weakness of the wooden bolts and wedges which clamped the pieces together, and the combination of strength and curvature which

[1] See *Samuel Pepys's Naval Minutes*, p. 352; *Catal.* I, p. 52.

was required in different places and could be produced only by certain pieces of timber, dictated within narrow bounds her qualities and performance; and for over a century it was almost impossible to distinguish the ships of one nation from those of another, as the favourite *ruse de guerre* of false colours showed from the wars of the Commonwealth to those of George III.[1]

These limitations were never overcome in practice. In the seventeenth century, their solution could not be satisfactorily envisaged in theory. The century, and particularly its later decades, was rich in scientific activity; it would be possible to enumerate a long list of books and experiments which bore upon ship construction alone. Throughout the last forty years of the century the best of this work was carried on under the aegis and within the membership of the Royal Society. Some of it was devoted to purely theoretical exposition, the most notable example of which was Sir William Petty's paper on the principles of ship's form;[2] but mostly it was harnessed to more specific ends.[3] The President, Lord Brouncker, designed a yacht for the King, Hooke tackled the project of a moving keel, Petty designed a double-bottomed boat, and the Society itself laid down the lines for a second-rate man-of-war.[4] The experiments, however, were distinguished by their failure. Petty's boat sank, and the Society's man-of-war, the *Katherine*, proved so unstable that she had to be girdled before she could put to sea. Outside the Royal Society, speculation took a more radical turn. The eccentric Marquess of Worcester patented a vessel which he announced could be propelled against wind and tide;[5] Dennis Papin, in the 1680's, was experimenting with a marine reciprocating steam engine, and claimed in 1707 successfully to have driven a boat by its means on the river Weser;[6] and in 1698 Savery published his *Navigation Improv'd*, with its

[1] In William's war, men-of-war were almost always issued with French colours.

[2] Sprat, *History of the Royal Society*, p. 220.

[3] There was some difference of opinion within the Society about its aims. Some members thought that the theoretical investigations should be put to practical use; others did not (G. N. Clark, *Science and Social Welfare in the Age of Newton* (1937), pp. 15-16).

[4] Sprat, loc. cit., pp. 240–1; *The Petty Papers*, IV, ed. Marquess of Lansdowne (1927), p. xiv.

[5] Marquess of Worcester, *Century of Inventions* (1663), no. lx.

[6] Robertson, loc. cit. p. 99.

less revolutionary proposal of a paddle-boat, operated by oars fixed to drumheads and geared by means of iron bars to a capstan, which relied upon a team of horses to start the paddles turning. But of all these and other experiments, only Savery's was taken up officially. It was tried out at Chatham in the 1690's where, with the aid of four horses, it managed to tow the biggest ships downstream against wind and tide.[1] For some reason, however, it was eventually rejected by the Navy Board.[2]

The failure of theoretical experiment may also be seen in another field, in the standard works on shipbuilding and naval architecture. The most ambitious work on shipbuilding at all near this period was William Sutherland's *The Ship-Builder's Assistant* of 1711, but this was merely a development of the handbooks which had preceded it, and broke no new ground. The earlier tradition of sea-dictionaries, with their lists of boatswain's and carpenter's tables, designed for the use of sea officers or naval officials in their day-to-day work about the ship, and deferring to theory only to the extent of a few cursory and introductory pages of Euclid, continued to appear in much the same form from the 1620's to the 1720's. Beginning in 1626 with Captain John Smith's *Accidence for Young Seamen*,[3] they included among their better-known examples Henry Bond's *The Boatswaine's Art*, *The Seaman's Dictionary* of 1644, Edmund Bushnell's *The Compleat Shipwright*,[4] Boteler's *Dialogues* and Narborough's *Mariner's Jewel*. The difference between them is small, as may be seen by comparing the successive editions of Smith's *Accidence*,[5] and with the exception of the papers to the Royal Society, some of which were available to a wider public in

---

[1] P.R.O.Adm. 3/10:11/5/94. Is this the origin of the term 'horse-power' in marine affairs? [2] Admty:Corbett, VIII, f. 40.

[3] I have placed these books in the order of their publication, not of their authorship. See *The Life and Work of Sir Henry Manwaring*, ed. G. E. Manwaring and W. G. Perrin (*N.R.S.* 1922), II, pp. 70–3; and also L. G. Carr Laughton, 'A Bibliography of Nautical Dictionaries', in *M.M.* I, no. 3, pp. 84–9, and R. C. Anderson, 'Early Books on Shipbuilding and Rigging', in *M.M.* X, no. 1, pp. 53–64.

[4] Bushnell's work is more concerned with mathematics than the others, but their frequent irrelevance is a better example of the lack of appreciation of their purpose even than the absence of such detail elsewhere.

[5] Those of 1626, 1636, 1653 and 1691.

Sprat's *History of the Royal Society* of 1667, they provided the only guide to marine construction.

This conservatism was the more marked in England because in Europe a whole new body of literature was springing up on the same subjects, with the work of the theorists affecting directly the more practical expositions of the designers. Pardie's *Théorie de la Statique* and Renaud's work on the same lines influenced the treatises which both published at much the same time on *L'Architecture Navale*,[1] while the latter and Paul Hoste's *Théorie de la Construction des Vaisseaux* of 1697 in France, and the comparable works by Nicolas Witsen[2] and Cornelis Van Yk[3] in Holland, were all very different affairs from the sea-dictionaries and handbooks of thirty years before, many of which were still appearing. The movement, however, does not seem to have affected England. None of the French or Dutch works mentioned above was translated during the century, whereas French and Italian works on gunnery,[4] and Dutch works on pilotage,[5] were available in English at this time. This, no doubt, was largely due to chance; but it also reflected an official attitude which, interested though it was in experiment, was not prepared, as in France, normally to accept its consequences.

For official investigation and action upon it were rare, and where taken applied more often to a familiar problem than to a new one. Sir Richard Haddock, the Comptroller of the Navy, conducted an inquiry in 1684 into the cubic contents of warships' hulls, which confirmed the growing opinion that the beam of the smaller rates

---

[1] A good example of the way in which the two lines of inquiry had become associated by 1700 is provided by the argument over Renaud's *L'Architecture Navale* of 1673. This was begun by Huygens with an article in the *Bibliothèque Universelle et Historique*, and continued during 1695–6 by the elder Bernoulli and Renaud himself in the *Journal des Savants* and the *Actes de Leipsic*.

[2] *Aeloude en Hedendaegsche Scheeps-Bouw en Bestier*. It is better known by the title of the second edition, *Architectura Navalis*.

[3] *De Nederlandsche Scheeps-Bouw-Konst open gestelt*.

[4] E.g. Gaya's *Traité des Armes*, translated by Harford; Tartaglia's *La Nova Scienzia*, translated by Henry Stubbe; and Moore's translation of Tomasio Moretii's work on artillery.

[5] E.g. Wagenaer's *De Spiegel der Zeevaert*, translated by Ashley as *The Mariner's Mirror* under Elizabeth, and often reprinted.

should be increased in proportion to their length;[1] Pepys used his personal influence to collect scientific information for the Admiralty, and to support the attempts of Sir Anthony Deane to alter the proportions of the lesser ships of the line; the Navy Board itself adopted the use of wooden scale models for all construction after about 1650[2]—and so important did the Commissioner at Chatham consider them, that when the Dutch came up the Medway in 1667 he removed them from the office as the most valuable information there;[3] and it was under naval direction that experiments were carried out with hull preservatives, from lead sheathing to tar and hair.[4] But this type of scientific investigation was more often the extension of traditional practice to theory than the application of theory to practice, and often significant of the development of organization around a problem rather than of an attack upon the problem itself. It differed radically from the action taken in France, where in 1681 a conference was held at Paris, under royal patronage, at which naval designers and scientists discussed the application to naval construction of the current theories of resistance and movement in water, and on which were based the relevant sections of the *Ordonnances du Roi* of 1689.[5]

But the difference between official attitudes was not in itself sufficient to produce very different results in France and England. Even where the user of the theories was willing to accept them, the theories themselves had to provide a foundation for development, and the object of their application—the existing practice of shipbuilding—had to be capable of profiting from them. In the later seventeenth century, neither was the case. Until the discovery of the metacentre in 1746 the formulae of marine architecture could do little to correct the basic

---

[1] Charnock, op. cit. II, p. 483.

[2] The earliest example of a scale model by an Englishman is in Sweden, by the royalist Sheldon, who fled there in 1648. Official models in this country date from a few years later (R. C. and Romola Anderson, *The Sailing Ship* (1926), p. 146).

[3] G. Callender, *The Portrait of Peter Pett and the Sovereign of the Seas*, pp. 29–30. The Admiralty in 1689 also had models made of some Danish men-of-war, to compare with their English counterparts (P.R.O.Adm. 3/1:5/12).

[4] P.R.O.Adm. 1/3577, ff. 113–14; 1/3578, f. 751; *The New Invention of Mill'd Lead* (1691) gives a full, though partisan, account of one of the ensuing controversies.

[5] John Fincham, *A History of Naval Architecture* (1851), p. xiii.

defects of instability and clumsiness; and even where, as in the case of the smaller rates in France, they corrected to some extent the earlier errors of proportion, their effect was largely lost by the inability of the shipbuilders to translate a draught plan into a correctly proportioned hull.

At the end of the century, Paul Hoste in France complained that the average shipwright still measured the angles of the stem and the sternpost by eye alone,[1] and throughout Europe the standard of their skill was much the same. They had changed very little from their predecessors of a century before. Skilled and experienced workmen, with a working tradition which in its way was admirable, they lagged far behind the requirements of the material with which they now had to work. The methods which built a satisfactory man-of-war of 700 tons were not enough for a man-of-war of 1500 tons. The difference was one of kind and not of degree, and this the shipwrights were reluctant to admit. In England they were local men, whose education was mostly, although not entirely,[2] confined to the practice of their yards, and few of them could read either the plans or the detailed specifications on which they were supposed to work. Illiteracy was the common factor of the profession: 'illiterate and supine to the last degree', 'illiterate and a great drinker', 'a very slow man of no learning', 'a very plain and illiterate man', 'illiterate and of no presence': so Pepys summed them up one by one, as he reviewed the depressing list of their disqualifications.[3] As a result, they frequently departed from their instructions, and it was seldom that the surveyors were able to allow that the dimensions which they produced were those originally intended.[4] Throughout the century they continued to turn out ships in a haphazard, approximate sort of way which was the despair of naval architects and officials, and which often made a mockery of the detailed programmes of construction.

The product of a limited and intractable material and a limited skill, the great ship emerged, therefore, almost fully fledged. This had a particular effect upon naval organization. In one step the ship of the line brought with her a new era of administration, which in turn was made

[1] In his *Théorie de la Construction des Vaisseaux*.

[2] Phineas Pett who built the *Sovereign* was a graduate of Emmanuel. (*Alumni Cantabrigienses*, compiled by John and J. A. Venn, pt I, vol. III (1924), p. 352.)

[3] *Catal.* I, pp. 77–8.

[4] See p. 76 below.

more complex and more revolutionary by the very conservatism of her type. For not only did her increased size and complexity make sharply increased demands on material and men, and on their organization for her different needs; her functions were such that her numbers were increased. It was not only that she was larger: it was also that she introduced larger fleets. Because her dimensions and equipment did not alter, because they were much the same whatever her country of origin, and because her size bore a fixed relation to her fighting strength, she was effective only when used in superior force to the enemy. Victory lay not with individual performance or equipment, but with numbers. The effect upon administration was thus cumulative, for beyond a certain point an increase in the degree of organization becomes an increase in kind. Before we can understand the precise effects of this change, we must first see the individual ship, no longer alone, but in the fleet which arose from her requirements, as

> Borne by each other in a distant Line
> The Sea-built Forts in distant order move.[1]

For of the various formations which lay open to the fleet, the line was the natural outcome of the great gun and the great ship. Their strength and their weakness alike contributed to its adoption. It was in its inception, as its name implies, a continuous line of ships, disposed astern of each other and, originally, beam on to the enemy. Such a formation was well suited to the performance of the component units. The larger ships of the seventeenth century, and the three-deckers in particular, were clumsy creatures. Their high sides and massive upper-works forced them easily to leeward in a breeze and kept them becalmed in light airs, while their sail plan and rigging emphasized rather than offset the limitations of the hull. Thanks to the practice of over-gunning, and in some cases to a tenderness which arose from a lack of scientific knowledge, they were under-canvassed for their size. It has been estimated that the *Sovereign* carried only 45% of the sail carried by a ship of equivalent dimensions two centuries later.[2] Their sail plan,

[1] John Dryden, *Annus Mirabilis* (1667), canto lvii.

[2] A. W. Johns, 'The Stability of the Sailing Warship', in *The Engineer*, August 1922, p. 133. This series of articles by a former Chief Constructor of the Navy, which begins in July 1922, is the best single authority on the subject.

too, was that of a square-rigged ship with few of the later modifications which improved its performance. Some recent additions had been made to the rig which had been inherited from the Tudor fighting ship; on each of the three masts the area of canvas had been increased by a topsail, a topgallant or a royal, according to the number carried before.[1] But these were alterations in degree, not in kind, and in any case were at their most effective in summer weather.[2] The sails were still square, so that they could be trimmed only approximately even with the introduction of the bowline and the brace into the larger men-of-war towards the end of the century,[3] which brought the ship's head to about three points off the wind.[4] The remedy lay in the fore-and-aft sail, to give direction to the power of the square rig; and of the three types which eventually appeared, the staysail and the jib at the bow, and the mizzen at the stern, only the latter had been fitted in the bigger ships by the end of the century. The triangular staysail was indeed known in smaller men-of-war from the later years of the Commonwealth, but it had not yet reached the ships of the line; while the jib on its jib-boom was not to replace the spritsail on its yard until the early years of the following century.[5] The development which most affected the ship of the line towards the end of the century was the reintroduction of the reef point, whereby the sail area could be adapted more quickly to the weather, but even this affected the topsails rather than the mainsails until the eighteenth century.[6] Finally, the whole immensely increased mass of timber and canvas was still controlled by the whipstaff, devised to steer vessels of a third or at best half the weight of the *Sovereign of the Seas* and her successors. In bad weather it had to be abandoned, and the steering done by a tiller, rigged with hand-lines and assisted by a pon-

---

[1] A. Moore, 'Rigging in the Seventeenth Century', in *M.M.* II, no. 9, pp. 268–71.

[2] Moore, 'Rigging in the Seventeenth Century', in *M.M.* III, no. 1, p. 7.

[3] William Sutherland, *The Ship-Builder's Assistant* (1711), p. 107. Before that, he stated, the ship was forced 'to go directly to leeward, or just as the Force of the Wind Drove'.

[4] Sutherland, loc. cit.; Moore, 'Rigging in the Seventeenth Century', in *M.M.* IV, no. 8, pp. 262, 265.

[5] Moore, 'Rigging in the Seventeenth Century', in *M.M.* III, no. 1, p. 11; R. C. and Romola Anderson, *The Sailing Ship*, p. 147.

[6] Moore, loc. cit. pp. 9–10.

derous and circumscribed manipulation of the sails to keep the ship's head on its appointed course. It was only in the first decade of the eighteenth century that the steering wheel was introduced, to relieve the helmsman of the more nightmarish of his difficulties.[1]

The manœuvrability which was the pride of the Elizabethan fighting ship had thus been largely lost a hundred years later, with the compensating accession of strength. The advantages which arose from the mêlée gave way to the advantages which arose from organized fire power. By the line, the former was prevented and the latter made possible, and it is not surprising that the English were the first to adopt the formation. Its principles, adumbrated as early as 1617 in the isolated example of Raleigh's fighting instructions,[2] and worked out in the course of the successive Dutch wars in the middle of the century, were simple: first, to gain the weather-gauge of the enemy, with its opportunities for taking the initiative and for firing unimpeded by the smoke of the guns; secondly, to range the line opposite to him, and to file past in unbroken succession, presenting so far as possible a continuous line of fire; thirdly, to prolong its continuity and to maintain a permanent line of ships by sending the leading units back to the rear to repeat the attack. On this foundation were built the two theories of the 'dashing' and individual manœuvre, favoured by Monck and Rupert, and the 'formal' and central control of Blake, Penn and James. The latter, represented most clearly in the Duke of York's 'Instructions' of 1665, 1672 and 1673, had triumphed by the close of the Dutch wars, and when war broke out again sixteen years later it was the Instructions of 1673 that Herbert and later Russell took as their model for the final and classic Instructions of 1691. It was, indeed, only through a well-organized and well-controlled formation implementing a formal and conservative plan of action, that individual initiative could achieve a useful object under the prevalent conditions. The flexibility which James has been accused of stifling posited an order which could be

[1] Anderson, loc. cit. p. 157; H. S. Vaughan, 'The Whipstaff', in *M.M.* III, no. 8, pp. 230–7.

[2] *Fighting Instructions, 1530–1816*, ed. J. S. Corbett (*N.R.S.* 1905), pp. 30–1, 42. These instructions in turn were doubtless based on spasmodic earlier practice. As with most tactical innovations, it is difficult to say when the line ceased to be an unconscious expedient and became adopted as conscious theory.

treated flexibly. 'Dashing' and 'formal' tactics had little meaning where the 'dash' was provided by such unwieldy agents as the ships of the line. It was not a choice between alternative types of order, but between order itself and chaos.

Nevertheless, it is sometimes difficult to follow the two schools of thought in action. Line tactics, although extremely well executed on some occasions, and sufficiently well carried out for refinements of squadronal activity to be added to the Instructions of the third Dutch war,[1] often remained merely an ideal. Apart from the limitations of the ships themselves, discipline in the fleet was still embryonic enough to upset a formation which relied so obviously upon it. It was doubtless unusual for a ship's officer in the fleet flagship to offer to throw the Admiral overboard in an argument over the conduct of the battle, as the Duke of Buckingham did to Albemarle off Lowestoft in 1666;[2] but a system which still sent men like Buckingham spasmodically to sea was no foundation on which to build a system of tactics. One of the objections, indeed, put forward by opponents of the line, was that the men who advocated its adoption also advocated the employment of the irresponsible 'gentlemen officers'.[3] But the 'tarpaulin officers', who had no social position to support them, were sometimes no better, and the traditional independence of the seaman was on occasions little less amenable to restriction than the vanity and bellicosity of a court favourite. When to the shortcomings of the commanders are added the normal chances of wind and weather acting on the square-rigged man-of-war, the set piece, whether of Monck's or James's devising, was apt to degenerate into an unregulated and haphazard dog-fight.

This was not only undesirable but dangerous. One of the most practical arguments for the line, which was recognized by its most uncompromising opponent,[4] was that in its absence a far higher standard of fire control would have to be observed than was in fact possible. The outstanding feature of the gun was its inaccuracy. Even at point-blank range, it could not be guaranteed to hit its target. In

---

[1] Article III in the Duke of York's Instructions of 1673 (ibid. p. 153).

[2] D. Ogg, *England in the Reign of Charles II* (1934), I, pp. 273–4.

[3] B.M.Addnl. 11602, ff. 37–8; 11684, ff. 30–1.

[4] Richard Gibson, in B.M.Addnl. 11602, f. 38.

1749, a 14-pounder (about the size of a culverin) was tested on land at ranges of 470 to 650 yards, with two degrees of elevation. It scored one hit.[1] Its predecessors were certainly no better. By 1750, gun barrels were generally cast solid, and the bore, even if not rifled, was ground out by machine; before 1700, they were cast hollow upon a core whose imperfections must be guessed rather than calculated.[2] Thanks to the unevenness of the internal surface and the unevenness of the surface of the shot, considerable clearance had to be allowed, and the diameter of the projectile was so much less than that of the bore that the shot actually bounded along the barrel, issuing from the muzzle in a direction often wildly divergent from that in which the piece had been laid. To this effect of windage must be added those of wear and tear, rust and temperature; between them, they reduced the force of the explosive by at best a quarter and at worst a half,[3] and combined to make the firing of an individual piece a hazardous and often valueless operation.

To these technological limitations were added the peculiar difficulties of firing at sea. In the first place the cannon, with their great weight, were placed as near the centre of gravity as possible, and consequently close to the water-line; and despite the objections of Deane and Pepys[4] their muzzles were seldom more than three, or at the most four, feet above the water.[5]

> With roomy decks, her Guns of mighty strength,
> Whose low-laid mouths each mounting billow laves,[6]

the ship of the line, like some of her successors in more recent days, was on occasions unable to use her main armament at all.

But all tiers were subject to the normal inconveniences of sea gunnery. The disadvantages of an unsteady platform and of the problems of relative movement—slight though this might be—which

---

[1] Ffoulkes, loc. cit. p. 98.

[2] The boring machine is generally taken as having been invented by the Swiss Maritz in 1739. There are, however, references to a boring process in England in 1713, and to a 'boring place' and a 'boring pond' as early as 1677 and 1680; but any such process was uncommon before 1700 (Straker, *Wealden Iron*, pp. 156–8).

[3] Robertson, loc. cit. p. 126.

[4] See Deane's remarks cited by Pepys throughout his *Naval Minutes*.

[5] *Catal.* I, p. 226.

[6] Dryden, *Annus Mirabilis*, canto cliii.

have always affected it, were not lessened at the time by the existing facilities for elevating and depressing the weapons, or by the state of ballistical knowledge or of mechanical mathematical aids. The greatest elevation attainable on any gun was about ten degrees; the greatest depression, six. And when it had been positioned and secured, and its muzzle was neither pointing into the sea nor at the sky, it was fired on the orders of a gunner who, superior though he might be to foreign rivals, relied for his technical qualifications on an experience of similar occasions, an ability to control his crew, and a trust in the good offices of St Barbara;[1] and who calculated his elevation and depression with the Gunner's Square—a quadrant with a plummet which he held to his eye[2]—his line of sight by the 'line of metal' (or by running his eye along the exterior of the gun barrel and allowing for its inclination to the axis of the bore),[3] his problems of relative movement by a ready-made maximum of one degree in five when the ships were broadside on opposing courses,[4] and his moment of firing by a knowledge of the thickness of metal at the touch-hole, whence he estimated the time taken by the powder in firing to the chamber.[5] His only tables were Streeter's Tables of Projection, published in Robert Anderson's *Genuine Use and Effect of the Gunne*,[6] and his only scientific equipment the Euclidean diagrams in the introductions to the manuals of gunnery. Under these circumstances, reliance on fire-power was a reliance on quantity to offset rather than to implement quality. Where one gun missed the target, ten guns discharged together might hit it. The converse, however, was equally likely. The shot which missed a foe might equally well hit a friend in his vicinity. For the achievement of

---

[1] E.g. Thomas Binning's *Light of the Art of Gunnery* (ed. 1689), where the protection of St Barbara is invoked in the 'mysteries' which the gunner must confront. This point of view lingered until Benjamin Robins's experiments in the middle of the eighteenth century offered a possibility of success that could be calculated mathematically.

[2] It is described in Moore, *General Treatise of Artillery*, p. 89.

[3] This accounts for the stress laid in the gunner's duties upon the importance of knowing the thickness of metal at the breech and muzzle (Moore, loc. cit. pp. 108–9).

[4] Ibid. p. 109. It is noticeable that in Streeter's calculations for sea ordnance (see n. 6 below) no allowance is made for inclination.

[5] Ibid. p. 108.

[6] Published 1674.

the first result, and the avoidance of the second, the line provided an equal solution.

By the end of the Dutch wars, these qualities of ship and gun had given to the sea battle some recognizable characteristics. Taken together they amounted to the achievement of an indecisive result at a considerable and sometimes disproportionate expense. The chances of a decision were slender. The vagaries of the weather and the tactical immaturity of the opponents combined to render destruction, in the Nelsonian sense, unlikely; for that, a favourable wind and a bold and well-organized plan were simultaneously required. In the absence of either—and frequently both were lacking—not even a clear-cut advantage could be depended upon. The full weight of both fleets might not be engaged, and individual squadrons alone might be damaged in single combat, or in an unequal action against greater odds conducted in full view but not within range of their consorts; if both sides were equally and fully engaged, line tactics did not encourage the seizing of opportunities, while if the line were broken its individual units could neither recover nor compensate for the advantages which had been lost with the formation; and even if an advantage were gained it could seldom be followed up, for a chase in which neither opponent enjoyed a decisive margin of speed over the other was liable to end, as indeed did almost all the battles, with their gradually losing touch. With such equality of performance, only overwhelming numbers or greatly superior tactics, combined with favourable weather, could achieve a result. Neither side enjoyed tactical superiority, and it was therefore in numbers that both sought the advantage. But precisely because they were the only criterion for success, numbers alone were not enough to ensure it. To force a result to its conclusion, they required in addition an assured tactical control, and this was to be obtained not through the performance of the ships but in spite of it. Only when the formation could offset, and need not depend upon the quality of its members, could victory become a matter of calculation rather than of faith; and for that, naval warfare had to wait until the advent of Nelson.

But the helplessness in face of conditions which sometimes kept the fleets apart, at other times embroiled them for hours at a stretch until exhaustion or lack of ammunition compelled them to desist. Favourable weather was the most certain guarantee of a stubborn engagement, and the heaviest actions took place in light breezes or in a calm. One carries away from the battle scenes of the Vandervelde a series of similar impressions: of a milky sea, a hot and hazy sky, and the great ships, their sails and flags hanging tattered and idle in the summer air, lying a few paces apart with their upperworks a shambles and isolated clouds of smoke issuing from their gunports as the pieces are spasmodically discharged. A few boats may even be seen, tugging the participants in or out of range. Under such conditions, it might be thought, a decision would be reached; and in fact, it sometimes was. But it was seldom achieved by the ships themselves. Once again we must take into consideration the performance of the gun. Assuming that it had been brought to within a few hundred yards of the target, and that it scored a hit at that range, it was still unable, except on rare occasions, to claim a sinking. In the absence of an incendiary or explosive projectile[1] the weight and penetrative power of the shot were not sufficient when faced with the thick sides and closely-knit construction of the larger ships. Even if the ball penetrated the hull at its vulnerable point 'between wind and water', it left a round and even hole with a maximum diameter of eight inches[2] which the surrounding fibres, swollen by salt water, themselves could partly close, and which offered no insuperable difficulties to the carpenter engaged on stopping it from within. The dangerous penetration was the large and jagged hole, and that came only with the short-range, double-shotted carronade in the second half of the eighteenth century. In the seventeenth century, despite experiments in double-shotting before 1700 to obtain the required effect,[3] the gunners were compelled to rely, as a more effective

---

[1] There were various attempts to introduce both during the century. In Harford's translation of Gaya's *Traité des Armes* (between 1678 and 1680) incendiaries are discussed at length; and Moore republished in 1683 the earlier *Of Artificial Fireworks* by Sir Abraham Dager, which sought to apply to defensive warfare the principles used in more harmless displays. Shell-fire was also discussed. Anderson devoted a chapter of his *Genuine Use and Effect of the Gunne* to 'the shooting of Granados out of Long Gunnes', and a certain Deschiens in 1690 claimed to have invented a method of firing bombs horizontally instead of parabolically from mortars which scared four English ships in the Channel (Robertson, loc. cit. p. 167). The mortar itself in the bombvessel was a feature of William III's war (see pp. 544, 572–3 below).

[2] Anderson, *Genuine Use and Effect of the Gunne*, p. 62.

[3] See Robertson, loc. cit. p. 128.

means of overcoming their disadvantage, upon the cumulative power of the broadside.

The control of a broadside, however, was not a simple affair. To load a cannon involved thirteen distinct manœuvres,[1] some of which, such as sponging, 'putting home your shot gently', and gauging the piece, took a considerable time; the piece had normally to be re-aligned after the recoil; and finally the action of the slow-burning match upon the slow-burning powder added a less remediable cause of delay.[2] What the highest, or even the average rate of fire was, is not certain. It formed one of the more closely guarded secrets of the profession which, whether well kept or not at the time, has successfully resisted later investigation.[3] It was certainly more rapid than on land,[4] but as the figures available for the latter are measured in rounds per day[5] that does not take one very far. It cannot, however, have been very rapid, for there were constant efforts to improve upon it; Pepys at one time had great hopes of the 'Punchinello'.[6] and the Marquess of Worcester of course had invented a wonderful gun which fired a 64-lb. shot every eighteen seconds.[7] It is doubtful, however, whether more than a few shots could be fired from a cannon in an hour, so that even if a broadside were successfully discharged its effect could not quickly be repeated.

The main engine of destruction was in fact not the gun at all, but the fireship. These small vessels, often converted merchantmen, sailed or were towed down wind under the lee of their weightier consorts, and at a suitable distance were ignited and allowed to drift down upon their victim. Their success was sometimes considerable and always dramatic, and they were in general the most dreaded form of attack. It is, indeed, ironic that an action which took its form from the gun should so often have had to be determined by other means.

---

1 Eldred, *The Gunner's Glasse*, cited in Ffoulkes, loc. cit. pp. 112–13.

2 E. W. Lloyd and A. G. Hadcock, *Artillery, its Use and Progress* (1893), p. 29.

3 Ffoulkes, loc. cit. p. 101.

4 Sir Jonas Moore, *General Treatise of Artillery*, p. 103.

5 They seem to be copied from each other, and do not differ from those originally given in Nicolo Tartaglia's *Quesiti et Inventioni Diverse*, book 1 (ed. 1553), which was a popular work in England under Elizabeth.

6 *Diary*, 20 April 1669.

7 Worcester, *Century of Inventions*, no. lxiv.

But if the cannon could seldom destroy, it could severely batter the hull of its opponent; and it was upon cumulative damage that the English relied for their results.[1] The position was well put in the previous century by the chief advocate of the heavy gun:

> The smaller shot passeth through and maketh but his whole [i.e. hole] and harmeth that which lyeth in his way; but the greater shaketh and shivereth all it meeteth...[and] worketh better effects, tormenting, shaking, and over-throwing all.[2]

If, after a long and spirited action, most of the participants were still afloat, they were often almost helpless from internal damage and strain.

They were liable also to be sadly short of men. While the cannon and full culverin were preparing their leisurely salvoes, the smaller pieces sustained the action with a more rapid and miscellaneous fire directed against the upperworks, spars and rigging of the enemy.[3] Different sorts of ammunition might be used, from the normal round shot to the langrel, the chain and the barrel shot used particularly against the crew.[4] The high casualties were perhaps the most outstanding feature of the sea fights of both this and the following century. By the time of the Napoleonic wars, indeed, the convention had arisen that the glory of a victory was to be measured by the numbers of killed and wounded. But in fact they bore little relation to the success of the action. Many a day's work ended in a combination of slaughter and indecision, and could be described as a contemporary described one such day in the Four Days' Battle:[5]

> And then began the most terrible, obstinate and bloodiest battle that ever was fought on the seas...we held on till 10 o'clock at night. In this day's work we came off indifferently on both sides, with no considerable loss, only 4 of theirs were blown up.

---

[1] B.M.Addnl. 11602, f. 38; Bodl.Rawl. D. 147, ff. 23–4.

[2] Quoted by Lewis, 'Armada Guns' (VII), in *M.M.* XXIX, no. 3, p. 164.

[3] There was a handbook dealing specially with the problems of this sort of gunnery: Robert Anderson's *To Cut the Rigging: and Proposals for the Improvement of Great Artillery* (1691). It was based on experiments carried out on Wimbledon Common.

[4] Cf. *Boteler's Dialogues*, ed. W. G. Perrin (1929), p. 201. Although this was written about 1640, it was up to date when published in 1685.

[5] Heron J. Roch, 'His Journal of Some Remarkable Voyages at Sea in the Years 1665, 1666, and 1667', in *Three Sea Journals of Stuart Times*, ed. Bruce S. Ingram (1936), p. 48.

This type of action set its own problems for policy and administration. The navy was faced with a series of sudden and large-scale demands on its resources, as the badly damaged ships with their depleted complements returned to port. Patching up could be done at sea, although until the establishment of sea-stores was laid down for the different rates in 1687 the necessary equipment was liable to vary, both in quantity and quality;[1] nor was the fleet regularly accompanied by storeships, as became more often the case in William's war.[2] But serious damage had naturally to wait for expert repair; and in the conditions which prevailed at the yards in the seventeenth century emergencies of this kind levied a heavy contribution upon supply and distribution, falling as they did on a system which was only gradually and with difficulty ensuring that the normal requirements of a campaign were themselves not treated as a series of emergencies, but as a matter of predictable routine.

The speed with which the yards could put the ships to sea again, manned and repaired, was only one of the factors bearing upon the effectiveness of a policy which had to be adjusted to meet the circumstances of sea warfare. The frequent disappointments, when the chance of a favourable action was missed or the possibility of victory seemed not to be exploited; the failure to force a fight when resources were plentiful, and its occurrence when they were not; the occasionally heavy cost, in money and material, of repairing a fleet when no apparent advantage had been gained by its effort, coming on top of the continuous cost of maintaining and increasing it in the hope of a victory; these were facts whose lessons, in any one war, could be learned only by a few, and whose immediate shortcomings were more obvious to the many than the causes that lay behind them. Except to those who live by it the sea is a strange element, and the ways of ships imperfectly understood. If the consequences are not to be relearned by every generation, and a valid standard is to be available by which to measure them, a continuous tradition of informed knowledge must be preserved and disseminated. In an age when the dividing line between politics

---

[1] *Catal.* I, p. 216.

[2] See J. J. Sutherland Shaw, 'The Hospital Ship, 1608–1740', in *M.M.* XXII, no. 4, pp. 422–6.

and administration was ill defined, when officials were often inefficient or corrupt, and when organization itself was uncertain, such a tradition was not readily available, and there was no standard by which unavoidable could readily be distinguished from contingent disappointment. To ministers, the arguments of the naval hierarchy too often seemed either interested or obstructionist: to naval officials the demands of ministers seemed too often irrelevant or impossible. Through the cross-currents of political animosity and administrative disorder, it was only gradually that the experience of the battles and, beyond them, of the campaigns could be generally accepted as a valid criterion, and that the directors of policy could be given the opportunity to appreciate the peculiar features of war at sea, and to apply to them the combination of patience, fortitude and single-mindedness which the exercise of sea-power demands.

While the sea battle had these effects on policy and administration, it also reacted upon the development of the warship herself. Its effect in this case was one of increasing definition, taking two forms: first, the differentiation of the ships which lay in the line from those which did not; secondly, the division of the former into classified rates, in which not only the size of the ship but her equipment and organization came increasingly under regulation. This process, although specifically concentrated on the ship, had its principal effect on the fleet. For while common technological factors produced the limits of naval architecture and performance, the emphasis which each navy placed upon the different types of ship within these limits differed according to the degree to which its resources, physical or scientific, were able to develop the lessons of the sea battle. The great ship of the line was much the same in England, France and Holland; but the fleets of the three powers were not the same, for each country produced some classes of ship better than others, and their facilities, combined with their rivals' efforts, moulded the composition of their navies.

The first result of the sea battle, the separation of the ship of the line from the smaller man-of-war, was an obvious consequence of the conditions under which she fought. The dividing line was placed, not at first rigidly but with general acceptance, at about 50 guns. This bore particularly hard on the Dutch, who in the middle years of the century had at their disposal a large number of medium-sized men-of-war well suited to their shoals and inlets, and a tradition of co-operation with their larger merchant ships which greatly augmented their fighting potential. Driven by their early defeats to adopt the tactics of their enemy, they were forced largely to exclude from their battle fleet the main strength of their navy, and to redesign its proportions on competitive lines laid down by a power which had very different facilities for construction. Between 1673 and 1689 they largely rebuilt their fleet. Out of a total of 102 ships at the end of 1688, 47 had been launched since 1680: of these, 27 were of over 50 guns, compared with 26 remaining from an earlier date, and eight of over 80 guns, compared with one 80-gun ship already built.[1] Faced with a heavy programme of construction after an exhausting series of wars, of a type unsuited to their means and alien to their traditions, the Dutch were unable in 1689 to put to sea either the numbers or the strength of the other two maritime powers.

The dividing line of 50 guns represented a real change of both size and function, which in England was represented by the difference between the fourth and fifth rates. It marked the difference between a ship of 500–600 tons and one of 200–300 tons, and between a complement of 250 men and one of only half that size,[2] with all that these figures implied in expense and organization. While, moreover, the duties which the smaller ship was called upon to perform remained much the same as before and demanded no increase in her size, the larger ship was big enough to become involved in the competitive programmes and manœuvres of the fleet. The difference between them, therefore, increased with the demands of the line; and where the earlier fourth and fifth rates were not always sharply distinguished either in tonnage or gun-power, those of William's war became quite distinct in both respects. The smallest fourth rate newly-built between 1689 and 1697 had a burden of 614 tons: the largest fifth rate, one of 438.[3] But both were launched in 1691, and in the programme of the middle years of the war the former rose in some cases to 60 guns and

[1] *Soc. Naut. Research, Occas. Publns*, no. 5, pt IV, *passim*.

[2] See Appendix I(B) below.

[3] The *Centurion* and *Adventure* respectively (*Soc. Naut. Research, Occas. Publns*, no. 5, pt I, nos. 704, 706).

over 900 tons, while the latter stayed at between 32 and 44 guns and 300 and 400 tons.[1]

The difference was not only to be seen in the men-of-war themselves, but was reflected in the naval employment of the merchant vessel. The initial separation of the fighting from the trading ship was complete by the end of the Civil War; the latter could no longer lie in the line of battle on her own merits. But until the end of the Dutch wars she could still be converted into the smaller unit of the line. With the next stage of separation, between the different classes of fighting ships themselves, that possibility was finally excluded. The ship of the line became a distinct species with requirements which no other type of vessel could satisfy, and it was only outside her ranks that the trading ship could still be used.[2] In the French war, of the 71 ships of the line acquired in all, none was converted from any other use;[3] and it is not without significance that as a complementary process the privateer—the merchant vessel used for irregular warfare against enemy trade—was first brought under statutory control in William III's reign.[4] In supplementing the fifth and sixth rates, however, and as fireships and storeships, the merchantmen still had a definite part to play.[5] In 1689, for instance, 21 of the 22 'convoys and cruisers' for the summer campaign were hired ships,[6] and the old *ruse de guerre* by which the smaller man-of-war took in her colours and behaved as a trader, continued to be practised until the coming of the frigate in the eighteenth century closed the gap which the merchant vessel had filled hitherto.[7]

---

[1] *Soc. Naut. Research, Occas. Publs*, no. 5, pt I, nos. 666–973.

[2] The East Indiamen were an exception to this argument; but no Administration would have been likely to demand their use.

[3] The one fourth rate shown as bought in Appendix II, p. 631, had been built as a fourth in New England (*Soc. Naut. Research*, loc. cit. no. 914).

[4] By 4 and 5 Will. III, c. 25. Privateers, of course, were by no means new; see the instructions given them by the Crown since 1543 in *Documents relating to Law and Custom of the Sea*, ed. R. G. Marsden (*N.R.S.*, 2 vols. 1895–6).

[5] It is in this sense that I take Corbett's remark, made *c.* 1740, that 'our Navy is very numerous: but if we wanted Shipping we could be furnished with many Stout Ships from the Merchants' (Admty: Corbett, VIII, f. 5).

[6] P.R.O.Adm. 3/1:22/3.

[7] Violet Barbour, 'English and Dutch Merchant Shipping in the Seventeenth Century', in *Ec.H.R.* II, no. 2, p. 263, n. 2.

The difference in size between the smaller ship of the line and the largest of the men-of-war outside it involved, as has been seen, a difference of development. The fourth rate grew larger, while the fifth rate remained much the same. Within the battle fleet itself, indeed, the classes had not yet assumed their final proportions, for while the upper and lower limits were fixed, in the medium-sized ships neither the exact relation of size to gun-power, nor their appropriate classification, had been satisfactorily settled. The definition of these classes was largely determined by the French, for it chiefly affected the smaller rates where the material limitations were not so pressing as in the great ships, and where superior scientific knowledge could therefore provide to some extent a superior performance. With their sharper lines and fewer guns to the deck, the French ships outsailed and were apt to outfight both English and Dutch, and the English thirds and fourths in consequence were enlarged in relation to their armament, and their proportions modified to obtain a better performance. But this process was not entirely satisfactory, carried out as it was without reliable knowledge. The results were often as unstable as before, and ballasted, furred or girdled,[1] the ships put to sea only too often with their original lines disguised and their performance, so far from being improved, still farther reduced. Still too narrow for their beam,[2] and excessively lofty for their size,[3] they chased after the French throughout the war in an unsuccessful effort to achieve superiority.

The English were thus faced with a situation which was largely dictated by their opponents,[4] and which involved a continuous modification of design in their lesser rates. It was upon such a process that the system of 'establishments' was imposed, with its attempt to standardize

---

[1] All three were methods of increasing stability: ballasting by means of increasing the internal weight at a point close to the water-line; furring by removing several strakes or planks near the water-line, packing pieces of wood inside them, and fastening the increased weight to the inner 'ceiling'; girdling—the most popular of the three—by adding strakes at the water-line to the ship's side. The last two methods increased the ship's beam without altering the centre of gravity.

[2] A. W. Johns, 'The Stability of the Sailing Warship', in *The Engineer*, July 1922, p. 133.

[3] L. G. Carr Laughton, *Old Ships' Figureheads and Sterns* (1925), p. 17.

[4] *Samuel Pepys's Naval Minutes*, pp. 351–2.

the dimensions and the armament of the ships of the line. The two movements, of change and of regulation, are not so opposed to each other as might at first sight appear. Both were directed towards the same object, and the difference between them was one of emphasis and not of kind. The former was pursuing and the latter defining a standard of which the embodiment was the class, satisfactory in itself and distinct from those above and below it. The answer was provided by the rated ship.

The first mention of the rate seems to have been early in 1653.[1] At that time its basis was the number of men carried, and its purpose merely one of administrative convenience; but as the need for symmetry increased with the battle fleet, what had originally been a method of identification became an instrument of standardization. The first establishment for the different rates was promulgated by Blake in 1655; but it was superseded in 1677, and it was to these dimensions that the newer ships in the fleet of 1689 were built.[2] More comprehensive than its predecessor, the later establishment catered for the proportions, the armament and the complement of the three largest classes of 100, 90 and 70 guns. Its provisions stood until 1706, supplemented but not contradicted by the establishment which intervening development had made necessary by 1691.[3]

But if the concentration on different rates at different times in England was directly the result of foreign competition, there were common factors which first turned the programme of both English and French construction in the same direction. Towards the end of the Dutch wars, the emphasis had been on the big ship: from 1667 to 1673, six first rates were built in England to four thirds. But when a programme of thirty new ships was laid down in 1677, it consisted of one first rate, nine seconds and twenty thirds. The only notable addition between the completion of these ships and the beginning of the French war was in the shape of four second rates, launched in 1687.[4] The war itself confirmed the process. Between the end of 1688 and the end of 1698 (the

---

[1] *Letters and Papers Relating to the First Dutch War, 1652–1654*, ed. S. R. Gardiner and C. T. Atkinson (*N.R.S.* 1906), III, p. 396.

[2] They are given in Charles Derrick, *Memoirs of the Rise and Progress of the Royal Navy* (1806), appendix 23.

[3] Ibid.

[4] See Appendix I (C) below.

later date seeing the appearance of the last of the ships from the war programme) no first rates, three seconds, 19 thirds and 36 fourths were built.[1] The French similarly, after providing themselves with the necessary nucleus of first rates, mainly in the 1660's and 1670's, concentrated on the two lowest rates of the battle fleet.[2]

The disfavour into which the big ship was falling may be seen in the arguments advanced against her. She was not, however, without her defenders. The most enthusiastic of these was Sir Henry Shere, James II's Lieutenant of the Ordnance, who spent his time in prison under William in composing the argument for a book of naval essays. His defence of the type is worth quotation, for it is the most logical argument for the big-gun ship:[3]

> Sea captains of all sorts have acknowledged (as being self-evident) that wherever there shall be found the greatest Fire in disputes by Sea or Land, there in all probability would be ye Odds of the Success. That, for Example, no Two-Deck-Ships could lie along on ye Broad side of a Three-Deckt-Ship in Fight....Now, if there be ye same Parity of Reason for ye Prevalence of a Battery mounted on Four Decks against One mounted on Three Decks... there will then remain no sound Objection to the Proposition, but the supposed Impracticableness with respect to their Structure and Navigation.... Ye Summ & Secret of my Proposal is a New Royall Rate of Ships...having four Decks, and mounting a quadruple Battery or Fire of Cannon compleat.

But this argument could be countered by others. The big ships were connected, in the minds of some of the veterans of the Commonwealth and their successors in the Country party, with the encouragement of gentlemen officers and extravagant administration. The most logical and best informed of these critics, the former purser and Navy Office clerk, Richard Gibson, put it specifically during the reign of William III. The sailing qualities of the ships were being spoilt by their galleries, carved work and 'Great Tafferills (like Ladys Topp-Knotts) not known in the Long Parliament and Olivers time';[4] and this profusion aft was required for the gentleman captain, who 'claimes the Sterridge for his Grandure, Quarter Deck for his Jarrs, Pidgeons, etc., and oft times all

---

[1] See Appendix II below.

[2] *Soc. Naut. Research*, loc. cit. pt II, *passim*.

[3] Bodl. Rawl. D. 147, ff. 23–4.

[4] B.M.Addnl. 11602, f. 58.

abaft the Main mast upon the upper Deck'.[1] The remedy was to cut down the ships to manageable size, and to 'stopp the spring head by vacating that Allowance made for Voluntier Gentlemen'.[2]

To such men, the whole conception of the line was pernicious. But even with those who accepted it, the first and second rates were becoming unpopular. Unlike the thirds—or at least the medium and smaller thirds—and the fourths, they could not keep the sea after September at the latest without grave risk of being lost, for their instability and their unhandiness exposed them to the dangers of winter, or even autumnal, weather. Throughout the war of William III, the Admirals at sea had continually to emphasize to their superiors ashore the impracticability of autumnal campaigns,[3] and in its later stages, when the French fleet seemed to have shot its bolt, they suggested that the great ships should be laid up and a fleet of third and fourth rates alone sent to sea.[4] Considering the cost in money, material and men, the two largest rates gave disproportionately little service.

For it was chiefly on the score of expense, both in money and material, that their construction, and even their employment, was attacked. In the first place, their absolute cost was considerable:[5]

		Price of hull						Cost of total fitting out			Timber loads	Plank loads
		Total			Per ton							
		£	s.	d.	£	s.	d.	£	s.	d.		
1st rate	1450 tons	21,750	0	0	15	0	0	33,391	0	0	2902	—
	1814 tons	31,110	0	0	17	13	0	38,400	0	0	2250	330
2nd rate	1150 tons	16,100	0	0	14	0	0	24,982	0	0	2300	—
	1438 tons	20,851	0	0	14	10	0	26,459	0	0	1950	280
3rd rate	850 tons	8,500	0	0	10	0	0	15,112	0	0	1383	—
	1064 tons	12,661	0	0	11	18	0	16,741	0	0	1370	198
4th rate	600 tons	4,800	0	0	8	0	0	9,152	0	0	880	—
	677 tons	6,228	0	0	9	4	0	8,853	0	0	760	105

1 B.M.Addnl. 11602, f. 40.

2 Ibid. ff. 58–9.

3 See pp. 319–20, 503 below.

4 See p. 611 below.

5 The first line of each set of figures in the 'price of hull', and those in the 'cost of maintenance for six months' are taken from Edward Battine's *The Method of Building, Rigging...Ships of War* (Pep:Sea MS. 977, ff. 105–11). This copy is dated 1684; the figures do not change in other copies, dedicated to other men, of 1687, 1688 and 1691 (B.M.Stowe 431, B.M.Addnl. 9957, Admty MSS. unnumbered). The second set of figures in the 'price of hull' is from B.M. Stowe 144, f. 12. Both these sets of prices and materials are theoretical estimates, and not accounts of ships actually built. The latter are available, but are subject to disadvantages which render them unsatisfactory

Cost of maintenance for six months

1st rate	£12,888 14*s.*
2nd rate	10,581 14*s.*
3rd rate	7,301 13*s.*
4th rate	4,558 2*s.*

The total annual expenditure of the navy in peacetime before the French war was in the region of £400,000:[1] the average total of oak timber and plank annually expended in the royal dockyards throughout the war, just under 11,500 loads.[2] To build one first rate and send her to sea for a summer campaign, therefore, cost about one-tenth of the normal annual charge of the navy, and consumed one-fifth of the dockyard timber in a busy year. In an age when money was limited and timber hard to get, and when the problems of manning and victualling were often acute, she represented an expenditure which could be justified only by results.

Her cost relative to that of the smaller rates was also high. The larger the ship, the more she cost per ton. The reason was to be found in the type of wood required for the larger hull. The cost of construction was based primarily on the price of timber, and this rose steeply the larger and more unusual the pieces required. It was thus not only the case that the big ship cost more per ton than the medium-sized ship: the more she cost, the harder she was to build. For perhaps the greatest argument against her construction arose from the type of material used. The 2900 loads of timber which went into the big ship made not only greater but also more difficult demands on the sources of supply than did the 1380 loads which went into the third rate. To see the peculiar difficulties which were involved, therefore, we must turn from the ship herself to her material and to the system of supply which lay behind her construction.

for this purpose. Delays in building, the rate of discount or interest, the rate of prices at particular periods, the difference of terms in different contracts and the wastage and mismeasurement of timber, all make even reasonably just averages difficult to achieve. The absence of these considerations, however, which makes a theoretical estimate more suitable here, must also limit its application to individual practice. If this is what ships were supposed to cost, it is not necessarily what they did cost.

[1] See p. 170 below. [2] Serg.Misc. III, f. 543.

CHAPTER II

MATERIAL AND SUPPLY

The ship of the line was larger than the average country house of the day, and her construction was far more complicated. Built entirely of wood, even to the pins that fastened the sections together, her hull had to withstand the external effects of sea and weather on the one hand, and on the other the internal effects of decay and the stresses which arose from the different types of wood. The builder and the agent of supply had to reckon with the exceptional size and shape of the timbers required for some of her parts, while the latter had also to allow for the problems set by her masts and spars, which were fashioned out of trees different from those already provided for the hull.

The problems confronting the shipwright were those of size and shape. In a great ship, the timbers required for the main beams, the keel, the sternpost and some of the ribs were massive indeed. The sternpost of a first rate might be some 40 ft. long and some 28 in. thick, and had to be of one piece, while other sections, such as the stem with its accurately defined curvature, the cathead for the anchor, and on a lesser scale the knees supporting the beams, the breasthooks, wing transoms and apron, demanded pieces of widely different shapes.[1] Of the two classes of straight and curved or, as it was known, compass timber, roughly twice as much of the latter as of the former went into the hull of a big ship,[2] although in normal repair work the emphasis was on straight timber;[3] and of the two it was compass timber that was the harder to obtain. The great trees from which the keels and sternposts were fashioned were by no means plentiful, for their growth and

[1] See R. G. Albion, *Forests and Sea Power* (1926), ch. I.

[2] William Sutherland, *Britain's Glory, or Ship-Building Unvail'd* (1717), pt I, pp. 117–23.

[3] One reckoning of the consumption of straight and compass timber in the royal dockyards from October 1688 to September 1697 placed it at 53,932 loads of the former to 30,722 of the latter (Serg.Misc. III, f. 543). I have included knees with compass.

care imposed sacrifices which their owners, often unwilling or unable to wait for a century or more to realize a profit, were reluctant to bear; but they were normally the products of parks or forests designed to furnish shipbuilding timber, whereas the crooked pieces were not. It was only when grown in isolation and, it was believed, when subjected to the unimpeded buffetings of the weather,[1] that the peculiar shapes required of compass timber could be provided; and it was from the hedgerows of the fields, and the ditches by the lanes, that it was largely procured. It came to a great extent not from land devoted to the supply of timber for the navy, or indeed to the supply of timber at all, but from farmland and wasteland where the peculiarities of tenure offered continual difficulties to the naval authorities. Throughout the age of the great wooden ship, such pieces demanded particular forethought and control from an administrative system which was often conspicuously lacking in both.

The number of trees which could answer the various requirements of the hull was limited. In practice, four alone were employed:[2] fir, beech, elm and oak. The proportions in which they were used may be seen roughly in the figures of wood used in the six royal dockyards in 1692:[3]

Ash	19	loads	10	feet
Fir	705	,,	96	,,
Beech	48	,,	17	,,
Elm	1129	,,	91	,,
Oak (of all sorts)	6789	,,	48	,,

The figures for fir may include some spars used in masting and not in building the ships, although normally these were not listed under the heading of timber. But the wood was often used in addition for deck deals, and sometimes for planking.[4] With its resinous bark, its pliability and its lightness, it could be quickly and easily worked, and was particularly suited—as the navy found in the eighteenth century—for building fast light hulls. On the other hand, opinion held that it

[1] Charnock, op. cit. III, p. 172.

[2] Ash, as may be seen below, was also used, but only for boats' oars, some trennels and various small items of equipment (P.R.O.Adm. 49/29, *passim*).

[3] Serg.Misc. III, f. 135.

[4] Planking consisted of the 'skin'—lengths of wood which covered the frames, sawn to 4–8 in. thick—and 'ceiling', sawn to 2–4 in. Deals were used for the decks.

splintered too easily in battle, and at this period it seldom formed part of the hull.

Beech was an unpopular wood, and was regarded merely as an inferior substitute for elm. Both were limited so far as possible to those parts of the ship that lay below the water-line, for neither was able to resist the effects of intermittent exposure; and they were thus to be found principally in the keel, in the lower parts of the stem, and sometimes in the lower wales of the planking. Cheap and strong, so long as its limitations were observed, elm in particular was a useful substitute for the more expensive and valuable oak.[1]

For oak, tough yet moderately pliable, resilient and hard to splinter, durable and well able to resist the effects of sea water, was incomparably the most important wood used in ship construction. It grew in various parts of England, but the timber of the northern counties was unpopular, and that of the west, thanks to the cost of transport, apt to be expensive. But the forests and woodlands of Hampshire, Kent and Sussex—and above all the latter—were supposed, and with some justification, to produce on the average the finest naval timber in the world. Its prosaic qualities became invested, as did those of the ships which it built, with a combination of patriotic affection and technical admiration[2] which helped in no small measure to lead to that excessive reliance upon it, and to the rejection of alternatives or substitutes, which landed the navy and the country in so dangerous a position in the later days of the wooden ship. Imported oak, therefore, was unpopular. The American variety was considered tender and liable to decay, and so far as possible was kept out of the yards,[3] while the Baltic and German oak was used mainly for merchant ships, having been finally judged, by a conference

[1] William Sutherland, *Britain's Glory*, pt I, pp. 35, 46; *The Ship-Builder's Assistant* (1711), p. 14; John Hollond, *Two Discourses of the Navy, 1638 and 1659*, ed. J. R. Tanner (*N.R.S.* 1896), p. 206.

[2] E.g. Sutherland, *The Ship-Builder's Assistant*, p. 28; *Britain's Glory*, pt I, p. 34; Charnock, op. cit. III, p. 171.

[3] *Cal.S.P.Col., Am. & W.I., 1696–7*, p. 10; P.R.O.Adm. 1/3581, ff. 101–3. This was largely due to the provisions of the Navigation Acts. The English based their opinion of American oak on the inferior white oak of New England, which was pushed on to the market because the colonial merchants had little else to export. In Georgia, on the other hand, where the superior *Quercus virus* grew, there were already alternative and more profitable exports, so that oak did not appear in the market (Albion, loc. cit. pp. 23–4).

of shipbuilders and naval officials in April 1686, to be more suitable for plank than for timber in all but the smallest men-of-war.[1] As planking, however, it was a popular and necessary import throughout William's war. Thus for the construction of the hull the timber came almost exclusively from English woodlands; only the plank and deals, after 1686, came largely from abroad.

The masting of the great ship was a very different process from the supply of timber for her hull.[2] There were over twenty masts, yards and spars in a first rate, ranging from the mainmast 38 yards long and 38 inches in diameter, and weighing about eighteen tons, to the upper yards seven and eight yards long and only a few inches in diameter. Their prices gave an indication of the requirements. A mast 38 yards long, with the correct diameter of an inch to a yard, cost three times as much as a correctly proportioned mast 32 yards long, which in turn cost just over half as much again as one of 28 yards; and the ratio was repeated at the next stage, where lower masts parted company with topmasts. For a mast was a much more valuable object than the amount of wood which it represented. Size and proportion were the twin deities of the timber merchant and the naval purveyor. A single rotten knot could reduce a potential mast worth £100 to £15-worth of timber.[3]

Apart from its size and proportions, the qualities required of a tree for masting were shape—a cylindrical straightness was the ideal—elasticity, strength and durability. Few woods could meet all these requirements, and in practice the choice was confined to three: fir, pine, and spruce. Fir was grown in Great Britain, particularly in Scotland, as well as in the great forests of northern Germany, Poland and Russia; but the Scottish trees were markedly inferior to their foreign rivals, and it was from the lands around the Baltic, and particularly from that part of the hinterland which was served by the port of Riga, that the greatest and most valuable supply was obtained. With their quick growth and a combination of suppleness and strength, Riga masts were recognized

---

1 Pepys, *Memoires*, pp. 72–9.

2 See Albion, loc. cit. and John Fincham, *On Masting Ships, and Mast Making* (1879).

3 Sutherland, *Britain's Glory*, pt I, p. 50; pt II, p. 204. No figures of prices have been reproduced, owing to their variety and the difficulties of comparing one source with another. But the ratio corresponds in the main in the different sources of P.R.O.Adm. 29/50, 49/29 and 95/13–14.

throughout Europe—in Spain, France and Holland as well as England—as the best available for their size.

They could not, however, provide the biggest masts of all. In the sixteenth century, fir-trees of over fifty inches in diameter had been known in Europe; but selective arboriculture no longer allowed the growth of such giants, and it was in the virgin forests of North America that the mainmasts and bowsprits for the ships of the line were now exclusively to be found. From the beginning of the Dutch wars, New England pine was regularly shipped to England from the colonial harbours of Portsmouth and Falmouth, and for the next century and a quarter the English men-of-war were saved from the composite fir masts which their rivals largely used and which they themselves were once more driven to use in the Napoleonic wars.

For the smaller masts and yards, the cheaper spruce was commonly used. With a coarse grain and a tendency to snap which disqualified it for the larger masts, by the 1650's it had been confined to spars below fifteen yards long. The masting of an English man-of-war, therefore, unlike her hull, was normally provided completely from abroad and, for the 'middling masts' and spars of up to about 28 yards' length, from the resources of foreign powers.

The wooden ship was particularly liable to two forms of attack: from without, through the activities of the sea worm, and from within, from its susceptibility to dry rot. The former was by no means a negligible factor in naval strategy. Only slightly discouraged by the tannic acid which was one of the more admirable qualities of oak, the worm bored its way through the wood literally eating up timbers and planking, particularly on southern stations; and one of the penalties which England had to pay for her West Indian and Mediterranean interests was the loss of whole squadrons from the *teredo navalis*.[1] Sheathing with tar, fir and hair proved useless, and the acid of the oak put an end to the experiment of lead. It was only with the adoption of copper sheathing during the war of the American Revolution that external decay was finally checked.

Dry rot was an even more serious matter, sometimes destroying whole fleets and completely upsetting naval policy. There were always

[1] Aptly called by Linnaeus *Calamitas navium*.

some men-of-war in harbour on its account, and there is little doubt that it sent others to the bottom at sea. A fungous growth, thriving on moisture from the air or from the sap of the wood itself, and penetrating the timber with white fluffy fibres, it appeared as a tough, leathery yet spongy cocoon as described by Pepys on his visit to the rotting ships at Chatham in 1684.[1] No satisfactory remedy was ever discovered for it. Only accurate supervision of the timber itself on receipt, sound construction and careful ventilation could save the wooden ship from her nemesis. The masts and yards, the results of whose defects were not likely to be on the same scale, were also subject to its attacks, working on the same element of moisture in the sap or in the conditions under which they were shipped; and unless adequate care had been taken to inspect them before they were stepped, they were liable in the stress of a high wind and heavy weather to break or splinter at sea.

The peculiarities of the material thus demanded in particular measure a well-organized and incorrupt system of supply. In the state of the timber business and of the naval contract system at the end of the seventeenth century this was simply offering hostages to fortune. The structure of the business varied according to the source of supply. Most of the trees which were suitable for shipbuilding were grown either in the royal forests or in the parks and groves of private persons. There were still 68 royal forests in the later seventeenth century, apart from the chases and parks,[2] but the term covered several types of land, from the open spaces of Exmoor Forest, which at one time was said to contain one oak, to the great timber preserves of Dean Forest, the New Forest and Alice Holt.[3] The navy was supplied almost entirely by the last three forests, which between them covered some 90,000 acres. Only some 35,000 acres, however, consisted of oak plantations, and much of that was exhausted.[4] The method by which timber was selected and supplied from these forests was the traditional one of past generations.[5] Their

---

[1] Pep:A.L. x, f. 100. [2] Albion, loc. cit. p. 107.

[3] I have included Wolmer Forest with Alice Holt for this purpose.

[4] *V.C.H. Gloucestershire*, II, pp. 271–2; *Sussex*, II, p. 313; *Hampshire*, II, pp. 441, 464; Serg.Misc. III, f. 542.

[5] See in general J. C. Brown, *Forests of England* (1883), and *V.C.H. Hampshire*, II, pp. 435–40.

administration, originally the responsibility of the Court of Exchequer, was now in the hands of the Treasury, whose permission had to be obtained before they were inspected.[1] In immediate charge of all royal woods was the Surveyor-General of Woods and Forests, under whom were placed the Lord Wardens, the individual heads of each forest whose posts dated in some cases from the eleventh century, with their bevy of medieval assistants—woodwards, verderers, regarders, and courts of woodmote and swanimote—who retained in some degree the attitude, as they enjoyed the titles of Plantagenet days. Representing the navy in this hierarchy were the naval purveyors attached to each forest, who inspected and selected the trees for naval timber and marked them with the broad arrow of naval ownership.[2] When the wood had been cut and brought to the waterside, the navy also transported it to the appropriate place.[3]

The supply of royal timber had certain disadvantages. Most serious was the temptation not to treat the forests as sources of supply at all, but simply as sources of profit, forming one element in the Crown's financial position. The widespread alienation and grants of their contents and rights, from Elizabeth to the Civil War, was a ruinous and short-term exploitation of long-term assets that could not be paralleled elsewhere, and it was this more than any reliance upon them that gravely reduced their value to the navy. This temptation to treat the woods uneconomically was repeated, as a feature of administration and not of policy, down the hierarchy of forest officials, thanks to the conditions of their appointment and tenure, which led often to absenteeism and almost always to indifference. The maladministration of the royal woods was notorious, nor did the divided system of authority between Treasury and navy help the latter to safeguard its interests. The naval purveyor, interested in the prevention of waste and decay and in regular re-afforestation, was faced, if he tried—as some did[4]—to represent his case, with the lethargy and often the opposition of the Warden's officials, and his superiors were faced with the indifference or even the anta-

---

[1] E.g. *Cal.Treas.Bks. 1685–9*, pp. 408, 427–9, 1116–17.

[2] *Cal.Treas.Bks. 1689–92*, pp. 948, 1967.

[3] P.R.O.Adm. 49/120, f. 13; Straker, *Wealden Iron*, p. 189.

[4] P.R.O.Adm. 1/3559, f. 752; 1/3564, f. 143.

gonism of the Treasury.[1] This difference of interest became a division of responsibility when the navy came to take its timber. To transfer a parcel of wood from a royal forest to a royal yard involved the master shipwright of the yard, the Navy Office, the Admiralty, the Treasury, the Surveyor-General of Woods and Forests, the Warden of the forest and the naval purveyor, in an ascending and descending series of cumbrous negotiations. The receipt for an oak from the King represented a far greater waste of time and effort than the receipt for an oak from a private owner.

On the other hand, royal timber had its advantages. In an age of frequent wars and uncertain credit, its supply, if urgent enough, could usually be relied upon, whereas the patience of country gentlemen and timber merchants could not. Moreover, hamstrung though the naval purveyor might be, he represented a definite naval interest in the forests which ensured that the fleet could not be entirely ignored in the competition from other consumers; while at the higher level, the King after 1660 was more concerned with naval requirements than the private owners, and could give more effective expression to his concern. The royal forests were regulated by ordinances and Acts of Parliament which attempted to safeguard the supply of ship timber,[2] and were occasionally subject to survey on its account.[3] Since the Restoration, the wholesale opportunism of the earlier Stuarts and the Commonwealth had been largely replaced by a policy of extensive replanting, and although this did not have any great results,[4] it at least showed an appreciation of naval needs which the attractions of rival demands were apt to blunt elsewhere. So far as their resources of timber permitted, the later Stuarts were willing to devote them in the main to the fleet.

But by the Restoration, and even more by 1680, these resources were distinctly limited. They had been steadily declining since the middle of

---

[1] E.g. in 1696 over the policy to be pursued in the New Forest (P.R.O.Adm. 3/13: 2/3, 16/5).

[2] The two outstanding Acts were 19 and 20 Car. II, c. 8 (for the Forest of Dean), and 9 and 10 Will. III, c. 36 (for the New Forest). For the Forest regulations, see Brown, loc. cit.

[3] E.g. Albion, loc. cit. p. 125: *Cal.Treas.Bks. 1689–92*, p. 1150.

[4] J. Nisbet, 'The History of the Forest of Dean, in Gloucestershire', in *E.H.R.* XXI, p. 453.

the sixteenth century, under the twin processes of sale and cutting and of failure to replant. There had been spasmodic scares over the position since Elizabeth's reign,[1] and Evelyn's *Sylva* of 1664 finally stirred government and landowners alike to concerted action.[2] The plantations then made in the Forest of Dean, for example, were to be the mainstay of the dockyards after 1740. But oak takes between 80 and 120 years to reach even moderate size for ship timber, and the Restoration fleets, and those of William and Anne, depended upon the forest policy of a generation which was only half aware of the recent decline of its resources. When in 1677 the construction of thirty ships of the line was undertaken, the royal forests could not supply enough compass timber, knees and standards to build even two first rates and six seconds in four years;[3] and the programme, coinciding as it did with a period of major repair after the misfortunes of the third Dutch war, left the King's woods almost bare.[4] By the end of the decade the naval demands could be met only, as Pepys wrote, 'if the gentlemen will fell'.[5]

But one of the disadvantages of relying upon private supply was that the gentlemen would not always fell, while at other times they felled too soon. The aesthetic demands of park and garden, and the economic pressure of a declining income, a daughter's dowry or an extravagant heir were apt to lead to a retention of timber beyond the proper time, or, more often, to a premature felling which bore particularly hard upon the largest men-of-war. The emphasis which the landowner put upon his trees as a source of profit, led him also to entertain demands from interests which rivalled the navy. The first of these was agriculture, always the most formidable alternative to arboriculture. Arable in particular made great demands. Corn was as important to the nation as oak, it produced a profit once a year instead of once a century, and it employed more men in a period of mercantilist argument. The rivalry was particularly pronounced since corn and oak both demanded the

---

[1] Albion, loc. cit. pp. 123, 125–7, 129; Nisbet, loc. cit. pp. 447–8.

[2] I have taken its claim at its own valuation (see the preface to the edition of 1679). Later works have disagreed on its effect.

[3] *Catal.* I, p. 49.

[4] E.g. the total amount of wood (oak and beech) received in the royal dockyards from the New Forest from 1691 to 1696 was only 6142 loads (Serg.Misc. III, f. 542).

[5] *Catal.* I, p. 50.

same type of soil—the rich, deep clay or loam which characterized the south-eastern counties.

This form of competition, serious as it was, had not reached the proportions by 1700 which it assumed so rapidly in the central decades of the following century. The more obvious alternatives to naval supply were provided by other industries requiring the same types of wood. Foremost among these were the private shipyards, engaged in building merchant ships. There were possibly 2000 trading vessels, excluding fishing vessels, in 1688, compared with 173 naval ships; and between two-thirds and three-quarters of these were estimated to be of English construction.[1] The Navigation Acts had not only encouraged more but also larger merchantmen to be built;[2] and the appearance of the East Indiaman in particular, backed as she was by the resources of a Company which could afford to bid against, or even to outbid the navy for the choicer oaks, provided a serious form of competition. But the average merchantman still weighed rather less than 100 tons, while almost half were fishing vessels and coastal craft of much less;[3] and their principal effect on the naval supply was not to compete for the same pieces, but to induce the owners of trees to fell them sooner than naval requirements preferred, and thus to reduce the numbers for which competition need not be feared.

Outside the shipbuilding industry itself, the most obvious danger came from iron, with its dependence on charcoal for the process of smelting.[4] Other rivals were to be found in the glass and lead industries, both of which required wood for their manufacture;[5] in the rebuilding and subsequent expansion of London throughout the later decades of the century, which made particularly heavy demands on Baltic and Norwegian fir and oak;[6] in the breweries, which demanded oak staves

---

1 Violet Barbour, loc. cit.; T. S. Willan, *The English Coasting Trade, 1600–1750* (1938), p. 14. Petty estimated the tonnage of English merchant shipping in the 1670's to be 500,000 tons (*Economic Writings*, I, p. 171). All such statistics are at best approximate.

2 22 and 23 Car. II, c. 11, art. 12.

3 Barbour, loc. cit. p. 262; Willan, loc. cit. pp. 11–13.

4 Nef, loc. cit. pp. 15–16.

5 Ibid.

6 T. F. Reddaway, *The Rebuilding of London after the Great Fire* (1943), p. 121.

for their casks;[1] in bridges and docks,[2] military fortifications,[3] and even the oak palings which surrounded so many parks. The navy may have been the largest buyer of timber; but the variety of its competitors, and the difficult nature of its own demands, did not make it inevitably the favourite customer.

Attempts were made by legislation to secure it that position. A long series of statutes restrained the owner of timber in the uses to which he might put his property, and his customers in the demands which they might make upon him.[4] But there was little guarantee that such a policy would be implemented in the existing method of purchase. The direct control which had been exercised in earlier decades by naval surveyors and purveyors, acting on the royal authority, had been dealt a succession of damaging blows by the Ship Money controversy, the Civil War and the reaction under Charles II to the arbitrary practices of the Commonwealth. The landowning interest was less amenable to control than it had been, and one expression of its increasing independence was the emergence of the middleman, who took the place of the naval purveyor in buying the individual lots and the place of the owner in selling them to the navy. In the last two decades of the century, naval purveyors confined their activities, outside the royal forests, to the remoter districts of England and to Ireland, where the timber merchant could not operate so well. This process was not altogether unsatisfactory to the navy. It saved it from most of the detailed work of bargaining and price-fixing, and enabled it to deal, in larger quantities and at more stable rates, with the middleman who had arisen to fill the gap left by royal power. In return for this work, the profits from individual bargains with landowners and petty traders went to the timber merchant,[5] who reconciled the prices of his different

---

[1] Albion, loc. cit. p. 120.

[2] In the last decade of the seventeenth century docks were built for the first time of stone; but the old wooden docks had still to be maintained (see, e.g., pp. 416–17 below).

[3] Albion, loc. cit. p. 120.

[4] Particularly 35 Hen. VIII, c. 17; 1 Eliz. c. 15; 5 Eliz. c. 21; 3 Jac. I, c. 13; and 15 Car. II, c. 2.

[5] A few landowners, whose properties were large enough, themselves acted as merchants, selling at flat rates like the rest: e.g., in particular, Richard Norton of Southwick in Hampshire (P.R.O.Adm. 49/29, *passim*).

purchases in the flat rates at which he sold to the navy, and which henceforth remained much the same from year to year, and even from decade to decade.[1]

The relations between these merchants and the navy can best be seen from the terms which they were able to command. These in turn may be divided into three sorts: the prices which they were paid for their goods, the value which they gave in return, and the conditions under which they were paid. It is difficult to say to what extent the merchants differed in the prices which they got for their timber, or how far they worked together to bring pressure upon the navy. The records of their contracts are preserved only by the navy itself,[2] and the necessary details of the size and, still more, the quality of their goods are not always shown; while apparently no evidence remains, in the form of diaries, letters or business documents, of their own activities. The prices of the different woods varied in different degrees, and no exact scale can be fixed, for the reasons already given, according either to quality or size.[3] A dealer might, however, gain an advantage over the navy and his fellows, not on his prices, but on what he gave in return.

When there was a demand for timber, he might deliver more than had been originally contracted for; or he might induce the naval officials to pass some wood of poor quality in a shipment of the right quantity; or deliver short and wait to make up the balance on a more favourable occasion.[4] To some extent, the merchants seem to have combined in these transactions.[5] It would indeed have been surprising if they had not done so. In the first place, they were able to take advantage of the circumstances owing to the fact that they had simplified

---

[1] I.e. the basic rate remained much the same. The rate of discount varied according to the state of naval credit (see pp. 162–3 below).

[2] P.R.O.Adm. 49/29.

[3] Oak plank in 1689 and 1690 cost anything between £1 and £5. 7*s*. 6*d*. a load, straight oak timber from £1. 10*s*. to £5. 10*s*., and compass oak from £2. 8*s*. to £5. 10*s*. Elm cost between £2 and £2. 10*s*. in comparison with the higher priced straight oak timber. Trennels varied between £1. 2*s*. 6*d*. and £8. 10*s*. a thousand, according to their size—12 to 36 in.—and according to whether they were oak, elm or ash (ibid.).

[4] The dockyard officials were warned against all these practices by their superiors in 1694 (P.R.O.Adm. 49/137, f. 29).

[5] Ibid.

the market, and could thus bring a pressure to bear upon their customer which the smaller men of earlier days, who sold directly to the naval purveyor, were often unable to do; and secondly, it was precisely at this level that they could persuade the naval officials, with their low wages and high opportunities for benefits in kind, to condone their practices. The many investigations of abuses in the last decade of the century, and the many pamphlets which attacked them, concentrated largely on the relations between the dockyard officers and the local timber merchants, and in this field at any rate left the higher levels of the naval hierarchy alone.[1]

The pressure which the merchants could exert upon the navy, which cannot be determined from the basic prices obtained, can however be suggested by the conditions of payment. This was the third way in which a dealer might gain an advantage over both customer and rivals, and here again most of them were able to raise the old problems of credit and discount more effectively than their predecessors. Some merchants, however, were in a better position to do so than others. The influence of a contractor with the navy depended either upon the degree of control which he exercised over the market, or on the degree to which he and his fellows were able to combine so as to present common terms to their customer; and in the absence of any evidence upon the latter point—and if any such combination had existed, its results, to judge from other cases, would almost certainly have been recorded in the navy's records—the extent to which the domestic timber merchants could hope to extract concessions of credit from the Administration may best be seen from the structure of the trade itself.

Few though they were in comparison with the landlords from whom they bought, the domestic timber merchants were numerous compared with the naval contractors for other commodities.[2] Between the middle of November 1688 and the end of 1690, 34 separate merchants dealt with the navy. Of these, one handled nine separate contracts, one handled eight, one six, and one five; three handled three contracts each, six handled two, and the remaining 21 one each. The largest amount of oak timber sold by one man—for oak was by far the most important

---

[1] See pp. 595–6 below.

[2] The following details are taken from an analysis of P.R.O.Adm. 49/29.

species dealt in—was 1664 loads, sold in eight lots; the two largest amounts which were sold singly were 1550 and 720 loads respectively, both sold by the same firm. Only five merchants sold amounts totalling over 1000 loads, and only another two amounts totalling over 500 loads: on the other hand, nineteen sold total amounts of under 100 loads each. Most of the dealers handled oak of various sorts, but two sold only trennels and wedges, one only wainscot board, while two dealt only in elm. A further ten dealers sold elm as well as oak, although in fairly small quantities. The trade was thus in the main composed of small men dealing in various and not in specialized goods. No single dealer could be said to dominate it either in the number of his contracts, in the amounts which he sold, or in the exclusive character of his goods. Compared with other industries which supplied the navy, its biggest men operated on a small—indeed a very small—scale; and it is not surprising to find that in William's war they were seldom able to get concessions from the navy until other and more powerful interests had successfully attacked it. The most formidable of these was the group of merchants which imported timber from abroad.

For the structure of the foreign timber trade was in marked contrast to that of its counterpart at home. The conditions under which it operated were entirely different. These may be divided into natural geographical difficulties and those imposed by the governments, English and Baltic, which respectively bought and sold the goods. Their joint effects could be seen in the cost and organization of transport, which rendered any small-scale activity unlikely. Transport was the most expensive item in the price of both domestic and imported wood. For the former, water carriage was less expensive than carriage by land, for a hoy could carry perhaps ten tons or more of timber, and a barge two or three, to a waggon's load of only one ton.[1] So far as possible the pieces were shipped either coastwise by hoy, as from the New Forest to Portsmouth and from Dean to Plymouth,[2] or by river, as from Alice Holt down the Wey to Chatham and London.[3] But even

[1] Which gave its name to the unit of measurement.

[2] P.R.O.Adm. 49/120, f. 13; Albion, loc. cit. p. 108.

[3] P.R.O.Adm. 1/3557, f. 577.

so, they had first to be taken to the water's edge, and carriage, dependent on the horse- or ox-waggon moving with its small load along the narrow, winding and frequently muddy lanes and roads,[1] was expensive and slow. The counties in which the timber was cut had therefore to bear the cost of its purveyance, provided that it was for the navy or ordnance, by Act of Parliament, for which they were paid only partly by the King. This imposition—the last remnant of the Ship Money controversy to which it had originally been related—was naturally highly unpopular, and the economy was often purchased only at the expense of further delay. In 1695 it was abolished, and thereafter the navy had to pay the full price for carriage by land.[2]

But in comparison with the cost of transport from overseas, that of domestic transport was low. It has been estimated that the price of English timber was often doubled between the time it was cut and the time it reached the yards, while that of Baltic timber was raised twenty times during the same process.[3] This remarkably high cost was mainly due to the complications of the voyage. The timber merchant had first to find the shipping for his cargo. English vessels were unpopular, for under the terms of the Navigation Acts it was uneconomic to compete with the Baltic powers in building the medium-sized, shallow and beamy vessels which the foreign timber trade demanded.[4] English shipping on the Baltic run therefore consisted normally of tramps and veterans: worn-out packets from the ocean trades, unsuitable and often decaying; Newcastle colliers which had seen their best days, or were merely varying their usual trip down the English coast, spoiling the wood with their black holds; and miscellaneous tramps, often manned by captains who had failed to hold their jobs elsewhere. Under these circumstances, the English merchants liked to deal so far as possible in foreign

---

[1] In 1698 an attempt was made by statute to widen the roads in general (8 and 9 Will. III, c. 16). Various private Acts were also passed to repair and improve particular highways.

[2] The Act in force in 1688 was 1 Jac. II, c. 11, prolonging 13 and 14 Car. II, c. 20. It was in turn prolonged to 1695 by 4 Will. and Mary c. 24, and then not renewed.

[3] Albion, loc. cit. pp. 151–2. For conditions of felling and transporting fir in the Baltic itself, before it reached the ports, see the review of Loudon's *Trees and Shrubs of Britain*, in *Quarterly Review*, no. 124, p. 354.

[4] For details, see Barbour, loc. cit. pp. 270–1.

shipping;[1] and cheaper and better though this might be on purely technical grounds, in the conditions of a war it involved constant delay and negotiation before the cargo was safely delivered, which only a trader of some standing and interest could count upon regularly overcoming.

The voyage itself might be a lengthy and hazardous affair. To get a cargo to England from the Sound or Norway in wartime involved the three antipathetic interests of the English Admiralty, which had to provide a convoy, the privateer, and the governments of the countries from which the cargo was shipped and through whose waters it passed. Any one of the three could prevent or delay the journey, itself limited to some extent by the weather. The merchants naturally preferred a summer voyage to what they called a 'winter adventure',[2] and normally tried to arrange for two such passages between May and October, to fulfil the contracts which were annually made in the spring.[3] But convoys were not always available, through diversions—largely caused by the privateering activities of Du Bart[4]—adverse winds or administrative inefficiency; and the Minute books of both Admiralty and Navy Board are full of complaints and petitions for an escort.

When the escort was provided, the regular convoy route which emerged from these difficulties involved a lengthy and interrupted passage.[5] If there were any ships ready to go to Hamburg, the whole Baltic convoy might sail first to that port, then up to the Sound, where the ships for Denmark and Riga were detached, and then by way of

---

[1] In peacetime it was estimated that not above half the trade was in English bottoms (*H.C.J.* XII, p. 432). For wartime examples of the extent of trading in foreign bottoms, see P.R.O.Adm. 1/3578, ff. 304–5.

[2] P.R.O.Adm. 1/3570, f. 301.

[3] See pp. 62–4 below.

[4] There was a difference between the attacks of the single privateer, which did comparatively little damage, and the deprivations of the Dunkirk squadrons, which became so serious that small allied forces of third and fourth rates, with an acting flag officer in command (see pp. 455, 572 below), had to be sent to blockade the port whenever intelligence suggested a sortie. In the first year of the war it was even suggested that the island of Heligoland should be rented from the Duke of Holstein and turned into a base from which small men-of-war could cover the route to the Sound against such attacks; nothing, however, came of this (Margery Lane, 'Heligoland in 1689', in *E.H.R.* XXX, pp. 704–5).

[5] The following details are taken from various instances in P.R.O.Adm. 3/1 and 3/2, not all of which are exactly alike.

Stockholm to Norway, where the mastships were left. The return voyage, if escorts were short or additional precautions necessary, instead of being made by the Norwegian and Baltic ships separately in different convoys, might also begin at Larsen, continue via Stockholm and Elsinore—where there was often a wait of a fortnight or more for various ships which either had not arrived from the upper Baltic or had not finished loading—to Hamburg, and possibly, if there were cruisers covering the Channel approaches, to Holland as well to pick up the canvas ships. From there, the convoy would make for the Downs, where normally some of it would be detached for Portsmouth, while the rest sailed for Chatham and the Thames. Each passage, with changing winds and changing intelligence of enemy movements in the North Sea, might take over a month, while the ships, even if they were not interrupted in their loading, needed another month at their various ports for the slowest of them to be ready for the return trip. If such interruptions occurred, the duration of a voyage became a matter of guess-work rather than of calculation.

The time which the ships took to load and to reach their rendezvous was determined by the prevalent attitude of the governments in whose countries they were trading. The two principal powers involved were

Iron	£70,000
Hemp	£90,000
Wire	£10,000
Pitch and tar	£15,000
Copper, masts, deals, furs, etc.	£20,000
Total	£205,000[1]

Sweden and Denmark, which themselves produced most of the material either from their own lands or from their respective dependencies of Finland and Norway, and which controlled the passage of what they did not produce through their possession of the two shores of the Sound. The other two powers which bordered the Baltic and exported timber were Prussia, with its port of Königsberg, and Poland, with the

[1] B.M.Harl. 1324, f. 38*v*. The same figures appear in the Board of Trade's report for 1698–9 in *H.C.J.* XII, p. 432. For other estimates during William's war, in which the value of hemp is given differently, see Duncombe's reports in G. N. Clark, *The Dutch Alliance and the War against French Trade, 1688–1697* (1923), appendix IV.

valuable port of Riga. But access to the west depended upon Sweden and Denmark, and the policy of the Baltic powers to the allies was formulated and carried out by these two countries. Their importance to England lay not only in the fact that they supplied the navy with timber and masts, but that they supplied it with other and equally necessary stores as well. Wood, indeed, was not their most valuable export. In 1697 the Board of Trade estimated the value of their trade into England on an average 'of late years' as shown in the table above. Not all of this went to the navy; but the proportion that did so in most cases amounted to its entire supply. Baltic imports, in fact, were essential before a ship could put to sea, and the relations between the interested governments were affected accordingly.

These relations remained delicate throughout the war. Despite the fact that Sweden and Denmark both belonged to the League of Augsburg, their traditional rivalry made it unlikely that any power outside the Baltic could enlist their joint support,[1] while domestic politics,[2] naval weakness,[3] disunity[4] and above all commercial

[1] See J. F. Chance, 'England and Sweden in the Time of William III and Anne', in *E.H.R.* XVI, pp. 676–711; 'William Duncombe's "summary report" of his mission to Sweden, 1689–1692', in *E.H.R.* XXXIX, p. 571; and Margery Lane, 'The Relations between England and the Northern Powers, 1689–1697; Part I, Denmark', in *Transactions of the Royal Historical Society*, 3rd series, vol. V, pp. 157–91.

[2] John Robinson, *An Account of Sueden* (1694), p. 80.

[3] The two fleets at the beginning of 1689 were as follows:

		Sweden	Denmark
First rate	(80–90 guns)	4	4
Second rate	(70–79 guns)	8	4
Third rate	(60–69 guns)	4*	3
Fourth rate	(40–59 guns)	13†	11
Fifth rate	(30–49 guns)	10	4
Sixth rate	(14–29 guns)	7	9
Total		46	35

* Two were being rebuilt in 1689. † Two were useless after 1680 and 1686 respectively.

Note that:

(*a*) Where alternative gunpower is given, the higher has been taken except where the variation exceeds ten guns. In such cases, the average has been taken.

(*b*) The rates are those given for Sweden after 1677.

(*c*) Danish floating batteries are not included. (*Soc. Naut. Research, Occas. Publns*, no. 5, pt III; 'Swedish Ships', compiled by H. J. Börjeson; 'Danish-Norwegian Ships', compiled by P. Holck.)

[4] G. N. Clark, *The Dutch Alliance and the War Against French Trade*, pp. 104–6.

advantage[1] made them neutrals, and often hostile neutrals at that. Although the Danes sent troops to Ireland in 1689, and the Swedes followed suit in Flanders in 1690 and 1691, these were merely mercenaries; while at sea, both powers confined themselves to sending observers with the allied fleet, in the manner of later neutrals.[2] Trading as they did in naval stores with both sides, they hesitated to throw their weight too heavily into the scales, and indeed their interest lay in an indecisive result and in the maintenance of an open trade. To the English government, however, the control of neutral trade was theoretically one of the chief weapons of war.[3] Unlike the Dutch burghers, with their maxim of 'free ships, free goods', many of the English merchants and William himself aimed at strangling French commerce by what amounted to a blockade; and thanks to their dominating position in the alliance they carried this point of view into the treaty with Holland of 1689, so that it represented, in theory at least, the policy of the maritime powers. Such a policy, as has been said, did 'not profess to exercise a belligerent right against neutrals, but in effect to forbid neutrality';[4] and it was bound to lead to trouble unless accompanied by overwhelming strength, which could not normally be spared for the Baltic during a hard-fought war. It was exacerbated moreover, at least in the case of England, by the vexed side-issue of the flag,[5] which furnished the lawyers with many a lucrative brief and the sea captains with many an excuse for an exchange of shot when the etiquette of the salute was not, in their opinion, exactly observed. At first the disputes were masked by an attempt of the English government in the winter of 1689–90 to con-

---

[1] Clark, loc. cit. pp. 99, 102; and see Robert Molesworth's remarks in his *Account of Denmark as it was in the Year 1692* (1694), pp. 226–7.

[2] The most notable of these missions was sent by Sweden in 1693, consisting of a vice-admiral and five captains (P.R.O.Adm. 3/8:7/7/93).

[3] For a full discussion on this point see Sir Francis Piggott, 'Ships' Timber and Contraband of War', in *Quarterly Review*, no. 468, pp. 93–111.

[4] John Westlake, *International Law* (1904), II, p. 226, cited by Clark, loc. cit. p. 33.

[5] See T. W. Fulton, *The Sovereignty of the Sea* (1911), particularly pp. 1–22, 517–20. The most recent statement of the issue at this time was Charles Molloy's *De Jure Maritimo et Navale* (4th ed. 1688); see also *The Petty Papers*, I, pp. 219–41. The question was still not dead in the middle of the eighteenth century; Thomas Corbett, then Secretary of the Admiralty, devoted considerable attention to it in his *Digests*, and discussed it before any other right or department of the navy (Admty: Corbett, vol. 1).

tract for all the Swedish tar available for export.[1] The negotiations dragged on for some months, but after they had fallen through the effort to provide an attractive economic alternative to the practice of open trade was abandoned in favour of a simple blockade by force. The results were soon to be seen. In 1690 and 1691 many arrests were made in the Downs and the Channel of Baltic shipping on its way to France;[2] in 1692, 34 Danish ships alone were cited as prize in the Admiralty Courts; in 1693, when Delavall held up an entire convoy bound for France, 71; and in 1694, 90 Swedes were similarly cited.[3] The seizures continued to the end of the war; one of the most notorious occurred in its last year, when in July 1697 Rooke brought in a whole convoy of ninety sail which had been under the escort of a Swedish man-of-war.[4]

The Baltic powers were not slow to retaliate. Their joint efforts were unimpressive, for their defensive alliance of 1690 and the joint conventions for the protection of trade of 1691 and 1693 were seldom implemented in practice, and were moreover disturbed by unilateral agreements which both governments signed with William, in 1691, 1693 and 1696, modifying the belligerents' rights of search.[5] But individually they proved on occasion more effective. In December 1690, the Danes confiscated six Dutch ships; they did the same again in 1691; and in November 1693 they stopped seventeen allied ships in the Sound and refused to let them go for the whole winter, with serious consequences to the naval stores.[6] Sweden did not resort to action of this kind,[7] but preferred to make use of her existing trade laws to penalize the allied merchants in that country. By a statute of 1617, any foreign merchant who did not become a burgher could at any time be forced to leave the country, under pain of heavy taxation on all his commercial transactions. Many of the resident Dutch traders were in the habit of becoming burghers, but the English were not and were thus always

---

1 Clark, loc. cit. p. 100.

2 E.g. P.R.O.Adm. 3/3: 18/5, 24/7; 3/4: 4/1, 18/2.

3 Clark, loc. cit. p. 113; *Cal.S.P.Dom. 1694–5*, pp. 290, 297.

4 Clark, loc. cit. p. 114.

5 Ibid. pp. 104–13.

6 P.R.O.Adm. 1/3574, f. 1157.

7 But it was feared that she might in 1693 (*Cal.S.P.Dom. 1693*, p. 60).

liable to the provisos of the Act.[1] These had seldom been enforced; but in October 1694 they were revived. English and Dutch merchants who were not burghers were then forbidden to stay in Sweden for more than two months in the year without paying the exorbitant taxes to the full, and the prohibition was not fully lifted for the rest of the century.[2]

This type of action, although not affecting the English importers themselves, crippled the agents who in many cases acted for them;[3] and even when not so directly expressed, the fluctuating course of Anglo-Swedish and Anglo-Danish relations was faithfully reflected in the difficulties which the agents encountered. Unlike earlier Baltic wars, on this occasion the war for supply was fought not by the navies themselves but by diplomats and traders. It might be thought that under such conditions the government could operate better through an agent or purveyor, who would be directly under its orders and armed with its direct support, than through a number of independent merchants whose interests at times might not coincide with its own; and in fact, in the early days of the trade this was how it had conducted its business.[4] But by 1660 the first of the great timber merchants, Sir William Warren, who at that time held virtually a monopoly of the domestic market outside the system of purveyors, had extended his activities to the Baltic,[5] and his initial success was soon followed by the appearance of rivals, of whom John Taylor was possibly the first, and who in the next thirty years first combined to defeat Warren and then divided the market more or less between themselves. Under these circumstances the royal agents in the Baltic ports became largely redundant, and in Charles II's reign they began to disappear.[6] The merchants who took their place were therefore affected by the state of diplomatic relations, not only as private traders, but to some extent as agents for their government; and they had to be men of some substance to withstand the vexations and delays which their official connexion imposed upon their business on both sides of the North Sea. The natural hazards of the

---

1 Robinson, loc. cit. p. 149.

2 Clark, loc. cit. p. 101.

3 Serg:Mins. XXXIV, 27/3; XXXVI, 21/4.

4 Albion, loc. cit. pp. 55–6; Sir William Beveridge, *Prices and Wages in England* (1939), I, pp. 610–12.

5 *H.M.C. Supplement to Lindsey*, pp. 116–54.

6 Albion, loc. cit. p. 56.

voyage, and the cumulative obstacles which were added to it, set a definite minimum of expenditure below which no business could hope to survive. An analysis of the foreign timber trade in 1689 and 1690, even before the full impact of these difficulties had been felt, accordingly shows a different type of merchant from the small man of the domestic market.

Compared with the 34 merchants who contracted with the navy during this period for domestic timber, fifteen contracted with it for Baltic masts and timber.[1] Of these, three dealt exclusively in Riga masts, three in plank, and three in deals; while one dealt exclusively in swathing board. The other five handled all types of wood, including masts.[2] The merchants trading exclusively in plank and deals were all small men, whose names do not reappear after 1690. Of the former the largest handled four contracts, all for under 100 loads of plank, one handled two and one handled one; of the latter, one handled two contracts and the other two one each. The largest was for 590 deals. The trader in swathing board had three contracts. The traders in Riga masts dealt mostly in larger quantities, although the number of their contracts was in each case small. Two of the three consisted of two partners each—John Taylor and Nathaniel Gould, and Grimble and Wray; the other merchant was Sir Benjamin Ayloff. He fulfilled only one contract, for a total of 52 Riga masts, while Taylor and Gould handled two contracts, amounting to 78 Riga masts and 525 Gothenburgh and Norwegian masts, and Grimble and Wray two, amounting to nineteen masts of different kinds. Of these three firms, one—Taylor and Gould—who later split into separate concerns, survived into later years.

Thus most of the smaller men, who traded in one commodity alone,

---

[1] And one for American masts.

[2] P.R.O.Adm. 49/29. I have described the relative importance of these men in terms of quantities and contracts handled and not, as might seem more reasonable, in terms of the monetary value of their contracts, because the figures for the latter, as given in this source, are subject to various qualifications which make it difficult to assess their value correctly. It is impossible to tell whether discount or interest is included in the rates agreed upon, and if so, whether they appear equally in all the figures or only in some; and it is equally impossible to discover the terms on which payment was made—a very important factor in assessing a dealer's importance.

were weeded out fairly quickly. The big contracts were handled from the beginning by a few of the general importers of timber. Of the five who did this type of business in 1689–90—Astell, John Butcher, the partners Sir William Warren and Francis Riggs, Sir Peter Rich, and Halfjar Samuelson—three—Butcher, Riggs and Rich—continued to do so later. Astell and Samuelson handled one foreign contract each, Butcher six, Warren and Riggs three and Rich eighteen. The latter was incomparably the biggest man in the trade, in the size as well as in the number of his contracts. It was not unusual for him to agree to deliver 500 spars and over 8000 deals, or thirty masts and 1000 loads of plank, in individual contracts. The contrast with the domestic market, even at this date, was obvious.

Soon, however, the tritons swallowed the minnows completely. In 1690 the Navy Board estimated that it would need 1728 Baltic masts for the following year. Of these, 998 were furnished by two contractors alone, John Taylor and Joseph Martin.[1] Again, when a large programme of war construction was approved by Parliament in 1691, and the Navy Board accordingly estimated the number of masts needed from the Baltic, it arrived at a total of 2586; and of these Taylor, Martin and Francis Riggs were able between them to supply 1567. In both instances Rich supplied a large proportion of the rest.[2] The case was much the same with plank, timber and deals. In the negotiations between the Navy Board and the Baltic merchants after 1690 the same group of men reappears every year, imposing its prices upon its competitors and in turn, particularly in the later years of the war when it was to the interest of big and small merchants alike to have standard rates and uniform conditions in the trade, representing them in the discussions with the Administration.

The same few merchants were concerned in the other naval stores from the Baltic. Apart from wood, the materials used to equip a man-of-war were hemp, canvas, iron, pitch, tar, tallow, rosin, oil and brimstone. The financial value of these stores in the total cost of a

---

[1] P.R.O.Adm. 95/13, f. 117.

[2] Ibid. ff. 197–8, 205. In neither case have small spars or bowsprits been included.

man-of-war is indicated approximately by the cost (given in pounds) of setting a new ship to sea:[1]

	Hull, masts and yards	Sails, rigging and stores for eight months
First rate	22,535	5,333
Second rate	16,550	3,938
Third rate	8,820	2,814
Fourth rate	5,010	1,889
Fifth rate	2,191	1,180
Sixth rate	1,216	527

Apart from canvas, tallow and oil, these stores came wholly or in part from the Baltic; and if we examine the structure of the trade, the importance of a few dealers is once more apparent.[2] The hemp merchants who dealt in the Baltic in 1689 and 1690 numbered twenty, of whom seven handled only one small contract each and four two contracts each. Four had three contracts, four had four and one had five. Most of the contracts were for between five and twenty tons of hemp, but a few men dealt in larger amounts. William Gore, Joseph Martin and Peter Joy each handled more than one contract for over 200 tons at a time, and the first two were among the four men who had four contracts each, while Joy had three. Others who operated in this trade on a smaller scale, were John Taylor and Nathaniel Gould. The other commodities—pitch, tar and rosin—were sold under one general heading. In this trade there were twelve merchants, of whom seven handled one contract each in 1689 and 1690. Two handled two contracts, two three, and one six, but there were no great variations in the amounts sold. No dealer disposed of more than ten tons of tar or rosin,

---

[1] Pep:Sea MS. 977, f. 105. These figures are not absolutely correct for two reasons. First, they include wages to workmen in each case, which introduces an unequal factor in the two columns owing to the different rates of pay for the different types of skilled men required in the two kinds of work. Secondly, some of the tar, pitch, tallow and rosin is included in the first column.

The proportions of the two columns remain the same, although the figures themselves have risen, in 1701, in N.M.M. MS., 'Tables, Wages, Estimates etc. 1692–1732', no. 4, and again in 1717, in William Sutherland's *Britain's Glory*, pp. xi–xii. The Navy Board estimated in 1690 that the respective figures for a fourth rate would be £4272 and £2200, in 1693 for a fifth £2970 and £1485, and in 1694 for a sixth £1625 and £650 (P.R.O.Adm. 7/169, nos. 3, 18, 31). None of the figures for equipment given above includes gunner's stores.

[2] P.R.O.Adm. 49/29, *passim*.

or of more than sixty lasts of pitch in any one consignment. Here again a few familiar names appear, although not in a dominating position. The man who had six contracts was William Fownes, unknown in the other Baltic trades; but Nathaniel Gould, William Gore and Peter Joy were among those who handled either one or two contracts. Indeed, if a list is made of the six or seven most prominent men in the different trades, two or three of them will usually be found to be concerned in more than one activity:[1]

	Wood and masts	Hemp	Tar, pitch and rosin
Fownes	—	—	Yes
Gore	—	Yes	Yes
Gould	Yes	Yes	Yes
Joy	—	Yes	Yes
Martin	Yes	Yes	Yes
Rich	Yes	—	—
Riggs	Yes	—	—
Taylor	Yes	Yes	Yes

Of these men, all but Riggs were creditors of the government on their private as well as their public account. Gore lent £8677, Taylor £5325, Martin £4450, Joy £3050, Rich £4700 and Gould £950 to the Crown between March 1689 and May 1690. The only other Baltic merchants who lent privately were Heathcote, who lent £4575, and Burrell, who lent £1200.[2] Such loans constituted a bond between the lenders, and an obligation on the part of the borrower, which might be reflected outside the immediate transaction. The first point is illustrated by the terms and the timing of the loans. It is particularly interesting to note that in every case except for a loan of £2700 from Joy and of £1200 from Rich, they were made on the same fund of government credit—the two shillings aid—and within three weeks of each other.[3] The navy had to reckon for most of its imported stores with a well-defined and apparently well-organized group of big merchants.

We are fortunately able to pursue the consequences of these facts, and to see to some extent what pressure these men were able to bring upon the navy, thanks to the way in which the contracts were drawn up. In view of the difficulties of the trade, the navy preferred to contract

---

[1] P.R.O.Adm. 49/29, 95/13.

[2] *Cal.Treas.Bks. 1689–92*, pp. 1971–2008.

[3] Ibid. particularly pp. 1194–5. The fund was guaranteed by the statute 1 Will. and Mary, sess. 2, c. 1.

for its Baltic stores annually in one large transaction as early as possible in the spring, to allow time for one or even two summer voyages.[1] To this end it advertised for tenders in the *Gazette*,[2] and also sent one of the clerks from the Navy Office to the Exchange to invite the better-known merchants to attend on a certain day.[3] There was thus every opportunity for concerted action on their part; and they were not slow to take it. The negotiations for the contracts of 1690 are a typical example of what took place in each of the early years of the war.[4] After the usual invitations had been circulated, on this occasion in the second week in May, the 'East Country merchants' attended the Navy Office in a body on Monday 19 May, to tender for hemp, pitch and tar. After discussing the manner of their payment, they were asked to send in their tenders on the following Friday, 'sealed up'. On Friday, therefore, they appeared in front of a full Board and, after hearing the terms of payment, withdrew 'to Counsell amongst themselves'. After an interval, they announced that they were not all ready, but would come again on the following Monday. Several, however—including Taylor, Gore and Joy—made private visits a few hours later to tender on their own, but after a preliminary argument over prices were asked to come in on the following Tuesday, the day after the general meeting. Over the week-end the Monday conference was postponed until Tuesday, and accordingly on 27 May, with most of the Navy Board present, all the merchants attended. The detailed bargaining then began over the sealed tenders. Each man was called in separately—first William Gore, then Martin, then Gould and then Taylor, followed by the others in order—and all the offers heard. At first all were refused, and Gore was then called in again, and at length agreed on a price for some of the hemp. The others who followed still refused, but when the whole assembly was once more summoned most of the dealers took the navy's offer, and the rest came in later individually to accept it. This, however, disposed of only some of the stores required, and the whole process began again at once for the rest. Throughout the next week, individual merchants

[1] The merchants were always anxious, but in the event seldom able to make two voyages (P.R.O.Adm. 1/3566, ff. 49–55; 1/3571, ff. 287–8).

[2] See *London Gazette*, normally in March of any of the war years.

[3] E.g. Serg:Mins. XXIII, 22/4; XXXIV, 22/4.

[4] The following account is taken from Serg:Mins. XXI.

called in from time to time to bargain over individual lots, until on 4 June, at another general meeting, the contracts were finally agreed upon. On this occasion, as had happened on 27 May, the dealers again acted together at the beginning and the end of the negotiations, first all refusing and later all accepting certain prices. The signing of the contracts followed over the next few days. The prices, in the end, were rather nearer those originally asked by the merchants than those originally offered by the navy.

In 1690, the war was still at an early stage, and the dealers could still be persuaded to some extent to act individually. Later, when the decline of naval credit had become really serious, and they seemed to be threatened with ruin, their unity was more marked at every stage. But even at the beginning of the war their negotiations were quite unlike those of any of the other naval contractors, and it is perhaps not without significance that the prices of their goods rose uniformly and sharply during its first year. With the exception of masts and timber, which offer peculiar difficulties in assessing prices, they were as follows:[1]

	Hemp:[2] shillings per cwt.	Pitch: shillings per ton	Tar: shillings per last	Rosin: shillings per cwt.
1688	25·83	124	124–210	13·33
1689	27	203·3	220–225	16·39

But if the Baltic merchants were able to bargain successfully, and to some extent collectively, with the navy, it must also be remembered that they in turn depended upon it to a considerable extent. What proportion of their total business its custom represented I have been unable to discover. To William Gore and Nathaniel Gould, who also dealt with the army, it was perhaps less than to some of the others; but many, including perhaps these two men, did most if not all of their business with the government in some form, even if not exclusively with the navy, and were involved accordingly in the stability of government credit. It was only in the last resort that most of them could afford to break with the navy, however badly it paid them; and to us the chief importance of the big East Country merchants lies in the fact that,

[1] Beveridge, loc. cit. pp. 673, 676.

[2] Presumably including hemp from sources outside the Baltic; but this was such a small proportion of the total that it may be accepted.

representing as they did the most powerful group of naval contractors, their protests and their concerted action at various stages of the war illustrate, more exactly than the action of their colleagues in other trades, the nature and the limitations of the pressure which the contractors as a class could put upon the navy in the difficult financial conditions of the war.

Although the Baltic supplied most of the naval stores, it could not produce them all. Iron, hemp and canvas came from other European countries. Swedish iron, although acknowledged to be better than English, was not so satisfactory as Spanish, which the navy demanded for the manufacture of anchors whenever possible.[1] The names of the iron merchants do not seem to be recorded.[2] Hemp could be procured from Russia as well as from Riga and Königsberg,[3] although it was acknowledged that Riga cordage had no rival for quality and, owing partly to disputes with Russia earlier in the century, was not in fact rivalled in quantity during the war.[4] Such Russian hemp as was imported for the navy, however, was handled exclusively by two of the Baltic merchants, Martin and Taylor.[5] In the later years of the war, efforts were made by legislation to encourage the growth of hemp in Ireland,[6] and some was also grown in East Anglia;[7] but this never supplied more than a fraction of the demand. Canvas came from Holland, France or Germany. The best material for sails was the Vitré canvas from France, but this fell under the ban on trading with the enemy which was imposed, as part of the intended blockade, before the outbreak of war. At the time there was no canvas manufactured in England, and despite attempts during the next few years to encourage it by legislation,[8] the navy continued to depend on imported material

---

1 Admty:Corbett, xv, f. 51.

2 I have been unable to find them in P.R.O.Adm. 49/29, 20/50, 95/113 or 95/114.

3 The latter was known at the time as 'Queenborough hemp'.

4 Serg:Misc. v, f. 409. See Ima Lubimenko, 'The Struggle of the Dutch with the English for the Russian Market in the Seventeenth Century', in *Transactions of the Royal Historical Society*, 4th series, vol. VII, pp. 27–51.

5 P.R.O.Adm. 49/29.

6 7 and 8 Will. III, c. 39.

7 Lord Ernle, *English Farming, Past and Present* (1926), p. 136.

8 7 and 8 Will. III, c. 10, art. 14.

in the form of 'Holland duck', and 'German' and 'Carroll' canvas. Five merchants contracted for these imports in 1689 and 1690, two handling one contract each, two handling two each, and one handling eleven.[1] The last of these, who then and later entirely dominated the market, was William Gore. The two men with two contracts each were Joy and Taylor, while Martin had one contract. In fact, the only canvas merchant who was not also a Baltic merchant was a man named Edmunson. With the convoy route from the Sound passing the Dutch and German ports, and with Hamburg, the main German timber port, also handling all the German canvas, the close connexion between the trades was perhaps not very surprising. As a result, the conditions for the purchase and sale of canvas, so far as the navy was concerned, were similar to those for Baltic stores.

Oil and brimstone came from farther afield. The first came from America and, apart from masts, was the only naval store imported from the colonies during the war. America for some two decades had been proposed as an alternative, or even a preferable source of supply to the Baltic on strategic and mercantilist grounds, for besides the constant threat of war England enjoyed an adverse balance of trade with the Northern Crowns.[2] But thanks to unfavourable reports of American wood, and to the conservatism of naval opinion, nothing was done in the course of the French war. The question of importing timber and plank from New England was raised many times by the colonial agents in London, and the Navy Board was asked to report;[3] but until 1696, when the Baltic stores seemed more likely than usual to be stopped, and when the agent for New England made a particularly vigorous effort to interest the government in the resources of the colonies,[4] no action was taken.[5] In that year, the government sent out four agents—two on

---

[1] P.R.O.Adm. 49/29, *passim.*

[2] David Macpherson, *Annals of Commerce, Manufacture, Fisheries, and Navigation...* (1805), II, p. 719. See also Clark, loc. cit. appendix IV.

[3] E.g. P.R.O.Adm. 1/3571, 22/2/9 (unfoliated); 1/3578, ff. 953, 1147–55; 1/3579, ff. 797–807; 3/11; 18/3, 14/5, 20/7.

[4] P.R.O.Adm. 1/4083, f. 1037.

[5] Jahleel Brenton had been sent out in 1691 as the Crown's agent general for woods and forests, and the same year the legislature of Massachusetts Bay was forbidden to fell any trees marked by him as reserved for naval use (P.R.O.Adm. 3/4: 4/3; Admty:Corbett, XV, f. 61). But these actions referred only to masts at the time.

behalf of the Admiralty, and two for the Board of Trade and the merchants—to report on the possibility of importing naval stores in general from America.[1] But their report, which was not received for five years, only confirmed the adverse reports on New England products which had already been made by the Navy Board,[2] and it was not until 1704, when the problem again became urgent in a new war, that colonial stores for the navy were assisted by legislation[3] and that they began to be regularly supplied. Brimstone came mostly from Italy, although a little came also from the Baltic.[4] Tallow was manufactured in England.[5] Both oil and brimstone were contracted for almost exclusively by William Fownes, who dealt chiefly in Baltic pitch and tar, but odd ships going to the Mediterranean were also requested from time to time to bring back brimstone, and even warships were engaged on the trade.[6] Tallow was supplied by a number of domestic dealers, including the celebrated James Whiston, editor of *The Merchant's Remembrancer* in which the first regular quotations were made of stocks and shares.[7]

As well as contracting for all its supplies of raw material, the navy also contracted in some cases for their manufacture. Apart from the ship herself, whose construction will be considered later,[8] some of her gear was made on standing contracts selected by tender. The goods so supplied were usually stores in regular demand, but involving processes in their manufacture which the average unskilled workman could not undertake. The terms were usually the same: to supply a particular dockyard with the items required 'for one year certain', with six months' notice on either side.[9] The system began about 1670,[10] and by

---

1 P.R.O.Adm. 3/13:20/8; *Cal.S.P.Col. Am. & W.I., 1696–7*, p. 542.
2 Albion, loc. cit. pp. 239–41.
3 3 and 4 Anne, c. 9.
4 P.R.O.Adm. 29/49.
5 Ibid.
6 Ibid.; P.R.O.Adm. 3/6: 14/7; 3/10:18/4.
7 P.R.O.Adm. 49/29.
8 See pp. 70–9 below.
9 P.R.O.Adm. 49/120. See also Beveridge, loc. cit. p. 613.
10 Ibid.

the beginning of the French war the standing contracts stood as follows:[1]

	Chatham since:	Deptford since:	Woolwich since:	Sheerness since:	Portsmouth since:
Anchor smith	3 Jan. 1683	3 Jan. 1683	19 Oct. 1686	23 Nov. 1688	2 July 1685
Ironmonger	9 May 1687	9 May 1687	9 May 1687	9 May 1687	25 May 1687
Glazier and plasterer	29 June 1687	22 June 1687 (Aug. 1683)	22 June 1687 (?)	29 June 1687	22 June 1687 (Aug. 1683)
Brazier	24 Jan. 1687	10 Dec. 1686 (July 1678)	10 Dec. 1686 (?)	—	13 July 1687
Plumber	11 May 1687	11 May 1687	11 May 1687	—	13 July 1687
Sailmaker	24 June 1686	24 June 1686	24 June 1686	—	24 June 1686
Cooper	1 June 1687	25 June 1687	25 June 1687	—	1 Oct. 1687
Compass and watch glassmaker	—	17 Nov. 1686	17 Nov. 1686	—	—
Colours (i.e. flags)	—	3 Jan. 1687	3 Jan. 1687	—	—
Painter	22 Feb. 1688	22 Feb. 1688	22 Feb. 1688	—	22 Feb. 1688
Tanner	15 June 1687 (Jan. 1677)	15 June 1687 (Jan. 1677)	15 June 1687	—	18 Aug. 1687
Turner	—	17 Nov. 1686	17 Nov. 1686	—	—
Tile maker	—	4 Nov. 1687	—	—	—
Blockmaker	—	—	—	—	4 Mar. 1687
Handscrews	—	18 May 1687	—	—	—
Lead and solder	Aug. 1676	May 1687	May 1687 (?)	—	—

The tradesmen who undertook these contracts formed a small group, which grew smaller as the war progressed. In many cases, one man contracted to supply more than one yard.[2] There were four anchor smiths to the five yards in 1688, but only two ironmongers, Robert Foley being ironmonger to all the eastern yards. Deptford, Woolwich and Portsmouth had the same glazier and plasterer, and likewise Chatham and Sheerness. Chatham and Woolwich had one brazier, and Deptford and Woolwich one plumber and one cooper each. The two Thames yards also shared a compass maker, a 'colours man', a painter, a tanner and a turner. One tradesman, the sailmaker, handled the work for the whole navy.[3]

[1] This list has been compiled from the individual contracts entered in P.R.O.Adm. 49/120. It will be found to differ in several respects from that printed in Beveridge, loc. cit. pp. 615–16. To what extent the source used here was consulted by the Committee on Price History it is difficult to say, but I see no reason to doubt its authority. Where Beveridge gives an earlier date than P.R.O.Adm. 49/120, I have put it in brackets. As Beveridge does not mention Woolwich, and as it was sometimes included with Deptford in contracts, I have put a query against that yard wherever Deptford is mentioned.

[2] The following two paragraphs are based upon P.R.O.Adm. 49/120.

[3] See also P.R.O.Adm. 3/10:23/4, 16/5, 6/7/94, when the sailmaker was changed. He was referred to throughout as 'the sailmaker of the navy'.

In 1688, the standing contractors seldom handled more than one type of business, although there was an exception at Portsmouth, where Thomas Brouncker was both brazier and plumber to the yard. But in the war years, and particularly in the provincial yards of Portsmouth and Plymouth, the tendency towards monopoly increased rapidly, and by 1698 most of the standing contracts were handled either by a London trader who monopolized one trade in all the yards, or by a local trader who monopolized the remaining trades in one yard.

Such a development was not surprising. Standing contracts led usually to standard rates, which always reacted favourably on the bigger man. The nature of the work, moreover, was such that it had usually to be carried out in the dockyard itself, where it was more convenient for one man to handle it all. The sailmaker, the 'colours man' and the compass maker worked in London, but other trades could only be carried on locally. If all ironwork, or painting, or blockmaking were to be handled by contract, the contractor must be included in the same organization as the other ships' trades. He himself might not be a naval employee, but his work could not be separated from kindred activities which were managed by naval employees. As one observer put it, he was 'not of the yards but a dependent of them'.[1] The smith's shop and forge, the blockmaker's loft, and the shops of the painter, the turner, the pumpmaker, the cooper and the glazier were part of the yard which they served. It is therefore time to turn from the supply of material to the use which was made of it: from the market to the shipyard, and from the merchant to the naval workman and official.

---

[1] Henry Maydman, *Naval Speculations and Maritime Politicks* (1691), p. 96.

CHAPTER III

SHIPYARDS AND DOCKYARDS

When the materials had been delivered to the navy, they had to be stored, and then used to build and to maintain the ships. The problems which these three processes raised were distinct. Administratively, it was easier to build a ship than either to maintain her or to store her materials. Ideally, her construction and her maintenance should be undertaken at the same place; but this was neither always practicable, nor indeed necessary, and although the tendency throughout the second half of the seventeenth century was to concentrate the three activities in one place, the limitations of both resources and organization ensured that, at the end of it, the process was still far from complete.

In comparison with other activities, shipbuilding towards the end of the seventeenth century was a large-scale affair. When all its processes are considered, it was indeed one of the first crafts which can be said to have earned the name of an industry.[1] But so far as the construction of the hull alone was concerned, its scale to later eyes remains small. The conditions, indeed, were simple. First, the site itself had to be on the coast or on the bank of a tidal river, with a reasonable depth of water and a hard, sloping shore. In their crudest form, these physical conditions might be supplied by a seashore itself; and the smallest naval auxiliaries, the pinks and hoys, were quite often built on open beaches, as shown in sketches by the younger Vandervelde. Ready access to timber and skilled workmen, good communications by land or sea, and a large extent of waterfront and hard ground were all subsidiary advantages, increasingly necessary as the size of the organization increased, but all of which could be and often were dispensed with. Secondly, there were the conditions set by material. The only raw material needed on, or at all near, the site was wood, and that only for timber. Planks and trennels, as well as bolts, anchors, tar, pitch and rosin, and the later additions of masts, rigging and sails, could all be

[1] Nef, loc. cit. in *Ec.H.R.* v, no. 1, pp. 20–1.

sent to the site if necessary, although obviously the less need there was to do so the better. The wood, moreover, could stand in the open without attention for months at a time, even after the keel, stern and ribs were in place. It was only when the planking was begun, and the deck beams laid and covered with deals, that delay was technically inadvisable.[1] The small man, therefore, who might be unable to work fast, or who got into financial difficulties, was protected to some extent by his material. Finally there were the conditions set by the numbers and types of the workmen required. These were also unexacting. The essential workmen were of four types—shipwrights, caulkers, sawyers and ordinary labourers—and their numbers, at least for the smaller and medium rates, were few. It was only with the bigger ships, with their great timbers, their complicated internal arrangements and their external ornamentation,[2] that the figures rose steeply and the conditions changed. The numbers which follow illustrate the position:[3]

	Shipwrights	Caulkers	Sawyers[4]	Labourers
First rate	120	6	7	10
Second rate	110	5	6	10
Third rate	75	4	5	6
Fourth rate	40	3	3	4
Fifth rate	15	1	1	—
Sixth rate	8	1	—	—

How small the organization could be for building one of the lesser rates, even at the end of the century, is well shown by an example of a ship built in 1696. At that time, shipbuilding facilities in England were strained owing to the heavy programme of war construction, and the Navy Board accordingly proposed that one of the new fourth rates, for which estimates had been prepared, should be built in the Isle of Wight. A contract was signed with a Southampton man, Richard

[1] A good contemporary description of the construction of an English man-of-war occurs in J. B. Colbert, *Lettres, Instructions et Mémoires* (ed. P. Clément, 1865), III, pt 2, pp. 328–32.

[2] For the great difference in ornamentation between the three highest rates and the rest, see L. G. Carr Laughton, *Old Ships' Figureheads and Sterns*. External ornament reached its climax in the reign of William III (ibid. pp. 23–4).

[3] B.M. Stowe 144, f. 12. I do not know what class of third rate this list refers to.

[4] The sawyers almost certainly are 'pairs of sawyers' as a sawpit needed two men to work the saw, and in other documents referring to workmen they are given in pairs. In that case their numbers should be doubled.

Herring, who instead selected a site on the mainland, in an unfrequented reach of the unfrequented Beaulieu river, about four miles to the west of Southampton Water.[1] The site enjoyed a hard which ran inland from the shore for about two hundred yards and along it for about a hundred. There was plenty of timber, but the nearest village was over two miles away, and the nearest road about half a mile through dense woods. There was no record of any shipbuilding there before.[2] Herring got protections from the press for forty shipwrights, sixteen sawyers (i.e. eight pairs), fifteen labourers and two 'timber hewers',[3] and cut a path from the hard through the woods to the road.[4] Using local timber, which he bought from the lord of the manor and which was felled for him by the tenants and manor workmen,[5] he proceeded to build a ship of 682 tons burthen, 134 feet long and with 34 feet beam.[6] The work went slowly, largely owing to financial difficulties, and eventually in the spring of 1698 the workmen, who presumably lived in the villages of the New Forest, left and the ship lay neglected for some months. In the summer, Portsmouth dockyard sent men and materials by water to finish her off, and she was launched later that year.[7] When she had left the river, the woods again grew over the little hard, the path disappeared, and forty years later, when a shipyard was set up on the same site, all trace of any activity had long since vanished.[8] In other parts of the country, near Bristol and at Hazell on the Humber, a few fourth rates and even a 60-gun third rate were built in similar conditions

---

1 P.R.O.Adm. 106/489: Herring to Navy Board, 27 Feb. 1696, and Board comment.

2 I am indebted for these facts to the kindness of the Trustees of Beaulieu Manor, who put contemporary estate maps at my disposal. The place, Bucklers Hard, became a well-known shipyard in the course of the eighteenth century, but no record of this fourth rate exists locally.

3 P.R.O.Adm. 106/489: Navy Board endorsement on Herring's letter of 27 Feb. 1696.

4 Estate maps of 1690 and 1701 compared.

5 P.R.O.Adm. 106/507: Herring to Navy Board, 22 Jan. 1698.

6 *Soc. Naut. Research, Occas. Publns*, no. 5, pt I, no. 967. The ship was the *Salisbury* of 48 guns.

7 P.R.O.Adm. 106/507: Herring to Navy Board, 8 Jan. 1698, 5 March 1698; 3/14: 19 Jan. 1698; 2/394, Bridgeman to Navy Board, 25 Feb. 1698.

8 Estate maps of early eighteenth century; and see Lord Montagu of Beaulieu, *Bucklers Hard and its Ships* (1909).

during the war.[1] But they represented the largest ships to be so treated, and then it was only at a busy time and under great necessity that such ventures were proposed and carried through.

Normally, the navy preferred to build its medium rates in properly constituted shipyards. These were all in England[2] and, although they were permanent and not *ad hoc* sites, were still not necessarily of any great size. They were controlled either by the navy itself or by merchant shipbuilders, the latter building on contract obtained by competitive tender, at a rate of so many pounds per ton.[3] Unfortunately, little is known about these merchants, for almost all their records have since disappeared and it is only from their letters to the navy, scattered over many volumes of its miscellaneous correspondence, that any picture of them can be obtained.[4] They were grouped mostly round the Thames. Of the English fleet in 1688, out of 21 ships of the first six rates built in merchant yards, fourteen came from the River:[5] of the rest, one was built in the Medway, one in Essex, two in Sussex, one in Hampshire, and two in Gloucestershire.[6] Of the Thames shipbuilders one was

---

[1] See p. 433 below.

[2] In 1693, the possibility of building third rates at Lübeck was examined; but, after considerable correspondence, it was abandoned (P.R.O.Adm. 3/8: 12 Dec. 1692; B.M. Lansdowne 1153, II, f. 16). In 1694, Taylor, the mast importer, built a fourth rate for the navy in New England, and in 1696 a Mr Partridge offered to build some men-of-war there. But Taylor's ship was built first and offered to the navy afterwards, and Partridge's proposal was turned down (P.R.O.Adm. 3/9: 4/1; 3/12: 18/3; Admty:Corbett, VIII, f. 4). In 1694 it was also proposed that some small men-of-war should be built in Ireland; but nothing came of it (P.R.O.Adm. 3/9: 9/3). Apart from these instances, there was no question of building any warships outside the country during the war.

[3] In 1691, Phineas Pett, the contemporary representative of the great shipbuilding family, offered to build two men-of-war on commission in his yard; but the proposal —so far as I know the only one of its kind during the war—was turned down (P.R.O.Adm. 2/171, f. 353; 3/6: 24/7).

[4] Some records of this period, belonging to the Shipwrights' Company, have now been destroyed by fire; and, apart from the miscellaneous letters mentioned, the only surviving collection of papers belonging to a merchant shipbuilder of the period appears to be the two volumes of Sir Henry Johnson's papers (B.M.Addnl. 22183–4) which, though interesting, are disappointing.

[5] See Appendix I(E) below. See also *Catal.* I, p. 224.

[6] Appendix I(E) below.

considerably larger than his rivals. This was Sir Henry Johnson, whose yard at Blackwall built five third rates for the navy between 1660 and 1688, almost double the number built by any of his contemporaries. Blackwall yard, indeed, was the only merchant yard capable of rivalling the royal dockyards in its facilities, and it provides an interesting contrast to the building sites which represent merchant shipyards at the other end of the scale. Founded at the end of the sixteenth century, it soon became associated with the newly constituted East India Company, from which in 1612 it took its name.[1] As the Company grew, so did the extent and the equipment of the yard. Houses were built for its officers at Poplar, next to the Company's almshouses, and lodgings for workmen followed in later decades. The Johnsons became connected with it in the 1630's, and by 1653 the elder Henry had bought it outright. The next year it began to build men-of-war for the navy. In 1679 its owner was knighted in his house at the yard by Charles II, and in 1683 he was succeeded in the business by his son, the younger Henry. The Johnsons were now substantial men: both Henrys and the latter's brother William represented Aldborough in Parliament, and William became Governor of Cape Coast Castle; the elder Sir Henry left money to build almshouses for 'six poore aged shipp carpenters' who, in the manner of the day, were to wear distinctive uniforms, designed by himself; and in 1685 the younger Henry in turn was knighted. By this time, Blackwall yard was one of the largest industries in the country. It had at least one dry dock, a large wet dock and a timber pond—facilities not available at all the royal yards—and a regular system of promotion for its officers which was not unlike that of the King's service. It still built most of the great East Indiamen, and its connexion with the Company as a port of discharge was very close; but its owner was now in close touch with the naval hierarchy as well, and even to its senior members he appeared as a patron rather than as a contractor.[2]

[1] The following account is taken from H. Green and R. Wigram, *Chronicles of Blackwall Yard* (1881). Green could trace a direct connexion with the Johnsons. The site of the yard is now swallowed in the East India Docks, the first of which was built in 1862.

[2] See the elder Johnson's correspondence with William Hewer and the younger's with Edmund Dummer, in 1678 and 1694 respectively, in B.M.Addnl. 22183, ff. 71–2, 209.

Without the connexion of the East India Company, Blackwall would never have risen to these heights. The other Thames yards—those of the brothers Castle and later of Edward Snellgrove at Deptford, of the younger Deane and later of James Taylor at Cuckold's Point, of Jonas Shish at Rotherhithe, of Haydon at Limehouse and of John Frame at Wapping[1]—were all far smaller affairs, though exactly how small it is difficult to say. Their limits were possibly fixed as much by space for storage as by space for building itself. Even Blackwall seems not to have held much in the way of stores, to judge from the admittedly slender evidence of one survey taken in September 1686, normally a busy month in any yard.[2] The stock at that time consisted of: straight oak timber, 59 loads; compass oak timber, 100 loads; elm, thirteen loads; knees of all sorts, sixteen; wale pieces, one; plank ($1\frac{1}{2}$ in. to 4 in.), 41 loads; sheathing board (1 in. to $1\frac{1}{2}$ in.), 46 feet; elm board ($\frac{3}{4}$ in. to 1 in.), two loads, 22 feet; and firboard ($\frac{3}{4}$ in. to 1 in.), two loads, 38 feet. In addition there were 82 shoars, four baulks and one new topmast.

The provincial yards seem normally to have been smaller than those of the Thames, but little is known either of their contents or their organization. Judging, however, by the speed with which some of them were founded in the war, and by the difficulty which the vastly superior naval yards experienced at the same time in erecting their more complex equipment and buildings, they were probably both small and crude, and in some cases possibly only one step removed from the *ad hoc* sites already alluded to on pp. 71–3.

The owners of these merchant yards in 1688, except for Sir Henry Johnson,[3] were all working shipwrights, and they suffered from the normal shipwright's lack of education. It was characteristic of many of them that they hardly ever seem to have written a letter to the navy in their own hand, but confined themselves to the signature.[4] The navy

---

[1] *Catal.* I, p. 223; B.M.Addnl. 9324, ff. 1–12.

[2] B.M.Addnl. 22184 f. 94. This list may, of course, have been made precisely because stores were low.

[3] 'An ingenious young gentleman, but above all personal labour, as being left too well provided for to work much' (Pepys's opinion of him, quoted in *Catal.* I, p. 78). In the context, 'work' means shipwright's work.

[4] Their letters are contained in the series P.R.O.Adm. 106/–.

professed to have a low opinion of their products, and this may not have been unjustified. It was a common charge that the dimensions of the warships built in private yards frequently differed from their specifications, and this seems to have had some substance. For of 69 of the third, fourth, fifth and sixth rates built by merchant yards during the war, only nineteen were as specified in the contract when surveyed by naval agents, and in several cases the discrepancies were considerable.[1] This, of course, does not mean to say that men-of-war built in the naval dockyards were built more exactly than in private yards, for on this point the tables are discreetly silent; but it is difficult at least to believe that they were built less exactly.

A second charge, that of waste, was also probably well founded, although the navy's accusations on this head were made, at least on occasion, in defence against similar allegations against itself.[2] According to one reckoning, the merchant shipbuilders wasted between a half and a third of their supplies,[3] and while this may have been an exaggeration there is no reason to doubt that ignorance as well as corruption led to a continual loss of material.

Months	Third rates	Fourth rates
10	—	2
11	—	1
12	—	1
13	3	—
14	1	—
15	1	2
17	—	1
18	1	—
24	1	—
29	1	—
31	2	—

Another and important charge was that men-of-war were built more slowly in merchant yards than in the royal dockyards. In this case, there are some figures on which to base the claim. It was usual to allow thirteen to fifteen months by contract for the launching of a third rate, and ten to twelve months for a fourth.[4] In the event, of eighteen ships

[1] B.M.Addnl. 9324, ff. 1–10. See also Appendix III below.

[2] E.g. the pamphlets of George Everett and Robert Crosfeild.

[3] Sutherland, *Ship-Builder's Assistant*, pp. 27–8.

[4] The individual contracts for ships which remain are contained in various bundles of P.R.O.Adm. 106/3069–71. Some of the details are given in P.R.O.Adm. 7/169, 175.

(ten thirds and eight fourths) built by contract in the Parliamentary programme of war construction during the French war, seventeen were launched in the times shown in the table above.[1] This, however, was not so bad a record as it might appear at first sight, for of the four ships which took over twenty months apiece, two were built at the new site of Hazell on the Humber, which turned out to be thoroughly inconvenient in every respect, and the other two at Harwich, which was no longer, as it had been in the Dutch wars, easy to supply. Similarly, the fourth rate built in seventeen months was a product of the site at Hazell.[2] The nine ships of the same programme built by the navy seem to have been launched no quicker than most of those above, although, with no date of contract to refer to, it is less easy to assign an exact length of time to their construction.[3]

The navy ignored one important factor in making its charges. For where the private builder failed to meet the terms of his contract, it was largely due to the paucity of the payments which he received. How far the various shipyards worked for the government to the exclusion of other business cannot be assessed without their records; but whether or not they turned out merchant vessels as well as men-of-war, the latter were in every case, except that of Blackwall, the largest and most expensive ships to be built, and the credit of the yard in many cases depended on them. At least one yard, moreover, had been started specifically to build men-of-war, and the treatment which its owners received from the navy involved them in the greatest difficulties from the start.[4] The private builders suffered a further disadvantage from the insecurity which at times threatened their workmen. Apart from the uncertainties of their attendance owing to lack of pay and to the mobile nature of their trade, which affected the royal yards in equal measure,[5] those

---

1 B.M.Addnl. 9324, ff. 2–3; Serg.Misc. IV, f. 141. I have been unable to find the date of the contract for the *Exeter*.

2 Serg.Misc. IV, f. 141.

3 The dates on which they were launched are given ibid.; the orders to set to work on them must be sought in the minutes of the Board of Admiralty.

4 The yard begun at Southampton by the brothers Winter in 1691 (P.R.O.Adm. 106/411, letters from the Winters to the Navy Board of 15/1, 12/2, 12/3). For their correspondence with the Navy Board in the following years, see P.R.O.Adm. 106 series, letter *W*.

5 See pp. 88–9, 90–2 below.

who worked for merchant builders were always liable to be pressed for the King's service whenever there was a shortage of men.[1] Normally, when contracting to build a man-of-war, the merchant yards were granted protections for a number of skilled men;[2] but these could always be revoked, and even so powerful a figure as Sir Henry Johnson occasionally found it impossible to keep his shipwrights and carpenters.[3] Unable to call on a general reserve of material to tide them over bad periods, frequently denied the money with which to buy the necessary supplies, and liable to lose their men to the royal yards, the merchant yards started at a distinct disadvantage to the navy.

The same factors largely accounted for the fourth and favourite charge which the navy liked to make against them, that of inferior material. Again, it is difficult to substantiate this complaint, but it was so widespread that there may well have been some truth in it. In so far as it was the case, it was partly the result of the navy's own treatment of the shipbuilders, in starving them of money with which to buy good material and in driving them into a state of indifference; although the yards themselves were no doubt ready to take a profit from the navy in ways which have always appealed to private contractors when faced with a government department.

An offshoot of this complaint was the charge that ships built in the royal dockyards survived longer than those built by contract. A statement of this sort is particularly difficult either to prove or to disprove. It depends on the quality of the repairs, the care devoted to maintenance, and the ways in which the ships met their end. The latter point alone has its own problems and, as may be seen from Appendix I(D) of this work, no conclusions of any great value can be drawn from such a charge.

The main importance of these complaints for us lies not so much in their contents as in the reason for which they were made. In so far as they were true, it was not so much because of a failure on the part of the merchant yards to comply with their standards, as because those standards themselves were low, and because the merchants' resources

---

[1] Admty:Corbett, VIII, f. 13.

[2] E.g. P.R.O.Adm. 3/1: 23/5; 3/2:25/2, 7/3; 3/9:2/11.

[3] P.R.O.Adm. 3/7:15/11.

were limited when faced with the requirements of a man-of-war and of the naval system of supply. When the shipbuilder supplied inferior material or delivered the ship late, or built to the wrong dimensions, it was usually because naval control or naval assistance was lacking. For while the average merchant shipwright could construct the hull of a warship, he could no longer complete her satisfactorily without expert guidance. The supply of gear to enable her to leave the yard for a naval port, and the uniformity of design which line tactics imposed, made external help essential for the small man to whom the primary task of turning out a hull could be assigned. The most compelling reasons for building men-of-war in the royal dockyards were not, except in the case of the largest rates, connected so much with the facilities for their construction as with its control.

This control was even more necessary after the man-of-war had been built than during her construction, for maintenance and repair demanded many more facilities, and a much closer and more constant supervision, than the existing type of private shipyard could supply. The maintenance of a warship was laid down on standard lines. Once a year she was supposed to be repainted and revarnished, and her bottom scraped and tarred; if she was a cruiser, it had in addition to be washed and tallowed every four months. Her masts and rigging had to be taken down, stored, and repaired or replaced if she spent the winter in harbour, and surveyed if she did not. After seven years, her iron work had to be taken out and surveyed, as well as part of her upper and lower decks, and her rudder removed for inspection. From time to time also her toptimbers, gratings and planks had to be examined.[1] In addition to these theoretically regular inspections and repairs, normal precautions had to be taken the whole time. The ship had to be ventilated in harbour to prevent dry rot, her gear constantly checked and replenished, and her stores kept up to standard. Finally, there were the exceptional occasions when, damaged by weather or battle, she had to be repaired. All these duties required more types of material and more and different types of workmen than did shipbuilding alone, and above all they

[1] For full details of this periodic maintenance, see Sutherland, *Britain's Glory*, pp. xv–xix.

required a different type of organization. It was not enough to be able to provide the right materials and men on occasions; they must be there the whole time, for the normal work of maintenance was never done and the extraordinary work of repair often came without warning.

The principal difference between the major yard, able to undertake all types of maintenance and repair, and the minor yard, used mainly for building, was marked, as indeed the name of the larger yard implied, by the dry dock. For although there were other ways of inspecting and repairing a ship under water, by careening her on a hulk or a hard,[1] docking was the most satisfactory method to avoid a waste of time and expense. A dry dock, however, was a serious undertaking. To build a dock large enough to hold a first rate man-of-war might cost between £9000 and £16,000,[2] and took about eighteen months.[3] Its advantages, moreover, led to further expense once it was built, for the fact that it enabled repairs of all types to be carried meant that stores and workshops had to be provided. These made their own demands on space and organization: the mast shops ideally had to be near the mastpond or foreshore where the masts themselves lay to preserve their sap; the timber store needed its saw-pits, and the plank store its 'stoving' space where the wood was moulded in the hot sand; the processes of converting hemp into rigging and cables demanded that the cordage store should be near the workshop, the pitch house and the tar kettle, and that the store and the workhouse themselves should be so subdivided that the material could be separated during the various stages of manufacture; while the canvas stores had to be fitted to protect the canvas against mildew, and the space for airing sails kept clear of the dust and heat of the workshops. A complete dockyard was an expensive and

---

[1] For a good account of how a vessel could be careened far from any shipyard, see Daniel Defoe, *The Farther Adventures of Robinson Crusoe* (ed. J. W. Clark, 1866), pp. 524–8.

[2] This is based on the cost of the only two large dry docks built in the 1690's, at Plymouth and Portsmouth. The estimates in each case were slightly less than the eventual cost (P.R.O.Adm. 7/169, no. 9: 95/3, f. 23).

[3] In the case of both Plymouth and Portsmouth it took much longer; but this was due to interruptions from lack of money, legal difficulties and administrative disagreements. Eighteen months was the time originally estimated for both docks (P.R.O.Adm. 3/6:8/1, 7/10).

complicated affair, involving not only a reasonable area of land—not always easy to come by, particularly near London—but also an initial and a recurrent expenditure, and a labour organization, which few private shipbuilders could command, and which indeed could not always be met by the navy itself.

At the end of 1688, there were five royal dockyards, disposed in three groups: the Thames yards of Deptford and Woolwich, the Medway yards of Chatham and Sheerness, and Portsmouth. Since the middle of Henry VIII's reign the centre of naval activity had been the Thames estuary, and the Dutch wars confirmed and enhanced its supremacy. All the activities of the fleet—its concentration as well as its maintenance and repair—were now centred there, and as contemporaries surveyed the new fortifications, from Hoe Fort and Gillingham to Upnor Castle overlooking the boom below Chatham and to Tilbury on the Thames,[1] it seemed to them 'that perhaps there may not be a more compleat Arsenal than this in the world'.[2] During the same period, the forts on the south coast were falling into disrepair. By 1689, Dover Castle was 'in a ruinous and unarmed state';[3] the Cinque Ports and Seaford had been largely disarmed;[4] and only the defences of Portsmouth were still in good order.[5]

This concentration on the Thames estuary raised its own problems. The yards were not easy to approach or to leave. The deepest first rate afloat in 1688 drew 21 feet;[6] from the Isle of Sheppey to the Nore the channels between the sands were nine feet deep at low water, while the entrances to the Medway through the West Swale, and to the Thames off Canvey Island, were navigable at all states of the tide only with the greatest caution.[7] Nor were their approaches well marked at all stages or under all conditions. From Dungeness to Harwich the lights were unreliable, thanks largely to the system, initiated by James I, of

[1] B.M. King's 43, unfoliated. Details of these and later fortifications may be found there. For the fortifications at the beginning of the third Dutch war, see Colbert, *Lettres, Instructions et Mémoires*, III, pt 2, p. 341.

[2] William Camden, *Britannia*, with additions by Edmund Gibson (1695), p. 219.

[3] *V.C.H. Kent*, II, p. 332.

[4] *V.C.H. Sussex*, II, p. 159.

[5] B.M.Addnl. 33283, f. 151; *V.C.H. Hampshire*, III, p. 190.

[6] See Appendix I(B) below.

[7] Grenville Collins, *Great Britain's Coasting Pilot* (1693).

farming them out to individuals,[1] while the Thames estuary itself was completely unlit until late in the eighteenth century, when Robert Hamblin introduced the first lightship.[2] The charts and sailing directions, moreover, did not compensate for these disadvantages. English hydrography, in the later seventeenth century, was poor compared with the Dutch or even with the French;[3] and until Grenville Collins published his *Great Britain's Coasting Pilot* in 1693—itself not particularly trustworthy—the standby for the average master was the 'plat', or at best John Seller's *Coasting Pilot* of 1675, in effect merely another edition of the standard Dutch 'waggoners' which were used all over Europe for most of the century.[4] Even these, superior to native products though they might be, were not particularly accurate, and it was on the local pilot or local experience that the man-of-war relied to get in and out of his base.[5] Under these conditions, the sands of the estuary, Black Deeps and Shivering Sands, Shipwash and Galloper, still often earned their names.

The rivers themselves were subject to other disadvantages. It was never easy for a large man-of-war to beat down stream against a head wind—and the prevailing direction of the wind throughout the first four months of the year is easterly in that area—from yards which lay several miles from the area of concentration at the Nore. Various towing devices were tried to overcome this difficulty, but none was finally adopted.[6] Two of the yards, Chatham and Deptford, lay, moreover, in particularly shallow reaches of their respective rivers, and the

---

[1] *V.C.H. Kent*, II, pp. 334–6; *Essex*, pp. 293–4. Apart from any other drawbacks, the system gave rise to lawsuits such as the case of the Forelands lights, which lasted from 1688 to 1717 and during which even less was spent upon their upkeep than usual.

[2] W. H. D. Adams, *Lighthouses and Lightships* (1870), pp. 50–2.

[3] *Samuel Pepys's Naval Minutes*, pp. 316–17, 324. The best French chart folio, the *Neptune français*, appeared in 1693.

[4] See Captain D. Gernez, 'Lucas Janszoon Wagenaer', in *M.M.* XXIII, no. 2, pp. 190–7; and 'The Works of Lucas Janszoon Wagenaer' by the same author, in *M.M.* XXIII, no. 3, pp. 332–50. For an example of Seller's own navigational information for the estuary without Dutch assistance, see David Ogg, *England in the Reign of Charles II* (1934), I, p. 256.

[5] The Dutch got up the Medway in 1667 with an English pilot and with the buoys still in position. In later scares Trinity House was ordered to take them up (P.R.O.Adm. 2/170, f. 296).

[6] *Samuel Pepys's Naval Minutes*, p. 231, and n. 3. See also p. 15 above.

latter was shoaling noticeably throughout Charles II's reign.[1] At low water, there was only one foot to spare for a first rate riding at anchor off the waterfront, while at Chatham she was liable to ground by four feet if caught at certain wharves on an ebb tide.[2] The rivers themselves were becoming more crowded. One observer reckoned that between London Bridge and Gravesend the wharves and warehouses, with their piers and steps, were covering 300 to 400 feet of new ground during each year of James II's reign;[3] and a few years later, a new parish had to be established in Wapping to meet the needs of the growing population.[4] As the waterfront was built over, so the river silted up off the new walls and landing stages, and by 1687 the Navy Board estimated that the channel of the Thames had been narrowed by one-fifth in the neighbourhood of the 'new encroachments'. The same applied, to a lesser degree, to the yards on the Medway, and early in the 1680's the dangers from the encroachments had become so great that the Admiralty seriously considered moving both sets of yards elsewhere—a threat which at once drew a petition to the Privy Council from the City of London to refuse the grant of any further licences to build on the river banks.[5] In 1684, and again in 1687, the Navy Board undertook surveys of both shores of the Thames, and Sir Jonas Moore supervised a similar work for the Ordnance Office.[6] But no official action was taken, or indeed was likely to be taken, on their reports.

By 1689, these difficulties had turned the bases near London into minor yards, used mainly for the construction of the medium and smaller rates. The dry docks at both Deptford and Woolwich dated from the reign of Charles I,[7] and no building had taken place at either yard, except for a few storehouses in the 1680's, since the Restoration. Their place had been taken by Chatham, which as a result of the Dutch wars had risen from an advance base on the Medway to the position of

---

[1] T.H. (Thomas Hales), *An Account of Several New Inventions and Improvements now necessary for England* (1691), p. 56.

[2] Ibid.

[3] Loc. cit. p. 109.

[4] Macpherson, *Annals of Commerce*, II, p. 685.

[5] Hales, loc. cit. p. 52, citing Brisbane, then Secretary of the Admiralty.

[6] The Navy Board's surveys, and Pepys's notes upon them, may be seen in Pep:Sea MS. 2997 and Bodl. Rawl. A 171, ff. 98–101 respectively.

[7] *V.C.H. Kent*, II, pp. 344–5.

incomparably the greatest dockyard in the country, and whose inconveniences were not so acute as its predecessors'. Its earliest surviving buildings dated mostly from James I's reign, when the Commission into naval organization of 1618 had inaugurated so extensive a programme that, although the buildings themselves were sparsely scattered, the area of the yard remained almost unaltered until 1860;[1] but in James II's reign, when the lessons of the recent wars had been digested, a fresh programme was carried out which turned it into virtually a new yard, in equipment if not in size.[2] Its place as an advanced base was taken to some extent by Sheerness, which had ousted Harwich for the purpose during the third Dutch war. Although shut down in the intervening years, with the possibility of a fourth Dutch war in the winter of 1688 it was again put into commission as a repair base under the control of Chatham,[3] and in the following year a serious effort was made to establish it as a properly equipped and permanent yard. On the south coast, the only base was that of Portsmouth, removed by the Dutch wars from the centre to the periphery of naval activity and, despite some additions in the past five years,[4] much the same as it had been thirty years before. In extent, however, it was second only to Chatham.

The equipment and the relative importance of the five yards are illustrated in their plans and in the views of their waterfronts, and by the tables on pp. 86–7.[5] The first impression to be gained from these views and figures is of the pre-eminence of Chatham. Its rated value was almost half as much again as those of the other eastern yards put together,[6] its

---

[1] *V.C.H. Kent*, II, pp. 344–5.

[2] Cf. Camden (i.e. Edmund Gibson) loc. cit. p. 219: 'The river *Medway*...glideth on to *Chatham*, which hath been...far advanced by the Kings, *Charles* and *James II*... with the large additions of new Docks and Storehouses, wherein are many conveniences unknown till of late.' And see p. 205 below.

[3] See pp. 217–18 below; and also *V.C.H. Kent*, II, pp. 353, 359.

[4] See p. 205 below.

[5] The views are reproduced, and the tables compiled, from B.M. King's 43, *passim*. The former represent the yards as they were in 1698, but the additions of the previous ten years may be seen in the plans below them.

[6] An exact comparison must take into account the conditions under which the land was held in each case. At Deptford, for instance, there was a long-standing legal dispute over the terms of compensation to be paid on part of the yard (*V.C.H. Kent*, II, p. 344).

effective waterfront more than double that of Portsmouth; it had four dry docks, three of which had been built in the last ten years, compared with the total of five in the other four yards; and the quality as well as the number of its storehouses and workshops was generally superior to those elsewhere.

But the second impression is of the inadequacy of all the dockyards to meet the demands made upon them. In the first place, they were badly placed for a French war. This was unavoidable in view of recent history. Advanced bases, which were set up when required, existed already at Harwich and Kinsale in Ireland, where facilities for storage and repair were available under the control of a naval agent who mustered the companies of the ships putting in there and acted as store-keeper and officer of the yard.[1] Other harbours existed which could be turned into such bases, or 'out-ports' as they were called: Yarmouth and Dover in the east, Weymouth and Falmouth in the south, Milford Haven and Liverpool in the west.[2] But these were of limited value, and could not offset the disadvantage of having the main concentration of dockyards in the wrong part of the country for the war in hand.

But secondly, even if they had been strategically convenient, the yards were technically ill-fitted for war. This was not altogether surprising. It was always easier to increase the size of a fleet than to increase the number or to improve the quality of the yards; and with only a limited amount of money available, the ships had benefited more than usual over the previous thirty years at the expense of their bases. As a result, the revolution in the character of the fleet which had marked the middle years of the century, had outstripped the capacity of the yards, and the efforts of James II had not been able entirely to redress the balance. A total of three double and six single dry docks was inadequate for a battle-fleet of 101 ships about to embark on a war. Nor were all the docks available for all uses. The dimensions of the *Britannia* in 1688 were 167 ft. 5 in. × 47 ft. 4 in.[3] There were thus only three dry docks that could take her in the royal yards, and all of these were at

[1] See the Instructions for such officers, in P.R.O.Adm. 2/1728.

[2] Sir William Petty, with characteristic ingenuity, played with a design for a floating harbour, so that the number of advanced bases could be indefinitely increased according to requirements. The plan may be seen in *The Petty Papers*, II, pp. 83–4.

[3] See Appendix I(B) below.

	Chatham	Portsmouth	Deptford	Woolwich (excluding ropeyard)	Sheerness
Total estimated value of ground and equipment	£44,940 4*s.* 5*d.*	£35,045 19*s.* 1¼*d.*	£15,760 15*s.* 2*d.*	£9669 15*s.* 0½*d.*	£5393 15*s.* 11*d.*
Waterfront of yard[1] (approx.)	3500 ft. (excluding Ordnance Office wharves for 700 ft.)	1430 ft.	1370 ft.	760 ft.	1150 ft. on south bank of Isle of Sheppey and 1150 ft. on north bank
Greatest depth of yard[1] (approx.)	820 ft.	1100 ft. (of which about 250 ft. was open ground)	1050 ft.	300 ft. (only 30 ft. longer than double-dock, which almost cut yard in two)	800 ft. (yard itself contained in 730 × 400 ft. Rest was open ground inside fortifications)
Number of docks:[1]					
Double	One (270[2] × 52[3]; 39[4])	One (260 × 45; 34)[5]	One (287 × 45; 30)	One (280 × 44; 22)	None
Single	Three (135 × 56; 38: 2–200 × 58; 36)	None	None	One (132 × 49; 27)	One (102 × 36)
Building slips[1]	One (95 × 42; 25)	One (162 × 40)	None	None	None
Wet docks	None	None	One	None	None
Mast docks	None	One	One	None	None
Cranes	1 'swinging' crane 3 'small' cranes	1 'double-wheel crane' 1 'middle' crane 1 'old' crane	1 'old' crane 1 'little' crane	1 'old' crane 1 'little' crane	2 'hand' cranes
Workshops and buildings[1]	1 ropewalk (365 ft. long) 1 boatyard 3 deal yards, with storesheds, including 1 joiner's shop and 1 forge 1 cordage house 1 spinning house 1 rigging house, with 14 sawpits beneath 1 trennel's house 1 pitchhouse 1 caulker's pitchhouse 1 boat pitchhouse 2 masthouses 1 building with 8 masthouses 1 taphouse 1 space for joiner's work 1 painter's shop 1 sawhouse 2 sawpits	1 ropewalk (250 ft. long) 1 trennel-mooters' shop 1 pitchhouse 1 boat pitchhouse – masthouses 1 taphouse 1 house-carpenter's shop 1 blockmaker's shop – 'old nail' shops 1 pumphouse 1 boatswain's house 1 boatswain's cabin 9 sawhouses	3 boathouses 1 mould loft and boathouse 1 sailroom and oar house 1 rigging house 1 pitchhouse 1 masthouse 1 taphouse 1 sheathing board house 1 reed house 1 pumphouse 1 smith's shop 1 wheeler's shop 1 teamer's stable and paint shop 2 sawhouses	1 rigging house 1 mould loft (in clock-house) 1 masthouse 1 smith's shop[6] 1 sawhouse	1 boathouse 1 pitchhouse 1 smith's shop

Storehouses[1, 7]	1 'long' storehouse (660 ft. long) 2 tar stores 1 store for blocks and colours 4 stores for rosin, pitch, tallow and old hammocks, with a sailmaking room 1 store for iron 1 store for cordage	1 'great long' storehouse (425 ft. long) 1 'great' storehouse (400 ft. long) 2 storehouses (unspecified) 1 store for blocks 1 store for hemp	1 'great' storehouse (405 ft. long) 1 storehouse (unspecified) – storesheds	1 'old' storehouse, including sail room, boathouse, engine house, brimstone house (185 ft. long)	1 store for cordage
Accommodation	Houses (10) for: Commissioner Clerk of survey Clerk of cheque Storekeeper Master shipwright Master attendant Second master attendant Master caulker Boatswain of yard Assistants Teamers Officers' stables Commissioner's coach-house	Houses (9) for: Commissioner Clerk of survey Clerk of cheque Storekeeper Master shipwright Master attendant Master caulker Boatswain of yard Porter Assistants Commissioner's coach-house Clerk of cheque's stable	Houses (7) for: Clerk of survey Clerk of cheque Storekeeper Surgeon Master shipwright His assistant Master attendant Porter	Houses (7) for: Clerk of survey Clerk of cheque Storekeeper Surgeon Master shipwright Master attendant Porter	Houses (8) for: Clerk of survey Clerk of cheque Storekeeper Master attendant Master caulker Master shipwright Porter Boatswain of yard Foremen's lodgings (over public bake-house) Workmen's lodgings
Offices not included in 'Accommodation'	Pay office Clerk of the rope-yard's office	Pay office 'New' offices, containing offices for clerk of the survey, clerk of the cheque, clerk of the ropeyard, storekeeper, master shipwright	None	Pay office	Clerk of the cheque's office Storekeeper's office
Extent of yard walls	3377 ft.[8] (brick)	Only officers' gardens walled	984 ft. (brick)	733 ft. (brick)	No wall

1 Dimensions from scale plans.
2 Length measured in feet, along the bottom of the dock, from apron to lowest end step.
3 Extreme breadth at top of the dock.
4 Breadth inside first step (approx. half way up dock).
5 This dock narrowed 170 ft. from apron, to an extreme width at top of 40 ft. and a width inside first step of 29 ft.
6 In one of the officer's houses.
7 These cannot be altogether distinguished from workhouses and other buildings, but I have followed the titles given in B.M. King's 43.
8 Given in rods and feet as 204 rods 11 ft.

Chatham. The double docks at Portsmouth, Deptford and Woolwich were just wide enough to take the small first rates with a few inches to spare, while the older single docks could accommodate only the smaller rates. All the dry docks, moreover, were built entirely of wood, and in 1684 the older ones were said to be virtually useless from moisture and decay.[1] Finally, their limited space was liable to be taken up for purposes other than under-water repair, for except at Deptford there was no wet dock or basin in which ships could lie before entering dry dock, and those undergoing repair above water had therefore either to stay in mid stream with the consequent administrative disadvantages, or else had to be brought into dry dock at once. In 1682, Sir Phineas Pett proposed that a wet dock should be built at Chatham, but the plan came to nothing[2] and the ships continued either to be stored and refitted afloat, or else were docked unnecessarily simply for the purpose of avoiding these delays.

The building facilities of the yards were likewise limited. In 1691 it was calculated that, at a time of normal activity, Chatham could build five rated ships at once, Portsmouth four, Deptford two, and Woolwich two.[3] In the event of a heavy programme of construction, therefore, the navy had to resort to the private yards. When such a programme was begun in 1691, of the 27 ships for which estimates had been made, eighteen were built outside the King's yards.[4]

The equipment of a dockyard was a permanent asset. The buildings and wharves, and the docks themselves, were not removed in slack periods and replaced when things were busy. They were not, however, always used at an equal rate. For long periods in peacetime, when money was scarce or when large fleets were unnecessary, some were wholly and others partly closed down. The efficiency of a yard in war, therefore, depended not only on its equipment but also on its organization, and particularly on the control which could be exercised over the workmen, who had to be recruited at a time of expansion and retained for so long as was required.

The dockyards not only provided more work in war than in peace,

---

[1] *V.C.H. Kent*, II, p. 360.

[2] Ibid.

[3] P.R.O. Adm. 3/4: 27/3.

[4] See Appendix III below.

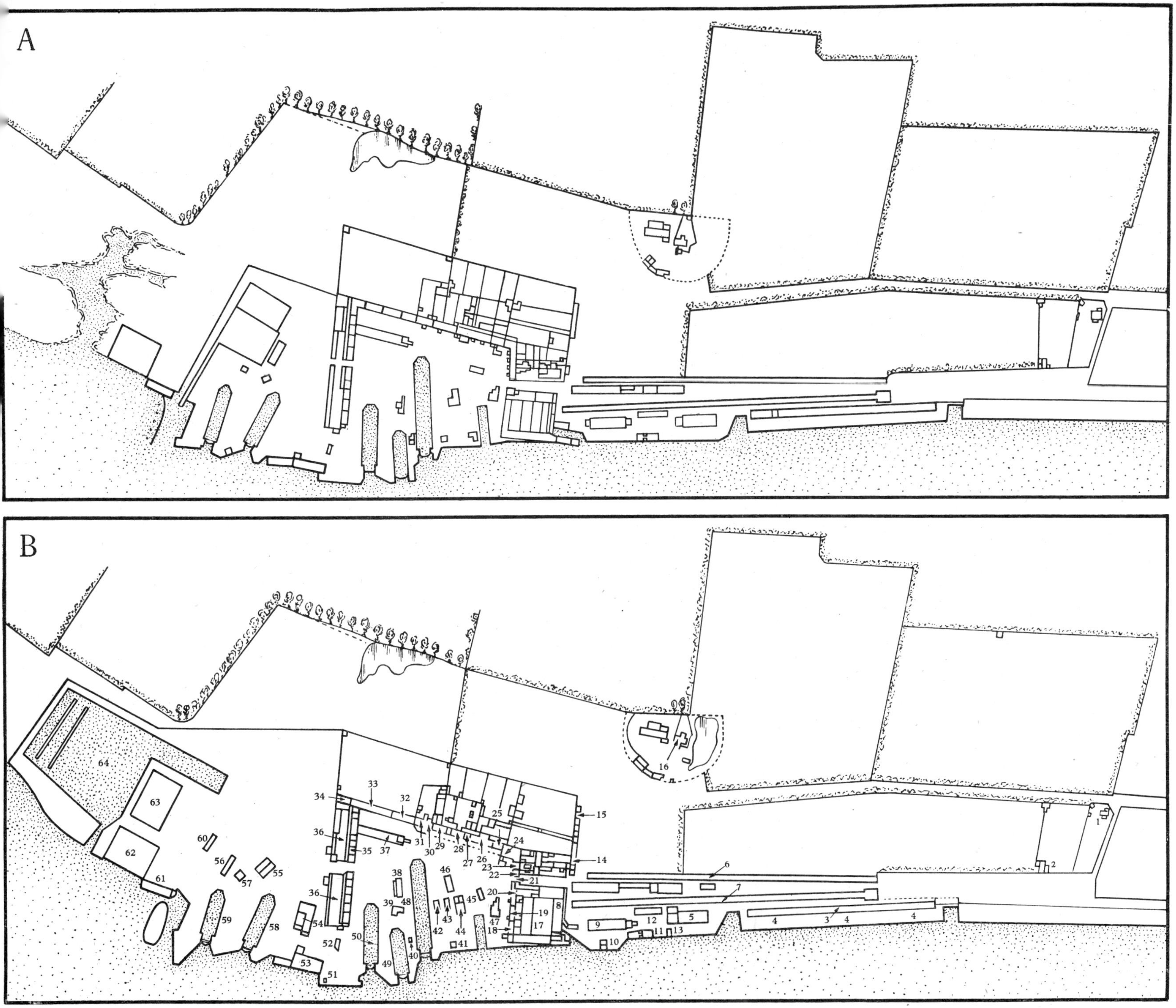

Fig. 1. PLANS OF CHATHAM DOCKYARD

THE DOCKYARD AT CHATHAM

View and Plans

A. The plan of the Yard before the Revolutio 1688.

B. The same plan showing improvements m since the Revolution, drawn in 1698.

REFERENCES

1. The hill house
2. A smith's forge
3. Long storehouse
4. Three cranes
5. A Cordage storehouse
6. Spinning house
7. Rope-walk
8. Clerk of the rope-yard's office
9. Another cordage storehouse
10. Capstan crane
11. The anchor forge
12. A storehouse for tar
13. Another capstan crane
14. Painter's shop
15. Officer's stables
16. Teamer's house
17. Boat yard and houses
18. Surgeon's house
19. Second assistants house
20. Clerk of the survey's house
21. Gatehouse
22. Clerk of the cheque's house
23. Storekeeper's house
24. Commissioner's house
25. Master attendant's house
26. Master builder's house
27. Second master attendant's house
28. Master caulker's house
29. First assistant's house
30. Clock house
31. Boatswain's ho
32. Storehouses for blocks
33. Storehouses for pitch
34. Storehouses for
35. Storehouses for iron and sails
36. Deal yard, etc.
37. The rigging-ho
38. Treenailer's hou
39. Caulker's pitch-house
40. Several cabins
41. A swinging cra
42. Saw pit, etc.
43. Saw pits only
44. The boat pitch-house
45. Porter's woodsh etc.
46. Joiner's shop
47. Tap-house
48. Double dock
49. Building slip
50. Old single dock
51. Another swing crane
52. Another saw-house
53. Old mast-house, etc.
54. Great smith's sh
55. Another saw-house
56. Assistant's office
57. Pitch-house
58. New single dock
59. Another single dock
60. Oar-maker's sho
61. Tap-house
62. Mast house
63. Mast house
64. Mast dock, etc.

VIEWS AND PLANS OF THE
DOCKYARDS AT

CHATHAM

DEPTFORD

WOOLWICH

SHEERNESS

PORTSMOUTH

PLATE II

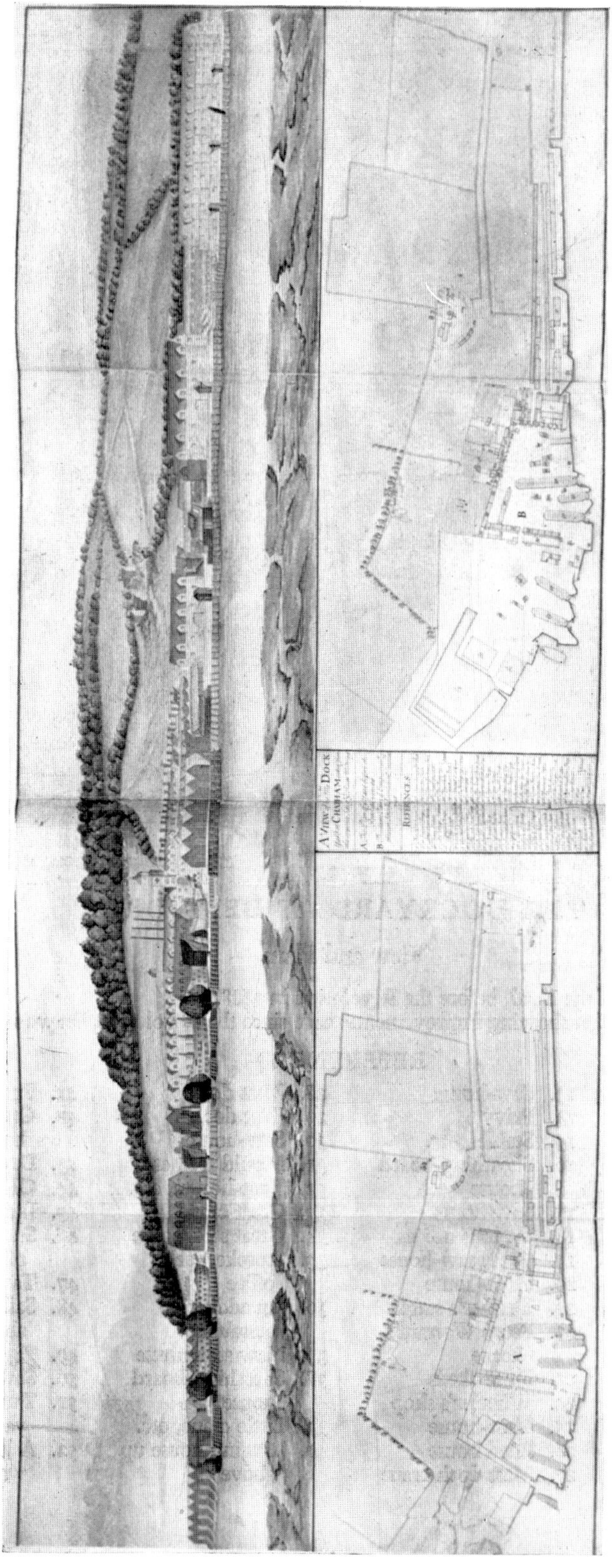

THE DOCKYARD AT CHATHAM

View and Plans

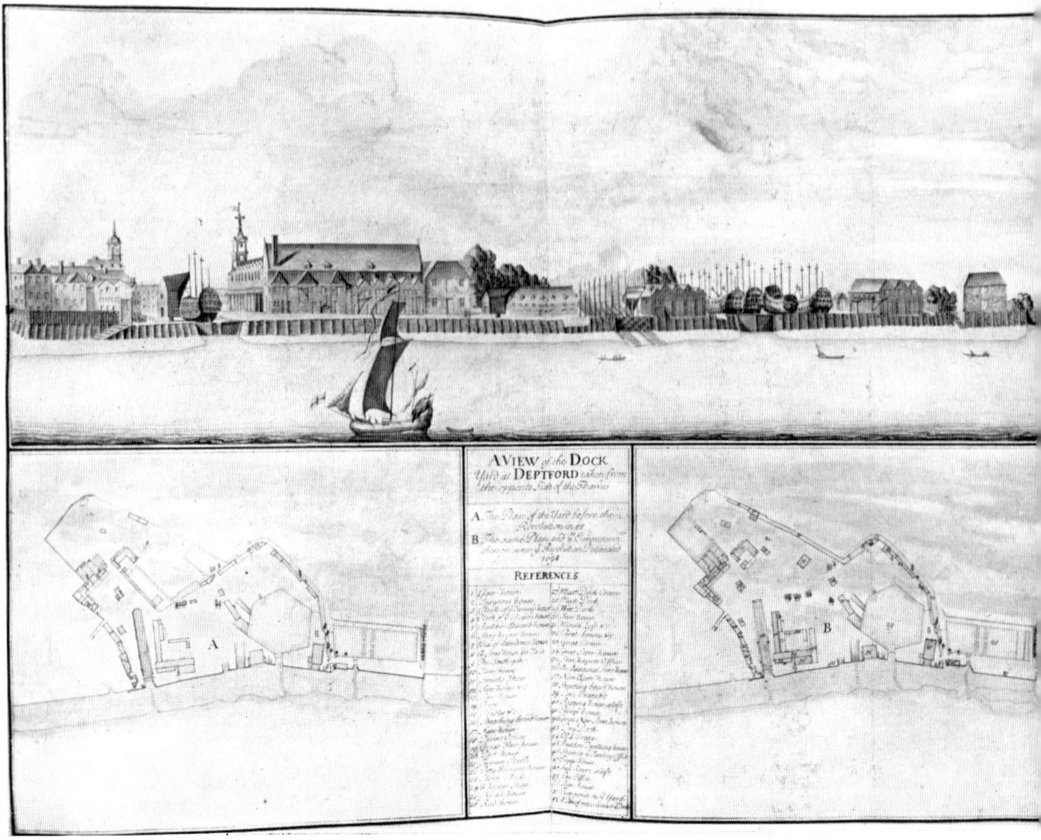

THE DOCKYARD AT DEPTFORD

View and Plans

A. The plan of the Yard, before the Revolution in 1688.
B. The same plan showing improvements made since the Revolution, drawn in 1698.

REFERENCES

1. Gate-house
2. Surgeon's house
3. Clerk of the survey's house
4. Clerk of the cheque's house
5. Builder's assistant's house
6. Storekeeper's house
7. Master of attendance's house
8. A storehouse for sails
9. The south gate
10. Saw-house
11. Smith's shop
12. Saw-house, etc.
13. Saw-house
14. Privy
15. Stables, etc.
16. Sheathing-board house
17. Saw-house
18. Various offices
19. Great saw-house
20. Pitch-house
21. Teamer's stable
22. Petty Warrant's house
23. Store-sheds
24. Wheeler's shop
25. Mast-house
26. Reed house
27. Mast dock crane
28. Mast dock
29. Wet dock
30. Saw-house
31. Mould loft, etc.
32. Boat-houses, etc.
33. Great crane
34. Great storehouse
35. Storekeeper's office
36. An additional storehouse
37. New storehouse
38. Sheathing-board house
39. Little crane, etc.
40. Rigging house up above
41. Pump house
42. Great new storehouse
43. Dry dock
44. Old crane
45. Builder's house
46. Stairs to the survey office
47. Tap-house
48. Sail room up above
49. Pay office
50. Saw-house
51. Two ponds in the yard
52. A lake of water to wash the docks

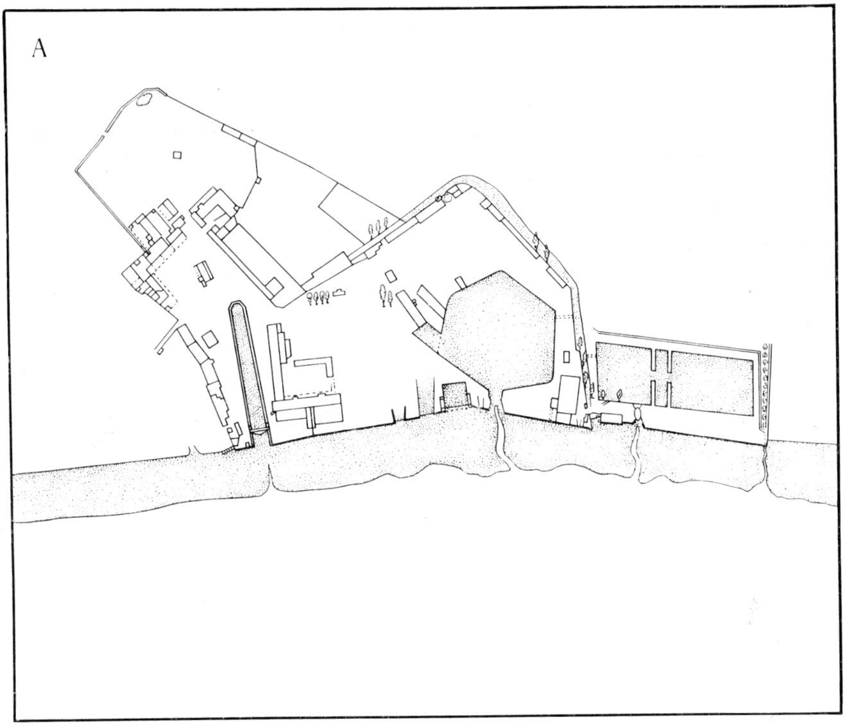

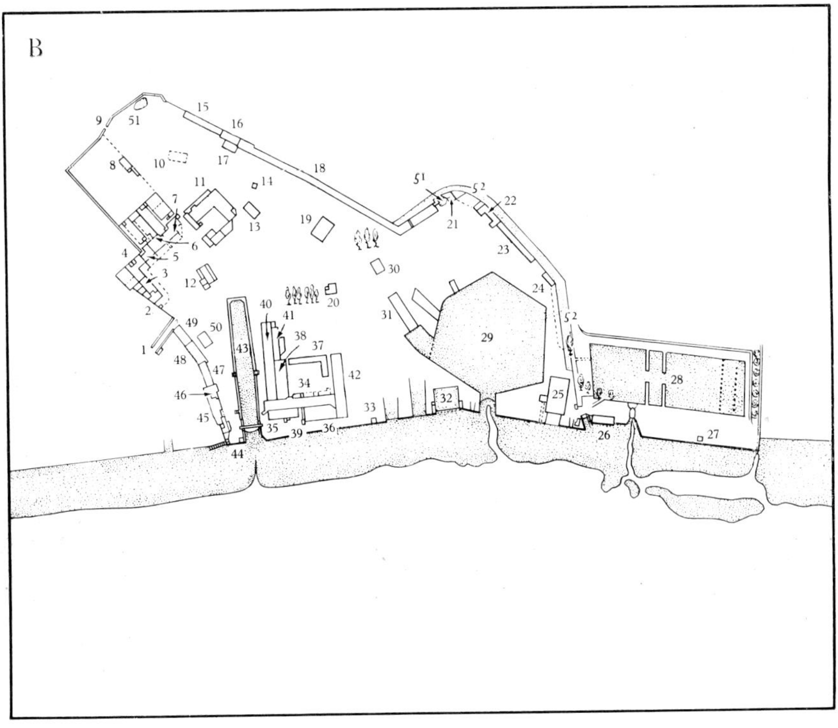

Fig. 2. PLANS OF DEPTFORD DOCKYARD

PLATE IV

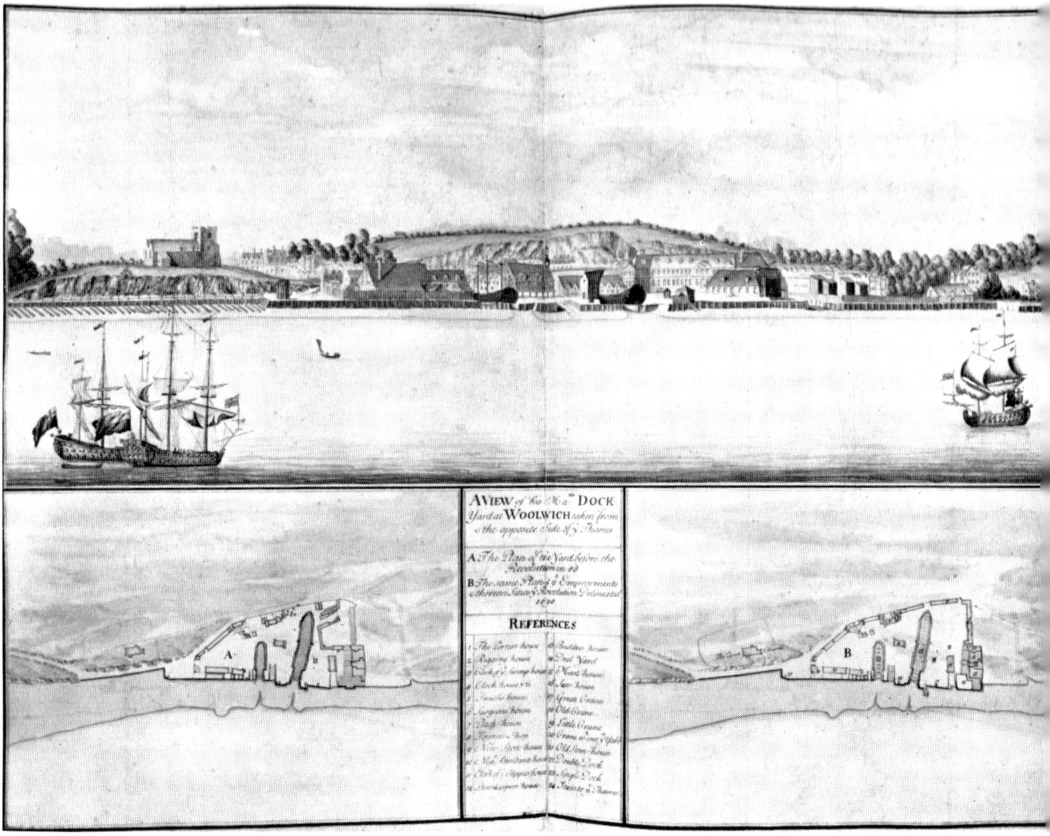

THE DOCKYARD AT WOOLWICH

View and Plans

A. The plan of the Yard, before the Revolution in 1688.
B. The same plan showing improvements made since the Revolution, drawn in 1698.

REFERENCES

1. The porter's house
2. Rigging house
3. Clerk of the survey's house
4. Clock-house, etc.
5. Smith's house
6. Surgeon's house
7. Pitch-house
8. Joiner's shop
9. New storehouse
10. Master attendant's house
11. Clerk of the cheque's house
12. Storekeeper's house
13. Builder's house
14. Deal yard
15. Mast-house
16. Saw-house
17. Great crane
18. Old crane
19. Little crane
20. Crane outside the yard
21. Old storehouse
22. Double dock
23. Single dock
24. Stairs to the Thames

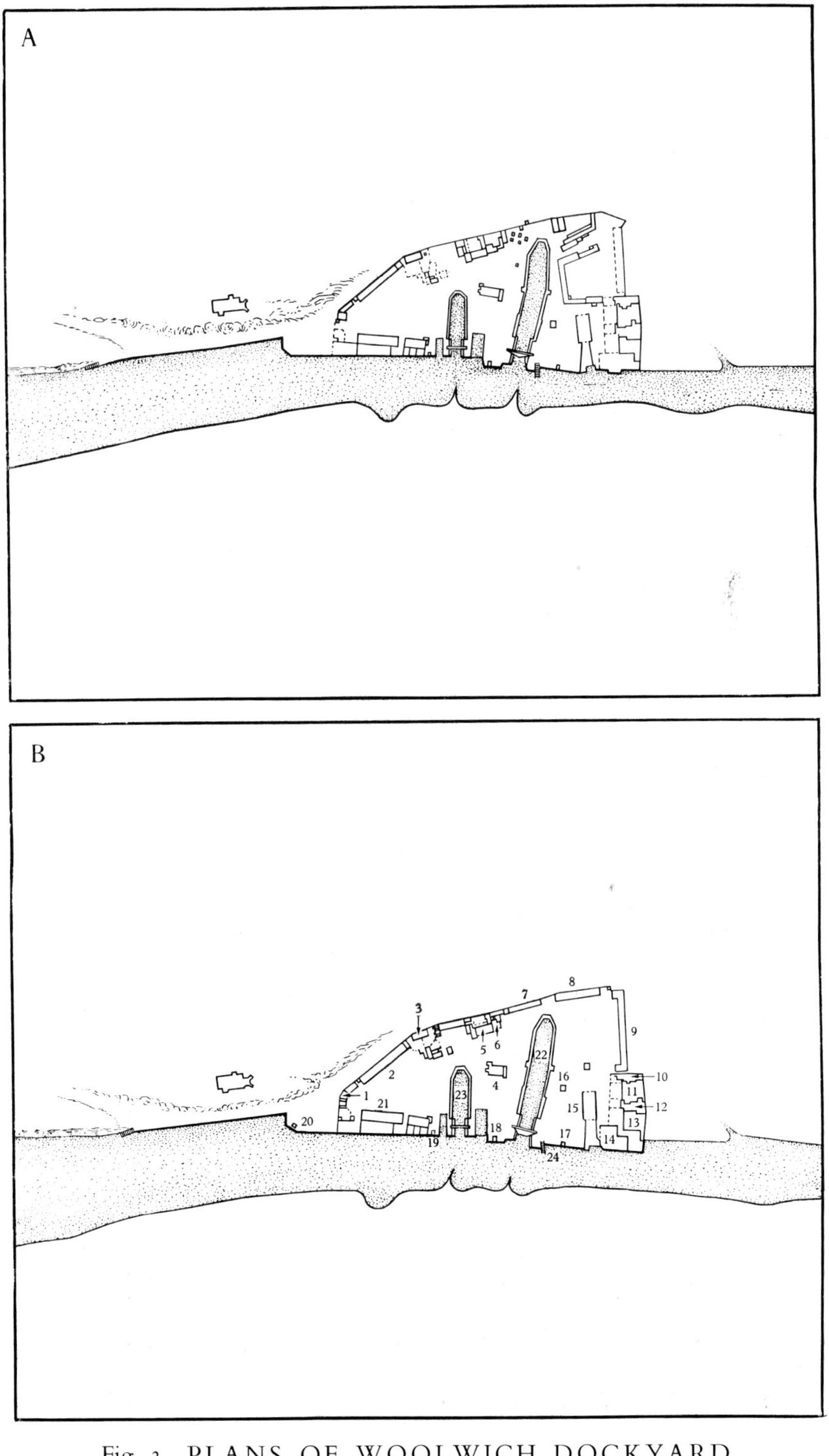

Fig. 3. PLANS OF WOOLWICH DOCKYARD

PLATE V

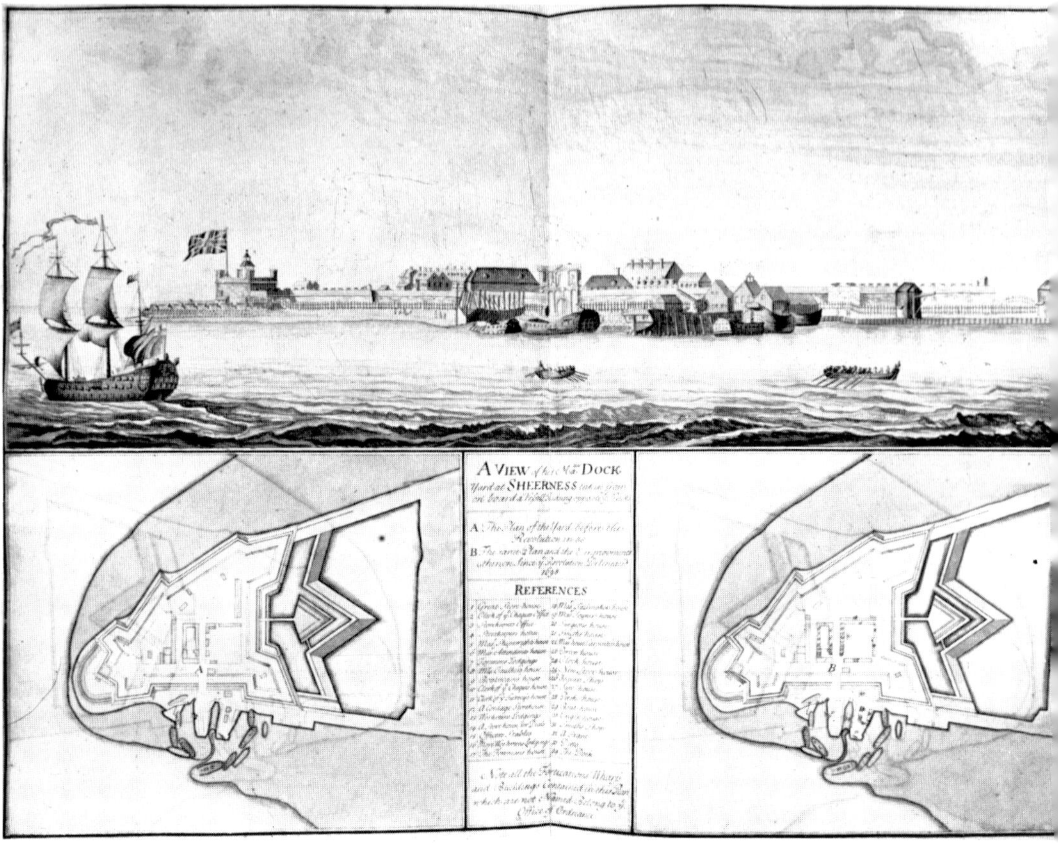

THE DOCKYARD AT SHEERNESS

View and Plans

A. The plan of the Yard, before the Revolution in 1688.
B. The same plan showing the improvements made since the Revolution, drawn in 1698.

REFERENCES

1. Great storehouse
2. Clerk of the cheque's office
3. Storekeeper's office
4. Storekeeper's house
5. Master shipwright's house
6. Master attendant's house
7. Foremen's lodgings
8. Master caulker's house
9. Boatswain's house
10. Clerk of the cheque's house
11. Clerk of the survey's house
12. A cordage storehouse
13. Workmen's lodgings
14. A storehouse for deals
15. Officers' stables
16. More workmen's lodgings
17. The foreman's house
18. Master sailmaker's house
19. Master joiner's house
20. Surgeon's house
21. Smith's house
22. Master carpenter's house
23. Porter's house
24. Clock-house
25. New storehouse
26. Joiner's shop
27. Saw-house
28. Pitch-house
29. Boat-house
30. Engine house
31. Smith's shop
32. A crane
33. A crane
34. The dock

Note: All the fortifications, wharfs and buildings contained in this plan, which are not named, belong to the office of ordnance.

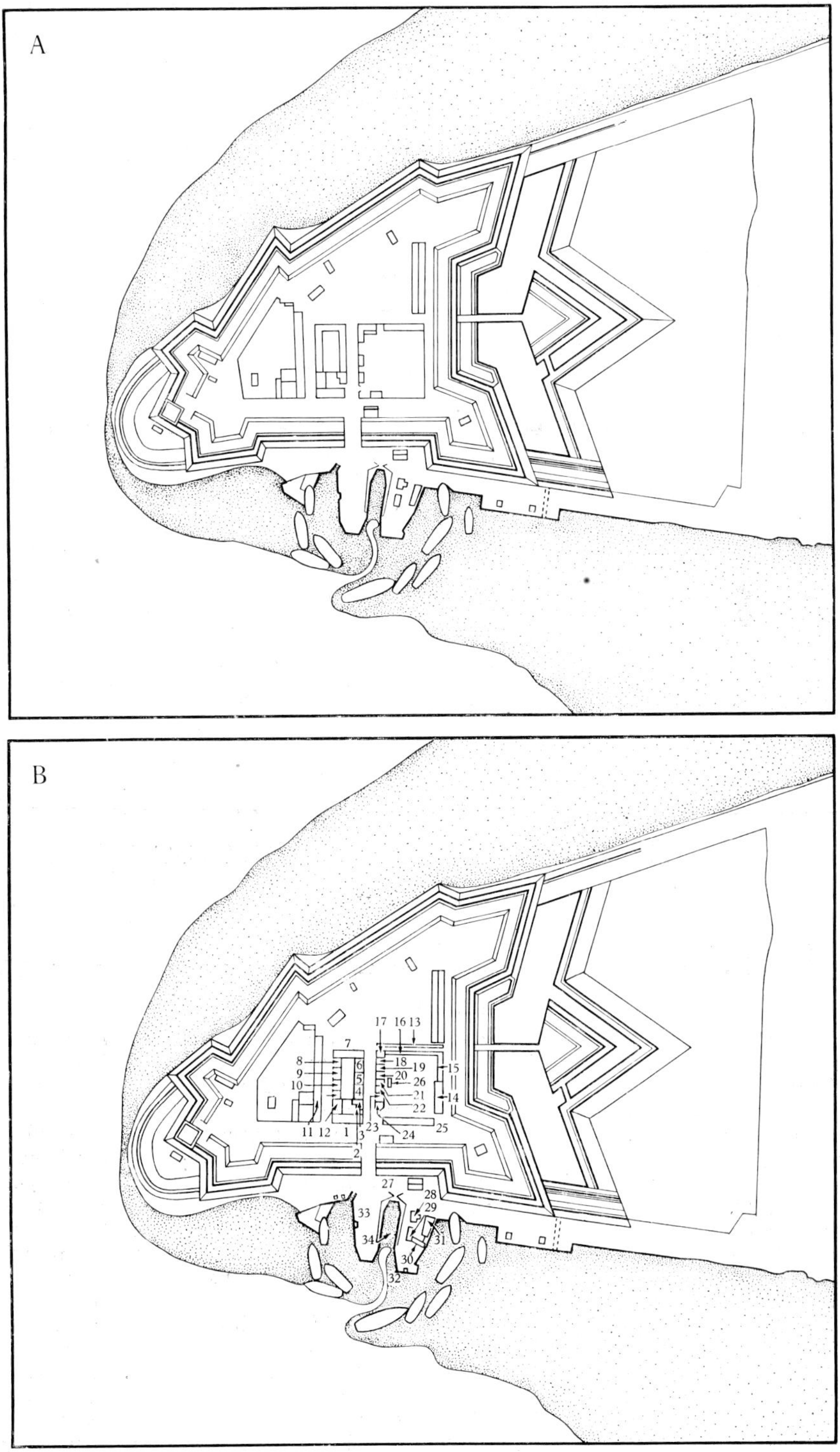

Fig. 4. PLANS OF SHEERNESS DOCKYARD

PLATE VI

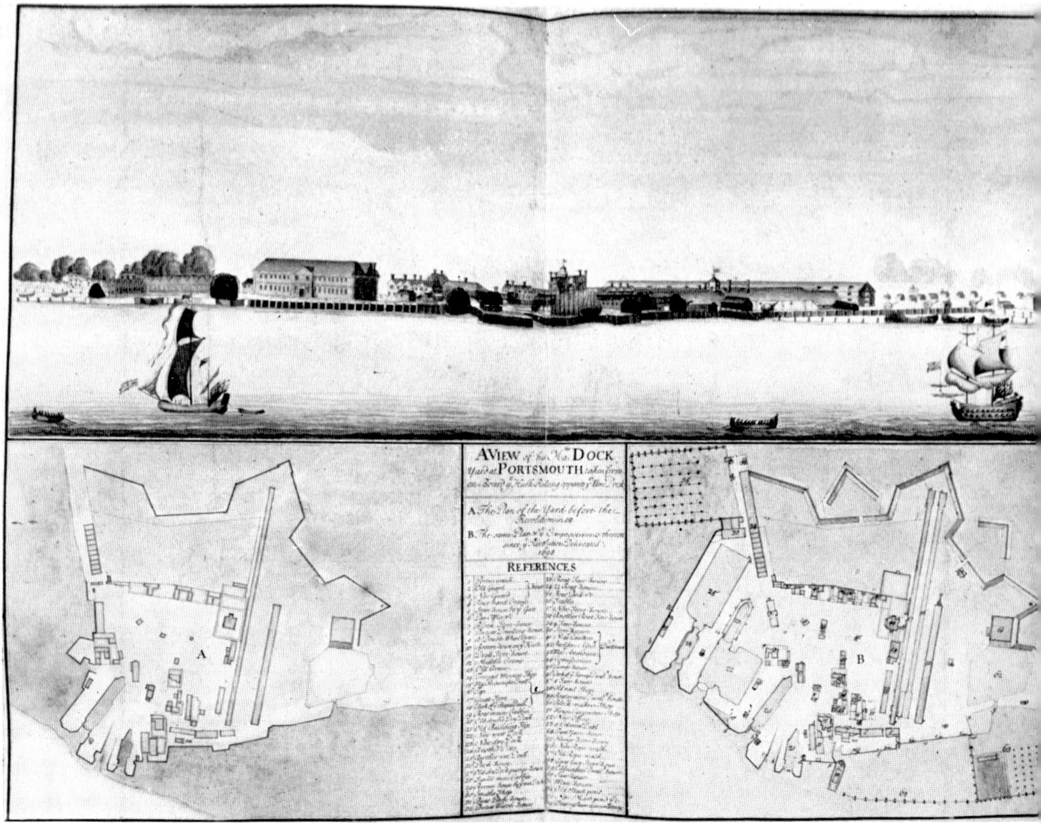

THE DOCKYARD AT PORTSMOUTH

View and Plans

A. The plan of the Yard, before the Revolution in 1688.
B. The same plan showing the improvements made since the Revolution, drawn in 1698.

REFERENCES

1. Porter's watch-house
2. Old guard-house
3. New guard-house
4. Four hand cranes
5. Storehouse by the gate
6. Pay office, etc.
7. Block storehouse
8. Porter's dwelling house
9. A double wheel crane
10. Broom-house on the hulk
11. Deal storehouse
12. Middle crane
13. Old crane
14. Treenail-mooter's shop
15. Master ship-wright's house
16. Tap-house
17. Great storehouse
18. Clerk of the cheque's house
19. Boatswain's cabin
20. Old double dry dock
21. Old building slip
22. New wet dock
23. New dry dock
24. Another dry dock
25. Another wet dock
26. Pitch house
27. Old dry dock pump-house
28. Scavel-men's cabin
29. Broom-house by the wet dock
30. Smith's shop
31. Boat pitch-house
32. Porter's watch-house
33. Boat saw-house
34. Twenty-two boat-houses
35. Boat pond, etc.
36. Stables
37. New storehouse
38. Another boat saw-house
39. Four saw-houses
40. Storekeeper's house
41. Master caulker's house
42. Builder's assistant's house
43. Master attendant's house
44. Commissioner's house
45. Pump house
46. Clerk of the survey's house
47. Five saw-houses
48. Old nail shop
49. Boatswain's house
50. Blockmaker's shop
51. House carpenter's shop
52. New offices
53. A column dial
54. Tarred yarn house
55. Hemp storehouse
56. New rope-walk
57. Old rope-walk
58. Great long store-house
59. Second assistant's house
60. Saw-house
61. Mast-houses
62. Old mast pond
63. New mast pond, etc.
64. A floating boom to secure lighters, etc.

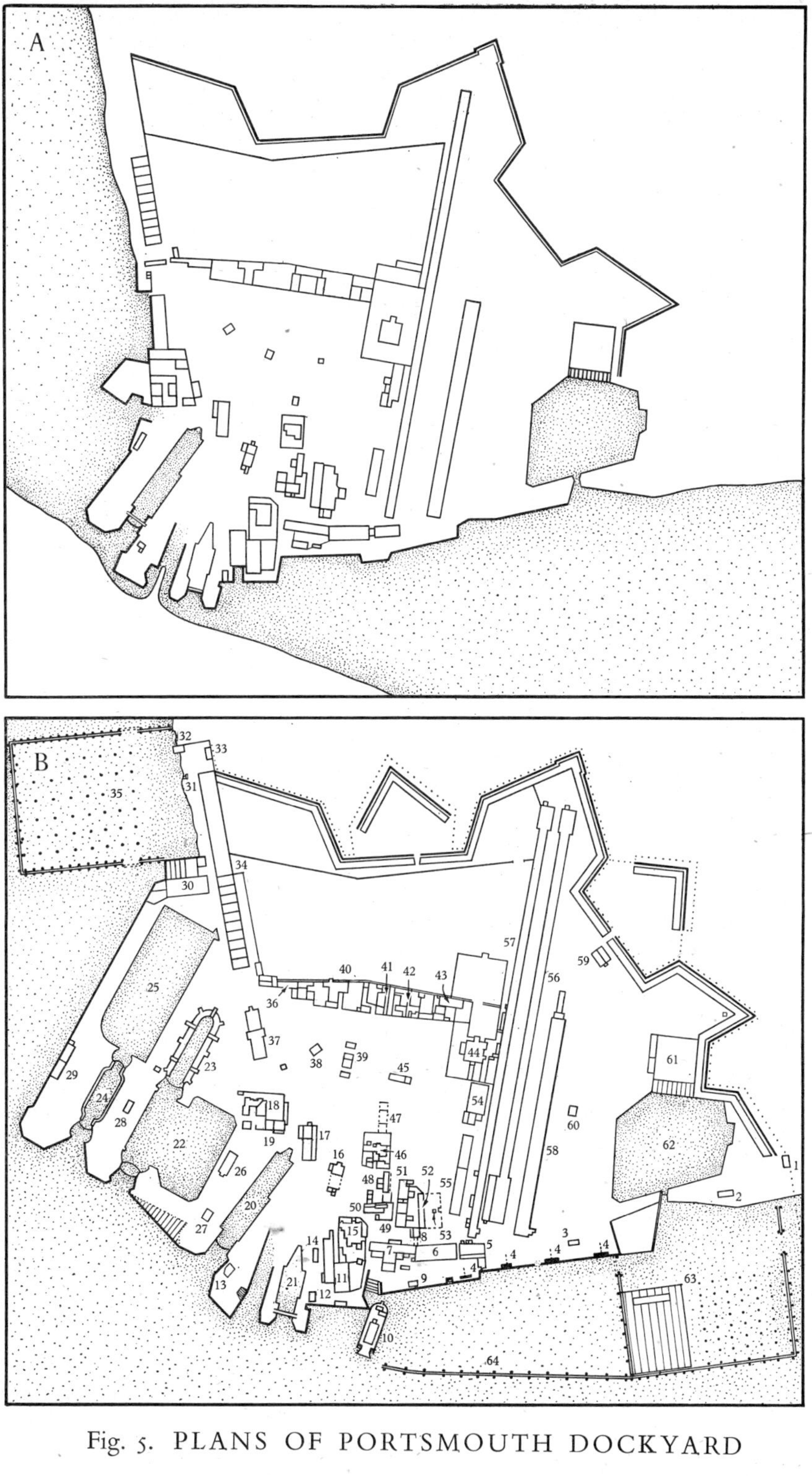

Fig. 5. PLANS OF PORTSMOUTH DOCKYARD

they provided it mainly at a different time of year. In peacetime, they were normally at their busiest in the summer, when the fine weather allowed more to be done on the ships as they lay in the open.[1] In war-time, on the other hand, they were particularly active in the winter, for it was then that the battle-fleet came into harbour to be refitted for the next year's service; and apart from battle repairs and occasional squadrons to be refitted from abroad, the yards in the summer of a war year were comparatively empty, so long as the main fleet was being employed. This difference is reflected in the numbers of workmen borne at the different seasons throughout the war. As will be seen from the graph in Appendix V (A) below, they varied considerably and regularly, rising each autumn, reaching their peak in the middle of the winter, and then declining equally rapidly to their nadir in the early summer.

The shape of this graph poses many, and answers only some, of the questions which the periodic nature of the work presents. The first point which strikes the observer is that the numbers involved were considerable. It was not just a matter of recruiting and dismissing a few score of men, but of organizing a labour force of some two to three thousand, and of changing anything between 200 and 800 men every few months. The navy, therefore, was not only one of the largest employers of skilled labour in the country, but an employer of labour in one of the most variable of industries, requiring a combination of permanent and temporary employees. Secondly, this fluctuation in numbers was a phenomenon common to all the yards, although in the smaller yards the proportion did not always seriously affect the total labour strength.[2] There are, indeed, variations between the graphs of the individual yards. In several cases these can be explained by external factors: Portsmouth, for instance, was used more than the eastern dock-yards during the summer, particularly in the later years of the war when its resources had been improved, because it was a base as well as a dockyard; Plymouth, which was built as a dockyard during the war, was faced with a different type of labour problem from the bigger yards, for it was expanding steadily winter and summer, and was thus not faced with the necessity of discharging its men; while Sheerness and

[1] Sutherland, *Britain's Glory*, pt 2, p. 131. [2] See Appendix V (B) below.

Kinsale, each of which was used purely as a base for storing and cleaning, were engaged upon a different kind of activity from the big yards, one which kept them more or less constantly busy and seldom required large additions of numbers. But the three great eastern yards and—subject to its expansion—Portsmouth, worked under similar conditions, and all produce the same sort of graph in varying degrees. The exact degree to which their labour force rose and fell depended on the extent to which they were used as repair yards, as opposed to shipyards mainly concerned with construction. Deptford and Woolwich came increasingly to be used for the refitting of the smaller ships alone, and otherwise for building; the great ships, and the majority indeed of all rates, went to Portsmouth and Chatham, and it is in the latter yard, unaffected as it was by the physical expansion which affected Portsmouth, that the graph assumes its most extreme form. The same result is reached if the types of workmen, and not their distribution, are examined. The two representative classes may be said to have been the shipwrights and the riggers, the one standing for the permanent employees, the other for those whose recruitment depended more directly on seasonal requirements. Too sharp a distinction must not be drawn between them, for obviously the shipwrights had to be augmented at busy periods, while the riggers could not be entirely dispensed with at any time. But an analysis of their numbers in all the yards during the war produces two distinct graphs, showing that the employment of the riggers, as might be expected, depended on the season of the year considerably more than did that of the shipwrights.[1]

But although the numbers of men naturally reflected the conditions for their employment, they also reflected the conditions of their treatment in that employment. These conditions in turn produce certain qualifications which must be applied to the figures themselves. It is useless to draw conclusions from the latter without recognizing that we know far too little about the men whom they represent. When it is said, for instance, that 941 men were employed at Chatham in January 1690 and 1062 in February,[2] what significance do these totals have? Were they composed of the same men in each case, or if not what proportion had changed? Did they include men employed by other

---

[1] See Appendix V (C) below.

[2] Serg.MS. A 123.

masters, like the workmen in the workshops of the standing contractors, and men loaned by other organizations, such as the Marines, and those who were already receiving pay from other sources, like the sailors set ashore by the fleet for the winter who were either on half pay or, before that system was introduced, were getting bounty money from the navy as volunteers for the next year's fleet? Did all the men entered in these figures work for the whole day at the dockyard, or did they put in some time elsewhere? Did they include men still on the pay books but temporarily absent, either on account of sickness or because they refused to work until paid? Did the fluctuations in the numbers represent merely the recruitment and discharge of additional men, without affecting a permanent corps of workmen, or did they involve the whole body of the yard? And how were the lists themselves compiled: from counting heads as the men went in and out of the yard, or from the yard pay books (which were extremely inaccurate), or from officers' reports? Some of these questions cannot be answered at all; others can be answered only indirectly. The figures, indeed, in many cases merely pose the problems which they are called upon to answer.

One thing, however, we know: the workmen were seldom paid on time. The methods of naval accounting, and the system for obtaining money from the national Exchequer, made it almost impossible, except in emergencies, to pay off the yards each quarter; and the wages for one quarter were thus automatically always in arrears. But the chronic state of naval credit usually ensured that more than that was owing. The means of redeeming this credit, moreover, did not necessarily ensure that the debts were paid off in the order in which they had originally been contracted. Thus it might be possible to pay the workmen for the past two quarters, but not for the quarter before that; and a change of régime, such as occurred at the end of 1688, was a particular incitement to neglect the more remote debts incurred by its predecessor. It might also be more convenient or more necessary to pay off the arrears in one yard than in another; and in general there was no guarantee how soon or in what manner the arrears of pay would be distributed.

When the men finally got their pay, it was often in the form of tickets upon the Navy Office rather than in cash; and except when clerks were sent down to the yards tickets could be exchanged for money only at the London office, so that many men were continually on the move to and from the city, while the rest who for some reason could not make the journey were in as bad a way as before. The tickets were therefore apt to change hands, as professional ticket buyers snapped them up cheap from the men in return for some cash, and took their profit at the Navy Office later. This shortage of money led the workmen to seek part-time employment elsewhere,[1] or sometimes to desert to other occupations or other parts of the country, or occasionally to down tools in the yard.[2] It led them also to supplement their wages by other means: by smuggling stores out of the gate, by working for officers of the yard—although they were also forced to do this without payment[3]—and by working slowly so as to receive pay for overtime.[4] There is no doubt that embezzlement of stores, in particular, was practised on a large scale. It has, indeed, been calculated that the daily loss of timber alone was nearly enough to build a sloop.[5] Hemp was particularly easy to smuggle,[6] but the greatest loss was in wood. By an ancient right, the 'chips', or shavings which were sawn off in the conversion of the log into the piece, were distributed amongst the workmen, and twice a week they and their dependants were allowed to take their quota out of the yard.[7] Naturally, this concession led to enormous abuse. A log which could be used for a large piece would be selected for a small piece, and the rest chopped up as chips; timber would be cut up for chips alone, on the plea that the wood was rotten; while the dockyard officers, who benefited from the practice as much as if not more than the men, accepted from the contractors logs of unsuitable shapes and sizes, or of inferior quality, with their own ends in view. It is no exaggeration to say that in the second half of the century, whole squadrons could have been built out of the wood which left the yards illegitimately; and it was indeed said in the early nine-

---

[1] See p. 328 below. [2] P.R.O. Adm. 1/3569, ff. 82–6; 1/3571, f. 421.

[3] Maydman, *Naval Speculations and Maritime Politicks*, pp. 85–6.

[4] *V.C.H. Kent*, II, p. 363.

[5] Albion, loc. cit. p. 87. For individual examples, see *Mr Williamson's Memoirs of a few Passages transacted by Mr Joseph Allen* (1717). Allen had been master shipwright at Deptford.

[6] B.M.Addnl. 9329, f. 164. [7] P.R.O.Adm. 7/633.

teenth century that the domestic architecture of Portsmouth was determined by the size and quality of the dockyard chips.[1] To the workmen, unpaid and often impressed, as to their superiors, the Administration was fair game; and the attitude towards a government service which has not vanished in later times, that it is meritorious rather than dishonest to smuggle out a piece of its property, seemed quite justifiable and was almost universal in an age when the government service failed to meet its commitments, and when the only person cheated seemed to all ranks of its hierarchy to be the King, whose connexion with themselves was of the slightest.

This behaviour was largely due to the defects in the treatment of the workmen. How far the terms of employment themselves were adequate, it is difficult to say. The men were paid at a daily rate, with extra wages for working nights and tides.[2] Their wages were as follows:[3]

	Per day[4]		Per tide	
	s.	*d.*	*s.*	*d.*
Shipwrights	2	1		7½
Caulkers	2	1		7½
Joiners	2	0		7
House carpenters	1	10		6
Plumbers	2	4		9
Riggers	1	6		4
Sailmakers	1	10		6
Bricklayers	1	8		5
Sawyers (per pair)	3	0		11
Coopers	2	0		7
Pitch heaters	1	3		4
Wheelwrights	2	0		7
Team of 4 horses and 1 man	6	0	1	8
Labourers	1	1		4
Quarter boys		8		2
Oakum boys		6		1

For these wages, the men worked from 6 a.m. to 6 p.m. in winter and from sunrise to sunset in summer, all time before or after that being

[1] Maria S. Bentham, *Life of Brigadier Sir Samuel Bentham* (1862), p. 143.

[2] A night consisted of five hours' work out of daytime, and a tide of an hour and a half's such work.

[3] P.R.O.Adm. 7/633; Serg.Misc. 1, f. 572; B.M.Addnl. 36784, f. 49. I have given several authorities for the same result in this case, because none of them is dated. From internal evidence, however, each would seem to refer to this period. Mr Norman McLeod, in an unpublished paper, 'Shipwrights' Wages, 1496–1788', which is based on dockyard books since destroyed, confirms these figures in one department.

[4] Night work was paid for at the same rate as day work.

included in nights and tides.[1] In the winter, that is to say from 1 November to 2 February, they got an hour for the midday dinner; in the summer they got half an hour for breakfast and, from 23 April to 24 August, an hour and a half for dinner. New Year's day, 30 January, Shrove Tuesday, Coronation day and 5 November[2] were normally holidays, unless there was essential work to be done.

There was one additional source of income for a few of the workmen. By the system of apprenticeship a 'deserving workman' was allowed to take one apprentice, whose wages he received in the usual fashion.[3] These ranged from 1*s*. 2*d*. to 1*s*. 10*d*. per day.[4] On the debit side of the balance, 2*d*. a month was deducted from the men to pay for the surgeon of the yard, which amounted to a form of medical insurance.[5]

But wages in this form are only one element in real wages. They assume quite a different value if the men are lodged and fed partly or wholly by their employer, and if they are adjusted to meet large fluctuations in prices, particularly of food. Lodgings for workmen at the beginning of the war were provided only at Sheerness, where daily travel to and fro was impossible.[6] The foremen and some of the men were housed on Sheppey Island itself, and the rest in hulks in the river.[7] The need for lodgings at the other yards was recognized by the local officials, and in two cases, at Portsmouth and Plymouth, some were provided by the end of the century.[8] But legal and financial difficulties in taking over new ground—for no yard wished to, and few could house their workmen inside their walls—prevented much from being done.[9] Most of the men travelled every day to their work and had to find their own lodging, receiving in lieu a lodging allowance of 2*d*. per day which is included in the wages shown above.[10]

---

1 P.R.O.Adm. 7/633.

2 And during the reigns of Charles II and James II, Restoration day.

3 See p. 97 below.

4 P.R.O.Adm. 7/633.

5 McLeod, 'Shipwrights' Wages' (unpublished paper).

6 See table on p. 87 above.

7 *V.C.H. Kent*, II, p. 359.

8 B.M.Addnl. 9329, ff. 167–8; B.M. King's 43.

9 B.M.Addnl. 9329, ff. 168–9.

10 At Woolwich, there may have been some lodgings near the yard which the navy rented; in the sixteenth century at least, three workmen were reckoned to a bed in these quarters (Oppenheim, loc. cit. p. 73). See also McLeod, loc. cit.

There is no indication that the workmen were fed officially by the navy. The only references to victuals being provided for them in the yards, are to the illegal habit of the yard porters of keeping beershops at the gates.[1] Part of the daily wages were originally cast under the heading of victuals, and this took the place of free meals at the yards.[2] No doubt, as always, there were ways of propitiating seamen coming ashore from the ships or, in yards where a victualling base was also established, of extracting a meal from the stores, particularly when provisions were being returned from ships in harbour. But theoretically it would seem that the workmen found their own meals; and certainly there is evidence, in the letters of the local officials, that at times some of them were literally starving to death.

For dockyard wages did not rise with the general rise in prices. It was not usual for wages to be flexible in the seventeenth century, and in any case, thanks to the perpetual debt which overshadowed all its activities, the navy could not afford to indulge in a sliding scale. It was far more concerned with delaying the payment of the wages which it owed than in considering how to raise them. The shipwrights' pay, to take one example, stayed at 2*s.* 1*d.* per day from 1660 to 1788,[3] and it is unlikely that other dockyard trades fared any better.

How far did these earnings enable the workmen to meet their necessary expenses? Taken all round, with chips and a little embezzlement, and allowing for extra work, a labourer probably made a maximum of 9*s.* a week, and a shipwright a maximum of 15*s.*[4] If we take the price of wheat to the navy in the late 1680's, it averaged just over 29*s.* a quarter, or about a fortnight's wages; in the 1690's it cost on an average anything between 33*s.* and 60*s.* a quarter, and after 1690 itself it fell below 45*s.* only twice.[5] When clothes and lodgings, and possibly a wife and a child or two—however little all these might cost—are taken into consideration, it is therefore not surprising that the ordinary workman embezzled as much as he could or that he is so often described in the letters from the yards as 'starving' or 'in rags'.

The question naturally arises of how his earnings compared with those of his counterparts in the private yards. The absence of records for

[1] P.R.O.Adm. 106/2507, no. 25 [2] McLeod, loc. cit.. [3] Ibid.
[4] Ibid. [5] Beveridge, *Prices and Wages in England*, I, p. 567.

the latter prevents a satisfactory answer. In the first half of the century, the royal yards paid better than most merchant builders,[1] and in 1652 the highest wages for shipwrights in the west country were 2*d.* a day lower than the standard rate in the dockyards.[2] By 1677, however, the private yards were paying better than the King, and it was for this reason that the dockyards resorted to impressment in that year.[3] Comparisons in our period are rare, but suggest that most merchant builders offered more than the navy, and the navy itself admitted as much early in the next century.[4] Compared with other trades, however, the shipwrights at least were not badly off, provided that they were paid. Taking their earnings at 15*s.* a week, they earned £39 a year. At the end of the seventeenth century, Gregory King estimated that artisans and craftsmen on the average earned £38 a year, shopkeepers and tradesmen £45, and men engaged in the liberal arts and sciences £60.[5] At the other end of the scale, it was calculated in 1713 that a family consisting of a man, his wife and three or four children would need to go on the parish if between them they earned less than £20 a year.[6] At this rate, a dockyard labourer just escaped charity on his own earnings.

The decline of wages in the royal yards compared with those in private yards indicated the growth of two factors, which in themselves were contradictory: continuity of employment, and impressment. So long as there was no regular employment in the naval yards, they had to adhere to the market rates for men; but with a prospect of permanent work many men came in on lower wages, and consciously or unconsciously the naval authorities used this fact to keep the rate of pay steady. When voluntary labour failed, the press was brought into play; and although it was applied only at certain times, when extra men were badly needed, its growth was a feature of the last twenty years of the century. In that case also, the inducement of high wages was not required.

---

[1] *The Autobiography of Phineas Pett*, ed. W. G. Perrin (*N.R.S.* 1918), p. xix.

[2] McLeod, loc. cit. [3] Ibid. [4] Ibid.

[5] *The Political and Commercial Works of...Charles D'Avenant* (ed. Sir C. Whitworth, 5 vols., 1771), II, p. 184.

[6] M. Dorothy George, *England in Transition; Life and Work in the Eighteenth Century* (1931), p. 10.

On paper at least, there was an organization for training and promotion in the dockyard service. A boy could enter a royal yard as an apprentice, either to an officer or to a 'deserving workman', the former being allowed a maximum of five and the latter one each. The total number of apprentices was not allowed to exceed one-fifth of the number of men in the yard.[1] The officers' apprentices were largely picked boys, often members of families with a tradition of shipbuilding from whom the future officers were chosen, and they received their training accordingly.[2] The workman's apprentice could rise after seven years to the position of workman,[3] and look forward, if he wished, to becoming a quarterman in charge of a group and then a foreman in charge of a body of workmen of the same class as himself. It was not impossible for him, at least if he were a shipwright, to rise above that to be a junior officer of the yard, in which rank again further theoretical possibilities of promotion came into sight. On paper, there was no obstacle to merit. In practice, of course, there were plenty. But at least the dockyard service under the later Stuarts offered in this respect a real inducement to its skilled workmen. They received no pension, however, until 1764.[4]

If a workman could stay in the dockyards, therefore, he had some reasonable prospects of advancement. But there was no guarantee of employment, and no valid distinction other than that of circumstance can be drawn between the long-service man and the pressed man. Both, though possibly in differing degrees, remained largely at the mercy of events, with no certainty of employment but on the other hand with no certainty of being able to avoid it. This type of labour, to which the navy had few obligations, was seldom able to gain concessions from it. Largely unorganized, and largely dependent upon what they could get from their employer, the workmen came low in the list of priorities for payment, and it was only by actually striking or deserting that they could induce the authorities to take notice of them. Throughout the war, they were seldom able to push their claims with sufficient force to satisfy their needs, and they remained, largely in the background, as

1 N. McLeod, 'The Shipwrights of the Royal Dockyards', in *M.M.* XI, no. 3, p. 286.
2 Ibid. pp. 285–7.
3 P.R.O.Adm. 7/633. Shipwright apprentices entered at the age of sixteen.
4 McLeod, 'Shipwrights' Wages'.

a constant problem to their superiors, embezzling, disappearing from time to time in little groups, laying down their tools to protest for wages or going slow on urgent work; generally hampering the pace of administration, but never actually stopping it, and occasionally even earning the congratulations of the ships' officers for their work. Seldom exercising so dramatic an effect upon administration as the contractors for the raw materials, they exercised an indirect effect upon it that was certainly more continuous and quite as important.

The organization which supervised the workmen of the royal yards is accompanied by none of the vagueness which attends the terms of the workmen's employment. Administratively, it represented quite a different problem, for however temporary and variable the nature of dockyard work, its management had to be permanent and consistent. While large numbers of workmen could be recruited and dismissed at short notice their officers were needed continuously, and the organization could not fluctuate with the numbers employed, but had to remain equal to the highest possible capacity of the yard. In this sense, therefore, the dockyard officers were less dependent than the men upon the material conditions of their employment. The duties remained, even when the conditions for their exercise did not. Within the limits set by the character of the yard itself, they represented a uniform hierarchy with well-regulated responsibilities and powers, although their status still remained to be settled in some respects.

The dockyard officers fell into two fairly distinct classes of junior and senior officers.[1] The former included those who had charge of the various dockyard trades, and the officers of the 'ordinary'. The master caulker, the master house carpenter and the master joiner, the master

---

[1] Their duties are given in 'The Duke of York's Instructions for the Commissioners and Subordinate Officers of the Royall Navy' of 1660 (P.R.O.Adm. 7/633). These appeared as the first printed instructions for naval officials in 1717, with the intervening minor modifications, under the title of *The Oeconomy of the Navy Office*. For an unofficial and very clear description of a dockyard at work see Henry Maydman, *Naval Speculations and Maritime Politicks* (1691), ch. III. Maydman himself was a disappointed purser, and his accounts of the theoretical duties of the officers are frequently followed by a description of their practice. For salaries, see P.R.O.Adm. 7/169, 7/173 and Serg.MS. A 133.

boat builder and master mastmaker, whose duties were sometimes combined, the master blockmaker and the master pumpmaker were borne on the books of the yard. The master ropemaker belonged to the ropeyard, which physically might be inside the dockyard walls. The officers of the 'ordinary', which referred to the maintenance and defence of the harbour and the ships in harbour,[1] were the boatswain of the yard, the purser, the gunner, the carpenter and the cook. Finally, there was the porter of the yard, who had charge of the gate where the men were checked in and out. Receiving much the same pay as the junior officers, but scarcely comparable to them in status, were the clerks of the senior officers.

There were six of these senior officers. They may be divided into two groups: first, the master shipwright, the master attendant and the clerk of the ropeyard; secondly, the clerk of the cheque, the storekeeper and the clerk of the survey. The master shipwright had 'the Oversight, and all the Direction and Contrivance of the Building all Ships...Docks, etc.' and for this purpose was placed over the junior officers of the different trades. In some yards he also had an assistant, who besides supervising the shipwrights more closely than he himself could do, helped him in his other duties. As master builder of the yard, by which title he was sometimes known,[2] he also had close connexions with his colleagues. It was his responsibility to sign for all issues from the stores, and to send the vouchers to the accountant of the yard; to check the carpenter's gear out of the ships; to assist in his expert capacity in all surveys of stores; and to check the workmen's wages, report their numbers to the head of the yard, and help the porter in preventing embezzlement. He was, as one account had it, 'a most material Officer of Trust'.[3]

While the master shipwright was in charge of the work in the yard, the master attendant was the head of the ordinary, in charge of ships' movements and of the harbour itself, with its berths and moorings, its

---

[1] The term was a financial one, to describe the peacetime maintenance of the navy as contrasted with those activities, whether in war or peace, which were financed by an 'extraordinary' Parliamentary supply.

[2] There seems to have been no rule as to when he was called master shipwright and when master builder (e.g. B.M.Addnl. 9329, *passim*; B.M. King's 43; Maydman, loc. cit. pp. 68–78).

[3] Maydman, loc. cit. pp. 70–1.

pilotage and the transport of stores and workmen to the ships. This involved him in the care of those stores which were not the responsibility of the shipwright, such as rigging, sails, cables and anchors. He checked their issue, distribution and maintenance, in the same way as his colleague.

The clerk of the ropeyard was technically not one of the dockyard officers, any more than the master ropemaker. He was the latter's superior, and in general charge of both the clerical and working branches of the ropeyard.

The second group of senior officials was composed of the clerical officers. The first of these was the clerk of the cheque. He had perhaps the most difficult of dockyard duties, to muster the workmen and ordinary and the companies of the ships in harbour. On the basis of these musters he made out the paysheets and indented for the necessary money. Although his own subordinates were entirely clerical, he was given disciplinary powers over the porter to ensure that the men were properly checked in and out, and he was also used as a general check on the behaviour of his colleagues to see that they did not employ the workmen of the yard for their own ends. As his musters of the yard involved him in other duties ashore, so also his musters of the ships led to kindred offices afloat. He made out the warrants which empowered the victuallers to put the ships' companies on harbour victuals, and issued imprest bills to the captains. He was also responsible for the contingent account of the yard. The authority and knowledge which he derived from these duties were used, in addition, to check the storekeeper's receipts and issues, and to countersign all bills already signed by his colleagues. One observer was so impressed by the responsibilities of the office that he concluded that 'this Officer is of that general Use, that he had need be endowed with as many good Parts, as can be found to be gathered into one Man; I mean, Endowments of the Soul; as, Faith, Justice, Charity, and all Spiritual Graces; and of the Mind; as Wisdom, Patience, Affability, and all the intellectual Graces; and of the Body; as, Temperance, Chastity, Labour, and Industry, Vigilance, and Carefulness'. As a necessary supplement to these virtues, he must also be 'a true Observer of the Method and Rules of the *Navy* and *Yards*'.[1]

[1] Maydman, loc. cit. p. 67.

The storekeeper's duties were those which his title implies. He received and issued all the stores, except those of the ropeyard. His responsibilities were thus entirely clerical, and their consequences financial; and he was the only officer who was obliged to give a security for his appointment. The receipts for his stores were checked by the clerk of the cheque, the master shipwright and his assistant, the master attendant and the clerk of the survey; his issues again by the clerk of the cheque; and his surveys by the officers concerned in the different stores.

The remaining officer was the clerk of the survey. He kept the accounts of the stores from the notes of receipt and issue passed to him by the storekeeper. He also surveyed independently all ships' stores returned to the yard, the better to pass their boatswain's and carpenter's accounts. He naturally acted as an indirect check, usually at a later date, on the officers drawing stores, and himself was checked by the quarterly examination of his books at the Navy Office. His duties, indeed, were merely those of a clerk of that office stationed locally rather than in London, and he was more directly under its control than were the other officers. For this reason, he gave no security for his post.

Finally, in charge of the dockyard was the resident Commissioner. His authority was sometimes more obvious outside the yard than within it. As its representative, he was usually made a Justice of the Peace in the county, and as such could keep an effective eye upon roving sailors and workmen. He could issue press warrants on the authority of the Navy Board, and as one of its members exercised a delegated authority over the dockyard personnel. But he had no powers of appointment or dismissal, or of punishment in the case of a dockyard officer. His relations with the sea officers were ambiguous, and were the cause of frequent trouble. Theoretically, he exercised a general supervision over their demands upon the yard and their compliance with the rules of the ordinary; in practice, he either submitted to them or quarrelled with them so long as they remained in harbour. His position in the naval hierarchy, indeed, was not entirely clear, and it reflected more clearly than did those of his subordinates, who were not brought into contact with the sea authorities in the same way, the uncertain status of the dockyard officers in their relations with other branches of the service.

For although the duties of the dockyard officers had been clearly promulgated in 1660, in such a way that they had hardly to be amended for almost a century,[1] their status was less clear at the end of the Stuart régime; and while full credit must be given to James for his clarification of the dockyard regulations, their significance cannot be understood unless they are related to the position of the officials who were to enforce them. Official regulations can be promulgated under two sorts of conditions. On the one hand, they may be the result of a period of administrative stability, in which function has conformed to a status which has itself been secure for some time, and where accordingly they serve the purpose of defining and partly modifying existing practice. On the other hand, they may be the result of administrative change, where new functions have to be organized and where the status of the agents follows upon the clarification of their duties. The latter was the position which arose from the appearance of the big ship and the big fleet in the middle of the seventeenth century. It was not surprising, therefore, that the organization of the dockyards in accordance with the new conditions preceded the formation of a stable and well-defined class of dockyard officers, nor that the late seventeenth century should have witnessed so great a discrepancy between the theory and the practice of their duties. The peculation and insubordination which were such a feature of Pepys's period and that which followed, were at least partly the result of a system in which the regulation of duties in the naval departments was matched by the vagueness of the status of their members.

The position of the dockyard officer may best be seen in his pay and in his prospects of promotion. The former in particular illustrates the direct connexion which still existed between function and status. Pay was not fixed at common rates throughout a unified dockyard service, but still varied with the establishment from yard to yard. At the end of 1688 the details were as given on p. 104.[2] The discrepancies in the

[1] Various additions to the original instructions had occurred by 1734, when the *Regulations and Instructions referring to His Majesty's Service at Sea* reached their second edition. Considerable changes came in the *Additional Regulations*... of 1756, which were incorporated in the ninth edition of the next year.

[2] This list is taken from P.R.O. Adm. 7/169, for 1689. The details do not differ from those given in *Catal.* I, p. 114, for 1684. I have included only those officers who have

different yards between the officers' salaries and allowances were the results of individual decisions, made at different times and as yet not comprehended by any one order or set of regulations. The tables reflect the relative importance of the yards so accurately because they reflect the varied status of the dockyard officials.

One branch, however, was more secure in its status than the rest. It is perhaps significant that alone among the seven senior officers, the master shipwrights should have received the same salary and fees at each yard.[1] They had been the first of the dockyard officials to be given the opportunity of permanent employment,[2] and the first to be given a formal training in their profession.[3] As a result, they were generally regarded as second in command to the Commissioner, and in his absence, as at Sheerness, and at Deptford and Woolwich for most of the century, they took his place.[4] Even after the emergence of other departments they retained their pre-eminence and, as Chief Constructors and later Managers of the Construction Department, they still take pride of place in the hierarchy of the twentieth century.[5] It is not surprising, therefore, that we should know more about them at the end of the seventeenth century than we know about the other officers, and the terms of their employment provide, as it were, the highest common factor for those of the whole hierarchy.

Exactly when the master shipwrights became full-time, as distinct from permanent, officers of the dockyards, is not certain, but it was probably not long before 1660.[6] A few years earlier they had been

---

already been discussed. Chaplains and doctors will be referred to later. For the differences in lodging enjoyed by the officers, which affected their rates of pay, see also the table on p. 87 above.

[1] The following account depends largely upon N. McLeod, 'The Shipwright Officers of the Royal Dockyards', in *M.M.* XI, no. 4, pp. 355–69.

[2] Oppenheim, loc. cit. pp. 73, 151–2.

[3] Ibid. pp. 162, 203–4, 208; Callender, *Peter Pett and the Sovereign of the Seas.* Perhaps the most notable example of this training was provided by the fact that the formula for measuring tonnage throughout the first half of the seventeenth century was produced by the shipwright Matthew Baker (Oppenheim, loc. cit. p. 266).

[4] McLeod, loc. cit. p. 357.

[5] They kept their title of Master Shipwright until 1895.

[6] For the evidence from the now irrecoverable dockyard books, see McLeod, loc. cit. p. 356.

	Chatham			Deptford			Woolwich			Sheerness			Portsmouth		
	£	s.	d.	£	s.	d.	£	s.	d.	£	s.	d.	£	s.	d.
Commissioner:															
Salary	500	0	0	500	0	0[1]	—			—			500	0	0
Paper money	12	0	0	—			—			—			12	0	0
Clerk of the cheque:															
Salary	120	0	0	80	0	0	70	0	0	80	0	0	80	0	0
Paper money	5	0	0	5	0	0	5	0	0	5	0	0	5	0	0
Clerks	120	0	0	104	0	0	80	0	0	30	0	0	110	0	0
Storekeeper:															
Salary	100	0	0	144	18	4	70	0	0	100	0	0	100	0	0
Paper money	6	0	0	7	0	0	2	0	0	1	0	0	5	0	0
Clerks	154	0	0	154	0	0	104	0	0	30	0	0	154	0	0
Clerk of the survey:															
Salary	100	0	0	60	0	0	50	0	0	50	0	0	50	0	0
Paper money	6	0	0	4	0	0	2	0	0	2	0	0	2	0	0
Clerks	50	0	0	50	0	0	30	0	0	30	0	0	50	0	0
House rent	10	0	0	—			—			—			—		
Clerk of the ropeyard:															
Salary	70	0	0	—			70	0	0	—			60	0	0
Clerk	24	0	0	—			24	0	0	—			24	0	0
House rent	10	0	0	—			—			—			—		
Keeping the gate	—			—			9	0	0	—			—		
Master shipwright:															
Salary	113	0	0	113	0	0	113	0	0	113	0	0	113	0	0
Exchequer fee	18	5	0	18	5	0	18	5	0	18	5	0	18	5	0
Clerk	30	0	0	30	0	0	30	0	0	—			30	0	0
Master attendant:															
Salary	100	0	0	144	18	4	100	0	0	100	0	0	100	0	0
Clerk	24	0	0	24	0	0	24	0	0	—			24	0	0
House rent	—			—			10	0	0	—			—		
Porter:															
Salary	18	0	0	13	6	8	13	6	8	17	10	0	17	10	0
Keeping the clock	3	6	8	4	0	0	3	0	0						
Master shipwright's assistant:															
Salary	(1) 70	0	0	70	0	0	—			—			46	10	0
	(2) 50	0	0	—			—			—			—		
House rent	10	0	0	—			—			—			—		
Master attendant's assistant	80	0	0	—			—			—			—		
Master bricklayer	31	6	8	31	6	0	—			—			—		
Master blockmaker	—			—			32	12	1	31	6	0	31	6	0
Master caulker	7	0	0	32	12	1	—			46	10	0	46	10	0
Master house carpenter				31	6	0	—			31	6	0	31	6	0
Master joiner				31	6	0	—			31	6	0	31	6	0
Master boatbuilder	163 (total)	5	0	31	12	1	—			—			31	6	0
Master mastmaker				32	12	1	—			—			42	12	1
Master pumpmaker				—			—			—			—		
Boatswain of the yard	60	0	0	60	0	0	60	0	0	40	0	0	60	0	0

forbidden to indulge in private business,[2] and this was strictly enforced later in the century. For instance, when Kinsale was again set up as an advance base in 1690, the master shipwright was found to be also a local

[1] One Commissioner was Commissioner for Deptford and Woolwich.

[2] McLeod, loc. cit. p. 356. In Charles I's reign, they were said to have spent two or three months a year away from the royal yards, looking after their own businesses (Oppenheim, loc. cit. p. 298).

builder, and his appointment was postponed until he had promised to dispose of his private yard.[1] In compensation for this loss of income, their salaries were raised in Charles II's reign to the uniform rate of £113 at every yard.[2] For a further three decades, however, they were paid partly as salaried officials and partly as wage earners. In addition to the Exchequer fees which they received until almost the end of the century, they were paid up to £150 a year in emoluments, as well as overtime for work done on nights and tides and wages for their articled apprentices. Nor were these last two items negligible: in the quarter ending Lady Day 1685, the master shipwright at Portsmouth was paid £3. 15*s*. 9*d*. for 21 nights and 54 tides, and a further £30. 14*s*. 4*d*. in wages for five apprentices.[3] Even when, in the middle of William's reign, their salaries were substantially raised, they continued to get emoluments in money, quite apart from what they received or took in kind. It was not until 1801 that dockyard officers as a class were given inclusive salaries.[4]

The recruitment of shipwright officers seems to have been chiefly from the ranks of the junior officers of the yard, but within that orbit the family connexion was strong. There was a large group of the shipbuilding fraternity with wide ramifications and powerful interests in both royal and private yards. This indeed had spread in the course of the century to include other naval officials and the sea officers as well. Sir Richard Haddock, successively an Admiral, a Commissioner of the Navy, and a Lord Commissioner of the Admiralty, was perhaps the best known of the officers who came of shipwright stock; but he was only an illustrious example, and there were many humbler cases. Dennis Lyddell, who was a member of the Navy Board during the reigns of William, Anne and George I, had shipbuilding connexions, and so had Sir Richard Beach and Benjamin Tymewell among the better-known dockyard officials, Sir John Berry among the Admirals, and Sir Anthony Deane and the Petts among the officers who went direct to the Navy Board.[5]

---

[1] P.R.O.Adm. 3/6: 3 July 1690.

[2] Oppenheim, loc. cit. p. 366.

[3] McLeod, loc. cit. p. 356.

[4] Ibid. See p. 598 below for some of these emoluments and perquisites.

[5] See Sir George Duckett's biographical notices in Sir G. Jackson, *Naval Commissioners...from 1660 to 1760* (1889); A. W. Johns, 'Sir Anthony Deane', in *M.M.* XI, no. 2, pp. 164–93.

Within this group of shipwrights, appointment to vacant posts was largely a matter of influence. Fathers recommended their sons and sons-in-law, and certain families like the Petts, the Furzers and the Hardings had many members in the naval service. William Sutherland, who wrote the two best books of the period on shipbuilding, was not an exceptional case, with 32 years' service as a shipwright and junior officer himself, his father 'and several of my relations' master carpenters and one of them a naval surveyor of contract-built ships, his uncle Bagwell master shipwright at Portsmouth, and his grandfather for thirty years a foreman of shipwrights at Deptford yard.[1] Patronage, however, did not exclude but was rather complemented by merit: appointment was by Admiralty warrant; candidates were theoretically selected according to their qualifications;[2] recommendations were sometimes refused; and the system of apprenticeship which has already been mentioned ensured that within the limits of the initial selection, ability could obtain its reward.

Once a man had reached the position of foreman shipwright his next step was to become a junior officer, as master caulker, master boat-builder, master mastmaker or one of the similar posts, in one of the yards.[3] He might then either remain there until a vacancy occurred for the higher posts of assistant master shipwright or master shipwright, or else go to some other and bigger yard in the rank which he already held. There was by now a considerable interchange of officers, and in the higher posts some approximation to a system of promotion by yards, with Sheerness at the bottom and Chatham at the top. Such a system cannot be said to have been either regularly or explicitly practised. It was nowhere laid down on paper. But combined to an uncertain extent with purely local selection, it was recognized as the orthodox means of promotion within the dockyard service. The prospects of rising beyond the rank of master shipwright, however, were slight. The highest post open to the profession was that of Surveyor of

---

[1] *The Ship-Builder's Assistant*, preface.

[2] There was no examination, but some notice was taken of the applicant's career, and a training in the dockyard service was an advantage.

[3] This paragraph is based on McLeod, loc. cit. and on many individual appointments discussed and listed in the minutes of the Board of Admiralty (P.R.O.Adm. 3/1–14).

the Navy, but it was rare for a shipwright to get beyond the rank of resident Commissioner at one of the yards.

Less is known about the other senior officers of the yards. The master attendant almost always came from outside, from the ranks of the ships' officers. He was often a senior captain, more attracted to money than to glory or else near the end of his active service; and during the war, complications arose when sometimes he had to accompany the fleet to sea as a sea officer.[1] His subordinate officers, including the boatswain of the yard, also came from the sea service. The clerical officers came partly from outside, but mostly from the subordinate clerks, who were encouraged as much as possible to stay in the service. Their prospects of promotion were good, for as juniors they were frequently although not regularly exchanged between the yards and the Navy Office in London, so that either they might hope to rise in the central office, or else eventually to enter the Navy Board by way of the post of clerk of the cheque or storekeeper at one of the yards. Sergison and Lyddell, who both had long service as officers of the Navy Board, were originally clerks in the London office and at Chatham respectively; and Samuel Pett may also have started as a clerk at Chatham.[2]

But the senior posts throughout the dockyard service were awarded by favour rather than by system; and in the matter of favour it was at a disadvantage compared with its rival, the hierarchy of sea officers. The clash came most directly at the rank of resident Commissioner. The four available posts were filled by seven men altogether during the French war. Of these, three—two of whom were employed at Chatham[3]—had probably risen within the dockyard service; one was appointed from outside, after serving the Navy Board as an agent at Liverpool;[4] and the other three had been sea officers of some distinction, one having reached the rank of Vice-Admiral and the other two that of captain.[5] In these appointments the relative status of the rival hierarchies could be compared; and the competition between them is of interest,

[1] P.R.O.Adm. 3/4:25/6; 3/5:14/1.

[2] See Sir George Duckett's biographical notices in Sir George Jackson, *Naval Commissioners...from 1660 to 1760*.

[3] Sir Phineas Pett, Sir Edward Gregory, Benjamin Tymewell. The latter's previous career is obscure.

[4] Henry Greenhill.

[5] Sir Richard Beach, Thomas Wilshaw and George St Lo.

not only for the reasons which withheld from the dockyard officers the monopoly of the higher posts in the dockyard service, but also because it illustrated one aspect of the conditions of service at sea which turned so many senior officers towards the land at a certain stage in their careers. Such uncertainty was bound to persist until the status of both the civil and the military branches of the navy had been more adequately regulated than was possible towards the end of the seventeenth century; as it was, they continued in the prevailing conditions to compete bitterly for the same uncertain prize.

CHAPTER IV

OFFICERS AND MEN

When the ship had been built and stored, the next stage was to man her. The former practice, whereby the numbers of men required were calculated on the basis of tonnage—one man to every four tons for ships of between 40 and 400 tons, one to every three tons in the larger ships[1]—had been replaced in 1677 by the establishment whereby the complement depended upon the gun-power. This method of reckoning had often been used before,[2] but it was now made universal and obligatory. The numbers carried by each ship were rated first according to her ordnance, and a proportion was then added, according to her size, to manage the ship herself. The details were as follows:[3]

	First rate	Second rate	Third rate	Fourth rate	Fifth rate	Sixth rate
Cannon of Seven 7 (or 8) men	182	—	—	—	—	—
Demi-Cannon 5 men	–130	130–110	130–	—	—	—
24-Pounder 5 men	—	—	–120	120–	—	—
Whole-Culverin 4 (or 5) men	112–104	104–	—	—	—	—
12-Pounder 4 men	—	—	104–	—	—	—
Demi-Culverin 3 men	—	–66	—	–60	54–48	—
Saker 3 men	84–78	72–42	48–72	66–54	30–24	48–20
Minion 3 men	42–30	24–18	–30	24–12	8	4–
3-Pounder 2 men	8–4	—	8–4	—	—	—
To carry powder to the guns	34–30	28–20	20–15	12–8	6	4–3
To fill and hand powder to the guns	15–10	6	6	5–3	2	2
Surgeon and crew	10–8	8	7–6	4	3	3–2
Carpenter and crew	8–6	4	4–3	3–2	1	1
Purser and crew	5	4	3–2	2–1	1	—
Men for the small shot	110–80	65–51	45–32	20–16	14–15	11–10
Men to stand by the sails	120–90	75–61	55–38	24–20	16–17	12
Men for the boats and tops	50–25	20	15–12	—	—	—
Total	780–600	540–410	445–340	280–180	135–125	85–50

From this table, the numbers required for any one year could be worked out, once the size of the fleet and of the detached squadrons

[1] *Catal.* I, p. 238. [2] *Boteler's Dialogues*, p. 65.

[3] *Catal.* I, pp. 239–40. The figures in brackets against men per gun are those allowed in the supplementary establishment for the thirty new ships begun in that year. The figures in the rate columns are those for the largest and smallest of each rate.

had been decided. Some idea of the wartime figures can be gained from the following table of the men theoretically borne each year at sea:[1]

1688	12,714	1693	43,827
1689	22,332	1694	47,710
1690	31,971	1695	48,514
1691	35,317	1696	47,677
1692	40,274	1697	44,743

These numbers did not remain steady throughout the year. As has been seen,[2] the larger ships could not safely stay out beyond September, nor could they go to sea before April; and thus the battle-fleets of both sides always spent between six and seven months of the year in harbour. The variation between the numbers required in summer and winter for the first two years of the war was of this order:[3]

January–April, 1689	16,362 men
May–September, 1689	24,164 men
October, 1689–February, 1690	21,740 men
March–October, 1690	33,573 men

The market from which these varied requirements could be met, was provided by the general seafaring population of Britain.[4] No satisfactory calculation has been made of its size. Two of the most careful statisticians of the later seventeenth century tackled the problem, but neither of them convincingly. Sir William Petty in the 1670's put the needs of the navy at 36,000 men, and those of trade at 48,000 of whom

---

[1] Admty:Corbett, XI, f. 108. The exact value of numbers such as these is discussed below.

[2] P. 36 above.

[3] 'A monthly abstract of all ships kept in Sea Pay, 5 Nov. 1688–1 April 1695', in N.M.M. MS. (uncatalogued).

[4] There was no regular system for attracting or impressing men from Ireland, possibly because, apart from the physical difficulties, Admiralty rights in that country were the subject of a long and acrimonious dispute throughout the war (see B.M. Egerton 744; B.M.Addnl. 38150). But there was a regular system of recruitment from Scotland. The men could not be pressed, but they got English rates of pay, equality with Englishmen in the exchange of prisoners of war and, in March 1693, permission to use English hospitals. The Scots had a small navy of their own, and several privateers, which had to be manned first (*The Old Scots Navy from 1689 to 1710*, ed. James Grant (*N.R.S.* 1914), p. 48, and see also texts of orders for seamen, *passim*).

only 24,000 were probably at sea at any one time; but he contented himself with remarking that neither navy nor trade could raise enough men to carry on simultaneously to their satisfaction.[1] Gregory King, working on the basis of twelve men to every 200 tons of merchant shipping, estimated that 11,432 men were employed in the ships of the overseas trades at the Revolution;[2] and, calculating the returns of the hearth money tax, that the total seafaring population was about 50,000.[3] But it seems likely that we shall never know with any accuracy the number of seamen in the country, for no organization existed at the time by which to compute it. In France, there was a registry which accounted for the greater part of the seafaring population; in Holland, it was comparatively simple to assess its size by geographical distribution; but in England, where the type of trade was not so directly determined by the physical distribution of the population, and where there was no register by which to assess its size, the number of skilled men could be calculated only on the theoretical basis of a trade which they failed fully to man.

Exactly what was a seaman, moreover, was not a simple matter to determine. Besides the regular sailors who gained their livelihood exclusively from the sea, there was a substantial fringe of men who came and went irregularly, making the odd voyage from time to time but taking other jobs in the interval. Many of these men were doubtless the 'landmen' who were entered aboard so many crews, particularly in wartime when the navy, which needed all the seamen it could get, often issued protections from the press on the basis of four landsmen to one seaman.[4] But although perhaps some of them were trained men

---

[1] In his *Political Arithmetick*, ch. II (*The Economic Writings of Sir William Petty*, ed. C. H. Hull (1899), I, pp. 276–7). The argument that there were fewer seamen in the country than its sea services required, seems to have been a common one later in the century as well, judging by the efforts of George St Lo (*England's Safety*... (1694), p. 52) to counter it.

[2] George Chalmers, *An Estimate of the Comparative Strength of Britain*... (1782), p. 3. This work depended for its figures of this period mainly upon Davenant and King himself. See also ibid. p. 30. I have taken this figure as applying to overseas trade because it is based on the tonnage of shipping which passed the customs (ibid. p. 5).

[3] *Works of*...*Charles D'Avenant*, II, p. 184.

[4] There are many examples throughout P.R.O.Adm. 3/1–14.

who were classed in this way to avoid the press, many of the landsmen were landsmen indeed, picked up for want of anything better from the boys and odd men of the seaport towns. It is impossible, however, to determine their proportions, for quite apart from the statistical confusion of the day, the term 'seaman', as any seaman knows, is largely a subjective term.

But these tentative estimates of the size of the seafaring population were made only by those interested in the science of measuring population. The navy itself normally concentrated on the markets which it knew to be most profitable rather than on any statistical information.[1] There were three obvious places to look for trained men. The first was in the ships, belonging mostly to the trading companies, which made the different voyages overseas. On the average, these were of over 400 tons burthen and carried one man to every four to eight tons,[2] so that more men could be found in fewer ships than in the European or coastal trades with their smaller vessels. A deep-sea voyage, moreover, was the most profitable voyage for the seaman as well as the owner and master—Edward Coxere and William Barlow as well as Robinson Crusoe sought to recoup their fortunes by this means[3]—and there was no shortage of trained men to sign on for a passage. Apart from the blue-water sailors there were the coastal seamen, and the fishermen and watermen. The former were to be found most easily in the Newcastle colliers which, with their high wages and regular employment, attracted the best of the men for the short passages.[4] The latter were regulated by chartered companies which were obliged, by the terms of their charters, to provide a quota of men when ordered to do so by warrant.[5] There were probably a third as many regular fishermen as

---

[1] The navy did make occasional efforts to find out the number of mariners in the country, but without success (Bodl. Rawl. A 171, f. 157). The Treasury also seems to have interested itself in the question, to judge from the lists of mariners contained in P.R.O. T. 64/298.

[2] Barbour, loc. cit. p. 263, n. 1; B.M.Addnl. 9764, ff. 8, 68, 70.

[3] See *The Adventures by Sea of Edward Coxere*; and *Barlow's Journal of his Life at Sea in King's Ships, East and West Indiamen, and other merchantmen, from 1659 to 1703* (ed. B. Lubbock, 2 vols., 1934).

[4] Willan, *The English Coasting Trade, 1600–1750*, pp. 11–12.

[5] Admty:Corbett, x, f. 61.

there were seamen,[1] so that theoretically they represented a certain and rapid supply in emergency; but in fact the companies seldom honoured their obligations, and in the event not more than a thousand men could be expected from this source.[2]

There were two ways in which the navy could get its men. It could attract them into the service by the conditions which it offered, or it could compel them to join, either indirectly by removing the possibility of finding jobs elsewhere at sea, or directly by impressment, or by a blend of both. In wartime, particularly when the main fleet was employed, there were seldom enough volunteers to man the warships, perhaps partly owing to the shortage of seamen in general, but mainly because the navy was the least profitable and in many ways the least pleasant of sea services. The gap had therefore to be met by compulsion of one sort or another. Three methods were used, individually or together. First, a nucleus for some of the crews could theoretically be collected from the chartered companies. This, however, only scratched at the problem. Secondly, an embargo could be imposed on shipping, preventing vessels from leaving port. This was not necessarily done only for naval purposes, although it was one of the standard ways of raising men for the service. Embargoes were ordered not by the Admiralty but by the Treasury, and sometimes served the purposes of trade policy, being imposed when no seamen were required or on occasion refused when they were. A three-cornered battle was constantly waged, when manning was involved, between the merchants whose trade was restricted, the navy which wanted the men, and the Privy Council whose policy had often to reconcile the conflicting claims. Unfortunately for the navy, the three sources which provided its best material were all able to bring considerable pressure to bear on the government to encourage the pursuit of their activities. The great trading companies by direct intervention, the coal merchants through the City of London and the fishermen through members of Parliament, all fought the navy, at times with considerable success; and few governments, when it came to the point, cared to disrupt trade on behalf of a well-manned fleet.[3] As a result, the total embargo that the navy would have liked was

[1] To judge from surveys earlier in the century (Oppenheim, loc. cit. p. 244).

[2] See pp. 230–1 below.

[3] See pp. 229–30 below.

seldom imposed, and a variety of measures was taken instead. An embargo might be placed upon the whole country for certain types of trade, or upon certain ports for all types of trade, or upon certain ports for certain types of trade. It might be regularly imposed upon some trades every year for given periods, or it might be imposed for a specific purpose with little or no warning and for an uncertain length of time. In all cases, its duration was determined by Order in Council.[1]

The selective process of the embargo was sometimes avoided and at other times paralleled by a selective control over the numbers of ships and men annually permitted to sail in certain trades. The two systems were alternative agents of the same policy. Thus, trade to New England, to Hamburg, to Portugal and to Bilbao was usually not restricted to any number of ships and was granted protections from the press for a standard proportion of its men, but was liable to be stopped completely by an embargo; while trade for the other Plantations, for the rest of Spain and the Mediterranean, for Africa and for the East Indies was usually allowed only a given number of ships per year as well as a given number of men per ship, but these could normally rely on being excepted from an embargo. The difference in method was partly the result of a difference in the wartime conditions of the voyage, and partly of the type of trade which it affected. As the approaches to the Channel became increasingly dangerous in the early years of the war, the Mediterranean and Plantation trades were confined almost entirely to convoys, which sailed at infrequent and irregular intervals: there were no convoys for over a year to the Mediterranean at one time, and only two a year to America. The Hamburg trade, on the other hand, although carried on largely by convoy, could operate more or less continuously, unlike the more complicated ocean passages. The New England mast trade, in contrast, was carried on largely by 'runners'—ships fast enough to stand a reasonable chance of outstripping the privateers[2]—and was important enough to the navy to demand more frequent sailings than the rest of the Plantations trade. The Spanish iron trade from Bilbao, and the Portuguese naval stores, were also carried to some extent by single ships. Thus where convoys were few and large,

---

[1] P.R.O.Adm. 1/5247–9, *passim*.

[2] See J. S. Corbett, 'Galleys and Runners', in *M.M.* VII, no. 5, pp. 133–4.

it was easier for the navy and the merchants to agree well beforehand, if possible on an annual basis, upon the numbers of ships to be allowed to each trade; where convoys were frequent, or where individual passages were possible or desirable, the periodic embargo was a more efficient system.

But neither method ensured that the men, thus prevented from earning money by other means at sea, would come into the navy. This could be brought about by one of two ways: by forbidding the seamen to leave the country, and by impressing them into the naval service. The first method merely reduced, in theory, the number of available employers, and did not prevent the seaman from leaving the sea altogether until things were easier again. It was, moreover, a peculiarly ineffective measure, and was usually employed only for political reasons. James II issued a Proclamation in 1688, aimed specifically at the Dutch, which forbade English seamen to serve under a foreign power, and William III forbade them to enter the service of the French.[1] Neither was in the least successful. In 1688 men continued to slip across the North Sea to Holland,[2] and English seamen continued throughout the war to serve under all colours, including those of the enemy. The interchange of seamen between the different maritime countries was too widespread and deep-rooted a custom to be prevented by an occasional proclamation. The complementary orders to all unemployed seamen to join the navy, which were sometimes issued in the spring,[3] were equally unlikely to produce enough volunteers to render compulsion unnecessary. It was therefore usually necessary to resort to the press.

The legal right of the navy to press had always been doubtful, and the discussion continued throughout the war.[4] The Crown claimed that the right was inherent in its prerogative, applying equally to ships, men and goods on land and at sea.[5] On these grounds the Letters Patent

---

[1] *London Gazette*, nos. 2178, 2450.

[2] Narcissus Luttrell, *A Brief Historical Relation of State Affairs* (6 vols., 1872), I, pp. 439, 441. [3] E.g. *London Gazette*, nos. 2450, 2455.

[4] Admty:Corbett, X, *passim*. See also *Harleian Miscellany* (1808), I, pp. 566–8; *Remarks on the Present Condition of the Navy...* (1700); John Dennis, *An Essay on the Navy...* (1702).

[5] The claims are set forth in Admty:Corbett, IV. Some of the works on the Dominion of the Seas also include a section on this right.

issued to the Lord Admiral authorized him to press seamen without hindrance by any authority other than the King.[1] The claims were also based on precedent, for impressment of all three types of material had taken place as early as the beginning of the thirteenth century, and a long and continuous list of examples could be given from the early fourteenth century. Even Parliament had impressed merchant vessels to serve in its fleet during the Civil War.[2] On the other side it was claimed that the practice was contrary to the fundamental rights of the subject, whose person and goods were free unless their owner had committed a felony. But in practice, while the legal and constitutional arguments were being conducted, the press was being put into operation.

Individual press warrants were issued to ships by the Lord Admiral or his Commissioners, and his or their order sufficed to cancel them. But they could not be put into force while there was a veto imposed upon impressment by the King, and this was normally, although not necessarily, the case when a general press was not in force.[3] The latter, which was a matter of policy, to be related to the course of trade and possibly to political feeling, was initiated and discontinued by the Council, acting theoretically as an alternative agent of the royal prerogative to the Lord Admiral.[4] In practice, individual warrants usually began to appear shortly before the general warrant was ordered, so that the press boats could collect as many men as possible before it was too widely known that a press had been ordered.[5]

The press warrant normally applied to the seaports and maritime counties alone, and then only to able-bodied seamen of between the

---

[1] His powers were comprehensive: 'to congregate, gather, retain, take, arrest, depute and assign as well war ships and boats, as any other ships and boats or vessels whatever, for whatever Our expeditions and business, or the discharge of the same. And also seamen, sailors, or pilots of ships, masters of ships, artillerymen, or bombardiers and mariners, and other the persons whomsoever apt and fit for ships and boats, or the like vessels, from time to time, as often as shall be necessary, in whatever places within Our realms and dominions...without any interruption or hindrance to be made by any others whomsoever to the contrary' (*Report of the Select Committee of the House of Commons on the Board of Admiralty, 1861*, p. 646).

[2] F. W. Brooks, *The English Naval Forces, 1199–1272* (n.d.), p. 140; C. N. Robinson, *The British Fleet* (1894), pp. 104, 322; Oppenheim, loc. cit. pp. 197, 234.

[3] Admty:Corbett, x, f. 111.

[4] P.R.O.Adm. 1/5247, *passim*.

[5] E.g. p. 229 below.

ages of eighteen and sixty. But when numbers were particularly low, or after the press had apparently exhausted these sources of supply, it could be extended to apply to seamen found anywhere in the country.[1] This was not particularly popular with the Admiralty, for the authorities of the inland counties were never very helpful, returning low numbers and apt to use the press warrant as an opportunity for claiming expenses which had never been incurred.[2] The men were collected by press boats sent ashore from the men-of-war, generally under the command of a lieutenant whose name was inserted in the warrant as the press officer, and by press gangs, paid by the navy but operating as private concerns, generally under the direction of a retired naval officer or seaman.[3] Either party could claim the assistance of the civil authorities: in the maritime counties and seaports, the Vice-Admiral of the county; in London, the Lord Mayor; and in the inland counties, the Lord Lieutenant.[4] The gangs made considerable use of the authorities near the coast, for the maritime counties had by now a well-organized system of collection through their own officers, which normally delivered the men at a convenient centre to the press gang,[5] although sometimes they did so to the men-of-war themselves or to the hulks where the men were held until called for. This was also the system which the inland counties were supposed to observe, but usually did not. The press boats, on the other hand, did a greater proportion of the collecting themselves—either for their own ship or, if orders were received from the Admiralty, for others[6]—without the co-operation of the civil officers.

The only seamen who could not be pressed, once the warrants were out, were those covered by protections issued by the Admiralty. These were granted to the naval departments themselves, to safeguard the workmen employed by the Navy Office, the dockyards, the Ordnance and the Victualling Office, and to merchant ships on the basis of so many 'seamen' and 'landmen' to each ship. The men were each given

---

1 Admty:Corbett, x, ff. 69–70, 74. 2 Ibid. f. 77.

3 Ibid. f. 30; J. R. Hutchinson, *The Press-Gang Afloat and Ashore* (1913), ch. III.

4 Admty:Corbett, x, ff. 70, 74.

5 For its details, see ibid. ff. 89–91.

6 Ibid. f. 77.

a printed 'protection' with their name inserted;[1] but these were often disregarded, and indeed the whole system of the press was liable to considerable abuse.[2] Even respectable merchants, naval captains,[3] and Parliamentary candidates[4] were not safe, and the humbler trades, to judge only from the accounts of those ordered to be released, were well represented in the fleet. Periwig-makers, organists, Westminster choir-boys, tailors, gentlemen's servants and coachmen were among those whose clients or masters had enough influence for them to be set ashore again.[5] Foreigners, too, were liable to be pressed, particularly Danes and Swedes whose ships were stopped for contraband or were boarded by an angry crew from a man-of-war, insulted by a failure to salute the flag; and the agents of the two countries were kept busy protesting to the Admiralty and the Court.[6] One qualification, however, must be made to this general behaviour. The unskilled and illegally pressed men were produced more by the press gangs operating ashore than by the press boats belonging to the men-of-war. One of the naval captain's greatest grievances, indeed, was the quality of the men whom he was forced to take, and for this he blamed particularly the gangs who were not under naval discipline.[7] Nor was the navy unique in pressing this poor material. The chartered companies, as the navy lamented, were only too apt to supply boys, old men, cripples and landsmen in place of fishermen and watermen.[8]

This supply of unskilled material was partly—although to what extent it is impossible to say—the result of a deliberate failure to produce trained and unprotected seamen. The sin of omission was probably

---

1 Reproductions of protections for a seaman and a dockyard workman may be seen in Laird Clowes, op. cit. II, pp. 236, 237 respectively.

2 Although not so inevitably as portrayed in Hutchinson, loc., cit., which although the standard work on the press, is misleading in this respect.

3 See *The Dear Bargain* (1689), p. 12.

4 For the case of alderman Burningham, see P.R.O.Adm. 3/9: 7/9, 8/9; *Cal.S.P.Dom, 1691–2*, p. 432.

5 P.R.O.Adm. 3/1–14, *passim*. Tailors seem to have been particularly easy to press, judging by the ballad *The Maidens' Frolick; Or, a Brief Relation how Six Lusty Lasses has Prest Fourteen Taylors....*

6 P.R.O.Adm. 3/1, *passim*.

7 P.R.O.Adm. 1/3563, f. 782.

8 *H.M.C.* 11th Report, appendix, pt. v, p. 200.

practised less than that of commission, but it was certainly not unknown. Orders not to take bribes were naturally frequent,[1] and at least according to one ballad they seem to have had occasional success;[2] but compensation to boat's crew and gang alike in money or in kind was a regular practice, particularly before 1693 when for the first time the larger ships were paid press money at standard rates to cover the expenses of their boats and tenders.[3]

The pressed men made up most of the fleet. There were also the volunteer seamen, and soldiers and Marines. Soldiers were seldom employed in the fleet once it was at sea, but it was not uncommon for them to help sail the ships from the Thames estuary to Spithead in the spring, and to make the passage back in the autumn when perhaps a large number of the crew had been removed to other ships. One of the reasons for their virtual disappearance from the fleet in the second half of the century lay in the formation of the Marine regiments, themselves a reflection of the growing specialization of naval warfare. The two Maritime regiments of Foot, as they were called at first, were established as part of the land forces in 1664. In 1688 one regiment was in active service, but this was disbanded at the end of the year and replaced in 1690 by the first two Marine regiments, raised by the Admiral commanding the fleet and the senior Commissioner of the Admiralty respectively,[4] and borne on the naval accounts. Their

---

1 Admty:Corbett, x, f. 29.

2 *The Sea-Mans Adieu to His Dear* (written towards the end of the century), where the maid says:

> 'I'll go thy captain and fall on my knee;
> Perhaps he'l take pity on me;
> If five or ten pounds will buy thy discharge
> He shall have it to set my love free';

and the Captain answers:

> 'Not ten pounds nor twenty will buy his discharge,
> Fair maid, you must patiently bear....'

(*Naval Songs and Ballads*, p. 102). Here as in some other ballads (e.g. *The Undaunted Seaman* of the same period) the seaman himself is eager to go.

3 Admty:Corbett, x, f. 30. A first rate was paid £80 in that year, a second £65, a third £50, and a fourth £40.

4 Arthur Herbert and the Earl of Pembroke.

maximum strength was fixed at 6000 men, divided into thirty companies. In practice, however, they seldom numbered more than 5000.[1]

The volunteers formed the nucleus of the crews.[2] It was the regular practice late in each winter for the King to issue a Proclamation, offering those who joined by a certain date, usually 1 March, a bounty of two months' wages to be paid during their first six months of service.[3] While the bounty was in force the press was discontinued, so that the two methods were regarded as alternatives.[4] The volunteers enjoyed certain privileges. They were not removed from their own ship to others without their consent, and they were discharged at the end of the season unless they volunteered afresh for further service.[5] It is indeed a curious reversal of later practice that the long-service men should be conscripts and the short-service men volunteers; but so long as there was not a standing fleet, there could be no naval seamen on any but a temporary or an opportunist basis. As a result, while the pressed men, to whom no concessions were necessary, could be kept aboard, the volunteers came and went intermittently as merchant seamen come and go to-day.

The low proportion of volunteers in the fleet, itself largely the result of the conditions of naval service, further affected those conditions; for the fact that the ships were filled mostly with pressed men reacted upon the way in which they were treated. The factors which affected the men in their service were first food, secondly clothes and medical treatment, thirdly rates of pay, fourthly the conditions of payment, and lastly their prospects of promotion and their treatment by their officers.

English seamen were renowned for the amount they ate. The administrative consequences were stated by Pepys:

> Englishmen, and more especially seamen, love their bellies above anything else, and therefore it must always be remembered, in the management of the victualling of the navy, that to make any abatement from them in the quantity

---

[1] L. Edye, *The Historical Records of the Royal Marines, 1664–1701* (1893), pp. 1, 304, 313.

[2] Their numbers varied, and are not always easy to find, for even when men had volunteered their captains often declared that they were pressed, in order to get press money for them (Admty:Corbett, XXI, f. 20).

[3] Ibid. ff. 1–2.   [4] Ibid. f. 2.   [5] Ibid.

or agreeableness of the victuals, is to discourage and provoke them in the tenderest point, and will sooner render them disgusted with the King's service than any one other hardship that can be put upon them.[1]

The navy was fully alive to this argument, and took care to cater for it. The diet of the naval seaman was more than adequate by contemporary standards.[2]

	Sunday	Monday	Tuesday	Wednesday	Thursday	Friday	Saturday
Biscuit (lb.)[3]	1	1	1	1	1	1	1
Beef (lb.)	—	2	—	—	—	—	2
Pork (lb.)	1	—	—	—	1	—	—
Peas (pints)	½	½	—	½	½	—	—
Fish (sized)	—	⅛	—	⅛	—	⅛	—
Butter (oz.)	—	2	—	2	—	2	—
Cheese (oz.)	—	4	—	4	—	4	—
Beer (gallons)	1	1	1	1	1	1	1

If fish were scarce, oatmeal was allowed instead.[4] The crews of ships going south of latitude 39 degrees north received a slightly different diet from those in home waters, with flour, raisins or currants in lieu of beef and pork, oil in place of butter or cheese, and wine or brandy in place of beer.[5] Ships in northern waters got four tons of water for every hundred men, and those bound for southern waters five tons.[6] The drink in particular was ample, and much appreciated; and when the Navy Board proposed in 1694 to reduce it by a quarter and to add the corresponding value to the seamen's wages, the plan was hotly resented as an attempt to remove 'the ancient liberty of resorting to the Beer at Pleasure'.[7] But the victuals in general were acknowledged to be more substantial than those received in the average merchant vessel, and indeed provided one of the few advantages which the navy enjoyed over its competitors.[8] The complaints against them, which were frequent, were made mostly on the score of quality,[9] and otherwise were

[1] *Naval Minutes*, p. 250.

[2] P.R.O.Adm. 7/639, f. 116.

[3] I.e. bread.

[4] Admty:Corbett, XIV, f. 41.

[5] *Catal.* I, p. 167.

[6] Ibid. pp. 168–9.

[7] Admty:Corbett, XIV, f. 45.

[8] William Hodges, *Proposals for the...Relief...of the...Seamen* (1695), p. 43; William Cockburn, *An Account of the Nature, Causes, Symptoms, and Cure of the Distempers that are Incident to Seafaring People* (1696), p. 5.

[9] The frequency of these complaints may be gauged by the fact that one of the crimes listed for punishment in the Articles of War was stirring up trouble over the quality of the victuals.

directed against the failure to provide the amounts laid down rather than against the amounts themselves. It was in its inability to maintain its theoretical standard, and not in the standard set, that the naval administration gave rise to unfavourable comparisons with other professions.

The seaman was fed free. He was clothed, and cared for when ill or wounded, partly at his own expense. There was no uniform at this time for either officers or men,[1] but the latter could buy certain slop clothes aboard which largely determined their appearance. These slops were limited, by an order of March 1663, to 'red caps, Monmouth caps, yarn stockings, Irish stockings, blue shirts, white shirts, cotton waistcoats, cotton drawers, neat's leather, flat-heeled shoes, blue neckcloths, canvas suits and rugs',[2] and could be bought from the purser at the mast.[3] Some of these articles tended to be of one type: most of the waistcoats were blue, and most of the trousers striped. The naval seaman of William's war was a distinctive figure, in his red cap, white kerchief, leather jacket and blue waistcoat, with striped drawers or breeches not unlike a kilt, stockings and flat-heeled buckled shoes.[4]

Since many of the pressed men came aboard in rags,[5] or certainly in clothes unfit for sea service, some provision of this kind was obviously necessary. The complaints which it occasioned were once more directed against the abuse of the terms rather than the terms themselves. The prices of the clothes were fixed, for most of the war, by the captain of

---

[1] This was a curious retrogression, for the mariners of the King's ships between the thirteenth and the sixteenth centuries were provided with a distinctive uniform (Oppenheim, loc. cit. pp. 76, 113, 134, 41, 68; Robinson, *The British Fleet*, pp. 486–7).

[2] G. E. Manwaring, 'The Dress of the British Seaman', III, in *M.M.* IX, no. 11, p. 326.

[3] The Rev. Henry Teonge, in his *Diary* (ed. G. E. Manwaring, 1927) gives a good picture of the proceedings in the 1670's.

[4] This description is taken from the illustrated title page of George St Lo's pamphlet *England's Safety, or a Bridle to the French King* (1693), where the striped breeches are prominent. The supporters to the arms which Arthur Herbert took on his creation as Earl of Torrington in 1690 (see p. 265 below) are interesting: 'Two mariners, proper, each habited in a waistcoat, buttoned, *azure*; wide breeches, *argent*, double striped crosswise crimson; hose and shoes, *sable*; neckcloth, *silver*, and cap, *gules*' (cited by Manwaring, op. cit. IV, in *M.M.* X, no. 1, p. 30).

[5] *M.M.* IX, no. 11, p. 327.

the ship with the assistance of the master, the boatswain and the gunner. The rates were laid down by the Admiralty, and theoretically the articles were put on sale only in their presence and in that of the whole ship's company.[1] These precautions were intended to act as a check upon the purser, and a further check was provided which enabled the dealer, in the event of an argument between himself and the purser, to entrust his goods to the master or to any other of the ship's officers.[2] The pursers, however, pleaded that they were in the hands of the dealer, owing to the system whereby the latter, as a standing contractor, held the monopoly of slopseller to the whole service. He was indeed apt to force articles upon the ships which were not in the regulations, and which were often more expensive than the men wished to buy. The prices of the regulation clothes were within the pay of the average man. A canvas suit and white shirt could not cost more than 5*s.* each; a blue shirt or a pair of shoes 3*s.* 6*d.*; a pair of drawers, a waistcoat, or a pair of yarn stockings, 3*s.*; a Monmouth cap, 2*s.* 6*d.*; a red cap, 1*s.* 1*d.*; and a pair of Irish stockings, 1*s.* 2*d.*[3] But the slopseller was liable to withhold some of these articles, and to substitute for them such extravagances as laced waistcoats at 14*s.* to 20*s.* each, kersey suits at 17*s.*, serge and dimity waistcoats at 10*s.* and 5*s.*, worsted stockings at 4*s.* to 6*s.*, and 'french falls' or linen collars—of much the same shape as the sailor's collar to-day—at 5*s.* In a list of clothes supplied, which one captain sent in towards the close of the century, there were ten articles not allowed by the list to eight so permitted.[4] Another practice of the slopseller's was to supply the right clothes but of inferior quality, which wore out quickly. This was made the easier for him by the fact that, although samples of his wares were checked from time to time by the Navy Office in London, no patterns were available at the ports with which his deliveries could be compared by the ships themselves.[5]

These abuses were the result of the slopseller's contract. There were others which arose aboard ship. The purser was allowed 1*s.* in the pound by the slopseller for his part in selling the clothes, and this commission

---

[1] Ibid. pp. 326–7. [2] Ibid. p. 327.

[3] Ibid. p. 326. These prices were altered slightly in 1696.

[4] Ibid. pp. 328–30.

[5] *M.M.* x, no. 1, p. 35. This was rectified in 1706.

led him to foist the more expensive items upon the seamen so far as possible, and to turn a blind eye to the dealer's irregularities. In his eagerness to sell as much as possible, he frequently disregarded another article in the regulations, which forbade a seaman to buy more than 10*s*. worth of clothes in the first two months of his service aboard ship, and more than another 10*s*. worth before the end of the voyage.[1] As a result, many of the men found themselves indebted to the purser to a degree which gave either himself or the navy a hold over them. With their pay often in arrears, they owed him money for months, even more, at a time, and the debts for slops provided one of the better means of keeping men aboard ship. With this in mind, and also because it was to their interest to preserve the men's health, the captain and the other officers, who were supposed to act as a check on the purser, were apt to overlook his peccadilloes just as the purser overlooked those of the slopseller; and one of the difficulties in disentangling the evidence of abuses in this department lies in the fact that those captains who were accused of them were often praised at the same time for clothing their men well, while those who forbade them were often accused of neglecting the men's health.

For naturally the seamen's health suffered in many cases from exposure. The incidence of sickness aboard a man-of-war in this period was very high. One contemporary estimated that for every man killed in battle, four died from other causes;[2] another, that after two years' confinement to their ship three men out of every four of her crew would have died from sickness.[3] It was disease which brought the English battle-fleet into harbour after the summer of 1689 and which drove the French from the Channel the next year, which largely ruined William III's Mediterranean policy in 1695, and which forced the West Indies squadrons home on every expedition which they undertook.[4] There was, indeed, no campaign of the war which it did not continuously and often decisively affect.

The origins of disease may be attributed to bad food and drink and

---

[1] *M.M.* IX, no. 11, p. 327.

[2] Cockburn, loc. cit. p. 17. Cockburn was physician to the Blue Squadron during the war (P.R.O.Adm. 3/10:9/4).

[3] Hodges, *Proposals for the Relief...of the...Seamen*, p. 30.

[4] See pp. 318–19, 353, 545, 609–11 below.

exposure aboard the ships, and to the presence of men already diseased before they were brought aboard, acting on crowded and often damp or overheated quarters;[1] its effects to the limited skill and knowledge of the ship's doctor, and to the long spells at sea of the ships themselves. Neither prevention nor cure could be achieved in these conditions by the immediate measures which alone could be undertaken. It required an improvement in naval architecture and in the administrative arrangements for supplying victuals and clothes, and an advance in medical knowledge and in the knowledge of the scientific preservation of food, before disease could be kept under control. In the late seventeenth century, naval architecture was largely experimental, naval administration largely chaotic, medical science rudimentary and the techniques for preserving food unknown.

The efforts to reduce the effects of disease, therefore, concentrated on cure rather than on prevention. It was, indeed, typical of the attitude towards sickness that no physicians, but only surgeons, were carried in the ships at the beginning of the war.[2] Their standard gave little hope for improving the treatment of the men aboard. Ships' surgeons were probably not much worse than those ashore, but their methods had to be drastic and their ignorance was considerable. The descriptions of the former which are given in John Moyle's text-book of 1702, *The Sea-Chirurgion*, are horrifying; but it was from the latter that the patient had most to fear. 'When I speak of *Abdomen*', wrote the author, addressing the ship's doctor, ''tis possible the young Surgeon...may not know what I mean.'[3]

The possibilities for improvement were therefore to be sought in administrative measures, and mostly ashore. A few attempts were made in the course of the French war to cut down the appalling rate of sickness in the worst case, that of the West Indies squadrons, by a more regular exchange of ships on that station;[4] and great care was taken to

---

[1] This was particularly the case in English men-of-war compared with French, owing to the excessive 'tumble-home' which English designers gave to their ships, and which made the lower deck, where the crew lived, far wetter in bad weather than it would otherwise have been.

[2] See p. 445 below.

[3] Loc. cit. p. 104.

[4] P.R.O.Adm. 3/10:4/4. See also Nathaniel Champney's report on the subject to Henry Priestman, then a Commissioner of the Admiralty, in 1696 (B.M.Harl. 6378).

stop the disease from spreading to England on their return by a thorough cleaning of vessels and men with vinegar.[1] But the main efforts concentrated on looking after the men from the fleet after they had already fallen ill; and despite its other faults, in this respect the navy was in advance of both the Dutch and French, and also of any other national authority in England itself.

In the foreign navies the men were cared for exclusively aboard the ships themselves, even when in harbour, unless the disease was recognized to be contagious; and the medical facilities were limited to the sea chests of the physicians and surgeons, and to the existence of surgeons at some of the dockyards.[2] In the English navy, these were likewise to be found: sixth rates and above were allowed surgeons, who in wartime were given an annual allowance, ranging from £6 to £20, for their equipment,[3] and surgeons were also to be found in the four largest dockyards.[4] Sick and wounded, however, were not necessarily kept aboard their ships, but could be sent either to hospital ships while the fleet was at sea, or to lodgings in the various coastal towns, where they were placed under the care of 'landladies'. Hospital ships had been known since James I's reign, although they were employed only on occasion.[5] They were always hired merchant vessels which could also be used for other purposes, such as taking stores between the yards or to the ships at sea, and acting as press ships between the hulks and the fleet.[6] They carried special medicine chests, and were allowed extra victuals.[7] The lodgings ashore were houses taken over by the navy, whose occupants were paid to look after the men for a month. After that they were supposed to report back to their ships if the latter were still in harbour, or if not to the Navy Office in London.[8] Besides the coastal lodgings, some provision was made for the men of the fleet in London by reserving for their use sections of St Bartholomew's and St Thomas's Hospitals;[9] and in 1689, the first exclusively naval hospital

---

[1] P.R.O.Adm. 3/10:9/8.
[2] Admty:Corbett, XIII, ff. 8–9.
[3] N.M.M. MS., 'Table of Officers' Wages and Allowances', no. 3.
[4] P.R.O.Adm. 7/169.
[5] Sutherland Shaw, 'The Hospital Ship, 1608–1740', in *M.M.* XXII, no. 4, pp. 422–6.
[6] P.R.O.Adm. 3/6:11/1, 15/2; 3/8:13/1.
[7] Cockburn, loc. cit. p. 5; Sutherland Shaw, loc. cit. pp. 424–5.
[8] Admty:Corbett, XIII, f. 15.
[9] B.M.Addnl. 11602, f. 15.

in England, and possibly in Europe, was set up at Plymouth, with a few beds for men set ashore when ships called there or at Torbay.[1] The foundation of Greenwich Hospital in William's reign was not merely a matter of chance, but rather the climax of a development which had been proceeding on a humbler level since at least the middle of the century, and which was accelerated by the war itself.[2]

In peacetime the medical system was run by a Chirurgeon General of the Navy under the Admiralty, but in war it became the practice, from the middle of the century, to appoint Commissioners for Sick and Wounded Seamen who supervised the arrangements ashore.[3] The appointment of surgeons afloat, their pay and allowances, continued to be managed directly by the Navy Board.[4] The Commissioners travelled around the country, inspecting the lodgings and trying to deal with the confusion which normally arose when large numbers of men were put ashore at one time;[5] but there were also resident agents at various places on the coast, who supervised the lodgings on their behalf.[6] On paper, the navy had made a real attempt to tackle the problem.

But the very fact that this attempt had to be concentrated on administrative measures, meant that it was unlikely to succeed. The system of lodgings, which was the backbone of the organization, would work only if there was enough money for the landladies to be paid, and good enough supervision to ensure first that the sailors were taken in, and secondly that their discharge was reported to the naval authorities; and if there had been enough money and adequate machinery for these purposes, it would have been possible to replace the lodging houses by hospitals. As it was, with only an intermittent demand for space and attention, the administrative response was intermittent and the arrangements rudimentary.

For both the navy and the seaman these arrangements had several disadvantages. The navy was faced with a new class of creditors in the landladies, who had to be paid before the men could be attended to,

---

[1] Admty:Corbett, XIII, f. 6.

[2] For the connexion of Greenwich with other and existing schemes, see Ch. XI below.

[3] *Catal.* I, pp. 132–3, 137.

[4] P.R.O. Adm. 7/169.

[5] Their travelling expenses during the French war in most cases came to over half their salaries (P.R.O. T. 38/615).

[6] B.M.Addnl. 11602, f. 15.

whose demands were peculiarly difficult to check,[1] and who often allowed the authorities to lose track of the men whom they were supposed to discharge. As a result, the leakage from the sick quarters was always considerable; for unless he knew that the landlady had reported him to the navy, the only inducement for the seaman to return to his ship was to get his pay.

This was particularly necessary after a stay in sick quarters, for the men had to pay some of their expenses there, for drink and for extra food, themselves. They could, of course, often get away with credit, but it was dangerous to let this run on for too long if they belonged to the district and had deserted, for then they could be arrested for debt, whereas if they went back to the navy they could not. A year after war began, another step was taken to persuade them to return by introducing the 'Q', or query, against their names in the pay book for the period while they were ashore, which automatically delayed their payment until they reappeared in person to claim it.[2] The 'Q's, as they were known, produced one of the most vociferous and prolonged series of complaints of the war. They were denounced as cheating the men of their pay while they lay sick ashore, unable to move for want of money to pay for their cure when the landladies refused to take them in, or while they journeyed to London to report for duty, or—and this was the real point of the grievances—when they were transferred on recovery to other ships from which they could not claim their wages.[3] The system, indeed, was a bad one, which attempted to prevent the result of administrative inadequacy by committing an administrative injustice. It was withdrawn after the war, and the seamen were discharged from the service when their month ashore had elapsed.[4]

---

[1] The allowance to the landladies for a month was 1*s.* per man per day for quarters, 6*s.* 8*d.* for his cure, and 10*d.* for his funeral. If he had smallpox, 6*d.* extra was allowed for twelve days (Admty:Corbett, XIII, f. 11).

[2] Ibid. f. 9.

[3] The pamphlets and petitions against the 'Q's are too many to enumerate. The most able and most vicious of the former are by William Hodges, *Humble Proposals for the Relief...of the Seamen of England* (1695); *Great Britain's Groans* (1695); and *Misery to Misery* (1696); the most persuasive of the latter, the seamen's petition to Parliament towards the end of the war (n.d.), in *B.M. printed* 816 *m.* 7, no. 58.

[4] Admty:Corbett, XIII, f. 9.

In one way or another, the physical well-being of the seaman was endangered by administrative inefficiency whose causes lay outside the processes which they affected. Theoretically, his food and drink were adequate, his clothes could be acquired under reasonable conditions, and provision was made for his treatment when he was ill or wounded. In practice, he often could not eat his food without the risk of poison, or clothe himself without sacrificing his freedom, or fall ill without losing the money due to him. The same symptoms of muddled administration were to be seen, in this case operating directly and not indirectly, in the payment of his wages.

The rates of pay of the naval seaman, unlike the provisions, the clothes and the medical treatment which theoretically he received, compared badly with those of most merchant seamen. A boy received 9*s.* 6*d.* per month, in all rates of ship; a gromet, 14*s.* 3*d.*; an ordinary seaman, 19*s.*; a barber, 19*s.*; and an able seaman, a swabber, a cooper, and a cook's mate all received 24*s.*[1] These rates had been fixed in 1653, and stayed the same throughout the century.[2] In contrast, the wages in merchant ships varied with the conditions under which the voyage was undertaken and with the competition for men in the particular trade. During the French war, ordinary seamen in the east-coast colliers were getting anything between 50*s.* and £3 a month, whereas in peacetime they got from 30*s.* to £2. In the Baltic, Dutch and German trades, where the seamen got about 25*s.* a month in peacetime, they got between £6 and £8 a voyage in war; and the same was largely true of the deep-sea trades.[3]

On the other hand, there were compensations in the navy. A man could earn prize money; he could get a pension if he was discharged owing to wounds or disabilities received in the service, and his family received a bounty if he was killed in action; while if his ship were damaged for any reason, he did not have to pay a proportion of the cost to repair her or to compensate the owner, as was the case in merchant vessels.[4]

---

[1] *Catal.* I, p. 150. [2] Oppenheim, loc. cit. pp. 226, 314.

[3] George St Lo, *England's Interest*... (1694), pp. 50–1; B.M.Addnl. 22184, f. 115. In naval finance the month was always reckoned at 28 days (i.e. a lunar month); whether that was the case in these various trades I do not know.

[4] St Lo, loc. cit. p. 18.

By custom, the right of the captors to a prize depended, until the passing of the first Prize Act in 1692,[1] upon the pleasure of the Crown: 10*s*. a ton was paid to the ship's company whether the prize were a man-of-war or a merchant vessel, and in addition £6. 13*s*. 4*d*. for every gun belonging to a merchantman and £10 for every gun belonging to a warship. The rest went to a fund for pensioning disabled officers and men, and relieving the families of those killed in action. Of the total, a third—again by custom until 1692—went to the captor's crew, a third to the captain and a third to the other officers.[2] The size of a seaman's share, therefore, depended on the size of his own ship as well as on that of the prize. Most prizes, however, from the nature of the action, were taken by small ships rather than large, and the distinction between 'glory' and 'profit', which gave rise to such rancour between the line of battle and the cruisers in Nelson's day, was already beginning to appear a century earlier. In all, 59 French men-of-war, mustering 2244 guns, were captured during the war,[3] and 708 merchant ships, both French and neutral, worth about £443,402.[4] But only some of the latter went to the navy, for a large number was taken by the privateers.[5] The average sailor, therefore, even if he were in a Channel cruiser, could not count on much in the way of prize money, and in any case by the time that the Admiralty Court had heard and judged the case, and the naval clerks had traced the members of the crew, it might be several years before he benefited from it.

The second positive advantage which the naval seaman enjoyed over his counterpart in the merchant ship was his claim on the navy for a wound or disability. Since Elizabeth's time the fund of Chatham Chest had existed for this purpose for officers and men,[6] supported partly by the navy itself from the prize money which was not distributed to the ships, partly by the officers, from a proportion of the fines which they paid for disobeying orders, and partly by a compulsory contribution of 6*d*. a month from the men themselves, with an addi-

---

[1] 4 Will. and Mary c. 25.

[2] *Law and Custom of the Sea*, II, pp. x–xii, 95; Oppenheim, loc. cit. p. 309.

[3] Charles Derrick, *Memoirs relating to the Rise and Progress of the Royal Navy* (1806), p. 110.

[4] Clark, loc. cit. p. 61.

[5] Ibid.

[6] Oppenheim, loc. cit. p. 145.

tional 4*d*. a month from the crews of those ships which by complement were allowed but did not carry a chaplain.[1] In return, the fund was supposed to pay £6. 13*s*. 4*d*. a year for life to a man who lost a leg or an arm, £13. 6*s*. 8*d*. for both legs, £15 for both arms provided that the man was unable to earn a livelihood, £5 for a permanently disabled arm, and £4 for the loss of an eye. Scotsmen and Irishmen could compound, if they wished, for two years' full pension at once, and waive the rest in return.[2]

The advantage of compounding for a definite sum lay in the uncertainty which attended all payments from the Chest. Throughout the century the fund was abused, sometimes failing to make an issue for years at a time, at others being rifled to fill the pockets of its managers. As with most branches of the navy, its practice differed from its theory; and of the many seamen stumping about the country on their wooden legs, with the familiar patch over one eye, it is safe to say that to few did the stump represent a steady £6. 13*s*. 4*d*. or the patch a steady £4 a year.[3]

The Chest was also partly responsible for the pensions to widows of officers and men killed in action. Here again, as was only to be expected when such large numbers fell in the sea battles, distribution was uncertain and payment largely dependent on influence.[4] Valuable as the pension system might be in individual cases, it cannot be taken for granted that all, or even most of those who were entitled to its benefits, in fact received them.

As against these problematical advantages, there were several disadvantages which the naval seaman suffered in comparison with the merchant seaman. The greatest of these lay in the manner of his payment. This indeed was the greatest scandal of the many which were

---

[1] Ibid. p. 246; *Catal.* I, pp. 205, 211. Chaplains, who were allowed to sixth rates and above, were appointed by the bishop of London, and paid from this contribution by all members of the ship's company (see A. G. Kealy, *Chaplains of the Royal Navy, 1626–1903* (1903)).

[2] *Catal.* I, p. 139.

[3] See Richard Gibson's remarks in B.M.Addnl. 11602, ff. 5–15.

[4] Bounties and pensions to widows were normally the responsibility of the navy, in such cases being charged on the ordinary. Occasionally, however, the King provided them from his own revenue.

raised about his service. The contemporary descriptions, particularly those of Evelyn, of seamen starving in the seaport towns or besieging the Navy Office for pay which had been owing to them for several years, are well known. They were not in the least exaggerated. It is indeed impossible to exaggerate the picture of misery which the arrears of payment to the seamen produced throughout the seventeenth and a large part of the eighteenth centuries. Perhaps the most adequate comment upon them was made by the Admiralty itself, when it invited Robert Adam to design a screen for its new building in Whitehall with the primary purpose not of adorning but of defending the forecourt against the seamen who came to London to clamour for their wages.[1] It was not uncommon for a man to remain entirely unpaid for several years, and to be owed some of his wages for a decade. In June 1695, when a real effort was made to clear up the outstanding arrears, one able seaman received his wages for January 1681 and another for January 1678, and in June 1698 an entire carpenter's crew was paid for February 1683. These were exceptional cases, but, taking an average of all the men who received arrears of wages from 1689 to 1698, the delay in payment was just over a year, and there were several instances of men receiving no pay from any ship for three or four years.[2] The bitterness of the seamen was exacerbated by the fact that they were often the only sufferers. Badly paid as were the naval contractors and officials, and the dockyard workmen, they were paid on the average with far greater regularity than the men at sea. The differences in treatment depended upon the pressure which each class could exert upon the Administration; when there was not enough money to go round, the terms and rapidity of payment became the test of the importance of the creditor. The impressed seaman, to whom the navy owed no obligation, over whom it had already demonstrated its control, who had only the one weapon of mutiny, which by its nature was occasional, with which to point his demands, and who was absent more often than any other class of

---

[1] Adam faithfully carried out the plan. The present screen on Whitehall, which has been restored to its original appearance, represents a strategic and not an initially aesthetic design (D. Bonner Smith, 'The Admiralty Building', in *M.M.* IX, no. 9, pp. 275–7).

[2] P.R.O.Adm. 30/2, *passim*.

creditor from the scene of payment, was the first to be ignored. The volunteer, who at least had to be paid his bounty if possible, and on whom the authorities liked to depend, had more influence; he was accordingly given priority in the payments to the fleet and, more important, was exempted from being turned over from one ship to another.

For the 'turn-over' was the navy's chief weapon for avoiding the necessity of payment. It was used for two purposes: to keep ships at sea, and to enable them to be laid up in harbour. In either case it was a particularly brutal measure, in that it often affected men just about to enter harbour or to be set ashore. The reason for its introduction lay in the difficulty of paying off the crew of a ship before it was laid up for the winter. A proportion of the crew was therefore turned over to other ships which needed more men to go to sea, and the rest could perhaps then be paid enough to induce them to go ashore quietly. Conversely, if a ship which was required for sea was short of men, and had no opportunity of pressing the rest, she would be informed by the Admiralty that a given number would be supplied from the crew of another man-of-war which either no longer needed a full complement, or needed it less. The captain of the latter ship—or there might be more than one—was then ordered to transfer the necessary men, who were accordingly entered on the books of their new vessel. There was no reason why a man should not be kept at sea in this way for years at a time, and many were. Meanwhile, his wages mounted with a decreasing possibility of payment, the greater the number of muster masters and pursers who reported on him. The system, according to its opponents, came in with the war against France in 1689; and although this is not entirely true, it was probably in that war that the turn-overs were first employed regularly and on a large scale.[1] As a reflection of the greater demands made upon the navy, of the greater size of the navy itself, and of the magnitude of the debts incurred by it as compared with any previous war, they were perhaps the clearest illustration of the bankruptcy of the traditional administration under changing circumstances.

[1] George Everett, *Encouragement for Seamen and Mariners*... (1695), pp. 15–16; Hodges, loc. cit. p. 26; *An Humble Representation of the Seamen's Misery*..., p. 3.

When the clamours against the turn-overs grew too great, the Admiralty provided for some priority to be given to the men affected when it paid off the arrears to the fleet.[1] This, however, merely put the payment of such wages in course, for once the principle was admitted whereby a pressed man could be kept aboard different ships indefinitely, all pressed men were equally subject to it and the delay in meeting their arrears was not diminished by this priority, but only put into some sort of order. When payment was made, moreover, it was seldom in money, but more often, as in the case of the dockyard workman, by ticket; and like the workman the seaman was often only too glad to sell his scrap of paper at a loss for cash to a ticket buyer. The discount varied a good deal, but was reported on occasion to have been as much as one pound in three.[2]

Finally, the conditions which delayed the payment and often reduced its value when finally made, also made it possible for some of the pay to be withheld altogether. This was due to the system whereby an 'R', standing for 'run', was put against a man's name on the pay book if he failed to appear on board for a month. In that case he forfeited his wages and became a deserter, subject by martial law to be condemned to death. 'R's were the complement of 'Q's, and were usually included in the same attacks. Reasonable in itself, the system was subject to abuse. In the first place, it was possible for a man belonging to one warship to be illegally pressed by another while ashore, or even occasionally while on board; secondly, a careless clerk—and there were many—might neglect to report that he had been turned over to another ship, and it might be some months, possibly more if his new ship was just off to the West Indies, before the muster lists from the second vessel were received in London; or thirdly, a dishonest clerk or purser might mark him as 'R' although he had been turned over, and then split the proceeds with the clerk who made the payment.

A seaman might also be cheated of his wages aboard his own ship. It was not unknown for warrant officers to extract a power of attorney from whole groups of men and to draw their wages or tickets for them, making their own profit in the negotiations with the ticket buyer.

[1] E.g. P.R.O.Adm. 3/1:17/4, 20/4.

[2] William Hodges, *The Art of Ticket-buying*... (1695), pp. 52–3.

Alternatively, a captain might defraud both the navy and the man's dependants by failing to report when he was killed in action, and then, at least for some time, draw his wages. The same, of course, applied if a man died normally at sea, or even if he were put sick ashore. Provided that the officers were prepared to act in this way, they could be prevented only with a good deal of trouble by an already overburdened clerical staff in London, and in any case it was often far too late to help the man himself.

The code of discipline under which the men lived at the Revolution had been drawn up in 1661, when James was Lord Admiral. It was embodied in an Act of Parliament[1] which followed closely the original articles of war promulgated in December 1652, themselves based on the ordinances of the House of Commons of 1649.[2] By the terms of the Act, various naval authorities, including the captains of men-of-war under the King's commission, were empowered to try certain offences committed aboard ship by court martial.[3] The death sentence, which could be imposed for such crimes as murder, desertion, mutiny, striking an officer, cowardice and aiding the enemy, required a court martial of at least five captains and, except in the case of mutiny, the confirmation of the Lord Admiral if the sentence were to be executed in the Narrow Seas, or of the Commander in Chief of the fleet or squadron if beyond them.[4] This Act, supplemented by a minor Act of 1664,[5] remained in force until 1750.

The punishments themselves were often hard: keel-hauling, ducking and the infamous 'pickling' had all come in by this time, and the ceremonious flogging round the fleet had been practised for thirty years.[6] But the extent to which they were indulged, and the use made of the

---

[1] 13 Car. II, c. 9. [2] *Catal.* I, pp. 183–4.

[3] The limitations of naval discipline, however, as the direct expression of an organized permanent service, were shown in 1691, when Admiral Russell questioned his right to court-martial two officers, one a Marine, who had fought a duel on a beach off which the fleet was anchored. The Secretary of State, to whom the matter was referred, decided that he could do so, but only on the ground that the beach in question was covered by the tide at high water, and was thus a foreshore which came within the jurisdiction of the Lord Admiral whose subordinate Russell was (Finch Transcr., Russell to Nottingham, 3/6; Nottingham to Russell 8/6).

[4] *Statutes of the Realm* (1819), V, pp. 311–14. [5] 16 Car. II, c. 5.

[6] Oppenheim, loc. cit. pp. 188, 357, 358.

articles of war generally, depended on the relations between the officers and men. In many ships these were good. Certain captains could always get men when they wanted them, and were allowed to take a proportion of their old crew when they joined a new ship.[1] On one occasion, after a ship had been wrecked, the crew volunteered in a body to man any other ship to which the captain might be appointed.[2] In other ships, naturally, relations were bad; and a bad set of officers could do a lot with the naval discipline Act. The only criterion which can be applied to these relations is to inquire into the nature of the officers. To do so, leads us to the last factor in the service of the seaman: his possibilities of promotion.

These were not uniformly good or bad. The absence of any regular long-service employment meant on the one hand that a man might remain in the navy for years without promotion, while pressed men or volunteers of a higher standing were entered above his head, but on the other that he might himself enter as a senior rating. Trained seamen, when men were scarce, could command a good rank on the lower deck in the same way that they could command good wages in a merchant vessel. The pay for the various officers' mates and skilled hands was still low compared with that outside the service, but some at least were not so likely to be defrauded of their wages. The monthly wages of the men other than seamen are shown on p. 137.[3]

It was possible for senior ratings to become junior officers. There was no system of promotion, for neither the higher rates of seaman nor all the junior officers were long-service men. But, for that very reason, the line between them was not a rigid one. Nor was there yet a sharp distinction further up the scale, and it was still possible for a cabin boy to become an admiral. In William's war, there were in fact two cabin boys who became admirals and knights, Sir David Mitchell and Sir Cloudesley Shovell. Between the skilled seamen and many of the officers there was indeed a closer connexion than there was between the former and the miscellaneous collection of pressed men and boys who formed most of the crew and whose prospects, of promotion or even of discharge, were at best fortuitous and more often remote.

---

[1] E.g. P.R.O.Adm. 3/1:17/7; 3/3:24/5.
[2] P.R.O.Adm. 3/2:14/11.
[3] *Catal.* I, p. 150.

	First rate			Second rate			Third rate			Fourth rate			Fifth rate			Sixth rate with over 50 men		
	£	s.	d.	£	s.	d.	£	s.	d.	£	s.	d.	£	s.	d.	£	s.	d.
Cook's mate	1	4	0	1	4	0	1	4	0	1	4	0	1	4	0	1	4	0
Sailmaker[1]		4	0		4	0		4	0		4	0		4	0		4	0
Steward's mate	1	0	8	1	0	8	1	0	8	1	0	8		—			—	
Steward	1	5	0	1	5	0	1	5	0	1	3	4	1	0	8	1	0	0
Armourer	1	5	0	1	5	0	1	5	0	1	5	0	1	4	0	1	4	0
Gunsmith	1	5	0	1	5	0		—			—			—			—	
Ordinary carpenters	1	6	0	1	6	0	1	5	0	1	5	0	1	5	0	1	5	0
Quarter gunners	1	6	0	1	6	0	1	5	0	1	5	0	1	5	0	1	5	0
Quartermaster's mates	1	10	0	1	10	0	1	8	0	1	8	0	1	6	0	1	5	0
Surgeon's mates	1	10	0	1	10	0	1	10	0	1	10	0	1	10	0	1	10	0
Trumpeters	1	4	0	1	4	0	1	4	0	1	4	0		—			—	
Master trumpeter	1	10	0	1	8	0	1	5	0	1	5	0	1	5	0	1	4	0
Coxswain	1	12	0	1	10	0	1	8	0	1	8	0	1	6	0		—	
Yeomen of the sheets	1	12	0	1	10	0	1	8	0	1	8	0	1	6	0		—	
Gunner's mates	1	15	0	1	15	0	1	12	0	1	10	0	1	8	0	1	6	0
Boatswain's mates	1	15	0	1	15	0	1	12	0	1	10	0	1	8	0	1	6	0
Corporal	1	15	0	1	12	0	1	10	0	1	10	0	1	8	0	1	6	0
Quartermasters	1	15	0	1	15	0	1	12	0	1	10	0	1	8	0	1	6	0
Carpenter's mates	2	0	0	2	0	0	1	16	0	1	14	0	1	12	0	1	10	0
Yeomen of powder	2	5	0	2	0	0	1	17	6	1	13	9	1	10	0	1	10	0

The dichotomy between theory and practice, which ran throughout the conditions of life aboard, makes it largely irrelevant to discuss the relative attitudes of different Boards of Admiralty and governments at different times towards the seaman. However brutal its measures, no Administration promulgated them out of brutality. The same benevolent phrases, genuinely meant, and the same well-phrased orders and good intentions are repeated by the Naval Boards, Lord Admirals and Admiralties of the Commonwealth, the Restoration and the Revolution; and the difference between their measures, and between the enforcements of them, was the result of their control, or lack of it, over factors which bore only indirectly upon the problems themselves, and not of any difference of feeling towards the men. In the same way, improvements in the treatment of the men on the whole came no more directly from benevolence than their ill treatment came from brutality, but were rather the result of more money, or of a temporary increase in control, or of easier strategic conditions, or of necessity. Greenwich Hospital, in its final form, is perhaps the only example in naval administration at this time of an unnecessarily benevolent act. In discussing the conditions of service, therefore, it is necessary to remember that theory and practice did not always coincide, and that where they did

[1] 'Above what he receives in another quality' (ibid. n. 2).

not the causes of failure lay not so much in the conditions of service themselves as in a lack of control over the general conditions for administration.

The sea officers,[1] recruited largely from the same seafaring population as the men, were not sharply separated from the higher rates in their pay. For the first five years of the war they received the monthly wages which had been laid down in 1686, and which followed those originally fixed in 1653. For ships' officers these were as follows:[2]

	First rate	Second rate	Third rate	Fourth rate	Fifth rate	Sixth rate	Large yachts	Othe ships
	£ *s.* *d.*	£ *s.* *d.*	£ *s.* *d.*	£ *s.* *d.*	£ *s.* *d.*	£ *s.* *d.*	£ *s.* *d.*	£ *s.*
Captain	21 0 0	16 16 0	14 0 0	10 10 0	8 8 0	7 0 0	7 0 0	7 0
Lieutenant	4 4 0	4 4 0	3 10 0	3 10 0	3 10 0	2 16 6	—	—
Master	7 0 0	6 6 0	4 13 8	4 6 2	3 17 6	(Captain is Master)		
Boatswain	4 0 0	3 10 0	3 0 0	2 10 0	2 5 0	2 0 0	2 0 0	2 0
Gunner	4 0 0	3 10 0	3 0 0	2 10 0	2 5 0	2 0 0	2 0 0	2 0
Purser	4 0 0	3 10 0	3 0 0	2 10 0	2 5 0	(Captain is Purser)		
Carpenter	4 0 0	3 10 0	3 0 0	2 10 0	2 5 0	2 0 0	2 0 0	2 0
Cook	1 5 0	1 5 0	1 5 0	1 5 0	1 5 0	1 4 0	1 4 0	1 4
Mates and pilots	3 6 0	3 0 0	2 16 2	2 7 10	2 2 0	2 2 0	2 2 0	2 2
Surgeon	2 10 0	2 10 0	2 10 0	2 10 0	2 10 0	2 10 0	2 10 0	—
Midshipmen	2 5 0	2 0 0	1 17 6	1 13 9	1 10 0	1 10 0	1 10 0	—

An increase in pay, however, is not a necessary consequence of an increase in power. Junior officers and senior ratings have never been sharply distinguished financially, and the latter sometimes earn more than the former. The difference is one of responsibility, one consequence of which is a difference of treatment, and in this respect the line was clearly drawn between officers and men.

To the naval authorities, the sea officers presented quite a different administrative problem from the seamen. Like the dockyard officers, they had to run the permanent service for which the men were only occasionally required, and in consequence they formed to some extent a distinctive corps. Compared with the dockyard officers, however, they were a less homogeneous and stable class. This was partly due to the conditions of their service, and partly to its importance.

---

[1] This was their contemporary title. The term 'naval officer' referred to the officers of the Navy Office, and was often used also to denote the dockyard officers and the naval agents at the out-ports. Here the term 'naval officer' will be used in its modern sense, except where it is likely to cause confusion.

[2] *Catal.* I, pp. 140, 150.

The sea officers could rely on being employed only in the event of a war, and then only for part of the year. In peacetime the fleet was almost certain to be laid up in harbour, and only a squadron in home waters, and probably two squadrons in the Mediterranean and West Indies, were likely to be in commission. Dockyards, too, might be reduced to skeleton staffs, and the smaller ones closed down; but apart from any construction that might be under way, there was often maintenance to be carried out, and it was in general more difficult to pay off a yard than to pay off a ship. Besides being paid off for years at a stretch in peacetime, most of the sea officers were required to serve for only eight or nine months in the year during a war, and were paid off with the men when the ships were refitted in the winter. Their terms of employment alone, therefore, were not such as to lead to a distinctive and permanent corps. Unless they could rely on frequent wars, or unless other inducements were offered, they were likely to remain on a purely temporary basis, and could not be expected to implement the long-term organization which went to the running of a fleet.

But during the second half of the seventeenth century both these conditions were largely fulfilled. No decade was entirely free from a major war at sea, and a system of half pay for unemployed officers and pensions for the disabled and superannuated gradually came into force. In July 1668, by an Order in Council, flag officers were allowed half pay during peacetime; in 1674 this was extended to the captains of first and second rates and the second captains of flagships; and in May 1675, to commanders of squadrons and to the masters of first and second rates.[1] The complementary system of pensions was also under construction. In 1672, pensions equal to the officer's salary or wages while employed, were instituted for all officers who had served for fifteen years 'where the employment is constant, such as that of boatswains, gunners, pursers, carpenters, etc.' and for eight years 'where it is not constant, such as that of masters, chirurgeons, etc.'[2] In the following year, the pension on superannuation was paralleled by creating the pension for officers wounded at sea. By the Revolution, however, this had only reached the stage of allowing all officers and volunteers a relief equal to their pay while actually under cure.[3] On the other hand, if they were

---

[1] *Catal.* I, pp. 145–8. [2] Ibid. p. 148. [3] Ibid. pp. 148–9.

disabled for a time but then recovered and could find no vacancy, by an order of 1676 they could return to sea as 'midshipmen extraordinary', a few of whom were allowed as supernumeraries to all rated ships. As such they got a wage similar to that of a lieutenant, and a servant.[1] In the same period, some inducement was offered to the junior officers to remain in the navy during the winter, by fixing a scale of 'rigging wages', in most cases equal to half the normal pay. This affected masters, boatswains, pursers, gunners, carpenters and cooks.[2] Taken together, these measures marked the beginning, on however small a scale and with whatever qualifications, of the class of long-service regular naval officers. The complicating factor in the process was that the importance of the navy which was leading to the emergence of a permanent class of sea officer, was at the same time leading the Crown to foster a different development by officering the fleet from outside, with nominees of its own choice designed to give the service that social importance which its function was leading it to deserve.

The officers drawn from the seafaring classes were thus confronted, at the very time when their organization was bringing them the possibility of regular employment and promotion, with the 'gentlemen officers', as they were called, who were frequently entered above their heads and were less subject in practice to naval discipline. Antagonisms inevitably arose, and even those who saw the necessity of both types were unable to reconcile their differences in behaviour. The dilemma of such men was well illustrated by Pepys, who simultaneously lamented the social unimportance of the naval officer, and fulminated against the conduct of those naval officers who were socially important.[3] To most of the protagonists, however, the argument was simpler. The champions of the 'tarpaulins', as the professional seamen were known, claimed that the gentlemen did not know their job and had to rely on the professionals to assist them,[4] that they brought the manners of the Court into the service,[5] that they prevented the trained sea officers from obtaining

---

[1] *Catal.* I, pp. 214–15.

[2] Ibid. p. 141. Masters received slightly more than half their full pay.

[3] *Samuel Pepys's Naval Minutes*, pp. 52–3, 194, 230, 405.

[4] Ibid. pp. 448–9.

[5] B.M.Addnl. 11602, ff. 58–61. See also Charles Shadwell's play, *The Fair Quaker of Deal* (1715).

the promotion which they deserved, and that they used their position to behave towards their professional superiors as they would never allow their subordinates to behave towards themselves.[1] The champions of the gentlemen replied, quite truthfully, that in matters of discipline there was often little to choose between the two types of officer, that the gentlemen, so far from maltreating the men, were more likely than the tarpaulins to prevent them from being defrauded, that there was nothing to show that they did not know their job, and that on the contrary they, with the background of an education in the art and practice of war, were often better qualified than the seaman to conduct a battle whether on land or sea.[2]

The remedy for these bitter feuds was seen by both Charles and James. While the gentlemen were undoubtedly needed in the new fleet, it was equally necessary for them to submit to the rules of the navy, to enter if not on equal at least on similar terms to the rest of the officers, and to rise with them, if at a greater pace, within a common service. There was no attempt to abolish the advantages of social status within the naval hierarchy—that would have been contrary to the very reasons for which the gentleman officer was encouraged—but simply to bring him within it as a regular member and to discourage the casual interloper. To this end, Charles II instituted in 1676 the system of 'volunteers', designed to encourage 'families of better quality...to breed up their younger sons to the art and practice of navigation'. These young men were to be at least sixteen years of age; they were attached to the captain, but were allowed no servants and only the ship's company's victuals, and their pay was fixed at only £24 a year.[3] This system paralleled the institution, at a lower social level, of the 'mathematical boys' of Christ's Hospital, founded by Charles to provide trained

---

[1] B.M.Addnl. 11602, ff. 76–7; *An Inquiry into the Causes of our Naval Miscarriages...* (1707), pp. 573–4; Hodges, *Proposals for the Relief...of...Seamen*, pp. 42–4.

[2] Bodl. Rawl. D 147, ff. 14–15. Many naval officers, particularly those of better family, held commissions in the army, and went on land service from time to time (see C. Dalton, *English Army Lists and Commission Registers, 1660–1700* (6 vols., 1894), introduction).

[3] *Catal.* I, pp. 213–15. One volunteer was allowed to a sixth rate, two to a fifth, three to a fourth, four to a third, and an unspecified number to first and second rates.

apprentices for future officers in merchant ships and navy alike.[1] But volunteers and mathematical boys, as an effort to combine different classes in a common service while retaining their difference in status, were important rather as an indication of the requirements than as an answer to them. Their numbers were small, and in the immediate future it was not by training and entry, but by disciplinary regulation, that a unified service was most likely to be formed out of the heterogeneous material of which it was still composed.

The reign of Charles II, therefore, also saw the framing of the officers' Instructions which remained more or less unaltered for almost a century. The duties of each rank were clearly laid down, financial as well as disciplinary penalties were imposed for neglect of duty or violation of the regulations, examinations were instituted for promotion to the rank of lieutenant and for appointment to the rank of master, and accommodation was regulated by establishment.[2] In James II's reign, one important addition was made to these orders, with the 'establishment about plate carriage' of 1686, which supplemented the existing orders forbidding ships to carry private merchandise for profit by raising the captains' table allowance, and thus indirectly their pay. But needless to say, all these orders, well framed as they were, were honoured quite as much in the breach as in the observance; for the regulations which were designed to discipline the officers, themselves depended for their observance upon the type of officer to whom they applied.

The position may perhaps best be seen among the higher ranks, in the appointment and employment of the flag officers. Although they were paid on a daily rate, the Admiral of the fleet getting £3 a day, with normally an extra £1 for table money, a Vice-Admiral of a squadron £1. 10*s*., and a Rear Admiral £1,[3] their half-pay, unlike that of the lower ranks, was fixed at annual rates.[4] But if financially their status was more

---

[1] See *The Present State and List of the Children of His Late Majesty King Charles II His New Royal Foundation in Christ's Hospital...by the Lord Mayor of the City of London* (1691). Naval officials from time to time considered the possibilities of recruiting the same sort of material from similar institutions already in existence (see, e.g., Pepys and Richard Gibson on the Charterhouse, in *Naval Minutes*, p. 159; B.M.Addnl. 11602, ff. 17–26).

[2] For the details, see *Catal.* I, pp. 183–205.

[3] See Appendix X below. See also *Catal.* I, p. 140.

[4] *Catal.* I, p. 145.

regular than that of their subordinates, their employment and promotion were not. Flag officers, whether of the fleet or of detached squadrons, were appointed afresh each year, with no reference necessarily to their employment of the year before. Command was an office, not a rank; it was quite possible for a Vice-Admiral of one year to be a Rear Admiral the next, or not to be employed at all.[1] While the Admirals were separated from the subordinate officers, in that they were never demoted from flag rank, at their own level their status was irregular and their employment uncertain.

This confusion was reflected in the flags which gave their name to the rank. Theoretically, there was an establishment of the flags which the different Admirals might wear under different circumstances.[2] But in fact practice varied indefinitely, particularly among the detached squadrons, and many indignant letters reached the Admiralty from Admirals in the fleet whose seniority had been threatened by unattached commanders wearing superior signs of rank.[3] The disputes which thus arose were significant, for they illustrated the uncertainty which existed over the relative importance of the different elements of command: of seniority by rank and seniority by function, of permanent status by length of service and promotion, and temporary status by *ad hoc* appointment. Seniority to a naval officer has always been the guarantee of regular employment. In the late seventeenth century, when the idea of a permanent service was being sedulously fostered in so many ways, this last barrier remained to a coherent and systematically graded hierarchy. It was in this direction, accordingly, that the greatest development took place in the status of the naval officer during the war of William III.

---

[1] See Appendix X below.

[2] It is given in W. G. Perrin, *British Flags* (1922), pp. 96–7.

[3] See ibid. ch. IV.

CHAPTER V

VICTUALLING

When the ship had been manned, her officers and men had to be victualled. The quantities of provisions which the navy consumed were impressive. The totals per man per week, which have already been given in detail by the day,[1] came to:

Biscuit	7 lb.	Sized fish	3/8th
Beef	4 lb.	Butter	6 oz.
Pork	2 lb.	Cheese	12 oz.
Peas	2 pints	Beer	7 gallons

In the first year of the war, the navy reckoned on having to cater for 10,000 men at these rates for twelve months, and in the event it had to feed over 20,000; for the next few years, it worked out its quantities on the basis of 30,000 men for twelve months. In other words, it had to feed a population larger than that of any town in England, except London, and almost half that of the capital itself within its walls,[2] at a higher and more uniform rate than that enjoyed by any urban population. These 30,000 men, moreover, were constantly on the move, coming and going for indefinite periods with little warning, and calling on different markets to meet their demands. With other populations of a similar size, such as those of Bristol and Norwich, the numbers to be catered for were fairly constant, and they remained in geographically the same position. But to feed a floating Bristol or Norwich, which had to store its food for long periods at a time, and was apt to turn up in different places upon the coast demanding to be victualled immediately, was a problem which no other organization in the country had to face.

---

[1] See p. 121 above.

[2] For the relevant figures see P. E. Jones and A. V. Judges, 'London Population in the late Seventeenth Century', in *Ec.H.R.* VI, no. 1, pp. 58–62; Daniel Defoe, *Tour through Great Britain*, I (ed. G. D. H. Cole, 3 vols., 1927); and G. Talbot-Griffith in *Royal Statistical Society Journal*, XCII, pt 2, pp. 256–63.

Food and drink were particularly difficult commodities to supply in this way, not because the country was not self-sufficient, for on the whole it was,[1] but because the different types of provisions set different conditions for supply. In the first place, they could not all be supplied equally well at the same time of year. The season for buying meat and pork was in the winter, for the animals were driven to market in the autumn, and killed in the following months. Butter and cheese, on the other hand, were produced for the most part in the summer, although they could be bought all the year round.[2] These seasonal limitations increased the difficulties of keeping the food fresh until it was consumed. Where it was salted—as were beef,[3] pork, butter and fish—the process was often inefficient, and other commodities could not be salted at all. The victuals had thus either to be bought long before they were needed, with the risk (considerable in this period) of deterioration before they were required, or else purchased only a short time before they were consumed, with the consequent administrative difficulties.

One of these lay in the variety of the sources of supply. The provisions were produced from all over England and Wales.[4] Beef came mainly from the west and north, from North Wales and Lancashire, Somerset and Glamorgan;[5] hogs from Hampshire, the Midlands and, to a lesser extent, Herefordshire; butter from Suffolk and the other eastern

[1] According to Gregory King, England had eleven million acres of arable, and ten million acres of pasture, at the end of the century. The latter produced a constant supply of 4½ million cattle and two million pigs, and the importation of cattle, flesh or fish was prohibited by law. The country also grew almost all its own corn by this time (see Lord Ernle, *English Farming, Past and Present* (1928), pp. 143–5; N. G. B. Gras, *The Evolution of the English Corn Market* (1915), p. 103).

[2] J. E. Thorold Rogers, *A History of Agriculture and Prices* (1887), v, pp. 337, 359, 363; B.M.Addnl. 11684, f. 69.

[3] But beef bought early in the autumn came from grass-fed beeves and not from stalled oxen, which were not ready for sale by then; and as such meat could not be salted without deteriorating, it was stored 'in its bloody pickle', which kept it fresh only for a short time (B.M.Addnl. 11684, f. 69).

[4] For a good table of agricultural produce by counties, at various dates throughout the century, see G. E. Fussell and V. G. B. Atwater, 'Agriculture of Rural England in the Seventeenth Century', in *Economic Geography* (Clark University, Worcester, Mass.), October 1933, pp. 382–94.

[5] Ibid. p. 381; and see also G. E. Fussell, 'A Western Counties Farmer, 1700', in *Journal of the Ministry of Agriculture*, XXXIX, no. 2, p. 128.

counties; and cheese mainly from Cheshire, but also from Wiltshire, Gloucestershire and Warwickshire.[1] Peas could normally be supplied locally, particularly in the south-east, and the south and south-east again were the principal wheat-growing districts,[2] at least for the London market. The principal fisheries lay off the east and south-east coasts. Kent provided most of the hops, and Kent and Hampshire most of the malt, for the beer.[3]

Many, if not most, of these provisions were transported by water, and most of them went by sea. Land transport over long distances was slow and uncertain, and with perishable goods this was fatal. The only victuals which could not be taken economically by water were cattle and hogs, and these were driven to their markets by well-established routes 'on the hoof'.[4] In wartime, this reliance on sea transport was liable to involve precisely the delay and expense which it was designed to avoid. Many of the coastal vessels, particularly those from the west, were either captured by privateers or, more frequently, forced to put into port from time to time when privateers were reported in the vicinity. Such interruptions might have disastrous results on the cargo, and as the war progressed the navy was forced to provide convoys for the regular traffic in victuals along the south coast. The basis for this system was provided from the beginning of the war by the escorts supplied for the salt trade, which was thought to be so essential for the preservation of food.[5] Salt was normally imported from France, but

---

[1] Willan, loc. cit. pp. 79, 83; G. E. Fussell and Constance Goodman, 'The Eighteenth-Century Traffic in Livestock', in *Ec.H.R.* XI, pp. 216–17, 222.

[2] According to the regulations which governed the quality of naval victuals, the biscuit had to be 'good, sweet, clean, sound, well-bolted with a horse-cloth, well-baked, and well-conditioned wheaten biscuit' (*Catal.* I, p. 166). Wheat was not the only, or even the most common type of bread in use at this time, although the bounties on the export of grain in 1689 led to its being consumed more widely than before (Sir William Ashley, *The Bread of our Forefathers* (1928), p. 5).

[3] Naval beer was supposed to consist of 18 quarters of malt and 18 of hops for sea beer, and 20 quarters of malt and 'a sufficient quantity of very good hops, to keep for the time of its warranty', for harbour beer (*Catal.* I, p. 166).

[4] *Ec.H.R.* XI, pp. 217–19.

[5] For one example of the importance attached to it, see the steps taken in 1689 and 1691 to legalize the use of salt captured from the enemy (*H.M.C.* 12th Report, appendix, pt VI, p. 349; 3 Will. and Mary, c. 4).

some was produced in Cheshire[1] and sent by sea to the east. It was convoyed down the coast from Liverpool, through the Bristol Channel and along the south and east coasts, until it was unloaded in the Thames.[2]

With its sources of supply widely scattered, and with this complicated system of delivery, it might seem that the best policy for the navy would have been to rely upon local supply so far as possible, rather than to have collected all the provisions in one place from which they would have to be redistributed to the various ports and bases. But there were several arguments against this. The distribution itself, as has been seen, was uneven. Only certain commodities could be supplied from certain areas, and even in those areas it was difficult to get enough from the immediate locality. The average farmer was a small man,[3] particularly if he dealt in cattle. It has been estimated that most livestock farmers had only about twenty beasts, and few more than sixty or seventy; and of these naturally only a given number was fit to be sold at any one time.[4] With contemporary methods of pasturing, the number of head which could be kept per acre was low and the beasts themselves were small and poor compared with later breeds,[5] so that more were required to obtain a given weight of meat than in later centuries while fewer were available for the purpose. There was in any case little incentive for the small farmer to grow or to breed more than could be disposed of in the small market provided by the local town; and if a larger market was sought, that would normally be London[6] and not a group of ships

---

[1] It was possibly the development of its salt works towards the end of the century that accounted for the rise in prosperity of Cheshire between 1672 and 1693 (Thorold Rogers, op. cit. v, pp. 75, 114, 116).

[2] E.g. P.R.O. Adm. 3/4:18/4.

[3] According to Gregory King's calculations, the average farmer's annual income was £44, which was less than that of a shopkeeper, tradesman or artisan. See also Richard Baxter's remarks on farmers in a pamphlet of much the same time. Both sources are quoted extensively in M. Dorothy George, *Life and Work in the Eighteenth Century*, pp. 5–8.

[4] G. E. Fussell and V. G. B. Atwater, 'Farmers' Goods and Chattels, 1500 to 1800', in *History*, xx, Dec. 1935, pp. 217–18.

[5] A deadweight of just over 5 cwt. for an ox seems to have been common (Thorold Rogers, op. cit. v, p. 331). A century later it was double.

[6] Ernle, loc. cit. p. 133. See also p. 242 below.

whose presence and numbers could not be foretold. The navy started at a disadvantage in the local market, unless the ships themselves could offer good terms for immediate purchase.

But the fact that the local farmers were mostly small men made it difficult for the ships to offer these terms. For the navy, dealing as it did in large quantities, and involved in the delays and disappointments of government finance, preferred to conduct most of its business on credit. This was of little use to a yeoman farmer. Even if the ships had been able to buy all that they needed locally, they would have had to pay for a good deal of it in ready money; and to deal with the provision merchants in cash would soon have proved impossible, not only because the amounts required could not always have been supplied, but also because the other dealers and creditors would have refused to continue on credit while ready money was being paid elsewhere.

But the greatest incentive to central purchase and distribution was the fact that to a large extent it already existed in the London market. In the sixteenth century the navy had acted, as in its other purchases, largely through purveyors or agents working on a commission;[1] but in the following century it was able, as in other fields, increasingly to make use of the middlemen who were already organizing the markets and who could thus save the Administration the trouble of doing so for itself. By 1688, the custom, and in at least one case the control, of provincial produce was concentrated in the capital. Some districts had a larger trade with London than with their local towns, and even where there was a well-established trade between two provincial centres, as between Hull and King's Lynn in butter and cattle, or between Chichester and Southampton in hogs, wheat and malt, it was less than between those centres and London.[2] The markets of the capital could meet a large proportion of the navy's demands more regularly and more simply than the regions of supply themselves. This concentration of facilities was particularly welcome in the middle years of the century, when it was conveniently placed to supply the fleets whose

---

1 Beveridge, loc. cit. p. 504.

2 Willan, loc. cit. ch. III, IV; Gras, loc. cit. ch. X, XI. See also G. E. Fussell and Constance Goodman, 'The Eighteenth-Century Traffic in Milk Products', in *Ec.H.R.* XII, pp. 380–7.

main bases were in the Medway and the Thames, and whose main area of concentration was at the Nore.[1]

The extent to which the London markets were controlled by groups of a few men may be seen in the contracts made by the navy in 1688 and 1689.[2] In a few cases, contracts were placed exclusively in the hands of a few big men. Butter and cheese were sold under one head by only two men, Joseph Herne and Thomas Rodband, and two-thirds of that came from the latter; and it would seem therefore that the well-known monopoly of the London 'cheesemongers' in the eighteenth century was already largely a fact by the last decade of the seventeenth century.[3] There was also a monopoly in fish, all of which was sold by one man, William Otber, and salt was sold to the navy exclusively by John Haggard and partner, except for one small lot handled by a certain Edmund Trimer.[4] The meat trades, too, were dominated by a few men, although not to the same extent as butter and cheese, salt and fish. Most of the beef was bought on the hoof, in the form of oxen, and only a small proportion was bought as meat. There were five contractors for oxen in 1688–9, but four of those sold 143 head between them while the fifth, Thomas Wright, sold 1228 head. Four dealers sold beef to the navy, but again three sold 802 cwt. while the fourth, Thomas Wright, sold 1469 cwt. The pork trade was less of a monopoly. There again most of the flesh was sold on the hoof, as hogs, and in this trade there were twenty dealers. Between them they handled 56 separate contracts, of which one dealer, John Bennett, had 22, one had eight, one, Thomas Wright, four, and five had two contracts each. The other twelve men had one each. The numbers of hogs sold in each contract varied between 632 (sold by Wright on one occasion) and twelve. Wright also made sales of 427 and 363 beasts in individual lots; but apart from these, there

---

[1] Beveridge, loc. cit. p. 514, does not indicate how far the victualling ports in different districts were self-supporting at this time.

[2] P.R.O.Adm. 20/48. All details of provision dealers are taken from the individual contracts recorded in this source. I have refrained from drawing comparisons in money, for the reasons already given in p. 59, n. 2 above.

[3] G. E. Fussell, 'The London Cheesemongers of the Eighteenth Century', in *Ec.H.R.* I, no. I, pp. 394–8.

[4] Currants, carried on southern voyages in lieu of a proportion of the meat, were also sold by one man, Robert Hawkins.

were only eight sales of over 200 hogs, while there were 22 of under 100 hogs each. There were ten dealers in pork, of whom three—Wright, Thomas Middleton and John Browne—also dealt in hogs. Middleton sold a total of 499 cwt. in two contracts, and Wright a total of 234 cwt., also in two contracts; the other eight men all handled one contract each, none of which was for more than 70 cwt.

Eighteen merchants sold peas to the navy, of whom one had five contracts and one two. The rest had one each. The amounts handled in each case were small, 32 quarters being the largest amount and sales being often made in bushels. Fifteen dealers contracted for oatmeal, and of these four dealers bore one name, Heathfield, and three another, Roades. The Heathfields handled ten contracts between them, two women having four each and two men one each, and the Roades ten, of which one man had five, another four and another one. Of the other dealers, one—also a woman, Mary Lucas—had four contracts, and two men three each. The other five contractors had one each. The amounts concerned ranged from eight to forty quarters, but there were only a few examples at either end of the scale and most sales were for twenty to thirty quarters.

Wheat was sold by six men, of whom one handled three contracts, two two each, and the other three one each. The amounts sold were considerable in most cases, being mostly from 300 to 400 quarters. Flour was contracted for by eleven dealers. Of these, one, Thomas Boles, handled seven contracts, two handled four each, one three, and two two each. The largest amount to be sold was fifty quarters, by Boles on one occasion; but this was exceptional, and ten to 25 quarters was more usual. Biscuit or bread, as a finished product, was sold to the navy by seventeen men, of whom four shared two names. Four of these dealers handled three contracts each and three handled two each. The rest had one each. The amounts varied a good deal, but no one dealer had any great advantage over his fellows. The sales were mostly reckoned by the bag, a bag containing 1 cwt., and the biggest individual sale was one of 919 bags. The next biggest was one of 600 bags; the smallest, one of 100.

There were twelve malt dealers, of whom one, Peter Hager, handled six contracts, one, Henry Ambrose, four, one three, two two, and the rest one each. Hager and Ambrose dealt mostly in amounts of between

100 and 250 quarters, and Ambrose had one large sale of 385 quarters. The rest dealt more often in lots of 90 to 100 quarters. Only four men sold hops, and only one had two contracts, the rest having one each. Apart from one large sale of 103 cwt. by this man, Henry Bartlet, no sale exceeded 30 cwt. Beer itself was sold by eight men, one of whom, Henry Rochdale, had seven contracts, one three, and one two. The rest had one each. The amounts sold were large. One dealer, who had only one contract, sold 385 tons; apart from that, there were five sales of over 100 tons, and the smallest amount sold in one contract was 56 tons.

Although there was thus a comparatively small group of dealers predominant in most of the provision trades, few of them dealt in more than one trade.[1] Thomas Wright contracted for all forms of flesh, Thomas Middleton for pork as well as hogs, and a certain Francis Zouch dealt on a small scale in both peas and malt. Otherwise no dealer handled more than one commodity except in the case of ships abroad, which were normally supplied by local agents, but occasionally by a victualling merchant in England who contracted for all the provisions, and who presumably acted as a second middleman.

This form of purchase was certainly the most convenient for the navy. It may also have been the cheapest. It is difficult to be certain of this, for our knowledge of contemporary prices is fragmentary. Purchase in bulk is normally cheaper than purchase by lot,[2] but in this instance there was a complicating factor. On the whole, London prices were higher than those in the provinces at the same time. Butter certainly cost less in Suffolk than in the capital, and so did cheese and cattle. Wheat prices did not necessarily respond in the same way, but on the average from 1691 to 1702 the south-west and the midlands grew wheat cheaper than the south-east, and the price was highest in London.[3] To what extent the London rates included the victuals sold to the navy, I do not know.[4] But it is possible that in so far as the navy

[1] See also Beveridge, loc. cit. pp. 515–16.

[2] Thorold Rogers, op. cit. v, p. 335, presupposes from this that naval victuals were probably cheaper than the same victuals sold to individuals.

[3] Gras, loc. cit. p. 119.

[4] They are usually taken from John Houghton's *Collection of Letters for the Improvement of Trade*, which is vague on this point.

paid standard London rates to its contractors, these were above rather than below the provincial prices.

But exactly how far it did pay standard rates is unfortunately impossible to say, for, as with naval stores so with naval victuals, the necessary details of quality are often not given fully enough to determine the causes for the differences in the prices paid. Oxen cost anything between 18*s.* and 27*s.* per cwt., and hogs between 23*s.* 6*d.* and 27*s.* per cwt. Wheat varied from 20*s.* to 24*s.* per quarter, peas from 18*s.* to 22*s.*, oatmeal from 27*s.* to 29*s.*, malt from 14*s.* 6*d.* to 16*s.*, and flour from 26*s.* to 38*s.* Hops cost anything from £2. 10*s.* to £3. 7*s.* per cwt. Of the monopolies, butter cost 4*d.* and cheese 2*d.* per lb., fish 6½*d.* each, and salt 50*s.* to 62*s.* 6*d.* per wey.

The most obvious advantage of the contract system arose from the possibility of controlling the dealers. If the navy wished to investigate complaints of quality, it was easier to check the source when only a few men were involved than if the provisions had been bought from any one of some dozens of local tradesmen. How far the navy managed to supervise their contractors it is once again difficult to say, for all records of naval victualling, except the lists of contracts which were drawn up outside the victualling department when the bills came to be checked, have since disappeared. Only miscellaneous references survive in the correspondence of other branches of the Administration, and these do not enable us to answer the question properly. But however slight the detailed supervision may have been, it was certainly closer than that obtained by the only other possible method of victualling the navy, which was to let out the whole process to contract. This had been done between 1660 and 1684,[1] and the abuses had grown so great that the navy itself took over the department in that year, with the appointment of Commissioners of Victualling.[2] This body survived throughout the war,[3] as an independent Board under the Admiralty in close touch with the other subordinate branches of the service.

The initial decision to let out the victualling to contract, and the subsequent creation of a Board of Victuallers, were both made for the

---

[1] *Catal.* I, pp. 152, 181.

[2] Ibid. p. 181. A Victualling Commission had been tried before, under the Commonwealth.

[3] See Appendix IX below.

same reason. Each seemed to offer advantages for the management of the later stages of the business after the provisions themselves had been bought. Three separate processes were involved. After purchase, the goods had to be converted or divided into suitable quantities for delivery and stowage aboard, they had to be kept wholesome so far as possible until they were consumed, and they had to be distributed to the ships.

The provisions as bought at the market were not automatically ready either for immediate storage or for immediate delivery. In each case they had to be packed, often after pickling or salting, to suit the peculiarities of stowage aboard ship, and this required an organization—particularly in the case of beef and pork, which if possible were bought in the form of oxen and hogs[1]—distinct from any other in the naval service. Material, in the shape of barrels, casks, iron and wooden hoops and staves, workmen—coopers, joiners, butchers and salters[2]—and amenities—slaughter-yard and slaughter-house, cutting-house, pickle-house, storerooms for the separate provisions, storehouse and workshops for the materials, and wharves and cranes for shipping the products—had all to be provided. A few offices and a house for the officer in charge were additional advantages.[3] Two of the commodities, moreover, demanded special treatment. In the case of biscuit and beer it was better to buy the ingredients for baking and brewing than to buy the finished products and see them go stale in the stores. Such biscuit and beer as was bought from contractors was designed normally to meet immediate demands from ships which the victualling yards themselves were unable to supply. To meet the bulk of the demands, the navy provided its own brewery and its own bakehouse, each with its buildings and organization.[4] Altogether, this branch of the victualling, including the purchase of materials, the payment of the workmen and the maintenance of the main victualling yard, cost £43,577 from November 1689 to March 1691, out of a total expenditure on victualling of £238,191.[5] On the one hand it was a temptation to avoid the

[1] B.M.Addnl. 11684, f. 68. [2] Admty:Corbett, XIV, f. 73.

[3] See the plan for a victualling yard at Chatham, in B.M.Addnl. 11643; and for the new yard in London after the fire of 1687, in Bodl. Rawl. A 186, f. 159.

[4] See ibid.

[5] P.R.O. T. 38/165, no. 1. There are no comparable figures for 1688.

additional complications and responsibilities which these processes entailed, by letting them out to contract; but on the other, it was difficult to supervise them at all economically without taking over the processes themselves.

This work had to be done if possible near the principal purchasing markets. The Victualling Office and the main yard were at Tower Hill, and it was from there that the supplies were distributed alike to the subsidiary victualling ports and to the ships. By 1688 the yard was most unsatisfactory, both for the processing and the distribution of provisions. Large enough when originally built by Henry VIII, it was now overgrown with tenements and small workshops which reduced its facilities for keeping cattle, thus leading to their premature slaughter when fresh supplies were brought in, and interfered unduly with the processing and storage of food.[1] These difficulties were increased by the fact that many of the yard buildings had been burnt down in 1687, and had not yet been replaced; while the site itself had only a limited access to the waterfront which made it impossible, particularly with the heavy traffic of the upper river, for the men-of-war to ship their provisions at the yard. Transport costs were thus high.[2] In the war with France, moreover, the yard was badly placed to serve the main areas of concentration.

Distribution was in any case bound to be complicated. In the spring, when most of the fleet was lying in the Thames and Medway, provisioning was done by boat from the ships; but in the summer the victuals had to be sent to the bases from which the ships were working, and if possible to the ships themselves to save them from having to leave their stations. The department thus needed a considerable fleet of provision vessels, many of them large enough to sail out to the Soundings and the western approaches. The hiring of these vessels, which sometimes numbered as many as fifty at a time, was a major commitment of the victualling office.[3] The boats were usually hired by the month, the navy feeding and paying the crews and furnishing guns and ammunition, and the owners finding the stores and maintaining and repairing the ships themselves.[4] When the victualling was under contract, the division of responsibilities between the contractor and the service

[1] Bodl. Rawl. A 186, f. 157.
[2] Ibid. ff. 157–8.
[3] B.M.Addnl. 9313, ff. 55–6.
[4] Ibid. f. 55.

became intricate. The contractor had to produce the vessels, and to see that they were ready at the right time for an escort to take them to their destination; the navy had to inform him of its requirements, and to ensure that his charges for freight and demurrage did not become excessive owing to a delay in providing the escort or a mistake over the time of departure. Once again, while apparently it would have saved the Administration a good deal of trouble to hand over its commitments to an agent, this would have involved it in the end in as much trouble and more expense than it met by itself doing the job.

As well as hiring vessels to distribute the provisions, the navy had also to maintain a group of victualling ports around the coast. These served as local storeyards, supplied to some extent locally but mostly from Tower Hill, and theoretically on the basis of the annual 'declaration', or estimate of men to be victualled in the coming year. In the 1680's, there were five of these ports—London, Dover, Portsmouth, Plymouth and Dublin[1]—but shortly after the outbreak of war they were increased to six, with the addition of Liverpool.[2] The ease with which fresh victualling ports were established throughout the war would seem to imply that they were not necessarily very large or complicated, and the figures of men to be victualled in 1688 and 1689 bear this out:[3]

	London	Dover	Portsmouth	Plymouth	Dublin
1688	1,600	300	200	50	20
1689	10,000	1,000	1,500	250	20

The smaller of these ports acted simply as store yards for the victuals with which they were supplied, and were managed by an agent who was usually also the muster-master.[4] In the cases of Portsmouth and Dover, the facilities for storage were sufficient to lead to limited facilities for processing, and a few junior officials were borne accordingly.[5] Both yards, however, were still supplied mainly from London.[6]

A proportion of the victuals for the year was also appropriated to victualling ports overseas. At the beginning of the war, these were

---

1 Pep:Sea MS. 2902, f. 79.

2 P.R.O.Adm. 112/68, figures of victuals for 1689.

3 B.M.Addnl. 9322, f. 150*v*; P.R.O.Adm. 112/68.

4 Admty:Corbett, XIV, ff. 74–5.

5 Ibid.

6 Portsmouth bought locally so far as possible, but was unable to rely more than slightly on local supplies (Beveridge, loc. cit. pp. 515–17; see also p. 242 below).

Gibraltar, which had been a victualling port with an agent for some years,[1] and the three new ports at Leghorn, Smyrna and Alexandretta or Scanderoon,[2] which had been established early in 1689.[3] The annual proportions assigned to each were: Gibraltar, provisions for 700 men; Leghorn, for 75; and Smyrna and Scanderoon, for 55 each.[4] The victuals were found locally by agents who were English merchants living at the ports.[5]

From the factors outlined above, it is not difficult to see why the victualling gave rise to more anxiety than any other department of the naval administration throughout the war. With large quantities of goods to be delivered at different places on the coast, in ships hired by the month and sailing from a port over a hundred miles from the main scene of action; with little possibility of supplying them locally, and no possibility of building up either a local or a central reserve of all the articles required, as could be done with other materials; and with the possibility that a voyage of perhaps a fortnight or more had seriously damaged the quality of the cargo, it is not surprising that the provisions could often not be provided when they were wanted. The fleet, as a result, had often to be put to short allowance of victuals, at which rate the normal rations for four days were made to last for six,[6] and the men were paid the balance in money. To prevent too much discontent, it was laid down that such an allowance should be paid in cash and by the month, and not permitted to stand over like the rest of the wages.[7] A shortage of victuals, therefore, not only reflected the existence of administrative difficulties but might often beget more, when an appropriation of ready money was required to meet additional payments shortly after the regular distribution of the available funds had already, in all probability, been upset by the victuallers' demands.

For the dislocation caused by a failure in the victualling was financial as well as material. The sudden heavy calls on the market meant either that the buyer had to have considerable reserves of cash at his disposal

---

[1] Pep:Sea MS. 2902, f. 79.

[2] P.R.O.Adm. 112/68.

[3] P.R.O.Adm. 3/1:12/4, 30/4.

[4] P.R.O.Adm. 112/68.

[5] Admty:Corbett, xiv, f. 80. See also H. Koenigsberger, 'English Merchants in Naples and Sicily in the Seventeenth Century', in *E.H.R.* lxii, pp. 304, 324–6.

[6] P.R.O.Adm. 7/639, ff. 120–1.

[7] Ibid.

or that his credit must be both reliable and flexible. The system of large-scale purchase made it possible for the navy to buy on credit, but even so only within limits which were fixed by the contractors' reserves of cash. For the problem of payment was removed only one stage further by the middleman; he in turn bought from the farmer, and to a far greater extent than the other creditors of the navy the latter demanded ready money. The seaman could live without cash payment for some time, because he was being housed and fed; the dockyard workman could also exist, although not for so long, for at least he was being given work and could extract some perquisites from his employer; the owners of domestic timber were on the average wealthy enough, and the owners of naval stores abroad powerful enough, to make use of the terms of their credit; but the small farmer, who provided so much of the agricultural produce for the navy, was neither supported by its credit nor able to make use of it in his business. He could not count on offsetting an immediate loss with a future profit, for he never knew what next year would bring, and the margin between subsistence and failure was small. The problem which he posed was always an immediate one, which the middleman might be able to veil but never to hide. Thus the department which was most likely to fail to meet its commitments suffered the most from failure, and the consequences could seldom be confined to itself. For once its credit was disturbed it was forced to borrow beyond its allowance, which could be done only at the expense of other branches of the service; and the repercussions soon disturbed their credit as much as the original demands had disturbed its own. In the financial conditions of the day, the material difficulties of the victualling were frequently the prologue to a general breakdown of administration.

CHAPTER VI

ESTIMATES AND ACCOUNTS

The financial position of the navy was a complex one. Possibly the largest employer of labour and the greatest consumer of material in the country, its obligations were varied and extensive. On the other hand, unlike other industries its capital, in ships and land, in buildings and material, yielded no income, and its finances were in a sense incomplete, in that it acted only as a paymaster and was supported entirely by subsidies from other sources. The results of its expenditure took place beyond its review, in the trade and industry which its custom or its protection encouraged and which in turn produced the wealth with which it was financed by Crown and Parliament.

With such varied commitments, the navy needed a common factor to which they could all be related. This was provided in the form of the individual seaman, and all figures of expenditure, of whatever nature, were translated into the cost of his maintenance per month. This in turn was calculated under the three heads of wages, wear and tear, and victuals. The subjects which each covered were listed as follows:[1]

Wages

Pay of all sea officers and men in ships
Bounties to widows and orphans not included in Chatham Chest
Pensions and relief not included in Chatham Chest
Three-fifths of costs for caring for sick and wounded seamen
Surgeons' necessaries in men-of-war
Wages of crews of hospital ships
Surgeons' necessaries in hospital ships
Wages of men in Fleet tenders
Costs of pressing seamen
Seamen's conduct money
Pilotage
Pay of muster-masters, and provost marshals in Fleet

[1] I know of no official list of this sort. The details given here were produced by Sergison in 1704 (Serg.Misc. VI, f. 28).

Pay of Flag Officers' secretaries
Bounty to volunteers
Clerks' expenses in paying off ships
Compensation for loss of clothes in action
Contingent money to Admirals of Fleet and commanders of squadrons
Surgeons' expenses in caring for soldiers transported in men-of-war
Expenses of courts martial
Discount on tallies for wages

Wear and Tear

Construction, maintenance and repair of ships and buildings
Transport of stores
Demurrage
Naval stores
Printing and stationer's ware
Expenses of Admiralty and Navy Office, and salaries
Salaries of officials and clerks
Travelling expenses
Freight of hired ships, and tenders, and compensation if taken by the enemy
Rewards for extra service
Press money to dockyard workmen
Wages of dockyard workmen
Interest on bills for naval stores and contracts
Lawsuits undertaken by Admiralty, against theft of stores, etc.

Victualling

Provisions of all sorts
Salaries and wages of officials in victualling service
Freight of hired vessels, and compensation if taken by the enemy
All stores used in victualling service
Building and maintenance of victualling office and yard
Office expenses
Interest on victualling bills
Two-fifths of costs for caring for sick and wounded seamen
Victualling of soldiers transported in men-of-war

The normal annual estimate reckoned wages at 30*s.* per man per month, wear and tear at 27*s.* 6*d.*, and victuals at 20*s.* In addition, a normal expenditure of 2*s.* 6*d.* per man per month for ordnance was added to wear and tear, bringing it to 30*s.* The total estimated rate per man per month was thus normally £4.[1] It was on this basis that the annual estimates were worked out.

The three heads of expenditure did not coincide exactly with the ways in which the money was actually spent. Wear and tear included certain wages as well as the purchase of stores; wages in turn included the purchase of certain stores and some external commitments; while victualling, necessarily following the administrative pattern already described, involved its own wages and stores as well as the victuals themselves. Each account was thus affected by financial conditions which did not by their nature attach to it. For the problems affecting the payment of stores differed from those affecting the payment of wages or victuals; both the method and the frequency of payment varied, according to the nature of the creditor and the nature of the material purchased. The reliability of the different estimates, therefore, was not the same; each was made on a different type of information, but each included to a varying extent the type of information affecting the others. The estimate for wear and tear, as an estimate purely for stores, had a different reliability from the estimate for wages or for victuals; but in its final form wear and tear was composed of material properly belonging to wages and victualling as well as to stores. The form of the estimates, therefore, was not entirely satisfactory.

The degree to which any one estimate might be expected to be reliable may perhaps best be seen by examining the type of control which its material required. Wages were the simplest form of expenditure to estimate correctly. The figures themselves were not attended by any complications: a monthly wage was a monthly wage, and a salary a salary, with no other conditions attaching to them. The accounts, therefore, were likely to be accurate, provided that the details of the men in pay were accurate. Unhappily, they were not. With the contemporary system of manning, the only possibility of keeping control lay in frequent and reliable musters whose details were sent regularly to a central pay office. On paper, an organization existed for this purpose: the clerks of the cheque were supposed to muster all ships in ordinary or in the yard, each squadron was allowed a muster-master at

[1] P.R.O.Adm. 7/169. The months are in each case the lunar month of 28 days, with thirteen of them to the year.

sea, and in detached ships the captain and purser were instructed to take musters; while ashore, the landladies and the agents for the sick and wounded were required to check the men in their care.[1] Each of these authorities was ordered to submit his muster lists to the Navy Office at regular intervals, and a printed form existed in the captains' Instructions which laid down the comprehensive details to be inserted. But in practice, the organization did not work. The clerks of the cheque were fairly reliable, but the muster-masters—provided that they were appointed, which often they were not[2]—were either the secretaries of the local flag officer, and apt not to be interested in that side of their duties, or, if they were appointed as muster-masters, were liable to find themselves the object of open hostility on the part of the captains of the ships. Often they were not allowed aboard, sometimes they were locked in the hold and kept there for days at a time, and sometimes their boat was taken from them so that they could not carry out their duties.[3] The reason for this attitude lay in the captains' dislike of supervision, which is easy to understand. Many ships unofficially carried more men, and others less, on deck than on paper; and in both cases the captain and the purser stood to gain in various unsavoury ways. Thus even when returns were made to the Navy Office their value was problematical. But more often it is safe to say that no returns were made at all. The Admiralty minutes and orders bristle with rebukes to muster-masters and captains, and to agents for sick and wounded, for failing to send in their lists; and in fact no musters for the navy as a whole could be submitted with the annual estimates for the first five years of the war.[4] While the figure of 30*s*. per man per month was therefore reliable, the estimated cost for the year, of which that figure was the multiplicand, was not. It too often represented simply the establishments of 1677, multiplied by the ships ordered for the next campaign and modified by scattered reports from press agents and from a few of the mustering authorities.

---

[1] P.R.O.Adm. 7/633, 7/639.

[2] E.g. p. 232 below.

[3] E.g. P.R.O.Adm. 106/478, 479, letters from Wilkins to Navy Board; Serg.Misc. IV, ff. 85–7.

[4] *Return of Public Income and Expenditure*, pt I, p. 693 (House of Commons, vol. XXXV, 1868–9). See also Admty:Corbett, XI, f. 108.

Naval stores and contracts set different problems. The details of the transactions were easier to check than the details of the complements aboard the ships. The terms of the contract might be evaded locally, on the lines suggested earlier, and in any case quality was hard to check satisfactorily on every occasion, so that the records might not be a true representation of the value of the transaction;[1] but at least they could be kept up to date and with some accuracy. The receipt and issue of stores over the signatures of more than one officer at the yard, although of course not foolproof, was at least a valuable check, while the dependence of the local storekeepers upon the central authority resulted in a fairly regular presentation of the accounts of material to the office of the Comptroller of the Storekeeper's Accounts.[2] There the bills were entered in course, that is to say in the order in which they had been acknowledged; and in that order they were paid, after examination by the Comptroller and three other members of the Navy Board.[3] Thus the accounts of the bills themselves on this head were normally reliable and up to date. The unreliability of the estimate lay in the terms of their payment.

When money was short, the interval between the registration and the settling of a bill might be as much as two or even three years; and even in the comparatively good years from 1689 to 1691 it was from four to eighteen months.[4] Contractors therefore often demanded interest or sold their bills to a discount merchant, who made his profit on the discount which the navy allowed for the delay in payment. The terms of interest and discount were constantly varying; shipbuilders were often given a regular rate of interest after either three or six months from the date of their individual payments on a contract,[5] but other contractors made their own arrangements, and the navy itself varied the rate of discount according to the pressure that was brought on it at different times. The extent to which the figures of the original bill were thus affected could seldom, under these circumstances, be noted in the

[1] In many cases, also, not enough details of quality are recorded to assess value, whether correctly or not, from the ledgers. See p. 49 above.

[2] See p. 182 below.

[3] This method of payment was known as 'the course', and will be referred to by that term in future. See Beveridge, loc. cit. pp. 623, 626.

[4] Ibid. pp. 626–7.

[5] E.g. in 1691. See Appendix III below.

ledgers;[1] and since discount on occasions stood at thirty or forty per cent, obviously it was of great importance in estimating the cost of wear and tear. As it was, the effect was incalculable from year to year, for not only might discount reach unforeseen heights in the period under estimate, but it was often being paid on bills which did not belong to that period at all.

The reliability of the estimates for wages and for wear and tear, therefore, are of different kinds, the one affected by external administrative conditions, the other by the internal difficulties of assessing the value of the figures themselves. The estimate for victualling suffers from both these defects. Victuals themselves were more difficult to measure accurately than other kinds of naval stores, and their processing led to further variations in weight and bulk. Meat, especially, was not always packed equally in the casks, for it was barrelled according to the shapes in which it had been cut, and the weight varied accordingly. But the greatest variation came in quality, and it was impossible to check this until the cask was opened aboard. Meat again was peculiarly subject to differences of quality, many barrels being full of bone, others full of meat with an excessive amount of fat, and others of meat which had gone bad; but the same applied to the other commodities, from the fish and the biscuit to the butter and cheese. The figures of provisions bought and issued meant little, therefore, without a close supervision at every stage of their conversion. On paper, for instance, a victualling port might contain a thousand sacks of biscuit; but 200 of these had possibly been baked some weeks before the rest and had gone bad, while not all the sacks might contain exactly the same amounts. The discrepancies were increased by the purser's activities aboard ship, in condemning good provisions, or in indenting for provisions for non-existent men and then selling them at a profit, or in varying his measures to the ship's company and reserving the proceeds to his own use. The fact that he was supposed to be checked by other officers was of little use if they themselves were involved in these transactions. The victuals might thus appear differently on the books according to the amounts recorded on purchase, on conversion, and by the ships themselves. It was little wonder that the

---

[1] Beveridge, loc. cit. pp. xxxi, 630. The ledgers themselves are contained in the series P.R.O.Adm. 20/49–.

different victualling authorities produced such different results from the same lists of stores.

The financial and material value of the victuals, therefore, by no means always corresponded, so that the financial position was continually upset by unforeseen expenditure. But even without such disturbances the position was not fully represented by the accounts at any time. Unlike the contracts for other stores and work, those for provisions were registered only intermittently in course. When urged to institute such a method, the victualling authorities always argued that the nature of their business made it impossible.[1] Faced with sudden and heavy demands on their resources, and dealing as they did with merchants who could stand only a limited amount of credit, their funds were continually being diverted to fresh and unexpected purposes. This process was accelerated when the stores which had been paid for in this way were found not to go so far as they should have done, and further calls at short notice had to be made on the markets. The victualling ledgers, in consequence, were usually in disorder, and it was often impossible to tell from them exactly what had been bought in any given period.[2] In addition, the same uncertainties of interest and discount that affected the estimate for wear and tear affected the victualling, if anything to a greater degree.[3] Thus while the Victualling Office made greater financial demands than any other department, it was less capable than any other of presenting a reliable estimate of what they were likely to be.

The annual estimates were in fact only an approximate hazard as to the requirements, even if the data on which they were based, of the numbers of ships and types of services proposed for the year, proved to be correct. In wartime, such data could only be approximate, and were seldom likely to prove less expensive than the original budget. It was perhaps impossible to allow for such uncertainties in the estimates themselves, particularly at a time when long-term planning hardly existed. Certainly no attempt was made to do so, and the rate of £4 per

---

[1] See pp. 481–2 below.

[2] They are contained in the series P.R.O.Adm. 20/48.

[3] Beveridge, loc. cit. pp. 519–20. The interest of 6% on bills from six months after the date of registration, which is noted ibid p. 519, seems to have been granted only on certain occasions and to certain men.

man per month continued for the first few years of the war irrespective of the varying margin of unforeseeable expenditure and of the fluctuations in prices. It was therefore essential for the executive to be able to check the estimates by the subsequent accounts and, where necessary, by regular statements of debt.

The naval system of accountancy was modelled on the Exchequer system of the 'declared accounts'. So far as it went, this served its purpose. The three accounts for wear and tear, wages and victualling were brought into a central account, for which the Treasurer of the Navy was responsible.[1] This was drawn up in two columns of charge and discharge, the former being an account of receipts and the latter of expenditure. In neither case, however, did these columns represent the financial position of the year. That indeed was not their purpose. They were intended to present the position of the Treasurer of the Navy as a creditor or debtor of the national Exchequer. To this end the discharge column showed not the total obligations of the navy, but only the sums paid out within the specified period by its Treasurer—which, as has been seen, were not all incurred in the course of it, and included the complicating factor of interest and discount—while the charge column showed his 'arrears and remains', which consisted partly of liabilities carried over from the previous account and partly of assets similarly recorded before, all expressed as a debt from the Exchequer. The account, in fact, was not intended to be used except for the domestic purposes of the Exchequer itself; and so closely did it follow that department's medieval system of accountancy that the amounts contained in it were presented in Roman figures, which would have to be converted into Arabic numerals before any calculations could be made.[2] It was, moreover, normally drawn up to cover a financial year ending

[1] See *Cal.Treas.Bks. 1685–8*, pp. lxi–lxv; ibid. *1689–92*, pp. cclxxxiv–cclxxxviii.

[2] The heads of the declared accounts are given in Arabic figures, ibid. The accounts themselves are contained in P.R.O. Audit Office, bundles 1718–21. Some are incomplete and may be supplemented by the Pipe Office accounts in P.R.O. Pipe Office, rolls 2322–32. The only discussion of the form of the declared accounts, so far as I am aware, occurs in J. Lane, *Reports of the Parliamentary Commissioners for auditing the Declared Accounts* (1787), a copy of which exists among B.M. printed books. *Income and Expenditure* (p. 331) discusses them in relation to the system of Exchequer auditing.

on Lady Day, 25 March, whereas the annual estimates were either for a year ending at Michaelmas, 30 September, or on 31 December.[1] There was in fact no balance sheet of the country's financial position in naval affairs, but only an account, in archaic form, of the Treasurer of the Navy's credit upon or indebtedness to the Exchequer.

This perhaps was not surprising, for in fact not all the money supplied for naval purposes passed through the hands of the navy. Thanks to the contemporary system of credit whereby supplies, particularly for war, were provided largely by individuals who had an early call upon the funds of Custom or Excise, some liabilities were met by the Treasury itself from funds diverted before they ever reached the Exchequer.[2] Thus not only were the declared accounts compiled in a form unsuitable for the purpose of checking the actual expenditure, but they did not entirely cover it.

The last check upon expenditure was provided by a regular statement of naval debt. Here again, the figures were subject to the same defects in the calculation of interest and discount as affected the estimates and accounts of expenditure; but at least such a statement could show the position at the moment, even if it could not estimate the same position when the debts actually came to be paid. To be of any use, however, statements of debt had to be drawn up regularly, and if possible at the same time as the other accounts. In practice, they appeared irregularly, neither every year nor on the same date in the years when they did appear.[3] This was partly due to the difficulty of compiling such statements, which had always to include a margin of estimate for the bills which had still to come into the central office.[4] But it was due far more to the type of demand made on the naval financial system by its sources of supply.

For while the orderly compilation of departmental estimates, accounts and debts was complicated by the technical obstacles to an

---

[1] *Cal.Treas.Bks. 1689–1692*, pp. cclxxxiv–cclxxxviii; P.R.O.Adm. 7/169, *passim*. In James II's reign, the declared accounts seem to have been submitted at various times of year (*Cal.Treas.Bks. 1685–8*, pp. lxi–lxv). [2] See p. 237, n. 3 below.

[3] See P.R.O.Adm. 49/173; Serg. A 133, *passim*; Appendix IV below.

[4] The standing contractors, in particular, made up their accounts over long intervals, and their bills were not always received regularly.

accurate and standard system of accountancy, the incentive for it was largely removed by the fact that their presentation was seldom demanded by any other authority. It was only occasionally, and for specific purposes, that the navy was required to submit an Estimate or a statement of debt, although the former were regularly drawn up within the Navy Office itself.[1] The authority responsible for supply acted, in fact, 'as a householder does whose only financial guide is his bank pass book'.[2]

That authority was the King's executive. Its resources were of two kinds: first, the hereditary and inalienable property and rights of the King himself; and secondly, the revenue which was granted him by Act of Parliament either for his reign or for a given period.[3] By origin and in theory, the second class of revenue, which by the second half of the seventeenth century was by far the larger of the two,[4] was simply an extension of the first, raised through the authority of the High Court of Parliament as an alternative to that of the prerogative or of private possession. This theory was reflected in the treatment of the revenue. Although levied by Parliament, in the form of taxation and dues, it was handed over completely to the executive as the standing revenue for which no accounts were required. Its amount and its collection were regulated by legislation, but its disposal rested entirely with the Crown. The King, in fact, controlled the whole of the national revenue which was not raised for specific *ad hoc* purposes: the only limitations to his control were the terms upon which the money was granted. In Charles II's reign, the Commons had on occasion used their financial authority as a bargaining weapon with which to argue national policy, and had confined their grants to a given period. But when James came to the throne on the crest of the Tory reaction, he was given the standing revenue outright for the whole of his reign, and thus for the

---

1 For details under the later Stuarts, see *Cal. Treas. Bks. 1689–92*, pp. cxiv–cxxiv.

2 Ibid. p. cxiii.

3 This paragraph is based upon W. A. Shaw's introduction to *Cal. Treas. Bks. 1685–8*, and ibid. *1689–92*, pp. x–xiii.

4 In the last two years of James II's reign, the average annual yield from Crown lands and hereditary rights was £26,351 out of a total standing revenue of £1,916'438 (*Cal. Treas. Bks. 1635–8*, pp. xxiv–xxviii). For the yield in the last decade of the century, see *Income and Expenditure*, pp. 5–18.

last three years before the Revolution no external authority was concerned in the way in which he distributed the national resources. Under these circumstances, the naval accounts could be included with other departmental accounts in a balance sheet which comprehended them all. The distribution of money and credit did not depend on any appropriation made by an independent body with independent powers of supervision, but rather on a system of internal allocations which could be continuously adjusted according to the general financial position. The interest centred less on the departmental balances than on the balance of the executive itself; and thus the checks upon departmental expenditure were provided by a statement of debit and credit with the Exchequer, which did not prevent that expenditure, rather than by a scrutiny of the accounts which ensured that it was limited to amounts reliably demanded in advance.

The flexibility of this system had one distinct advantage for the departments. The fact that money was not allocated to specific purposes by an external authority, but only by the Treasurer of the Navy on receipt,[1] made it easier to distribute as the occasion demanded between the different branches of the service. If, for example, the contractors were pressing for payment, money could be diverted to them at once which in the accounts was distributed among the three heads. Such a form of distribution was more difficult to control by external appropriations for given purposes, which could be made only on the basis of the estimates and thus devoted to wear and tear, or wages, or victualling, rather than to creditors who might not all be covered by the generic term employed. When such appropriations were introduced with the growth of Parliamentary financial control, the naval estimates thus provided an unsatisfactory basis for their operation.

But the very flexibility which thus favoured a ready allocation of funds to meet the demands as they arose, was largely responsible for the fact that they had to be met in this way. If it provided a partial answer to the problem, it also indicated the problem itself. In the absence of any accounts, Parliament had only an approximate idea of the expenditure for which it was making provision, and the standing revenue was not always equal to its commitments. Moreover, in the contemporary

---

[1] Or more occasionally by the Treasury (e.g. p. 331 below). See p. 166 above.

state of statistical inquiry, the yield from the taxation and dues which were imposed was difficult to calculate at all exactly, and the rate at which it could be collected varied indefinitely.[1] There was in fact seldom enough money to meet the demands, and the executive had to work mostly on credit. But regarding the departmental finances as it did merely as elements in the total balance sheet, the Crown declined to appropriate the different funds of revenue for different and publicly defined purposes, and its credit was thus based simply on the general credit of the Exchequer. The creditors of the navy were not able to rely upon their demands being met from a specific source of supply on which they had a specific claim, but had to fight for priority with the creditors of other departments upon a general source of supply which was known to be inadequate to satisfy them all. Credit, instead of being a source of strength to the creditor, was a source of weakness. The tally which was the government's substitute for money[2] could not be made into a negotiable instrument, for normally it carried no interest and no guarantee of payment within a given time. It did not circulate, but remained simply a token to be changed as soon as possible into money.[3] Under these circumstances, a flexible manipulation of the funds led to confusion, and the only remedy lay in a rigid system of appropriation. This was later to be provided by Parliament; but at the beginning of the French war, the navy was largely financed by a form of credit which it was unable to control and its creditors unwilling to trust.

The uncertainty over the actual rate of expenditure which was engendered by this system of supply, became particularly serious in the event of a war. For it was not clear exactly where the financial responsibilities of the executive then stopped, and those of Parliament began.[4] The standing revenue which the latter granted to the Crown was designed to cover its standing expenses. Extraordinary expenses

---

[1] See introduction by G. N. Clark to *Guide to English Commercial Statistics, 1696–1782* (1938).

[2] The tally was a wooden stick inscribed with the amount for which it stood and the date of registration, of which the creditor took one half and the debtor kept the other half. On redemption the creditor brought his half to the debtor, and was paid his money in return.

[3] The effects of this type of credit in particular cases are examined on pp. 336–7, 489–90, 542–3 below.

[4] See *Cal.Treas.Bks. 1689–92*, pp. xiii–xvi.

had to be met by extraordinary grants, and war was an extraordinary occasion. But with no accounts of the standing expenses to guide it, Parliament found it difficult to separate the two kinds of expenditure. The extraordinary supplies were almost always insufficient to meet the case, for neither executive nor legislature could estimate accurately the gap between peacetime and wartime expenditure. The annual cost of the navy in peacetime was estimated at about £400,000,[1] and this comprised the ordinary of £100,000 to £130,000,[2] the maintenance of the dockyards, repairs to the ships, and the expenses of a winter and summer squadron for the Channel.[3] Outside this figure, the expenses of war became the subject of an extraordinary grant. Until the Commons could be provided with the necessary data on which to calculate these expenses, by reliable estimates and accounts of expenditure, the supplies were inadequate; until they could improve upon their estimates of yield and methods of collection, they remained largely unreal. The executive found itself faced with an outlay which far exceeded its income, and a system of credit which increased rather than narrowed the gap. The most urgent problem in the first few years of the war was not material but financial; not so much the organization of resources, real though this was, as the organization of wealth.

As we look back on the conditions for naval policy and administration, we may wonder how, with the rudimentary organization and the chronic lack of money and credit, they were able to operate at all. To examine them in detail is to chronicle a series of failures, until the obstacles to success appear to be insuperable. But in fact, administration never completely broke down, and there was in consequence always a basis for policy. The seamen were badly treated, but they continued to go to sea, and to fight very well when they got there; the dockyard workmen often starved, but they never stopped working entirely; the contractors were often on the verge of bankruptcy, but some at least were always willing to supply the stores. The fleet was put to sea year

[1] *Cal.Treas.Bks. 1685–8*, p. xciii.

[2] P.R.O.Adm. 7/169, no. 9; *H. of L. N.S.* I, p. 12.

[3] *H.C.J.* x, p. 80, where the total fixed for the peacetime expenses was rather higher, coming to 'ordinary' £130,000, 'ships and men' £366,080.

after year, and after a war which lasted almost nine years the navy emerged as the greatest of the sea powers of Europe. How, it may be asked, can this be reconciled with the picture of almost unrelieved gloom which has been painted?

Two answers may perhaps be given. In the first place, the very disorganization which appears so overwhelming meant that unorganized effort had a valid contribution to make. If the margin between administration and chaos was narrow, it required only a narrow margin to separate administration from chaos. The scale of naval organization was still small, however large it might seem in comparison with other small-scale organizations, and the factors which militated against a successful form of central control were not necessarily a feature of local activity.

But the real strength of the navy lay in the foundations for these activities. England survived the war because her resources were well adapted to war. Her navy was the product of a peculiar combination of national power and national wealth, in which the one element complemented the other in the demand not only for a large but for an expensive fleet. As a maritime power whose interests to an increasing extent were concentrated upon foreign trade, she required as strong a navy, in a period of national rivalry, as her rivals. But while trade might demand a navy, trade might not necessarily be able to support it. The appearance of the big ship and the big fleet, with their new demands on material, meant that in the last analysis the ability to win a war at sea depended on the ability to fight an expensive war. England possessed that ability. Maritime war did not merely help her to gain wealth, its progress directly increased wealth, and the expensive fleet stimulated and did not exhaust trade and industry. The substance of the country was largely in the hands of those interests which could not operate without a navy; which could directly support a navy, either by supplying it with imported goods or by developing the trades on which it could draw for men; and which provided the money and the spirit to develop the domestic resources and the general circulation of wealth which increased with the cost of the war. Power and wealth reacted upon each other, and increasing costs were met by increasing resources.

The expensive war not only suited England: it favoured her in comparison with the other two great maritime powers of Holland and

France. Holland, indeed, had possessed a similar combination of wealth and power; but applied originally to a less complex type of warfare, and circumscribed by the physical peculiarities of the country, it was now on the decline. In France, such a combination did not exist. The French navy was not an integral part of the French economy, but, like the German navy at the beginning of the twentieth century, was the product of its rival. In 1651, at the beginning of the first Dutch war, it had consisted of only 25 sail of the line, one frigate and three storeships, with a number of lightly armed rowing galleys.[1] Four years after the end of the third Dutch war, it consisted of 12 first rates, 17 seconds, 56 thirds, 43 fourths, 30 fifths, and 21 sixths, with 30 galleys—a total of 209 ships excluding auxiliaries, mounting 9384 guns,[2] and leading directly to a counter-programme of construction in England. The organization of this navy excited the apprehension and admiration of its rivals. It became the fashion in England to compare the native administration with the French, usually to the former's disadvantage,[3] and the sign of a conscientious official was to have Louis XIV's *Ordonnances du Roi pour les Armées Navales* translated for his private use.[4] But impressive as this achievement was, it was imposed by the state and did not grow from a national demand. The very organization which contemporaries so greatly admired was made necessary by the natural poverty of the resources, and while the former might operate successfully in the early stages of a war, it was liable to be offset by the latter as the war progressed. French sea power was brittle, and as its resources were progressively extended by the demands of war they were exhausted beyond recovery. In contrast, after the end of the war the English marine was more active than before. Where in 1688 285,800 tons of shipping were cleared in and out of the English ports, of which 190,533 tons were English, in 1699 a total of 337,328 tons was cleared, and of this the English accounted for 293,703 tons.[5] As one observer

[1] *Soc. Naut. Research, Occas. Publns*, no. 5, pt II, nos. 1–91.

[2] *Catal.* I, p. 55.

[3] *Samuel Pepys's Naval Minutes*, pp. 33–4, 227, 316, 361–3.

[4] Both Pepys and Charles Sergison had copies made of the translated French instructions (Pep:Sea MS. 693; Serg.MSS., unnumbered).

[5] George Chalmers, *An Estimate of the Comparative Strength of Britain...* (1782), pp. 5–6.

remarked a century later upon these figures, 'the commerce of England...may be aptly compared to a spring of mighty powers, which always exerts its force in proportion to the weight of its compression'.[1] It had not 'always' been so; and that it was so at the time at which he wrote was due in no small measure to the French war of William III, during which, the further their resources were extended, the more firmly the navy and the country entered upon their European supremacy.

[1] Ibid. p. 6.

CHAPTER VII

THE LORD ADMIRAL'S DEPARTMENT AT THE END OF 1688

The fact that the navy in 1688 was the most comprehensive, and in some respects the largest industry in the country, had its effects on the organs of naval government. While to the various interests which it affected it appeared as a substantial importer of raw material, as the biggest shipbuilder, both in its own right and by contract, in England, as one of the two biggest purchasers of agricultural produce and clothing material, as a large medical institution, and—with 15,000 men on its pay roll in 1688 and treble that number a few years later—as one of the biggest employers of labour in the country; to its own hierarchy the departments which controlled these activities 'represented', as has been said of their successor, 'practically all the departments of state rolled into one', and indeed 'discharged, in addition, most of the functions of an inscrutable Providence'.[1]

At the end of 1688 there were three of these departments, under the general supervision of the Lord Admiral. They were the Navy Board, the Commissioners of Victualling, and the Ordnance Board. A fourth department, which was not in existence at the time but which was a recognized part of the organization and was re-formed in the following year, was the wartime medical branch of the navy, the Commission for Sick and Wounded Seamen. In addition, after the war began in 1689, an allied body was established in the Commissioners of Transport, to relieve the Navy Board of its responsibilities for transporting troops in vessels other than men-of-war. This last body, however, will not be considered in the remarks which follow.

The other four bodies were all subordinate to the head of the naval department, the Lord Admiral, but not each to the same degree. The Ordnance, indeed, was related to the navy by function alone and not by any constitutional tie. For a century it had been a separate depart-

[1] Sir Oswyn Murray, 'The Admiralty, I' in *M.M.* XXIII, no. 1, p. 14.

ment which supplied army and navy alike, with complete control of the guns and ordnance stores for both services.[1] The system, despite frequent complaints against its impracticability,[2] lasted until 1887,[3] enjoying an inefficiency which was never denied but never seriously tackled. The Board of Ordnance was created directly by the Crown, with no reference to the departments of state which it served and with its own Instructions which were issued on the counter-signature of a Secretary of State, and without the formal participation of either the Captain General or the Lord Admiral.[4] In 1688 the Instructions in force were those promulgated by Charles II in July 1683, and amended in some particulars by James in February 1685.[5] They provided for a Master General of the Ordnance—both then and in 1688, the naval officer Lord Dartmouth—with a Lieutenant General, a Surveyor, a Clerk of the Ordnance, Storekeeper, Clerk of the Deliveries and Treasurer; an establishment of local storekeepers, clerks, engineers and armourers; and a similar staff together with purveyors, messengers and a few skilled officers (a firemaster, a proofmaster, and some furbishers of arms), at the central armoury in the Tower.[6] Their rates of pay corresponded on the whole to those of their counterparts in the navy. The estimates and accounts, the contracts and receipts, and the maintenance and issues of guns and stores were entirely the concern of this organization.[7] The navy confined itself to specifying the amounts and types of ordnance required, and to taking receipt of them aboard the ships: even their delivery was supposed to be the responsibility of the Ordnance. This division of duties naturally led to constant friction between the two departments, the Ordnance accusing the navy, often

---

[1] Oppenheim, loc. cit. pp. 85–6.

[2] Ibid. p. 289; Sir R. Vesey Hamilton, *Naval Administration* (1896), pp. 79–81.

[3] Vesey Hamilton, loc. cit. pp. 92–4.

[4] B.M. King's 70. How far the Lord Admiral vetted the Instructions before they were issued I do not know; certainly his successors, the Commissioners of the Admiralty, seem to have had no say in the few additional Instructions issued in William's reign (for which see B.M. King's 70). The Admiralty, of course, held a copy of them (*Catal.* I, p. 242).

[5] A copy of all the 'Rules, Orders and Instructions for the future Government of the Office of the Ordnance' from 1683 to 1751, is contained in B.M. King's 70. Another copy of the Instructions of 1683 may be found in P.R.O.Adm. 7/677.

[6] B.M. King's 70. [7] See ibid. in the instructions of the senior officers.

with justice, of failing to give due warning of its requirements, and the navy accusing the Ordnance of failing to deliver the guns and stores.[1] With this division of responsibility, it was unfortunate that one of the partners should have been notoriously inefficient. From the sixteenth to the nineteenth century the Ordnance enjoyed an unbroken reputation for procrastination and corruption, attracting the attention of Marlborough as of Hawkins, and of Wellington as of Pepys. Throughout the French war, the inevitable failures on both sides were emphasized by the acrimony of their relations.

The other subordinate bodies were all purely naval departments, and in each case their legal status was the same. The Commissions were appointed by Letters Patent under the Great Seal,[2] and those members who joined a Commission after its appointment, by royal warrant. Their constitutional position was also in some respects the same. Each received its Instructions signed by the King and countersigned by the Lord Admiral, and each received its orders from the latter. Within this common framework, however, the relations of the Commissions with their superior differed according to the nature of their members, itself the result of their activities. Neither the Commissioners for Sick and Wounded nor the Victuallers were so exclusively subordinate to the Lord Admiral as the Navy Board, for neither was a permanent board as the Navy Board was permanent, and neither was so closely related by the nature of its duties to the permanent hierarchy of senior officials. The Commissioners for Sick and Wounded appeared only during a war, and their responsibilities, while of immediate naval concern, were not such as to attract naval officers into that service. Their temporary nature did not offer any prospects comparable to the other shore posts, while on the other hand it removed the holders from sea at a time of promotion and prize money. Sea officers and dockyard officials or clerks, therefore, seldom found their way into the service during a war. None of the Commissioners for the third Dutch war—Sir William Doyley, Colonel Reymes, Henry Ford and John Evelyn[3]—or of those appointed in 1689 for the French war—Thomas Addison, Edward Leigh, John Sharkey and Anthony Sheppard[4]—was a naval

[1] For examples, see P.R.O.Adm. 3/1–14, *passim*.

[2] See the Patent Rolls. [3] *Catal.* 1, p. 133. [4] P.R.O. T. 38/615.

official, but all were members of Parliament or placemen. Their background, therefore, was not such as to lead to any marked dependence upon the Admiralty, and during the war they were often in touch with the Privy Council as well as with their immediate superiors.

The Victuallers were likewise connected with other authorities besides the Admiralty. In their case again the nature of the Commissioners led to a certain independence, for although the replacement of the contractors by a Commission in 1683 was designed to tighten the Lord Admiral's control of the department, this was achieved by retaining at least some of the contractors themselves to manage the processes which they knew already from professional experience. For victualling demanded expert supervision, and with no tradition of trained officials in this branch, the members of the Victualling Commissions continued to be recruited largely from outside the ranks of the naval hierarchy. When a new Commission was appointed in 1688, only one of its four members, Sir Richard Haddock, had climbed the professional ladder,[1] and when William was searching for an experienced man to save that Commission at the end of 1689, he found him again outside the ranks of the naval hierarchy.[2] The idea of a Commission, indeed, was still a matter for dispute. It was still possible for the business to revert to contract, and in fact a scheme for the regular alternation of contractors and Commissions was proposed and seriously considered in 1686, and again in 1700.[3] This administrative independence was strengthened during the war by the Victuallers' financial dependence on another government department. For by the nature of their work the Commissioners were tied almost as closely to the Treasury as to the Admiralty, and the former, with its frequent inspections of their accounts and its close interest in their proceedings and their appointments,[4] acted from the first not merely as a complementary authority to the latter in supervising the victualling arrangements, but often as a court of appeal from its decisions. The two Commissions, therefore, which cared most directly for the physical well-being of the navy, were by tradition and membership still partly independent of the naval administration.

The third body, the Navy Board, was in contrast entirely subordinate

[1] See Appendix IX below. [2] See pp. 315–16 below.

[3] B.M.Addnl. 11684, f. 65; *Remarks on the Present Condition of the Navy, And particularly the Victualling...* (1700), p. 15. [4] E.g. p. 316 below.

to the Lord Admiral. Its history, its work and its membership were quite different from those of its colleagues, and were reflected in its status not only in relation to its superior but also to them. For although by the terms of their appointments all three bodies were constitutionally equal, in practice the Commissioners for Sick and Wounded and the Victuallers were partly subordinate to the Navy Board. The draft of their Instructions was often sent to the Navy Office to be checked and if necessary modified before the final version was promulgated;[1] and while they could sometimes appeal successfully to external authorities in the quarrels which followed, it was precisely because the Navy Board was so integral a part of the naval hierarchy that the balance which was thus redressed was initially tipped in its favour. In comparison, the Victuallers and the Sick and Wounded were temporary agents, and it was in this light that the Navy Board generally regarded them.

The relations between the three bodies were further defined by the fact that some of the work of the first two was already being done by the third. If the Commissioners for Sick and Wounded looked after the sick quarters ashore, the Navy Board appointed the surgeons and looked after the sick afloat; while the Victuallers' accounts, before they reached the Treasurer of the Navy, were scrutinized by a member of the Navy Board, the Comptroller of the Victuallers' Accounts. For just as the Navy Board itself had originally grown out of the Lord Admiral's office, so the other two bodies had grown out of the Navy Board, which still retained an immediate interest in some aspects of their work as well as a general concern in it all.

At the end of 1688, the Navy Board consisted of the following members, shown with their salaries per annum:[2]

Treasurer of the Navy	£3000
Comptroller of the Navy	£500
Surveyor	£500
Clerk of the Acts	£500
Five Commissioners of the Navy	£500 each

[1] E.g., P.R.O.Adm. 3/7:26/11; 7/639, f. 116. As no records appear to survive for either the Sick and Wounded or the Victuallers, it cannot be said whether they did the same for the Navy Board. But, both from the nature of the work and the tone of their mutual relations, it is more than likely that they did not.

[2] P.R.O.Adm. 7/169, no. 9.

Behind this membership lay a considerable historical process. The genesis of the Navy Board lay in the first quarter of the sixteenth century, when the original Keeper or Clerk of the Ships, the predecessor and later a subordinate official of the Lord Admiral, was reinforced first by a Keeper of the King's Storehouses, or Comptroller, and then, as that office grew more complex, by a Comptroller and a Treasurer of Maritime Causes. In 1545, a fourth officer, the Surveyor and Rigger, made his appearance,[1] and about that time the four seem to have worked together as a body.[2] The Board itself was appointed by Letters Patent on 24 April 1546 under the direction of the Lieutenant of the Admiralty, a subordinate of the Lord Admiral's appointed for this purpose, and was composed of the four Principal Officers, as they were now known.[3] This nucleus, with the exception of the Lieutenant of the Admiralty,[4] remained the same for almost three centuries, the Treasurer of Marine Causes soon becoming Treasurer of the Navy and the Clerk of the Ships the Clerk of the Acts. In 1832 it was amalgamated with the Admiralty and its officers gave their functions to three of the five Sea Lords who exist to-day. The Navy Board thus drew its authority entirely from the Lord Admiral and was attached entirely to his service. Its duties were purely administrative. It was not consulted on policy, except when that was directly affected by administration, and it had nothing to do with the movements of ships at sea.

The duties of the Principal Officers were defined by Elizabeth, and thereafter remained much the same. Those of the Treasurer of the Navy are implied in his title. He drew the money from the Exchequer, represented naval requirements to the Treasury, checked all naval departmental accounts and distributed money to those departments.

---

1 A. W. Johns, 'The Principal Officers of the Navy', in *M.M.* XIV, no. 1, pp. 32–42.

2 E. S. de Beer, 'The Lord High Admiral and the Administration of the Navy', in *M.M.* XIII, no. 1, pp. 45–50.

3 M. Oppenheim, loc. cit. p. 85.

4 The Lieutenant of the Admiralty disappeared in 1564, but his office was revived in the seventeenth century. In 1672 he became known as the Vice-Admiral of England, in 1707 as the Vice-Admiral of Great Britain, and in 1801 as the Vice-Admiral of the United Kingdom, which title he still holds. After the Restoration the duties were honorary, although the fees remained (see W. G. Perrin, 'The Vice-Admiral and Rear Admiral of the United Kingdom', in *M.M.* XIV, no. 1, pp. 26–31).

His accounts were checked by two other officers, of whom the Comptroller had to be one. In the course of the seventeenth century, however, he drew further apart from the rest of the Board. This was due principally to the struggle between the Lord Admiral and the Lord Treasurer for the control of the navy during the reigns of James I and Charles I,[1] in which he was necessarily and closely involved. As the Great Officers made their bids for power, his status was progressively enhanced at his colleagues' expense. His salary was increased over theirs until it settled at £2000 in 1660,[2] and he was allowed the additional advantage of poundage, by which he received 3*d.* on every payment made to him from the Exchequer; his office was removed from the Navy Office itself and set up in Broad Street with its own establishment; and in the French war, unlike any of his colleagues, or indeed any naval authority except the Board of Admiralty, he was allowed a barge and a bargemaster of his own.[3] In the Restoration period, this position was reflected spasmodically in the Treasurer's Instructions. In those of 1662 he was made responsible for the naval finances to the Lord Admiral alone, and although his payments still required the counter-signatures of two of his colleagues, he was given a personal right of veto. These powers were curtailed in 1671, restored in 1673 and again curtailed, following the example of 1671, in 1686; but the Treasurer's pre-eminence was restrained rather than abolished, and throughout the French war he stood apart from the rest of the Board, attending its meetings only when the business affected him directly, and enjoying his own relations with authorities whom it never met. The status of the office may indeed be seen in the names of the men who held it.[4] Sir George Carteret, the Earl of Anglesey, Sir Thomas Osborne, Sir Thomas Littleton and Lord Falkland were figures of a very different stamp from the other Principal Officers. None of them was a naval official; all either used the place as a political stepping-stone or were given it as a political reward. In William's reign, the distinction was marked even more clearly, when Edward Russell filled the post while

[1] For the details of this development see Murray, 'The Admiralty, II', in *M.M.* XXIII, no. 2, pp. 139–47.

[2] Increased to £3000 in 1681 (*Catal.* I, p. 8, n. 3).

[3] P.R.O.Adm. 7/169, no. 9. Whether this had been the case before 1689, I do not know.

[4] See Jackson, *Naval Commissioners*.

at the same time acting as Commander in Chief of the fleet and senior Lord of the Admiralty.[1]

The Surveyor of the Navy was responsible for the construction and maintenance of ships and dockyards, on which he was supposed to submit a monthly report to the Lord Admiral and which from time to time, in company with the Comptroller and the Clerk of the Acts, he surveyed. His clerical duties were to supervise the indents of stores for the ships. The Comptroller acted as head clerk of the navy, with no department under his charge but associating with the other officers in the supervision of their departments: signing the warrants for money with the Treasurer and passing his accounts, surveying material with the Surveyor, and checking departmental accounts before they were incorporated in the general declared accounts of the navy. The Clerk of the Acts was in charge of contracts, kept the petty cash account and was responsible for the domestic organization of the Navy Office. In this capacity he arranged the order in which business was taken, kept the records and was head of the office staff.

This nucleus of four officers had grown to a Board of nine by the beginning of the French war. In 1660, after the experiments of the Commonwealth, the traditional organization had been restored, but with the addition of three new members known simply as Commissioners of the Navy; and from that time its full title became the Principal Officers and Commissioners of the Navy. Of these three, one was appointed to reside at Chatham, but the other two had no specific duties and were designed 'for the understanding the defects of the whole, and applying their assistance where it may be most useful'. In 1662, another extra commissioner was appointed, and another in 1664, bringing the total of the Board to nine.[2] In that year also the practice was revived which had begun under the Commonwealth, of appointing resident Commissioners to dockyards other than Chatham.[3]

In 1667, two of the extra Commissioners were assigned to particular duties, to assist the Treasurer in passing his own and the Victuallers' accounts, and for these purposes were known as the Comptroller of the Treasurer's Accounts and the Comptroller of the Victuallers' Accounts.[4]

---

[1] See Appendices VI, VIII, X below.
[2] *Catal.* I, pp. 7, 9, 13.
[3] Ibid. pp. 14–15.
[4] Ibid. p. 17.

In 1671, a third Commissioner likewise became Comptroller of the Storekeeper's Accounts.[1] During the following decade the Comptroller of the Treasurer's Accounts disappeared,[2] and at the end of 1688 the five Commissioners were: the Comptroller of the Victuallers' Accounts, the Comptroller of Stores, and the resident Commissioners at Chatham, Portsmouth, and Deptford with Woolwich.[3]

The Instructions issued to the Navy Board were those promulgated by the Duke of York on 28 January 1662.[4] They remained the basis of subsequent orders until well into the following century, and some passages from them were still to be found in the regulations under which the officers of the Navy Board were acting at their dispersal in 1832. The Instructions themselves were not original, but derived from some issued by the Lord Admiral in 1640.[5] But they improved upon them in many ways, regulating the arrangements for Board meetings, defining more closely the duties of the several officers in purchasing stores, increasing the punishments for illegal dealings in naval stores, and modifying certain phrases which before had been loose or obscure. With the addition of the Instructions of September 1671 which redefined the Treasurer's duties,[6] the regulations for the Board were complete.

Within this organization there was no system of regular promotion from office to office. The resident Commissioners sometimes moved up the scale from the smaller to the larger yards—during the French war, Tymewell went from Kinsale and Henry Greenhill from Plymouth to Portsmouth, and early in the next century St Lo went from Plymouth to Chatham[7]—and in general they were regarded as the junior Commissioners of the Board.[8] Occasionally a resident Commissioner found his way on to the central Board. In 1668 Middleton moved from Portsmouth to the post of Surveyor, and his successor Tippetts had also been at that yard; and in 1696 Benjamin Tymewell went from Portsmouth to become an Extra Commissioner.[9] But transfers of this kind were rare, and among the senior Commissioners there was also no

---

[1] *Catal.* I, p. 17.

[2] He reappeared in 1691.

[3] See Appendix VIII below.

[4] *Catal.* pp. 20–1. A copy may be found in P.R.O.Adm. 7/633.

[5] Ibid. p. 20.

[6] P.R.O.Adm. 7/633.

[7] See Appendix VIII below.

[8] Jackson, loc. cit., introduction.

[9] Loc. cit.; see also Appendix VIII below.

system of promotion. Extra Commissioners were not graded in any order, and seldom if ever became Principal Officers.[1]

The appointments to the Board, indeed, were of various sorts. They might be made from the dockyard service, from the clerical staff of the Navy Office, or from sea. The latter source was responsible for more members of the Navy Board than either of the other two. Between 1688 and 1698, of the 25 men concerned in such appointments, thirteen came straight from sea, three from the local yards, three from the staff of the Navy Office, one from Chatham Chest, one from an out-port, and four from outside the naval hierarchy.[2] The clerical staff naturally graduated to the clerical posts, as Clerks of the Acts and Comptrollers of the accounts;[3] the dockyard men to the post of Surveyor and to some of the resident Commissionerships. The other posts were filled mostly by the sea officers, usually senior captains with no prospect of a flag, or with a preference for a steady salary and a shore billet to the hazards of a life afloat. With few exceptions, however, the Board was well served with experience: of the men cited in the figures above, only two, Falkland and John Hill, had no qualifications, unless to be Shovell's father-in-law, as Hill was,[4] counted as a qualification; while of the other men appointed from outside, Samuel Pett, presumably a member of the shipbuilding family, had apparently been occasionally employed as an independent observer on dockyard inspections, and Tymewell had been in the Victualling Office before going to Kinsale.[5] Although to the junior naval official the selection of the Board appeared largely arbitrary, to its superiors and to the world it represented a body of experts, the more experienced and reliable because of the varied professions which went to its composition.

---

1 No such event occurred during the last twenty years of the century (ibid.).

2 Those from sea were Ashby, Aylmer, Beach, Berry, Booth, Greenhill, Haddock (originally), Priestman, Rooke, Russell, St Lo, Shovell and Wilshaw; those from the dockyards, Dummer, Phineas Pett and Tippetts; those from the staff of the Navy Office, Lyddell, Sergison and Sotherne; from Chatham Chest, Edward Gregory; from the out-port at Deal, St Michel; and from elsewhere, Falkland, Hill, Samuel Pett(?) and Tymewell.

3 But not all Clerks of the Acts came from the clerical staff. Pepys, for instance, had arrived through patronage, and the habits of the preceding generation still often held good at the Revolution.

4 Luttrell, op. cit. IV, p. 327.

5 Jackson, loc. cit.

The traditional type of Navy Board, with which the French war was fought, was revived only a few months before the end of 1688. From 17 April 1686 to 13 October 1688 it had been replaced by a Special Commission of twelve members,[1] whose duties were defined on different lines. This body was the result of an administrative crisis. It consisted of two groups, a 'Commission for current business', whose title explains its duties, and a 'Commission for bringing up the old accounts', which were in a sorry state when the previous Commissioners had finished with them. Unlike earlier and later Boards, it had no Principal Officers and made no distinction between its members, except in the case of the resident Commissioners, of whom there were three. As an emergency body, appointed to redeem a serious situation, this group of Commissioners centred on personalities rather than on titles; and it was on the energy and the reputation of its members—Narborough and Berry, Godwin and Booth, Hewer and above all the great shipbuilder and ship designer Sir Anthony Deane[2]—that James placed his hopes. The other group, to settle and pass the accounts outstanding from the old Board, was composed of three of the four former Principal Officers, the offending Treasurer being omitted.[3]

This was not the first time that the Principal Officers and Commissioners had been replaced by Commissions on other lines. But there was a significant difference between this and earlier occasions, for in 1688 the office establishment was unaffected by the change of Boards. Before 1660, the absorption of a Board by another Commission meant that its business was carried on in a different building, quite possibly by different clerks and with a different system of keeping records. Administration itself was still on a small enough scale for continuity in the methods of business and personnel to be of only minor importance. But with the advent of the big fleet these conditions began, slowly and unevenly, to change. Administrative processes were respected, even if the administrative hierarchy was not. After thirty years of increasing organization and stability, the Navy Office had achieved a status as well as functions of its own.

The establishment for 1689 shows the stage which its organization

---

[1] See Appendix VIII and Ch. VIII below.

[2] Pepys, *Memoires*, pp. 47–55.

[3] B.M.Harl. 7476, f. 17.

PLATE VII

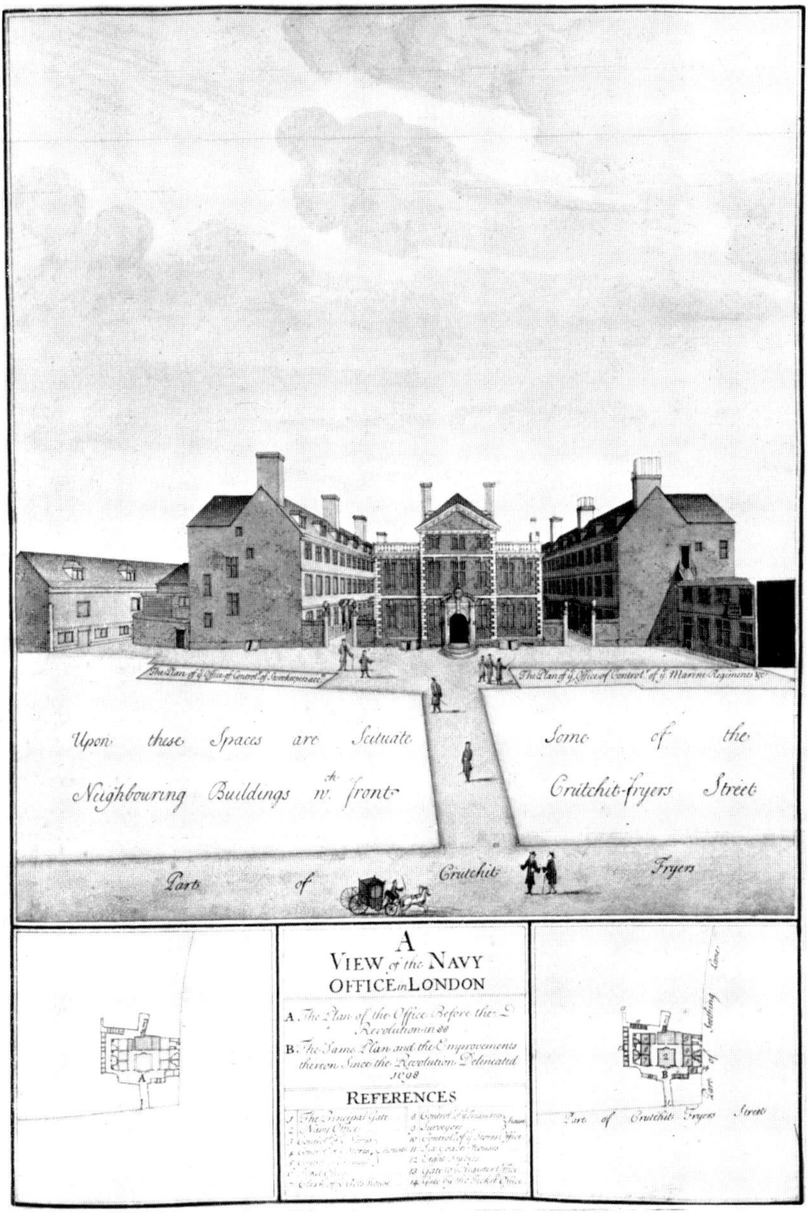

THE NAVY OFFICE IN CRUTCHED FRIARS

View and Plans

1688–1698

had reached. The office itself had been in the same place since 1654, when it had moved from Tower Hill to Seething Lane, where it remained until its removal to Somerset House in 1780.[1] The buildings, with an annual rent of £600,[2] were quite substantial, as may be seen from the plan opposite.[3] The office, facing Crutched Friars, consisted of a hall, a board room, separate offices on the ground floor for the Comptroller, the Surveyor, and the Comptroller of the Victualling, and on the first floor for the Clerk of the Acts and, when he existed as such, the Comptroller of the Treasurer's Accounts. Outside the board room was a 'withdrawing room for persons attending at ye Board', where, among others, the Baltic merchants conferred among themselves in the annual negotiations for their contracts. The Comptroller of Stores had an office in an adjoining building. The ticket office was housed on the other side of the main entrance, with a separate entrance from Seething Lane. The two wings of the main building consisted of officers' houses: one range for the Comptroller and his two assistants, the Comptrollers of Victualling and of Stores; the other for the Clerk of the Acts, the Surveyor and the Comptroller of the Treasurer's Accounts. A porter lived over the gate. At the back of one of the ranges of houses stood eight stables for the officers. There were gardens behind, where in the 1660's Pepys, then Clerk of the Acts, and his enemy Sir Edward Batten, the Surveyor, were almost able, as they chatted over their dividing wall, to forget the feud which business and their wives had forced upon them. The land was enclosed by a wall, a very necessary precaution in a period when the office had to keep a small magazine of arms to defend itself against the seamen demanding their pay.[4]

The staff of the office consisted of:[5] one assistant each to the Surveyor, the Clerk of the Acts and the Comptroller of the Victualling, each at £300 a year; seven clerks for the Comptroller, two at £100, one at £50, two at £40, and two at £30; three clerks for the Surveyor, one at £100, one at £50, one at £30; four clerks for the Comptroller of the Treasurer's Accounts,[6] one at £100, two at £50, one at £40; three

[1] *Catal.* I, p. 23, n. I.
[2] P.R.O. Adm. 7/169.
[3] Reproduced from B.M. King's 43.
[4] *Catal.* I, p. 119.
[5] P.R.O.Adm. 7/169, no. 9.
[6] Still borne as such despite the absence of the Comptroller himself.

clerks for the Comptroller of the Victualling, one at £100, one at £50, one at £30; five clerks for the Comptroller of the Stores, one at £100, three at £50, one at £40; a messenger, at £50; a housekeeper, at £40; a labourer, at £12; two watchmen, and a warden on Sundays, at £39 12*s.* all told; and a porter, at £25.

The office of the Treasurer of the Navy, with a rent of £120 a year, had a staff of: clerks and juniors (unknown number), at £800 a year all told; three watchmen, and a warden on Sundays, at £57. 7*s.* all told; and a doorkeeper, at £20.

The two offices paid £2000 a year between them in parish dues and taxes, and for their equipment of paper, pens, firewood and the like. Between them, they represented a substantial item in the ordinary of the navy, and an administrative investment which represented a complex and permanent organization.

Above the subordinate boards, and at the summit of the naval hierarchy, stood the Lord Admiral, as the representative of the King in naval affairs. In this capacity, his authority and functions were defined entirely by Letters Patent, issued under the Great Seal on the authority of a royal warrant. The Admiralty to-day still represents a Great Officer of State, deriving his powers by virtue of a delegated authority from the Crown. 'In theory', it has been said, 'we might any morning wake up to find that His Majesty had been pleased overnight to substitute a Lord High Admiral for the Lords Commissioners of the Admiralty.'[1] Since 1688 the primary source of authority of the patent has been reinforced by statute[2] and by Order in Council, so that at the present date the Admiralty, like other departments of state, is not in fact administered entirely in accordance with the instrument which gives it warranty to act;[3] but at the Revolution, these accretions had not yet appeared. The patent was the sole authority both for the creation and the administration of the Office, and the attributes of sovereignty

[1] Murray, 'The Admiralty, I', in *M.M.* XXIII, no. 1, p. 20; cf. 52 and 53 Vict. c. 63 (the 'Interpretation Act' of 1889).

[2] See Ch. X below.

[3] *Preliminary report of the select committee of the House of Commons appointed to enquire into the civil and professional administration of the Naval and Military departments* (1890), p. ix.

which Bagehot was able to display as theory in 1872,[1] at that time found adequate expression in this exercise of the royal power. Lord Admiral, Commissioners of the Admiralty, or the sovereign in person are three equal possibilities for the government of the navy; and in fact all three had been tried in the eight decades of the seventeenth century before the Revolution.

The patent itself is still essentially the same as in 1688, and the patent then in force hardly differed from that issued by Henry VI in the middle of the fifteenth century.[2] Its survival with so little alteration has been largely due to its vagueness. When a Commission of Admiralty replaced the Lord Admiral in 1689, its patent was divided into two sections, empowering it to act for that officer 'as well in and touching those things which Concerne our Navy and Shipping as those things which concern the Rights and Jurisdictions of or appertaining to the Office or Place of High Admiral of England'.[3] The 'things which Concerne our Navy', however, were specified no more exactly in the patent of the Lord Admiral himself than in that of his Commissioners. The only authority for his control lay in the original phrase of Henry VI's patent, constituting him 'Magnus Admirallus...necnon praefectus generalis classicum et marium'.[4] The rest of the text deals with the territorial limits of this jurisdiction, and with the juridical functions of the Office. Nothing is said of the Admiral's duties, or of his relations with other Officers of State.[5] The authority of the patent itself, in fact, was

---

[1] 'She [the Queen] could dismiss all the sailors...she could sell off all our ships-of-war and all our naval stores....In a word, the Queen...could by disbanding our forces, whether land or sea, leave us defenceless against foreign nations' (*English Constitution*, p. xxxvi). This passage does not occur in the first edition of 1867.

[2] The form of the present patent was settled in 1872. It merely abbreviated the older form, particularly by reducing the list of foreign territories to which the instrument applied. This read 'Jamaica, Barbadoes, St Christopher, Nevis, Montserrat, Bermudas and Antigoa, in America, and Guiney, Binney, and Angola, in Africa'; and the reading of the patent before a new Board of Admiralty used to be known in the department as 'the reading of Guiney-Binney' (Murray, loc. cit. p. 25).

[3] See Appendix XI below.

[4] G. F. James, 'Admiralty Administration and Personnel, 1619–1714', in *Bulletin of the Institute of Historical Research*, XIV, p. 172.

[5] The text of the Patent may be seen in *Report of the select committee of the House of Commons on the Board of Admiralty* (*H.C. 438* (1861), pp. 644–8).

supplemented by custom. Sir James Graham, an authority well qualified to judge, stated before a committee of the House of Commons:[1]

> The more I have investigated the matter, the more I am satisfied that, like the common law in aid of the statute law, the power exercised by the... Admiralty...rests more upon usage than upon Patents, uninterrupted usage, from a very early period....It is clear that the powers of the Lord High Admiral himself, and of the local admirals who preceded him, were exercised by virtue of usage and of the power exercised by the Crown in maritime affairs.

The omissions of the patent, however, were supplemented from time to time by regulations or statements of the duties of the Office, which came to be accepted as binding upon its incumbents with almost the force of a legal instrument. Most of these were drafted in the seventeenth century; and the most recent of them in 1688 was the list of 'duties of the Lord High Admiral' of 1673, which was drawn up, not for the guidance of a Lord Admiral, but of a Commission of Admiralty.[2]

The division of the patent into the two sections of administrative and judicial powers illustrates the development of the Admiral's Office. This involved three distinct, if connected, processes: the emergence of the Admiral as an administrative officer, his emergence as a fighting officer, and his emergence as a legal officer. It was as an administrative officer that he seems first to have appeared, with the establishment by John of the 'custodes galliarum' or 'custodes portuum' as a central authority for the government of the King's galleys, and with the emergence of one of them, William de Wrotham, as the principal guardian of the royal ships.[3] His position, which like the precocious system of which he was a part soon disappeared for a time, was paralleled in Henry III's reign by the creation of the Lord Warden of the Cinque Ports, who outstripped in importance the 'Keeper of the King's Ships', by then the sole survivor of John's

[1] *H.C. 438* (1861), pp. 653–4.

[2] For its full text, see James, loc. cit. pp. 178–9. An incomplete text is given in *Catal.* I, pp. 36–7.

[3] For the early history of the Admiral of England, see F. W. Brooks, *The English Naval Forces, 1199–1272*; Sir N. C. Nicholas, *A History of the Royal Navy*, I (2 vols. 1847); and W. G. Perrin, 'The Lord High Admiral and the Board of Admiralty', in *M.M.* XII, no. 2, pp. 117–44.

'custodes' and a comparatively uninfluential member of the royal household. But as the number of the King's ships increased under Edward I, the 'Keeper' was joined by a 'Captain of the sailors of the realm' or 'Captain of the King's mariners', with whom the second element in the subsequent Admiralty patent originated; and shortly afterwards, the coasts were divided into two areas for administration and command, with the same officers performing both duties in each. The precedent of John's reign existed for this distribution of organization, but the combination of command with administration was new. Appropriately enough it produced a new title, when in 1297 William de Leyburn, the Captain of the King's mariners, was placed in charge of both areas as 'Admirallus magnus Angliae'. The dual title was never discarded. It persisted through the later middle ages after a single Lord Admiral appeared, and, so long as the office was held by an individual, through the sixteenth and seventeenth centuries into the first decade of the eighteenth; and even reappeared in the nineteenth century for a last time during the comic and ill-fated interlude of the Duke of Clarence.[1] When there was no Lord Admiral, the term Captain, or Captain-General as it later became, was still used on occasion for the Admiral of the fleet, as in the land forces it was used for the commander of the troops.[2]

During the fourteenth century two Admirals were invariably appointed, one for the north and east and one for the south and west of the Thames, and the Office gained rapidly in importance. This was due less to the Admirals' combined military and administrative powers than to the emergence of their legal responsibilities.[3] It was only occasionally that they were called upon to put ships to sea, but the jurisdiction of maritime cases and the emergence of a distinctive maritime law involved them in regular and indeed continuous duties. Early in the fifteenth century an Admiralty Court was founded; despite the lawyers' quarrels

---

[1] See Buckingham's patent of 1628 in *M.M.* XII, p. 128; and those of George of Denmark and the Duke of Clarence in *H.C. 438* (1861), appendices II and III.

[2] E.g. for Arthur Herbert in 1689 and Edward Russell in 1694 (P.R.O.Adm. 2/377, 6/6; see pp. 546–7 below).

[3] See *Select Pleas in the Court of Admiralty, 1390–1602*, ed. R. G. Marsden (2 vols., 1894–7); *Documents relating to the Law and Custom of the Sea*, ed. R. G. Marsden; *The Black Book of the Admiralty*, ed. Sir Travers Twiss (4 vols., 1871–6).

which it occasioned and which lasted for three centuries after its creation, its jurisdiction and its perquisites were soon a reality, and in 1412 it was followed by the amalgamation of the two Admiralties into the single Office of Admiral of England. The first holder of this Office was Thomas Beaufort, Duke of Exeter, and in him was found the type of great noble who was thenceforth to occupy the position and enjoy its profits. In the course of the century, the Admiral became the ninth of the nine Great Officers of State, no longer exercising a personal command of the King's ships, but lending his authority to the maritime jurisdiction and enjoying the fruits of the Office. The three processes had met, and the legal instrument which followed in Henry VI's reign embodied the fact in sufficiently flexible terms to satisfy any later changes of emphasis.

The powers which the Lord Admiral had thus gained were put to the test on various occasions in the seventeenth century, acquiring in the process the form and the limitations which the Board of Admiralty in 1689 inherited both from the Admiral and from the early, and largely unsuccessful, Commissioners of Admiralty. By the end of the sixteenth century the Great Officer, like several of his peers, had abandoned the tradition of a profitable sinecure and had come to represent an administrative department upon a revised and more powerful Privy Council. The title of the Office altered, by custom rather than proclamation, from Admiral of England to Lord Admiral, High Admiral or Lord High Admiral;[1] and while the legal duties and position of its occupant remained the same as before, his new administrative duties involved him in the struggle for political power.

The result of the first stage of the argument may be said to have been the creation in September 1628 of the first Commission of Admiralty, 'granting [the Commissioners] or any three of [them] full power and authority to do, execute, exercise and perform all and every acts, matters and things which to the Office of a Lord Admiral of England...

[1] The title Lord Admiral was already in use in the Admiralty Court when it was found necessary to translate 'magnus admirallus'. The first official reference to a Lord High Admiral occurs in the patent of 1628, where the text was English instead of Latin. English versions of sixteenth-century patents, which include that title, are in fact translations made in later centuries (Perrin, loc. cit. p. 117, which should be used to correct Murray's statements in *M.M.* XXIII, no. 2, pp. 136–7).

appertaineth and belongeth'.[1] This was the outcome of the prolonged and increasingly bitter feud, already noticed in its effect on the status of the Treasurer of the Navy, between the Lord Admiral and the Lord Treasurer, which ended in favour of the Admiral when Buckingham was appointed to the Office in 1618. On his assassination in 1628 a Commission was set up, partly to redeem his debts by the collection of the official perquisites but partly marking the resumption of power by the Lord Treasurer. Its members included the Treasurer himself, who now virtually managed the Admiralty's affairs, the Great Chamberlain, the Lord Steward, the Queen's Chamberlain, the Vice-Chamberlain and the Secretary of State.[2] As well as an Admiralty Commission, the quarrel produced two supplementary declarations of the rights and duties of the Lord Admiral.[3] The first of these, in 1611, confined itself to the terms of the patents; but the second, in 1630, set out to define those powers to which the patents merely alluded, and in its course remarked, significantly in view of later developments, that the Crown need not necessarily delegate its maritime powers to a Lord Admiral or to his Commissioners, but could reserve some, if it chose, to itself. This report came at a time of increasing friction between the King and the Treasurer, and after a series of deadlocks over the next few years, a Lord Admiral was reappointed and Charles reserved the place for the Duke of York as soon as he was old enough to fill it.[4] Despite a temporary reversion to a Board under the Treasurer in the 1640's,[5] when the Civil War began the Lord Admiral had regained control of the department. In the interregnum, the traditional establishment was replaced by Commissions of various kinds, in which the distinctions of Admiralty and Navy Board disappeared;[6] but at the Restoration, it was the Lord Admiral who was put in charge of the navy and, as intended by Charles I, it was the Duke of York who was appointed to the post.[7]

The fortunes of the Office after the interregnum were of a different nature from those before it. Although the alternatives of a Lord Admiral

---

[1] The full text is given in *M.M.* XII, no. 2, pp. 129–31.

[2] *M.M.* XXIII, no. 2, pp. 139–45.

[3] Quotations are given from the first of these documents, and the second is given in full, in James, loc. cit. pp. 174–6.

[4] *M.M.* XXIII, no. 2, p. 146.

[5] Ibid.

[6] Ibid. pp. 146–7.

[7] *Catal.* I, p. 6.

and a Commission continued to be used by the Crown, with the additional complication, which had been adumbrated in 1630, of a partial reservation of their powers on occasion by the King himself, the issues were different and the connexion between political and administrative control less direct. Seen from the point of view of administration, perhaps the chief legacy of the Civil War and the interregnum was to turn the political interest of the executive away from itself in another direction. When the different elements within the executive henceforth disputed the control of administration, they did so on an administrative rather than on a political basis, and when their struggle was political it was waged through the external agency of Parliament. The Commonwealth and Protectorate put an end to effective conciliar government, where politics and administration were the subject of the same body, and distributed political rivalries over a wider field. Where the earlier administrative expansion had led to a fight between the members of the executive, the administrative expansion of the 1660's and 1670's led to a political fight between the executive itself and the legislature.[1] The last stage, which came after the Revolution, was the effective entry of the legislature into the administrative sphere.

---

[1] I have ventured to place a different interpretation on the development of the Admiral's Office in these years from that put forward by Murray in 'The Admiralty, III', in *M.M.* XXIII, no. 3. As the only statement which exists of the constitutional issues involved, this article is important, and its point of view should be stated here. Murray argued that 'the unusual interest of the King and his brother in the Navy began before long [i.e. after 1660] to have less satisfactory results. Naval administration became the favourite object of attack...with those who desired to discredit James...and with those who wished to oppose Charles himself. It was dragged into the political arena, as in the days of Buckingham....Moreover the King's personal intervention in the affairs of the Navy greatly restricted the Lord High Admiral's normal sphere of activity. More and more of the questions, even his minor questions, which the Navy Board submitted for the Duke's decision, had to be reserved for settlement by the King in Council, or by the King of his own motion.'

I am unable to agree that Charles's interest in the navy detracted from the power of the Lord Admiral under the circumstances. It did not shift that power to another member of the executive, as had been the case in the transference of the Admiral's powers to a committee of the Council in the reigns of James I and Charles I; and although the particular interest of the royal family in the navy doubtless increased the attacks upon it, under the material conditions of an expanding fleet naval administration was bound to be of Parliamentary concern, and a connexion with the Crown had

The Lord Admiral remained in office from 1660 to 1673. But as a result of the Parliamentary debates upon the Test Act, James was driven to resign in that year, and in June a Commission of Admiralty was again appointed.[1] It consisted almost entirely of members of the Household and of the Privy Council,[2] and Charles himself not only attended its meetings but transacted much of its business. He inserted indeed a new clause in the patent, reserving to himself the disposal of the places and offices in the gift of the Lord Admiral and of the Admiralty dues. As Pepys put it, 'His Majesty was pleased to put several parts of the said office into commission, retaining the rest in his own hands'.[3] At the same time, as had happened during the earlier arguments, a report appeared on the Lord Admiral's duties, particularly on his relations with the Navy Board, which was so comprehensive that both at the time and later it was taken as a statement of the responsibilities of the Office almost as authoritative as the patent itself.[4]

---

its uses as well as its disadvantages. The basis for Murray's argument is the sentence 'It [naval administration] was dragged into the political arena, as in the days of Buckingham'. It has seemed to me throughout that the political arenas of 1610–30 and 1660–80 were not of the same kind.

[1] *Catal.* I, p. 36. [2] Ibid. p. 38. [3] Ibid. n. 4.

[4] Here again, I must venture to disagree with Murray. He states (loc. cit. p. 324): 'The drafts...of "Instructions for ascertaining the Duty of the Lord High Admiral of England" met the King's wishes entirely....In it the Lord High Admiral was unblushingly represented as an official whose functions in administration did not extend beyond supervising with diligence the work of the Navy Office, especially on the financial side, assisting in wringing the money required for the service of the Navy out of the Treasury, and acting as the channel by which submissions from the Navy Board passed to the King or the Council, and decisions and instructions from the King or the Council passed to the Navy Board. The functions of the Board of Admiralty having been thus minimized, the King proceeded to preside over it.....' It is difficult to see how something that had not been defined before, either by patent or in the reports of 1611 or 1630, could be minimized. Moreover, it was the duties of the Lord Admiral's Office, and not its powers, that were defined. For this purpose, the 'Instructions' of 1673 were concerned to define an administrative practice that had existed, in varying degrees, since the formation of a Navy Board, and was certainly not the product of the personal intervention of Charles II.

I have referred to these statements of Murray's because his articles form the only (and an excellent) constitutional history of the Admiralty, and because I am much indebted to them (for the circumstances under which they were published, see Bibliography, p. 688 below).

The Board of 1673 lasted innocuously until 1679. In that year, when his power was at its lowest and Parliamentary faction at its height, Charles was forced to replace it with a Commission of a very different character. In place of the office-holders who had left the control largely in his hands, he was faced with a Board of seven members of Parliament.[1] The patent under which they acted was at first that of 1673, but 'being ..dissatisfied with the limitations of power under which the last commissioners acted, reserving several parts thereof to his Majesty's own execution, [they] did insist upon having their commission to run in the fullest terms of any lord high admiral',[2] and on 14 May a new patent was accordingly issued to that effect. The senior Commissioner, Sir Henry Capel, was sworn a member of the Privy Council, and the first Parliamentary Board of Admiralty with access to the royal executive had been established. The Commission was renewed with a change of members late in the same year, and a further innovation was then made, although not of immediate significance. Hitherto the members of an Admiralty Commission had ranked in seniority according to their seniority as Privy Councillors. But now, when few if any were Councillors, seniority went by the order of the names in the patent. At the end of 1679, Daniel Finch, who had been second Commissioner earlier in the year, became senior member of the new Board on the removal of Capel, and was made a member of the Privy Council.[3] In practice the honour was an empty one, for Lord Brouncker, another member of the Board, insisted successfully that he took precedence as a peer;[4] but a precedent had been established which could not be entirely ignored when Commissions came regularly to include members of Parliament without seats on the Council.

The Board of 1679, with its membership of Parliamentary Commissioners, may be said to have been the precursor of the later Boards of Admiralty. Although its final patent was modelled on that of 1628, its real power derived from the external authority of Parliament, and the combination was something new in the history of the Office. The Board itself, however, did not last for long. In 1684, on the wave of

---

1 *Catal.* I, p. 57. 2 Pepys's remark, in ibid. pp. 57–8.

3 Murray, 'The Admiralty, III', in *M.M.* XXIII, no. 3, p. 328.

4 Ibid. pp. 328–9.

popular reaction to the excesses of the Popish Plot, the King was able to restore James to his post as Lord Admiral; and when the new King succeeded in the following year, he retained the Office with which he had been associated in name or deed since 1638. It was as Lord Admiral as well as King that he prepared to defend the throne in 1688; and it was the Admiralty as well as the throne which William was required to fill at the beginning of 1689. When he came to do so, he had before him a legal instrument and a series of constitutional precedents which were sufficient to meet the case and to sustain the innovations of the following century and a half.

The relations of the Lord Admiral with other authorities affected his relations with his subordinates. Those with the fighting service were regulated by martial law, the consequences of which had been defined by statute and have been mentioned already.[1] The duties of the Admiralty's legal officers were clear, and their details are not relevant here. It may suffice to say that in this capacity the Lord Admiral was served by a Judge of the High Court of Admiralty, a Register who registered its acts, a Marshal, an Advocate General, a Procurator General, a Solicitor and Comptroller of the Perquisites, and a Councillor of the Admiralty and Navy. All these were appointed by warrant.[2] A local organization was also required, to inform the Admiral of matters affecting his jurisdiction and where necessary to execute the decisions of his Court. This was provided by the Vice-Admirals of the maritime counties, a creation of Henry VIII. Like the Admiral himself they were appointed by patent,[3] and were normally local noblemen of eminence and of the right political colour, who corresponded for maritime affairs to the Lord Lieutenants of the counties. Their duties, however, were as much administrative as legal, and they corresponded as much with the clerks as with the Judge or the Register of the Admiralty.[4]

It was, indeed, through the administrative department of his Office that the Lord Admiral exercised his greatest powers. In this sphere his chief assistant was the Secretary of the Admiralty, and in 1688 this post was

[1] See p. 135 above.
[2] Admty:Corbett, v, ff. 48–160.
[3] Ibid. ff. 3–4.
[4] See, e.g., p. 117 above.

held by Samuel Pepys. His position provides the clearest illustration—a clearer illustration, indeed, than does that of the Admiral himself—of recent developments. The title of Secretary of the Admiralty first appeared only in 1660; but the occupants of the post, Sir William Coventry, Matthew Wren and Sir John Werden, were not recruited from the navy and were still the personal secretaries of the Lord Admiral. Pepys, however, came from the Navy Board, where he had been Clerk of the Acts, and his career as Secretary went far to secure the identification of the post with the department. During his tenure of office, from 1673 to 1679 and again from 1684 to 1688, a great advance was made in the three main tasks of administration, in the regulation of business, the classification of records, and the accommodation of a permanent staff; and while this would no doubt have occurred without such active intervention from Pepys himself, the precise form which it took and the lines on which his successors were trained were undoubtedly the result of his personal activity. He concentrated functions which might otherwise have remained dispersed, and ensured on the one hand that the execution of naval policy was carried out in a form that was common to all branches of the Lord Admiral's department, and on the other that the makers of policy, whatever their nature, could rely upon the service of an identifiable and to some extent a stable organization.[1]

This administrative activity had constitutional consequences. The wider its scope, the more powerful the Secretary became in relation to other departments of government, and when James became King as well as Lord Admiral Pepys became virtually a third Secretary of State,[2] whose importance extended beyond the limits of the navy and who came to be regarded within its ranks as no Secretary had been regarded before. The very increase of administration, which was characterized by the absence of political considerations, led the agent of administration to assume a political character. While the emergence of the Secretary as a departmental official had been made possible by the removal of the political struggle to beyond the confines of administration, the fact that he was now, through his administrative activities,

---

[1] For details of the office organization after his retirement, see Ch. IX below.

[2] He himself deplored the absence of a naval minister (*Naval Minutes*, p. 120).

associated with the level of policy, involved him in the political struggle. In consequence, when the Lord Admiral was removed at the Revolution, the Secretary of the Admiralty went too: not, like his predecessors, as the personal secretary of the office holder, but on the contrary as a political Secretary of State.

But if Pepys by his administrative energy had set a constitutional problem, he also bequeathed to his successors a problem of administration itself. In his hands, the demands of the time had been amply met, and as a result the Admiralty Office by the Revolution had many of the characteristics of a permanent department. The fact that the Secretary was directly responsible for the co-ordination of the different levels of administration, and for putting the accepted policy into practice, had led to a radical reorganization of the records, which now numbered some hundreds of volumes,[1] and to an increase in the clerical staff of the office. The department, in fact, was fast outgrowing its former arrangements, and also the sort of buildings in which it had hitherto been housed. Throughout the Restoration period, it had continued in traditional fashion to change its abode according to the nature of the body in authority. During James's first spell as Lord Admiral, business was done in the royal palace of Whitehall; but in 1673 the office moved to Derby House, which it had formerly occupied for a time during the Commonwealth and which was then the residence of one of the new Commissioners of the Admiralty, the Duke of Ormond.[2] It remained there until 1684. When Pepys returned to the Secretaryship in that year the office moved in the usual way to the house which he occupied in York Buildings, at the river end of Buckingham Street. There it stayed until 1689, the connexion between residence and department of state being displayed, as on many a consulate to-day, by the official Admiralty anchor which hung on the wall of the house.[3] When the

---

[1] See John Ehrman, 'The Official Papers surrendered by Pepys to the Admiralty by 12 July 1689', in *M.M.* XXXIV, no. 4, pp. 255–70.

[2] D. Bonner Smith, 'The Admiralty Building', in *M.M.* IX, no. 9, p. 273.

[3] D. Bonner Smith, 'Samuel Pepys and York Buildings', in *M.M.* XXIV, no. 2, pp. 226–31. The seventeenth-century water-gate may still be seen at the lower end of Buckingham Street, at the head of the Savoy Gardens. The naval anchors on its northern face, however, were not placed there in Pepys's day, but while Buckingham was living in the same street as Lord Admiral in the reign of James I.

Board of Admiralty of that year replaced the régime of James and Pepys, it was thus faced with an Office of State which had grown into a permanent department, but still with no departmental building in which to house it. The anchor on the private house reflected accurately enough the position of the Admiralty itself at the time. It was the function of James's and Pepys's successors to disentangle its more recent developments from the encumbrances of an earlier age which still existed when they entered office.

PART TWO

THE WAR IN PROGRESS

CHAPTER VIII

THE PEPYSIAN LEGACY AND THE MOBILIZATION OF 1688

I

When Samuel Pepys reflected, after his retirement, on the misfortunes which had dogged the navy since the beginning of the war with France, he was invariably struck by the contrast between its present state and that in which he had left it only a few years before. Such a change, he recognized, was nothing new; throughout the reigns of Charles II and James II its fortunes had varied from Administration to Administration, and had no sooner been mended than they were again reversed. In the process, two peaks emerged, from which the better to observe the surrounding inefficiency. 'The navy', he concluded, 'will never be found to have been once in the good condition I have had the leaving of it twice, viz. in April 1679 and December 1688.'[1]

The two occasions were separated by a dramatic interval. When Pepys was removed to the Tower in 1679, he left in sea pay a total of 76 ships, manned by 12,040 men, and a reserve of stores worth £60,000.[2] When he returned to the Secretaryship late in April 1684,[3] he found 24 ships at sea, with 3070 men, and the value of the reserve down to £5000.[4] At the same time, the naval debt had risen by over a quarter, from £305,000 to £384,000, and although the Parliamentary supply had been irregular, there had been only the evacuation of Tangier and the activities of the Mediterranean squadron to account for the expense

---

1 *Samuel Pepys's Naval Minutes*, p. 273.

2 Pepys, *Memoires*, pp. 6–8. And see *Catal.* I, p. 68, n. 2.

3 The Admiralty Commission of 1679 was ended only on 19 May, from which day Pepys's salary began. But, as was so often the case in this period, the incoming office-holder was at work two or three weeks before his patent was passed (A. Bryant, *Samuel Pepys, the Saviour of the Navy* (1938), p. 85).

4 *Memoires*, pp. 14–15.

at sea in a time of peace.[1] Nor had the activities of the Administration ashore been such as to justify the increase. On the contrary, ignorance and faction in the Admiralty Commission had allowed the administrative and material obstacles to take charge, which always arose so easily in the conditions of the time, and the work of the previous six years had been largely undone. At the Navy Office, the Commissioners were irregular in their attendance, and unable to provide even a reasonably plausible account of the money which had passed through their hands; in the yards, more men were kept in pay than could be employed, while the duties of maintenance, which alone were required, were barely observed; and the fleet itself was rapidly falling into a state of complete disrepair.[2] Most serious of all, on the slips and in the basins, the thirty new ships of 1677, the backbone of the reconstituted Line, completed only five and six years before, were sinking at their moorings without ever having got to sea. As they lay rotting in the river, their ports open to the rain, their holds alternately steaming neglected in the summer heat and mouldering in the winter damp, so that the toadstools grew as big as a man's hand; their trennels charred and splintered, their timbers powdering away and the adjacent planks hanging loose from their sides; their holes patched with board and canvas until they appeared to have just come in from an action at sea; they represented the bankruptcy of a policy which had only recently applied to the battle-fleet the lessons learnt in the most expensive and stubborn series of maritime engagements ever fought, and of an achievement which had cost the nation more than a third of its total annual income.[3]

To the solution of this by now familiar chaos, Pepys brought a vigorous, coherent and ambitious plan. After almost two years' spade-work along the orthodox lines, and able, for the first time since 1660, to count on an assured and substantial Parliamentary revenue for the

---

[1] *Catal.* I, p. 68.

[2] Bryant, loc. cit. p. 93; *Catal.* I, pp. 61–2. The Surveyor estimated that it would cost about £120,000 to get the fleet afloat in May 1684.

[3] *Memoires*, pp. 18–19. As Macaulay pointed out, Pepys's account, although undoubtedly prejudiced against his predecessors, can be checked against Bonrepaux's report to Louis XIV (*History of England*, I, ed. C. H. Firth (1907), p. 289). It is also substantiated by Deane's report of 4 November 1685, summarized in Bryant, loc. cit. pp. 139–40.

realization of his scheme,[1] he put forward five proposals:[2] (1) to maintain the ordinary of the navy ashore and in harbour, and to repair the offices, storehouses and dockyard equipment where necessary; (2) to repair fully by the end of 1688 the 'extraordinary decay under which the body of your fleet now in harbour labours', and within the same period to add to it three new fourth rates; (3) to supply the whole fleet with sea stores for six months, 'separately laid up and preserved for use'; (4) to put to sea in 1686, 'instead of the three small ships assigned...to your whole Channel guard...a squadron of no less than ten ships', involving 1310 men instead of the 275 contemplated; and (5) to supply two 'nimble' frigates each year, to rectify the shortage of such craft. The whole programme was to be carried out at a cost of £400,000 per annum, paid in equal quarterly instalments. To effect it, a Special Commission was to be set up, composed so as to supervise more closely those departments which had particularly declined under the previous régime, and to give to the genius of one of its members, Sir Anthony Deane, the support and the scope which his special responsibilities for the repairs demanded. In addition, a separate branch was to be established, with some of the former Commissioners, to settle the outstanding accounts. The plan, after some difficulty, was passed by the Lord Treasurer, and soon afterwards approved by the King; and when the negotiations and intrigues for the necessary men had been concluded, the new Commission was able to begin its work. That work lasted from 17 April 1686 to 12 October 1688.[3]

In the disappointments that followed under its successors, the achievements of this emergency Administration were brought into the heat—one can hardly say the light—of partisan debate. On the one hand, the first engagement of the war, fought only seven months after its close and only three and a half after the disappearance of Pepys himself, revealed a misdirection and an apparent lack of material which inevitably

---

1 *Cal.Treas.Bks. 1685–9*, pp. x–xviii.

2 *Memoires*, pp. 33–41. They were originally set out in a Memorial to the King of 26 January 1686 (*Catal.* I, p. 67).

3 For the composition of the Commission, see p. 184 above and Appendix VIII below; for the circumstances of its appointment, and the negotiations with Deane, see Bryant, loc. cit. ch. VII; for the dates of the patents inaugurating and concluding it, *Memoires*, pp. 56, 128.

seemed to reflect upon their labours, and of which the Secretary's opponents both within and outside the navy were quick to take advantage; on the other, the defenders of the former régime were not reticent in the comparisons which they drew with later Administrations, and the age of Pepys was to many a standard regret in the dark days of the war.[1]

The argument, as was to be expected, often confused what had with what had not been attempted, and drew comparisons which should never have been drawn at all. When in 1691–2 the Parliamentary Commissioners for auditing the public accounts turned their attention to the finances of the Special Commission, the confusion extended from the general debate to the official inquiry, for the political flavour of the case prevented some of the participants from distinguishing between the programme laid down and the fate which awaited it.[2] Pepys himself, in his private minutes, sometimes failed to do so, reading into the former more than had been there, and often thus seeing in the latter a contradiction to what had been done, instead of a partial consequence of what had not.[3] It is necessary, therefore, to confine our attention to the original five propositions, and to see how far they were realized before seeing how the whole range of naval administration bore the test of mobilization and war.

Of these proposals (4) does not concern us, and (5), owing to the labour and the space which it would occupy in an already full programme, was allowed to drop, and the money earmarked for it was not demanded.[4] The other three objects were vigorously attacked. The maintenance and reform of the ordinary, involved as it was in the measure for repairing the fleet, was a straightforward process. It was to some extent codified in the Yard Orders, of which thirteen survive

---

[1] For responsible and irresponsible examples of accusation, see B.M.Harl. 7476; and 'A Dialogue between Whig and Tory' (1692) in *A Collection of State Tracts Publish'd during the Reign of King William III*, vol. II (1706). For examples of defence, see Sir Henry Shere's remarks in Bodl. Rawl. D 147, f. 8*v*; John Evelyn, *Memoirs*, II (ed. W. Bray, 1818), p. 18; and 'The Dear Bargain' (1689), in *Somer's Tracts*, vol. x, which makes use of the argument for the purposes of pamphlet warfare.

[2] Sir Benjamin Newland would not sign the Commissioners' report on political grounds; and Robert Harley, who had been unable to attend their meetings through illness and so also did not sign, later criticized its findings (*Catal.* I, pp. 96–7).

[3] *Naval Minutes*, pp. 271–2, 291.

[4] *Memoires*, pp. 147–8.

for this period;[1] and to judge from their evidence, its concerns were first for the supervision to be exercised over the watch in the ships under repair, and secondly for the observance of the prescribed method of naval accounting, evaded apparently by all departments of the dockyard staff.[2] In one instance the supervision of the yards was more directly enforced, by appointing a Commissioner (Pepys's unstable brother-in-law, Balthazar St Michel) to Woolwich and Deptford, hitherto directly under Chatham. But the more obvious achievement of the Commission under this head was the large-scale erection of dockyard buildings —21 storehouses at Chatham, twenty at Portsmouth, twelve at Deptford, one at Woolwich,[3] apart from the minor storesheds and in some cases the encircling walls, all of which, as has been seen, formed so great and so valuable a proportion of the yard facilities at the time of the Revolution.[4] It was a fine monument, and Pepys's claim, that more had been done in this respect in two and a half years 'than had ever been before, by all the *Kings* of *England* put together',[5] was, when the quality as well as the extent of the programme is considered, not very far beyond the truth.

The creation of a reserve of stores to fill the new storehouses, distributed by type and size to supply the fleet for six months, was a more difficult process. Pepys, however, asserted that in the event not six but eight months' stores were left for each ship, and that in addition a further reserve was provided of the eight principal commodities—hemp, pitch, tar, rosin, canvas, iron, oil and wood—worth over £100,000.[6] The exact value of a statement of this sort is difficult to assess; in the cases of most of the materials the quality as well as the quantity in store must be known before its accuracy can be checked, and the measurement which enabled the figures to be produced was not necessarily always the same. The reserve, moreover, and even the basic magazine, turned out not to be sufficient in all respects to answer the demands of the first two—let alone the first eight—months of the ensuing mobilization, and it is possible that Pepys displayed the same

---

[1] P.R.O.Adm. 49/132, nos. 76–87; 106/2507, no. 69.

[2] P.R.O.Adm. 49/132, nos. 77, 79, 80, 83, 85.

[3] *Catal.* I, p. 95. [4] See p. 84 above. [5] *Memoires*, p. 144.

[6] Ibid. pp. 139, 142. So far as I can understand his statement in *Naval Minutes*, p. 359, he there estimates the reserve at a minimum of £60,000.

optimism about its state as did those later officials whose ignorance he was so quick to remark. Nevertheless, the concentration on a reserve produced some results. Of the most important commodity, wood, there remained in the four yards on 5 November 1688, after two and a half months of fitting-out preparations, 5640 loads of timber, 957 loads of plank, and 262,689 of the indispensable trennels;[1] and it says a good deal for the Administration that, of this reserve, the timber and the trennels were more than double the amounts expended in the repair of the fleet over the previous two and a half years.[2]

The outstanding work of the Commission, however, lay in this programme of repair. Its success rested upon three distinct achievements. First, the repairs were fully and efficiently carried out; secondly, they did not exceed the original estimate of their cost; and thirdly, they were completed in less than the original estimate of the time required. All these facts were later questioned, but all were finally established by the Parliamentary inquiry of 1691–2, in its elicitation of a defence of their work from Deane and Hewer, the two men principally concerned, and in the detailed acknowledgment of its validity by the Parliamentary Commissioners themselves.[3]

Altogether the Special Commission repaired 69 ships and rebuilt twenty. It also built the three fourth rates promised, and a hoy and two lighters. By the time it came to a close, only four ships still remained with their repairs not completed, and four more with their repairs not begun. In addition to the work on these 96 ships, a further 29 were repaired which had been at sea when the Commission was inaugurated, and had not been included in the original programme.[4] Pepys's inten-

[1] B.M.Harl. 7476, f. 51.

[2] The figures were:

	Timber (loads)		Plank (loads)		Trennels (no.)	
	In store	Spent	In store	Spent	In store	Spent
Chatham	2,400	1,700	454	446	92,660	60,200
Portsmouth	2,803	339	97	155	102,350	34,247
Woolwich	403	154	139	83	29,320	8,600
Deptford	34	108	267	43	38,359	4,830

[3] Deane's and Hewer's defence, of which more than one copy exists, has been taken from B.M.Harl. 7476; the report of the Parliamentary Commissioners from the full summary in *Catal.* I, pp. 92–7.

[4] *Catal.* I, pp. 94–5. Pepys, in his *Memoires*, p. 133, states that only three ships had still not been begun at this date.

tions were therefore more than fulfilled in the number of the vessels which were tackled.

Repairs, however, vary in quality. In William's reign, it was hinted by some discontented members of the late Commission—by Tippetts and Haddock in particular—that many of the ships had had to come in from sea after only a few months, for further work on their hulls.[1] But, as will be seen later, those ships which returned to port during the first months of 1689, did so to store or to convert for new services, and their stay in harbour was in every case a brief one.[2] In fact, no serious repairs were carried out on any of the units under discussion for at least two years after the end of the Commission, except where damage in battle made it necessary;[3] and in the case of the thirty ships of 1677, where subsequent work was done between October 1688 and November 1691, of £2524 spent on them, only £624 was devoted to the maintenance or the repair of their hulls.[4] The negative evidence of silence also bore witness to the good condition of the ships in 1689; for in the investigations of July and August by the Commons into the misfortunes of the spring, no objections were raised, even by such a hostile witness as Falkland, an old enemy of Pepys and Deane, or by such interested witnesses as the new Commissioners of Admiralty, to the state of the fleet at the beginning of the year.[5]

Positive evidence to the same effect, however, was to be had in the certificates signed by the carpenters of the repaired ships, that they were satisfied with the work. Here again the validity of the statements was later questioned, and it was asserted that they had been extorted by threats from the Navy Office. But the objections were found, on inquiry, to come from a distinctly suspect source, that of the master shipwright at Chatham, Robert Lee, and his assistant, Edmund Dummer,[6] between whom and Deane relations had long been bad. According to the latter, Lee had deliberately ruined no less than eleven ships to cover up his own defective construction; Dummer, whom Lee had brought in as his assistant, was so inexperienced that an ordinary shipwright had to be provided to do his work; and their joint report 'carryes on it deeper characters of Remisness, Ignorance, and

---

1 B.M.Harl. 7476, f. 58.
2 See pp. 262–3 below.
3 B.M.Harl. 7476, f. 59.
4 Ibid. f. 47.
5 Ibid. f. 89.
6 *Catal.* I, p. 92.

Unfaithfulness, than Wee believe can be shewne to have ever met in any one Account of ye Navy, since England had a Navy, or (we hope) ever will againe'.[1] For their part, the two shipwrights asserted—and in this they had the more considerable support of Tippetts, Haddock and Sotherne—that Deane and Hewer had used their authority and their power to override local objections and, in their surveys, to disregard the normal procedure by which different interests were represented.[2] The latter statement was easily disproved,[3] and the Parliamentary Commissioners finally upheld Deane and Hewer.[4] Although there may have been some truth in the complaints of arbitrary practices, those practices were just as well at the time; and the combined evidence strongly suggests that the repairs were carried out with considerable efficiency.

More surprising, and even, as Pepys concluded, more important,[5] they were effected with economy. The full cost of the Commission's work, although covering a wider field than had been anticipated, was less than the estimate for the original programme, although the receipts were less than had been expected. On the assumption that the Commission would last three years, it should have received £1,200,000, and it was on this sum that Pepys based his calculations in 1686. The Commission, however, came to an end six months before this time, and for the period while it lasted it should have been paid the sum of £1,015,384.[6] In the event only £849,670 was paid from the fund allowed, but a further £82,893 was received from other sources, so that a total of £932,563 altogether was put at its disposal. A sum of £82,821 thus remained unpaid. On the other hand, Pepys had budgeted for an expenditure of £1,290,787,[7] an excess of £90,787 over the estimated, and of £358,224 over the actual, receipts, while in the event the

---

[1] B.M.Harl. 7476, ff. 22–3, 38. For Pepys's opinion of Lee and Dummer—admittedly given with the ulterior motive of getting a job for Deane—see *Catal.* I, p. 77.

[2] *Catal.* I, p. 93; B.M.Harl. 7476, ff. 17, 19, 25.

[3] B.M.Harl. 7476, ff. 19, 74.

[4] *Catal.* I, p. 93.

[5] *Memoires*, p. 146.

[6] The figures in this paragraph, except where otherwise stated, are those given in B.M.Harl. 7476, ff. 1–3; cf. *Catal.* I, p. 94.

All financial figures, except where otherwise stated, are given throughout to the nearest pound.

[7] *Catal.* I, p. 71.

Commission finished its work after spending only £909,979. The excess of receipts over expenditure in this time was thus £22,584. Other items, arising from the activities of the Commission but after it had come to an end, amounted to £19,892,[1] so that the total expenditure came to just over £929,871. On this basis, a sum of £270,129 had been saved on the original estimate.[2] Pepys, working with a different end in mind, and thus including in both debit and credit accounts 'extraordinary works and services' not chargeable on the annual appropriation of £400,000, calculated the saving at £307,570.[3] In terms of monthly wear and tear, these figures represented over the period a reduction from the traditional expenditure of 30*s.* per man per month, to one of 22*s.*;[4] and in this achievement they set a standard to which future Parliaments constantly referred in their provision for the annual requirements of the navy.

Finally, the work was completed, with the exception of the four ships already mentioned, in two and a half instead of in three years. As early as the spring of 1688 the restoration of a normal Navy Board was being discussed, and on 20 June Pepys was able to present a memorial in which these suggestions were embodied.[5] By August the work of the Commission was done,[6] and under the pressure of events in October its patent was revoked on 12 October, after the approbation and the gratitude of the King had been expressed.[7] A month before, in a letter to its members announcing the probability of this step, Pepys had been able to remind them 'that the last command you had to execute from the King was upon a warrant for fitting forth of ships presented him by me with blanks for their numbers to be filled at his pleasure....God grant that this, which I take to be the first instance to be met with of the kind since England had a navy, may be within the power of your

[1] This figure is given in a different way in *Catal.* I, p. 94.

[2] I have been unable to deduct the money previously saved on the frigates, as the original estimate of expenditure does not give their cost separately (*Catal.* I, p. 71).

[3] *Memoires*, pp. 153–4; *Catal.* I, p. 94.

[4] *Memoires*, pp. 41, 146.

[5] Bryant, loc. cit. p. 256, citing Bodl. Rawl. A 176, ff. 215–16. On the evidence of ff. 217–18 of the same volume, the plan would seem to have been first drawn up on 6 April.

[6] *Memoires*, pp. 99–100.

[7] Ibid. p. 128; B.M.Harl. 7476, ff. 77–8.

successors to follow you in.'[1] In this first contribution to the mobilization of the autumn the measure of the Pepysian régime found a fitting expression.

II

Hitherto the naval administration has been seen, as it were, at rest; and no true verdict can be given on its efficiency without first considering the verdict of events. Such a test, however, must distinguish between the normal technical results to be expected from an administrative machine in operation, which form the true criterion of its success, and the modifications which may be imposed upon them by considerations of financial, political or diplomatic necessity. The mobilization of 1688 was a particularly good test of administration, precisely because the circumstances under which it was carried out allowed the material factors to operate almost undisturbed by the extraneous influences either of financial restriction or changes of policy. The technical business of fitting out the ships, of storing, victualling and manning them, may be observed, as it were, in a vacuum as it could never be again during the following nine years, when it was deflected by conflicting political, financial or strategic considerations. Before attempting to describe its progress, therefore, it is necessary to describe the conditions in which it took place, and which protected it from such external interference.

The mobilization began in the middle of August. It was not the first sign of naval activity that year, either in England or abroad.[2] Through-

---

[1] *Catal.* I, p. 91: letter of 12 September.

[2] I have relied for my account of diplomatic events throughout the late summer, autumn and winter, on Leopold von Ranke, *History of England, mainly in the seventeenth century*, vol. IV (1875 ed. of the English trans.), particularly for Dutch affairs, and on F. A. J. Mazure, *Histoire de la Révolution de 1688 en Angleterre* (1825); on the documents published in Sir John Dalrymple, *Memoirs of Great Britain and Ireland*, vol. II, appendix (1773 ed.), and on the eighteenth-century historians White Kennett, *A Complete History of England*, vol. III (1706); Laurence Eachard, *The History of England*, vol. III (1718); John Oldmixon, *The History of England during the Reigns of the Royal House of Stuart* (1730); Nicholas Tindal's trans. of Rapin de Thoyras, *The History of England*, vol. XV (1731); and James Ralph, *The History of England during the Reigns of K. William, Q. Anne, and K. George II*, vol. I (1744). Macaulay, *History of England*, vol. III (ed. Firth, 1914), should be corrected by Sir Charles Firth, *Commentary on Macaulay's*

out the spring, William of Orange had been laying the foundations for an intervention in England which had been in the air for almost twelve months, since Dykveld's 'embassy to the opposition' in 1687. The secret, however, was well kept, and the intention possibly not yet definite. There were good reasons other than the English domestic scene for the Dutch preparations, and James himself was reported to have believed at first that their measures were directed against the French. The warnings of Barillon, the French ambassador, met therefore with little response. His overtures for the formation of a joint squadron to lie in the Channel were first accepted only with the proviso that it must be confined to a demonstration, and finally rejected altogether. On his side James's preparations were slight, despite his open annoyance with William's overtures to English faction and English seamen, and it may be doubted whether his fear of the Dutch fleet went much further at this time than to serve as a convenient pretext for postponing the summoning of Parliament in the spring.

The scale of the preparations themselves does not support the idea of a serious mobilization. A normal Summer Guard had been envisaged in the winter, and exactly when orders were given to fit out a more powerful force is not certain.[1] But their effect was felt in April and May,[2] and they culminated by 14 June in a concentration in the Downs of about twenty of the lesser rates and four fireships.[3] Pepys later called this squadron an 'ordinary *Summer-Guard*',[4] and although this was an understatement—he himself had reckoned on one of only twelve rated ships[5]—it was not a very bellicose gesture. Nor did the activity which preceded it suggest anything but a local mobilization. The normal peacetime routine of course came under greater pressure. The number

---

History of England (1938). M. V. Hay, *The Enigma of James II* (1938) provides an alternative point of view to Ranke and Macaulay, and F. C. Turner, *James II* (1948), a good summing up of the problems of this short but difficult period. For J. S. Clarke, *Life of James II* (1816), see Ranke, op. cit. vol. VI, pp. 29–45, and p. 385 below.

[1] Some orders were given in February, but these may have been for the Channel Guard already decided on.

[2] J. R. Tanner, 'The Naval Preparations of James II', in *E.H.R.* VIII, p. 272.

[3] Luttrell, *Historical Relation*, I, p. 443; P.R.O.Adm. 8/1, 1 June.

[4] Pepys, *Memoires*, p. 131. Burchett described it as 'a small squadron' (p. 2).

[5] Bodl. Rawl. A 186, f. 191.

of workmen in the royal yards rose from 1506 in April to 1601 in May,[1] stores and ammunition were in public demand,[2] and early in May James visited Chatham and the Thames defences.[3] But once the decision had been taken to fit out the squadron, things again became normal. No reinforcements were ordered for two and a half months after the ships had left port, and their supply of men, food and stores followed the familiar peacetime pattern, with none of the usual signs which heralded an emergency.[4] Nor, when the squadron assembled, was its programme exceptional. After a concentration in the Downs for a month[5] under the Catholic Rear Admiral Sir Roger Strickland, with scouts out to the eastward, it proceeded on two cruises, to Solebay and off the Suffolk coast, which it broke by a visit to the Nore in the middle of July, and ended by returning to the Downs on the last day of the month.[6] On 1 August Pepys came to the conclusion that no greater force would be needed at sea for the rest of the year, 'but that on ye contrary it will be much lessen'd by ye discharging sev^al^... Shipps... in one, 2, or three Months at furthest'.[7]

---

[1] Serg.MS. A 123. The corresponding figures for 1687 were 1205 and 1248, and for January to March 1688, 1421–1459–1498.

[2] Luttrell, loc. cit. p. 437.

[3] Ibid. p. 439; Pep: MSS., Miscellanies XI, f. 913.

[4] No embargo was laid on shipping, and Strickland was forbidden to press men (Burchett, p. 11). It must be remembered that the flow of stores to the ports was heavy at this time, owing to the efforts of the Emergency Commission to build up its reserve.

[5] From the end of May to 5 July (E. B. Powley, *The English Navy in the Revolution of 1688* (1928), pp. 15, 17).

[6] Ibid. pp. 16–17. Mr Powley quotes James's order of 18 June to Strickland for the scouting frigates, and cites a passage from the *Memoirs Relating to the Lord Torrington*, in support of the view that he was at this time actively alarmed at the Dutch preparations. The former, which does not mention the Dutch by name, should be compared with the orders of 21 August to Captain Cotton (Tanner, loc. cit. p. 273) for the difference between a state of precaution and a state of alarm. The latter, written after 1721 by an anonymous author, who is still unknown, cannot be regarded as an authority for June 1688, where the remark represents only the writer's view; while the evidence of Byng himself (later Lord Torrington), who was at this time an, admittedly influential, lieutenant is of greater value for the attitude of the Orange faction in the fleet in the autumn than for the King's state of mind in the summer.

[7] Pep:A.L. XIV, f. 304.

But three months later, so far from being reduced, the force in the Channel had risen from 25 rated ships to 41.[1] The first days of August saw a recrudescence of Dutch activity which now had to be taken seriously. A rapid succession of reports of extraordinary financial and military preparations was followed by the diversion of the inbound Dutch East India ships from their normal passage up Channel to the safer route around the north of Scotland, and by the detachment of a Dutch squadron to escort them through the North Sea. The preparations had indeed been harnessed for almost a month to the definite intention of invasion, ever since Herbert had handed to William the invitation of 30 June, without which the latter had refused to sail. When on 12 August Louis wrote to James, through Barillon, to prepare by land and sea against a descent,[2] he was for once addressing willing ears. James's reaction was swift. On the 16th he countermanded the orders already sent for the squadron to go to the westward and directed it to remain in the Downs. On the 20th all leave for its officers was stopped, and for the first time the Dutch were specifically mentioned in the order.[3] The same day Pepys was instructed to victual the ships to 1 November.[4] On the 21st Captain Cotton, commanding one of the royal yachts, was ordered to sail for the coast of Holland, to observe the movement of the Dutch fleet or any of its men-of-war,[5] and the complements of Strickland's ships were directed to be brought to war strength. On the 22nd the Navy Board was instructed to convert six fifth rates into fireships, to fit out one third and six fourths, rig a further seven thirds, and take up and fit out eight more fireships and six small vessels for scouts, 'and all to be dispatched as for Life and Death'.[6] With the drafting of fresh orders for Strickland the same day, the fleet embarked on the first stage of its preparations for hostilities.

This week of 16–23 August was decisive for the navy. For in it James's brief spell of determination was embodied in measures which his subsequent retreat into indecision did not affect. That retreat soon came. Already on the 25th he was beginning to lose sight of the danger to himself in his preoccupation with the neutrality which he still

---

[1] P.R.O. Adm. 8/1; 1 August, 1 November.

[2] Dalrymple, op. cit. II, p. 283.

[3] *E.H.R.* VIII, p. 273.

[4] Pep:A.L. XIV, ff. 345, 356.

[5] *E.H.R.* VIII, p. 273.

[6] Ibid. p. 274.

professed, complaining 'that the French and the Dutch were to fall out, and that we were pressed on to declare speedily which to take'.[1] One is reminded of his grandfather's capacity for delivering judgements so admirable in themselves and so fatal in their context. On the 26th Barillon thought him still impressed by the imminence of the descent,[2] but on the 30th he was not so sure.[3] Up to 18 September he continued to report that neither the King nor his ministers believed that Orange dare invade at this time of year.[4] Possibly the personal but soothing assurances of Van Citters on the 12th had had their effect; possibly the enigmatic influence of Sunderland was in the ascendant. But of the men around James in the first half of September, only the sailor Dartmouth was said to believe in the certainty of a descent.[5] It was not until the last week of the month that he was finally convinced that danger was upon him.[6] By 8 October he was expecting the Dutch to embark in a week, and then to sail with the first easterly wind.[7] And in fact the first, and unsuccessful, departure was made from Helvoetsluys on the 19th.

Various explanations have been offered for James's conduct throughout the year. But with this evidence it cannot be said either that he suspected a descent for the first time at the end of September,[8] or that he never suspected it at all until it was under way,[9] or on the contrary that he suspected it consistently from at least the middle of August.

[1] Sir John Reresby, *Memoirs*, ed. A. Browning (1932), p. 506.

[2] Dalrymple, op. cit. II, appendix, p. 283. [3] Ibid.

[4] Ibid. pp. 283–4. [5] Clarke, *Life of James II*, II, p. 177.

[6] The dramatic story of D'Albeville's dispatch from the Hague, which is supposed to have opened James's eyes, is given in Macaulay, *History of England*, III, p. 1105. Dalrymple and Laurence Eachard, alone of the eighteenth-century historians, give the same story. Macaulay's authority was the latter (*History of England*, III, p. 888 in the 1718 ed.). Eachard himself gives no authority, other than a general indebtedness in the preface to the volume, to Bohun (presumably to his *History of the Desertion*), to an anonymous 'Life of King William III', and to 'several Manuscripts and private Accounts from Persons of unquestion'd knowledge and Credit', probably from Tory and High-Church sources (see *Conduct*, pp. 3–19). Macaulay does not give the date on which James read the dispatch; according to Eachard it was the 23rd. But whether the story is true or not, all the evidence points to the period between 18 and 25 September as the turning point in the King's attitude to the invasion.

[7] G. N. Clark, *The Later Stuarts* (1944), p. 131.

[8] Macaulay, *History of England*, III, pp. 1105–7.

[9] M. V. Hay, *The Enigma of James II*, ch. v.

Apart, indeed, from the measures taken then, his statements were contradictory and his moves uncertain. Why, then, were his naval measures not interrupted after August, as were his other policies, but on the contrary pursued with considerable energy irrespective of his later shifts of position? The answer would seem to lie in the close and peculiar relation which they bore to a foreign policy, in every other sphere leading to inconsistency and disaster, but in this respect to a clear and unaltered line of action. The mainspring of this policy was a reluctance on James's part to commit himself to either side in the European struggle, a desire for neutrality which was expressed in his actions from the early days of June, when he finally declined to join forces with the French, to his recall of Skelton in August for attempting to identify the English with the French attitude to Holland, and his complementary snub to Van Citters for a similar attempt to identify the English and the Dutch attitudes to France. The force of circumstances sometimes drove him from this position, but it was one to which he always returned so long as it was at all tenable. That in the end it proved not to be so, was due to the interaction of foreign and domestic interests; that on the other hand James continued to think that it was, was due to his peculiar capacity for ignoring this interaction, and his consequent inability to reconcile his attitude with a changing situation in which, as the year went by, European interest was transferred from what England would do to what would happen to England. But despite the confusion which it led to in national affairs, such an attitude, resting as it did upon a firm belief in his own strength if properly deployed, was not likely to interrupt the prosecution of the naval measures upon which it consciously depended. The only doubt was whether it could be sufficiently disturbed by events for them to be inaugurated. Such had not been the case in the spring; but with the alarm in August, and with the orders once given, Pepys and his colleagues could get to work unhampered by changes of policy from above, and secure in the knowledge that they enjoyed the support of a King who, professionally and personally, was interested in their success.

The mobilization itself lasted from the third week of August to the end of October, by which time the fleet was ready to put to sea. Its objective was a simple one. On 22 August, Strickland's squadron consisted of 26 ships; by the end of the month, orders had been given for him to be reinforced by a further 35, exclusive of scouts and auxiliaries. The proportions of the two forces were as follows:[1]

	Strickland's squadron	Reinforcements
Third rates	1	10
Fourth rates	16	11
Fifth rates	3	—
Sixth rates	2	1
Fireships	4	13
Total	26	35

The task of the Administration was to re-store and revictual Strickland's ships, and to get the reinforcements to sea, before the Dutch were able to put out.

It was able to pursue its objective undisturbed by any changes of strategic intention. On 27 August, Strickland was ordered to take up his station between the North Sands and the Kentish Knock,[2] and these instructions held until 1 October, when the fleet was directed to concentrate at the Nore.[3] It stayed there until the third week of the month, when it was ready to sail again to the Thames approaches. The area of concentration thus remained the same throughout the mobilization, and the administrative preparations were not deflected by a change of rendezvous or of purpose.

Nor were they thrown out of proportion by amendments to the earlier orders. The reinforcements were supplemented only once before the end of October, when on the 10th of that month 'some' third and fourth rates were directed to set their rigging and to stand by in reserve.[4] Otherwise, the supply system was able to operate along lines which, once laid down, were not subsequently altered to any extent.

The preparations might also have been delayed or misdirected by opposition, either to measures or to men, on the part of the fleet. But relations with the Admiral, which had been normal in August, were in fact improved in October, thanks to a change of command. On 24 September the Catholic Strickland was replaced by the Protestant

---

[1] Burchett, p. 3. [2] Ibid. p. 9. [3] Ibid. pp. 12–14.

[4] *H.M.C.* 11th Report, appendix, pt v, p. 154. According to Serg:Mins. XVIII; 13/10, the order applied to six thirds, and to all the fourths as yet unfitted.

Dartmouth,[1] and with the advent of this efficient and powerful figure the correspondence between Secretary and Navy Office on the one hand, and Admiral on the other, became possibly more cordial and certainly more intimate than before. Dartmouth's popularity with the fleet, moreover, ensured a greater measure of support for the administrative preparations than they were likely to have been accorded in the atmosphere of mistrust and incipient mutiny which was characteristic of Strickland's last weeks in command;[2] while his loyalty ensured that the individual disappointments to which the mobilization gave rise, did not sour his relations with those officials ashore whom he knew to be doing their best.

The preparations were concentrated upon a familiar as well as a clear policy. The early identification of the Dutch as the enemy ensured that they would be mounted once more in the traditional nexus of ports and regions of supply which had Chatham, Deptford and Woolwich as its foci, and Ipswich and Harwich, Deal and Dover as its perimeter. The south and west coasts did not enter into the calculations. Early in August it had been agreed that the port of Kinsale in Ireland no longer required a clerk of the cheque, in view of the unimportance of the area which it served[3]—a decision which was never questioned later—and throughout the rest of the year no reference was made to the use of any port in the west of England. Even Portsmouth itself, the second greatest dockyard and much nearer the probable scene of action, was not mentioned as a possible base until 14 November, by which time 'ye expectacon of Action in the West' was being considered.[4] The change of emphasis from east to south was, in fact, a last-minute affair; and the policy which had dominated the measures of the autumn was never expressed more cogently than on the very day on which William turned down Channel from his original objective of the east coast. A few hours before the expedition altered course, the Navy Board recommended that, in the event of a fourth Dutch war, Harwich and

[1] *H.M.C.* 11th Report, appendix, pt v, p. 255. This reference will be abbreviated, in future notes, to *H.M.C.* 11, v.

[2] Ibid. p. 261; *Life of Captain Stephen Martin*, ed. C. R. Markham (*N.R.S.* 1895), p. 6.

[3] Serg:Mins. XVII; 8/8.

[4] Ibid. XVIII; 14/11.

Sheerness should be revived as naval ports;[1] and in the latter case, its suggestion was put into effect.[2]

The machinery of administration was well suited to the circumstances. A system of authority, in which direction of policy and of execution were each concentrated in one man, was faced with an unambiguous and immediate objective, and unhampered by external pressure either from the Closet or from a Parliament in session. It was a situation for which the naval administration of the Stuarts had been created; and Pepys and the Commission of 1686 were the men to take advantage of it. In their hands the blue-print of an Administration was made to work; decisions were passed from King and Cabinet, or King alone, to Secretary, from Secretary to fleet or Navy Office and from Navy Office to yards and ships, with regularity and with despatch. The linch-pin of the system was Pepys, representing to the higher levels of policy the detailed requirements of administration, and to the multifarious, diffuse interests of administration the co-ordinating influence of an informed policy. In the early days of the mobilization he was constantly on the move, following the King to Richmond or Windsor. He was at Richmond on 5 August, at Windsor on 16 and 18 August. He spent the whole of the next week travelling to and fro, sometimes at night, between the Castle and the Admiralty; and again in the first six days of September he made at least four such journeys.[3] In the later months of the year, for which his correspondence to the fleet survives, he seems to have attended the King in Cabinet in London between once and three or four times a week, and out of Cabinet, on occasions, several times a day.[4] Meanwhile a quorum of either three or four members of the Navy Commission was meeting at least five mornings and four afternoons a week at Seething Lane, with Deane, Hewer and Berry the most regular in attendance.[5] From this core of activity, the orders, reproofs and, occasionally, commendations flowed to the local officials and the ships. Exhortations fell impartially on commanders absent from their

---

1 Serg: Mins. XVII; 2/11, A.M.

2 By the order of 8/11.

3 Pep: A.L. XIV, ff. 316, 345, 362–4, 366–70, 387–94.

4 *H.M.C.* 11, v, pp. 147, 159, 178, 188, 191, 193, 196, 212, 216; 141, 162, 165, 168, 176, 217, 226–7.

5 The busiest days were Mondays and Tuesdays, Thursdays and Fridays (Serg: Mins. XVII and XVIII, August and September, *passim*).

commands,[1] on officers irregularly demanding stores,[2] and on subordinates failing to make the proper returns;[3] while Pepys tackled the bigger game—the Ordnance Office for failing to send guns,[4] the Post Office for delays in the mail,[5] the London Companies for withholding men who should have been sent to the fleet,[6] and even, on one memorable occasion, the King in Cabinet for allowing an officer to be seen at Court who should have been with his ship in the Thames.[7]

An enumeration of meetings held and letters written, however, does not describe satisfactorily the degree of control exercised by the central authority. Some of the greatest disorders of the ensuing war were preceded by a spate of orders, quite as excellent as those of Pepys, but none of which was followed in the event. Beyond a certain point, indeed, the more meetings and letters, the greater the proof that control has been lost. What distinguished the mobilization of 1688 from many of its successors was that many of the Admiralty instructions had the intended results; and the process can be seen better in these results than in a list of the instructions, or of examples, however widely chosen, that show the working of the machinery itself. But when the machinery does not work satisfactorily, its operation may with profit be examined independently of the material upon which it works. Such a case arose when the central authority was required itself to supervise the local control of the preparations.

For as the mobilization progressed, it became clear that exhortations from London were not in themselves enough to support the labours of the officials on the spot. A more powerful and more mobile control was wanted to force the local efforts to their conclusion. The resident Commissioners at Chatham and Deptford, in particular, were in need of help. An effort was made to provide it. On 25 August, Pepys recalled two members of the Navy Commission, Booth and Berry, from the Downs, where they had been paying Strickland's ships, and sent them to hasten the work at Chatham.[8] This proved satisfactory,

---

[1] *H.M.C.* 11, v, pp. 140, 142, 145, 148, 166.
[2] Serg:Mins. XVIII; 1/10.
[3] Ibid. 10/9, 26/10.
[4] See pp. 224–5 below.
[5] Pep:A.L. XIV, f. 392.
[6] See pp. 230–1 below.
[7] *H.M.C.* 11, v, p. 179.
[8] Pep:A.L. XIV, f. 369. Berry may have been recalled initially for a conference with the King on the 26th (Burchett, p. 10).

and when the fleet was taking to the water towards the end of September, they were given Flag appointments in it, partly to continue their administrative labours—for, as Pepys wrote, 'notwithstanding their sea commands, [they] are not less Commissioners of the Navy than they were before'.[1] But the attempt to identify two different functions, so often identified in the past, was not in this case a great success. The removal of Booth and Berry left a gap of which Dartmouth was beginning to complain early in the following month, and which soon led him to demand that two of the Commissioners in London should be sent to help him, particularly in checking his stores. This request came at an awkward time. By 4 October, Deane and Hewer were suffering from the effects of overwork, and if St Michel had not been sent up to the Navy Office, there would not have been enough members there to make a Board.[2] The Admiral was therefore asked to use the two Rear Admirals as Commissioners, and was reminded that they were in any case the most useful officials available for his particular requirements.[3] On 7 October, however, he was loaned the master attendant at Deptford, Captain Wilshaw, whom, to the dismay of the Navy Board, he retained until towards the end of the month.[4] At the same time, more serious efforts were under way to meet his demands. They seem, indeed, to have been responsible for the end of the special Commission of 1686. Despite the earlier agreements that it would end some time in the autumn, no exact date had been fixed; but as the necessity for some reorganization grew more obvious, arrangements were made to free some of its members by replacing it with a smaller Navy Board on the traditional lines. On 7 October, Pepys informed Dartmouth of this, remarking specifically 'that in a very little time, the few of the present members that are remaining here will be relieved, and consequently some to spare to assist you, in your affaires'.[5] On the 12th the order constituting a new Board was sent to the Commission, and at about noon on the 15th Pepys read the patent to its assembled members at the Navy Office.[6] But the gap was not thereby satisfactorily filled, and, as soon as the new Board was in being, the Secretary proposed to the

---

1 *H.M.C.* 11, v, p. 147.
2 Ibid. pp. 142, 147, 152.
3 Ibid. p. 147.
4 Ibid. p. 146; Serg:Mins. XVIII; 19/10.
5 *H.M.C.* 11, v, p. 147; see also ibid. p. 156.
6 Serg:Mins. XVIII; 13/10, 15/10.

King that either its Comptroller or Surveyor should be sent at once to the fleet. In the meantime, however, after further complaints about the lack of assistance,[1] Dartmouth had sailed for the Gunfleet, and the idea was therefore dropped, 'it being respited only till you come next in the way of its being useful to you'.[2] The problem of controlling ships, not yet in company with the fleet, but no longer immediately affected by the organization of the yards, still awaited a solution other than an extension of the central authority which was merely personal and therefore opportunist.

It is time to turn to the material results of all this activity which alone give it reality. These may be grouped under the four headings of ships, stores, food and men. In the first instance, that of ships, the preparations began with the advantage of the work of the Special Commission behind them. The ships themselves were available, and the process of repairing them had moreover bequeathed another legacy which could be appreciated only after the mobilization had begun. This lay not in the hulls which had been restored, but in the organization which had restored them, capable as it was of expansion, or of serving a variety of purposes, without suffering excessive strain. The task of fitting out 35 men-of-war did not unduly embarrass a group of yards in which the numbers of workmen had been steadily increasing since the beginning of the previous year.[3] The figures for the autumn are significant:[4]

	Total	Chatham	Deptford	Woolwich	Portsmouth
August	1749	836	320	213	380
September	1818	859	336	239	384
October	1809	863	338	246	362
November	1845	886	305	292	362

All the Thames yards show a definite rise followed by a month of stability. The numbers for November may be influenced by an external factor, the strengthening of the ports by armed bands of workmen for their defence, which took place during October;[5] but the total increase from the end of August to the third week of October is remarkably small. Indeed, although the numbers themselves are

[1] *H.M.C.* 11, v, p. 257.
[2] Ibid. pp. 166–7.
[3] See Appendix V below.
[4] Serg.MS. A 123.
[5] *E.H.R.* VIII, pp. 275–6.

larger, they repeat almost exactly the development of the same period in 1687, when the total figures were: August 1371, September 1434, October 1437, November 1446.[1] It is curious that there should not have been a greater dissimilarity between the two years in view of the different circumstances. It cannot be ascribed to indifference or to failure, at a time of such obvious vigilance, and when such satisfactory results were achieved. Rather, when coupled with the marked lack of correspondence on the subject of workmen in a period of epistolary activity,[2] it suggests that the yards, already under considerable pressure, were able quickly to absorb the increase of work, and that the increase itself did not have to be very great.

The effort was devoted entirely to fitting out the reinforcements, for, unlike all subsequent mobilizations, there were no ships to be repaired for damage either from battle or weather, and the June squadron, although no longer so clean as might have been wished, was still able to keep the sea.[3] Nevertheless, its results were not at once apparent. No steady flow of reinforcements reached Strickland's squadron during September. On the 24th, with his fifth rates still converting into fireships, there were only 22 ships at sea in the Channel command, and only 26 on 1 October.[4] By the 7th, Dartmouth was getting worried, and envisaged having to sail against a strong Dutch force with a small and foul squadron.[5] The delay, however, was not attributable to the yards. Most of the ships were by this time out of their hands,[6] and awaiting their stores and many of their men, and in some instances their commanders. When these had been provided, they soon began to join the fleet. On the 12th, many of them had already done so.[7] On the 17th the ships from Portsmouth were on their way round, and the Admiral had with him 31 of the 37 ships of the line which he could

---

[1] Serg.MS. A 123.

[2] On 29 August, eighty soldiers were loaned to dispatch the works at Chatham. Otherwise the Navy Board minutes have little to say on the subject (Serg:Mins. XVII, XVIII, *passim*).

[3] See *H.M.C.* 11, v, p. 156, for one exception.

[4] I have followed P.R.O.Adm. 8/1 for the first figure, and Powley (loc. cit. pp. 29–30, and 30 n. 1) for the second.

[5] *H.M.C.* 11, v, p. 256

[6] Ibid. pp. 150–1.

[7] Ibid. p. 257.

expect.[1] The next day, the Admiralty disposition list gave 59 of the 61 units 'At Sea',[2] and although this was anticipating some which still lay in the river, the fleet was ready to sail to its appointed station. On the 24th, Dartmouth wrote to the King from the Gunfleet that, though he could have wished for a stronger force in view of the latest enemy intelligence, he had with him 'as good a winter squadron as ever England put to sea', adding—accurately enough in view of the miscarriage of William's original departure—'we are now at sea before the Dutch with all their boasting'.[3] The concentration was not quite complete, for two ships were still in the Downs, and four away cruising. But only three, the *Woolwich*, *Newcastle* and *St Albans*, still lagged behind, the first two delayed by lack of stores and then by head winds, the latter, as Pepys was quick to note, by the laziness of her captain.[4] The last of them finally sailed down river on 8 November, and with her departure the original orders had been fulfilled.[5]

As the work on the ships' hulls and rigging came to an end, most of the stores were put aboard. On the whole, this was done with comparatively little delay, for in this sphere again the effects were felt of the labours of the previous two and a half years. The creation of a reserve had left an active supply system, as the repairs had left an active labour organization in the yards. But the former was not so successful as the latter. It had not achieved so uniform a result. The large reserve of timber which was most frequently mentioned, and of which the Commissioners of 1686 were particularly proud, was not altogether typical of the general position. The imported naval stores could not be accumulated so fast, and the repairs had in some cases eaten into the reserve more quickly than it could be replaced. There was, in particular, not enough hemp and tar by the autumn to maintain both the current service and a magazine, thanks largely to the difficulties experienced during the spring and summer by one of the most considerable of the Russia merchants, Joseph Martin, in honouring his contracts.[6] Figures, unfortunately, are not now available, although they were at the

---

1 Ibid. p. 259; Powley, loc. cit. p. 56.

2 P.R.O. Adm. 8/1; 18/10.

3 *H.M.C.* 11, v, p. 261.

4 Ibid. pp. 264; 179, 181.

5 Ibid. p. 182. The achievement is summed up in a complementary survey, five days later, of the ships not at sea, ibid. p. 199.

6 Serg:Mins. XVII; 10/8, 24/8; *Cal.Treas.Bks. 1685–9*, pp. 1913, 2029, 2039.

time;[1] and it must be remembered that descriptions of the stores referred equally to those used in fitting out the ships in the yards and to those used aboard them when fitted, which alone were the immediate concern. But at any rate, Dartmouth, who was never quiescent when delayed, did not complain much on this score. His captains were not so satisfied as their commander, but, as Pepys remarked, that was nothing new, 'for I hardly ever remember a shipp that could not find something or other to ask within tenn days after they went out';[2] and he congratulated the Admiral on managing to reduce the flood of requests to some semblance of necessity. On the whole, the amounts in store seem to have been enough for the job in hand, while the work of building up a reserve, both of native and imported materials, went on throughout August and September.[3]

In two respects, however, the captains had a legitimate grievance. When the fleet sailed for the Gunfleet, the men were still short of slop clothes, and the ships of signal flags. In neither case had the preparations been made soon enough. The Navy Board first contracted with the slopseller on 8 October, after Dartmouth's initial complaint had been received, but by the 19th enough clothes had been collected to supply only twelve ships. The rest came in slowly, and by the 20th the Board was buying up what it could all over town.[4] Over the failure to supply flags, a discreet silence reigns. Some other stores had also inevitably to be shipped aboard at the last moment or sent after the fleet. But in the main, the immediate problem had been solved. How far the effort had dislocated the general balance of supply remained to be seen in the next few months.

One branch of supply, however, was badly mismanaged. Throughout the autumn, there was a steady stream of complaints about the delay and the poor quality of the guns, ammunition and ordnance stores. This was of course outside the jurisdiction of the naval administration, and one advantage which had been hoped for from Dartmouth's appointment was that he also held the post of Master General of the Ordnance.

---

[1] Deane and Hewer left with their successors a list of the principal stores remaining in the yards on 1 September (Serg:Mins. XVIII; 2/11). I have been unable to trace it.

[2] *H.M.C.* 11, V, p. 163.

[3] Serg:Mins. XVII, *passim*.

[4] *H.M.C.* 11, V, pp. 151, 154, 160, 168–9, 177; Serg:Mins. XVIII; 18/10.

It was in this capacity that Pepys addressed to him some of his most passionate letters, and, even allowing for the fact that the Secretary often liked to have a poor opinion of other men's work and for the bad relations that had existed for some time between the navy and the Ordnance, it is clear that he was abundantly justified in his protests. Early in October, he was hinting that the officers of the Ordnance should be hastened by their own superior rather than by further letters from himself, and he followed this up on the 8th by passing on to the Admiral the information from Portsmouth that the guncarriages just received there did not fit the guns, and that most of their retaining tackles had not arrived.[1] This seems to have had a temporary effect; but the complaints soon began to come in again.[2] The supply of ordnance stores continued to vary while their quality unfortunately did not, and on 20 October Pepys could restrain himself no longer. 'However matters may be represented to you from the [Ordnance] Office', he wrote to Dartmouth, 'there is not one shipp now behind you, from whose Comander I doe not daily hear of want of gunns, carriages, shot or something else relating thereto, notwithstanding (as the captains averr) their gunners' daily attendances for them.' These grievances, he continued, were being aired at a higher level, and he had been questioned that very morning at the Cabinet whether the ships now had all their guns and ordnance stores.[3] Rival demands from the field army and the coastal forts doubtless complicated the task of the Ordnance, although the former at least was not much better supplied than the navy; and, however great the reserve of gunners' stores and ammunition, their distribution, necessitating as it did their transfer, by land or water, to the centres of naval supply, involved a stage more than did that of naval stores. But the ordnance was delayed principally because its supply was mismanaged, and because the inefficiency played into the hands of a mutual jealousy always only too liable to prevent co-operation between the Navy and Ordnance Offices.

In the supply of ships and stores, therefore, where the direct impact of the past two and a half years could be felt, the mobilization went quite smoothly. Its difficulties arose in the other two spheres, and the

---

[1] *H.M.C.* 11, v, pp. 140–1, 151. [2] Ibid. pp. 156, 167, 174.
[3] Ibid. p. 169.

most intense anxiety was caused by the victualling arrangements. The Victuallers had not been active during the summer. Apart from their normal responsibilities of supplying the odd ships for the Plantations and the Straits, their only commitment had been to victual Strickland's squadron, and that could be done out of the annual declaration. The sudden demand in the autumn for four months' provisions for an additional 35 ships, coming on top of an order to continue those already at sea for a further two and a half months, involved them in a task for which, by the nature of the commodities in which they dealt, they had been largely unable to prepare; and when the time came to put the food aboard, in many cases they could not do so.

It is an indication of the nature of the danger, and of the experienced vigilance of the Administration, that it was upon this situation that Dartmouth and Pepys at once focused their keenest attention. The former was apprised of the backward nature of the victualling as soon as he arrived in the fleet on 2 October, and wrote at once to Pepys that it was likely to be the most probable source of delay.[1] The latter acted energetically. On the 4th, he held a conference with the Navy Board and the Victuallers at the Navy Office—one of the few visits on his part which is recorded in the Navy Board minutes—which lasted for about three hours, and at which he pressed the Victuallers to furnish him with a state of the provisions as it then appeared. His eloquence must have stirred them, for 'they promised him a state of ye whole affaire this afternoon at 4, and that a Minnits time should not be lost, but every moment improved towards ye supply of what remains behind'.[2] By five o'clock he had the list, and it accompanied the evening letter to the Admiral.[3] By that time Pepys had been with the King, and it had been agreed that the ships fitting out should be victualled for three instead of for four months.[4] With this prompt revision of the original plan, the centre of interest again shifted to the Victuallers.

In the days that followed, they continued to work very hard. They managed to supply the fleet with water and water-boats, and on the 6th sent an agent to it to supervise the delivery of their stores.[5] Pepys

[1] *H.M.C.* 11, v, pp. 140, 142. [2] Serg:Mins. xviii; 4/10.
[3] *H.M.C.* 11, v, p. 142. The list is missing from Dartmouth's papers.
[4] Ibid. p. 140.
[5] Serg:Mins. xviii; 12/10; *H.M.C.* 11, v, p. 147.

acknowledged their industry.[1] But the provisions still failed to appear in the quantities expected, and the week went by with Dartmouth remarking on the distinction between promise and performance.[2]

The disappointment was partly due to an annoying external commitment to victual the garrisons in some of the coastal forts, which by the 7th had consumed enough food to supply three third rates for two months, and which should not have been made a naval responsibility.[3] But apart from this, Pepys found it difficult to account for the delay. There was no lack of assurances, nor of figures to support them. On the evening of the 7th, the Victuallers informed the King in Cabinet that the ships at Portsmouth and those of Strickland's squadron were all fully provisioned, and presented him with an account of how the rest stood that day. On the 8th they submitted another account, by which it appeared that the whole fleet had been fully supplied, except for four ships which would be ready in a few days, and two more which were not yet advanced enough to take in provisions.[4] The assurances (for so they remained) were repeated on the 11th,[5] but on the 14th Pepys confessed himself baffled by their unreality. As he said:

> Soe many papers have been given already, and more are like to bee for ought I see, both on one side and other, without the satisfaction that should arise from them, till some expedient bee found to render them more effectuall.... This evening at the Cabinett...the Commissioners by way of reply presented his Majestie with some papers that carried with them such an account of the provisions said to bee now actually shipped off, for supply of your fleete, as could have no other present exception made to it, then that their former papers were in noe degree less cleare, and yet in noe wise (as your Lordshipp observes) made good by the state of provisions.[6]

It was the same story, of figures contradicted by facts and of apparently reliable figures contradicting each other, which was to perplex his successors. The 'expedient' to make them 'more effectuall' had not yet been found, and the remedies proposed were largely irrelevant. In

---

1 Ibid. pp. 154–5.
2 Ibid. p. 257.
3 Ibid. p. 147. Pepys's concern over this question may be seen in his notes on the state of the victualling in four of these forts on 24 September (Bodl. Rawl. A 186, f. 455).
4 *H.M.C.* 11, v, pp. 147, 150.
5 Ibid. p. 155.
6 Ibid. p. 159.

this instance, the cause of the delay was thought to be the lack of supervision over the victualling vessels on their way down river, and Pepys got the King's approval for the Victuallers to send one of their number to hasten them to the fleet. But in his argument he touched upon the underlying cause of the disappointments, although his allusion referred it to a different context and an inadequate solution. For what he requested of the Commissioner of Victualling was that he should, by his arrival with the truant vessels, 'present...not only...his account in paper, but...the only visible evidence of the truth of them, namely, the victuall itself spoaken of in those accounts'.[1] Pepys contemplated this result solely from the appearance of the provision boats, but in fact, although the authority of the Commissioner was needed to hasten the vessels to their duty, it was more important that his experience should be available to ascertain the relation which the victuals as bought by the Victuallers bore to the same victuals as measured by the ships. This was a different problem from that of producing the initial quantities demanded, and it required different treatment. Now, as later, it was not clearly appreciated that more than one question was involved; and as the problem shifted from one of purchase and supply to one of measurement and control, the remedies applied to the first situation were continued in the hope that they would satisfy the second. On this occasion they did so, temporarily and to a limited extent, for the presence of an experienced Commissioner was necessary on either account. With his arrival, the position began to improve; and apart from some beer which had still to come, the ships were well enough stocked by 24 October for Dartmouth to be able to devote his attention to the Dutch, unhampered by having only a few days' provisions aboard.[2] But the presence of a senior official was neither always applicable nor possible, and the real solution lay in the acceptance of a discipline which did not require personal intervention, but which enabled a more precise standard of book-keeping and measurement, and a better-regulated disposal of the victuals themselves, to obtain in both the civil and the executive departments of a common service.

The victualling crisis was a brief one, but the difficulties of manning the fleet were prolonged. To find men for 35 ships simultaneously put

---

[1] *H.M.C.* 11, v, p. 159. [2] Ibid. p. 261.

into pay was in itself a hard enough task; but it was complicated by the existence of an earlier problem, of the same type although on a smaller scale, that of completing the manning of the ships already at sea. Strickland's squadron, like most summer guards in peacetime, had not been allowed to press, and at the end of August its actual numbers were well below its complement on paper.[1] When, on the 23rd, the latter was increased by warrant to a war establishment,[2] the competition between the original squadron and its reinforcements increased. The machinery to deal with the problem was inadequate, consisting as it did of the traditional means of press and bounty, enforced and stimulated through the traditional agencies which had proved so ineffective on similar occasions. An attempt, one of many, had been made in July, to discover to what extent the Lord Admiral was entitled to inquire into the number of ships and seamen available in the kingdom; but the Admiralty Solicitor had returned an evasive answer,[3] and when the time came the men, as usual, had to be found without a register, collected without proper supervision, and retained without any adequate inducement.

The machinery, moreover, was set in motion neither soon enough nor extensively enough to meet the case. Although individual press warrants were granted in the last week of August, and the boats were at work before the end of the month,[4] the Order in Council for a general press was issued only on 25 September, when Dartmouth received his appointment to the fleet.[5] It is true that the ships fitting out were only then reaching the stage at which they could take all their men, but to delay their supply until the week in which most of them were required was at marked variance with the vigilance displayed by the Administration in other fields. Nor did it employ the alternative method of the bounty, with its addition to the standing wages of the volunteers. Indeed, apart from the restraints upon seamen enlisting with foreign powers,[6] no general official action was taken before the third week of September to control their destination in any way.

The explanation is to be found in James's unwillingness to disturb the

---

[1] Burchett, pp. 8, 11.

[2] Pep:A.L. XIV, f. 362.

[3] Bodl. Rawl. A 171, f. 157.

[4] Luttrell, op. cit. I, p. 457.

[5] Powley, loc. cit. p. 25.

[6] *London Gazette*, no. 2326.

normal trade of the nation. This extended even to the Order in Council for a general press, in which outward-bound merchantmen were protected from the navy. In the latter half of October, their freedom of movement was partially restricted by embargoes for France and Holland, placed first on the 19th upon the port of Harwich, and then, on the 22nd, on the whole coast from Berwick to the Thames.[1] But, unlike later measures of the same type, these were imposed not to facilitate the manning of the fleet, but to prevent the spread of intelligence of English movements and to deprive William of the transports which he was then known to need.[2] The navy itself did not oppose, but rather supported the demands of the trading interest:

> The King [wrote Pepys to Dartmouth on 1 November] has been all allong...much of your Lordshipp's mind...touching the keeping of trade on foot, at the same time with the fitting forth of his own shipps....And for passes and protection, they will cease of course, especially if the ships that shall hereafter be sett out find noe other expedient of manning themselves than those that are now behind in the river are dayly complained of to doe, namely, out of merchant ships outward-bound upon trade, with his Majesty's own hand to protect them against pressing.[3]

It was the only instance throughout the autumn of the naval preparations being subordinated, and with naval support, to another national interest.

The sources of supply were therefore restricted, and the concentration upon those remaining was all the greater. These may be divided into two main types: the professional Companies—of Fishermen and of Watermen—who by the terms of their charters were responsible for producing a given quota on demand, and the local, unregulated supply of unprotected seamen picked up in the seaports and coastal districts and from incoming merchantmen. The former were naturally approached as soon as possible, in view of the theoretical certainty and quality of the supply. A few days after the Order in Council appeared, the Fishermen were called upon to provide 500 men, and the Watermen 200.[4] But the orders produced more excuses than men. The Fishermen

---

[1] Powley, loc. cit. p. 76.
[2] *H.M.C.* 11, v, p. 182.
[3] Ibid. See also *H.M.C. Downshire*, 1, pt 1, p. 302. The embargoes were in fact soon removed (*E.H.R.* VIII, pp. 277–8).
[4] Serg:Mins. XVIII; 27/9, 28/9.

pleaded that their members were themselves engaged in pressing for the navy, as crews of the press-smacks, while the Watermen, after the usual preliminary skirmish, asserted on 4 October that they had already delivered their full quota, and they could not subsequently be induced to admit that they had in fact done nothing of the sort.[1] Unfortunately, the Navy Office had neglected to ensure that the men were collected and shipped down river together, so that the Company's ruse of giving them their tickets individually instead of entrusting them all to an officer, had enabled most of them to disappear before they reached their destination.[2] On the 11th, a further 200 were demanded, and this time Pepys provided a vessel for their collection.[3] But even when they were secured, the men proved to be of very poor quality, the watermen 'for the greatest part very raw young men', and the fishermen 'persons of all sorts, but that only which they should be of; namely, fishermen, or at least seamen'.[4]

Even, however, if all the right men had reached the ships, they would have amounted to only 900 all told. In September, the fleet at sea and fitting out needed over 12,000 men,[5] and of these 6013 were required for the earlier reinforcements and for a few of the worse-manned units of Strickland's squadron numbering 33 ships in all.[6] On 9 September these ships had 2886 men aboard and by 4 October 4553, leaving on that day a shortage of 1460 for themselves alone.[7] The professional quota did not go far, and most of the men came from the ordinary activities of the press. They were collected from as far afield as Yorkshire and Sussex, with the west supplying the Portsmouth ships so far as possible but, if the activity bore any relation to the results, with the majority coming in—often unwillingly enough—from the area of the Thames and Medway.[8] In addition, there were some volunteers,

[1] *H.M.C.* 11, v, pp. 141–2, 149, 154.

[2] Ibid. p. 142.

[3] Ibid. p. 157.

[4] Ibid. p. 200.

[5] P.R.O.Adm. 8/1, 1 September, gives a total of 12,245, including a few ships in the Channel not intended for the fleet. Pepys, *Memoires*, p. 132, estimates that 12,303 were required for the fleet itself.

[6] Bod. Rawl. A 186, f. 65. I have concluded that these 33 ships included some of the ships at sea, since fifteen fourth rates are mentioned, four more than were ordered to fit out at the time.

[7] Ibid.

[8] Serg:Mins. XVIII, 14/10; Luttrell, op. cit. I, pp. 463–4; *H.M.C. Frankland-Russell-Astley*, p. 68; *Le Fleming*, p. 216; 11, v, pp. 143, 146.

perhaps more than usual owing to the personal popularity of the Admiral,[1] and also 300 soldiers, whose demands for bedding caused a slight flurry.[2] By 31 October, with these assorted contributions aboard, the fleet was pronounced officially to be manned.[3]

It was no mean feat on the part of the Administration to have reached this conclusion, for it had no figures on which to base it. Its information was contained in the pressmasters' lists of men delivered to the ships, which were thoroughly unreliable, and in Dartmouth's general reports, which contained no figures.[4] While the ships were still in the yards, the resident Commissioners could muster them,[5] but once they left for the Nore the only reports were those of the captains, undisputed by any other authority and in any case in literary rather than numerical terms. A muster-master to the fleet should have been appointed with the new Admiral,[6] but the weeks passed without any of the various applicants being selected. The post remained vacant until at least the end of October, and it was finally settled upon the Admiral's secretary, Phineas Bowles.[7] No more musters, however, were produced by the presence of a muster-master than by his absence. At the end of January 1689 Pepys declared that 'not any one Muster has (to my knowledge) been taken by that Officer from ye first day of the Fleet's Setting abroad till this; nor by any body else but the Clerke of the Cheque at Portsmth. at ye Fleet's comeing last in'.[8] The figures on which the Admiralty worked throughout this period were those of 'Men in Pay',[9] which consisted of the ships' establishments, modified so as to conform to the manning policy in force, and to absorb so far as possible the miscellaneous collection of press lists, Admiral's surveys and captains' complaints which together made up its statistical information. It was upon this system of inspired guess-work that it relied for its reports of the manning situation to the King and the Council, and demanded from the Treasury the money with which to pay the fleet's wages.

Its difficulties, however, were not confined to numbers. The fleet of 1688 was like many before and after it, neither better nor worse, and

---

1 *H.M.C. Downshire*, I, pt I, p. 302.
2 *H.M.C.* 11, v, pp. 142, 152.
3 Serg:Mins. XVIII; 31/10.
4 *H.M.C.* 11, v, pp. 149, 167.
5 Pep:A.L. XIV, f. 407.
6 Serg:Mins. XVIII; 24/9.
7 *H.M.C.* 11, v, pp. 164, 173, 227.
8 Pep:A.L. XV, ff. 559–60.
9 P.R.O.Adm. 8/1, *passim*.

the behaviour of its men in the last months of the year followed much the same course as usual. It was not a particularly happy one. There were some desertions, how many it is impossible to say—Sir William Booth lost some, and Sir Francis Wheeler the whole of his ship's company in this way[1]—captains found it difficult to get men, and even more difficult to replace them,[2] while the usual disappearance from their quarters of those put sick ashore continued throughout the period. It was a familiar foundation for the political unrest which arose towards the end of the year and which, although not the real, provided the immediate cause of the widespread dissatisfaction and occasional mutiny that broke out, and had to be pacified by Proclamation, in the early months of the following reign. For to the sailor, the change of régime was significant mainly as a threat to his wages, the payment of which he still awaited from the previous reign, and the disturbances of January and February 1689 were not a consequence of, nor to be contrasted with, his behaviour in the previous three or four months, but rather, in the atmosphere of temporary instability, gave point and a rare articulation to the normal conditions of his employment, which remained unaffected by whatever Administration was in office.

III

The unsatisfactory state of the manning is the link between the autumn and the winter of 1688. Apart from that, the problems of the earlier period were exceptionally self-contained. Unaffected by diplomatic, political or financial complications, they can be examined as an isolated example of the material which at other times influenced and was influenced by such considerations. In the later period, the administrative problems were no longer purely technical; they were centred on the maintenance of a fleet at sea, and were therefore determined by decisions not themselves taken on administrative grounds. They came to an end, not with the solution of their material difficulties, but with the end of a campaign and a policy which they in turn influenced but did not exclusively control, and which is associated not with a technical process but with a government and a reign.

---

[1] *H.M.C.* 11, v, pp. 161, 200. [2] Pep:A.L. xv, ff. 265–6.

The campaign which dictated the administrative measures did not exercise them unduly. Its direction was decided on 2 and 3 November, when the Dutch, prevented by a north-easterly wind from continuing towards the east coast, altered course to the westward, leaving the English windbound behind them in the Gunfleet. Their luck held. The wind, after bringing them safely to the Devonshire coast, veered to the south on the morning of the 5th and dropped to a light air, turning a navigational error on the part of the leading ship into a perfect landfall at Torbay and, by its continuation until the afternoon of the 6th, enabling William to land most of his troops in a calm that could never have been expected at that time of year. It then continued to veer to the south-west, and rose to a gale during the night, forcing the English ships, by now coming down Channel in pursuit, to turn back for the Downs. The fleet on which James had placed all his hopes had, through sheer misfortune, lost the first round.[1]

It continued to lose the rest, though from now on the Protestant wind was not alone responsible. The initial reverse was followed by ten days of indecision, during which Dartmouth stayed in the Downs with an exaggerated idea of the enemy's strength, while James hesitated to give him any definite orders. It was not until the 12th that it was at last agreed that the fleet should again attempt to engage the Dutch, using Spithead as a rendezvous and Portsmouth as a base. After a few more days, during which head winds prevailed, it sailed on the 16th for the west.[2] But once again, the weather was against it. On the afternoon of the 19th, it was within sight of the Dutch masts in Torbay, but a few hours later a repetition of the earlier south-westerly storm forced it first to lie to and then to bear away to the east. On the 22nd, battered by the gale, and with at least eleven of his ships not in company, the unfortunate and despondent Admiral came to anchor in Spithead.[3]

He returned to a situation which had changed in three respects in the last week. At the Court and at the Admiralty unrelieved gloom had replaced the pugnacity of ten days before, and James, in the flood of

[1] The possible strategic disadvantages of its original station cannot be said to affect this as a statement of the position on 7 November. See Powley, loc. cit. pp. 91–4.

[2] Ibid. pp. 79–91, 98–108.

[3] Ibid. pp. 110–14, 121–2. *Memoirs relating to Lord Torrington* suggests (p. 30) that with more skill the fleet could have ridden out the storm at sea, and stayed in the west.

disasters that now seemed irresistible, was concerned only to keep the fleet intact.[1] But in the fleet, disaffection to his cause was beginning to spread. Until now it had been confined to a group of officers working influentially but not altogether successfully for the Orange cause,[2] and most of the officers and men, if not active supporters of James, had been loyal to traditional affections and hatreds which the first broadside against the Dutch was more than likely to revive. But failure had done its work, and the prospect of a stay near the land while repairs were under way was calculated, on the 22nd, to stimulate an interest in precisely those political and personal questions which an engagement on the 20th might well have allayed.[3] Finally, the Administration was becoming worried by the cost of maintaining the fleet, particularly in a season of recurrent gales.

Its subsequent history was the result of these three factors in combination. In a state of depression and indecision, it lay in Spithead and Portsmouth until Dartmouth surrendered it to William on 12 December,[4] and it passed, intact as James had hoped it would be, into the hands of his opponents. With this act a new chapter began, in different circumstances from those of its predecessor, for James's policy and the disaffection to his cause disappeared with James. But the business of maintenance did not. It would not have done so even if the campaign had gone otherwise. It is indeed worth imagining for a moment that this had occurred: that Dartmouth had in fact been able to meet the Dutch on the 20th and had gained a decisive victory. In that event, James's attitude and that of his sailors might well have been very different; but the difficulties of the Administration would have been the same. In fact, the more hard-fought the victory, the more they would have grown. To see the legacy of the mobilization and the campaign, therefore, it is necessary to look beyond the two factors which disappeared with its close to the third factor which survived, and briefly to examine the material and financial cost of maintaining the fleet.

---

[1] Tanner, *E.H.R.* VIII, pp. 282–3; *H.M.C.* 11, V, pp. 211–12.

[2] *Memoirs relating to Lord Torrington*, p. 30, shows the change after the 20th.

[3] Burchett (p. 19) and, possibly following him, *Memoirs relating to Lord Torrington* (p. 29) think that disaffection would have made an action impossible as early as 5 November. I have followed Powley's comment on this (loc. cit. pp. 87–8).

[4] Powley, loc. cit. pp. 120–49.

The question of expense has so far not been touched upon, because it did not in fact affect the autumn preparations in the least. When it arose, it was as a result of events which, as outlined above, were not themselves likely to be particularly expensive. No action was fought, and the fleet as a body spent more of its time at anchor or in harbour between the beginning of November and the end of the year than it did at sea;[1] and while it may be true that it was thereby in a position to demand more stores and to carry out more minor repairs than it would otherwise have done, it was on the other hand less likely to sustain serious damage from winter wear and tear—the worst enemy, as Dartmouth remarked, that it had to face.[2] Nor was there an expensive programme of reinforcement for it at this time. Only four rated ships were ordered to fit out after it had left the Gunfleet.[3] Nevertheless, an increasing anxiety soon began to be felt in London about its supply. At first this centred on the scarcity rather than on the price of stores. 'It is to be feared', wrote Pepys on 20 November, 'if the present action continues or grows...navall commodities will...be out of the power of money to purchase, at least for some species of them, and for many within any reasonable time.'[4] It was a bad season of the year for the supply of imported goods, which were particularly in demand. Individual shipments came in from time to time, but the unpopularity of the winter voyage from the Baltic prevented more than an occasional delivery.

The argument, however, changed from scarcity to expense a few days later, when the strategic implications of the storm of 20 and 21 November had already inclined the King towards an abandonment of the campaign. The economies soon came. On the 29th, Dartmouth was instructed, for financial as well as material reasons, not to fit out any ships unless they were absolutely required to replace others, and six fireships which had been ordered were to be cancelled unless their contracts had already been signed.[5] More followed on 10 December, when the press came to an end, and when work was stopped on one of three rated ships which had been ordered to fit out a month before.[6]

[1] It stayed at Spithead from 22 November to 30 December. Individual ships, of course, put to sea from the fleet during that time.

[2] *H.M.C.* 11, v, p. 200.

[3] Ibid. p. 194.

[4] Ibid. p. 208.

[5] Ibid. p. 218.

[6] Ibid. pp. 194, 227.

The motif of economy ran through the short remainder of the reign, leaving its imprint upon the early decisions of its successor.

The navy was not alone in its growing financial difficulties. The other services, indeed, were in a worse state. The disorganization in the army had by now spread to the pay department,[1] and the Ordnance was in desperate straits. On 22 November, according to Musgrave, there was not a penny in the office in cash, and by 1 December 'the great weight of debt upon them, the impoverishment of their best and ablest creditors, merchants and artificers...and the exhaustion of their stores, render them incapable of furnishing the least part of the land forces or the smallest squadron (nay ship) of the fleet'.[2] The forces, as they complained, were not getting sufficiently large or frequent payments from the Treasury. It is not difficult to see why. The national revenue which reached the Exchequer in the financial year 1688–9 was £1,979,650; in 1687–8 it had been £2,233,220.[3] It had therefore decreased by £253,570 in a year of military expansion, and, with the financial methods at its command, the government could not meet all its increased commitments out of a falling or even a stationary income. Nevertheless, it tried to do so. Its Exchequer payments amounted in 1688–9 to £2,125,831, an excess of £146,181 over its receipts, and only £10,089 less than its corresponding payments in 1687–8, when there was a proportionately higher revenue.[4] In these conditions, any expansion was difficult to finance, but a sudden expansion was particularly difficult. Thanks to their technical requirements, the increase of both the army and the Ordnance was of this nature, and both could not therefore be satisfied. The payments to the former increased from £321,135 between Easter and Michaelmas 1688, to £621,426 between that Michaelmas and the following Easter; but those to the latter, so far from increasing, fell from £62,551 in the first period to £58,355 in the second.[5]

---

[1] J. W. Fortescue, *A History of the British Army* (1910), I, p. 335.

[2] *H.M.C.* 11, v, pp. 211, 222.

[3] *Cal.Treas.Bks. 1685–9*, p. xxx. These figures do not cover the total revenue and may not represent an equal proportion of it in both cases. An unknown, and probably variable amount, was diverted before reaching the Exchequer. William Lowndes, the Secretary of the Treasury, left figures which are possibly more accurate, but which unfortunately do not cover the periods required (see ibid. p. xxxi).

[4] Ibid. [5] Ibid.

The payments to the navy for the same periods show the difference between its case and that of the other two services. They rose from £213,976 to £232,068—a comparatively slight increase to a figure which was itself less by £2138 than the corresponding figure for the year before.[1] Compared with the payments to the army, these were small; unlike those to the Ordnance, they bore some relation to the increase in expenditure. For in this case Peter was not being robbed to pay Paul. Although payment was not complete, it was regular and, throughout the summer and early autumn, more substantial than the payments to the other services.[2] A weekly sum from what remained of the annual allocation of £400,000, usually amounting to £7000, was regularly paid until the middle of November,[3] and the correspondence of the autumn is remarkably free from references to financial difficulties.

The moderate nature of the increase was due not so much to any financial manipulation on the part of the Treasury as to the moderate nature of the naval requirements themselves. The fact that the preparations in the autumn were based on a programme of repair and supply already in existence, enabled them to be supported by money which had been spent over the past two years. The good state of the ships, the small increase in the numbers of dockyard workmen, the use of stores already in the sheds, meant that the Administration was not faced with sudden and heavy demands for cash.[4] The danger confronting it lay

---

[1] *Cal.Treas.Bks. 1685–9*, p. xxx.

[2] Cf. the figures in *Cal.Treas.Bks. 1685–9*, pt IV, for May to September. They may be found through the index, on pp. 2202, 2496 and 2511.

[3] Ibid., through p. 2496.

[4] Shaw, in his introduction to *Cal.Treas.Bks. 1685–9*, remarks that the tables of expenditure (i.e. Exchequer payments) of James's reign 'show that the greater part of the additional revenue which James enjoyed [over that of Charles II] was spent on the Army. In view of the statements which are widely made as to James's solicitude for the Navy and in view of James's own language on the subject when addressing his Parliament, we should have expected that whatever excess of revenue he received over and above that enjoyed by Charles II he would have spent on the Navy. The...tables do not bear this out at all.' (Ibid. p. xciii.) This statement completely ignores the different technical requirements of the army and navy, and the different purposes for which they were used. The navy, as has been seen, did not require unlimited money to achieve its objects. Nor were those objects themselves unlimited; they were related to foreign competition and to national resources of which money was only

rather in the future, if the expansion continued beyond a certain length of time, and its attention was fixed therefore not on the lack of money with which to finance a new burden, but on the threat to its credit which would come later if that burden were prolonged. The expenditure of 1686–8, which had largely paid for the mobilization, was designed to come to an end while that was in progress. Retrenchment, therefore, was necessary as soon as possible if future embarrassment were to be avoided; and it is for that reason, rather than because money was plentiful, that the emphasis in the references to the problem was on credit rather than on want.[1]

The problem was faced on 10 November, at a meeting of the Treasury and the Navy Board in the King's presence. A scheme was then agreed upon, for preserving the good credit of the navy, by applying £1000 a week for seven weeks to the payment of arrears for stores, workmanship, freight and wages.[2] In the event, most of the money went to the merchants, who must be kept quiet if they were to refill the rapidly emptying magazines in the spring, and they soon found that a threat to stop supplies would bring immediate relief.[3] The workmen in the yards came second, and were paid, if possible, when delay might otherwise ensue. The sailor, and the officer afloat, had to take his chance. The total of their wages was the one branch of expenditure, falling under the review of the Navy Office, which had risen suddenly and rapidly. Its payment was completely neglected. In the summer, the most regular allocation of the weekly payments had been made to clear the arrears of wages to the fleet still outstanding from before March 1686,[4] and by the end of 1688 these had been reduced to a sum of £4797, compared with the £9421 still owing to the yards and ordinary for the same period. But at the same time the wages to seamen still unpaid for the period since March 1686 amounted to

---

one. To expect the King to spend 'whatever excess of revenue he received...on the Navy' is to disregard both the economic and the diplomatic reasons for such expenditure, and to make a comparison with another service which is entirely unreal.

[1] Pep:A.L. XV, ff. 555–6; *H.M.C.* 11, v, p. 218.

[2] *Cal.Treas.Bks. 1685–9*, p. 2120.

[3] Serg:Mins. XVIII; 24/12.

[4] *Cal.Treas.Bks. 1685–9*, pts III and IV, *passim*. The last one was on 25 September (p. 2080). For those between pp. 1845 and 2080 see p. 2496.

£85,244, compared with £5403 to the yards.[1] It was therefore apt to convey a false impression, although no doubt strictly in accordance with the facts, to say, as did Pepys, that:

not a *Penny* [was] left unpaid to any *Officer*, *Seaman*, *Workman*, *Artificer* or *Merchant*, for any *Service* done in, or *Commodity* delivered to the use of the *Navy*, either at sea or on shore, within the whole time of this *Commission*, where the Party claiming the same was in the way to receive it, and had (if an *Accountant*) done his part, as much, towards entitling himself to Payment.[2]

To a seaman turned over from an incoming to an outgoing ship, or abroad in the Mediterranean or the West Indies, such a statement would not have been of much comfort.

The concentration on the payment of the merchants and, to a lesser extent, the workmen, achieved its immediate object. The credit of the navy still held in the spring of 1689, when new plans demanded a fresh effort of supply. This cannot be ascribed solely to the satisfaction of the merchants' claims, for in fact that was not complete,[3] but largely to the fact that they needed the navy as the navy needed them. Provided that its credit was at all reasonable, they would continue to deal with what was for some of them their biggest customer; and their willingness to do so was shown particularly at the end of the year, when business was temporarily at a standstill in the prevalent confusion, but when their tenders continued to come in despite the knowledge that no agreements could be made.[4] The standard of credit demanded by contractors and workmen was not, in fact, a high one; and the real weakness of the naval finances is to be seen not in this type of business, but in those activities which resembled the problems of the other armed forces, when a sudden increase in expenditure was demanded to finance the imposition of a new burden. The manning of the fleet was such a problem, but, as has been seen, that could be temporarily shelved; and it was in the victualling that the essential instability of naval finance was revealed.

1 Serg.MS. A 133; Navy Office estimate of debt on 31 December 1688.

2 *Memoires*, p. 148.

3 I cannot substantiate this remark with any figures, for I have not found a statement of the debt due to contractors at the end of 1688. References, however, are made throughout the Navy Board minutes of January to March 1689 to back payments and arrears (Serg:Mins. XVIII, XIX).

4 E.g. Serg:Mins. XVIII; 31/12, 9/1.

The Victuallers, unlike the Navy Board, had got into difficulties in the autumn. Their supplies of money had been calculated on the basis of the annual declaration for a force of 10,000 men, and failed to meet the initial demands of the mobilization. By 29 September, they were asking for £10,000 to enable them to carry on.[1] They were given £3000, and a further £5000 on the 17th. For the next three weeks they were paid regularly, and received £9000 in all. But their difficulties continued. On 9 November they appeared at the Navy Office to tell the Board that they could not carry on without immediate assistance. The weekly payments were therefore kept up—£2000 on the 16th, £3000 on the 23rd—but presumably their complaints had by now gone beyond the Treasurer of the Navy, for at the end of the month the Treasury intervened directly to ensure that they should not be neglected. On the 28th, £5000 of the weekly payment to the navy was specifically allocated 'for the victualling', and the Navy Office was docked accordingly. A further £2000 followed in the same way on 4 December.[2] This may have satisfied the Victuallers, for no more payments were made to them for five weeks after this. With the fleet now theoretically provisioned for three months, and the problem therefore merely one of maintenance, the crisis may have been thought to be over.

In the middle of November this replenishment was already under way.[3] By 1 December, however, no results were as yet visible in the fleet. Dartmouth was apparently already getting worried, for Pepys assured him that the King himself, and his ministers, were concerned in getting more supplies to the ships.[4] It is surprising, in view of the expressions of satisfaction from the fleet only five weeks before, that in the first week of December there should have been serious anxiety over the amount of food aboard.[5] The explanation would seem to lie in those discrepancies between the Victuallers' and the pursers' estimates of the quantities supplied, and between the latter and the quantities actually consumed, which have already been mentioned. As Pepys remarked, 'the service may meet with disappointment...if the commissioners of

[1] Ibid. 1/10. The rest of this paragraph, except when stated, is based on this authority, and the references will be found under the appropriate dates.

[2] *Cal.Treas.Bks. 1685–9*, pp. 2136, 2138.

[3] *H.M.C.* 11, v, p. 201.

[4] Ibid. p. 221.

[5] Ibid. pp. 227, 232, 273.

the victualling here goe by one reckoning and the men eat by another'.[1] The short measure was particularly serious in view of the fleet's distance from its source of supply. Portsmouth was unable to provide more than a month's food, and, after the arrival of some vessels from the Thames by the 6th, the ships received no further replenishments, for westerly winds kept those that had been collected by the middle of the month immobilized in the river.[2] By the 20th Dartmouth was so short that he was considering sailing for the Nore, and James's last, mysterious note to him referred to this possibility.[3] In the end, after an anxious month, the wind changed and by the close of the year the fleet was again adequately provisioned.

Much worry might thus have been avoided if the ships could have been supplied from the Portsmouth area. If there had been any money, Haddock assured Pepys, this could have been done, but as it was he advised Dartmouth to put the fleet to short allowance.[4] The experiences of December, indeed, had plunged the Victuallers back into the financial morass from which they had only just emerged, and the circle of lack of money and shortage of provisions was becoming a vicious one. The succession of appeals began again, but at their height a stop was put on all payments to the navy, owing to James's departure, and this lasted until early in January 1689. Not until the 9th did the Victuallers receive any money at all.[5] By that time, they were well in debt, and pledging their personal credit to maintain supplies.[6] In January and February, therefore, a determined effort had to be made to restore the situation; £26,000 was allocated to them by the end of the first month, of which £23,000 was designed to help clear the arrears, and a further £34,000 followed in the second. In March, the more normal rate of £4000 for the whole month was again reached.[7]

It is impossible to say how much the mobilization and the campaign cost altogether. That would require a detailed statement of the full naval debt as it stood at the beginning of August and of the following

---

[1] *H.M.C.* 11, v, p. 218. [2] Powley, loc. cit. p. 153; *H.M.C.* 11, v, p. 238.

[3] *H.M.C.* 11, v, p. 240. [4] Ibid.

[5] Serg:Mins. XVIII; 18/12, 14/1; P.R.O.Adm. 49/173, f. 3.

[6] Pep:A.L. XV, f. 527.

[7] *Cal.Treas.Bks. 1685–9*, pp. 2148, 2153, 2157, 2161, 2165; P.R.O.Adm. 49/173, ff. 3–4.

January, as well as an account of the money received during that time from the Exchequer. But statements of debt were seldom drawn up more than once a year, and it is not known how much the deficit increased in the last five months of 1688. It is not even quite certain how much it amounted to at the end of that year. The Navy Board first estimated it at £162,830. 19*s.* and later, in October 1689, at £159,537. 16*s.* 7*d.*; but this did not include the debt for victuals or stores.[1] The former came possibly to £27,853. 6*s.* 5*d.*[2] and if an overall figure of £200,000 is taken, perhaps that is not very wide of the mark.

If, therefore, we agree with Pepys that the navy in December 1688 was in a better condition than it had ever been before, except in 1679, we may do so for different reasons. After a mobilization and a campaign lasting four and a half months, and undertaken in favourable conditions, largely of his own making, the navy was in debt to approximately half of its annual expenditure, its stores were unevenly distributed and in some cases uncomfortably low, its victualling recently proved to be a costly and only partially redeemed failure, its men deserting, unpaid and—as it proved in another few weeks—occasionally mutinous, and the loyalty of its officers profoundly disturbed. That despite all this, it was undoubtedly in a better state than it had been five years before, or was to be one year later, is a sufficient commentary on the conditions in which it operated. The fact that such contrasts could so easily be

---

[1] P.R.O.Adm. 1/3558, f. 235; Serg.MS. A 133, loc. cit.

[2] The only statement of the victualling debt on 31 December, which I have been able to discover, is contained in P.R.O. T. 1/3, no. 3. Unlike the brief reference to it in *Cal.Treas.Papers*, I, p. 31, this is not a clear account. It contains three lists of debts: (1) 'Moneys owing at the Victualling Office for victualling H.M. Navy', which are given as £21,650. 6*s.* 10*d.*; (2) 'An Account of Money due for Victualling their Majesties' Navy before the 31st December 1688 and since paid', which comes to £27,288. 18*s.* 5*d.*; (3) 'Money due for Victualling their Majesties' Navy before the 31st December 1688 and not yet paid', which comes to £564. 8*s.* Some of the items given in (1) correspond with those in (2), others do not; (1), however, would seem to have been compiled while James was still on the throne, and 'moneys owing at the Victualling Office' is an obscure phrase. It has seemed to me that this list is a statement of debt which is given more fully and clearly, although possibly not in the same form, in the two later statements (2) plus (3). It must be remembered that a complete list of debts was probably impossible at the end of the year to which it referred, which would account for the difference between the respective totals.

drawn, and that the state of a department and of a fleet could apparently show such variation in so short a time, is evidence precisely of the compelling and unchanging circumstances which demanded so great a contribution from personal management. It was by the exercise of individual forethought and energy that Pepys and his associates were able to achieve as much as they did; with their disappearance, the obstacles which they partially overcame again appeared to dominate the scene, and to emphasize for contemporaries the contrast, and for ourselves the similarity, between the last months of James and Pepys and the first months of William and the Board of Admiralty.

CHAPTER IX

THE BOARD OF ADMIRALTY AND THE FIRST YEAR OF THE WAR JANUARY 1689–APRIL 1690

I

On 7 May 1689, after almost a month's open hostility, England declared war upon France. By that time, the scene of five months before had almost completely changed. The head of the naval administration had become a fugitive on enemy soil, and the form of naval government had changed from a Lord High Admiral to a Commission of Admiralty; the Secretary of the Admiralty, with whom the achievements of the past five years had been identified, had been replaced by a minor official who, at the earlier date, had been out of work and soliciting him for a job; the fleet had come under the command of an Admiral who, a few months before, had been commanding the enemy force; and that enemy itself had become an ally, and had concluded a naval treaty which was to form the basis of maritime co-operation for the next twenty-five years. It was an important and a confused period, in which the foundations for the conduct of the ensuing war were being laid. But to contemporaries, its interest lay less in its long-term possibilities than in the immediate misfortunes by which it was distinguished.

For the activities of these months ended in a natural climax, when on 1 May the first engagement took place between the English and the French at Bantry Bay, on the Irish coast; and for us, as for the men at the time,[1] their significance falls into a perspective determined by this result. It was not an encouraging one. The numbers and strength of the opponents were as shown on p. 246.

[1] *H.M.C.* 12th Report, appendix, pt VI, pp. 134–92; 'An Impartial Inquiry into the Causes of the Present Disasters' (1692), in *A Collection of State Tracts Publish'd during the Reign of King William III*, II (1706), p. 224.

	French[1]	English[4]
Third rates	18[2]	8
Fourth rates	6[3]	10
Fifth rates	5 frigates	1
Sixth rates		—
Fireships	10	3
Total ships	39	22
Total guns	1266	1094

It was a depressing comparison. But it could be paralleled by another. On 1 May, the English squadron consisted of 22 ships: on 31 December there had been at sea a fleet of three times that size. The question to be asked was obvious: what had happened in the intervening months to turn the former well-organized concentration which faced the Dutch into the weak and miscellaneous collection of odd ships which later had to face the French?

The problem seemed the odder in that no units of the fleet had been laid up and paid off during that time. But this continuity was more apparent than real. There were in fact three distinct periods between the middle of December and the end of April, in each of which a different policy was pursued. The first was marked by William's initial decision to lay up the fleet; the second, by his abandonment of that intention for a limited objective of three small squadrons; the third, by his announcement of the final and more ambitious policy for the year. In all three periods, the factors to be considered were the same: on the one hand, there was William's overriding interest, which had brought him to England, the employment of her resources in the war against France; on the other, the material condition of the fleet as a result of the activities of the autumn and winter; and thirdly, operating upon these two constant factors, were the variable and contingent circumstances of domestic interest and personal inclination.

Although the original invitation to William of 30 June 1688 had concerned itself exclusively with domestic affairs, it was understood and generally accepted that his successful intervention would mean the

---

1 Roncière, op. cit. IV, pp. 47–8; *Soc. Naut. Research, Occas. Publns*, no. 5, pt II, *passim*; Laird Clowes, op. cit. II, p. 328, with which cf. Burchett, pp. 21–2. I have given the total number of French ships available; some failed to engage.

2 One sometimes counted as a second rate (*Ardent*), and one as a fourth (*Fendant*).

3 One sometimes counted as a third rate (*Neptune*).

4 Laird Clowes, op. cit. II, p. 328.

replacement of the neutrality practised by James by an overt hostility to France. But such a step could not be taken immediately, and William's first orders to the English force were merely the continuation and, as it seemed, the completion of his predecessor's. The Dutch ships in Torbay had received instructions early in December, suitable to the state of war that had existed, on Louis's side, since 26 November: they were to attack French men of war and to seize French merchantmen whenever encountered. These orders, moreover, were extended to apply to such English ships as should declare for the Orange cause.[1] But by definition this committed the English rebels, and not the English forces. When Dartmouth surrendered the fleet on 12 December, William's first orders were for it to sail from Spithead to the Nore, leaving a squadron of only thirteen sail behind from which cruising frigates might be sent 'to prevent any affront that may be committed by the French or others'.[2] His other arrangements for this force were purely precautionary. On the 25th he protected the Harwich packets with a group of four frigates stationed between Harwich and Flanders, and Dover and Calais; he forestalled a French occupation of the Channel Islands by sending a few of the lesser rates to cruise off Guernsey—a step apparently recommended by Dartmouth;[3] at the end of the year, he used some men-of-war on trooping duties to the Isle of Wight;[4] and he rounded off his dispositions by despatching two frigates to Chester and two small fourth rates to the Irish coast.[5] By 1 January, when his small winter guard had risen to eighteen sail,[6] his initial arrangements were complete.

Meanwhile, in the orders to the main fleet, the emphasis, as under James, lay on economy. As early as 26 December, according to Pepys, William was talking of retrenchment.[7] By the 29th, he took the serious step of deciding to lay up and pay off all the third rates and the larger fourths, and all those smaller fourths and below which had not already been reserved for the winter squadron.[8] By 3 January, the detailed list of ships to be laid up had been prepared, and that night it was sent to

[1] E. Maunde Thompson, 'Correspondence of Admiral Herbert during the Revolution', in *E.H.R.* I, p. 533.

[2] *H.M.C.* 11, v, p. 283; orders of 16 December.

[3] Ibid. p. 239.

[4] Ibid. p. 246.

[5] Ibid. pp. 243, 246.

[6] Ibid. p. 243.

[7] Ibid. p. 241.

[8] Ibid. pp. 242–3.

meet Dartmouth as he passed through the Downs on his way to the Thames.[1] But the next morning the orders were cancelled, and the fleet was directed to remain at the Nore until further notice.[2] In the event, they were never put into effect.

The cancellation was due to the successful issue of William's appeal for a loan from the City of London. At the end of December he had asked for £200,000 to meet the immediate demands of the army, the navy and Ireland. It was subscribed in four days, and the large individual amounts from some of the bigger merchants showed that the new régime had the backing of some powerful financial interests.[3] This afforded a relief from the most pressing demands upon the Exchequer, and enabled the complete demobilization of the fleet to be avoided; but it was not a supply that could be regularly repeated, and the orders to the fleet continued throughout the first half of the month to stress the need for economy. Complements, where possible, were reduced to a minimum; ships were put into Petty Warrant victuals;[4] and the new dispositions themselves did not depart from the limits which seemed to have been inherited by William with the previous Administration.

They did not, however, like the earlier orders, originate from that Administration. Until the early days of January its influence, as represented by Pepys, seems not to have declined so much as might have been expected. If the Secretary did not serve his new master with enthusiasm, at least he continued to serve him, with the efficiency which was by now a second nature to him. On his side, William was prepared to use any instruments that lay to hand, particularly when they were of this calibre; and it may not be fanciful to see in the similarity of his first with James's last measures, the presence of an administrator to whom the preservation of recent achievements and the maintenance of future credit were as important as any change of régime and of policy. But at the beginning of the new year, Pepys was joined in London by Arthur Herbert, the English commander of the Dutch expedition to Torbay. Herbert had stayed in the west until the last week of December,

[1] *H.M.C.* 11, v, p. 248. [2] Ibid. p. 249.

[3] Luttrell, op. cit. I, p. 496; Sir James Mackintosh, *A History of the Revolution in England in 1688* (1834), p. 581.

[4] Pep: A.L. xv, f. 528.

but with the dispersal of the Dutch ships on the 26th his responsibility there came to an end, and on that same day William was hoping to see him in town.[1] Exactly when he arrived is not certain, but he was certainly there by the 12th, for on that day a conference was held between the Prince, himself, Pepys and Edward Russell, the other prominent English sailor who had sailed in William's expedition.[2] At this meeting, and mainly on Herbert's initiative,[3] the details of the new dispositions were worked out and were sent off to the Navy Board on the same day. They provided for three squadrons, for the Mediterranean, the Channel and Ireland, the composition of which was as follows:

	Mediterranean	Channel	Ireland	Total
Third rates	4	1	—	5
Fourth rates	8	5	6	19
Sixth rates	—	—	2	2
Total	12	6	8	26

The Mediterranean squadron was to be manned with its middle complement, and victualled wet for four months and dry for six; the squadrons for the Channel and for Ireland were to have their highest complements, and the former was to have at least two months' victuals and if possible more. The remaining 35 of the original 61 ships were to come into port, there to stay in reserve. None was to be laid up or paid off, but all were to be reduced to their lowest complements.[4] On the 16th, three fireships were added to the squadron for the Mediterranean.[5]

The extent of these preparations was not perceptibly different from those of the previous spring, when a total of 26 ships was also put to sea. In this case, however, almost half the force was designed for the Mediterranean, and a bare fourteen ships were left for home waters. But the limitations of the programme corresponded with a situation which was still undecided; in which neither approval for a foreign alliance, nor parliamentary financial support had yet been secured, and in which the authority of William himself was still legally ambiguous. It is not surprising that the dispositions of 12 January were limited in their scope. But it is surprising that they were not modified for the

[1] Powley, loc. cit. pp. 159–60.
[2] Pep:A.L. xv, f. 527; Bryant, loc. cit. p. 370.
[3] Pep:A.L. xv, f. 554.
[4] Bodl. Rawl. A 186, ff. 122–5.
[5] Pep:A.L. xv, ff. 537–8.

next two months, which were vital to William's security, and during which there might have seemed every reason for him to act energetically.

When the final orders came, it was on 16 March.[1] They provided for a total strength at sea of 87 men-of-war, and ten fireships. The main fleet was composed as follows:

Second rates	1
Third rates	17
Fourth rates	32
Smaller rates	15
Total men-of-war	65
Fireships	8

Of these 65 ships, 30 were designed for the Mediterranean.[2] The remaining 22 men-of-war and two fireships were allocated for convoys and cruisers, and, apart from the third rate *Mountague*, were all hired ships.[3] With these orders, the country embarked upon the first year of the war with France.

Neither the date on which they were promulgated, nor the orders of 16 March themselves, were the result of purely English developments. It is true that only four days before, on the 12th, James had landed at Kinsale;[4] but the news had not yet reached London, while rumours of it had been circulating for several weeks,[5] and as early as 27 February William himself had mentioned its probability to Parliament.[6] The final strength of the fleet was no more symptomatic of domestic events than the date on which it was announced. Both were solely the result of an external process, the negotiations for a naval treaty which were at that time under way with the Dutch.

As early as 20 December, William had been making arrangements for the States General to send over a mission to discuss the nature of Anglo-

1 *Cal.S.P.Dom. 1689–90*, p. 27.

2 P.R.O.Adm. 3/1: 21/3.

3 Ibid. 23/3.

4 *H.M.C. Buccleugh*, II, pt I, p. 36.

5 Luttrell, op. cit. I, p. 519. According to Lord Wolseley, *The Life of John Churchill, Duke of Marlborough to the Accession of Queen Anne*, II (1894), pp. 89–90, William received the confirmation of the news only when dressing for his coronation, on 11 April. For rumours, see *Memoirs of Sir John Reresby* (1932), ed. A. Browning, p. 562; *The State Letters of Henry Earl of Clarendon...and...Diary*, II (1763), p. 171.

6 White Kennet, *Compleat History of England*, III, p. 517.

Dutch co-operation.[1] The deputies arrived in England on 18 January, and began, slowly and with many disappointments, to work out the details of an alliance. But technical naval matters did not fall within their scope, and on the 24th William asked for a mission of experts to be sent, representing the five Admiralty Colleges. This mission arrived early in March, and stayed until the middle of April to conclude its arrangements. It then went home, leaving the original deputies to sign the naval treaty on 21 May.[2]

The contents of this treaty were suggested by the Dutch. The estimates of the enemy's strength, and the detailed proposals for allied co-operation, came from them and were in the main accepted. They were not indeed new to all the English negotiators, for these consisted of Nottingham, the newly appointed Secretary of State for northern affairs, within whose province the treaty fell, Edward Russell, Arthur Herbert and later, when Herbert went to sea in April, Lord Carbery, a member of the recently created Admiralty Commission. Of the three original deputies, therefore, two had come from Holland, where they had discussed, and probably evolved, the general plans for the joint fleets with William and Hiob de Wildt, the secretary of the Amsterdam Admiralty;[3] and the other was not himself in a position to modify the main lines of a scheme which had been worked out under the personal supervision of the Prince.

The alliance itself, moreover, was not new. It existed already in the Treaty of Westminster of 3 March 1678, which provided for assistance, with a minimum of twenty ships, on the part of one power when the other was attacked by a third party, and in the supplementary Treaty of 26 July of the same year, according to which the proportions of a joint force were to be three English ships to two Dutch. But in 1689 the Dutch, working on an estimate of a French fleet of eighty and a

---

[1] The following account of the negotiations is taken from G. N. Clark, *The Dutch Alliance and the War against French Trade* (1923), and J. C. M. Warnsinck, *De Vloot van den Stadthouder Koningk, 1689–90* (1935). The text of the ensuing treaty is given in *European Treaties bearing on the History of the United States and its Dependencies*, ed. F. G. Davenport (1929), II, pp. 332–3.

[2] It was dated 29 April, presumably to suggest that agreement had been reached before England declared war (Clark, loc. cit. p. 40).

[3] J. C. De Jonge, *Geschiedenis van het Nederlansche Zeewezen*, III (1858–62), pp. 194–5.

Dutch force of thirty rated ships, proposed that the existing proportions should be altered from three to two, to five to three, so as to enable the allies to face their enemy on equal terms. At the first meeting on 9 March they accordingly asked for an English quota of fifty men-of-war, and at the same time suggested the dispositions for the joint fleet. Fifty men-of-war were to be provided for the Channel and Irish Sea and thirty for the Mediterranean, with an additional ten frigates to cruise for the protection of commerce between Dover and Holland. The Mediterranean squadron was a heavy one, and it has been maintained that its size was due to William himself.[1] Certainly the emphasis on such a squadron in the original dispositions of 12 January would seem to support the view that, even at this early date, he had in mind the advantages to be gained from a strong force operating in that sensitive and diplomatically vital area. The proposals were all accepted within a week, and the orders of 16 March followed.

Two minor Dutch proposals met with opposition and eventual defeat. The first was a plan for a joint expedition to American waters, for the protection of the Plantations and, presumably, the expansion of mutual interests in that area. But the English refused to acknowledge the existence of such interests, and although the idea was later revived it was never accepted. The other disagreement arose over the question of command. By the Treaty of Westminster, the joint forces were to be under the direction of the power which had been first attacked by the mutual enemy; but in 1689 the English claimed the right of permanent control over the allied fleet by the senior English officer present, whatever his rank. On this point all the English deputies agreed. Herbert indeed had already debated it when he insisted on commanding William's expedition in November 1688,[2] and it gave rise to more trouble during the following summer.[3] Bentinck considered that the lengthy wrangles which it engendered were of trivial interest; but to the Dutch deputies with their eyes on opinion at home the outcome was evidently of importance, and for us, if not important, it is at any rate significant. Questions of allied seniority often reflect, better than wider measures of strategy and organization, the true

[1] Warnsinck, loc. cit. p. 22.

[2] Gilbert Burnet, *History of My Own Time*, III (1823), pp. 285–6.

[3] *H.M.C. Finch*, II, pp. 214, 219; P.R.O.Adm. 2/169, f. 159.

relations of the partners; and in an age when etiquette was still an embodiment of function, it is not surprising that in its technicalities should be found the suspicion, and the memories of recent antagonism, which were sublimated in the weightier clauses of the treaty. In the end the English got their way, and the alliance was drawn up. With its conclusion, the lines had been laid down on which the co-operation of the 'Maritime Powers' was to continue throughout the two long wars of William and Anne.

But if the character and date of the English preparations were thus determined by the negotiations with the Dutch, this does not itself account for the passivity which marked the two months after 12 January. It would still have been possible to reinforce the original three squadrons on a purely domestic basis, and to modify their original dispositions in the light of changing events. But it was only about 11 March that they were combined into one force under the command of Herbert,[1] and only on the 20th that this was augmented by some of the ships ordered to fit out on the 16th.[2]

In view of this, the first question to be asked is whether William was given adequate and early warning about the Irish situation. According to witnesses in the summer of 1689, he was. From the end of December, deputations and letters, many from credible sources, followed each other at frequent intervals across the Irish Sea.[3] They were not, moreover, disregarded. William promised his support on several occasions,[4] and reminded Parliament three times—on 28 January, 18 February and 8 March—of the necessity for subduing the Catholic rebellion,[5] which as early as 30 December he had connected with the possibility of a French landing with James at its head.[6]

---

[1] I have been unable to discover the exact date of this order. On the 11th it was already known to Herbert, but it must then have been fairly recent (*H.M.C. Finch*, II, pp. 194–5).

[2] See p. 262 below.

[3] *H.M.C.* 12th Report, appendix, pt VI, pp. 137–41, 143–4. This will henceforth be referred to as *H.M.C.* 12, VI.

[4] Ibid. pp. 137, 139, 143.

[5] *H.C.J.* X, pp. 9, 30, 45.

[6] H. C. Foxcroft, *The Life and letters of...Halifax*, II (1898), appendix to ch. XIII, pp. 201–2. This appendix consists of Halifax's 'Spencer House Journals'. Where references are made to it in future, they will be to 'Spencer House Journals'; where they are made to other parts of the book, they will be in the usual form.

An attempt, indeed, was made during this period to settle the problem by negotiating with James's viceroy in Ireland, the Duke of Tyrconnel. It ended in disaster. The parts played by the various actors—the duplicity of Richard Hamilton and of Tyrconnel himself, the gullibility of Richard Temple, the possible gullibility of William—have been discussed in detail by historians from Oldmixon and Ralph to Macaulay. Two arguments have been pursued: first, that William, following the advice of Halifax, deliberately prolonged negotiations which he knew must fail, to ensure his own indispensability in the ensuing confusion; secondly, that he was completely misled by them, that he pinned all his faith upon them, and that consequently when they failed he was unable to enter Ireland with an adequate force until it was too late.

The first possibility is unlikely. It comes from the suspect source of Danby, the Lord President of the Council and the great opponent of Halifax, who in any case was not at this time one of the inner circle where the decisions were known and taken.[1] It was not, moreover, an argument likely to appeal to a Prince whose main, indeed whose only, concern was to settle all confusions which might interrupt the prosecution of his policy to bring English strength into the quarrel with France.

The second possibility must be taken more seriously. William undoubtedly lent himself to the negotiations, and was thus involved in their collapse. But it is unlikely that he stood or fell by them. He did not completely abandon his preparations while they were in progress, although, for various reasons, these did not amount to much. Precisely because of this, however, he had every incentive to wish for the success of a peaceful alternative; and perhaps the most that can be said is that he pinned his hopes, even if not his entire faith, upon it.

It is not in the negotiations themselves, but in the factors which induced William to embark upon them, that the reason for the ineffectiveness of his measures is to be sought. These factors were of two kinds: first, the difficulties of material and of opinion, which frustrated his preparations; secondly, the existence of objectives other than Ireland, which constantly tended to divert them from that campaign.

The frustrations which William experienced were both naval and national. In the first place, it was doubtful whether the fleet would

---

[1] Foxcroft, op. cit. II, pp. 76–9.

fight, and if so whether it could. On the first point he himself was explicit. Danby noted at the turn of the year that 'when...I would have a squadron of ships to have been sent thither [i.e. to Ireland], I was answered by the Prince that hee durst not trust the fleet, but had putt that business into a very good way'.[1] Allowing for the mistrust which Danby himself aroused in the Prince just then, the remark is probably true enough. It was not so long since the fleet had been on its way to sink the man who was now its master, and there was no reason to suppose that it had since become entirely reconciled to the new order. The men were suspicious that they would be defrauded of their back pay,[2] while the officers were not likely to have recovered as yet from the conflict of loyalties to which they had only recently been subjected.[3] The average sea officer was not good at changing sides quickly: many of them, like Ashby, were apt to argue 'that in their profession they were not wont to turn against the King';[4] and in any event, the cabals of the previous months had been involved too much in questions of professional rivalry, apart from those of loyalty and affection, for them easily to be composed. An attempt to employ the fleet in a civil war, even though all Papist officers had been removed during December,[5] might have ended in abrupt and dramatic failure; and that was a luxury which William could not yet afford.

Nevertheless, that does not completely explain the naval inactivity. It cannot have been a paramount objection, judging by the later preparations for the employment of the fleet in March, when its attitude was still much the same as it had been in January and February, although some of the sailors had by then received their back pay. But a more useful comparison can be made with the army at the beginning of the year. Feeling there was no better than in the navy, and there were

---

[1] A. Browning, *Thomas Osborne Earl of Danby*, II (1939), p. 159. No date for this remark is given by Danby, but it appears in a memorandum of events 'att my first coming out of the North to the Prince att St. James'. This was during the last ten days of December (*H.M.C. Duke of Leeds*, p. 28; *Lindsey*, p. 455).

[2] Pep:A.L. xv, ff. 544–5.

[3] There were in fact occasional attempts by captains throughout the spring to take their ships over to James (*Cal.S.P.Dom. 1689–90*, p. 119; Luttrell, op. cit. I, pp. 530, 532).

[4] *Memoirs relating to Lord Torrington*, p. 28.

[5] Powley, loc. cit. pp. 145–6.

greater incentives to rebellion. The sight of Bluecoats at St James's was not one that appealed to London pride, and moreover while the fleet had only tried to fight the Dutch, some of the troops, however ineffectively and briefly, had fought them. A mutiny in fact took place, when on 8 March William ordered some battalions of the Guard and Line to embark for Holland.[1] But the military preparations went on, in spite of the mass desertions which took place,[2] because they were considered important. The attitude of the navy affected the argument, because the argument allowed it to do so.

The same can be said of its material condition. It may be asked whether William could afford to act in the financial circumstances of the first quarter of 1689. Faced with a naval debt of approximately £200,000 at the beginning of the year, his only income throughout January and February came from City loans.[3] The House of Commons did not begin to debate supply until 26 February, and it was 11 March before an inadequate personal revenue was settled upon the King and Queen, and 25 April before a grant was made for the maintenance of the navy itself.[4] Between 12 January and the end of March, the Exchequer paid the navy a sum of £100,377, but of that £58,377 fell between 16 January and 6 February, and after that nothing was received until 12 March; while of the £42,000 received between then and the end of the month, £37,000 was from private sources.[5] Despite these payments, in the middle of March £44,773 was still owing to the yards, and £37,150 alone to the turned-over men immediately required for sea;[6] the naval stores were in many respects still low; and there were only enough beer, biscuit and butter to last 10,000 men for one month.[7] Similar difficulties were met with in the military preparations. The magazines were so exhausted that fresh equipment had to be procured from Holland; about two-thirds of the 10,000 men disbanded by Feversham had not returned to the colours, and there was not enough

---

1 J. W. Fortescue, *History of the British Army*, I, pp. 336–7.

2 Wolseley, op. cit. pp. 98–9; *H.M.C. Portland*, III, p. 435; cf. Falkland's remark in Cobbett, *Parliamentary History*, V (1809), p. 156.

3 *Conduct*, p. 54, n. 35.

4 *Cal.Treas.Bks. 1689–92*, pp. xvi–xxxvi, cxxvii.

5 Ibid. *1685–9*, pp. 2153, 2157, 2161, 2165; ibid. *1689–92*, pp. 6, 9.

6 P.R.O.Adm. 1/3558, ff. 135–6; P.R.O.Adm. 3/1: 11/3.

7 P.R.O.Adm. 1/3558, ff. 54–5.

money to levy fresh troops; and complaints poured in every day from the counties of the thefts and indiscipline of the army.[1] But although financial disability rendered William's military policy useless, nevertheless there was a policy; while, however true it may be that naval preparations were equally handicapped, there is no indication that the Admiralty or the Navy Board were ever urged to surmount the difficulties, or indeed asked if they existed.[2] If such considerations affected William, they did so because rather than in spite of his attitude to the employment of the fleet.

The difficulties were not only naval but national. Despite the indication of Parliamentary approval on 22 January when the Convention met, and again on 4 March, when the House of Commons resolved to assist the King in the support of his allies abroad and in the reduction of Ireland,[3] its precise extent was in doubt. The debates were bitter and often inconclusive, while outside the House William's popularity was appreciably on the decline between December and March. On 13 March, indeed, Halifax remarked that if James were a Protestant he could not be kept out four months, and Danby reduced the period to a day.[4] But James did not turn Protestant, and in so far as William enjoyed the support of Parliament it was precisely for the defence of the kingdom against a Catholic return. That alone united the different interests of the Revolution, and however inadequate its appreciation of the measures involved, public concern was fixed primarily upon the outpost of that defence in Ireland. The suspicion and procrastination of the Commons, which delayed the possibility of early action there, were themselves increased by that delay; and they had originally arisen, and were not lessened by the fear that William's foreign interests were not committed so deeply as those of the nation to an immediate campaign in the west.

---

[1] C. Walton, *History of the British Standing Army 1660–1714* (1894), pp. 61–2.

[2] The authorities consulted, in none of which any such orders or questions appear, are for the Admiralty, Pep:A.L. xv, ff. 527–98, and P.R.O.Adm. 3/1, to the end of March; for the Navy Board, Serg:Mins. XVIII, XIX, January to March, P.R.O.Adm. 1/3557, ff. 847–1086, and ibid. 1/3558, ff. 1–136; and for the Secretaries of State and the Council, *H.M.C. Finch*, II, pp. 194–7, *H.M.C.* 12, VI, pp. 160–78, and *Cal.S.P.Dom. 1689–90*, pp. 1–47.

[3] *H.C.J.* x, pp. 12, 41.

[4] Reresby, loc. cit. pp. 564–5; see also ibid. p. 566.

Nor was such a fear entirely groundless. For William's idea of how the war should be fought differed from that of his subjects. An expedition to Ireland satisfied neither his diplomatic requirements nor his personal inclination. In the first place, he was constantly beset by the fear that the Confederates, and even the Dutch themselves, would desert him if his new resources were not visibly employed on their behalf;[1] and in the second, his military experience and his lifelong ambition led him to seek Louis upon his chosen and familiar ground. As soon as possible, he began sending troops out of the country to Holland;[2] and although, as King of England, he was forced to do so by the terms of the Treaty of Nimuegen,[3] as Stadtholder of Holland he was undoubtedly delighted to receive them. His objective, in fact, was France; and his intention, to reach it directly by invasion and not indirectly by a defensive war in Ireland. In his speeches to Parliament, his theme was constantly of the danger from the west, and it was to that cause that most observers attributed his impatience with the delays.[4] But in private conversation he revealed his preoccupation with a European campaign. He 'said', noted Halifax, 'that if it would be rightly understood he would land in France to save Ireland'; and slightly later 'said there was but one reason to appoint the Rendezvous to Milford, and that was not to bee told; viz. more convenient to go from thence to France'.[5] 'Hee hath such a mind to France', was Halifax's comment, 'that it would incline one to think, hee took England onely in his way'.[6] Later, on 6 and again on 24 June, he returned to the charge.[7] The difficulty of reconciling all his actions in the first half of 1689 to a common standard, lies not only in the distortion of the evidence and the intricacy of the political manœuvres of those around him, but also in the conflict with which he himself was faced, between his foreign commitments and personal intentions on the one hand, and on the other a domestic interest in which he saw a constant threat

---

[1] 'Spencer House Journals', pp. 212, 224.

[2] Pep:A.L. xv, ff. 594, 597; P.R.O.Adm. 3/1, *passim*, where references to troop convoys to Holland occur constantly from early in March.

[3] Sir Charles Firth, *A Commentary on Macaulay's History of England*, pp. 155–6.

[4] Reresby, loc. cit. p. 546.

[5] 'Spencer House Journals', pp. 218 (and n. 6), 219.

[6] Ibid. p. 219.

[7] Ibid. pp. 220, 222.

to their success and whose importance, by a process of wishful thinking, he undoubtedly underestimated.

But if this explains William's emphasis on military preparations, it does not account for his neglect of the navy. An invasion of France might have been thought to require the presence of a fleet more, and not less, than an expedition to Ireland, to protect the lines of communication against the inevitable French concentration. We are finally led to conclude that William's naval preparations were inadequate because his conception of sea power was inadequate. In his references to Ireland, he dwelt exclusively on the number of troops required;[1] the idea that James might be prevented from landing at all was never mentioned. It cannot, however, be said that he disregarded sea power altogether. His attitude towards neutral trade, with its insistence on the right of search, relied entirely on its possession; and his emphasis on a Mediterranean squadron, perhaps purely personal at this stage, showed the value which he attached to it as a diplomatic agent. But neither of these examples is particularly satisfactory. It would be rash to say whether the control of contraband was supported by a true conception of sea power, or whether an assumption that sea power would be available followed from the desirability of controlling contraband; while in the emphasis on a Mediterranean squadron may be seen William's real conception of its role—not as an indispensable but as an alternative factor in a campaign. At the back of his mind seems always to have been the idea that the best way to use a fleet was to send it where armies could not be sent. In the Mediterranean it could make a specific contribution to the campaign; in the Irish Sea or in the Channel, beyond which a campaign on land was already possible, it could be virtually disregarded. Events were later to modify this attitude. But it is curious that a war in which combined operations played a major part should have been fought under a King who, at any rate at the start, thought of the relations between land and sea warfare in this way.

Nevertheless, despite William's lack of policy, by 22 March 45 ships had been ordered to fit out for the fleet. Another nine were instructed

[1] *H.C.J.* x, p. 45.

to join between then and the end of April. Thus at one time or another, 54 ships were designed for Herbert's flag; but only 22 were present on 1 May. Within the limits of their instructions, the failure to provide a greater force would seem to rest with the administrative authorities. They had had over three and a half months in which to fit out the original three squadrons, and almost six weeks in which to do the same for the first and most considerable reinforcements. What, therefore, had happened to the missing 32 ships?[1]

As early as 2 February, things were not going according to plan. On 11 January, the main body of Dartmouth's fleet had anchored at the Nore, and the rest were on their way back to Portsmouth after accompanying him as far as the Downs.[2] Following the orders of the 12th, the supplementary instructions were given quickly, and by the 16th the yards and the ships knew where the latter were to refit.[3] On 2 February, however, only four of these 29 ships were refitting; and of these, two had been in harbour for over a month, and the other two, as it happened, were later taken for other purposes and did not reach the fleet. Of the remaining 25, five were able to keep the sea until May without coming into port, and two of these were already on their way to the Irish Sea; eleven were waiting to go into harbour; and nine were cruising and convoying in the Channel and the North Sea.[4]

These last duties continued, throughout the first four months of the year, to drain the squadrons and then the fleet of their more advanced units. The trouble lay in the failure to reinforce the original winter guard left out in December, as its commitments grew in January and February. Of this guard, nine ships had been taken for the three squadrons, and the increase in trooping and in the activities of the

---

[1] Several disposition lists exist for this period, which are supplemented by remarks on individual ships in P.R.O.Adm. 3/1 and 2/169, and Serg:Mins. XVIII. The lists are contained in P.R.O.Adm. 8/1, 1 January, 2 February, 1 and 13 April; S.P.Dom. 8/5, no. 8; P.R.O.Adm. 2/169, ff. 30, 86; P.R.O.Adm. 3/1: 12/3, 20/3; *H.M.C.* 12th Report, appendix VI, pp. 166, 172, 186–7; Bodl. Rawl. A 186, f. 22.

The following paragraphs are based on an analysis of this evidence, which in some cases is confused.

[2] Powley, loc. cit. pp. 157–8.

[3] Serg:Mins. XVIII, 14/1; P.R.O.Adm. 1/3557, ff. 847–8; Pep:A.L. XV, ff. 537–8.

[4] P.R.O.Adm. 8/1, 1 January, 2 February; *H.M.C.* 12, VI, pp. 186–7; Bodl. Rawl. A 186, f. 22.

French privateers,[1] and the escorting of Mary from Holland,[2] threw more work upon the remainder than they alone could sustain. It would have been reasonable to reinforce them from the ships going into reserve, most of which were thought—and as it proved rightly[3]—to be in good condition. But, either from reasons of economy or from neglect, no such orders were given; and the borrowing of ships which were already designed for sea continued to delay and sometimes to prevent their joining the fleet. Of the nine so borrowed in January, five had later to refit, while the other four were retained until the middle of February. In the event, five had not joined the fleet by the time it reached the Irish coast, and four were not present at Bantry Bay.[4]

Thus on 2 February, three-quarters of the ships immediately intended for service in the squadrons had not begun to refit, and of the rest only three were available at once if a concentration was required. In view of this, it is not surprising that on 13 March, the day after James landed at Kinsale, only four units should have been ready at Spithead, where the squadrons had been ordered to assemble.[5] But 17 of the 29 were by now either in the Downs, or on their way there for the rendezvous. It seemed as if an adequate force would very soon be available, and the next day the Admiralty was ordered to make out a Commission for Herbert to command the fleet.[6] On the evening of the 18th he arrived at Portsmouth.[7] But by that time, the four sail at Spithead had risen only to six,[8] and the two reinforcements had come, not from the Downs, but one from Jersey and the other from Portsmouth.[9] The trouble lay with the wind, and when on the 22nd it veered from west to north the squadrons were able to move down the coast.[10] The

1 *Cal.S.P.Dom. 1689–90*, p. 6; Luttrell, op. cit. I, p. 527; Pep:A.L. xv, ff. 575, 585.

2 Four of the Straits ships were taken for this, and their refits delayed (Pep:A.L. xv, ff. 546–7).

3 By the survey begun on 4 February (Pep:A.L. xv, ff. 569–70), and concluded by 13 March (P.R.O.Adm. 1/3557, f. 1011).

4 Only one of these—the *Phoenix*—was not intended later to join the fleet.

5 S.P.Dom. 8/5, no. 8; *H.M.C.* 12, vi, p. 166.

6 P.R.O.Adm. 3/1: 14/3.

7 According to Burchett (p. 20) he got there on the 20th. But a letter of Herbert of the 19th mentioned his arrival 'the night before' (P.R.O.Adm. 3/1: 20/3).

8 *H.M.C. Finch*, II, p. 196.

9 S.P.Dom. 8/5, no. 8; P.R.O.Adm. 2/169, f. 30; *H.M.C.* 12, vi, p. 172.

10 P.R.O.Adm. 3/1: 22/3.

crisis seemed almost over, and on 1 April the Admiralty hopefully declared that the fleet consisted of 23 men-of-war, one fireship and two yachts, with a further five fireships and bombvessels on the way.[1] On the 4th Herbert set sail for the west.[2]

But when the Admiral's first letter was sent from the coast of Ireland on the 17th, he still had with him only twelve men-of-war, one fireship and two yachts, with two smacks.[3] The Admiralty, in their reply of the 23rd, were surprised at these numbers, and estimated that twenty sail, excluding smacks, should have been in company by then; but they had been too optimistic about the progress of some ships which were, in fact, still in the west of England.[4] Meanwhile, William on the 20th ordered all units of the fleet of 16 March, which were in a state to do so, to join Herbert's force as soon as possible, if necessary sailing singly.[5] As a result, six more names were added on the 29th to the list of those soon ready to depart. But none of the six had gone by the end of the month, and when Herbert entered Bantry Bay on 1 May he had only increased his numbers by four since the 17th, and there were only a further four on their way and at all near him at that time.[6]

What, therefore, had happened to the rest since 22 March? To answer this question, it is best to take in turn the two groups of ships which failed to appear in time; those from the original squadrons and those ordered to join on or after 20 March.

The first group consisted of nine ships, three of which were ready in time to have been present on 1 May, but had by then been diverted elsewhere. The remaining six were all in the Downs on 22 March, waiting for the change of wind to sail to Spithead. None was still in dockyard hands. It is not therefore to such delays that we must look for an explanation. Indeed, the contrast between the comparative speed with which the ships were refitted, and the amount of time which they spent to no purpose out of harbour both before and after their refits, is remarkable. Of the fifteen ships supposed to be in port by the middle of January, eleven arrived only after 2 February, as has been seen; but

[1] P.R.O.Adm. 8/1, 1 April.
[2] *London Gazette*, no. 2443.
[3] Burchett, p. 21; P.R.O.Adm. 3/1: 22/4.
[4] P.R.O.Adm. 2/169, f. 72.
[5] P.R.O.Adm. 2/377, 20/4 (Secretary to Navy Board).
[6] P.R.O.Adm. 2/169, f. 186, states that by that time 26 ships had sailed to the fleet. I am giving the *Kingfisher Ketch* the benefit of the doubt.

eleven out of the fifteen were out within five and a half weeks, and of the other four, one had been found to be rotten, one awaited only victuals and men, and two were out nine days later. Yet of these eleven, only five had reached the fleet within a month of leaving harbour, and only four were actually present at Bantry Bay.[1]

The second group consisted of sixteen ships, of which two were yachts, and one was diverted to other duties. Of the thirteen which otherwise failed to join, none was still in harbour; all had in fact been out by 29 April, and several a fortnight before. At the end of April, four were on their way to their rendezvous, and the rest were either waiting for them before sailing in company or else were still hanging around the English coast, theoretically on their way to the Irish Sea as they had been for a fortnight.[2] Although in their case the contrast between time spent in harbour and time spent aimlessly out of it is naturally less noticeable than in the case of the earlier ships, the way in which both spent the time after their refits is the same.

In both cases they were delayed by manning troubles, operating either directly thanks to the shortage of men aboard the ships, or indirectly, thanks to the necessity of paying them their back wages if the ships were to sail at all. In January, the feeling over the arrears of pay which had been inherited from the previous régime grew dangerous, and the Navy Board was kept busy distributing copies of William's Proclamation of reassurance.[3] Nevertheless, two mutinies took place early in March, in the *Ruby* and the *Greenwich*,[4] and at the end of the month Herbert was asking for a Judge Advocate and a Marshal to deal with the further trouble that he expected.[5] An effort was made to meet the men's demands. On 16 March the Treasury allowed £37,000 for wages to ships and yards, of which £20,000 were ear-marked for the turned-over men.[6] £17,000 had already been sent down to Portsmouth, and by the time that Herbert arrived a set of clerks and tellers was at work among the ships at Spithead.[7] But the men were not satisfied, and the progress

---

[1] Bodl. Rawl. A 186, f. 22; *H.M.C.* 12, VI, pp. 172, 186–7; P.R.O.Adm. 8/1, 2 February, 1 April, 13 April; P.R.O.Adm. 2/169, f. 30; S.P.Dom. 8/5, no. 8.

[2] P.R.O.Adm. 2/169, f. 86.

[3] Pep:A.L. xv, ff. 540, 544–5, 549.

[4] Ibid. f. 540.

[5] P.R.O.Adm. 3/1: 1/4; P.R.O.Adm. 2/377, 2/4.

[6] P.R.O.Adm. 49/173, f. 4; P.R.O.Adm. 3/1: 15/3.

[7] P.R.O. Adm. 3/1: 15/3, 20/3.

was slow. In his first letter, the Admiral demanded two months' pay for the whole fleet in addition to the payment already under way, and remarked that otherwise he saw it being held indefinitely at Spithead.[1] In reply, the Admiralty hoped to send him another £30,000 and promised another set of clerks and at least 1100 pay tickets.[2] At length, a fortnight after Herbert's arrival, he sailed with just over half the ships, while the payment of the rest continued.[3] The later reinforcements were affected in the same way; even on 23 April the *Warspite* was ordered not to proceed from the Downs until all her turned-over men had been satisfied, and this delayed other ships which had been ordered to sail with her.[4] At the eastern end of the Channel, this overdue and desperate payment of the seamen was steadily nullifying, as day succeeded day, the work of the yards and the hopes of the Administration.

But by the last week in April there was a group of ships at the western end of the Channel ready, as it seemed, for the last lap of the journey, but yet unable to get away. These were still held by actual lack of men.[5] The volunteers were coming in very slowly[6] despite government propaganda to the contrary,[7] and with the ill-feeling in the fleet William refused to apply the press.[8] Captains requesting permission to press got short shrift, and were simply told to attract volunteers.[9] It was not until 15 April, when an embargo was imposed upon shipping for France, that the complementary step of a general press was at last ordered,[10] but this was too late either to help the ships already at sea or to get the nearest reinforcements away in time. Between 20 and 25 April most of the latter left Plymouth,[11] but on 1 May it was an undermanned as well as an undersized squadron that sailed in to engage the French.[12]

This is a sufficiently depressing list of misfortunes. Nor is the word 'list' chosen inadvisedly, for the succession of failures is distinguished principally by the fact that it is simply a succession. The most obvious

---

[1] P.R.O.Adm. 3/1: 20/3. [2] Ibid. [3] Ibid. 24/4.
[4] Ibid. 23/4. [5] *H.M.C. Finch*, II, p. 201.
[6] P.R.O.Adm. 2/377, 26/4 (Bowles to Herbert).
[7] *London Gazette*, nos. 2454, 2461; see also *H.M.C. Le Fleming*, p. 242.
[8] 'Spencer House Journals', pp. 206, 216.
[9] P.R.O.Adm. 3/1: 19/3.
[10] Ibid. 15/4; *H.M.C. Finch*, II, p. 201.
[11] P.R.O.Adm. 2/169, f. 86. [12] Burchett, p. 23.

difference between the events of the last quarter of 1688 and those of the first quarter of 1689 is the absence over the latter of a controlling purpose. The constant diversion of units to duties for which they were not originally intended, and the failure to bring any significant pressure to bear on the various delays affecting the ships both before and after their refits, handicapped the administrative measures as effectively as the procrastination and inconsequence of the orders had originally delayed them. The progress of James's last mobilization had shown that only the impact of a vigorous and coherent policy could affect the material difficulties inherent in the task; in the absence of such a policy under William, the odds against success, always heavy, became overwhelming. The machine operated as before, but the cogs failed to engage, and William was fortunate to escape with as indecisive a result as he did, when the first-fruits of his administration were put to the test.

The skirmish at Bantry was an inconclusive affair, and as is usual upon these occasions both sides claimed the advantage, the French because they had suffered less loss than they had inflicted, the English because their opponents had returned to Brest.[1] Herbert himself retired to his rendezvous off the Scillies to await reinforcements, but as none arrived he made his way to Spithead, where considerable efforts were being made to prepare for him.[2] On his arrival, he was hailed as a conqueror. The fleet was visited by the King, and the men rewarded with the promise of 10*s.* apiece;[3] two of the successful captains, Ashby and Cloudesley Shovell, were knighted aboard the flagship; and Herbert himself was made Baron Herbert of Torbay and Earl of Torrington.[4] When he came to London, he received the thanks of the House of

[1] The English losses were 94 killed and about 270 wounded: the ships were only slightly damaged. The French lost 40 killed and 93 wounded (*London Gazette*, no. 2451, reproducing the official account from which Burchett's and later accounts were mainly taken; Roncière, op. cit. VI, p. 50).

[2] Burchett, p. 23; P.R.O.Adm. 3/1: 8/5, 10/5

[3] *London Gazette*, no. 2454. Characteristically, many of them had still not been paid a year later (P.R.O.Adm. 2/379, f. 527).

[4] Ibid. nos. 2454, 2458. He will be referred to as Torrington from now on when events after June 1689 are mentioned.

Commons for 'one of the bravest Actions done in this last Age'.[1] But these were gestures to confirm public faith in the régime and to conciliate the seamen. Although William remarked in public that Bantry was the sort of action that was necessary at the beginning of a war,[2] in private he was thoroughly dissatisfied with it;[3] Herbert himself did not regard it as a victory;[4] and perhaps its most valuable result was the speech that he made in reply to the Commons' address, in which he pleaded the cause of those killed or wounded at sea, and their dependants, and forced the House into appointing a committee to examine the existing facilities for their care and treatment.[5] The outcome, however, did not depress the public,[6] although the more knowledgeable were sceptical of its value,[7] and it provided the Administration with a spur which was long overdue. An energetic programme of repair and replenishment was put in hand,[8] and on 15 June the fleet sailed again for the west, over forty strong and with eleven Dutchmen in company.[9] During July it was joined by Russell and Killigrew, and by about another twenty Dutchmen, until on the 13th it was, as the former wrote, 'fit to fight any strength that can be put out'.[10] For the rest of the summer it cruised, between sixty and seventy strong,[11] in the western approaches to the Channel, until at the end of August it returned to Torbay.

---

[1] *H.C.J.* x, p. 142.

[2] Thomas Lediard, *The Naval History of England* (1735), p. 624, n. *g*.

[3] *Conduct*, p. 51.

[4] *H.M.C. Finch*, II, p. 219.

[5] *H.C.J.* x, p. 142.

[6] '...At the breaking out of this French War, the English, especially in London, were so sanguine that Odds were laid in many hundred Wagers, that King William would be at Paris before Christmas' (John Oldmixon, *History of England During the Reigns of King William and Queen Mary, Queen Anne, King George I* (1735), p. 11).

[7] *State Papers...of Clarendon*, II, p. 186; *Samuel Pepys's Naval Minutes*, p. 216.

[8] The numbers of the workmen in Portsmouth dockyard rose from 426 on 1 May to 507 on 1 June; the greatest increase was in the number of caulkers, which was almost doubled, from 42 to 77 (Serg.MS. A 123).

[9] *London Gazette*, no. 2463; *H.M.C. Finch*, II, p. 219.

[10] *H.M.C. Finch*, II, p. 227.

[11] P.R.O.Adm. 8/3, 1 August.

II

The emphasis throughout this chapter has been upon the policy of William himself, because, in the conduct of the war, William was the only figure whose decisions were at this stage of any importance. The attention of the political world was fixed primarily upon his health,[1] his habits[2] and his intentions; and the conduct of affairs followed, and was seriously affected by his choice of residence.[3] This is not surprising, when it is remembered that he was the central figure and indeed the embodiment of a revolution. Subject to their guidance by the principles and circumstances of the occasion, men behave much the same in any revolution, even in a peaceful revolution like that of 1688. As the Duke of Wellington remarked, it was only after doing business with the French politicians of 1814 that you could appreciate the activities of Sunderland and Marlborough.[4] Those whose fortunes or loyalties are heavily involved in the cause, tend to become its extremists; those who, for either reason, can sit loose to it, to remain its moderates. As usual, there were both sorts in 1689. But the Glorious Revolution was unusual in that it was brought about by the latter alone, to the exclusion of the former. It was not the Jack Howes and the Wildmans, but Danby and Halifax, Shrewsbury and Nottingham, who were responsible for its success and whose imprint it bore. It had, therefore, in a peculiar measure the defects of its qualities. While the contributions of different interests and different theories gave it a national and moderate character, none of the individuals responsible for those contributions was irrevocably committed to its cause. The extent and the manner of their commitment varied according to the reasons for their support: some who, like Halifax and Churchill, had acted, in their different ways, for personal as well as political reasons, did not entirely relinquish their personal connexions with the former régime; others, whose contributions to its downfall had been, like Danby's, the result

---

1 Reresby, loc. cit. pp. 571, 577; Burnet, *History*, IV, p. 2 (Dartmouth's note).

2 Reresby, loc. cit. p. 571; Browning, op. cit. II, p. 159; 'Spencer House Journals', pp. 210–11.

3 Reresby, loc. cit. p. 577; Burnet, *History*, IV, p. 3.

4 Cited in Firth, *Commentary on Macaulay's History*, p. 266, n. 1.

of political animosities, transferred these to its successor; others again who, like Nottingham, had found that on balance they could not support James, were able only on balance to support William. There was no Bentinck in England in 1689; there was not even a Fagel. No English minister could or wished to be identified with all the consequences of the settlement which he had helped to bring about.

The distrust and contempt which their manœuvres inspired in William increased his addiction to a secrecy to which he had always inclined. He had long been accustomed to reserve to himself the direction of foreign affairs and, in that high region where diplomacy and strategy meet, of war. He allowed of no alternatives to his ultimate authority, but only in the choice of his associates, whose responsibility it was to execute his policy; and his experience of Dutch politics and of war combined with his temperament to keep his confidential advisers and his public utterances to a minimum. He was reserved when he came to England; the delicacy of his position and the anfractuosities of English politics soon turned that reserve into a secrecy which no Englishman was able entirely to penetrate. Unable to trust any of the great figures, and with the various minor figures from whom confidants are often made impossible for personal reasons, he turned again to his Dutchmen, who were accustomed to these questions and from whom he knew what to expect.[1]

The official hierarchy of State, therefore, was largely irrelevant to William's main purpose. Its Offices were filled with the adherents of the different groups which had brought him to power, so that from the great posts of Lord Steward and Lord President to the seats on the administrative Commissions the balance was evenly maintained. But however satisfactory this counterpoise might be in the interest of political amity, it made the theoretical and the actual responsibilities of the Offices at best parallel and more often divergent, for those posts which were designed to meet an executive purpose might well be occupied by a political nominee to whom it was undesirable to entrust

[1] See 'Spencer House Journals', pp. 201–27, for William's opinion of the great men of 1689, apart from Halifax. Of the minor figures, one has only to think of the most likely names—Henry Sydney, Mordaunt, Lumley, Godolphin—to see that the last alone could fill the post; and he was too cautious to do so.

a particular executive design. In these circumstances, William's habitual reliance on his chosen individuals increased. He had always shown a liking for the short cut, a disregard of the usual channels. This was now intensified by the discrepancy between his requirements and the provision made for them by a system of domestic politics which seemed to impinge only erratically upon them. He liked to work through men, and not through their Offices; now he was apt to work through men in spite of their Offices. The constitutional development of the departments of State in his reign can be understood only if it is realized that to William it was not a constitutional question at all, but one of personal efficiency and military security.

This was particularly the case with those departments which were immediately concerned with the war: the army, the navy and the Treasury.[1] Like his predecessor, William refused to let any of them fall into individual hands other than his own.[2] There was no question of this happening with the army, for it was obvious that he would take command of that himself. About naval and financial matters, however, he knew and cared less.[3] He did not indeed regard them both in the same way: he took considerable interest, in particular, in Treasury business. But he was not prepared to manage either in person, and his requirements from the office holders were thus much the same in both cases. For the Treasury at least there was considerable competition;[4] but the dangerous choice was avoided, and the Office put into commission, the places being filled with political candidates. The Admiralty was treated in the same way. But in both cases this merely removed a danger; in neither did it supply an answer to the problem. A political Commission could not, and was not designed to give William what he wanted from the department: a group of efficient administrators, capable of implementing a policy which their political interest did not oblige them to question and of advising upon its efficacy on technical, and not on political grounds. When he found such men, he relied upon them

[1] For this purpose I have bracketed the ordnance with the army.

[2] 'Spencer House Journals', p. 221.

[3] But, as ruler of Holland and England, he took good care to follow the direction of the wind. The weathercock which he installed at Kensington Palace, with a dial over the fireplace of the Presence Chamber, may still be seen.

[4] 'Spencer House Journals', p. 205.

almost completely for day to day business, for he himself had no head for detail. His indifference to it indeed was his subordinates' main complaint throughout the war: even in his chosen subject of military affairs, he was more of a strategist than an organizer. But in two of the three departments he was fortunate. At the War Office, he found the perfect instrument for his personal supervision, in the unimaginative but meticulous Secretary at War, William Blathwayt—one of the most competent civil servants that England has ever had; and at the Treasury, where his control was less direct and the issues more complicated, he was equally fortunate in finding the experienced and reliable Godolphin, 'never in the way', as Charles II had said, 'but never out of it'.[1] Only at the Admiralty did his luck desert him, and the history of naval administration during the first year of the Commission is the history of William's failure to discover a naval Godolphin. Pepys, the obvious man, was too deeply implicated in the previous régime, and in any case was unwilling to continue; Dartmouth was similarly out of the question; there was no suitable alternative among William's recent opponents; and his active supporters in the fleet were all comparatively unimportant. Early in January, however, a possible substitute seemed to be available from his own retinue, in either of the two sailors who had been attached to his cause and had sailed in his fleet, Edward Russell and Arthur Herbert.

Edward Russell[2] had been attached to William's cause at least since 1686, and for four years before that he seems to have been disaffected to the Court, probably since the execution of his cousin William, Lord Russell. He had played an important and indeed a prominent part in the preparations for the Revolution, making throughout the summer a series of journeys to Holland through which the arrangements were gradually brought to the point, signing the famous invitation of 30 June, and sailing in a private capacity in November with the expedition. On the march to London he had acted as the Prince's secretary. At the time of the Revolution he was 35, with eleven years of active service in the navy behind him, from 1671 to 1682. He had

[1] For William's opinion in 1689 of Blathwayt and Godolphin, see 'Spencer House Journals' pp. 226, 205; and also Reresby, loc. cit. p. 564, for the latter.

[2] For details of his career, see *D.N.B.*, corrected by *Bulletin of the Institute of Historical Research*, XIV, p. 56.

fought at Solebay as a lieutenant, and as a captain had served in the Mediterranean under Narborough and Herbert. His professional experience was nothing exceptional, and certainly did not warrant the references to its length and severity which he made later in 1689;[1] but he had seen as much service as most gentlemen commanders of the same age, he had learned his navigation and seamanship from Sir David Mitchell, the Scots fisher-boy who rose to be an Admiral,[2] and he undoubtedly knew his job. He had not, naturally enough, held any political office; and his importance is attributable, not to professional attainments or to political experience, but to his name and his connexions. The nephew of William, first Duke of Bedford, he was related to several and companion to all the members of the aristocratic opposition to James. He spoke specifically for a great house—the most necessary support that William could have—and for the sea officers, with whom he had kept up relations and to whose cabals he brought the reassurance of a powerful connexion. As such, he was entitled to a major share in the favours of the successful revolution.

It is difficult to describe his character, not because it is excessively complicated, but because certain aspects of it emerge only in their results. Taken all round, he was not a pleasant man. As he stares from his portraits, with his fresh complexion, his heavy jowl and his choleric expression, he seems the embodiment of the typical sea-dog. Placed against the portraits of other captains of his day, he differs from them only in the degree to which he reproduces the high colour and the prominent eye which Channel weather and heavy drinking gave to so many. Contemporary lampoons emphasized his physical appearance. 'The cherry-cheekt Russell', one called him,[3] and in another:[4]

> He has a quick eye, and sprightly glance,
> His face a map of jolly ignorance.
> The lilies and the roses so disposed
> Should not by careful thought be discomposed.
> Pity the fat, round, pretty, blushing thing
> Should e'er be thus condemned to counseling!

---

[1] Anchitell Grey, *Debates of the House of Commons*, IX (1763), p. 418.

[2] *Memoirs of the Secret Services of John Mackey* (Roxburgh Club, 1895), p. 108.

[3] *Naval Songs and Ballads*, ed. C. H. Firth (1908), p. 112.

[4] Quoted from a pamphlet in the Huntington Library, in *Conduct*, p. 66, n. 68.

But Russell was not 'condemned' to counselling: it was his *métier*. Despite a certain laziness and, at times, a want of self-confidence,[1] his advice and his protests were seldom lacking, and were given with an extraordinary disregard for the rank or the political opinion of the recipient.[2] He brought to his official correspondence an aristocratic freedom of speech which it is a delight to read now, but which must at the time have been a burden and, on occasions, a bore; and the concerted efforts of the Admiralty and the Secretaries of State, of his fellow officers and his private friends, and even of the King himself, failed to stifle or even to control the unending flow of impassioned but seldom irrelevant observation. When really roused, he was capable of a wilfulness amounting to treachery, as when, in the summer of 1695, he sent a protest from Cadiz to Flanders about the strategic employment of his fleet by the overland route through France.[3] But his advice could not be dismissed, even when it was opposed. Amid the abuse and the lamentations the argument was usually to the point; and even if that could be disregarded, the position of its author could not.

For Russell became the great naval figure of the war. Simultaneously Commander in Chief of the fleet, senior Lord of the Admiralty, Treasurer of the Navy, Treasurer of the Chamber[4] and a member of the Privy and inner Councils; with his former secretary as Secretary of the Admiralty, and his own creature a member of the Board; disposing in his flagship in the Mediterranean of the perquisites of an ambassador, and author of the only great naval victory of the war; at the height of his power he was without a rival in the conduct of naval affairs.

It is the more curious that nothing should be known of the basis and the results of this power: of the political activities by which it was gained and later exercised, and of the financial activities which accompanied it and thanks to which he was able to purchase and to maintain one of the finest estates in Cambridgeshire.[5] Their products were to be

---

[1] *Supplement to Burnet*, p. 289.

[2] E.g. his quarrel with Herbert in the Mediterranean, in *Samuel Pepys's Naval Minutes*, p. 113.

[3] See p. 551 below.

[4] *Cal.S.P.Dom. 1693*, p. 82.

[5] On Chippenham, Russell's estate, see *The Journeys of Celia Fiennes*, ed. C. Morris (1947), pp. 36, 153–4; and Daniel Defoe, *A Tour through Great Britain*, ed. G. D. H. Cole (1927), I, p. 75.

PLATE VIII

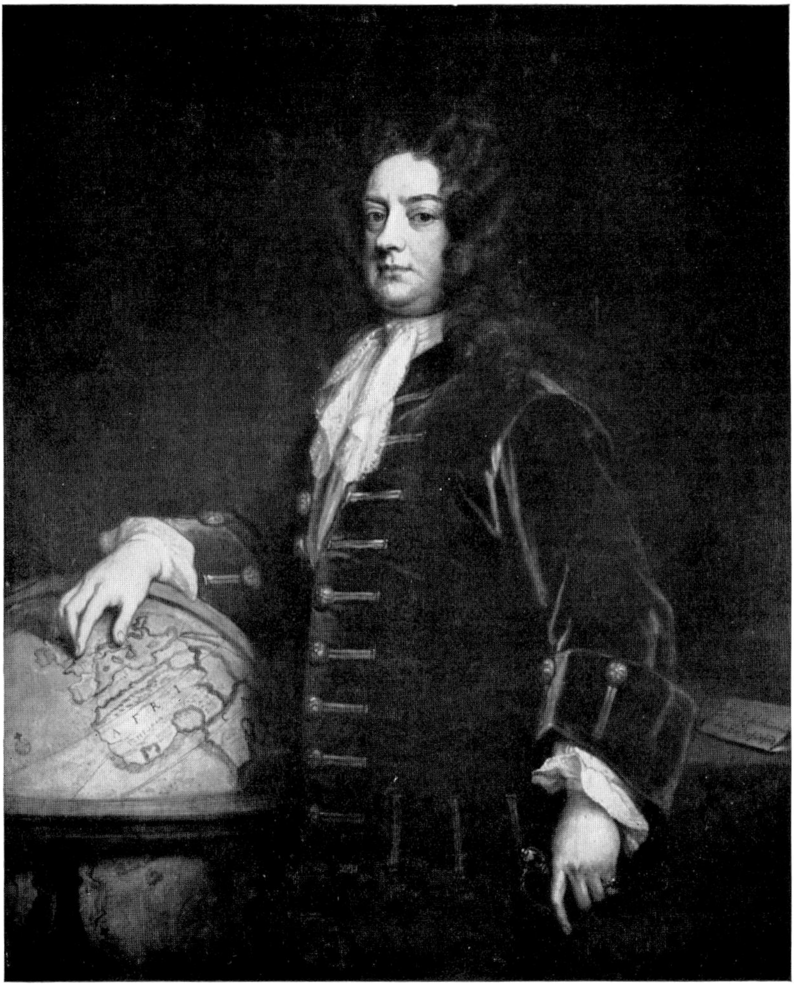

EDWARD RUSSELL, EARL OF ORFORD

[SIR GODFREY KNELLER]

seen, outside his profession and beyond the end of the reign, in an important and varied career. A member of Mary's Council in 1690, claimed by the Jacobites as a secret adherent to James's cause throughout the war, created an Earl by William in 1697, and impeached for naval mismanagement and peculation three years later; one of the Junto under Anne, and a minister again under George I; after thirty years of intrigue and high office, his actions still remain largely a mystery, of which the fruits alone are to be discerned. It is only occasionally that we see him at work—attending a meeting of the leading Whigs at Somers's house;[1] supplementing his plan of a register for seamen by appointing his own steward as receiver of their contributions;[2] speculating in privateering, while a Lord Commissioner of the Admiralty, as part owner in the *Adventure Galley* commanded by Captain Kidd[3]—and then it is from the remarks of others. His own private papers have never been found;[4] and while it is dangerous to deduce from evidence that does not exist, it is curious that he, who in his correspondence from sea was so unusually indiscreet, should have left no trace of his activities ashore. When we return to his portrait and remember, as we look at the bluff and stupid face, that it belongs not to a simple Admiral of the Blue, but to a prominent politician who weathered the storms of three reigns, and who contrived at the same time not unsuccessfully to feather his nest, we discern behind the lilies and the roses, and associated with the seaman's ready bellicosity, a sharp brain and a pronounced capacity for intrigue in the service of a resourceful and well-informed ambition.

But in 1689 Russell had not yet the experience to fill William's requirements. Nor probably did he wish to do so. Even if there had been no one else, it is doubtful, in view of his refusal eighteen months

---

[1] *Private and Original Correspondence of...Duke of Shrewsbury*, ed. William Coxe (1821), p. 417.

[2] See p. 600, n. 5 below.

[3] I am indebted for this fact to Dr G. N. Clark.

[4] Only his letters on public affairs are to be found in the national archives or the private libraries catalogued by the Historical Manuscripts Commission. Miss Gladys Scott Thomson has kindly supplied me with transcripts of those private letters of his which exist in the Bedford archives; there are only six of them (Bedford MSS. L. v, nos. 30, 101, 121; L. vi, nos. 90, 98, 102), and they are of no importance.

later,[1] whether he would at this stage have accepted high office, and he was well satisfied with his appointment on 18 March to the important but politically second-rate post of Treasurer of the Navy.[2] But there was some one else. The obvious choice for naval confidant was Arthur Herbert.

Herbert[3] was professionally in a different category from Russell. Although only six years older, he was not only the senior naval officer who had come over to William; he was the most obvious choice in the whole navy for Admiral of the fleet. Had it not been for his quarrel with James, he might well have commanded the English force in the winter of 1688; as it was, he commanded the Dutch. In view of his family and his career, this was surprising. The second son of Sir Edward Herbert, the lawyer who had gone overseas with Rupert in 1648, and the brother of Edward Herbert, the Lord Chief Justice of James II who followed his father overseas forty years later, Arthur Herbert himself had been a favourite of the Stuarts. In February 1684, he had been made Rear Admiral of England and Master of the Robes, and had been found a seat as member for Dover in James's solitary Parliament of 1685. But much to everybody's surprise, including the King's, he had refused to agree to the repeal of the Test Act, and had in consequence been dismissed from all his employments. In July 1688 he crossed to Holland, and returned to England with William in November.

His appointment as Rear Admiral of England was not unmerited. Born in 1647, he had entered the navy at the age of seventeen and had seen a great deal of service throughout the Dutch wars, most of it in command. He was present at Solebay, and at the action of 28 May 1673, but for most of those years, in 1666, from 1669 to 1672, and from 1674 to 1675, he was in the Mediterranean. In 1678 he returned there under Narborough with the local rank of Vice-Admiral; and when in May 1679 Narborough left for England, he remained in command, receiving his commission as Admiral and Commander in Chief in July of the following year. He stayed in the Straits for a further three years, managing in that time to bring to a close one of the many Algerine

---

[1] See pp. 356, 357–8 below.

[2] *Cal.S.P.Dom. 1689–90*, p. 29. The patent was issued on 4 April.

[3] For details of his career, see *D.N.B.*

wars of the period, and to conclude a treaty with that elusive power which proved rather more successful than any of its unsatisfactory predecessors. When Dartmouth came out in the summer of 1683 to evacuate Tangier, he returned to England; and it was shortly before he left that Pepys encountered him there, living ashore in the town, waited upon by his captains 'to the meanest degree of servility', and spending his time upon his rogueries and his debaucheries.[1]

For there are no subtle shades to Herbert's character. He was almost a professional bad man. He himself seems rather to have enjoyed his reputation. Burnet, who was assigned to the unenviable task of keeping him in good humour during William's march to London, was constantly referring to it in his correspondence with elephantine roguishness. 'You are a strange bad man', he began one letter, and another, 'As bad a man as you are'.[2] Of the exact nature of his badness there is also no doubt: his contemporaries were unanimous about it. He drank to excess, even by the standards of his profession and his age, and even by those standards he was excessively licentious.[3] It was this last trait in particular that the ballads and the pamphlets seized upon in his downfall, although his pride and his financial rapacity were also hymned at length and with some vigour.[4] Pepys, who hated him more than any other man he knew, attributed to him all the other vices as well: besides immorality, cruelty, laziness, peculation, vanity and bellicosity.[5] 'Of all the worst men living', he concluded, 'Herbert is the only man that I do not know to have any one virtue to compound for all his vices';[6] and James, on hearing that he had resigned his posts on a point of conscience, remarked that he did not normally appear to set much store by it.[7] He must have been a repulsive figure, with his one eye—the other had been lost during a fight with an Algerine, by the accidental

---

1 *The Tangier Papers of Samuel Pepys*, ed. E. Chappell (1935), p. 138.

2 *Supplement to Burnet*, pp. 530, 528. 3 E.g. B.M. Egerton 2621, f. 77.

4 *Naval Songs and Ballads*, p. 111; see also ibid. p. 112, and *The Parable of the Bear-Baiting* (1691).

5 *Tangier Papers*: the references, in the order of these qualities, are pp. 200, 121–2, 113, 216, 101, 182–3, 122, 152, 245.

6 Ibid. p. 225.

7 *Supplement to Burnet*, p. 211; and cf. William's opinion of him, in 'Spencer House Journals', p. 243.

explosion of some cartridges—his drunkenness, and his incessant stream of foul language. Nevertheless, he was genuinely popular with many of his captains, and apparently with many of his men. Even in his downfall, when his power was at its lowest and his life in danger, some of his adherents in the fleet continued to support him;[1] and it cannot have been only for professional reasons that, on his acquittal by a court martial after his defeat at Beachy Head, all the vessels in the river manned ship and cheered him as he passed.[2] His most obvious vices, as Macaulay noted, were not unpopular vices,[3] and to balance them he had the most popular virtue of a seaman, that of personal courage.

More to the point than his bottle and his ladies was the last shortcoming noted by Pepys—his bellicosity. In William's circle in 1688, it was believed that the root of Herbert's quarrel with James's cause lay in a personal quarrel with Dartmouth, who appeared to be displacing him in the royal favour[4] and whom he challenged to a duel at Ostend during his short absence abroad.[5] His disagreements had their roots in suspicion, for, with the one possible aberration of 1685, his whole career was a pilgrimage towards the seat of power, from which he could seldom bear to be absent and upon which he concentrated the burden of his correspondence from sea during 1689. When transferred from personal to administrative questions, this suspicion showed itself in a pessimism which eventually drove him to leave office and, according to his enemies, to throw away his chances of a victory at sea. For Herbert had the melancholy satisfaction of seeing his forebodings come true. He is one of that unenviable class of commanders who are the instruments of the disaster which they themselves have prophesied. He was suspicious of Russell: and he saw his own disgrace clear the way for Russell's success. He foresaw the inadequacy of the Admiralty of which he was the nominal head: and its consequences ruined himself while leaving his fellow Commissioners unscathed. To a later age his grasp of tactical theory,[6] which was displayed even in the implications of the

---

1 B.M.Addnl. 15857, f. 261.

2 B.M.Addnl. 17677, LL, f. 9*v*. I am indebted to Mr James for this reference.

3 *History*, IV, p. 1764.

4 Burnet, loc. cit. p. 261.

5 B.M. Egerton 2621, ff. 9–10.

6 It is possible that he was the author of the additions to the Duke of York's Fighting Instructions of 1673, which Corbett has argued were 'the earliest known attempt to

PLATE IX

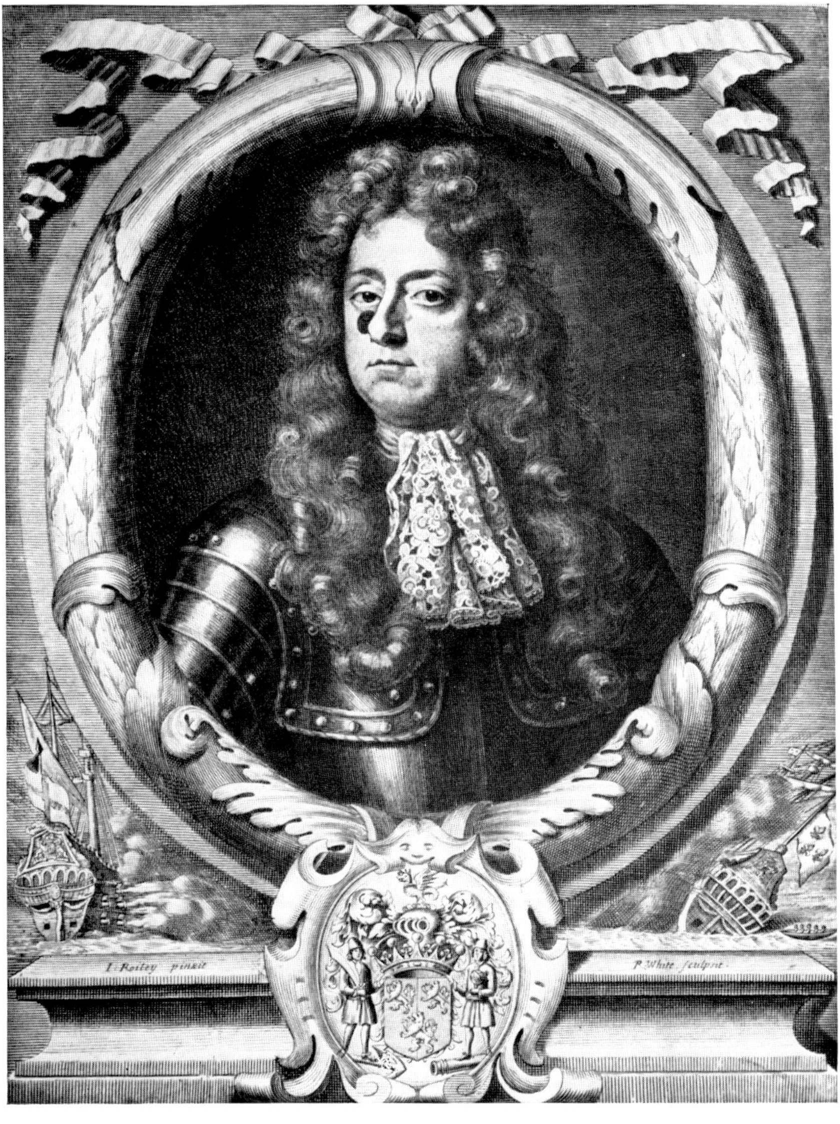

ARTHUR HERBERT, EARL OF TORRINGTON

[R. WHITE *after* J. RILEY]

phrase 'the fleet in being' with which he justified his defeat, has compensated for the bad seamanship, the corruption and the indecision of which his enemies accused him.[1] After being condemned by his contemporaries, he enjoys the dubious revenge of being rehabilitated by posterity. But in a war, and particularly at an early stage of a war, it is not enough to foresee the consequences of an unsatisfactory policy; and Herbert's nemesis lay not in a defeat whose effects he in fact largely contrived to mitigate, but in allowing himself to be involved in a situation of which he disapproved, of which he had foretold the result, and for which he could offer no remedy. He had lost his battle before it began, and the decisions which he took in it, and which were afterwards subjected to such close investigation, were those of a commander whose choice had already been made, and whose character and experience had already deprived him of confidence in his superiors and in himself.

All this, however, lay in the future, and when Herbert arrived in London it was, as he hoped, to be made Lord High Admiral.[2] But although he had William's ear, he had to remain content with the position of head of the new Commission. On 22 February its warrant was issued,[3] and to fill the interval while the Letters Patent were preparing, he was empowered on the 28th temporarily to act in its place.[4] He had already begun to do so on the 26th, and until 1 March he was busy tidying up overlapping details with Pepys.[5] From that date he

---

get away from the unsatisfactory method of engaging in parallel lines ship to ship' (*Fighting Instructions*, pp. 140–5). It also seems likely that Russell's Instructions of 1691, taken by Corbett as probably the most important single document in the history of naval tactics (ibid. p. 175), followed very closely Torrington's two sets of Instructions to the fleet of 1689 and 1690 (R. C. Anderson, 'Two New Sets of Sailing and Fighting Instructions', in *M.M.* VI, no. 5, pp. 130–5). His defeat at Beachy Head, and his defence of his conduct there, are discussed briefly on pp. 350–1 below.

[1] He was supposed to be so ignorant of the terms of his profession that when he wanted a rope or a sail hauled up, 'he will say "Haul up that whichum there", with a kind of jest to disguise his not knowing the name for it' (*Tangier Papers*, p. 225). For his corruption, see ibid. pp. 147, 210.

[2] *Supplement to Burnet*, p. 312; cf. the later account in Burnet, *History*, IV, pp. 8–9.

[3] *Cal.S.P.Dom. 1689–90*, p. 6.

[4] Ibid. p. 11.

[5] Pep:A.L. XV, ff. 596–9.

acted alone,[1] until on 8 March the Admiralty patent was ready, and on the morning of the 9th the Board met to hear it read and to begin its work.[2]

Apart from Herbert, none of its members was of the first importance, and most of them had been appointed, as in the other Commissions, for political reasons. They were, indeed, an average cross-section of the available Parliamentary material. In addition to himself, they consisted

---

[1] There is a curious incident at this time to which I have been unable to find an answer. When the House of Commons, in the summer of 1689, came to investigate the miscarriages of the spring, its committee asked Herbert's secretary, Phineas Bowles, 'who acted between Mr. Pepys's time and the time of the Admiralty, about 17 days, viz from 20 Feb. to 8 March? He says he is not prepared to answer now. Thinks L. Clarendon was directed to act for some few days. His Lordship employed witness as his friend.' He was then directed to bring an account in writing. Accordingly, a few days later, he delivered a paper to the Committee 'which he says is all the account he can give while E. Clarendon was concerned' (*H.M.C.* 12, VI, pp. 142, 144). This account consisted of orders given by Herbert from 2 to 8 March, concerning naval movements to Ireland and the provision of troop transports for the same purpose. It was endorsed 'Mr Bowles' paper relating to Irish affairs whilst E. of Clarendon was concerned', and dated 13 August 1689 (ibid. p. 191). This is distinctly curious, for Clarendon is the last person to have had anything to do with the government at this time. A former viceroy of Ireland, he had been the first great figure on whom the dispossessed Protestants had pinned their hopes, and had communicated a list of their officers to William at the beginning of the year (*State Letters of Clarendon*, II, diary, p. 133). But disappointed in his hopes of employment, he quickly reverted to his initial attitude of opposition to the new régime. As James's brother-in-law he was in any case suspect, and his behaviour during the days in which Bowles said he was working for William did nothing to lessen that suspicion, which eventually in 1690 landed him in the Tower. On 18 February he had absented himself from the House of Lords when William went there in state; on 1 March he argued at length with the bishop of St Asaph against taking the new oath, and on the 4th he left town to avoid a summons to the Lords; he returned on the 7th, but stayed at home on that and the following days (ibid. pp. 172–5). He was thus actually absent for a part of the time specified, and when he was in London he attended no meetings of the Council Committee for Ireland (*H.M.C.* 12, VI, p. 167). No trace of any official activity on his part appears anywhere else; on the contrary, he was notoriously on bad terms with William throughout this period. I can only conclude that the affair was in some way connected with the complicated intrigues in which Bowles was then involved for the vacant Secretaryship at the Admiralty (see pp. 291–2 below) and that for some reason it suited his book in August to mention Clarendon in this way.

[2] Patent Rolls; P.R.O.Adm. 3/1: 9/3.

of the Earl of Carbery, Sir Thomas Lee, William Sacheverell, Sir John Lowther, Sir Michael Wharton and Admiral Sir John Chicheley. John Vaughan, third Earl of Carbery,[1] was a strong Protestant 'exclusionist', with a long career in the Commons before he succeeded to the title, and some record of colonial office—as chequered as that of many a public figure of the age—behind him. He had considerable estates and influence in Wales, which he brought to the support of his Whig activities and which, as much as any personal merit, were responsible for his prominence in the Kit Kat Club, among whose portraits his may still be seen. Despite, or perhaps because of his early schooling at the hands of Jeremy Taylor, he was, even in his fiftieth year, one of the gayer figures of the town; but he had also a certain inclination for patronage, was President of the Royal Society from 1686 to 1689, and had long been one of Dryden's protectors. By his second marriage he became Halifax's son-in-law. At the Admiralty, thanks to his rank, he was regarded as Herbert's deputy, succeeding him, as has been seen, in the Dutch negotiations, and taking precedence of his most formidable colleague, Sir Thomas Lee.[2] The latter,[3] although now an old man and by no means well, was still, as member for Buckinghamshire, an important House of Commons man, one of the stalwarts of the old Country party, and a former Commissioner of the Admiralty in 1679. He was, when he chose to be, one of William's most reasonable and convincing supporters,[4] and, with his long experience and power of debate, was to prove the ablest defender of the naval administration in Parliament. William Sacheverell[5] was chosen on the same grounds, but with different results. At first, indeed, he seemed the greater catch, for

---

[1] *D.N.B.*

[2] 'I mov'd that Lord Carbery might be of the Council, he [i.e. William] said, then Sir Thomas Lee would expect it, I shew'd the difference, he said, he would think of it' ('Spencer House Journals', p. 233).

[3] Rev. F. G. Lee, *Genealogy of the Family of Lee* (1884); F. A. Blaydon, *Genealogica Bedfordiensis, 1538–1700* (1890). I am indebted for these and some of the succeeding references to Mr James.

[4] But only when he chose. His name figures in a confidential list of William's of 'Comoners eminent in Parliament, useful men, but not to be trusted' (S.P.Dom. 8/6, no. 56).

[5] *D.N.B.*; Sir G. Sitwell, *Letters of the Sitwells and Sacheverells* (1900), and *The Story of the Sitwells* (galley proofs only, Oxford, 194–).

with his prominence in the House as member for Heytesbury, and his long connexion—in the Test Act, the Exclusion Bill and the activities of the Green Ribbon Club—with the Country party, he had always been shy of office. But as one of the Board he proved himself as independent in the House as when he was a private member, and outside it he took virtually no part in Admiralty business during the few months in which he remained a Commissioner. Lowther,[1] a close friend of Lee, a moderate Tory and equally opposed to extremes, was appointed for his territorial influence rather than for his personal ability. A member of the great family which dominated Cumberland and Westmorland, and a cousin of the more famous Sir John who later became the first Lord Lonsdale,[2] he himself founded the port of Whitehaven, from which he exported his coal and which he represented in Parliament as member for Cumberland. Wharton,[3] 'the rich Wharton', said to be worth £15,000 a year, stood for a different, though a kindred interest. Member for Beverley, where he had large estates, his influence lay in the East Riding and the port of Hull, where William had originally intended to land. His politics were those of Danby, his principal friendship that of Dartmouth. Lastly, Chicheley,[4] Herbert's sole naval colleague on the Board, represented the more influential professional interest. A veteran of the Dutch wars and a former member of both the Navy Board and the Ordnance, he also belonged to the richest family in Cambridgeshire, and was brother-in-law to Halifax. In Parliament, he sat for the Lancashire borough of Newton. It was a typical and not ill-chosen example of the contemporary solution, composed of the adherents of the more important Parliamentary groups, proportioned satisfactorily with territorial and personal influence,

---

[1] *D.N.B.*; R. S. Ferguson, *M.P.s of Cumberland and Westmorland* (1871).

[2] Both Macaulay (*History*, III, p. 1330) and Professor Keith Feiling (*History of the Tory Party, 1640–1714* (1924), p. 257) confuse the cousins and place Sir John Lowther of Lowther, later first Lord Lonsdale, at the Admiralty as well as at the Treasury. The Admiralty Commissioner was Sir John Lowther of Whitehaven.

[3] *Beverley Borough Records, 1575–1812*, ed. J. Dennett (1933); G. R. Park, *Parliamentary Representatives of Yorkshire from the Earliest Parliament...* (1886).

[4] *D.N.B.*; W. F. C. Chicheley Plowden, *Records of the Chicheley Plowdens* (1914); Benjamin Buckler, *Stemmata Chicheleana* (1765); W. Duncombe Pink and Rev. A. B. Bevan, *Lancashire Parliamentary Representatives* (1885).

and provided with a quorum of capable members to tackle such business as must unavoidably be entrusted to its charge.

But, despite the unexciting auguries, the appointment of this Commission was a turning point in the history of naval administration. For, unlike its predecessors of the previous thirty years, the political expedient of 1689 proved the constitutional solution which has survived, with only two exceptions, until the present day. From January 1702 to November 1709, and again from May 1827 to August 1828, the Office of Lord High Admiral was revived; but the nineteenth-century interlude of the Duke of Clarence was not to be taken seriously by anyone but himself, while in the eight years of the earlier revival, which might be thought to constitute a more important break in continuity, the Admiral acted for over six of them through a Council which was, in effect, a Board like those of William's reign.[1] It is, however, difficult to relate the event immediately or clearly to its results. It was marked by no alteration in constitutional procedure, for, as before, the Admiral derived his authority from the royal prerogative, exercised in this case through a Commission and not through a Great Officer of State, and expressed as usual by the issue of Letters Patent under the Great Seal. The patent itself, moreover, was textually that of 1679,[2] and thus no innovation was made upon the traditional divergence between the theory and practice of the Office. With the Admiralty, as with other departments at the end of the century, it is not in constitutional form that the constitutional changes are to be found.

But if they were not embodied in legal form, the changes themselves cannot be used to point the argument. They came about slowly, unevenly, often ambiguously. The road was seldom marked by signposts, and its stages fell into proportion and its direction became clear only when the journey was seen to have an end as well as a beginning. For constitutional change—the change of balance between organs of government—is not an autonomous process. It is the synthesis, over a longer period, of political and economic events which, in so far as

[1] D. Bonner Smith, 'The Lord High Admiral's Council', in *M.M.* XVII, no. 2, pp. 181–3; G. F. James, 'The Lord High Admiral's Council', in *M.M.* XXII, no. 4, pp. 427–9.

[2] For its text, see Appendix XI below.

they contribute to a development other than their own, do so as much in spite as because of their immediate significance. Seen from the vantage point of the result, they are fragmentary, often contradictory, and often endowed in their own context with an importance quite different from that with which they must later be invested. If, therefore, the creation of a Board of Admiralty in 1689 is of constitutional significance, this cannot be demonstrated by a constitutional development which is either immediate or obvious, but only by reference to a result itself to be explained by the unforeseen and detailed interaction of events. But if this significance cannot be seen directly, it can be seen in reflection: not in the events themselves, but in their documentation. For it is in the preservation and arrangement of its records that the process finds expression whose agents may only gradually and with some difficulty be observed.

Our identification of periods in history is largely determined by the material at our disposal; and viewed in the light of naval records, the year 1689 marks the change from one period of naval administration to another. Before that date, Admiralty papers hardly exist as a generic class: such as there are under that name in the Public Record Office were partly transferred later from the State Papers, partly transcribed from documents no longer to be found or retained in other hands,[1] and in only a few cases were probably brought direct from the Admiralty office itself.[2] After that date, most of those that have ever existed were preserved in the department of their origin and, for the most part, with their contemporary classification.[3] For any section of the earlier period, therefore, the history of naval administration must be pieced together from miscellaneous groups of records, of which only a minority is in its proper setting. In these conditions, we must apply to it the same methods of inquiry that we apply to quite different but contemporary subjects, and be content with the external view that alone can be expected where materials as well as events must be reconstructed. But in the later period, the former themselves assist in the

[1] See Hubert Hall, 'The National Study of Naval History, II', in *Transactions of the Royal Historical Society*, XII, pp. 95–101.

[2] For details see John Ehrman, 'The Official Papers transferred by Pepys to the Admiralty by 12 July 1689', in *M.M.* XXXIV, no. 4, pp. 255–70.

[3] For exceptions, see ibid.

reconstruction of the latter. In their continuity of content and—hardly less important—of arrangement, the records are, as it were, the mummy of the events, and the task under these circumstances is to bring to life again the institution whose corpse is thus embalmed, its features and its lineaments intact and already discernible.

This contrast is the reflection of an administrative change. But to see what the latter was, it is necessary to see first what the former was not. It is easy to exaggerate the very real change that took place into a complete and abrupt break with the recent past, particularly when the preservation of documents at the Admiralty after 1688 is compared with their retention for the preceding years by Pepys. Such a comparison cannot be avoided. If we wish to examine the history of the navy during the Restoration period, we do so in the Pepysian Library at Magdalene College, Cambridge, rather than in the Public Record Office. But this is not because the Admiralty was denied the custody of these papers, but because it has since largely managed to lose them. Two lists exist of the official documents surrendered by Pepys to his successor between the middle of March and the middle of July 1689, and from them it is clear that the transfer was a full one, and that the records themselves were, on the whole, well preserved from 1660, and in some cases since the Commonwealth.[1] Indeed, shortly after Pepys's retirement the history of most years of the Restoration navy could have been studied more profitably in the Admiralty library than in his own. The arrangement of the papers, moreover, was much the same as it was in William's Admiralties: Board Minutes (when there had been Boards), Secretary's In and Out Letters, Lord High Admiral's Orders and Warrants, all existed and the classification, so far as it went, closely resembled the later classification of the French wars and therefore, allowing for the necessary expansion, of the eighteenth century. It would seem, indeed, that on the one hand the new régime adhered to its predecessor's arrangement of the records, while on the other hand it failed to equal its success in preserving them.

Nevertheless, the change in the treatment of papers was profound. In the first place, there were some gaps in the lists of the records

[1] N.M.M., Bibl. Phill. uncatalogued. They are reproduced in full in Ehrman, loc. cit.

transferred by Pepys. Apart from some unimportant documents which he himself did not bother later to retain,[1] he withheld some of the materials for James II's reign, the most important of which were his own letter books from 1684 to 1688; and despite a correspondence on this point which lasted until 1700, only a selection of them—and that possibly a later transcription—has found its way into the national archives.[2] In contrast the only letter book outside the Public Record Office of any Secretary in William's reign is one of William Bridgeman's for the years 1694–7, the contents of which are in any case partly private.[3] Where there are gaps in the later official series, they would seem to be the results mainly of fire, from which the Admiralty was no more immune than other buildings in the neighbourhood;[4] occasionally of loss[5] or of deliberate destruction;[6] but never of deliberate removal.

In the second place, Pepys had transcripts made of most of the papers which he surrendered, for his own periods of office, as well as copies of others for earlier and intervening years which he included in his private 'Miscellanies'.[7] It is not, indeed, certain which series held the originals and which the transcripts;[8] but for our purpose, it is less important to know whether he retained the papers themselves, than that he openly retained their contents. In contrast again, no duplicates were made on a comparable scale for any Secretary after 1689.[9] Where

---

[1] Bodl. Rawl. A 186, ff. 2–5 contains a list of papers which were neither surrendered in 1689 nor are included in the library at Magdalene. They were mainly cancelled passes and printed Instructions, but also included some officers' journals between 1684 and 1688.

[2] *Private Correspondence and Miscellaneous Papers of Samuel Pepys, 1679–1703*, ed. J. R. Tanner (1926), II, pp. 168–9, 354, and 168, n. 3.

[3] B.M. Lansdowne 1152 B.

[4] E.g. *Cal.S.P.Col. Am. & W.I. 1717–18*, p. 313; *Historical Register*, I, p. 550.

[5] Possibly in the first half of the nineteenth century, when some of the records were moved first to Deptford, then to the Tower, and finally to Chancery Lane (*2nd* and *17th Reports of the Deputy Keeper of the Public Records* (1841, 1856)).

[6] The volume of court martial records containing the account of Torrington's trial in 1690 would seem to have disappeared in this way.

[7] Pep:Sea MSS. 2869–79.

[8] Dr Tanner thought, to begin with, that Magdalene held the originals (*Catal.* IV, pp. vii–viii); later he was not so sure.

[9] Bridgeman had some transcripts made, but they are on a small scale compared with those of Pepys (Bodl. Rawl. A 447–54).

papers were transcribed, it was for the official purposes of the senior Commissioner, and with the full knowledge and approval of the Board.[1] The significance of the Pepysian Library, indeed, lies not in the fact that it is now unique, which is largely adventitious, but precisely in the fact that at the time it was not.

Lastly, it was only with some difficulty that Pepys was induced to surrender the papers. By an Order in Council of 23 June 1673, he was theoretically bound to hand over all official correspondence on his retirement,[2] and the first move to secure it was made by the new Board on 9 March, when the Secretary was directed to write 'for all Books, Papers and things belonging to the affairs of the Admiralty'.[3] This seems to have met with little success; but later a compromise was reached, whereby one of the clerks, by name Pett, was sent to fetch individual books and to sign the receipt. After several demands for specific papers,[4] Pepys on 6 May stated that he was ready to hand over all the documents required,[5] but it was only on 12 July, for whatever reason, that the original demand of 9 March was satisfied to the extent that it was, and the final receipt signed by his successor.[6]

There were thus two aspects to Pepys's attitude towards his official papers, the one professional and disinterested, the other personal and political. Their combination was inherent in the nature of his Office. His career has been described on the one hand as that of the first of civil servants;[7] and so, in its professional aspect, it was. But it has also and equally correctly been seen as the climax of a tradition, stretching from Buckingham to Pepys and from the Spanish wars to the Dutch, in which administration was personal and the line between the direction and the execution of policy ill defined.[8] The dichotomy was not confined to the Admiralty. It was a problem of government itself, affecting throughout the later seventeenth century the relations of the

---

[1] Finch Transcr., Lord Cornwallis to the Queen, March 1692.

[2] G. F. James, 'Admiralty Administration and Personnel, 1619–1714', in *Bulletin of the Institute of Historical Research*, XIV, p. 168, where the relevant passage is quoted in full.

[3] P.R.O.Adm. 3/1: 9/3.

[4] P.R.O.Adm. 2/377, 19/3, 9/4, 16/4, 26/4; Bodl. Rawl. A 170, ff. 75, 77.

[5] Bodl. Rawl. A 170, f. 73.

[6] N.M.M., Bibl. Phill. lists.

[7] A. Bryant, *Samuel Pepys, the Saviour of the Navy*.

[8] Hubert Hall, loc. cit.

departmental officials with their political masters, and thus, since the solutions were different, the relations between the different departments themselves. For Pepys the professional administrator was not an isolated phenomenon. He came of a generation which also produced Downing, Williamson and the younger Southwell,[1] in whose hands the technique of organization, as an aspect and a prerequisite of government, was being overhauled and extended. Their departments bore witness to their activities. At the Treasury, standing orders began to appear upon lines not unfamiliar to ourselves;[2] in the office of the Lords of Trade, the Secretary was applying, at his own expense, the modern system of a classified index; and in 1689, after several years of argument, was held the first civil service examination, with the setting of mathematical papers for the appointment of landwaiters in the Customs.[3] Government, in fact, was getting more complicated. Files of papers and departmental buildings were becoming increasingly necessary, as the constantly increasing scale of the wars began to transform the paternalism of the seventeenth century into the oligarchic control which was the characteristic of the eighteenth. And in response to its demands, there was emerging a new class of professional administrators, the forerunners of the Permanent Secretaries, already coming to be noted in the contemporary books of reference;[4] forming at this early stage their own hereditary alliances,[5] and inheriting to some extent the traditional confusion of official with personal servants;[6] but nevertheless developing an *esprit de corps* at once different from that of the clerks in the old Offices of State at whose expense they were gaining ground, and at variance with the personal and proprietary attitude to office that still distinguished their masters.

---

[1] Born 1623(?), 1633 and 1635 respectively. Pepys was born in 1633.

[2] G. A. Jacobsen, *William Blathwayt* (1932), p. 25; Doris M. Gill, 'The Treasury, 1660–1714', in *E.H.R.* XLVI, pp. 600–6.

[3] Jacobsen, loc. cit. pp. 24, 414.

[4] They were first mentioned in Edward Chamberlayne's *Angliae Notitia* in the fifth edition of 1671, in which the long-projected second part first appeared. But although most of them were also mentioned in the later and rival *The New State of England* of Guy Miège (2nd ed. 1693), the Secretary of the Admiralty was not.

[5] For instance the Poveys.

[6] Blathwayt included in his 'family' his office clerks, as well as his footmen and coachman (Jacobsen, loc. cit. pp. 409, 422).

But Pepys, the political official, was also not an isolated phenomenon. The very independence of external interference which advanced his administrative measures was political in origin. With direct access to the royal will, and complete responsibility under it, he was virtually a Secretary of State on his own account; and to that extent he shared the tradition of the Secretaries' offices, where the official repository of documents—the State Paper Office—was largely ignored, and the principal actors continued to remove the evidence of their activities. The inconsistencies in his treatment of the records reflect with peculiar clarity the prevalent confusion, faced as he was with an expansion of business possibly greater than that of any other department, but obscured by the identification—at first virtual, and later explicit—of the head of the department with the King, and by the consequent elevation of its Secretary above the normal level of his colleagues, particularly of War and of the Treasury. It was, indeed, a position which in its uniqueness was typical of contemporary developments. Seen from its point of view, the problem of the age was not Parliamentary, but executive and administrative. In the Admiralty under Pepys, this problem had been met by the performance of both functions at one level; with the disappearance of the régime for which he stood it could be met only by their separation. And if we look back to the Admiralty of 1689 as the first of the modern Administrations, it is because that step was then taken, and the administrative work of the office then began to emerge from the cocoon of political interference in which it had hitherto been enveloped.

But this was only a step. If it was necessary to separate the functions of policy and administration, it was only in order to reconcile them on a basis other than that of personal government. This second stage was not reached during William's reign; for, upon different premises and with different limitations, his government was as personal as that of his predecessors. His answer to the problem lay, like theirs, within the confines of the executive, and where with them the identification of functions had overloaded Pepys with business, with William the Board of Admiralty, thanks to the separation of those functions, was largely starved of work. The connexion between the two levels had merely changed from one which was personal and intimate to one which was personal and tenuous. The same confusion of policy with administration often persisted, in a form which was suitable to the change of emphasis. The Admiralty Commissioners, appointed to pacify Parliament, were not the men to consult on policy: in consequence they found often enough that they were forbidden to carry it into effect. For, within the closed circle of the executive, there was no intrinsic constitutional guarantee that the nature of an Office would be respected in the nature of its employment. Indecision at Cabinet level involved progressive confusion throughout the hierarchy, and a change of confidential advisers might well be reflected in the routine of a permanent department. While administrative routine was developing along independent lines, administration itself was still subject to political pressure. The solution lay not in adjustments to the internal relations of the executive, but in the extraneous impetus of Parliamentary development, providing as it did the alternative of party to personal government, and preventing an expanding administration from either invading the domain or eluding the interest of the makers of policy. Under these circumstances, the Parliamentary nature of the Admiralty Commissioners would not involve their complementary exclusion from both levels of government, but would protect their employment at the lower level by regulating their access to the higher. It is indeed the triumph of party government that it enabled the political Commissioner to be replaced by the professional. But for that final reconciliation both Parliament and the executive had to wait beyond the end of the reign, the century and the wars with Louis XIV.

The details of this confused situation were worked out at the Admiralty in the months following Pepys's resignation on 20 February. In the subordinate departments, however, the change of régime involved hardly any change in administration or personnel.[1] Throughout the upheaval of James's flight, their work had continued with a minimum of interruption. Some of the effects of the Revolution had of course been felt. The stop of Exchequer payments between Christmas and 9 January had frightened the Navy Board into a refusal to make any

[1] Or in the treatment of official papers. The minutes of the Navy Board from 1673 to 1718 were later removed by its Clerk of the Acts, Charles Sergison, to his house in Sussex, where they remained until this century.

contracts, which continued spasmodically until well into the next month.[1] But on the whole things had gone smoothly, and the subordinate Boards and officials, immobilized by the Proclamation of 31 December which retained them in their jobs,[2] continued to work for their new master much as they had worked for the old. With the advent of a war,[3] certain additional duties had always to be assumed, and these were catered for in the course of the year. On 13 June Commissioners were appointed for regulating the exchange of prisoners of war; on 11 July the office of Surgeon General, whose incumbent, Richard Pearse, was suspected of Jacobitism, was replaced by a Commission for Sick and Wounded Seamen, on the lines of those of the Dutch wars which Evelyn's *Memoirs* have made familiar to later generations;[4] on 19 June Commissioners for Prizes were appointed, and on 25 October Commissioners for appeals in prize matters; and on 29 August one James Herbert was made Receiver General of all prize moneys.[5] With these appointments, the necessary additions to the peacetime Administration had been made.

The personnel of the existing Boards, of Victualling and of the Navy, was hardly affected by the war. It was no time to change the members of the Victualling Commission, and they survived accordingly until the autumn. The Navy Board also continued as before, except for a new Treasurer in Edward Russell, and for the loss of its Comptroller of Storekeeper's Accounts, Sir William Booth, who after trying unsuccessfully to persuade the crew of the *Pendennis* to sail for France under his command, managed himself to leave the country and to join James in exile.[6] His place was taken by Captain Henry Priestman.[7]

But at the Admiralty, both within the office itself and in its relations with other authorities, the implications of a new régime were soon evident. The final organization of the office was the product of three

---

[1] Serg:Mins. XVIII; 31/12, 4/1, 12/1, 18/2.

[2] *Bibliography of Royal Proclamations of the Tudor and Stuart Sovereigns, 1485–1714*, ed. R. Steele (1910), I, p. 475.

[3] *Cal.S.P.Dom. 1689–90*, p. 146.

[4] P.R.O. Privy Council register, 2/37, f. 180.

[5] These three appointments are entered on the Patent Rolls.

[6] *D.N.B.*; *Cal.S.P.Dom. 1689–90*, p. 119.

[7] Jackson, *Naval Commissioners*, pp. 2–3, 10–11.

factors: the growth of a permanent secretariat, the existence of a larger building in which to house the results of its work, and the presence of a purely departmental Secretary to supervise it. The emergence of a properly organized staff was a feature of the later years of William's war, and is discussed elsewhere.[1] It was also not until 1695 that the office moved finally to a building which had been designed specifically for it, and to the site which, with one short break, it was thenceforth to occupy until the present day. When the Admiralty Commissioners met on 9 March 1689, it was at Herbert's lodgings in Channel Row, Westminster, an unsatisfactory house of which he was neither the landlord nor the householder.[2] It is not, therefore, surprising that already on the 6th his secretary had approached Pepys with a view to taking over the old office in Buckingham Street.[3] Pepys, however, merely referred him to Hewer, and despite the unpopularity of the former Secretary and his successors' attempt to dispossess him, the absence of any legal connexion between house and office defeated their efforts.[4] Business continued to be done at Channel Row until 21 May, by which time Herbert had been out of London for over two months and the position must have been getting increasingly awkward. On the 22nd, however, the Board moved to a new office, near Pepys in York Buildings.[5] It may have hoped by this to bring pressure to bear on him, but the building was in any case popular with official bodies. The Commissioners for Prizes moved there in 1690, and the Parliamentary Commissioners for auditing the public accounts, before whom some of the Board's more unpleasant moments were to be spent, made it its headquarters from 1692.[6] There the Admiralty remained, further negotiations with Pepys having broken down in the spring of 1690,[7]

---

[1] See Ch. XIII below.

[2] G. F. James, 'The Admiralty Buildings, 1695–1723', in *M.M.* XXVI, no. 4, p. 357. 'Channel Row' was a corruption of Canon Row, which ran parallel with King Street (now Parliament Street) on the river side. The Secretary called it 'an unfit place' for an office (P.R.O.Adm. 2/377; 13/5, to Herbert).

[3] Bonner Smith, 'Samuel Pepys and York Buildings', in *M.M.* XXIV, no. 2, p. 232.

[4] According to the *L.C.C. Survey of London*, XVIII, p. 71, the arrangement between Pepys and Hewer had probably been made to meet just such a contingency (cited by James, loc. cit.).

[5] P.R.O.Adm. 3/1: 22/3.

[6] *London Gazette*, no. 2470.

[7] The Board had hoped to move in March (P.R.O.Adm. 3/3: 7/3).

until on 9 May it took the lease of Judge Jeffreys' former house in Duke Street, Westminster. By the beginning of June it had moved in. The house, a comparatively new one, lay at the southern end of the street, with a good view over its garden wall into the depths of St James's Park. The office stayed there for five years, until in June 1695 the new buildings in Spring Gardens were ready for it to make its last move of the century.[1]

Of more immediate importance was the change in the status of the Secretary, which became evident with the replacement of Pepys by Phineas Bowles. It was not, of course, at once complete. In some respects, Bowles behaved much as Pepys had done, and his appointment itself was a good example of the traditional methods of patronage. Five months before, he had been out of a job, and applying to Pepys for a post on the Victualling Commission, which it was rumoured Haddock was about to leave on his appointment as Comptroller of the Navy.[2] As a former victuallers' agent in Tangier and Lisbon, his qualifications might not have been inadequate; but Haddock had no intention of resigning, and Bowles had to be content in October with the humbler and less remunerative post of secretary to the Admiral of the fleet.[3] Keenly alive to the possibilities of the times, from this vantage point he watched closely the increasingly rapid swing of power away from his master, Dartmouth, first towards the Orange faction in the fleet and finally to the associates of Orange himself. His precise activities unfortunately remain as obscure as he himself could have wished; but towards the end of December, when Dartmouth sent him to London to spy out the land, he seems, after his false cast in the direction of Clarendon,[4] to have recognized the rising star. After contriving to embroil his two immediate superiors, the Admiral and the Secretary, in an argument on his account,[5] he disappears from view, to re-emerge towards the end of February as Herbert's secretary.[6] The two were old acquaintances from Tangier days, and the knowledge of recent politics which Bowles was able to supply was no doubt useful to a

[1] James, loc. cit. pp. 358–9. [2] Bodl. Rawl. A 186, f. 173.

[3] *H.M.C.* 11, v, p. 160; *Records of the Bowles Family*, ed. W. H. Bowles (1918), pp. 35–9.

[4] See p. 278, n. 1 above. [5] *H.M.C.* 11, v, pp. 242, 245, 247.

[6] P.R.O. Signet Office Dockets, March 1689.

master who had been out of touch with the fleet for some months. When Herbert was appointed as head of the Admiralty Commission, Bowles came in on his coat-tails. On 9 March, by one of its first resolutions, the new Board appointed him as Secretary of the Admiralty.[1]

Bowles was not backward in acknowledging his debt. 'This Post', he wrote to Herbert of the Secretaryship, 'wch by yor interest and favour I am established in';[2] and the corollary followed. ''Tis morally impossible', he confessed, 'that I should omitt any injunction from yor Lo^{p}.'[3] Nor did he. When his patron had left for the fleet, he supplied him with a series of long and confidential letters, complementing his official correspondence from the Board, which reached an average of almost two a week over a period of six months.[4] Sometimes, indeed, so well recognized was the relationship, these took the place of the Board's letters, while in return Herbert often duplicated his observations to both,[5] and occasionally omitted the Commissioners altogether. His account of Bantry Bay, for instance, which Aylmer brought to London, was addressed not to the Admiralty but to Bowles.[6] It was to the Secretary, too, that he communicated the suspicions and personal disappointments which beset him,[7] while in return Bowles confided his family worries, where there was a possibility of their being eased, to his superior.[8] The closeness of the relationship was finally to be seen in the disappearance of the Secretary a month after the Admiral had resigned from the Board.[9]

At the same time, Bowles built up other connexions. Among the Commissioners, he cultivated particularly Lowther and Lee, the former

---

[1] P.R.O.Adm. 3/1: 9/3. [2] P.R.O.Adm. 2/377, 1/4.

[3] Ibid. 13/6 (first of two letters).

[4] P.R.O.Adm. 2/377, 2/378, 1/4 to 21/9, *passim*. He announced his intention of forwarding news and rumour in his letter of 13 April.

[5] P.R.O.Adm. 3/1, April and May, *passim*. Herbert's official correspondence has entirely disappeared, but the Board minutes contain a précis of the contents of the letters between him, itself and Bowles. A particularly good example of his duplication lies in his letters of 30 March to the Board and 31 March to Bowles.

[6] Ibid. 8/5. [7] P.R.O.Adm. 2/378, 1/9.

[8] Ibid. 6/7, 9/7; P.R.O.Adm. 3/2: 15/18, 11/12.

[9] Bowles was dismissed in the middle of January 1690 (Luttrell, op. cit. II, p. 10).

mainly for the latter's sake.[1] When Lee was ill during July and August, he sent him, by order, the minutes of the Board, and supplemented them with news and conjecture on his own account.[2] He also performed more personal offices, drawing his salary for him, seeing that he got the Gazette, and supplying him with a coal merchant in the shape of his brother.[3] In the fleet, too, he had his contacts and a certain influence, although the latter was only a shadow of the searching and pervasive interest of Pepys. He was on particularly friendly terms with Shovell and Berkeley among the flag officers, and with Delavall and Stafford Fairborne among the senior captains;[4] and while the first two conferred rather than received honour, with the captains he savoured the pleasures of patronage. 'Ye Com.^rs^', he wrote to Fairborne, with his usual unctuousness, 'are jestingly pleased (sometimes) to terme you my Captain.'[5]

These personal connexions sometimes cut across the orthodox channels of communication, and private and public business were liable to go hand in hand. But the office organization itself was not strictly defined. Matters which called for a Board letter on one occasion, were answered on another by the Secretary; both wrote equally to officers at sea, to their subordinate departments, and to external authorities. Sometimes, indeed, their correspondence strays, without incongruity, into each other's letter books,[6] and in only one instance is it possible to distinguish any difference between them. When it was necessary to correspond with the Ordnance, the Commissioners addressed its Master; the Secretary confined himself to the Lieutenant or to the officers of the Board.

Nevertheless, despite this personal activity, Bowles occupied a position in the Admiralty which was very different from that of Pepys. He was, as he recognized, the servant of the Board,[7] and his relations with external authorities extended only to the communication and never to the initiation of business. For this purpose, he sometimes visited the

---

1 P.R.O.Adm. 2/377, 12/6 (Bowles to Lowther); 2/378, 16/8 (Bowles to Lee).

2 Ibid. 1/7, 13/8, 20/8, 24/8, 31/8.

3 Ibid. 16/8.

4 P.R.O.Adm. 2/377, 15/3, 23/3, 23/4, 4/6.

5 Ibid. 4/6.

6 There are several examples in P.R.O.Adm. 2/169, and 2/377, 2/378 and 2/379.

7 P.R.O.Adm. 2/377, 1/4 (Bowles to Herbert).

King on behalf of the department;[1] but he was never granted an audience like his predecessor. Such importance as he possessed was reflected importance—influence with the Board and knowledge of its decisions—and if his appointment and his behaviour were not always those of a subordinate official, the nature and still more the limitations of his work undoubtedly were. It was in what he could not do, rather than in what he did, that he appears as the genesis of that line of permanent salaried administrators to whom his methods and his contacts would have seemed so foreign and repugnant.

The Board worked him hard. Within a week of its appointment, he was complaining of the pressure of affairs,[2] and throughout the spring and summer he regaled Torrington with accounts of the long hours and varied business which his duties entailed. 'Ye Board has set early and late for some days past', he wrote on one occasion, excusing a gap in his letters;[3] a fortnight later, thanks to its 'continually setting twice a day from Morning till nere 2 and sometimes longer, & from afternoon till Midnight...it is allwayes morning ere I can get to my Bedd; so that I may say in truth I am almost harrassed out of my little senses'.[4] The same story was repeated in the following months;[5] and indeed many of his letters were signed near midnight, or even at two or four o'clock in the morning. In May 1690, after his dismissal, he submitted a memorandum concerning his duties which enumerated his different activities.[6] He had to wait on the King,[7] the Council, the Secretaries of State and the Treasury; to attend 'frequently' the sessions of the Navy Board and see the numerous sea officers who came to the Admiralty; and to prepare agenda for the Board, 'minutely attend' its meetings and often take the necessary action upon its decisions. In his opinion, the work called for two Secretaries, so that 'while one is employed in the common business...the other may apply himself to think of what may

---

1 P.R.O.Adm. 2/377, 23/5 (Bowles to Navy Board); 2/378, 1/9, 16/9, 14/10, 21/11 (all to Torrington).

2 P.R.O.Adm. 2/377, 14/3 (to Berry), 15/3 (to Shovell).

3 Ibid. 30/4.

4 Ibid. 13/5.

5 P.R.O.Adm. 2/378, 4/6, 26/6, 24/7, 10/8.

6 P.R.O.Adm. 2/170, ff. 225–7. It is reproduced as Appendix XIII below.

7 The memorandum states 'frequently if not daily'. The Admiralty records do not confirm this.

be for the welfare and better government of the navy in general and prepare drafts for the amending and altering several things in the economy of the Navy'.

The Board meetings themselves must have occupied a good deal of the Secretary's time.[1] Except for Sundays,[2] there were only five days on which one was not held in the first six months of its creation.[3] On the other days, the Board met on 93 occasions once, and on 59 occasions twice a day; and during the busy weeks from the middle of April to the end of June the proportions were 20 of the former to 43 of the latter. Business was taken as it came. Petitions and contracts, protections from the press and officers' peccadilloes, letters from merchants and justices of the peace, and memoranda for the Council and for the King jostle one another without distinction in the closely-packed pages of the daily minutes. In the autumn, one day a week was reserved for the attendance of the Navy Board, at first Fridays and then Wednesdays.[4] Occasionally also something would be put aside, when only a few members were present, to await the attention of a full Board; but after the first few months, when full Boards had become the exception, this procedure followed suit.[5]

But exactly what was a meeting it is difficult to say. It was apt to be an informal and fluid affair. Members came and went throughout, so that it was not unusual for the personnel to have changed almost completely between its beginning and its end. The business sometimes stretched, in a haphazard sort of way, over six or seven hours, and the only difference between a day on which one meeting, and a day on which two or even three were recorded, seems often to have been that on the former occasion most, while on the latter all, of those present at the start had left the room after a certain time. Another difficulty, no doubt, when there were perhaps only two Commissioners in the office,

---

[1] The following three paragraphs are based on P.R.O.Adm. 3/1 and 3/2, for the period 9 March to 9 September.

[2] Minutes are recorded for Sunday, 9 June, but there are no names of those present. It is possible that the Secretarial business for the day was inserted in error.

[3] 28 and 29 March, 2 April, 5 and 27 June.

[4] P.R.O.Adm. 3/2: 10/8, 31/10.

[5] Certain Orders in Council continued to require the attention of a full Board (P.R.O.Adm. 2/379, f. 101).

was to distinguish between resolutions taken formally at a Board and decisions arrived at in conversation; and it was usually safest to include everything, under the heading of one comprehensive meeting. Unfortunately, no details are known of the buildings in which the Admiralty worked during the first six years of the war; for domestic architecture has a definite if minor effect on procedure. In the Board Room at the later Admiralty, for instance, the size of the table undoubtedly influenced the way in which its occupants approached their task. Its enormous size[1] enabled the Commissioners not only to work, but to take their meals at it—and in one case to write a book at it—when things were slack.[2] The separate heads of the departments who were in the building, were thus in one room; when a particular matter demanded the attention of a Board, a Board was convened by rapping on the table; and when it had been settled, the Board automatically dissolved. The minutes were written up at the end of the morning and the afternoon, and a semblance of unity was given to what had in fact often been a lengthy and disconnected affair.[3] Something of the sort may well have happened in the earlier years. But with all this there was a difference between individual or informal decisions and those taken officially by a Board, for the latter were recorded, under the names of those present, by the Secretary or by a clerk in attendance; and the precedents accumulated, under responsible authority, in a constitutionally recognizable manner.

One of the contributory causes for the flexibility of procedure was the fact that the average attendance soon dwindled to three or four. A quorum, of course, was necessary, but its exact strength was never recorded. Bowles, in May, remarked that Carbery, Lowther and Chicheley, 'remained to make a quorum for despatch of immediate Ord^rs';[4] but business was sometimes officially done with only two members present,[5] and once by Lowther alone.[6] In the first two months

---

[1] It may be seen in Pugin and Rowlandson's print of the Board Room in 1808.

[2] See Admiral Sir John Berkeley's evidence before the Select Committee on the Board of Admiralty in 1861 (*H.C. 438* (1861)).

[3] Ibid.

[4] P.R.O.Adm. 2/377; 13/5, to Herbert.

[5] 13/5 p.m., 17/5 a.m., 8/6 p.m., 26/6 p.m., 28/6 p.m., 29/6 a.m., 12/7 p.m., 26/7 a.m., 1/8, 3/8, 14/8, 24/8.

[6] 2/7 p.m.

attendance was good, and there were seldom less than five Commissioners present; but as the summer wore on, two of the total of six (Herbert being at sea) fell away, and from June to September the names of Carbery, Lowther and Chicheley appear regularly and almost exclusively at the head of the agenda, with the addition of Lee in the last month, after he had recovered from his illness. Wharton and Sacheverell, indeed, not only did not take any part in business, but also failed to draw their salaries:[1] the latter, probably because of his old disinclination to have anything to do with the executive, the former—it can only be conjectured—out of a lack of interest or a caution which a small loss of income was not sufficient to overcome. Their absence caused rumours of their resignation throughout the summer and autumn, and was probably responsible for William's intention to appoint another Commissioner at the end of August.[2] But in the event, the first changes came only at the end of the year.

Within the executive, the position of the Board of Admiralty was unstable. The Revolution settlement has been looked at in the past more from Parliament's point of view than from that of the executive, and where the latter has been considered it has usually been at the highest level, where the influence of Parliament was most direct and considerable. But seen from the point of view of an administrative department, its immediate importance lies in its effect on the relations between the different levels of executive authority. This is difficult to describe in general terms, precisely because decisions, and action upon them, were taken on the same subjects in different ways at different times. A problem which concerned authorities at different levels was being approached, from the highest level, in an attitude which frequently confused one with the other. Such a confusion had two complementary results in naval affairs: first, the Admiralty was denied access to the higher levels of authority; but secondly, and at the same time, its own level was

[1] Wharton drew his only until 25 March, and Sacheverell not at all (P.R.O. Audit Office 1/17; Declared Accounts, Treasurer of the Navy). In August, however, there was an agreement that the latter could draw £200 salary for 'a broken Quarter' (P.R.O.Adm. 2/378; 13/8, Bowles to Sacheverell).

[2] P.R.O.Adm. 2/377, 13/5; 2/378, 29/6 (both to Torrington); 'Spencer House Journals', pp. 233, 238.

invaded by those authorities. The first result has already been seen from the point of view of the highest authority, the King; it may also, with the second result, be observed from the levels of his subordinates.

Throughout the campaign of 1689, the Board of Admiralty seldom saw the King as a Board. According to its records, it attended him, with other members of his Council, twice in April, once in May and twice in June;[1] and it is not surprising that it noted, among the subjects to be raised at the first of the June meetings, 'That his Ma^{ty} be acquainted, That the Board attending his Ma^{ty} frequently will be for his Ma^{ty} service'.[2] Whether or not this suggestion was in fact conveyed, it had little immediate effect. Two audiences are recorded again for July,[3] one for August, two for September, and one for October.[4] During the winter, the arrangements were greatly improved, probably as the result of the increasingly grave financial situation, the necessity for humouring Parliament and the controversies of the autumn which led William to turn from Torrington as his confidant on naval affairs.[5] Beginning in the third week of November, a regular series of conferences was held on Sunday, normally at Whitehall but occasionally at Hampton Court, with the more prominent members of the Council. These continued until the end of the year, and were renewed for a short time in the first quarter of 1690.[6] But their *ad hoc* character was shown when they stopped after March of that year, and no system developed at all comparable to the relations which existed between William and the Treasury, whose meetings he frequently attended and whose business was often conducted in his presence without the intervention of his ministers.[7] In contrast, he never attended the Admiralty, nor did he ever hear the Commissioners alone.

---

[1] P.R.O.Adm. 3/1: 8/4; 2/169, f. 82 (Board to Navy Board); 2/337, 8/5 (Board to Herbert); 2/169, f. 145.

[2] P.R.O.Adm. 2/169, f. 145.

[3] Possibly three; a reference on the 27th is obscure. The other two were on the 17th and 27th (P.R.O. Adm. 3/1).

[4] P.R.O.Adm. 2/169, 15/8 (Bowles to Torrington); 2/378, 12/9, 28/9 (to Torrington); 3/2: 31/10.

[5] See pp. 308–40 below.

[6] P.R.O.Adm. 3/2: 24/11, 1/12, 8/12, 15/12, 22/12, 29/12, 25/1/90, 23/2, 9/3. Other meetings were held on 24 November, 19 January 1690, 25 January and 3 March.

[7] See *Cal.Treas.Bks. 1689–92*, pp. 26–78.

There were other and less formal contacts. Sometimes a memorandum was sent by the Secretary instead of by a messenger, and sometimes individual Commissioners were summoned to Hampton Court or Whitehall. Carbery, Lowther and Lee were all sent for at different times, although the latter's illness prevented him from attending as often as either of the other two.[1] The other three junior Commissioners were never summoned, for the King disliked Chicheley,[2] and Wharton and Sacheverell were obviously of no account outside Parliament. But until the middle of April, and again when he was in London in the last half of May, the most, and indeed the only effective link between William and the Board was Herbert.

So far as the Admiralty was concerned, Herbert represented the orthodox channel of communication with authority. When he was available, the number of points to be submitted to the personal attention of the King immediately increased, and if he failed to attend the office for any length of time a vigorous search would be made for him, for he did not always bother to inform his colleagues of his whereabouts.[3] He was also supplied with all information when he was with the fleet, and the more important matters were dispatched by advice boat to the Soundings or to the French coast for his decision. On 30 March his colleagues resolved that he be sent 'an account of such other matters as hee thinke fitt for his knowledge', and two days later that 'Our Secretary send him the Minnits of the Board from time to time'.[4] While cruising in the chops of the Channel, he was asked to settle the disposition of 'convoys and cruisers', to draw up a scheme for a West Indies squadron, and to recommend the composition of the winter guard.[5] But on his side Herbert did not always respond as the Admiralty would have liked. Condemned as he was to be absent at sea, he was determined to keep in touch with events on shore, and for this

---

[1] P.R.O.Adm. 3/1: 25/7; 2/377, 2/7; 2/378, 1/9, 30/10 (to Torrington); 'Spencer House Journals', p. 206.

[2] 'Spencer House Journals', p. 213.

[3] E.g. the fuss when he stayed at Weybridge during the third week in May (P.R.O.Adm. 2/377, 22/5, 24/5), and near Walton in November (P.R.O.Adm. 2/378, ff. 453–4, 469, 474, 476).

[4] P.R.O.Adm. 3/1: 30/3, 1/4.

[5] P.R.O.Adm. 2/169, ff. 113, 256; 2/378, 24/7.

purpose the Board was of little use to him. He turned, therefore, to the authority which was able both to deal with his affairs and to act on his complaints; and while he omitted at times to write to the Admiralty at all for some weeks,[1] it was with regret that the latter occasionally found him finishing business, which it had initiated, through the more convenient and influential agency of a Secretary of State.[2]

For the Secretaries of State emerged rapidly after the Revolution as a factor in naval affairs. Under James II, when Pepys was at the height of his influence, they had little connexion either with the Admiralty or with the fleet. Dartmouth, in the mobilization of 1688, received only one order from Middleton,[3] and none from Preston. In Charles II's reign, however, when the navy had at times been directly administered from outside the Admiralty, by committees of the Council or by the Council itself, the Secretaries had been more closely in touch with the service. They were, indeed, the obvious means of communication with it when government did not work through departments. But the peculiar nature of their relations with the navy under William arose from the fact that they enjoyed a greater authority in its affairs than ever before, precisely at a time when departmental administration was itself expanding.

The gradual replacement of conciliar by departmental administration affected the Secretaries of State in two ways. In the first place, they improved their position at the expense of the Council. For under such a system, whereby the direction and the administration of affairs were largely carried out by the same body under different forms, the Privy Council's loss of control in one sphere, thanks to the emergence of the administrative department, was accompanied by a loss of control in the other; and the Secretaries, by origin the personal servants of the King and connected with the Council only as his ministers, were not necessarily involved in its decline. But at the same time some of the new departments were themselves unable to satisfy the personal requirements of the King, and in these cases the Secretaries of State, again as his personal agents, were able to exercise a direct influence upon

[1] P.R.O.Adm. 3/1: 4/5; 2/378, 24/7; 2/169, ff. 240, 275.

[2] P.R.O.Adm. 2/377, 13/5; 2/378, 2/7.

[3] *H.M.C.* 11, v, p. 198.

them on his behalf. The fact that the Admiralty was losing in administrative authority at the same time that it was gaining in administrative technique, enabled them, thanks to their independence of the Council which the latter development supported, to take advantage of the former and to intervene between the department and the King. Under William's system of personal government, this meant not only that they supervised but that to some extent they absorbed the departmental functions. Their activities were the product entirely of other factors; in them was found a solution to the relations between their superior and subordinate levels of personal and departmental authority.

These activities can best be seen through the Secretaries' correspondence with the different naval authorities. Their responsibilities to King and Council, and the functions of the latter, appear in their letters to the Admiralty; their relations with that department, in the letters which they received from the Admiralty and in their correspondence with the commanders at sea. When writing to the department they appear, thanks largely to the form of the transaction, merely as a channel of communication for higher authority. An order to the Admiralty could be made in one of two ways: either under the sign manual of the King, or by an Order in Council, the former being always and the latter often conveyed by a Secretary of State. These alternatives corresponded to the alternative means of action possessed by the sovereign, of his own volition and of his formal advisers. Either might be employed to determine and to promulgate any subject of policy. On one occasion, the King might convey his intentions by warrant; on another, by Order in Council; on a third, by word of mouth. In naval affairs, there was no criterion of subject or of circumstance by which one mode of action might be distinguished from the other; but, in fact, the Council had for some years been a theoretical alternative. Its full assembly by the Revolution had come to be used merely for the formal recognition of policy, while its component Committees could be made to mean almost anything that was required. Two of these, in the early years of William's war, had definite naval functions and a distinct power of their own. The Committee for the Affairs of Ireland in 1689 was directly in charge of the arrangements for transporting troops to that country, and in that connexion was placed over the Admiralty and the War Office, and empowered to order escorts for the convoys and to regulate the dispositions of the ships which the King had made available in the Irish Sea.[1] So close, indeed, was its connexion with the day-to-day preparations for the campaign, that the Admiralty started a separate letter book for its correspondence.[2] The Committee for Trade and Plantations also exercised some authority over the Admiralty, but less directly and consistently. It took a hand in drafting the Instructions for the commanders of squadrons to the West Indies[3] and in arranging for the transport of troops there by warship,[4] and it sometimes attempted to regulate the convoy system in the Channel.[5] As a permanent Committee until 1696, when it was replaced by the Board of Trade, it was in immediate authority over the Admiralty on the detailed arrangements for colonial expeditions, and remained as a standing check on its relations with the merchants at home. But although its correspondence was included with that of the King and Queen and of the Secretaries of State in one volume of 'important In-letters',[6] its letters and orders were in fact few.[7] Apart from these two Committees, the Privy Council itself, formidable as it was in theory, had little actual power.[8] It had become simply a bag into which those of its members who were the real government of the day, dipped to provide themselves with the appropriate constitutional apology for their actions; and although, after the Revolution, many of the decisions on which the Admiralty was required to act continued to be conveyed on its authority[9]—sometimes

---

[1] Its orders to the Admiralty are reproduced in *H.M.C.* 12, VI, pp. 160–80. The correspondence of its Secretary, William Blathwayt, is alluded to constantly in P.R.O.Adm. 3/1 and 3/2 *passim*.

[2] P.R.O.Adm. 2/169; 30/10 (Board to Committee).

[3] P.R.O.Adm. 2/378, f. 378; 3/7: 12/8. [4] P.R.O.Adm. 3/1: 30/5.

[5] P.R.O.Adm. 3/1: 15/5.

[6] See the title to P.R.O.Adm. 1/4080, and contents.

[7] It also had relations with the Admiralty through the relations of its local officials with those of the Admiralty in the colonies themselves (see G. L. Beer, *The Old Colonial System*, I (1933), pp. 260, 264).

[8] Cf. Halifax on William's reluctance to increase its numbers. 'In that hee committed a mistake. Double the number would have done no hurt, and would have ingaged men of quality. [He] had a wrong notion of the Privy Councell; thought the Gov^{t} was to reside there' ('Spencer House Journals', p. 204).

[9] Professor M. A. Thomson, in his *Secretaries of State, 1681–1782* (1932), p. 78 and n. 3, states that Orders in Council on naval matters were not common during this

over the signatures of a full Council, sometimes over those of a Committee, and sometimes over those of some of its members, who in number did not form a full Council nor in function a Committee—many of these had already been taken at an earlier stage, and with the knowledge of the Secretary of State in whose letter they were officially enclosed.

As the King's ministers, and as such connected with the Council, the Secretaries of State conveyed many of its orders; as the King's servants, they conveyed all his personal directions to the Admiralty. Throughout 1689, their letters to the department on this score were restricted to enclosing the royal warrants, in which the Secretary's signature remained merely a countersign to his master's sign manual.[1] It was only in 1690 that there began the regular succession of letters over the Secretary's hand alone. But while his personal authority might seem small from this correspondence, he nevertheless appears in it as the normal and recognized channel of communication between two authorities which had previously corresponded direct with each other. As the historian of the Office has observed, 'it cannot be a mere coincidence that both the extant Secretarial entry books (naval) and the extant Admiralty entry books of in-letters (Secretary of State) begin in 1689'.[2]

The Secretaries' importance, however, is seen more clearly in the reverse correspondence, from the Admiralty to its superior authorities. For if at the higher level they appear as a convenient medium of communication, from the lower, within four months of James's flight, they have come to be regarded with Herbert as the normal last stage in any administrative process, and thus assume explicitly an authority which is implicit in their conveyance of the King's instructions. Close to the King, they were, particularly in Herbert's absence, in constant demand. From 23 March, when the Admiralty was requesting a Secretary 'To move his Majesty to consider whether more small ships should not

---

period; but in the context, I take it that he refers to Orders to 'naval officers who held independent commands'. I am not sure exactly what he means by 'independent commands', but Orders in Council to the Admiralty, as a class, were by no means uncommon between 1689 and 1698; see P.R.O.Adm. 1/5247–9.

[1] P.R.O.Adm. 1/4080, ff. 1–20; and see Thomson, loc. cit. p. 78, n. 4.

[2] Thomson, loc. cit. p. 78, n. 2.

speedily be built',[1] they were recognized as an intermediary step between William and the Board. But at the same time, they appear not only as a superior but as an alternative authority to the Commissioners, alluded to in references to business which concerned the latter but of which they had not been directly informed. Indeed, the ignorance of the Admiralty at times astonishes a later age. It had even, on occasion, to inquire the whereabouts of its own ships, or the nature of their instructions, when a Secretary of State had neglected to inform it of the latest news.[2] In August, the limits of its knowledge were shown even more sharply, when the Board was obliged to confess that:

> The Admirals of their Majesties' fleets have lately written hither to be... supplied with soe many of the maritime articles of peace between their Majesties and their allies as may be sufficient to dispose of to the several commanders, but we having no knowledge of the said treatise do desire your Lordship will take care that the Admirals be furnished with such of them as shall be thought fitting.[3]

This ignorance was often due to the alternative arrangements which existed for sending orders to the Admirals at sea. These could take one of two forms: they could be either instructions from the Admiralty, in which case they need not be signed by anyone but the Commissioners, or warrants from the King, signed by himself and countersigned either by the Commissioners of the Admiralty or, as in the case of any other warrant, by one of the Secretaries of State. On 15 March, Herbert was instructed by the Admiralty to obey any orders received direct from the King, which came with the countersign of a Secretary.[4] It was the first of many such instructions, continued throughout the remainder of that and most of the following century,[5] by which a parallel system of command to that of the Admiralty was created. Within the drastic limits thus imposed, the Admiralty tried to maintain its rights against external interference. It defeated one attempt on the

---

[1] *H.M.C. Finch*, II, p. 196. [2] P.R.O.Adm. 2/170, f. 256; 2/171, f. 51.

[3] P.R.O.Adm. 2/169, f. 370. Nevertheless some of the contents, even if not the text, must have been known officially, for they had been communicated to the House of Commons, on William's command, on 2 July (*H.C.J.* x, p. 203). In November, however, the Admiralty still professed ignorance of both (P.R.O.Adm. 2/378, f. 503).

[4] P.R.O.Adm. 2/3, f. 19. [5] Thomson, loc. cit. p. 79.

part of the Privy Council to deprive it of power to grant protections from the press, and another to send instructions from the Council direct to the fleet.[1] Nor did the commanders at sea entirely neglect the letter even when they complied with the spirit of the law. Ten days after he had received the order of 15 March, Herbert was writing to a Secretary of State, with reference to some directions which he had received from the Council Committee for Ireland: 'I am not empowered to obey any orders but theirs [the Admiralty's] unless immediately signed by the King... [I] am seeing the orders executed, but for the future desire that they may come in the proper way.'[2] It was a good comment on the situation: the Council's orders were obeyed, the authority of the Admiralty was protested, and the redress was left to the Secretary of State.

The order of 15 March enabled the latter to embark on a correspondence with the commanders afloat which reveals fully and clearly the extent of his power. It is possible to read the papers of the Board of Admiralty without gaining any idea, except through orders from above, of the policy to be pursued. But it is impossible to read the letters between the Secretaries of State and the Admirals in the fleet without realizing that here the decisions are being made, and their consequences discussed on grounds other than that of their effect upon administration. In the relations of the principal actors which appear there, a pattern may be traced which is often markedly absent from the minutes and letters of the Board; and simultaneously, on the level at which the latter alone should be operating, the impact of a higher authority may be observed, at once limiting and confusing its responsibilities.

In 1689, one Secretary alone conducted this correspondence. Shrewsbury, the Secretary for the southern department, had little to do with naval affairs. The Admiralty approached him occasionally over its Mediterranean or West Indian interests; the wording of passes for ships trading to North Africa, the diplomatic consequences of the King's intention to use Port Mahon and Gibraltar for the supply of his squadron in the Straits, and the provision of advice-boats to Bermuda

[1] P.R.O.Adm. 2/337, 4/5 (Bowles to Sotherne).

[2] *H.M.C. Finch*, II, p. 196.

involved his personal attention; while, like his colleague, he also took an interest in the safe arrival of the North Sea packets which were under naval protection.[1] But apart from these particular responsibilities, he took no share in the day-to-day conduct of naval business or in the private correspondence which accompanied the orders to the fleet. These were the exclusive concern of the Secretary for the northern department.[2] This can be accounted for to some extent on official grounds, since the northern department included the Netherlands, and thus the negotiations for the naval treaty with the Dutch. But naval affairs as such did not necessarily fall under either department, and in any case the Secretaries' work often overlapped their provinces and the distinction was ill defined. The Secretary for the north conducted the naval correspondence not because he was Secretary for the north, but because he was the Earl of Nottingham.

Daniel Finch, Earl of Nottingham[3] is, with Herbert, Russell and William himself, one of the four great *dramatis personae* of the naval scene in the first half of the war. Aged 42 at the time of the Revolution, he had over half a lifetime of public service behind him.[4] He had had some experience of naval business, for he had been a Commissioner of the Admiralty from 1679 to 1684, and in 1683 had been head of the Board. He prided himself, thereafter, on his knowledge of its affairs—occasionally to the annoyance of professional sailors, who were brought up against political and, as they claimed, amateur opposition disguised in professional terms;[5] and it was as Bolgolam the Lord High Admiral, who piqued himself upon understanding sea affairs, that Swift satirized him in *Gulliver's Travels*.[6] His politics were those of the High Church Tories who had accepted the Revolution, and, as their leader, his

[1] P.R.O.Adm. 3/1: 23/4, 3/3, 15/5; *Cal.S.P.Dom. 1689–90*, pp. 68, 87.

[2] In P.R.O.Adm. 1/4080 (In-Letters to the Admiralty from the Secretaries of State) there are only two letters from Shrewsbury.

[3] For his career, see *D.N.B.* and *Conduct*.

[4] He was first returned to Parliament in 1673; but it is possible that he did not sit until 1679 (*D.N.B.*).

[5] Cf. Dartmouth's remark in Burnet, *History*, II, p. 95.

[6] C. H. Firth, 'The Political Significance of *Gulliver's Travels*', in *Proceedings of the British Academy, 1919–1920*, pp. 242–3.

attitude and his votes upon its different problems were of crucial importance in deciding its form. When he accepted office as a Secretary of State, it 'had', according to a contemporary who by no means saw eye to eye with him, 'so good effects that I reckon I do not exceed the severe rules of history when I say that Nottingham's being in the ministry...first preserved the church and then the crown'.[1] In the ministry, he acted conscientiously as the King's servant on executive matters without compromising his political beliefs. While a strong opponent of faction,[2] he continued to vote Tory in the House of Lords to an extent that occasionally alarmed William,[3] and openly advised him against the more extreme Whigs.[4] William, despite the suspicion with which most of his other advisers regarded Nottingham, liked and trusted him,[5] and as a self-claimed expert on the navy his power became considerable. Provided that on domestic grounds he could remain in office, he was, with his honesty, his experience and his high notions of the prerogative, a strong candidate for the unofficial post of minister for naval affairs.

In person he was dark, thin and solemn. Formal in manner, long-winded in debate, old-fashioned in his clothes, he was the sort of man who naturally attracts nicknames. 'Don Diego' he was called by Steele, and 'Dismal' by Swift,[6] although in fact he was not so solemn as all that. If he had been brought up strictly, he had also been brought up liberally. Busby was his master at Westminster and Richard Allestree at Oxford; he had a deep and almost gay affection for his first wife,[7] and in the manner of his peers he enjoyed his hunting and his local duties in Rutland, where he built his great house of Burley. In his patriotism,

---

[1] Foxcroft, *A Supplement to Burnet's History of My Own Time*, p. 314.

[2] *Conduct*, pp. 129–30.

[3] 'Spencer House Journals', p. 230; *Supplement to Burnet*, p. 315.

[4] *Supplement to Burnet*, pp. 314–15.

[5] *Memoirs of Mary Queen of England*, ed. R. Doebner (1886), p. 30; 'Spencer House Journals', pp. 202, 206.

[6] *Conduct*, p. 6; *The Tatler*, no. 121; *The Poems of Jonathan Swift*, ed. Harold Williams (1937), I, pp. 141–5.

[7] Their occasional letters, while he was in Holland, are a welcome relief from those between himself and Russell. They were obviously devoted to each other (Finch Transcr. 1691–2, *passim*).

his churchmanship and his love of country pursuits, he was the finest type of a class that the Revolution badly needed. But his character was not altogether fitted for the task of naval minister at such a time. As Professor Feiling has said, he was 'apt to make moral and political indignation coincide',[1] and in his disgust with Torrington's morals and later with Russell's morose and uncontrollable temper, he was apt to lose sight of the former's grasp of strategy and of the latter's knowledge of his job. Strongly conscious of his own rectitude, he could, as was proved in 1690, be blindly obstinate on matters in which it was in fact not at all involved. While no one can deny his honesty, his professional knowledge was not so great as he was apt to think, and it cannot be said that he was either prescient or adroit enough to compensate for its absence. His character was soon to influence naval affairs; for when the first great argument of the naval war arose in the autumn of 1689, it was through Nottingham that it was mainly conducted, and it was to him that the participants addressed their orders and protests and confided their ambitions and their fears.

III

The circumstances in which the argument arose formed one of the main issues of contention in what had been a contentious session of Parliament. The Admiralty Commissioners, selected from among its members and intended to balance, if not to guide the naval debates, were seldom able to do either. This was not because they did not attend the House. Their absences from the Board on its account were a feature of which the Secretary had regularly to take account.[2] Parliament was sitting throughout the spring and summer, from 22 January to 20 August 1689, and, after a prolonged adjournment, again from 19 October until its prorogation on 27 January 1690; and apart from the debates and the Committees of the whole House, the Admiralty members sustained throughout the period a good deal of committee work, only some of which was connected with their official business. Sacheverell, Lowther and Lee, in particular, were heavily involved in such work; and, from 9 March to 9 April alone, in the first month of the

[1] *A History of the Tory Party, 1640–1714*, p. 259.

[2] E.g. P.R.O.Adm. 2/377, 2/4, 4/4 (to Herbert); 2/378, 3/8 (to Torrington).

PLATE X

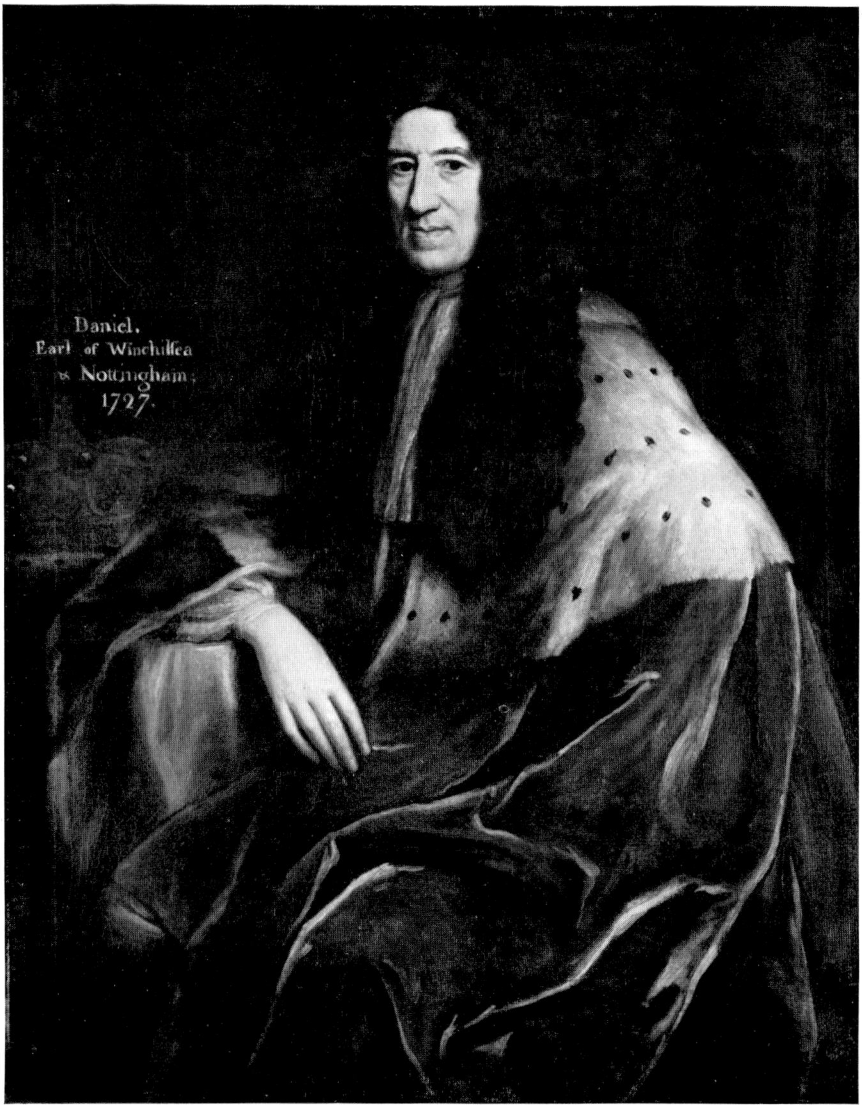

DANIEL FINCH, 2ND EARL OF NOTTINGHAM

[Artist unknown]

Board's life, its members were on twenty committees other than those on naval affairs.[1]

The committees on naval affairs usually, though not always,[2] included all the Admiralty Commissioners, and sometimes in addition the members for all the seaports by definition.[3] The matters which were referred to them were of two types: those which arose from individual incidents, and those which were the result of a full-scale debate on policy. The former included the mutiny in the *Greenwich* early in March, as a result of which the seamen presented a petition to the House, and also Torrington's plea for better quarters and attention for the wounded and disabled seamen.[4] No acrimonious party debate accompanied either of these events,[5] and—a testimony to the interest which non-political measures aroused—no resolution of the House resulted from the report of either committee. In contrast, the debates were confused and the resolutions fierce when the discussions turned on the conduct of the naval war itself.

These debates took three main lines: concern over the Dutch contribution to the joint effort, dissatisfaction with the victualling, and suspicion of the direction of the war. All three were raised during June in the first two major arguments of the year on the naval miscarriages: the debate on the failure to provide an earlier relief for Londonderry on 1 June, and the debate on the neglect of the outlying island garrisons on the 18th.[6] The suspicion of the Dutch, inherent in an attitude which placed the emphasis of the war on England's naval and not on her military contribution, found a paradoxical expression in complaints of their delay in joining the English fleet. These seemed, indeed, to be justified. The first contingent arrived at Portsmouth only on 7 June,

---

[1] *H.C.J.* x, pp. 35, 45–84, 121, 127, 162, 183, 225.

[2] The only Commissioner on the committee to determine the size of summer and winter guards for which money should be voted, was Sacheverell. It also included Russell (ibid. p. 56).

[3] E.g. on the committees to investigate the mutiny in the *Greenwich* (ibid. p. 47) and to inquire into the facilities for providing for sick and wounded seamen (ibid. p. 154).

[4] Ibid. p. 47.

[5] So far as can be judged by the negative evidence of silence in Grey, Cobbett and the Admiralty Out-Letters and Minutes.

[6] Anchitell Grey, *Debates of the House of Commons*, IX, pp. 276–80, 833–6.

and, despite the efforts of the Dutch deputies in England to hasten the departure of the rest, it was not until 18 July that the full quota was at sea and the allied fleet a reality.[1] According to the Dutch the delay was caused by lack of money with which to restock their stores after William's expedition, and at the beginning of the year they had declared that the speed with which they could meet their obligations depended on the speed with which the English contributed to the repayment of their expenses.[2] The amount demanded of Parliament was £663,752, and after a vigorous debate £600,000 was voted on 15 March;[3] but payment was not made until the following October,[4] and meanwhile the Dutch had to foot the bill themselves. By the end of the summer, however, the appearance of their ships had temporarily deprived the opposition to William of this excuse to air its views on Dutch trade and Flanders mud.[5]

The contribution of the Dutch squadron was again attacked in the winter, but on this occasion it served the purposes not of those who wished to discredit the Dutch alliance, but of those who wished to attack the domestic conduct of the war.[6] The summer campaign at sea had fallen below expectations. Although the presence of the fleet in the western approaches had helped to prevent any large-scale reinforcement of the French troops in Ireland, this negative achievement was less obvious to most observers than its failure to prevent the French Mediterranean squadron, which left Toulon on 9 June, from slipping

[1] Warnsinck, loc. cit., pp. 25–7; H. J. van der Heim, *Het Archief van den Raadpensionarus Antonii Heinsius* (1867), I, p. 15. There were premature reports of their arrival earlier in the month (e.g. *H.M.C. Le Fleming*, p. 244; Luttrell, op. cit. I, p. 540).

[2] De Jonge, op. cit. III, p. 735. For a detailed statement of the Dutch bill, see B.M.Addnl. 17,677, ff. 281–301. The printed statement in *H.C.J.* X, pp. 47–8, confuses pounds with guilders.

[3] Grey, op. cit. IX, pp. 161–4, 169; *H.C.J.* X, p. 50.

[4] *Cal. Treas. Bks. 1689–92*, pp. 273–4, 1990.

[5] The Commons' Committee appointed on 3 July to inquire 'why the Dutch Fleet were out no sooner to join the English Fleet: and also why the English Fleet were laid up' (*H.C.J.* X, p. 204), in fact concentrated solely upon the second half of its task. The whole affair was largely a pretext to discredit Nottingham, who was wrongly held to have been partly responsible for the delays (*H.M.C. Finch*, II, pp. 208–9; *H.M.C. Portland*, III, p. 437).

[6] Grey, op. cit. IX, p. 389.

into Brest to join the Atlantic squadron,[1] and to protect the inbound trade from being captured in the Channel approaches. It was estimated that almost a hundred vessels had been taken by privateers between the Scillies and Plymouth alone, and the West Indies and Mediterranean trades were at a standstill.[2] The influential and vocal resentment of the merchant interest was aroused, while public opinion in London was excited by the more dramatic junction of the enemy squadrons, with its implications for the Irish campaign. As the summer drew to a close, a series of Parliamentary attacks began upon the measures and, in some cases, the men responsible for the recent disappointments.

The protagonists in the Commons, where the main discussions took place, were the same throughout the debates: on the one side, Clarges, Garroway and Birch of the old Country party, Guise and Sir Edward Seymour, Jack Howe and the younger Hampden; on the other Lee, supported at first by Sacheverell, later by Russell, and sometimes by other members of the Administration outside the Admiralty, such as Ranelagh and Goodricke. The issues raised were twofold: the shortcomings of the naval officers, and the shortcomings of the ministers and of the Administration itself.

The first attack upon the officers came in mid June, but was soon dropped after Lee had intervened with a personal defence of Torrington. But it was revived on 13 November, when the merchants' losses were discussed. For some time inbound merchant ships had been complaining of extortion on the part of their escorts, who sometimes refused to follow their orders unless suitably rewarded by the convoy. The merchant captains alleged that they had been asked to give eight and ten guineas apiece, and in some cases up to £40, for the protection which was their due.[3] In one instance, the charges were proved. Captain George Churchill, younger brother to the more famous John, was found guilty of demanding money from merchants in Plymouth, and of illegally pressing their men. After a sharp debate, in which the morals of naval captains came under general discussion, he was committed to the Tower.[4]

---

[1] Roncière, op. cit. VI, p. 62; Warnsinck, loc. cit. p. 38; *H.M.C. Finch*, II, p. 228.

[2] *H.C.J.* X, p. 285; A. C. Wood, *History of the Levant Company* (1935), p. 108.

[3] Ibid. p. 413.

[4] *H.C.J.* X, p. 289; P.R.O.Adm. 2/378, f. 454.

The debates, however, concentrated less upon abuses than upon the alleged inefficiency of the fleet. In one discussion during June,[1] and again in November, it was roundly affirmed that the navy did not know its job. The last debate drew from the Admiralty the only reasoned and determined defence which has been recorded, in which Russell dealt with the charges against the commanders of the fleet. They had lain, as he remarked, for six weeks upon the enemy coast, mostly within three leagues of Ushant, and had established a blockade which was evaded by the Toulon ships only because of those natural hazards of the sea—foggy weather and a favourable breeze—which seamen alone appreciated and which no one could prevent. 'Unless', he is reported to have concluded, 'we should pull the French out of port by the ears, I know not how to have fought.' Lee followed up with a defence of the existing convoy system, a further defence of the Admirals and a general appreciation of the effect of war upon trade. He finished by welcoming an examination of the Admiralty's order books, which would show in their true light the precautions that had been taken.[2]

This last remark removed the dispute to a different plane. So long as the Administration was content to bandy words with its opponents on the relative merits of its Admirals with those of Cromwell's day, and to answer detailed accusations with a general and usually cloudy defence on technical grounds, its arguments remained as inconclusive and ineffective as those which it was attempting to counter. Under such circumstances the debates could proceed no further than the premises with which they began, and could be expected only to record and not to remove dissatisfaction. For behind their irrelevance lay the real problem of Parliamentary discussion: the ignorance of the Commons, and the determination to keep them ignorant on the part of the executive, which made the observations of both sides almost equally irresponsible. The shadow of this problem lay over all the disputes; at times, particularly in the debates of June upon the defence of Ireland, it emerged into the light of open argument.

For unlike the arguments over the fleet, those on the Irish miscarriages have a consistent and developing theme. They were raised in three debates: that of 1 June over the neglect in the relief of Londonderry,

---

[1] Grey, op. cit. IX, p. 335. [2] Ibid. pp. 415–20.

that of 22 June on the Irish miscarriages, which led to further debates on the consequences of the resolution which it initiated, and that of 11 November on the state of Ireland. On 1 June, after a preliminary skirmish over the victualling, Tredenham and Howe went straight to the point. The former declared that to examine the officers directly responsible was to strike only at a branch of the evil; the real trouble lay with the root in London. The latter carried the argument to the stage at which it was taken up three weeks later, and demanded a detailed inquiry to discover who was responsible for the orders.[1] As a result of the debate, a resolution was passed to send for papers and persons, and a committee of investigation appointed.[2] On the 22nd, the attack developed. Seymour demanded copies of all relevant orders,[3] and Sir Thomas Littleton suggested that the King be asked to allow a committee from the House to examine and to take copies of the Admiralty's order books.[4] A petition was accordingly presented, and granted. The Admiralty was instructed to submit its records, and the Commons appointed four members to examine them.[5] But it was soon obvious that the answer did not lie wholly within their pages; and on 3 July a second address was made to the King, for permission to examine the books of the Council Committee for Ireland.[6] On the 12th, William's reply was received. He would take the address into consideration.[7]

The Commons, however, were now in full cry. A debate was immediately held on the reply, and a resolution passed, *nemine contradicente*, that those who had advised His Majesty to defer giving his permission were enemies to the King and the kingdom. The discussion then moved to a debate for the removal of Halifax and Carmarthen from the Council, which continued until the House adjourned.[8] Irritated and alarmed, the executive gave way. On the 16th, William gave permission for the offending records to be examined,[9] and on the 29th the long process of investigation began.[10] But the result was disappointing. The Council books revealed the miscarriages, but not

---

1 Ibid. pp. 279–80.
2 *H.C.J.* x, p. 162.
3 Grey, op. cit. IX, p. 355.
4 *H.C.J.* x, p. 193.
5 P.R.O.Adm. 3/1: 22/6; P.R.O.Adm. 2/169, f. 199.
6 *H.C.J.* x, p. 204.
7 Ibid. p. 217.
8 Ibid.
9 Ibid. p. 224.
10 *H.M.C.* 12, VI, p. 137.

their causes, and the Commons, who had scented an impeachment at the beginning of their task, were still inconclusively examining witnesses when the investigation was brought to an end by the prorogation of Parliament on 20 August.[1] When it met again, the subject was raised once more. On 11 November, the Commons were again asking for an investigation of the fleet to get to the bottom of the miscarriages of the summer,[2] and the year ended with the same talk of treachery in high places and of criminal negligence with which the discussions had begun.[3] But in spite of all efforts, the causes of the misfortunes remained unsolved, and faced with hostility at the highest level of the executive and with ignorance at those levels to which it was given access, the first Revolution Parliament proved no more successful in enforcing the consequences of responsibility, and rather less successful in identifying it, than its predecessors before 1685.

In one instance, however, and on a lower level, the Commons were able to take conclusive action. The debates on the victualling were brought to a satisfactory conclusion for Parliament, even if not for the victualling itself. Throughout the year, as in the campaign of 1688, the Victuallers' shortcomings had jeopardized, and in this case finally ruined, the intentions of the Administration. No sooner had their debts been settled in February than fresh trouble arose in the west, where the navy was provisioning the troops for the passage to Ireland through its agent at Chester, Matthew Anderton.[4] Appalling reports of the quality of the victuals began to circulate. The beer was said to be so bad that the men preferred to drink salt water, or their own urine, some of the biscuit had been in Chester Castle since Monmouth's rebellion, and officers and men were dying before they ever reached the Irish coast.[5] The trouble, as usual, was lack of money. Throughout the spring Anderton was chronically short of cash, and he had raised the first and

---

[1] *H.M.C.* 12, VI, p. 144. [2] Grey, op. cit. IX, pp. 404–6.

[3] *H.C.J.* X, pp. 309, 317.

[4] Anderton's position was anomalous, in that he received orders from the Council Committee for Ireland as well as from the Admiralty and the Navy Board. Most of his instructions for the hiring of transports and the provisioning of troops, however, came from the latter (*H.M.C.* 12, VI, pp. 164–5; P.R.O.Adm. 1/3559 *passim*, particularly f. 983).

[5] *H.C.J.* X, p. 263.

the last £2000 on his own credit.[1] But serious as it was, this was a local failure. Anderton alone was responsible to the Navy Board for supplying the troops, and the Victuallers were called upon to provide only for the men-of-war in the area, and then only with money upon credit and not with food itself.[2] But later they were implicated in a more serious failure, when the fleet, whose ill success was already giving rise to such anxiety, was forced to leave its station at the end of August through the shortage and bad quality of the provisions. Two months later, when they met again, the Commons proceeded to examine witnesses who could throw light on the reason. On 9 November, they appointed a committee to investigate the Victuallers' activities, and on the 23rd, after a virulent debate, the latter were arrested by order of the House and summoned to answer in their defence.[3] Even Haddock, a favourite of the Country party and generally respected by all sections of the House, was included in the order.[4] The attack seized on a point which had already been raised, although without advantage, in the arguments upon the higher conduct of the war: the employment of James II's servants to carry out the policies of William. The fact that the Victualling Commission had not been changed in the spring, but was still that of 1688, was repeatedly stressed, and it was useless for Lee to explain that fresh appointments in that business at that time would probably have meant even greater inefficiency. The Commons were deaf to excuses and, regardless of the contradiction in its terms, they proceeded to pass a resolution which condemned the Administration for supplying the fleet corruptly and inefficiently, and the Admirals for not bringing the French to action.[5] It was only on 5 December, after another debate, that the Victuallers were allowed out on bail.[6]

William had already taken his own steps to end this crisis. Late in October he dismissed the old Commission, and at the end of the month he attempted to put the victualling out to contract. Two groups applied for the business, one headed by the shipbuilder Sir Henry Johnson, the other by three of the old Commission; but by 14 November the idea had been dropped, and at a meeting in the Treasury on that

[1] Ibid. [2] Ibid. p. 282.

[3] Ibid. p. 293; Grey, op. cit. IX, pp. 441–6; *H.M.C. Le Strange*, p. 110.

[4] *Camden Society Miscellany*, VIII, pp. 51–2; Grey, op. cit. IX, pp. 44–6.

[5] *H.C.J.* X, p. 309. [6] Ibid. p. 302.

day of the Lords of the Treasury and Admiralty and the Treasurer of the Navy, in the presence of Carmarthen, Halifax and both Secretaries of State, the composition of a new Commission was discussed, and a ballot taken to choose its members.[1] By that time, William had approached one of the most prominent Whigs and experienced victualling contractors in London, Thomas Papillon, with the offer of the leading post. Papillon at first asked to be excused on account of the appalling condition of the service; but the King was determined to get him, and eventually, by raising his salary from £400 to £1000 a year, was able to announce his appointment.[2] It was a notable success on his part, for Papillon was well suited to the job; and although the victualling continued to give serious trouble, his reputation outside the House and his popularity within it prevented the Victuallers from being attacked so bitterly again for the rest of the war. Despite his age (he was nearly 67 at the time of his appointment) and his numerous requests to be relieved of office, William refused to let him go for the remainder of his reign, and he died still in office in 1702. The most difficult of all administrative problems had been put into hands of which Parliament could approve, and although it could not be foreseen at the time, one source of Parliamentary trouble had been finally removed.

But if the victualling fiasco provided the Parliamentary attacks with their one satisfactory solution, it also precipitated, before its repercussions had attracted Parliamentary attention, that first major disagreement within the executive which has already been mentioned. When Torrington returned to Torbay with the fleet, it was to face a long and stubborn quarrel with the King. The ground had been well prepared for it during the summer. As the dissatisfaction with the fleet became more widespread and, in certain quarters, more vocal, the demands upon it steadily and correspondingly increased. When it had proved

---

[1] *Cal.Treas.Bks. 1689–92*, pp. 60–1, 63, 65.

[2] *Memoirs of Thomas Papillon, Merchant of London, 1623–1702*, ed. A. F. W. Papillon (1887), pp. 353–5. Mr James points out that the account given there of Papillon's reluctance to accept the post is supported by the dates of the Admiralty warrants for the patents of the new Commissioners. The warrant for the other four is antedated to 24 October; the warrant for Papillon is dated 21 November (P.R.O.Adm. 2/4, ff. 386, 462).

itself unable to maintain a reliable blockade of Brest, its cruisers were taken from it for the protection of commerce;[1] when it was obviously incapable of protecting commerce, it was ordered to send reinforcements to the Irish Sea.[2] At the same time the inadequate appreciation of sea warfare which was responsible for these incompatible demands, was diverting badly needed resources to an unbalanced Irish squadron[3] and reserving some of the lesser cruisers for the immediate service of the Secretaries of State. Torrington was faced with competing claims from different interests working with some success upon the technical ignorance of the various political authorities, and was forced to oppose to them the claims of a fleet which he could support only by illustrating its limitations. To achieve any success in this difficult task, he required the confidence of his superiors ashore and the support of his immediate inferiors afloat. Thanks to the activities of Edward Russell, bringing his political interest to bear on his reports from sea, and his professional status to secure their acceptance ashore, he ended by lacking both.

Russell had been appointed Admiral of the Blue on 20 May, and by the end of the month he had begun to write to Nottingham from his command.[4] His reports, while seldom contradicting Torrington's, managed to convey a rather different impression. Where Torrington, as was his way, was gloomy, Russell—for the only time in his later career—was cheerful. While the former complained about the Dutch, the latter alluded to their achievements;[5] while the one constantly demanded reinforcements, the other remarked on the satisfactory state of the fleet;[6] and while the senior Admiral incurred William's displeasure by failing to write for three weeks,[7] the junior maintained a regular correspondence.[8] By September, Nottingham was openly criticizing

---

[1] P.R.O.Adm. 2/170, ff.168–9; 3/1: 10/7; 3/2: 8/8.

[2] P.R.O.Adm. 8/2, 18 July.

[3] In mid July, this was composed of seven fourths, two fifths, and three sixths, and was being further strengthened by three more fourths. According to a note left by the late Admiral Sir Herbert Richmond, this was a waste of small ships of the line which should have been with the fleet.

[4] *H.M.C. Finch*, II, p. 222.

[5] Ibid. pp. 219, 222.

[6] P.R.O.Adm. 2/169, f. 240; *H.M.C. Finch*, II, pp. 227, 232.

[7] *H.M.C. Finch*, II, pp. 236, 250.

[8] Possibly even with William himself. At all events, at the end of August William was writing privately to him ('Spencer House Journals', p. 235).

Torrington to Russell,[1] and the latter, in return, forwarded to the Secretary a memorandum about winter service which his superior had drawn up, but had not liked to submit to the authorities ashore.[2] During that month, while guardedly supporting the Admiral of the fleet in his professional capacity, Russell sent his own reports to London through the agency of Priestman;[3] and towards its close, when the King ordered Torrington to come to London for a conference, his main anxiety was to go there himself as soon as possible.[4] Early in October he got his reward. On the 6th he was ordered to attend the King, and by the 10th he was on his way, with Priestman waiting to meet him in Godalming with the latest news.[5]

Torrington was thus already in a difficult position, when on 29 August he put in to Torbay. He was quite sure of the propriety, indeed of the 'necessity',[6] of his action. The French were reported to be at Belleisle, so that any immediate sortie towards Ireland seemed unlikely, while his own fleet was falling to pieces with disease. The effects of bad food and drink were more serious even than the reports to the Commons suggested. As early as 31 July, Russell had reported that the seamen were refusing to eat until forced to do so by hunger, and that many of the ships were 'extremely sickly'.[7] To judge from his own description of the provisions, this was not surprising. 'The beafe proves full of gaules...and no longer agoe then yesterday, in severall of the buts of beare, great heapes of stuff was found at the bottom of the buts not unlike to men's guts, which has alarmed the men to a strange degree....'[8] Inevitably, they began to talk of papist treachery and to refuse their duties. By the third week in August, the disease was spreading at such a rate that ships were submitting a daily death roll to the flagship, and by the time that they returned to the English coast the sick-list amounted

---

1 *H.M.C. Finch*, II, p. 236.

2 Ibid. p. 254.

3 Priestman was sent down to the fleet, officially to Torrington, at the beginning of September, and arrived on the 7th (ibid. pp. 242–3). On the same day Russell wrote to Nottingham, 'I can say nothing now concerning the fleet, but by the person that came down you shall know it at large' (ibid. p. 243). In view of Priestman's later dependence upon Russell, it seems likely that he was 'the person'; see also ibid. p. 244.

4 Ibid. pp. 250, 256.

5 Ibid. pp. 254–5, 256–7.

6 His own word (ibid. p. 235).

7 Ibid. p. 232.

8 Ibid. p. 241.

to 530 dead and 2327 sick.[1] A week later, these totals had arisen to 599 and 2588 respectively.[2] Approximately one man in four was out of action.[3] The season moreover was getting late, and under the circumstances Torrington, with the consent of a council of war of English flag officers, considered that the fleet should be rested and then reduced to a winter guard before its further employment hazarded even the ships required for that service.[4]

William, however, did not agree.[5] Until the French concentration at Brest was laid up, it seemed to him to constitute a standing menace to Ireland. At the same time, he had committed himself, for obvious diplomatic reasons, to another project which he wished to support in force. On 28 August the Princess Anna Maria of Neuberg had been married by proxy to the king of Spain, and he had promised to convey her to her new kingdom by sea, for the overland journey was now impossible. Torrington tried hard to get the intended convoy reduced to a squadron of small ships, with a small third rate or even a fourth for flagship; and in this he for once had strong support from Russell, who had been chosen to command the expedition and who was vainly attempting to evade the responsibility. But after trying to get a Rear Admiral appointed in his place, Russell had to resign himself to the dangerous honour of conveying the queen in midwinter through the Channel and the Bay of Biscay in a second rate, with four third rates, two fourths and two yachts in company.[6]

Besides providing in this unsuitable way for one of the winter expeditions, William ordered the fleet to put to sea again at once and to take up its old station before Brest. Torrington was now genuinely alarmed at the King's disregard of technical objections and of the opinion of his technical advisers.[7] But William remained firm. On 15 September the Admiral was again ordered to sail,[8] and ten days later

---

[1] Ibid. p. 234. [2] Ibid. p. 238.

[3] P.R.O.Adm. 8/2, 1 September. At that time there were supposed to be 13,847 men in the fleet, excluding men on their way to join.

[4] *H.M.C. Finch*, II, pp. 238–9.

[5] See his immediate reaction to Torrington's letter of 24 August, in 'Spencer House Journals', p. 235.

[6] *H.M.C. Finch*, II, pp. 242–3, 245; Burchett, p. 35.

[7] *H.M.C. Finch*, II, pp. 243–5. [8] Ibid. p. 246.

the King's project for the winter services followed. Apart from the convoy for the queen of Spain, a squadron of 25 sail (of which fifteen were to be Dutch) was intended for the Mediterranean; a further 25 English men-of-war for the Channel, six for the Irish Sea, and four for northern waters; and small squadrons for the West Indies and for the Canaries.[1] Torrington was still in Torbay when these orders arrived, for the weather had achieved what he himself had failed to do, and had kept the fleet at anchor. On the 26th he was accordingly summoned to town to discuss the situation. Sensitive as always to a hostile atmosphere, and apprehensive that he would be journeying to his dismissal, he delayed his departure, and Nottingham had to write again to hasten him on 3 October. By that time, however, he was on his way, and he reached London on the 5th.[2] William by now was at Newmarket, and the next day Shrewsbury, who had accompanied him from Hampton Court, informed Nottingham of the King's wish to see Russell and the Dutch Admirals as well.[3]

Reports from all interested authorities were now required, for William was beginning to be impressed by the weight of professional opinion; and at the end of September the Admiralty Commissioners were asked for their advice.[4] Unaware that Torrington had been called to London, they immediately wrote to him in the fleet, assuring him that they would not act until they had heard his views.[5] Unfortunately, there is no record of any reply, nor does there appear to be any record of the discussions between the Admirals and the King. Little enough, however, came of them. Although the first and second rates were ordered to Spithead, William, influenced possibly by the prevalent rumours of a French sortie and of Jacobite successes in Ireland,[6] still insisted that two substantial squadrons under Berkeley should embark some troops and sail at once for the Irish Sea.[7] But the arrangements came to nothing. The ubiquitous westerly winds kept the ships where they were, and the troops did not go aboard. Berkeley sailed at last with one squadron, and from the evidence of prisoners whom he

---

[1] *H.M.C. Finch*, II, pp. 249–50. [2] Ibid. pp. 249, 252, 254. [3] Ibid. p. 255.

[4] P.R.O.Adm. 2/169, f. 302. [5] Ibid.

[6] *H.M.C. Finch*, II, p. 257; *Portledge Papers*, ed. R. J. Kerr and I. C. Duncan (1928), pp. 64–5.

[7] *H.M.C. Finch*, II, p. 257.

picked up from stray privateers and from the number of these in the Channel, it became clear that the enemy fleet was not, and had not for some time been at sea. On Christmas Eve he returned to Plymouth, leaving Russell alone, grumbling and disconsolate, to represent the original design.[1] Delayed by the weather, the Spaniards and the Dutch, he waited with increasing impatience at Flushing and later at Spithead, until on 7 March 1690 he finally managed to leave.[2] After a bad passage, in the course of which his flagship ran ashore off Corunna, he returned to Portsmouth on 28 March.[3]

As a result of the prolonged quarrel in the autumn, the personal relations of the participants altered decisively. William did not forgive Torrington for his obstinacy,[4] and with his removal from favour the balance, already weighted against him by his long absence at sea, tilted finally in Nottingham's favour. During the winter, the Secretary of State established himself as the chief confidant on naval policy and as the undisputed means of communicating it to Admirals and Admiralty alike. When William crossed to Ireland in 1690, he was in virtual control of the daily business, subject only to Mary's Council of which he was a member. Russell, too, benefited at the expense of his superior. With no constitutional status through which to exercise a personal power similar to Nottingham's, and without the experience to replace Torrington either at the Admiralty or in the fleet, he consolidated his reputation as a professional adjutant to the former and as an alternative adviser to the latter; and when William came, in the following year, to pick the names of Mary's Council, he had the satisfaction of seeing his included. The two great figures were moving, one directly and the other by a devious route, into the positions which they were to assume in the central and decisive years of the war.

In this tale of personal gain and loss, the Admiralty was directly involved. The defeat of Torrington, declining though his power had been during his summer absence, meant also its final exclusion from the determination of policy. Even if he had remained at its head, and had been content to identify himself with it, his relations with the King and

---

1 Ibid. p. 264; Luttrell, op. cit. I, p. 615.

2 *H.M.C. Finch*, II, pp. 267–72.

3 Burchett, p. 36.

4 'Spencer House Journals', p. 228.

with the inner Council were unlikely ever again to be so close. But he did not do so. Towards the end of the year, when the Brest project had finally been dropped, he resigned from his seat on the Board.[1]

His action placed William in an awkward position. For however annoyed he was with Torrington's professional advice, the resignation came at a time of political difficulty. The uncomfortable coalition through which the King liked to work was rapidly giving way under the strain of a disappointing war and of dissatisfaction in Parliament. The signal for its collapse was given at the beginning of January, when Sacheverell attempted to rush through his clause to the Corporation Bill, excluding from office for seven years all those who had been concerned in the confiscation of the municipal charters under James II. It was an explicit threat on the part of the Whigs to revive their old stalking-horse of the Popish plot, and to upset the uneasy compromise of the past year. After a long and acrimonious debate, William and the Tories combined to defeat it. It is fortunate that one of the few remaining division lists of the period survives for this occasion.[2] Of the Admiralty Commissioners, Wharton, Lee, Lowther and Russell were among those who supported the clause which the King so heartily detested. His reaction was swift. On 20 January, a new Admiralty patent was issued in which the names of Wharton and Sacheverell were omitted.[3] Their places were not filled, and for the time being the Board consisted of five members. The only new name was at the head of the list, as Torrington's successor. It was that of Thomas Herbert, Earl of Pembroke, one of the more moderate 'Regency' Tories, popular with all groups and generally regarded as sound, relatively disinterested and moderately capable.

More than domestic issues lay behind his appointment. The Dutch alliance was in almost as much jeopardy as the English coalition. The

---

[1] The exact date of his resignation is not certain. The earliest mention of it is on 14 December ('Spencer House Journals', p. 240), but he attended the Sunday meeting of the 22nd, although possibly in his capacity as a Privy Councillor (P.R.O.Adm. 3/2: 22/12). He had attended the Admiralty very rarely in October and November.

[2] R. R. Walcot, 'Division Lists of the House of Commons, 1689–1714', in *Bulletin of the Institute of Historical Research*, XIV, pp. 25–6.

[3] Patent Rolls. The warrant for it was issued on the 6th, during the fight on the bill (*Cal.S.P.Dom. 1689–90*, p. 399).

ill feeling which had been expressed in the Commons had been reflected in Torrington's attitude towards his foreign colleagues, and was fully reciprocated by them.[1] Pembroke, on the other hand, had only recently returned as a successful ambassador from The Hague, and so popular had he been there that William at the beginning of 1690 had considered sending him over to attend the forthcoming Congress.[2] At the Admiralty, he could serve the same purpose, for Hiob de Wildt was on his way over to discuss the plans for the ensuing campaign.[3] As a warning to the extreme Whigs, as a sop to the Dutch, and as an unexacting but respected colleague for Nottingham, he was an excellent choice at a difficult time. As an administrator, he proved conscientious, attending the Privy Council and the Admiralty regularly throughout the year. With the more obvious absentees of 1689 removed, the Board was generally a full one in the spring, only Lee being sometimes away as his illness returned from time to time.[4]

It was not only on account of the political situation that William resented Torrington's 'quitting'.[5] The specific cause of the Admiral's resignation had been the material difficulties of the Administration. He told the House of Commons later in the year:[6]

Not seeing things go as well as the service required, and [as] it was not in my power to prevent it, I humbly begged and obtained the King's leave to

[1] Warnsinck, loc. cit. p. 139.

[2] 'Spencer House Journals', pp. 241, 245; *Correspondentie van William III en Bentinck*, I, p. 75.

[3] According to De Jonge, op. cit. III, pp. 194–5, he remained in England until the end of June or the beginning of July.

[4] P.R.O.Adm. 3/2, *passim*.

[5] 'Spencer House Journals', p. 240. The extent of his annoyance may be measured not only by his own remarks, but by Russell's. That weathercock was echoing the King's words in January, in a far more extreme strain than his remarks of the previous September (*H.M.C. Finch*, II, pp. 269–70).

[6] *The Earl of Torrington's Speech to the House of Commons, in November 1690* (1710), p. 12. This pamphlet provides the only complete version available of Torrington's speech in his own defence in Parliament (see p. 364 below). Some of its passages can, however, be checked against a manuscript account of the same occasion, given in N.M.M., Bibl. Phill., Admiralty Papers, vol. IV, ff. 101–8. This report of the speech refers only to the course of the battle of Beachy Head, and does not include the passage quoted above; but where the same ground is covered, the sense and often the words

be dismissed from that Commission and giving any further attendance at that board; that since I could not prevent the mischief, I might have no share in the blame.

To William it seemed simply that the Admiral was running away. But to Torrington's naturally pessimistic disposition the situation in December appeared intolerable. The Administration had only a few weeks before been repeatedly attacked upon every aspect of its conduct, and the members of one of its Boards thrown into custody, by a Parliament to which it would soon have to apply for its annual financial support; he himself had just been defeated on a major question of policy, and his influence was less than ever before; and as the ambitious projects which he had opposed began to be prepared, the objections to them which he had foreseen began increasingly to make themselves felt. Deficiencies of policy and of material seemed to him to supplement each other; and it was hardly surprising that he should wish to leave a post where he was peculiarly exposed to attack upon matters which he was peculiarly ill-fitted either to influence or to defend.

For the programme for the winter seemed likely to lay a considerable strain on the available resources. The winter guard of assorted squadrons and cruisers amounted in all to sixty English ships, or two-thirds of those at sea in the summer.[1] It thus departed from the traditional conception of a radically smaller force for these months, which could be relied upon to keep the annual expenditure within the traditional limits, and in particular it made a heavy demand on the manning situation, which normally became easier at this time of year. Coming on top of the mens' dissatisfaction in the autumn, when the numbers were in any case not up to complement,[2] it seemed to be asking for trouble. Beyond it,

---

of MS. and pamphlet are the same. No date is given in the former, but it is included with some of Blathwayt's correspondence for the same period. The only other account I have found, which is likely to be contemporary, is contained in some almost illegible notes, in a contemporary hand, in S.P.Dom. 32/3, no. 41; and these correspond closely with the MS. already cited. Assuming both MSS. to have been written before the printed pamphlet, and the correspondence between some sections of them all to indicate a probable correspondence between others, then the pamphlet may be regarded as genuine.

[1] P.R.O.Adm. 3/2: 12/10. There were also 24 Dutch.

[2] P.R.O.Adm. 1/3559, f. 623.

moreover, lay the project for 1690, with its variegated demands not only on men but on materials, victuals and finance, all of which were being directly complicated by the heavy programme already under way. The fleet for the following year had been under review since 26 October, when William had outlined his ideas to the Admiralty;[1] and after two months' work by that Board and the Navy Office, under the supervision of Nottingham and Halifax,[2] the names were found for the numbers and strength required. On 5 January, a summer fleet of two first rates, six seconds, 25 thirds and seven fourths, with 27 of the smaller rates and auxiliaries and twenty fireships, was decided upon.[3] Cruisers and escorts remained to be settled.[4] At the end of the year, it was estimated that the total force for the following summer would require 32,842 men.[5]

To balance this programme there was a formidable and rapidly increasing list of debts. On 30 September these amounted in all to £567,543—almost three times the size of the debt of nine months before—of which £68,819 was still owing for the period before 25 March 1686. The details were as follows:[6]

	Before 25 March 1686			Since 25 March 1686			Total		
	£	s.	d.	£	s.	d.	£	s.	d.
Stores	14,600	0	0	16,226	5	8	30,826	5	8
Victuals	—			68,057	11	8	68,057	11	8
Wages and salaries in offices	40,000	0	0	—			40,000	0	0
Wages to yards and ordinary	9,421	10	0	75,736	0	7	85,157	10	7
Wages to seamen afloat	4,797	3	5	321,637	1	4	326,434	4	9
Freight for hired ships and tenders	—			17,067	6	3	17,067	6	3
Totals	68,818	13	5	498,724	5	6	567,542	18	11

1 P.R.O.Adm. 3/2: 26/10. The details at this stage, for which space was left in the minutes, were unfortunately never inserted. They must have been fairly full, as a page and a half were reserved for them.

2 P.R.O.Adm. 2/169, f. 383; 2/378, f. 535; 2/379, ff. 71, 92.

3 P.R.O.Adm. 3/2: 29/12; *Cal.S.P.Dom. 1689–90*, pp. 395–8; cf. the list of 22 December, which gives a total of 82 ships for the Channel and Mediterranean, as well as a West Indies squadron of 12 ships (*H.M.C. Finch*, II, p. 263).

4 An estimate was made that 46 ships would be needed for these services (*H.M.C. Finch*, II, p. 263).

5 Ibid.

6 Serg.MS. A 133; estimate of Navy Office, dated 19 October 1689. P.R.O.Adm. 49/173, ff. 12–19, gives the same individual totals for the period since 25 March 1686, excluding stores.

£404,005 of this debt had been contracted since the beginning of the year, and unless receipts could overhaul expenditure in the near future the effects of the reverse process were soon likely to be seen. At the beginning of October, the Navy Board reported that it had no money to pay for stores, victuals or wages for the yards; that a weekly payment of £15,000 would be needed to settle the contractors' arrears of pay by the end of the year, and £2000 a week to settle those of the seamen; and that the workmen in the yards were in such a state that two weekly payments of over £9000 and £5000 respectively were alone likely to satisfy them.[1] There was only one way to redeem the situation before the winter. The navy must be given a high priority in the weekly payments from the Exchequer to the departments. Its receipts from this source for October, however, were not satisfactory. The first £9000 was paid, as requested, to Deptford and Woolwich; but apart from that, there were five payments of £12,000, £5000, £8720, £10,176 and £5500 respectively[2]—amounts sufficient neither to clear the arrears, nor to meet the unusually severe requirements of the current service. By the end of the year, the naval debt had risen to £782,970, and the situation was becoming desperate.[3] On 3 January the Navy Board summed it up. The debts on current bills in the office alone were now £99,074, and would soon be 'much increased' when the quarterly bills for standing contracts came in. To meet this, there was only the weekly money received 'for current services', and none had in fact been received since 29 November. The seamen were embarking on a large-scale sale of their tickets to get ready money. The yards and ordinary were still a year in arrears, and Portsmouth had also not been paid for one quarter before that. Many of the men were almost starving, 'and by their great Labour (often times by Night as well as by Day, in this time of Extraordinary Action), and want of fitting Sustenance, the Workmen are so Weakened as that they cannot do their Work as they ought to do. If something be not done, we expect the works at ye yards to come to a standstill in a very few days.' Eleven fireships had lately been contracted for on William's orders,

[1] P.R.O.Adm. 3/2: 30/9; 1/3559, ff. 379–81.

[2] *Cal.Treas.Bks. 1689–92*, pp. 274, 280, 282, 288, 291.

[3] P.R.O.Adm. 1/3560, f. 497.

and the builders were already beginning to worry about the first payment for them, although it had been due for only a few days. Lastly, the owners of the ships which had been hired to take the army to Ireland, and for which the navy had to pay, were getting restive and were liable at any moment to remove them from that service. If they did so, the office doubted whether it could find any others.[1]

The Victuallers were financially in just as bad a state; and in the excitement of turning over to a new Commission their organization had completely broken down. Apart from producing the routine establishment of provisions for the following year,[2] they relapsed after the end of October into unqualified chaos. They lost track of the distribution of their victuals, and even of the amounts in store;[3] and, badgered out of their wits by their creditors, they spent the last two months of the year in desperate attempts to get the highest priority in the distribution of Exchequer payments, or, if they still failed to meet the case, to appropriate money from the Treasurer of the Navy which had already been ear-marked for other services.[4]

The only department which at this time had any assets to set against its liabilities was that of naval stores. During the autumn it received over £46,000 worth of goods, and if these could not be paid for at least they could be used.[5] The system of paying in course, moreover, in this case sustained the naval credit until March,[6] and in January the Navy Board had actually been able to hold out hopes of a settlement and of an assured scheme for future weekly payments.[7] But when at last it became obvious that these were not to be realized, and as their arrears of payment steadily increased, the merchants showed their hand. The big importers of Baltic and Norwegian stores, always better organized and more powerful than the smaller domestic contractors,

---

1 Ibid. ff. 33–6.

2 P.R.O. Adm. 3/2: 20/11.

3 The last account of the year of quantities in the different ports was made on 1 October (P.R.O.Adm. 112/68), and when asked by the Treasury on 3 November what was in store, they were unable to say (*Cal. Treas. Bks. 1689–92*, p. 62).

4 P.R.O.Adm. 1/3560, f. 931; *Cal. Treas. Bks. 1689–92*, pp. 62–3, 66, 68–9, 70, 79.

5 P.R.O.Adm. 1/3559, ff. 379–81.

6 P.R.O.Adm. 1/3560, f. 499.

7 Ibid. f. 498. The Admiralty had been very hopeful of this around the 20th, after consultation with the Treasury (P.R.O.Adm. 3/3: 16/1, 20/1; 2/379, f. 165). But nothing came of it.

were the first to take concerted action. In March they announced their intention of refusing to tender for the forthcoming annual contracts unless they were paid some of their arrears,[1] and on 15 April they carried out their threat. In a body they attended the Navy Office and refused to deal any more without a guaranteed weekly settlement.[2]

This came as the last of a series of calamities in the new year. During 1689, although the situation had obviously been getting out of hand, the machine had continued to run as before. But now it was jamming fast. Throughout the first three months of 1690, reports from Chatham and Portsmouth continued to emphasize the desperate necessity of the yards. Edward Gregory at Chatham, in particular, wrote almost weekly upon the straits to which he was reduced. By the end of 1689 his workmen were hard pressed by their creditors, and during the next few months they were deserting in large numbers.[3] At Portsmouth, in addition to those who disappeared permanently, others were absenting themselves for two or three days at a time to earn some money elsewhere, and it was only with difficulty that in February Beach managed to persuade the entire yard not to go on strike.[4] Driblets of money and copious promises kept the organization going,[5] but when at last, at the beginning of March, one quarter's arrears were received, the men only asked what had become of the rest, and Gregory himself remarked that he wanted it 'more than I did a playday when a schoolboy'.[6]

Some effort had been made, if not to reduce the debts to the yards, at least to prevent them from increasing.[7] But in the effort to clear these arrears, the current services were entirely starved. No money had been received for them since the end of November, and at the end of March the debt upon them had risen to £145,000. The shipbuilders in whose hands the new fireships lay, had refused to launch them, and timber merchants all over the country were defaulting on their promises.[8] Only the standing contractors were still willing to supply

---

[1] P.R.O.Adm. 1/3561, f. 74. [2] Ibid. ff. 153–4.

[3] P.R.O.Adm. 1/3559, f. 847; 1/3560, ff. 169, 219–20.

[4] P.R.O.Adm. 1/3560, ff. 170–2; 2/379, f. 247.

[5] P.R.O.Adm. 2/379, ff. 165, 239, 269, 293.

[6] P.R.O.Adm. 1/3560, f. 849.

[7] Cf. the lists of debts on pp. 325 above and 329 below.

[8] P.R.O.Adm. 1/3561, ff. 74, 189; 2/170, ff. 146–8.

goods regularly. Local officials, as one of them complained, were living 'upon tick';[1] the Victuallers, despite the personal efforts of William to set them on their feet, had almost trebled their debt of six months before; and the Commissioners for Sick and Wounded could not even induce the landladies of Portsmouth to look after the seamen who were put ashore, nominally in their care.[2] In all, the naval debt had risen over fifty per cent since the end of September 1689, and now stood at £867,203. In comparison with its predecessor, its proportions were as follows:[3]

	Before 25 March 1686			Since 25 March 1686			Total		
	£	*s.*	*d.*	£	*s.*	*d.*	£	*s.*	*d.*
Stores	54,600	0	0	98,625	0	0	153,225	0	0
Victuals	—			177,422	17	9	177,422	17	9
Wages and salaries in offices, pensions and expenses	2,797	3	5	10,884	0	0	13,681	3	5
Wages to yards and ordinary	—			99,994	19	4	99,994	19	4
Wages to seamen afloat	2,000	0	0	378,915	2	9	380,915	2	9
Freight for hired ships and tenders	—			41,164	0	0	41,164	0	0
Sick and wounded	—			800	0	0	800	0	0
Totals	59,397	3	5	807,805	19	10	867,203	3	3

As Torrington had foreseen, the refitting of the fleet was inevitably affected. Many of the ships at the beginning of the winter were in need of an overhaul after over a year out of port,[4] and the necessity for getting the squadrons for the Mediterranean and the West Indies to sea as soon as possible, in order to convoy the trade, delayed those other units which were known to be required for the Channel in the following year.[5] Supposed to be out of harbour by the middle and the end of November respectively, the two squadrons were still not ready at the end of January, and none of the main fleet began refitting until the end of December.[6] The Navy Board, replying in January to questions about their probable date of completion, stated that if money were not received 'It is not to be depended on that ye ships Ordered for the Sea wilbe gott ready',[7] and on 26 February, when forwarding a state of the fleet, it repeated that no money for the current service had been

[1] P.R.O.Adm. 1/3560, f. 765.
[2] P.R.O.Adm. 2/170, f. 71.
[3] P.R.O.Adm. 49/173, no. 2.
[4] P.R.O.Adm. 2/378, f. 409.
[5] P.R.O.Adm. 2/379, f. 167.
[6] P.R.O.Adm. 1/3559, ff. 497–8; 3/2: 13/12; Burchett, p. 34.
[7] P.R.O.Adm. 1/3560, ff. 127–8.

received for four months, and that the delay was incalculable. If two weekly payments of £50,000 could be made, one to the yards and the other to the contractors, and if £10,000 a week could be guaranteed after that, they should all be ready within five weeks, except for six third rates at Portsmouth and one fourth at Deptford.[1] But in fact it was not until 9 May that Torrington was able to go to the Nore to take command,[2] and only six weeks later that the fleet finally put to sea.

Most of the ships in the Navy Board's list of 26 February had left the yards by 1 April,[3] and the main reason for delay thereafter lay in lack of men. Throughout December and January they were deserting,[4] and perhaps the only good result of the chaos of the winter was the consequent attention given by the Admiralty to the problem of manning in general, and to the revision of complements in particular; for although no action was taken on any of the suggestions put forward, they were not without their effect at a later stage of the war.[5] But despite attempts to pay the men some of their wages during February and March,[6] there was a poor response to William's proclamation of the latter month offering a bounty to volunteers,[7] and a general press was accordingly put into force. With the usual illegality and muddle the men were collected at last, but when they sailed in the third week of June they were still largely unpaid. By that time the stores were exhausted,[8] the distribution of victuals for the year already in disorder,[9] and the naval credit lower than it had been for seventeen years.

The inadequacy of the Exchequer payments to meet the demands of the navy cannot be attributed to Treasury inefficiency. So far as conditions permitted, allocations were regularly and carefully made.

---

[1] P.R.O.Adm. 1/3560, ff. 800–1, 807–8.

[2] P.R.O.Adm. 2/379, f. 546.

[3] P.R.O.Adm. 8/2; 1 April.

[4] P.R.O.Adm. 2/170, f. 12; 2/379, f. 160; 1/3560, f. 351.

[5] See pp. 447–9 below.

[6] Cf. lists of debts on 30 September and 30 March above. See also P.R.O.Adm. 2/170, f. 68.

[7] P.R.O.Adm. 2/379, ff. 459–60.

[8] P.R.O.Adm. 1/3561, f. 73.

[9] Only partial returns were made for May, and these showed a most uneven distribution of stores both within and between the ports (P.R.O.Adm. 112/68; lists of 20, 24 and 30 May).

One of the results of the crisis, indeed, was to increase the detailed control which the Treasury exercised over naval finance. Instead of assigning sums simply to the Treasurer of the Navy, as had mostly been the case hitherto, the Board now appointed specific amounts for specific purposes,[1] as it had occasionally done between November 1688 and March 1689, and it did not again revert to the former practice. The allocations were realistic and flexible. During the period from 8 March to 30 September 1689, when £327,388 was paid to the navy,[2] they were mainly devoted to the current service; from 1 October 1689 to 31 March 1690, when £369,073[3] was paid, to wages and arrears.[4] There were few weeks in which no allocation was made,[5] and the Lords of the Treasury themselves supervised the proportions. During the winter these were several times under review. When the Victuallers collapsed in November, they were given a priority which lasted to the end of the year,[6] and their complaints in April and May 1690 quickly produced the same result;[7] the necessity of meeting some of the arrears of wages was similarly followed by a reallocation of the available supplies;[8] and in January, and again in March, more thoroughgoing efforts were made to arrive at a satisfactory scale of priorities.[9] But lack of money ruined the plan of January, and it was only some weeks after the scheme of March had been settled that it could be put into effect.

Why was there such a shortage of money in 1689, to frustrate the intentions of the Treasury? The expenditure was not greater than had

---

1 Ibid. no. 1; *Cal.Treas.Bks. 1689–92*, pt 1, *passim*.

2 This does not include imprest money paid direct to naval contractors and others, without going through the hands of the Treasurer of the Navy, which amounted to £13,382.

3 P.R.O.Adm. 49/173, nos. 1, 2.

4 £123,217 was assigned to the current service in the earlier period, as compared with £81,429 in the later.

5 Particularly during 1689. The only weeks between March and September in which no allocation was made were the last in March, the first in April, and the third in June.

6 They were paid £79,564. 6*s*. 6*d*., out of a total of £142,740. 5*s*. 6*d*. between 1 October and 31 December; and only £15,000 of this was paid in October (P.R.O.Adm. 49/173, no. 2; *Cal.Treas.Bks. 1689–92*, pp. 274, 280, 291).

7 P.R.O.Adm. 1/3561, ff. 161, 201, 229.

8 *Cal.Treas.Bks. 1689–92*, pp. 274, 288, 356.

9 Ibid. p. 359; P.R.O.Adm. 3/3 : 19/3.

been foreseen. The Navy Office estimate on 12 April put it at £1,215,600 for the period from 1 January to 31 December, excluding ordnance and reckoning wages, victuals and wear and tear per man per month at the accepted rate of £4.[1] During that time, the navy actually spent £581,626[2] received from the Exchequer, together with £13,382 which passed from the latter directly to the merchants, while it increased its debt from about £200,000 to approximately £782,970, or by about £582,970. This expenditure, exclusive of ordnance, was therefore in the region of £1,177,978. It does not represent the whole of the expenditure during the year, for the amount of the debt at the end of December was known not to include the bills on standing contracts, and in any case a portion of it was only estimated; nor does it represent the expenditure which eventually took place for the year, since portions of the debt were subsequently paid at different times and at varying rates of interest. But the latter consideration does not affect the debit column as seen at the time, while the additional expenditure on the standing contracts is unlikely to have exceeded £40,000. Within these limits, therefore, it may be said that the naval expenditure did not exceed the naval estimate.

But this estimate was never submitted to the House of Commons, and the provision made by Parliament for the navy in 1689 was based on a different set of figures. These were the results of the confusion which existed for the first two years of the war, between the financial responsibilities of Parliament and those of the Crown.[3] Under the existing arrangements, whereby the King paid for his own out of his own revenue—most of which was originally granted to him by Parliament—the latter was called upon only to supply the money required to finance extraordinary expenditure, the object of which

---

[1] P.R.O. Adm. 7/169, no. 4.

[2] This amount is taken from the lists of individual Exchequer payments throughout the year, in P.R.O.Adm. 49/173. Two different amounts are given elsewhere: (1) £488,240. 16*s*. 1*d*., in *H. of L. N.S.* VII, p. 225; (2) £490,332. 16*s*. 3*d*., in *H. of L. N.S.* I, p. 12. But both these are for the period 5 November 1688 to 30 September 1689, although in the latter case the sum is balanced against a grant for a different period.

[3] I have followed W. A. Shaw (*Cal. Treas. Bks. 1689–92*, pp. xvi–lix, cxxvi–cxxvii) for this argument.

it approved but which could not be met out of the ordinary resources of the Crown. When war seemed likely in 1689, therefore, the Commons' first step was as usual to request from the executive an estimate of the total expenditure, its second to estimate for itself the expense of the navy in peacetime, and its third to vote a sum which it thought reasonable to meet the gap between the two. On 19 March, the Admiralty was ordered to submit an estimate of the charge of the navy for the ensuing year.[1] On the 23rd this was followed by a request to the King for an account of the fleet considered necessary for the summer.[2] But already on the 21st William had ordered the Admiralty to prepare an estimate of its charge 'to be presented to the Parliamt.',[3] and on the 26th this was submitted. It was calculated on the basis of the fleet ordered a week before, plus the 22 escorts and cruisers which the department had just recommended to the King; but in both cases the charge was worked out for a full year, and to this extent replaced the alternative estimate, which as has been seen was demanded but was never submitted, for the total naval expenditure for the ensuing year. It did not, however, include the ordinary. Allowing £4 per man per month, the total cost came to £1,128,140.[4]

The House then proceeded to estimate the cost of the normal peacetime summer and winter guards, and of the peacetime ordinary.[5] The former came to £366,080,[6] the latter to £130,000. Both these amounts, therefore, were chargeable to the King on his standing revenue; both were accordingly deducted from the total expenditure for the purpose of making a grant, and in their place £600,000 of the King's standing revenue was allotted to the navy and Ordnance.[7] The House accepted—reluctantly, because it had not the means of checking the figures—the numbers of men for whom the Administration had budgeted in the fleet and the cruisers, and including an extra 5*s.* per man per month for ordnance, arrived thereby at a total cost of £1,198,649. Subtracting

---

[1] *H.C.J.* x, p. 53.

[2] Ibid. p. 63.

[3] P.R.O.Adm. 3/1 : 21/3. Shaw's statement (*Cal.Treas.Bks. 1689–92*, p. cxxvi) that William ordered this estimate verbally, is incorrect.

[4] *H.C.J.* x, p. 65.

[5] Ibid. pp. 80–1.

[6] Not £336,080 as Shaw states (loc. cit. p. cxxvii, n. 2).

[7] *H.C.J.* x, p. 104. The Commons' estimate for the peacetime charge of the ordnance was £22,600 (ibid. p. 80).

£366,080, it was faced with a sum of £832,569.[1] Against this, it voted a sum of £700,000 'towards the Occasions and Service of the Navy'.[2]

On the grant alone, it would thus seem that the Commons failed to satisfy a demand which they had recognized as reasonable. But later they claimed that, when the £600,000 on the standing revenue was taken into consideration, they had more than met it.[3] If the latter amount had in fact been available to the King, their argument would have been valid. But, by their own calculations, it was not. On 20 March, they had resolved that the revenue to be settled upon the Crown for its annual peacetime expenditure should be £1,200,000.[4] On 25 April, they unanimously voted £600,000 as the maximum charge of civil government,[5] leaving the rest for the support of the armed forces. But on 5 April, after making all possible retrenchments, they had already calculated the peacetime charge of the latter as £718,680.[6] Their own figures thus showed an annual expenditure of £1,318,680 to be met out of an annual revenue of £1,200,000. To reserve half of that revenue to the navy and Ordnance alone was a gesture which, in the conditions of 1689, meant nothing. When the Crown was almost certain not to be able to meet even the expenses for which the Commons had budgeted, they saddled it with an extra £81,000[7] for two of the armed forces, while themselves defaulting by over £132,000 on their own obligation.

The provision for the navy's requirements, therefore, was to a certain extent illusory, and it would not have been surprising if the service had never received a large proportion of the extra-Parliamentary supply of £600,000. But in fact, as has been seen, the Parliamentary grant itself was not met. The total amount received by the Treasurer of the Navy during the year was £581,626 out of an intended £1,300,000.[8] The

---

1 *H.C.J.* x, pp. 80–1. 2 Ibid. p. 104. 3 *H. of L. N.S.* I, p. 13.
4 *H.C.J.* x, p. 56. 5 Ibid. p. 104. 6 Ibid. p. 80.
7 Subtracting the ordinary of the army from the total ordinary of the armed forces.
8 When the Commons came to debate in November why the grant of April was proving insufficient, they did so without the guidance of the actual issues to the armed forces, which were made available to them only in 1707. They were therefore confused. The reason for this confusion has been attributed by Shaw to the fact that the establishments could be altered by the executive without the knowledge of Parliament, and thus the calculations of the latter could be upset without the possi-

trouble lay in the discrepancy between the calculations of the national revenue made by the Commons and the revenue actually received. Even if the former were correct, the results could only slowly be seen. As early as April, an observer had noted of one of the Parliamentary grants that the money 'could not be raised soon enough for the uses to which it was given'.[1] The defect was not overcome. A system of credit had to be built upon the expectation of revenue; and, thanks in the first place to the paucity of statistical information and the uncertainty how to use it, and secondly to inadequate methods of collection,[2] the revenue usually failed to answer these expectations. The Treasury thus had difficulty in distributing the money to the departments, particularly as some of it was diverted to encourage or to repay loans before it ever reached the Exchequer. Unfortunately, it is not possible to say what proportion of the national revenue the payments to the navy represented in 1689, for no statement remains of national income and expenditure either for that or the following year.[3] It is, however, possible to estimate the proportion of those payments that was made in cash.

In the first half of the year, out of a total of £230,676, £24,251 was probably issued in ready money; in the second half it was only £6891,[4]

bility of correction on its part (*Cal.Treas.Bks. 1689–92*, pp. cxxxiii–cxxxiv). But he has not shown that the fleet originally proposed by the executive had been augmented, and in fact it was not; while the expenditure, as has been suggested, was not outrunning the original estimate. The confusion certainly lay in the absence of data, which arose from a lack of co-ordination between the executive and Parliament, but not on the grounds argued by Shaw.

[1] Reresby, loc. cit. p. 570.

[2] G. N. Clark, *Guide to Commercial Statistics 1696–1760* (1938), pp. 33–42.

[3] One auditor's declaration exists, for March 1689 to March 1690, but its form—that of a declared account—makes it useless for this purpose. The first of the later series of 'Income and Expenditure of Great Britain' (P.R.O. T. 30/1) is drawn up for the period 5 November 1688 to Michaelmas 1691.

[4] The individual issues of ready money have been taken from *Cal.Treas.Bks. 1685–9* and *1689–92* for the period, after checking the respective totals with those given in P.R.O.Adm. 49/173. There are, however, many instances in the former where no designation is given to the issue, and it is possible that some of these were in cash. But where payment was made in ready money, it attracted attention and seems to have been looked on as unusual. I have therefore included the ambiguous issues with the more normal issues of 'unappropriated money'.

and when in March 1690 a new Treasury Commission came into office, its spokesman declared that 'the Navie had not received anything for a quarter of a year'.[1] Almost 95 per cent of the payments during 1689 therefore had to be made in tickets or tallies. There were various types of these tallies. Some, issued on the expectation of revenue from specific sources, were redeemable on those sources: such were the tallies issued on the Present Aid, the first Poll Act, and the first twelvepenny aid or Land Tax.[2] These were mostly issued in return for loans by individuals to the Treasury. Others were redeemable only on the general credit of the Exchequer, or of the Treasurer of the department concerned.[3] Among the latter were all payments made on 'unappropriated moneys', which at this time meant issues that were not made on any specific fund and not, as later, issues that were made for no specific purpose. These tallies went mainly to the ordinary creditors of the government, and it was with them that most of the payments were made to the navy between March and December 1689.[4] Not negotiable, carrying no interest which might make them a source of profit, and not guaranteed by any individual source of revenue, they awaited merely a general promise of cash repayment which made them a liability until it was met, for their value depended upon the quantity of ready money issued by the Exchequer, and as it decreased they depreciated. It was, in fact,

---

[1] 'Memoirs of the first Lord Lonsdale', in *E.H.R.* XXX, pp. 94–5. 'Anything' obviously means 'any cash'.

[2] 1 Will. and Mary c. 3; 1 Will. and Mary c. 13; 1 Will. and Mary c. 20.

[3] The method varied. In the spring and summer of 1690 the credit of the Treasurer of the Navy was increasingly used. He, in turn, sometimes made loans to the Treasury, possibly to shift some of the onus of redemption (*Cal. Treas. Bks. 1689–92*, pp. 657, 706, 723, 778).

[4] From Michaelmas 1688 to Lady Day 1689, only £35,000 were paid from this source, compared with £33,000 from the Customs, £10,000 from Excise, £28,000 from the Linen Duty Act and over £42,000 from the duties on wine and vinegar. Again, from Michaelmas 1689 to Lady Day 1690, while most of the payments, amounting to £190,904, were made from the 'unappropriated moneys', over £27,000 were paid from the Customs, £24,000 from Excise and £5000 from the Land Tax. But between Lady Day and Michaelmas 1689, there were no payments except from the 'unappropriated moneys' and the small amount of ready money noted (*Cal. Treas. Bks. 1685–9* and *1689–92*, for individual issues concerned; checked against P.R.O. Adm. 49/173).

a *reductio ad absurdum*. Precisely when tallies were designed to replace money, their validity depended upon money. Under these circumstances, the only men who would accept tallies after a time were those who could afford to buy them at a discount from their holders, and could wait to be repaid in full by the Exchequer or could persuade it to redeem them at an early date. Among these men were the recipients of the registered tallies on the individual funds, who had a particular claim on the government. The original holders of the tallies of assignment were therefore faced with two alternatives: to stop dealing with the department which thus loaded them with wooden sticks, or to force up their terms to compensate for the discount at which they could get rid of them. This was happening increasingly throughout 1689, and while the process had not reached the stage by the end of the year at which it actually increased the total of the naval debts, in the early months of 1690 this was becoming the case.

It was thus not only because the payments fell short even of the minimum to be expected from the muddled provision made for them, but because they were made in such an unsatisfactory way, that there was financial chaos by the end of the winter. It was for this reason that during March 1690 a proposal from some of the naval contractors attracted so much attention from the Admiralty and Treasury. On 18 March the builders of the fireships that were ready to be launched, who had not yet received any payment, demanded to be paid as in the case of a loan to the Treasury, by tallies on a definite fund. They proposed for this purpose the first twelvepenny aid.[1] By that time, however, all unrepaid loans on that tax had been transferred to the second aid, and after a week the contractors were granted their tallies on the Excise, payable from the ensuing 1 October, and carrying six per cent interest from the time the money was due by contract.[2] It was the first case of a group of merchants, who had not lent money to the government, being paid on demand by registered tallies with a Parliamentary guarantee and a fixed rate of interest behind them.

If Parliament's money was to be directly involved in this way in the Exchequer payments to the navy, Parliamentary control of its allocation

---

[1] P.R.O.Adm. 2/170, ff. 146–8.

[2] P.R.O.Adm. 1/3560, f. 1043; *Cal.Treas.Bks. 1689–92*, p. 378.

was likely to follow. This, in fact, was happening at the same time, but by a different process. The debate of 2 November 1689 had shown that the Commons were dissatisfied with the apparent inadequacy of the earlier grants for the war,[1] and a month later it was moved, in the debate on providing the land tax, that a clause should be considered for appropriating some money 'for the paying of the Seamen, and providing Victuals and Stores for the Navy'.[2] Sacheverell and the Solicitor General were ordered to prepare the bill accordingly, and on the 9th it was introduced. The amount in the appropriation clause, which had been left blank, was then filled in as £400,000, and penalties were prescribed for those who misapplied the money. On the 16th the bill became law.[3] The relevant articles are worth some examination, for they set the pattern for all future Parliamentary appropriations during the war.[4] In article 45, the £400,000, 'part of the Moneys to be raised by vertue of this Act', was to be applied to the speedy payment of seamen in the navy, and to the payment of stores 'supplyed and to be supplyed' to it. It was to be 'applyed and appropriated out of the First Money which shall be Leavyed and Paid by vertue of this Act into the Receipt of the Exchequer as well upon Loane as otherwise', except for the money allowed as payment to the collectors of the tax, and for the repayment of loans registered by tally on the Act's predecessor between 1 November 1688 and 21 December 1689. Of the £400,000, half was to be reserved for the payment of the seamen, one-quarter for the purchase of victuals, and one-quarter for that of stores. Article 46 enumerated the penalties for collectors of the money and for the Receiver General to whom it was paid for transfer to the Exchequer, if any of them misappropriated it. A collector would be mulcted £5 for each offence, the head collector £20, and the Receiver General £500. By article 48, the officers of the Receipt of the Exchequer were directed to keep the accounts of this appropriation 'distinct from all other Moneys and Accounts whatsoever'; the Commissioners of the Treasury to sign warrants and orders for its issue only to the Treasurer of the Navy or his deputy; and the Auditor of the Receipt to draw orders

---

[1] Grey, loc. cit. pp. 388–94. [2] *H.C.J.* x, p. 303.

[3] Ibid. pp. 304–5, 310.

[4] *Statutes of the Realm*, VI (1819), pp. 140–2: 1 Will. and Mary sess. 2, c. 1.

for it, and to instruct his subordinates to make payments on it, only in favour of these officers. By the next article, the Treasurer of the Navy, in his turn, was to keep a distinct account of the appropriated money, and to pay it out only on a warrant signed by at least three Principal Officers of the Navy, stating that it was for one of the above purposes and no other. Article 50 instructed the Principal Officers and Commissioners to the same effect, and articles 51 and 52 prescribed the penalty for any officer who, entitled by the Act to receive or apply any of the money, retained it or diverted it to unauthorized uses. He was to forfeit it and, if necessary, to stand his trial by law. Finally, article 55 specified that an account should be given to the House of Commons of all the uses to which the money levied by the Act had been put.

So far as the £400,000 was concerned, Parliamentary control was assured. But it was only an individual instance of what was later to be the general rule. The normal division between the ordinary expenditure of the standing revenue and the extraordinary supply continued as before, with all its opportunities for confusion, and the main Parliamentary supply for 1690 was given for the war in general, without any particular appropriations.[1] Nor was the intention of the appropriating clauses of the earlier Act entirely clear, when the Treasury came to consider them. On 10 February, at a meeting with the King and the Admiralty, the opinion of the law officers of the Crown was taken, whether the wording by which different sums were reserved for different purposes implied any priority in their use.[2] The law officers thought not, and neither did the two Boards. But the opinions of the Navy Board and of the Treasurer of the Navy were also required, and an argument developed which was settled only at the end of the month.[3] It was not until April, when a list of priorities had been drawn up by the Navy Board on the basis of the debt at Lady Day, that a proper distribution of the money could be made. Nevertheless, although only on a small scale and not drafted entirely to the satisfaction of those who had to put it into effect, the Parliamentary appropriation was clearly a step in the right direction. This could be seen by the way in which it was used in the first quarter of 1690, even while the legal

[1] *H.C.J.* x, p. 362. [2] *Cal.Treas.Bks. 1689–92*, p. 367.
[3] Ibid. pp. 368–72.

queries remained unsettled. Of the £198,333 issued to the navy from the Exchequer in that period, £135,000 came from the appropriated money.[1] Nor was it without significance that the first suggestion to set up Parliamentary commissioners to audit the public accounts occurred at this time, when on 14 April, during the third reading of a new Poll bill, a rider was proposed for their appointment. It was withdrawn, and the bill passed without it.[2] But it was a commentary on the development of a new sense of financial responsibility on the part of the Commons, thrust upon them by events, limited to a specific purpose and viewed only in the light of immediate necessity, with no thought of its significance or its consequences, or even of its general application to national finance, but containing within itself the solution not only to the problem of financing the war, but to those other problems of executive responsibility which at the time seemed to bear little relation to it and which no member of the House in that session contemplated as being settled by its development.

[1] P.R.O.Adm. 49/173, no. 2.

[2] *H.C.J.* x, p. 377.

CHAPTER X

BEACHY HEAD AND THE DISGRACE OF TORRINGTON[1]

The Revolution settlement was put to a hard test in 1690. Benefiting by the concentration of their resources and their singleness of strategic purpose, the French were able to resume the offensive which they had taken less effectively the year before; and with Ireland still unsubdued, with disaffection apparently increasing at home and faction threatening to wreck the unity of the previous year, with both army and navy unpaid and the fleet notoriously behindhand in its preparations for sea, and with William himself rumoured to be crossing the Irish Channel, the country at the beginning of the campaign was in poor shape to resist. A defeat, either in Ireland or at sea, might prove decisive; and in the summer there was a complete defeat. On 30 June, the English and Dutch fleets were beaten by the French off Beachy Head. The action seemed, moreover, to carry every attribute of disaster. The allies had put to sea only just in time to meet the enemy; their handling during the battle, as allies, was particularly unfortunate; they retreated right out of the Channel at once, leaving the French unchallenged masters of that sea; and the subsequent inquiry revealed, not only to the authorities involved, but to Parliament, public and ally alike, that the Admiralty had been incompetent and the Admiral at sea irresolute, and that the ministers had disagreed first with the Admiral, then with the Admiralty and lastly among themselves. With the quarrels of 1689 in mind, these events may be seen as a climax to the earlier period; looking forward to the administrative reorganization of 1691, they may be viewed as a prelude to what followed. But the fact that the years before and after fall into these distinct periods was due to their own peculiar character, which was itself quite different from that of any other phase of the war. For in 1690 national pride was outraged, and popular anger

---

[1] Some of the material and much of the treatment for this chapter depend upon Mr James's work on the same subject, to which I am particularly indebted here.

and apprehension aroused, to a degree which made earlier and later reverses seem insignificant, and which caused the summer of that year to be remembered as a period of crisis long after the immediate event. With the years of the Armada, of Barfleur, of 1779, of the Trafalgar campaign and of the evacuation of Dunkirk, the year 1690 was one of the few occasions in four hundred years when invasion seemed both intended and close; and on that occasion, unlike any of the others, the way for it had been directly laid open by defeat at sea, and was accompanied by open disunity within the government and by open disagreement between itself and the commander on the spot.

The year had begun badly, and Torrington was not alone in fearing the worst. Towards the end of January, Russell also voiced the fears which many naval officers must have been feeling. 'For God's sake, my Lord', he wrote to Nottingham, 'cast your eye sometime towards the next summer's fleet. I dread the French being out before us. If they are we shall run hazard of being undone....I see all matters relating to the Navy go on so slowly that I am in amaze.'[1] In February he was so apprehensive of their outcome that he declined the appointment of Admiral of the Blue, which had just been announced,[2] on the ground of ill health;[3] and although this did not prevent him from enlisting Nottingham's interest to secure his election as a member of Parliament for a seaport,[4] nor from accepting seats on the reconstituted Board of Admiralty and on the Queen's Council in June, it continued throughout the year to dissuade him from accepting a command afloat.[5]

It may also have been concern over the way things were going that induced Chicheley, the only remaining naval member of the Board, to resign in May.[6] The Commissioners were now reduced to four, and on 5 June, before he left for Ireland, William appointed three new members, Russell himself, Captain Henry Priestman and Sir Richard Onslow. Russell and Priestman were obviously designed to replace the two naval members who had resigned, Onslow to represent the moderate Whigs to whom the King was again making overtures after

---

1 *H.M.C. Finch*, II, pp. 269–70.

2 *D.N.B.*, corrected by *Bulletin of the Institute of Historical Research*, XIV, p. 56.

3 *H.M.C. Finch*, II, p. 270.

4 Ibid.

5 See pp. 356, 357–8 below.

6 *D.N.B.* No reason for his resignation has been discovered.

the discovery of a Jacobite plot in the early months of the year. Aged 36 at this time, Onslow had been in the Commons for twelve years as member for Guildford and Surrey, and was already well embarked on the Parliamentary career which he was to end as Speaker. Reliable, uncompromising, rather stern, 'Stiff Dick' continued the tradition which William had tried to begin with Sacheverell and Lee, as a representative of the more experienced and influential Whigs, and himself began the tradition which was afterwards pursued for the rest of the reign, of associating the merchant interest with the Administration. A grandson and son-in-law, through his mother and his wife, of two Lord Mayors of London, he prided himself on his connexions with several of the trading companies and ended by being Governor of the Levant Company.[1] Priestman came straight from the Navy Board, after a not particularly distinguished career of sixteen years at sea. His only distinction came later, when as member of Parliament for Shoreham he became noted for his attacks on the merchant captains, whom he accused in the House of ruining the convoy system by their eagerness to get into port.[2] His appointment was probably due to Russell, who was generally regarded as his patron and whose interest he was later able to safeguard on the Board. In politics he was a Whig like his chief.[3] With these accessions, the Board of 1690 was completed.

Meanwhile, as the weeks passed and the fleet was still not ready for sea, Torrington continued to protest. Early in May he threatened to resign his commission as Admiral of the fleet,[4] but fatally for himself he did not do so. In June, the ships at last began to appear,[5] and by the 22nd, when he received his sailing orders, he had with him fifty English ships and twenty Dutch. But the same day he heard that a French

---

[1] *D.N.B.*; Arthur Collins, *The Peerage of England*, v (1812); *H.M.C.* 14th Report, appendix, pt. IX, pp. 487–94.

[2] See p. 410 below.

[3] John Charnock, *Biographia Navalis*, I (1794), pp. 400–2; E. Chappell, 'Henry Priestman', in *M.M.* XX, no. 1, pp. 115–19.

[4] James, loc. cit., citing a dispatch of 5 May from Van Citters, the Dutch Ambassador in London, to the States General. This series of dispatches (B.M.Addnl. 17677) contains some valuable information on the events of 1690. I have only looked at them briefly myself, and have taken most of the passages cited from Mr James's work.

[5] *H.M.C. Finch*, II, pp. 284, 293; N.M.M., Bibl. Phill., Admiralty Letters, IV, f. 106.

force of 77 ships had been sighted off Falmouth.[1] Profiting by the concentration of their whole fleet at Brest during the winter, the French had indeed put to sea on 13 June, under the command of Tourville, with a total strength of 77 men of war, six frigates, and twenty fireships mounting over 4000 guns, and with instructions to attack Portsmouth and then to blockade the Thames so as to prevent the English and Dutch fleets from joining.[2] As they moved slowly up Channel, in the light summer breezes of June, they were accompanied by a crop of rumours and reports—from fishing vessels and merchantmen, and from watchers on the cliffs of Devon and the Isle of Wight—which by a sort of natural law seemed to gravitate, according to their tenor, to those quarters most ready to receive them: the comforting reports to Nottingham and the Council in London, those of overwhelming numbers to Torrington in his flagship at the Nore.[3] As the enemy drew nearer, the disagreement between the two authorities increased. To each, the other seemed unaware of the real situation. Torrington complained incessantly, of the delays in embarking the Marines and in reinforcing the ships, and of the procrastination of the Dutch.[4] When on the 23rd he finally put to sea, it was with the gloomiest forebodings. 'The ods are great', he wrote to Nottingham that day, 'and you know it is not my fault...lett them tremble at the consequence whose fault it was the fleet is noe stronger.'[5] In London, however, the position seemed different. From the beginning Nottingham had been optimistic. 'Our Fleet here', he wrote to William on the 17th, four days after Tourville had sailed, 'is stronger than any the French can sett out from Brest';[6] and the events of the next week did not seriously modify his

---

[1] P.R.O.Adm. 2/170, f. 206. This contradicts Torrington's later statement that 'we had no account of ye ffrench preparations or setting out till ye appeared nere the Isle of Wight' (N.M.M., Bibl. Phill., Admiralty Papers, IV, f. 106).

[2] Roncière, op. cit. VI, p. 64, n. 4. They mounted either 4210 or 4502 guns. The unexpectedness of the move was shown by the fact that on the 17th orders were sent to Killigrew, who was thought to be at Cadiz, to remain there until further notice, and not to return home. A few days later it was hoped that he had missed the order, and would soon be in the Channel (*H.M.C. Finch*, II, pp. 299, 313).

[3] *H.M.C. Finch*, II, pp. 307–8, 318–19; *Cal.S.P.Dom. 1690–1*, p. 38; P.R.O.Adm. 3/3 : 18/6.

[4] *H.M.C. Finch*, II, pp. 296, 308; P.R.O.Adm. 3/3 : 21/6.

[5] *H.M.C. Finch*, II, p. 308.

[6] Ibid. p. 299.

view. The Council did all that could be done. Orders were sent to the two largest detached squadrons—to Killigrew returning from the Mediterranean with the home-bound convoy and now thought to be in the Channel, and to Cloudesley Shovell in the Irish Sea—to join Torrington immediately; Haddock was dispatched to Portsmouth, to speed the laggards to sea; the senior commander in the Downs was instructed to hasten to the westward any Dutch ships that arrived; and the Navy Board to prepare all the ships in harbour for service and to renew the general press for the necessary men.[1] With these precautions taken, Nottingham was able to write to the King on the 24th, when he enclosed Torrington's letter of the previous day, 'nothing is neglected to re-inforce the fleet or repair any misfortune... [and] we may expect that one way or the other Lord Torrington may be considerably strengthened; but', he concluded, 'if Mr. Russell, Sir Richard Haddock and some others can judge of the uncertain events of war, your Majesty may expect very good success from the ships now together.'[2]

The discrepancy between the two attitudes grew even stronger when the fleets first came in sight, and began to manœuvre for position. On the 26th, Torrington wrote to Nottingham from his flagship off the Isle of Wight that he had seen the enemy and tried, unsuccessfully, to engage. 'I do acknowledge', he wrote, 'my first intention of attacking them a rashness that will admit of no better excuse then that though I did beleeve them stronger than wee are, I did not beleeve it to so great a degree....Their great strength and caution have put soberer thoughts into my head, and has made me very heartily give God thanks they declined the battle yesterday, and indeed I shall not think myself very unhappy if I can gett ridd of them without fighting.'[3] He had had, he continued, a pretty good view of the enemy, and they consisted of almost, if not quite, eighty men-of-war 'fitt to lye in the line' and thirty fireships. Nottingham, however, continued to rely on his own sources of information in the Isle of Wight, who, in the haze that enveloped the area,[4] could hardly be expected to send such reliable reports as the Admiral on the spot. On the 27th, after receiving Torrington's letter,

---

[1] Ibid. pp. 312–13; P.R.O.Adm. 3/3: 20/6, 21/6, 23/6.

[2] *H.M.C. Finch*, II, pp. 312–13.

[3] Ibid. p. 315.

[4] Ibid.

he replied that 'those who were very near, and often counted their fleet say there were not. . . above 60 that could stand in a line'.[1] At the same time he wrote to the King that it was thought the French were not so strong as the Admiral conceived them to be, but that on the contrary they were much surprised to find so great an allied fleet opposed to them.[2] He enclosed the order sent, as a result, by the Queen to the fleet, not to retreat but to engage the enemy.[3]

From such an account Nottingham's attitude may seem, as it seemed to Torrington, fantastic. In the face of the strongest evidence, and 'with that strange fascination for self-deception which sometimes affects people',[4] he was obstinately persisting in an attitude which had been proved wrong when the French sailed from Brest a fortnight before; and now, as a result of it, the Admiral on the spot had been specifically ordered to stand and fight, and his choice of action removed on the evidence of a crop of second-rate reports.[5] It was indeed, and has since often been taken as, a classic example of direct interference by the statesman with the local commander—the first and golden rule of

---

[1] *H.M.C. Finch*, II, p. 318. I have taken Nottingham's sources of information to be Sir Robert Holmes, the governor of the Isle of Wight, Edmund Dummer, who 'had been very near the French fleet' (*Conduct*, pp. 68–9), and some English prisoners of war whom the French had taken on their way up Channel and set ashore in the island. His letters at this time and his memoirs later point exclusively to them. None of these sources, it might be thought, should have been preferred to the testimony of the Commander in Chief of the allied fleet, unless Nottingham had already concluded that they were likely to be more reliable.

[2] Ibid. pp. 318–19.

[3] The text of the order read as follows: 'Her Majesty does not doubt his [Torrington's] skill and conduct in this important conjuncture, but thinks the consequence of his withdrawing to the gunfleet would be so fatal, that she rather chooses he should, upon any advantage of the wind, give battle to the enemy. But in case he finds it necessary to go to the westward to join any ships from that direction, he is by no means to lose sight of the French fleet, whereby they may have opportunities of making attempts upon the shore, or in the rivers of Medway or Thames, or gett away without fighting.' It was signed by Mary and countersigned by Nottingham (ibid. p. 318).

[4] Sir Herbert Richmond's description of his attitude at this time, from some unpublished notes on the events of Beachy Head.

[5] Nottingham never changed his point of view. In the notes which he wrote later in his long life about the events of this year, his figures and his judgements are again those of June and July 1690 (see *Conduct*, pp. 68–91).

failure in war.[1] But while its lessons may have universal application, the causes of such interference spring from particular conditions. They arose on this occasion from the composition of the Queen's Council which had been formed early in June.

William had intended to go to Ireland in May, to conduct the campaign there in person. But the delay in the naval preparations forced him to stay in London until 4 June,[2] and in the interval he was busy choosing a Council to assist Mary in his absence. In the spring he had selected a Council of nine, composed of Carmarthen, Dorset, Devonshire, Pembroke, Nottingham, Shrewsbury, Lord Chief Justice Holt, Thomas Wharton and Sir John Lowther of Lowther;[3] and privately he had recommended to Mary that she should rely in particular on Shrewsbury. The latter, however, who had for some time been unhappy in office,[4] was talking throughout May of resigning; and finally did so on 3 June, much to William's annoyance,[5] leaving Nottingham as sole Secretary of State until December. On 2 June, the Council of nine was formally announced, but with several changes. Besides Shrewsbury, Holt and Wharton had gone, and in their place Monmouth, Marlborough and Russell came in.[6] Russell, although officially holding only a minor position, was an obvious choice, representing as he did on the one hand the Whigs of Shrewsbury's group even though Shrewsbury himself was absent,[7] and on the other the element of professional advice in a Council concerned largely with sea affairs.[8]

Expert opinion on the Council was thus weighted against Torrington.

---

1 The clearest statement of this argument is in P. H. Colomb, *Naval Warfare* (1895), pp. 112–20.

2 *Memoirs of Mary Queen of England*, ed. R. Doebner (1886), p. 29. He left the country on the 8th (*H.M.C. Finch*, II, p. 293).

3 *Memoirs of Mary*, pp. 23–4. Wharton and Lowther were the Comptroller and Vice-Chamberlain respectively who are mentioned there. Burnet (*History*, IV, p. 86) states incorrectly that it had eight members.

4 Ibid. p. 28.

5 T. C. Nicholson and A. S. Turberville, *Charles Talbot, Duke of Shrewsbury* (1930), pp. 48–9.

6 *Memoirs of Mary*, pp. 28–9. Where the word 'Council' is used henceforth in this chapter, it will refer to Mary's Council. Otherwise reference will be made to the 'Privy Council'.

7 Shrewsbury had returned the seals through him (ibid. p. 28).

8 Burnet, *History*, IV, p. 86.

Nottingham, who had lost faith in him the previous year and had assisted in his defeat in the autumn, as sole Secretary of State was managing all business;[1] and Russell, who had been recommended to Mary by William 'for sincerity', and who after an initial hesitation was coming to take a part in affairs,[2] was now openly his rival. The other members were indifferent but unlikely to favour the Admiral. This was not because they supported Nottingham or Russell, nor because they were particularly united among themselves, but on the contrary because they were not. Nottingham, with his uncompromising Toryism, was a nuisance to Carmarthen's group and suspect to the Whigs on the Council;[3] Russell was beginning to incur the jealousy of Carmarthen, who was using his influence to try to get him out of London;[4] and the two main groups of Whigs and Tories were preserving merely an uneasy truce. The unity of the Council rested purely upon negative causes, and it was on these that Torrington was condemned, as a not particularly popular scapegoat whom it was to nobody's interest to support. On this point, if on no other, Mary's advisers were unanimous.

These antagonisms, which had existed for several months, had a direct effect on sea affairs thanks to the power which the Council enjoyed. It was not new for Nottingham to dislike Torrington, or for Carmarthen to dislike Nottingham, or for the Whigs to distrust Carmarthen and each other. In 1689, however, the presence of William had prevented this faction from immediately affecting the direction of the war. In 1690, the importance of the Council of nine lay in the inexperience of the Queen whom it was appointed to advise and who was forced to rely heavily upon it. Conscientious[5] and moderately capable though Mary was, she knew herself to be without experience and was perhaps excessively conscious of her dependence on others.[6] Every circumstance that summer led her to distrust Torrington.

[1] *Memoirs of Mary*, p. 30.

[2] Ibid.; Dalrymple, op. cit. II, appendix to pt II, p. 122.

[3] *Memoirs of Mary*, p. 30.

[4] Dalrymple, loc. cit. p. 122.

[5] *Cal.S.P.Dom. 1690–1*, p. 38.

[6] *Memoirs of Mary*, pp. 22–3, 28; Dalrymple, loc. cit. p. 122. Her sense of her own inexperience had been fostered by William's poor opinion of her capacity (see 'Spencer House Journals', pp. 246, 248).

Devoted to William's intentions and fully accepting his views, she knew of the King's disappointment in the Admiral's judgement and of his resentment at his resignation. Her Secretary questioned Torrington's information, her naval adviser was optimistic about the fleet's chances, and both united with the rest of her ministers in condemning his irresolution. He seemed to her to be wasting time before putting to sea, while he drank and entertained, and to be throwing away his opportunity of a badly needed victory.[1] She needed little inducement, accordingly, to overrule his decisions. When urged to do so by Russell and Nottingham, with the approbation of the rest of the Council, she had no hesitation in sending the order of 27 June.[2]

It was in such hands that events now went quickly forward. There was little opportunity for William himself to intervene even if, as there is no evidence, he wished to do so. He had landed in Ireland on the 14th, and by the 22nd he was in touch with the French.[3] During the last week of the month, he was fully engaged in manœuvring for position, and was content to approve the measures taken in London,[4] while between 28 June and 4 July, by which time the battle of the Boyne had been won, neither he nor his secretary, Southwell, had time to refer to naval affairs at all. It was only on the latter date that he was able to approve Mary's orders to Torrington of the 27th.[5] Even had he been in London there is no reason to suppose that he would have acted differently from the Queen at this time, for her decisions were largely determined by what she knew to be his attitude; but events were

---

[1] Dalrymple, loc. cit. pp. 118, 125; *Memoirs of Mary*, p. 30. The accusation that he 'lay drincking and treating his friends till the French came upon the coast' was admittedly written later. Burnet, Mary's champion, repeated it in almost the same words (*History*, IV, pp. 86–7).

[2] On Russell's part in this decision, see Dalrymple, loc. cit. p. 123. 'Mr Russell drew up a pretty sharp letter for us to sign; but it was softened, and the only dispute was whether he [Torrington] should have a positive order to fight: at last it was made in such terms as you will see, to which all agreed' (Mary to William, 28 June).

[3] *H.M.C. Finch*, II, pp. 297, 307.

[4] Ibid. p. 307; B.M.Addnl. 38146, f. 56. E.g. also, 'His Majesty being returned... sayd, he could not now (being weary) answer the points of your Lordshipps letter which I was then exposing to him...but would only write a little letter to the Queen' (Southwell to Nottingham, 28 June; *H.M.C. Finch*, II, p. 321).

[5] *H.M.C. Finch*, II, p. 336.

in any case moving too fast for his authority to be effective. On receipt of the Queen's orders, and with no alternative but to fight,[1] Torrington engaged on the 28th off Beachy Head, with 56 ships of the line against 75. It was a calm day, but with a breeze from the north-east, so that the allies had the windward gauge of the French and could, if they wished, come to grips.[2] The Dutch, grouped together in the van, did so at once, but Torrington held back the English throughout the day, and the brunt of the fighting fell on his allies. At the end of the day, with only one Dutchman lost, but with several badly damaged and with some fireships sunk, he decided to retreat to the Gunfleet at the mouth of the Thames, as he had all along wished to do; and taking advantage of the ebb-tide which was sweeping the opponents to the westward, he anchored his fleet and let the enemy drift out of range. In the retreat up Channel, three more Dutch ships of the line and one English, all of them damaged in the battle, were lost. The next morning the French found themselves in command of the Channel.[3]

It is not within the scope or the competence of this work to discuss the wisdom of Torrington's decision. It should, however, be noted that it was taken with the consent of a full council of war of English flag officers.[4] He himself summed up the reasons for his action in a famous phrase: 'Most men were in fear that the French would invade, but I was always of another opinion, for I always said that whilst we had a fleet in being they would not make the attempt.'[5] Expert opinion

---

[1] No less than four copies of the orders were sent to the fleet, by different routes (endorsement on one of them in Torrington's hand, B.M. Egerton 2621, f. 91). This is confirmed by *Conduct*, p. 71.

[2] Torrington's description of the battle is contained in N.M.M., Bibl. Phill., Admiralty Papers, IV, ff. 106–8; the evidence of the English and Dutch officers called as witnesses at the court martial is in B.M. Stowe 143, ff. 90–7, and Stowe 305, ff. 184–5; Ashby's and Rooke's despatches in *An Account given by Sir John Ashby, Vice-Admiral and Reere-Admiral Rooke of the Engagement at Sea...June the 30th, 1690...* (1691); and two accounts by participants in *Memoirs relating to Lord Torrington*, pp. 43–51, and *Conduct*, pp. 72–3.

[3] The French did not lose any ships. Their casualties amounted to 344 killed and 811 wounded (Roncière, op. cit. VI, p. 78).

[4] B.M. Stowe 143, f. 95.

[5] *The Earl of Torrington's Speech to the House of Commons, in November 1690* (1710), p. 49. For the authenticity of this pamphlet, see p. 323, n. 6 above.

within the last fifty years has inclined to the view that he acted correctly.[1] For our purposes, his strategic theory is less important than his attitude when he began the fight. As has been said, 'A commander will go into battle in one of two minds: either with a determination to beat the enemy or with a determination not to be beaten, and between them there is a wide difference. Torrington's outlook was the latter.'[2] Apart from its own merits, the concept of 'the fleet in being' was closely related to the quarrels of the previous six months.

The news of the fleet's retreat caused a panic in London. There had already been suggestions that the Admiral should be removed. On the 26th, on receipt of his first letter off the Isle of Wight, Carmarthen had proposed that someone should be sent to the fleet to share the command, and Monmouth, whose impetuosity was leading Mary to think him mad,[3] offered to go if he could have the expert assistance of Sir Richard Haddock. The Queen had been able to stop other members from following suit only by reminding them that it was the King's wish that none of them should leave London during his absence.[4] On the 28th, however, the Council got its way, and Russell was sent to Dover in case the orders of the previous day had miscarried, with instructions to go aboard the fleet if it should pass that way, and take over the command. But when Torrington's acknowledgement of Mary's instructions arrived on the 29th, he was pursued, overtaken at

---

[1] Colomb, *Naval Warfare*, pp. 112–20; Admiral Sir Herbert Richmond also took this view (in an unpublished note). It has not been confined entirely to later ages. On 31 July 1690 Shovell wrote to Torrington: 'Nothing could be more to your Lordship's honour nor to our country's safety than your keeping out of reach of them' (*Naval Chronicle*, IV (1801), pp. 116–17); and Haddock's first reaction was also to commend his wisdom in avoiding battle (B.M. Egerton 2521, f. 67). Nottingham, on the other hand, took the view that a hard-fought action, even if ending in defeat, would have had the same effect on the French as a 'fleet in being', for they would then have been too weak to attempt anything (*Conduct*, p. 70); and this has been upheld by Laird Clowes (op. cit. II, p. 342). Possibly neither side has reckoned sufficiently with the administrative weaknesses of the French, who in the event failed to follow up their victory because their men were falling sick and their ships were running short of supplies.

[2] Unpublished note on the battle by Admiral Sir Herbert Richmond.

[3] *Memoirs of Mary*, p. 30.

[4] Dalrymple, loc. cit. pp. 122–4.

Canterbury and recalled.[1] When the news of the battle and the retreat reached London, therefore, Mary had no option but to send representatives of the Council to the fleet. The members could not agree among themselves who should go, and she herself finally selected Devonshire and Pembroke,[2] probably the wisest choice that could have been made. The two Earls accordingly met the fleet off Deal, but on finding that the council of war of English officers was unanimous in its opinion that it was impossible to continue the action, they returned to London and the retreat went on towards the Thames.[3] Meanwhile, the panic spread throughout the south of England. The rumours multiplied fast: Torrington was secretly a Jacobite, he had actually gone over to the French; there was going to be a landing in the Romney marshes, or in Sussex or on the Exe; there was going to be an attack upon Portsmouth or Plymouth.[4] The Admiralty sent arms to the dockyards, where the workmen were being organized into companies,[5] and ordered Trinity House to take up the buoys in the river;[6] while all over the country the orders went out for the militia to be raised, for troops to be sent to the coastal districts, for the horses of papist gentlemen to be seized,[7] and for the leading papists and disaffected notables to be sent to the Tower. Clarendon, Dartmouth and Pepys were among those who were clapped up in this way.[8] The situation seemed indeed to be very bad. The fleet could not be refitted for at least three weeks, and Killigrew's squadron could not be counted upon when it arrived, for it was bound to be foul; the regular troops which could be assembled numbered under 6000, and the militia was not to be taken seriously.[9] The principal danger lay in an attack on the transports in the Irish Sea, with the possibility of cutting off the King from England; and Council and Admiralty spent

---

[1] Dalrymple, loc. cit. p. 126; *H.M.C. Finch*, II, pp. 331–2. William himself appears to have had this plan in mind before he left, if the worst came to the worst. See *Cal.S.P.Dom. 1690–1*, pp. 58–9.

[2] Dalrymple, loc. cit. p. 127.

[3] *H.M.C. Finch*, II, p. 342.

[4] Anthony à Wood, *Life and Times...*, III, ed. A. Clark (1894), p. 333; *H.M.C. Hastings*, II, p. 215; *Le Fleming*, pp. 277–9.

[5] P.R.O.Adm. 3/3: 9/7, 18/7.

[6] P.R.O.Adm. 2/170, f. 296.

[7] *Cal.S.P.Dom. 1690–1*, pp. 51, 55–6, 66–7; *H.M.C.* 13th Report, appendix, pt II, p. 163; *Conduct*, pp. 79–80.

[8] *Cal.S.P.Dom. 1690–1*, p. 65; Luttrell, op. cit. II, pp. 63–4.

[9] Nottingham to William on 15 July; Dalrymple, loc. cit. pp. 109–10.

an uneasy week trying to guess the enemy's intentions.[1] But as William had accurately guessed,[2] the French could not follow up their opportunity. They had not the troops available to attempt any sort of invasion, while to the disgust of Seignelay, the minister of marine, the fleet found itself unable to pursue the enemy. With sickness growing in his ships and a shortage of stores aboard, Tourville sailed back down the Channel and contented himself with burning the fishing village of Teignmouth in Devon before he returned to Le Havre.[3] On 7 July Killigrew arrived at Plymouth,[4] and by 5 August, when the French left the Channel, the panic had died down.[5] The garrisons returned their emergency victuals to store, and the militia, whose members were needed for the harvest, went back to their homes.[6] The relief that no invasion had been attempted, and the good news of William's victory at the Boyne, prevented the full consequences of popular anger and dismay from being realized.

Nevertheless they had been fully roused. The Dutch, in particular, were furious. All their feeling of inferiority to their recent enemy, and their dissatisfaction with the way in which the war was being fought, concentrated on the discrepancy between the Dutch and English contributions to the action. Torrington himself they regarded as a coward, and his retreat as sheer desertion, and they demanded reparation for their damage and revenge for their disgrace.[7] The first public indication of the Council's attitude was revealed in the measures which it took to pacify its ally. Nottingham wrote to the English ambassador at The Hague that Torrington's failure to support the Dutch was the sole cause of the disaster,[8] and on 7 July the Queen sent a personal message to the States General which has been described as one of the

[1] N.M.M., Bibl. Phill., Admiralty Papers, IV, f. 37; *H.M.C. Finch*, II, pp. 347–8.

[2] See his letter of 9 July to Marlborough, in Winston S. Churchill, *Marlborough, His Life and Times*, I (1930), p. 325, n. 1.

[3] He had anything between 3600 and 8800 sick by the time he re-entered Brest (Roncière, op. cit. VI, p. 80, n. 3).

[4] Luttrell, op. cit. II, p. 72. [5] Burchett, p. 50; P.R.O.Adm. 3/3 : 2/8.

[6] N.M.M., Bibl. Phill., Admiralty Papers, IV, f. 101.

[7] See the pamphlets printed by Warnsinck, loc. cit. pp. 130–1, and the letters from Dursley and de Wildt to Nottingham in S.P.For. 84/221 and 222, cited by James, loc. cit.

[8] 'My Lord Torrington is wholly and only guilty' (*H.M.C. Finch*, II, p. 339).

most humiliating addresses ever delivered to a foreign government.[1] After admitting English responsibility for the defeat, it assured the Dutch that their sick and wounded would be looked after and their ships repaired at English expense, that immediate reinforcements would be equipped for sea, and that those responsible for the allied defeat would be quickly punished.[2] The first two conditions were fulfilled. Arrangements were made for housing the Dutch,[3] and the dockyards were set to work to put the fleet to sea again. Russell was sent to Portsmouth and Priestman to Chatham to hasten the preparations, and on 2 August the Admiralty was able to report that thirty English ships were again ready to sail.[4] With the seventeen Dutch available, this was sufficient to patrol the Channel for the rest of the month, for the French were back at Brest and Tourville himself, like Torrington, had been dismissed.[5]

But the third condition, that those responsible would quickly be punished, proved less easy to satisfy. The demand for Torrington's trial, which was thus initiated by the Dutch, was echoed in England. On 12 July a commission had been sent down to the fleet, composed of Pembroke and the Earl of Macclesfield, Sir Robert Howard, Sir Henry Goodricke and Sir Thomas Lee, to investigate the course of the battle. A week later it reported that in the general opinion Torrington's behaviour alone had been responsible for the defeat.[6] This further exacerbated feeling, which was already running high, and the Admiral's life itself was thought to be in danger.[7] But for the ministers it was not

---

1 Warnsinck, loc. cit. p. 133.

2 B.M.Addnl. 1152A, ff. 106–8.

3 P.R.O.Adm. 3/3: 4/7, 16/7; *London Gazette*, no. 2575.

4 P.R.O.Adm. 2/170, ff. 336–8; *H.M.C. Finch*, II, p. 341.

5 Roncière, op. cit. VI, p. 80. Torrington remarked at his subsequent trial that it seemed odd for the French Admiral to be dismissed for not destroying the English fleet, and for the English Admiral to be dismissed for not allowing it to be destroyed (B.M. Stowe 143, f. 95 *v*.).

6 *Cal.S.P.Dom. 1690–1*, pp. 62–3; James, loc. cit. p. 79, citing B.M.Addnl. 29593, ff. 3–8. *D.N.B.* states incorrectly that the Admiralty Commissioners were sent down. On 27 July they asked for a copy of the report (P.R.O.Adm. 3/4: 27/7).

7 Dalrymple, loc. cit. p. 131; *H.M.C. Le Fleming*, p. 276; *Conduct*, p. 77. See also *Camden Miscellany*, II, pp. 155–6. The ablest of several pamphlets which have survived for this occasion was *A Plain Relation of the Late Action at Sea*... (1690), by Edward

simply a question of placating opinion. Both to punish and to replace the Admiral involved political and constitutional problems which in the event, after splitting the Council and antagonizing the Admiralty and the fleet, prevented his punishment, delayed the appointment of his successor and finally led to a solution which failed to satisfy ministers, their opponents, and the Dutch.

To the government, the question of who was to succeed Torrington in command of the fleet was even more urgent than that of his punishment. Raising for the first time a positive problem in place of the negative unity provided by his disgrace, it first split the Council and then brought its members into conflict with the Admiralty. In the events surrounding Beachy Head, the latter had taken little part other than to ensure that its organization at the ports was ready to deal with emergencies. This was not surprising, for the quarrel between Torrington and Nottingham, and the Queen's intervention, were subjects for the Council to consider. But the visits of the Councillors to the fleet, and the proposals that they should take over command, were different matters. At first, in the heat of the moment when constitutional niceties went by the board, the Admiralty did not complain, but by the middle of July it had come to feel that it was faced with a constitutional principle.

The legal position was not a simple one, for it was itself the product of a constitutional ambiguity similar to that which it had to try to solve. By the terms of its patent, the Board of Admiralty had control only over 'divers offices and places and employments...properly in the gift and disposal of the Lord High Admiral', and the Crown was not bound either to accept its nominees or even to ask its opinion. On the other hand, custom and precedent decreed that the Admiralty's recommendations should be sought. The legal position reflected the status of the sea officers whom it affected. The Crown was free to select its professional servants without interference from a professional department, and

---

Stephens, which took the opportunity to relate Torrington's behaviour to the system of promoting gentlemen captains in the fleet. It elicited an unconvincing answer, *Some Modest Reflections upon Mr Stephen's Late Book...* (1690) which probably came from the hired pen of one Rashdall Taylor, an employee in the Treasurer of the Navy's office and, interestingly enough, later known to be connected with Russell (see his *Observations on a Pamphlet touching the Present Condition of the Navy...* of 1700).

could, and did, choose its Admirals regardless of rank or seniority. On the other hand, the development of the sea officers as a professional body over the past forty years meant that, in default of such appointments, rank and seniority counted. There were alternatives, but while to our mind the conception of office is subordinate to that of rank, at the time the conception of rank was subordinate to that of office. The trouble in 1690 arose from the fact that the Council, unlike William in 1689, was unable to fill the office with a personal nominee, but at the same time ignored the alternative of consulting the professional department on the standing of the professional candidates. Having failed to select a commander on grounds that were not purely professional, it attempted to apply these criteria to the professional hierarchy. The Admiralty's insistence on its right to recommend was justified by the collapse of other standards.

The first proposal in the Council, made by Carmarthen, was that Russell should take the command. Although this may well have been suggested in order to get him out of town,[1] it was, on other grounds, the obvious suggestion. Russell, however, did not feel confident of his ability to occupy the post, and, reluctant to hazard his career in these dangerous waters, declined.[2] With this refusal the Council turned to consider others of its own members, and its debates over the next few days are possibly the last example of an attempt to return to the old practice of the amateur nobleman in nominal command, assisted by professional subordinates. Monmouth again proposed himself, and even Shrewsbury, taking the waters at Tunbridge Wells, offered to go accompanied by 'two able and mettled seamen'.[3] Fortunately, both offers were turned down, for even if the Council was not interested in professional advice, it was not foolish enough to appoint amateurs in

---

[1] Dalrymple, loc. cit. pp. 122–3.

[2] Ibid. pp. 127, 131. Shrewsbury, who was possibly Russell's closest political associate at this time, described him on 12 July as 'not being confident enough of his own experience to desire the command alone, nor yet willing to undergo so much trouble and danger as such a business requires when he is only to share the honour'. See also Carmarthen's view in *Cal.S.P.Dom. 1690–1*, p. 53.

[3] Dalrymple, loc. cit. p. 131; S.P.Dom. 8/7, no. 48. Shrewsbury's offer is wrongly calendared in *Cal.S.P.Dom. 1690–1*, p. 31, as 12 June, and addressed to the King. It was actually dated 12 July, and addressed to 'My Lord', whom Dalrymple (loc. cit. pp. 172–3) takes to be Carmarthen, as President of the Council.

command. But the disputes which had hitherto been held in check by events now began to appear as the rival groups pressed their claims, and as Mary refused to make any decision until she had learnt William's views.[1] These were not the same as the political proposals of the Council. In May, when Torrington threatened to resign, it was rumoured that the King had been in favour of a Commission of more than one Admiral;[2] but later he had decided on Sir Richard Haddock—long retired from sea, but generally respected and senior enough to be free from the rivalries of the fleet—as the prospective Commander in Chief.[3] In July, however, Haddock had one great drawback, for he had recently quarrelled with the Dutch on some administrative questions. William therefore resorted to his original idea of a Commission of professional sailors, but left the choice of names to Mary and the Council.[4] This was merely the signal for renewed argument. The names of Sir John Ashby, Sir Cloudesley Shovell, Killigrew and Haddock himself were mentioned, but no decision could be reached, and eventually the latter, to solve the problem of seniority, again suggested that two seamen and a peer—he proposed Devonshire or the Earl of Grafton—should be appointed.[5] The possibility of an amateur once more led to such disputes that Carmarthen wrote privately to William urging him to return secretly from Ireland, as the only possible solution to the chaos that was fast developing.[6]

A deadlock seemed to have been reached, and on 22 July the Board of Admiralty, which presumably knew of what was going on through Pembroke and Russell, itself intervened. It was thought by then that Haddock was bound to be one of the joint Admirals, and, unaware that he was William's choice, the Commissioners concluded that he was Nottingham's.[7] Resenting what they regarded as an unconstitutional violation of their rights by the Secretary of State, they determined to make a stand. At a meeting that day, at which Russell was present, they overruled his objections and decided to recommend him for the

---

[1] Dalrymple, loc. cit. p. 131.

[2] James, loc. cit. citing B.M.Addnl. 17677, KK, f. 93.

[3] Dalrymple, loc. cit. pp. 107–8. [4] Warnsinck, loc. cit. pp. 154–6.

[5] *Cal.S.P.Dom. 1690–1*, p. 53. William at first seemed likely to accept this advice (B.M.Addnl. 38146, f. 58), but eventually did not.

[6] Dalrymple, loc. cit. p. 132. [7] Ibid. p. 148.

command;[1] and in the evening, with only Russell himself and Priestman absent, they went to Kensington and protested that a Commission would be intolerable. Pembroke, 'for form's sake', opened the argument; but according to Mary Sir Thomas Lee was obviously the man behind it, and he soon took it over.[2] As a result of the meeting the Queen again approached Russell; but he again refused,[3] and thereupon the Council summoned all the Admiralty Commissioners and informed them that it had decided to choose Killigrew, Ashby and Haddock as joint Admirals. The result was an open quarrel in Mary's presence.

Sir Thomas Lee grew pale as death, and told me [i.e. the Queen] that the custom was that they were used to recommend, and that they were to answer for the persons, since they were to give them the commission, and did not know but that they might be called to account in Parliament...and at last Sir Thomas Lee came to say plainly, Haddock was the man they did not like....I might give them a commission if I pleased, but they could not. I said I perceived then that the King had given away his own power, and could not make an admiral which the Admiralty did not like; he answer'd, No, no more he can't. I was ready to say then that the King should give the [Admiralty] commission to such as would not dispute with him, but I did not though I confess I was heartily angry.[4]

Russell withdrew before the meeting ended, but Carbery, Priestman and Onslow supported Lee. Pembroke, who as a member of the Council knew William's views, in the end declined to do so, and despite their objections the Commissioners were ordered to prepare the warrant for a Commission to the joint Admirals. But the order had to be given again on 18 July, and yet again on 5 August,[5] before they would complete the details; and when the document was finally ready on 8 August, Lee, Carbery and Onslow excused themselves from signing, while the rest of the Board insisted that a clause be inserted which stated that the appointment was 'by the King's particular command'.[6]

The course of the arguments over the command of the fleet had

[1] P.R.O.Adm. 3/3 : 22/7.

[2] Dalrymple, loc. cit. pp. 145–6; see also *H.M.C. Finch*, II, pp. 377–9.

[3] Dalrymple, loc. cit. p. 147.

[4] Ibid. pp. 147–8. See also *H.M.C. Finch*, II, pp. 382–3.

[5] Dalrymple, loc. cit. p. 152; P.R.O.Adm. 3/4 : 6/8.

[6] P.R.O.Adm. 2/6, f. 232.

shown the limitations of political appointments; for the keener the political rivalry, the less political the appointment could be. In their later stages, however, they hinged on the Admiralty's relations with Parliament. The department's quarrel with the Council was the direct result of the Commons' attacks of the winter before, for the Commissioners appreciated that, whatever their relations with the King's ministers in fact might be, the latters' failure might be followed by their own dismissal. As the easiest target for Parliamentary criticism and as an easy scapegoat for a government which they represented on naval affairs in the House, but of whose measures, for that very reason, they were ill informed, their only alternatives were to influence events within the ranks of the executive, or publicly to avoid responsibility for them. In the discussions on Torrington's successor, they had tried to do the former; on the other great question which arose from his defeat, that of his trial and punishment, they strenuously attempted to do the latter. The argument thus shifted on this last question from the comparative secrecy of the executive to the platform of Parliamentary politics; and the domestic disagreements of the groups within the Council, and its antagonism to the Admiralty, were now recorded in the votes and debates of the two Houses.

In the process, the Admiralty was led along some curious paths. Where, in the discussions over the command of the fleet, its relations with Parliament led it to claim a direct authority over the fate of the professional officers, it later, for the same reasons, was led strenuously to deny that authority. The ministers, on the other hand, at first the opponents of such control, later tried hard to prevent Torrington from exercising his rights as a peer to evade it. The connexion of the executive with Parliament was far from straightforward, and both sides at times took their stand upon arguments which, viewed from the later development of their relations, seemed to weaken, or even to contradict, the claims for which they were fighting so vigorously.

Torrington himself on 10 July had joined his predecessor Dartmouth in the Tower, on a general charge of 'high crimes and misdemeanours'.[1] No specific charge had as yet been preferred, and on the 21st the law officers of the Crown were ordered to consider the relevant papers and

[1] P.R.O. Privy Council Register, 2/73, f. 475.

to report on the manner of his trial and on the type of warrant needed to justify his continued imprisonment.[1] The last problem was not of immediate importance, for the Admiral's friends were quite relieved to see him protected from the crowd in this way;[2] but the question of his trial raised both legal and political difficulties.[3]

One point of view, which found its way into the pamphlet warfare then at its height, was that Torrington should be impeached by Parliament,[4] if only because the state of allied relations demanded a trial by the highest court in the land. The proceedings would then be public, and removed from the influence of naval faction. They would also, added the pamphleteer in a typical passage, help to discover who were the true friends of England in Parliament. But this did not appeal to ministers. As Carmarthen wrote to William and the Prussian ambassador to his own government, trial by Parliament meant trial by faction,[5] and the alternative of a court martial was decidedly preferable. The Admiralty, however, disagreed. Opinion in the navy itself was hardening against the way in which the Admiral was being made the scapegoat for Dutch resentment and ministerial apprehension. Nottingham's letter to the English ambassador at The Hague had been published, without his permission but without his subsequent disapproval,[6] and had increased the feeling in the fleet that the navy was being betrayed by the government. It was, indeed, obvious by now that Torrington alone was intended to bear the blame. Rooke, whose conduct as Rear Admiral had also been criticized at the preliminary inquiry, was escaping all censure.[7] If naval officers were to be the judges the chances of an acquittal were now considerable, and if they returned a verdict of 'not guilty' the issue would shift from the handling of the fleet

---

1 P.R.O. Privy Council Register, 2/73, f. 492.

2 Bonnet's dispatch of 10 October in Ranke, *History of England mainly in the Seventeenth Century*, VI, p. 148.

3 A good account of the former is given by J. McArthur, *On Naval and Military Courts Martial*, I (1813 ed.), pp. 107–11.

4 See *Reasons for the Trial of the Earl of Torrington by Impeachment by the Commons in Parliament rather than by any other way* (1690).

5 *Cal.S.P.Dom. 1690–1*, p. 95; Ranke, op. cit. VI, p. 148, n. 1: 'Les Whigs voulant le perdre, cela suffit aux Tories de tacher de le sauver.'

6 *Conduct*, p. 79; see also *H.M.C. Finch*, II, p. 355.

7 He was formally cleared on 8 August (P.R.O.Adm. 3/4: 9/8).

during the battle to the circumstances of its weakness beforehand, and the Admiralty itself would once again be subjected to a severe political attack. To the Commissioners, it seemed better to submit the question at once to Parliament on an issue which did not directly affect them, rather than to risk an eventual debate there upon an issue which did so. Late in July they refused to sign a commission for a court martial, asserting in support of their action that they had no legal power to do so,[1] despite the fact that they and their predecessors had been issuing such warrants since the beginning of the war.[2] With this refusal, their disagreement with the Council was brought dramatically into the open.

The Admiralty's legal argument was that the power to call a court martial lay by statute[3] with the Lord High Admiral alone, and that despite the authority of their Letters Patent the terms of that statute were still law.[4] The law officers were therefore consulted, and on 25 July Lord Chief Justice Holt reported their unanimous decision that a power vested in the Lord High Admiral could be exercised by a Commission appointed to execute his duties.[5] The Board was accordingly directed to issue a warrant for a court martial, charging Torrington with 'keeping back and not engaging and coming into the fight and not relieving and assisting a known friend in view', which, by the articles of war, was a capital offence.[6]

This order came while the Commissioners were fighting their losing battle over the question of the command of the fleet. Their first reaction was to submit. But before signing the warrant they again consulted the officers of the Admiralty Court, and after hearing their further opinion that the warrant was illegal decided after all not to do so.[7] On 9 August, they were again ordered to sign and to commit Torrington to the

---

1 *Cal.S.P.Dom. 1690–1*, p. 95.

2 P.R.O.Adm. 1/5253, *passim*. I do not know of any statement by or on behalf of the Admiralty Commissioners which gives their reasons for acting as they did. I can only conclude that they must have thought along these lines, as no other explanation seems possible.

3 13 Car. II, c. 9, art. 34.

4 G. F. James, loc. cit., citing Bodl. Carte MS. 79, f. 335.

5 *H.M.C. Finch*, II, p. 385. For the individual opinions, see *H.M.C.* 13th Report, appendix, pt V, p. 93.

6 13 Car. I, c. 9, art. 14.

7 P.R.O.Adm. 3/4 : 28/7.

custody of the marshal of the Admiralty Court.[1] A week later they were summoned by the Council to explain why they had done neither. Lee, answering once more on behalf of his colleagues, replied that they were not convinced of the validity of the warrant, despite the decision of the law officers of the Crown;[2] and on their return they again consulted their own legal officers. As a result they once more refused to take any action.[3] The deadlock appeared to be complete.

Throughout September nothing was done, the lawyers of both sides taking good care not to meddle too far in such a dangerous case,[4] and the position when Parliament assembled on 2 October was still the same. Two days later Torrington himself complicated the issue, by a petition to the House of Lords claiming that his commitment to the Tower was a breach of privilege the consequence of which as a precedent he asked the House to consider.[5] This raised problems which were not confined to himself, but which extended to the other peers under confinement, and a motion that the Earls in the Tower should be discharged was defeated only by 29 votes to 21, Shrewsbury and Carbery voting with the majority and Nottingham with the minority.[6] The Whigs then asked how Torrington could be kept in the Tower without being charged with treason, and the question of privilege was referred to a committee.[7] With the whole affair fast becoming political dynamite, it was clear that a solution to the legal arguments over a court martial would quickly have to be reached.

The lawyers were therefore consulted again, both on the original issue of the powers of the Board of Admiralty, and on the new problem of whether Torrington could claim privilege as a peer or should be treated and tried on his behaviour as a naval officer. The second problem

---

[1] *H.M.C. Finch*, II, p. 405. [2] James, loc. cit.

[3] Ibid., citing B.M.Addnl. 17677, KK, f. 242.

[4] 'Our Common and Civill Lawyers make so strange a Galimatias of the Process agst my Lord Torrington, (as they do indeed of most things where there is any danger) that He is not like to come to any tryall at all. The Lawyers of both Sorts avoid as much as they can to have to do with his Lop' (Blathwayt to Southwell, in N.M.M., Bibl. Phill., Admiralty Papers, IV, f. 94).

[5] *H.L.J.* XI, pp. 517–18; *H.M.C.* 13th Report, appendix, pt V, p. 93. This will henceforth be cited as *H.M.C.* 13, V. [6] S.P.Dom. 8/8, ff. 3–4.

[7] Ranke, op. cit. VI, p. 152: *H.L.J.* XIV, p. 519.

in turn involved two distinct questions, for both his commitment and the manner of his trial had now to be considered. On the second question the judges decided that as an Admiral subordinate to the Admiralty he could be tried according to the articles of war,[1] and the Lords thereupon resolved that he had no privilege as a peer to be exempt from a court martial.[2] The Admiralty was now compelled to realize, by this devious route, that a court martial could no longer be avoided, and Torrington was accordingly committed on 16 October to the custody of the marshal of the Admiralty Court.[3] Four days later, after a long debate, the Lords resolved by 32 votes to 17 that his original commitment to the Tower had been a breach of privilege.[4]

The initial argument over the powers of the Admiralty was still not satisfactorily settled, and moreover, in appealing to the statute of 1679, the Board had raised questions that went far beyond the immediate dispute. All rights and powers granted to a Lord High Admiral by Act of Parliament could be similarly argued when occasion arose, and there was a mass of such legislation still in force dating back to the time of Richard II.[5] To settle the immediate problem, and to prevent any such objections from being raised again, a bill was introduced in the House of Lords on 24 October declaring that all rights and powers legally enjoyed by a Lord High Admiral were, and had always been enjoyed by the Commissioners for executing his Office.[6] A fierce discussion at once arose over the purpose of this bill. Its proposers and the lawyers regarded it as purely a declaratory measure 'for avoiding all...Doubts and Questions'. No attempt was made to re-define existing powers, for the bill merely mentioned authorities vested 'by any Act of Parliament or otherwise', but simply to confirm by statute the terms of the Letters Patent which in the first instance had been challenged by statute. Its opponents, however, claimed that the bill was retrospectively granting powers which had not specifically existed at the time of the events which it was designed to regulate. It alone, they stated, debarred Torrington from being granted the privilege of being tried by his peers,

[1] *H.M.C.* 13, v, p. 93.
[2] *H.L.J.* xiv, p. 521.
[3] P.R.O.Adm. 3/4: 16/10.
[4] *H.L.J.* xiv, pp. 525, 527.
[5] See *Statutes relating to the Admiralty... from 9 Henry III to 3 George IV inclusive*, ed. John Raithby (1823).
[6] *H.L.J.* xiv, p. 531. For the text of the bill and the Act, see Appendix XII below.

and as such it was a gross example of the injustice of retroactive legislation.[1] The close connexion between the two problems, between the Board's relation to the Lord High Admiral and his relation to his subordinates, was shown by a point raised during the second reading: whether, by the terms of the bill, the Commissioners of Admiralty could give leave for a sentence of death to be carried out if such were the decision of a court martial authorized by them.[2] The lawyers were once more consulted; but on this occasion their report was not unanimous, for six of the judges, including the Lord Chief Justice, declared that the Commissioners possessed such a power by virtue of their function, while the other six declared that they did not.[3] The bill was therefore modified in committee, and on the 29th it was accepted in the Lords without further amendment, the dissenting peers recording their protest.[4] The next day it was sent down to the Commons.[5] On 11 November it was read there for the third time; after a fierce debate lasting for two days, in which Torrington's friends again raised the original point of trial by Parliament, it passed the House, and on the 18th received the royal assent as 2 Will. and Mary, sess. 2, c. 2.[6] Its connexion with the personal fate of the Admiral was emphasized during the third reading, when a message was received that he desired to be heard at the bar of the House; but by the time that he was allowed to appear the bill had been accepted, and instead of speaking on the course to be adopted for his trial, he therefore confined himself to defending his conduct during the engagement.[7]

Thus, arising from the political disagreements and argued on party grounds, two important constitutional decisions had been made in both of which, despite itself, the Admiralty had been granted the verdict. In the teeth of professional opposition, the professional status of the sea officer had been advanced. A peer who was also a naval officer must be tried as a naval officer. At the same time, the department had been confirmed, to its dismay, in the constitutional exercise of its powers, and the sanction of Parliament had been obtained despite all its efforts

1 *H.L.J.* XIV, p. 535. 2 Ibid. p. 533. 3 *H.M.C.* 13, V, pp. 147–8.

4 *Complete Collection of the Protests of the Lords with historical introductions*, I, ed. J. E. Thorold Rogers (1875) pp. 100–1.

5 *H.L.J.* XIV, p. 535. 6 *H.C.J.* X, pp. 461, 463, 467.

7 Ibid., p. 470; N.M.M., Bibl. Phill., Admiralty Papers, IV, ff. 101–8.

to prevent it. The Board's authority now rested, not only on the Letters Patent which created it, but in a secondary degree on the confirmation of their validity by statute.[1] Around the unfortunate figure of Torrington, the only two legal decisions which affected the navy during the war had been evolved, and while at the time they did not satisfy the Admiralty, the ministers or the Dutch on whose behalf the discussion had largely been started, their importance for the future lay in the precedents which they set in a development itself to be decided on other grounds.

With the passing of this Act, the business was now in its final stages. Sir Ralph Delavall was appointed commander in chief in the Thames and Medway for the purpose of presiding at the court martial, and the only issue still remaining was the composition of the court.[2] This was solved by taking the judges from the commanders of those ships which were in the Thames at the time—a large proportion of the fleet—and limiting them to men who had been present at the action. Despite the fact that the resulting court is supposed to have been hostile to the Admiral,[3] Delavall informed Nottingham shortly before it sat that an acquittal could confidently be expected.[4] There were still delays, for the trial was at first fixed for 30 November;[5] but some of the Dutch witnesses were away on convoy,[6] and it was 10 December before the proceedings opened. The trial itself was short.[7] The witnesses for the

---

1 Sir Oswyn Murray, in his first article on 'The Admiralty', in *M.M.* XXIII, no. 1, p. 27, adduces another important result from the passing of the Act. 'The Act', he argues, 'referred to "powers vested in the Lord High Admiral by Act of Parliament *or otherwise*", so that it may be regarded as giving a general Parliamentary recognition to the practice (then already over sixty years old) of appointing Commissioners to execute the office.' This was certainly not its intention, nor did any of the parties concerned regard it in this light, either at the time or later.

2 This question seems actually to have been under discussion since July (*Conduct*, pp. 89–90).

3 *D.N.B.*

4 *H.M.C. Finch*, II, p. 193.

5 P.R.O.Adm. 3/4: 24/11; *H.M.C. Portland*, III, p. 454.

6 B.M.Addnl. 17677, KK, f. 347.

7 The minutes of the court martial are missing from P.R.O.Adm. 1/5253. The fullest account, with the names of the members of the court, is given in B.M.Addnl. Stowe 145, ff. 90–7, and the evidence of the Dutch Rear Admiral Schey in B.M. Stowe

prosecution turned out to be almost useless, while in contrast Torrington defended himself competently. The Dutch, as was to be expected, made some vehement charges, and their senior witness left the court in a rage. It was clear which way the verdict was going to go, and after only a few hours the Admiral was acquitted *nemine contradicente* and discharged. On his return up-river he was saluted all the way with guns and cheering.[1]

The verdict made no difference to his future. His commission as Vice-Admiral of England was revoked on 12 December,[2] and although his name remained on the list of the Privy Council until 23 June 1692,[3] William never forgave him[4] and he was not employed again. He retired to his home at Walton-on-Thames, where he was able to watch his former colleagues and their successors 'without envie of the senate'. 'I wish them', he wrote from this retreat some years later, 'eternally confounded, that wee poore country farmers mought injoy our innocent diversions in peace and quiet, and the nation its trade, and more prosperitie, then possibly it can under the management of sutch insipid ignorants, as that Commission is composed of....'[5] Grumbling and loquacious as ever, he passed into obscurity. With his disappearance, the first and most dramatic phase of the war had come to an end.

305, ff. 184–5, of which another copy exists in B.M.Addnl. 38176. Part of this evidence is given in *H.M.C. Portland*, x, pp. 29–32, and in *Life of Sir John Leake*, I, ed. G. Callender (*N.R.S.* 1920), p. 39.

[1] B.M.Addnl. 17677, LL, f. 9*v*.; *An Impartial Account of Some Remarkable Passages in the Life of Arthur Earl of Torrington together with some Modest Remarks on His Tryal and Acquitment* (1691), pp. 16–18.

[2] *Cal.S.P.Dom. 1690–1*, p. 186.

[3] P.R.O. Privy Council Register, 2/76, f. 1. [4] *H.M.C. Portland*, III, p. 454.

[5] *Epistolary Curiosities...illustrative of the Herbert Family, Series I*, ed. Rebecca Warner (1818), p. 157.

CHAPTER XI

THE MIDDLE YEARS, 1691–1694

I

The first phase of the war has been examined in some detail, for it was a confused and intricate period. But after 1690 it is possible to take longer periods through which to follow the development of naval administration, and to concentrate on certain events within them as illustrating the complementary development of policy. In each of these periods the activity was as full and as varied as in the years which preceded them; but the proportions of this story must be determined not by the amount of effort engendered by events, but by its significance. The activity during a particular campaign may be intense, and the course of naval policy intricate, without either being modified by its progress. The middle years of the war were full of incident; but much of it, for our purposes, was repetitive. Their unity is a broad unity, and it is only by taking them as a whole that a change may be seen between one year and another.

It is not only chronologically that the years 1691 to 1694 are the central years of the war; they also formed its climax, and appear at once as its central period. They witnessed the developments which distinguish the war of William III from its predecessors, and which associate it as much with the wars of the eighteenth as with those of the seventeenth century. Before them, the foundations were being laid; after them, the problem became simply one of survival, as the defects of the new developments threatened their own existence. But the failures of policy and administration after 1694 were not the same as the failures of 1689 and 1690, for the factors which threatened them were not the same. In the interval, new strategic considerations, and new problems of organization and finance had appeared, with a consequent alteration in the direction of policy and with some change in the methods of administration. The similarities between the first and the last phases of the war were due largely to the fact that organization changed more slowly than the demands made upon it; the differences, to the fact that these demands had changed. And while to contemporaries the dislocations of the later years pointed to a steady decline of control over familiar problems, to ourselves they may indicate the failure of traditional methods to deal with problems which were largely new.

The data for naval policy at the beginning of 1691 were much the same as they had been a year before. The two factors which had been present at the outbreak of war still existed: an unsubdued Ireland to determine the direction of English strategy, and an unsubdued French fleet to provide the obstacle to its success. In the years that followed, both factors disappeared. Ireland was conquered, and the French fleet soundly beaten. But these events did not occur in the same year, and the reorientation of policy thus took place at different times for William, with his personal strategy for the war, and for the navy which had to carry it out. To the King, the turning point came at the end of 1691, with the final reduction of Limerick and the consequent possibility at last of using English resources directly to help the allied plan in Europe; to the navy, and to much of the nation, the main objective at sea remained, as always, the major fleet action which had become the more desirable since the reverse of 1690. The campaign of 1692, therefore, which successfully provided this action and thus reconciled the two objectives, led at the same time to a period of confusion in which the strategic weapons did not altogether fit the strategic intention. For the fleet had by then been built up for a certain purpose—that of a great action—the success of which left it unable to follow up its consequences. With the disappearance of the familiar conditions in which it had hitherto operated, it faced a new situation for which it had not been developed.

The defence of Ireland and the pursuit of the fleet action were also linked in a more immediate and positive way. This was to be seen almost immediately after Beachy Head. In July, with that defeat only just behind it, the government was paying little attention to the campaign in the west. As Blathwayt pointed out to William, the Council Committee for Ireland had not been given any directions for some time, and indeed hardly met any more. 'The reason indeed of this mistake', he concluded, 'is as of many others that nobody has a particular charge of generall matters so as to watch and pursue the dispatch of them in the severall places.'[1] Ireland itself, despite the battle of the Boyne, still lay at the mercy of the French provided that they could take advantage of their victory at sea. But the material factors behind the campaigns were common to all the combatants alike, and inefficiency and indecision were not a monopoly of the English government. In the following months, indeed, the victors were more at a loss than the defeated. While the French fleet was recouping its stores and discharging its sick, poisoned by their victuals as their opponents had been the year before, and while the French court was hesitating over its next step, the English acted imaginatively and with dispatch. A month after Blathwayt wrote in this strain, Irish affairs were far from being neglected. In the middle of August, Marlborough submitted a proposal to the Council to send an expedition to attack the harbours of Cork and Kinsale, which were still in James's hands.[2] Most of his colleagues, naturally perturbed at the idea of losing the bulk of the few troops still in England with the threat of invasion only just behind them, opposed the plan; but William, who had never believed that an invasion of England was

[1] Blathwayt to Southwell, 27 July; N.M.M., Bibl. Phill. Papers, IV, f. 71.

[2] Mr Winston Churchill gives the credit for this proposal to Marlborough (*Marlborough, His Life and Times*, I, p. 326). Nottingham later claimed that he had first put the idea into Marlborough's head: 'But now...the clouds of fear [i.e. after Beachy Head]...were all dispersed...for the prospect of having a fleet at sea opened a very agreeable scene....The Earl of Nottingham, therefore, proposed to the Earl of Marlborough an attempt upon Cork and Kinsale...and urged that if any number of troops could be spared from hence, they might straightway be embarked on board the men-of-war....His lordship was extremely pleased with this overture, and they both waited on the Queen to acquaint her with it....This Her Majesty approved and ordered them not to mention it to the Cabinet Council till there came an answer from the King. In the meantime the Earl of Marlborough, in confidence of His Majesty's approbation, disposed all the troops designed for this expedition in quarters as near to Portsmouth as possible' (*Conduct*, pp. 86–7). This passage, unlike some in *Conduct*, is from Nottingham's own notes, in which he always referred to himself in the third person (textual notes A and B to ch. II; ibid. p. 154). In view of his persistent optimism throughout 1690, it seems possible that his claim may be justified, although Marlborough would seem to have been thinking along the same lines at the same time. In such cases, it is often difficult to award the credit exactly, for men in similar positions and with full knowledge of the facts are, after all, often working on their own towards the same end.

likely, approved of it, and towards the end of August the Admiralty was working out the details of the escort, and the naval victuallers were busy laying in provisions for the troops on their passage to the west.[1] On 17 September, the convoy sailed from Portsmouth, and after a well-executed campaign of only a month both ports were taken.[2] Although William was unable to finish off the campaign, as he had hoped, by reducing Limerick, the prospects for the next year seemed brighter than usual, with the southern flank protected by the two harbours nearest to France.

The possession of Cork and Kinsale was important not only for its effect on the Irish campaign, but also because it provided advanced bases for the fleet in the west.[3] The coast of Brittany and the Soundings provided the normal cruising ground for the summer, to spy out the French fleet and to give a general protection to the inbound trade from the Straits and the Plantations. In the later years of the war, there was a distinction between the two activities, and escorts and cruisers to cover trade were regarded as an alternative to the battle fleet. But in its middle years, the main fleets themselves were engaged directly in both activities; and in 1691 the connexion between the fleet action and the protection of trade was particularly close, thanks to the events of the previous year. For while the English were anxious to stage a major engagement, to remove the disgrace of Beachy Head and to put an end, if possible, to the constant accusations of mismanagement that plagued the Administration, the French, depressed by their inability to follow up their advantage in 1690 and by the large numbers which it was known the English were putting to sea despite their defeat,[4] were as anxious to avoid it. Committed to a large fleet by the action of their opponents, but unwilling to put it to the test, they therefore turned from the idea of a fleet action to the alternative but hitherto untried plan of

---

[1] P.R.O.Adm. 3/7: 23/8.

[2] Churchill, op. cit. I, pp. 328–33.

[3] There is, however, no evidence to show that the expedition to capture them was undertaken with this in mind.

[4] An accurate but unauthorized list of the fleet for the summer had been printed and sold publicly in the spring, and in May the Admiralty was trying to find out how the leakage had occurred (P.R.O.Adm. 3/6: 8/5). Russell was very disturbed by its appearance (Finch Transcr., Russell to Nottingham, 6/5).

using the fleet in a *guerre de course*.[1] Tourville, who had been reinstated in the spring, was sent out with instructions to evade the allies and to cruise in search of trade along the main Atlantic and Mediterranean routes, where these converged in the area between the Bay of Biscay and the south-west coast of Ireland.[2] It was a comment on the limitations of a victory at sea under the prevailing conditions that the initiative could thus pass so swiftly to the loser.

With one side determined to avoid an action, the chances of its taking place became at once remote. It would require a combination of exceptional luck and good management to bring the one fleet into touch with the other, and even better handling to force a battle when contact had been gained. And in fact, despite some exciting moments, nothing happened in 1691. On the other hand, so long as one side wanted a battle, both sides would have to continue to put large numbers to sea. Until an action had been fought, and probably until a decisive victory had been won, the war at sea seemed likely to persist on a large scale. Apart from a major defeat, the only end to such a process that could be contemplated was the financial or material collapse of one of the protagonists. In the event, the impasse was ended by battle and not by financial decline, when Russell won the great victory of the war in May 1692 at Barfleur. The period between July 1690 and May 1692 is therefore self-contained, beginning with a defeat and ending with a victory. It may be defined as the period of the great fleet.

This type of warfare was expensive. The fleets themselves, their stores and provisions, and the facilities for their maintenance and repair, had to be kept ready for a major action when such an action was improbable. They were a constant expense, likely moreover to be increased as the fleets themselves increased under the competition which such warfare entails. As has been seen,[3] the expensive war at sea in general favoured England, whose objectives and resources complemented each other, in comparison with Holland and France. The significance of the years between Beachy Head and Barfleur lay in the

[1] It might perhaps be said that this plan approximates more closely to the 'fleet in being', as seen by later writers on strategy, than did Torrington's definition of 1690. For whereas he had in mind an inferior fleet, in 1691 the French threat lay in the threat of superiority.

[2] Roncière, op. cit. VI, pp. 89–90.

[3] Pp. 171–3 above.

way in which this comparison turned into a contrast. While the size and organization of the navy was steadily increasing in England, it was stationary, and even slightly on the decline, in Holland and France. Where Beachy Head had proved the end of the beginning for the English fleet, it was the beginning of the end for the French. To the former it acted as a spur, for the latter it was a climax. In England, a defeat of the fleet led at once to the construction of a greater fleet; in France, a fleet victory led to the avoidance of fleet actions. Having failed to beat their enemy on his own terms, the French turned to their natural recourse of a war against trade, as the result not of an open defeat but of a recent and apparently decisive victory.

The expansion which characterized these two years in England was begun almost wholly within the twelve months after Beachy Head, and followed familiar lines. Between July 1690 and July 1691 the foundations were laid for the most important shipbuilding programme of the war, and for all the developments in naval organization that were undertaken before its close. Within that year, apart from the construction referred to, a new dockyard was established and a new base set up, the first two naval hospitals were founded, an establishment for a new class of ship promulgated, and investigations begun—into the seamen's diet and their officers' pay, into the system of naval accountancy and into the organization of the Victualling Office, into the problems of manning and into the question of promotion in the fleet—in all of which the results were to be seen within the next three years. These achievements marked the culmination of the Restoration navy. For the last time, the organization bequeathed by the Stuarts was increased upon Stuart lines, with the definite prospect of a fleet action unimpeded by the conflicting claims of combined land and sea operations, and through the agency of a financial system which, in its essentials, was as they had left it. It was the familiar type of reorganization and expansion after a defeat; but in this case, the scale on which it was conducted made it the last of its type, and its end was marked by different conditions from its beginning, when under the pressure of new strategic problems and of new forms of financial supply and control, there emerged from the naval administration of the Stuarts the organization which, with little change, was to support the wars of the eighteenth century.

While these campaigns demanded an administrative reorganization, their progress enabled the direction of policy to settle down. In the early months of 1691 there seemed little chance of this. It was generally expected that the French would try to land as soon as possible,[1] and when William left in January for the allied conference at The Hague, the Council which he had chosen for Mary soon began to quarrel more bitterly than ever and some of its members, in the general insecurity, to correspond with the exiled court at St Germains. Godolphin, who in December had been appointed head of a new Treasury Commission and who was now reluctantly one of the Council, and Marlborough, jealous of William's Dutchmen in the army and opposed to the domination of Carmarthen in the government, almost certainly did so. Domestic and foreign intrigue flourished throughout the year. But the French never felt able to invade without risking a major naval engagement; and despite some of the most virulent faction of the war, the ministry was composed of the same men at the end of the campaigning season as it had been at the beginning.

Throughout this season, naval affairs were managed as before by Nottingham. But since he accompanied William to The Hague for the three preceding months, from 18 January to 13 April, the King then appointed a second Secretary of State to fill the place which had been vacant since Shrewsbury's resignation. To everybody's surprise—and it was a testimony to the bankruptcy of English politics—he chose Henry Sydney, his amiable but thoroughly lazy favourite from before the Revolution, whose part in the negotiations of 1688 had so far been officially rewarded only with the post of gentleman of the bedchamber. To Sydney, therefore, fell the supervision of the preparations for the naval campaign; but Nottingham kept a close eye on them throughout the period,[2] and maintained from the Netherlands a constant and parallel correspondence with Russell.[3] The new Secretary was not in

---

[1] *Memoirs of Mary*, p. 36.

[2] Finch Transcr., Nottingham to Sydney, 30/1, 20/2, 13/3; Nottingham to Pembroke, 13/2. See also *Cal.S.P.Dom. 1690–1*, pp. 268, 288, where Nottingham's personal interest may be seen beyond his demands for information on the King's behalf.

[3] Finch Transcr., Nottingham to Russell, 26/1, 6/2, 26/2, 13/3; Russell to Nottingham, 20/2, 27/2, 3/3.

fact required to do very much, for unlike the preparations of the two previous years those of 1691 were well managed, and the fleet was out, in greater numbers than ever before, by the middle of May.[1] In April William paid a short visit to England; when he returned to Flanders on 2 May he took Sydney with him, leaving Nottingham at home. From that time until the fleet finally returned to port in September, the Secretary reigned unchallenged as the minister for naval affairs.

The Board of Admiralty itself was changed in January. Carbery had resigned immediately after Torrington's court martial,[2] and a month later Russell was removed, possibly because on 23 December he had finally been induced to accept the post of Admiral of the fleet for the coming year,[3] and had not yet the influence to retain his hold on both positions at once. Certainly he was annoyed at his removal, and in May was openly complaining that he had received little reward for all his services.[4] The two places were filled by Lord Falkland and Colonel Robert Austen, who may be described as respectively a Tory and a Whig. The appointment of Falkland,[5] grandson of Clarendon's Lucius, caused no surprise and had a certain poetic justice, for it had been rumoured for over a year as a reward for his supersession as Treasurer of the Navy by Russell.[6] Austen[7] was a veteran of the Country party, as member for Winchelsea since 1666. He was himself a Kentishman, living at Tenterden, and in April 1687 was made a Baron of the Cinque Ports. He had some links with trade, and usually formed one of the Board when petitions were heard from any of the merchants. The new Commission was dated 23 January. Almost immediately, the Board was again reduced by one, for on 20 February Sir Thomas Lee died.[8] There were several claimants for the vacancy,[9] of whom Sir Robert Rich

[1] See pp. 472–3 below.

[2] Luttrell, op. cit. II, p. 144; *H.M.C.* 12th Report, appendix, pt VII, p. 307.

[3] P.R.O.Adm. 3/4: 24/12.

[4] *Cal.S.P.Dom. 1690–1*, p. 367.

[5] G.E.C., *Complete Peerage* (1926); *The Devon Careys* (privately printed, New York, 1920).

[6] 'Spencer House Journals', pp. 238, 240.

[7] *Archaeologia Cantiana*, XVIII, p. 371; *Sussex Archaeological Collections*, XV, p. 209.

[8] Luttrell, op. cit. II, p. 179. He had actually attended business for the last time on 8 December (P.R.O.Adm. 3/4: 8/12).

[9] *Cal.S.P.Dom. 1690–1*, p. 290.

was rumoured to be the favourite;[1] but William was by now in Holland, and was content to leave the Commission as it was until his final return in the autumn. Despite a strong rumour in the spring that Anne's husband, George of Denmark, was to be appointed Lord High Admiral[2]—possibly connected in some way with the intrigues with St Germains, which received a fillip when the princess was persuaded to seek a reconciliation with her father at about this time—the members of the Admiralty were not disturbed; while Prince George himself managed only to be accepted as a volunteer aboard a man-of-war, and then only to find at the last moment that his baggage had been put ashore on the Queen's command, and himself forbidden to embark.[3]

The first problem for this Administration arose in May, when a French convoy with important reinforcements set sail from Brest for Galway. The expedition had been rumoured since February, and was confirmed in the middle of April.[4] On 24 April the fleet received its sailing orders, to proceed to the coast of France leaving a squadron to watch Dunkirk; but on 7 May these were altered, and those ships which could be sent at once were directed to sail to Galway to intercept the French squadron, the rest of the fleet following as fast as it could.[5] Again on the 13th and the 14th, the necessity of destroying the reinforcements was stressed, but on the 19th the news came that the French were already off the Irish coast, while the English, delayed by contrary winds, were still in the Downs.[6] No further information arrived in the ten days that followed, during which the fleet still hung around Dover and the Kentish coast, unable to get away; but in the last week of the month William himself intervened from Holland, and directed the ships to sail for Brest.[7] The French had once again reached their goal before

---

[1] Luttrell, op. cit. II, p. 187.

[2] *H.M.C.* 12th Report, appendix, pt. VII, p. 320.

[3] Luttrell, op. cit. p. 225; *Memoirs of Mary*, p. 38.

[4] Finch Transcr., Nottingham to Sydney, 27/2; intelligence from France, 11 (O.S.)–21 (N.S.)/3, 1/4. In future, where the documents give dates in both O.S. and N.S. in this way, only O.S. will be referred to in these notes.

[5] Ibid., Nottingham to Admiralty, 24/4; Queen's orders to Russell, 7/5.

[6] Ibid., Queen's additional orders to Russell, 13/5; Queen to Russell, 14/5; Portland to Nottingham, 19/5.

[7] Ibid., Nottingham to Sydney, 22/5; Russell to Nottingham, 28/5.

their opponents, and the first disappointment of the year had taken place before the campaign had even begun.[1]

It was not a propitious opening for Russell. On 5 May he had gone down to the Nore to join the *Britannia*,[2] which was to be his flagship whenever he was in command for the next four years. At first, his relations with Nottingham were most cordial. After taking leave of the Secretary before his journey, he wrote, in a farewell note, 'I am not sorry to have the occasion "of acknowledging the thousand obligations I have to you for all your favors...for I am realy, without expressing my self to be a Courtier, most sincerely, my lord, your lordship's faithfull humble servant"'.[3] His earliest remarks on the strategic situation were also restrained, although he had his doubts about the wisdom of sending a squadron to Galway, and disliked the thought of dividing the fleet perhaps for several weeks at this important time of year.[4] But by the 20th he was becoming exasperated with the long delay in the Downs, and at the first sign of misfortune his habitual, and not unfounded, suspicion of intrigue was aroused. When Nottingham, following the agreement which he seems to have made with Russell before the latter left town, acquainted him of the speculation which his delay was now causing,[5] he replied at once with the first of that long series of embittered letters, with their curious mixture of abuse and common sense, which were to become so familiar to successive Secretaries of State. As became almost a convention, it contained an offer of resignation.[6] The Secretary at once sent a soothing reply, but the Admiral was now in the full tide of self-pity and irritation. His answer of the 26th is worth quotation, for it is a typical example of his peculiar combination of personal rancour and sound strategic judgement. It also contains the only acknowledgement, so far as I know, which he ever made of his own shortcomings:

"I found uppon my being forced back to this place [i.e. the Downs], a letter from your Lordship of the 22nd, in which you are soe kind to give

[1] Finch Transcr., Nottingham to Portland, 5/6.
[2] P.R.O.Adm. 3/5: 6/5.
[3] Finch Transcr. 5/5. As I have used, in all my quotations from this source, the transcript made by the *H.M.C.* of the original manuscript, I have followed its indications of what is précis and what original, the latter being always given within double inverted commas.
[4] Ibid. 9/5.
[5] Ibid. 20/5.
[6] Ibid. 21/5.

me good advice, to expect and bare censur, with patience. Since I am not conscious to my self of any neglect of duty, that is all I feind I have to comfort my self with, but 'tis a mellincoly prospect to know a man's best endevors for the good of his country must be rewarded with reproches. I am not naturaly a sanguin man but have rather too much fleame, and yet that won't keepe me from lamenting the misfortune of having enemyes when to the best of my remembrance [I] never gaive the occasion to create any; but that which puts me past all patience, is the litell servis I can hope to render my King and country this summer with soe powerfull a fleate, for the best judgment I can make of the paper you sent me,[1] I conclude the French will not come to sea this summer, and thou I am very farr of loveing fighting, twas for that purpose only I undertook this Campaigne....I am affraide all this is an amusement to keep ous upp to the topp of expence, and at last do nothing but force ous to spend our mony."[2]

Characteristically, on being asked by Nottingham in future to send any remarks that were meant for his private ear under separate cover, he replied that he was quite agreeable for the whole of the letter to be shown to the Queen and the Council.[3] Within four weeks of the Admiral's joining the fleet, the Secretary had been given a good idea of the sort of man with whom he would now have to do business.

But apart from his personal rancour, the Admiral had good grounds for his dissatisfaction. As he explained again early in June, he did not know what to do with the fleet, if the French were determined to avoid him. The only alternative to a battle, so far as he could see, was to '"burne some foolish towne on the coast"'.[4] Nottingham agreed that '"barely to burn a France [i.e. French] Tingmouth is too mean a project for such a fleet"',[5] but admitted that he could offer no positive advice. He was insistent, however, that it must sail to the westward, if only to prevent the enemy from attacking the Smyrna convoy that was on its way home at that moment;[6] and both Council and Admiral agreed that, even if nothing else happened, it could assist the campaign in Ireland from time to time.[7]

---

[1] Ibid., Nottingham's letter of 22 May. [2] Ibid. 26/5.
[3] Ibid., Nottingham to Russell, 29/5; Russell to Nottingham, 2/6.
[4] Ibid. 2/6. [5] Ibid. 4/6.
[6] Ibid., Nottingham to Portland, 5/6.
[7] Ibid., Russell to Nottingham, 2/6; Nottingham to Russell, 4/6.

Accordingly, with no detailed instructions, but with the general intention of seeking out the French, of covering the entrance of the trade into the Soundings and of preventing further French reinforcements from reaching Ireland, Russell sailed from the Downs on 9 May.[1] After again being held at Torbay by bad weather, he reached the Soundings in the third week of the month.[2] On the 22nd he got '"the welcome news"' that the French were out with eighty sail, and for some days a battle seemed likely.[3] But nothing happened, and for the next two months the fleet cruised rather aimlessly between Ushant and Cape Clear, now led one way by a rumour that the enemy had been seen, now another by the approach of some merchant vessels or by the scare that the French were slipping arms and men through to Ireland.[4] With the capture of Athlone by the English on 30 June, Ireland became less important, for only Limerick remained to be captured;[5] and Russell was able accordingly to devote his main effort to protecting the trade. The Smyrna convoy got in safely, but another from the Bahamas was taken, and a considerable number of individual merchant ships was captured before reaching the Soundings.[6] It was with increasing bitterness that the Admiral viewed the results of his cruise, as he heard fresh stories of the dissatisfaction that now existed in London over the conduct of the fleet, and considered mournfully that he had foretold the results which were now being attributed to his incapacity, or even to his treachery.[7]

---

[1] By a good piece of seamanship. There was no appreciable breeze, so he weighed anchor on the floodtide and drifted in soundings until the ebb, when he again anchored. He continued to work down the first few miles of coast in this way until a favourable wind arose. With a large fleet, this cannot have been easy; and it had not, in any case, been often, if at all, tried before (Finch Transcr., Russell to Nottingham, 9/6).

[2] Ibid., Russell to Nottingham, 21/6, 22/6, 28/6.

[3] Ibid. 22/6.

[4] The course of events can be followed adequately on the English side in Finch Transcr. and more briefly in Burchett, pp. 90–109, and on the French in Eugène Sue, *Histoire de la marine française au dix-septième siècle, 1653–1712*, IV (5 vols., 1835–7).

[5] The Lords Justices of Ireland were anxious for a squadron from the fleet to help the army in the assault, but Russell successfully withstood this incentive to weaken the main concentration (Finch Transcr. Lords Justices to Nottingham, 3/7; Russell to Nottingham, 31/7).

[6] Ibid., Russell to Nottingham, 22/6, 31/7.

[7] Ibid., Russell to Nottingham, 31/7, 15/8. The question of his treachery is discussed below, on pp. 382–90.

The campaign came to an end in the familiar way. On 5 August Russell decided to put back to Torbay to water and revictual. Five days later he informed Nottingham that the fleet was 'very sickly', about 2000 men being down with scurvy. His own ship's company fortunately had only lost two men, '"but I observe (generally speaking) God Almighty comfort the afflicted in some kinde or other"'.[1] This news served to initiate the usual discussions which took place at this time of year, about the latest date at which the fleet could stay at sea. On the 14th, the Admiralty was asked for its opinion,[2] and on the 19th a council of war of English and Dutch flag officers was held in Torbay. This made its usual report that the fleet could not with any safety stay at sea in a body after the end of August, and must on no account be out after 10 September.[3] With only a short time left, therefore, the Council considered whether even now a battle might not be forced, and on the 21st, on receipt of the news that the French had put into Camaret Bay, it recommended that the fleet should attack them there while at anchor.[4] Russell agreed that a battle was desirable, but doubted whether an attempt of this sort was practicable so late in the year. The matter was clinched on the 25th, when a council of war decided that, in view of the lateness of the season and of the shortage of provisions, no attempt should be made upon the enemy, and that for the short time remaining the fleet should cruise to the south-west of Scilly.[5] When it sailed again, it accordingly confined itself to trailing its coat off Ushant. Russell continued to point out the uselessness and indeed the danger of these proceedings, and on 2 September he urged once more that the large concentration should be sent home, and a strong squadron for the protection of trade alone left to cruise in the Soundings. At present, he argued, this modest objective, which alone was practicable, was being obstructed by the continuation of the more ambitious plan, for there were not enough provisions to victual both a large fleet for another two weeks and a strong squadron thereafter. '"Upon the

---

1 Ibid. 10/8. See also ibid., Russell to Nottingham, 11/8.

2 Ibid. 14/8; P.R.O.Adm. 3/7: 15/8.

3 Finch Transcr., resolutions of the council of war, enclosed in Russell to Nottingham, 19/8. 4 Ibid., Nottingham to Russell, 21/8.

5 Ibid., Russell to Nottingham, 24/8; 25/8, enclosing resolutions of the council of war.

whole matter"', he concluded, '"this is my opinion: that if there bee a prospect of doing service, your fleet ought to bee ventured. 'Tis for that purpose they were built, and not to bee looked on or talkt of; but unless there bee such hopes, the lesse they are hazarded, in order to make a shew or a bravo, the better. I won't pretend"', he continued in his usual strain, '"to be much of a seaman, since I have been at the trade only from the fourteenth year of my age, but this I dare allmost affirme, that what I have writ...relating to the fleete, not a seaman in England contradict, at least if hee had beene one of the acters."'[1] The next day he followed it up with a note to the same effect: '"Pray God send the nation has not cause to lament that unhappy day we sayled from Toor Bay."'[2] Nine days later, his fears proved to have been justified. Running in a westerly gale towards Plymouth Sound, one second and one third rate were wrecked in the approaches, the former with the loss of her captain and most of her crew, while several others were severely damaged in their hulls or their rigging.[3] It was a depressing end to an unsatisfactory campaign.

Unsatisfactory though it was, a negative campaign of this sort had its own importance in the conditions which it inherited. It provided a much-needed breathing space after the excitement of 1690; for however disappointing the fleet's cruise had been, nevertheless it had prevented any reinforcements from reaching Ireland after May and had indirectly contributed to the fall of Limerick on 13 October, thus freeing William from the necessity of keeping a large proportion of his troops locked up in this defensive warfare, and giving him the opportunity to embark upon new plans. But strategic possibilities were of little value without the political incentive to undertake them, and this in turn depended on the continuation of a government which had already been weakened by the failure of the earlier campaign. Another reverse—perhaps not even a defeat—might well have seen the breakdown of William's settlement at any time during the summer. The different political groups seemed to have reached the limits of concilia-

---

1 Finch Transcr., 2/9.

2 Ibid. 3/9.

3 Russell's first account gave the *Harwich*, *Oak* (i.e. *Royal Oak*), *Northumberland* and *Coronation* lost (ibid. 14/9). But the *Oak* and *Northumberland* were later salvaged (Burchett, pp. 102–3).

tion, and their antagonisms were by now open and uncontrolled. One serious reverse was indeed suffered, when the King was defeated at Mons; but this did not seem to threaten the safety of the country itself, and affected neither its western bastion, the army in Ireland, nor its immediate shield, the fleet. As it was, the preservation of both throughout the year ensured that the government at the end of it could plan for the ensuing campaign, and that it could still control sufficient support in Parliament to get the money with which to do so.

Early in 1692, therefore, William was able to propose his cherished plan of an invasion of France. Exactly when he communicated this to the inner Council it is hard to say, but by 11 March both the latter and the Treasury had been informed.[1] The ministers' first reaction was to oppose the plan. They argued that there would not be enough troops in England to carry out a descent without ten battalions being sent from Flanders, and it seemed doubtful whether these could or should be spared. Those who supported the scheme did so principally because William had told Parliament in the previous October that he intended to 'annoy the common enemy, where it may be most sensible to them',[2] and had then allowed his Privy Councillors in each House to let it be known that this meant an invasion. The army estimates, accordingly, had been examined by the Commons on this assumption; the supplies had been voted for this specific purpose; and it therefore seemed politic to proceed with the plan. In the event, the Council agreed after some discussion to prepare the victuals which would be required, but nothing was said about the transports, and Nottingham himself felt that little would be done unless the King made it clear that he wished the preparations to be vigorously pursued. Mary, too, warned William that the ministers would not be content to know only the outline of his plan, but would want to be informed of its details.[3] William thereupon hastened to provide the ten battalions from Flanders,[4] and by the 22nd the Council was making detailed arrangements for the transports

[1] Finch Transcr., Nottingham to William, 11/3. The inner Council had by then already discussed it on several occasions, but from the tenor of the letter the Treasury had only just been told.

[2] *H.C.J.* x, p. 538.

[3] Finch Transcr., 18/3.

[4] Blathwayt to Nottingham; B.M.Addnl. 37991, f. 9*v*.

and for the rendezvous for the troops.[1] The time for the invasion was fixed for the end of May or the beginning of June, and the preparations went ahead from the last week of March.[2]

But similar preparations were being made on the other side of the Channel. If the survival of the political balance allowed the plans for invasion to go ahead in England, its precariousness encouraged identical plans in France. The very absence of a battle in 1691 which had possibly saved a crisis had given rise to widespread dissatisfaction by the end of the year. William's government stood, but it was profoundly unpopular. The Jacobite cause seemed at last to be really gaining ground, and in January 1692 James composed a memorandum for Louis on the general position.[3] The time, he emphasized, had come to invade. Morally and materially, the English Administration was bankrupt: Parliament was dissatisfied and demoralized, and almost all the prominent members of the government were by now committed to his cause; there was every reason to rely on the sympathy of the country gentry once the army had landed, and in any case the militia was not a formidable obstacle; and the real obstacle and first line of defence, the English fleet itself, was unlikely to prove a danger. In the first place, he was reliably informed that it could not put to sea before June; and in the second, that when it did so neither officers nor men would fight wholeheartedly for William. This memorandum, unlike its predecessors, had its effect, for the French court, while unlikely to act solely on Jacobite reports of disaffection, was itself receiving much the same intelligence of widespread dissatisfaction. The time seemed indeed to have come, and in the spring the preparations were put in hand for a large-scale descent upon England.[4]

Before proceeding to describe the effect of these similar preparations on each other, we must examine the validity of James's assurances that English ministers and the English fleet were prepared to assist his cause, either actively or by their neutrality. Definite proof on questions like

---

[1] Finch Transcr., Nottingham to Blathwayt, 22/3.

[2] Ibid., Nottingham to Blathwayt, 29/3.

[3] It is reproduced in James Macpherson, *Original Papers*, I (1775), pp. 408–11. It was the last of several similar memoranda during the winter (see ibid. pp. 394–408).

[4] Roncière, op. cit. VI, pp. 96–9.

this is usually impossible, for the evidence is by nature scarce, and partial evidence in such matters is often more misleading than no evidence at all. In this case, it is doubtful whether a satisfactory answer can ever be given. Without the discovery of important new material—and judging by what has already been found there would seem to be little chance of that—the problem must remain as it does at present, a matter of inference so far as many of the facts are concerned, and at best of probability when it comes to pronouncing upon them. It may be said, however, with some confidence that James exaggerated the value both of his agents' reports and of the professions of regard which he constantly received from England. Exiled monarchs are peculiarly prone to live upon hope; not only are the inevitable intrigues of which they hear the only signs by which they can measure their chances of returning to their former country, but in many cases they also provide them with their only reason for claiming the continued hospitality of others. James, moreover, was more prone to optimism than most; even in power, it had been his besetting weakness. With every incentive to hope for such signs, the professions of loyalty from the great figures of William's government were too often taken at their face value by the exiled court.

Nevertheless, while it would be a mistake to accept them as James was inclined to do, as all equally encouraging, it would possibly be just as great a mistake to deny them equally any value at all. Their value may well have varied according to the position of the author. Some letters were no doubt sent merely as a form of insurance against a dark future, which no sensible man would neglect to take. It is even probable that some were sent with the permission of William himself.[1] But others—and it was only to be expected—were possibly more dangerous. The motives which lead men to collaborate with an enemy are seldom easy to disentangle; to ourselves, who have seen the varied forms which

[1] Cf. Earl of Ailesbury, *Memoirs*, II (1891), p. 31: 'It is very certain that the King gave leave to the Earl of Marlborough, my lord Godolphin, the Duke of Shrewsbury and Admiral Russell to correspond with my lord Middleton at St Germains. They infused into the King the great advantage that might arise to him by it, and on my conscience I believe it.' That, however, is not to say that they did not take advantage of William's permission—by which he stood to lose nothing, and possibly to gain something—for their own ends.

such collaboration can take, and have experienced the difficulties of distinguishing truth from half-truths, the conduct of the leading statesmen at that time seems almost familiar. Nor must it be forgotten that collaboration itself, apart from the motives which lead to it, is not a simple process. It may start as one thing, and end as another. Perhaps all that can be said about William's ministers in general is that, after making full allowance for personal differences of temperament, their attitudes to the sort of connexion which they fostered with the old King were likely to have been influenced not so much by their attitude towards himself as by their attitude at that time towards his successor. If William's most genuine supporters were insuring themselves against his defeat, it is only natural to suppose that others were not unwilling to assist in it. It is quite likely that Godolphin and Shrewsbury were not actively plotting with James; but it is equally likely that those with a stronger motive to do so were doing precisely that. Our concern, however, is with Russell and the fleet. If he was committed to James's cause, or if it was disaffected, his behaviour in 1692 must be explained on those grounds alone, for once treachery can be proved in one instance it cannot be excluded in any instance; and in that case, the arguments which arose between the fleet and the ministers throughout the summer become largely unreal. The question may be approached from two points of view: first, we may take such direct evidence as exists, in the letters which Russell sent to St Germains, and try to infer from them what in fact were his intentions; and secondly, we may apply to them the indirect test of his actions and the correspondence which he held upon his actions, during this period. It cannot be pretended that any conclusive proof of his innocence or guilt is likely to result; but this is all that we can do with the evidence at our disposal.

The direct evidence that Russell corresponded with St Germains is contained in three sources: first, the 'Nairne Papers' in the Bodleian Library, transcribed from Jacobite papers in the Scots College in Paris during the eighteenth century by Thomas Carte;[1] secondly, transcripts taken partly from those papers in the Bodleian Library and partly, if

[1] See p. 385 below, and also *Report to the...Master of the Rolls upon the Carte and Carew Papers in the Bodleian and Lambeth Libraries* (1864), by T. D. Hardy and J. S. Brewer; and *The 32nd Annual Report of the Deputy Keeper of the Public Records*, I (1871), pp. 25–6.

we are to believe the editor, from the original papers in Paris, and published by James Macpherson in 1775 as *Original Papers containing the Secret History of Great Britain*; thirdly, a life of James II, reputed to be an autobiography, edited by the Reverend J. S. Clarke as *The Life of James II...collected out of memoirs writ by his own hand*, and published in 1816. It is not necessary to examine the validity of these three sources, for that has already been done convincingly by Mr Winston Churchill.[1] It may be taken for granted that they are in each case largely a repetition of the same material, and that for the most part they are forgeries—Macpherson's *Papers* being to some extent forged by himself, as might be expected from the creator of *Ossian*, while Clarke's *Life*, although honestly reproduced as genuine, was in fact entirely the product, for this period, of a Jacobite called Dicconson in about 1714. Carte's transcripts, also made in all honesty, suffer from the same defect. It may also be assumed for our purposes that all subsequent authorities, including the two greatest authorities, Macaulay and Mr Churchill, have been concerned principally with these Jacobite sources of evidence.

It may seem strange to call as witnesses documents that are known to be largely forged; but the forgers in this case had every motive to discredit the great figures of William's reign, and we may therefore take them as the most hostile and prejudiced evidence that can be produced against Russell. On examination, however, they are found to contain little that damages his reputation, and indeed they make a certain distinction between him and the other prominent men whom they mention—a greater distinction, in fact, than has subsequently been implied either by those who have reached an adverse verdict upon his conduct, or by those who have been favourable to him.[2] In neither

[1] Op. cit. I, ch. XXI.

[2] It is necessary to remark here that in the two greatest authorities on this subject—Macaulay and Mr Churchill—who came to different conclusions on Russell's honesty, this distinction between himself and the other figures cited is blurred. A curious muddle, indeed, exists in both upon his account, possibly because neither was really interested in him as both were in Marlborough, and tended to include the lesser figures under one head as being in the same case as the latter. Macaulay (*History*, IV, p. 2222) says that 'Lloyd (one of the Jacobite agents) conveyed to James assurances that Russell would...try to effect by means of the fleet what Monk had effected in the preceding generation by means of the army'; and in support he cites a letter of Russell's to William of 10 May 1691, as given in 'Dalrymple's Appendix, Part II, Book vii', and

Clarke nor Macpherson is there any report about Russell during 1691,[1] and his name first appears in the former source early in 1692. At that time, according to the report, very little could be got out of him. He

> express'd an earnest desire to serve the King [i.e. James], sayd the people were inclined to be of his side again if his Majesty took a right way to make them so...[but] If he met the French Fleet he would fight, even tho the King himself were on board, but that method he proposed to serve the King was by going out of the way with the English Fleet, to give the King an opertunity of Landing, or els by makeing choice of ships for a winter Squadron, whose Officers he could influence and by that means do as he pleased.[2]

The account from this source is not likely to err on the side of pessimism; when referring to the other supposed adherents of James's cause, it most certainly does not do so. Its own conclusion on this behaviour of Russell's may therefore be quoted: 'This resolution of fighting even against the King himself, was an od method of restoring him, and tho he might pretend an impossibility of influenceing the whole Navy to

---

also the '*Memoirs of Sir John Leake*'. The former is an odd authority to give, as it has nothing to do with Lloyd (Dalrymple, op. cit. II, appendix to pt II, pp. 227–9), nor is there any letter of Lloyd's in book vii of that appendix. The latter is presumably Stephen Martin-Leake's *Life of Sir John Leake*. Macaulay does not give the edition which he used of the 'Memoirs', but in Sir Geoffrey Callender's edition of the 'Life' (2 vols., *N.R.S.* 1920) no mention appears of any conversation or transaction between Russell and a Jacobite agent, let alone Lloyd. The work, however, contains some adverse comments on Russell's character, which allude to his ambition, his avarice and his laziness (loc. cit. pp. 37, 45), and it may be to these that Macaulay was referring. Mr Churchill (op. cit. I, pp. 368–9) in his argument against Macaulay's remarks about Marlborough, and with naturally only a side glance at Russell, repeats his opponent's error, and gives the impression that Russell, as well as the other three figures mentioned—Godolphin, Halifax and Marlborough himself—was approached by the Jacobites at the beginning of 1691. Furthermore, by taking in this context a different passage of Macaulay's in which the latter states that he has relied upon Clarke's *Life of James II*, II, pp. 444–50, he makes it seem that Macaulay's authority on this occasion was Clarke. As has been seen, it was not. Nor was it likely to be; for, in fact, Clarke makes no mention of Russell at this time.

[1] But according to Clarke, Russell in the spring of 1692 'still' pretended to be in James's interest. By inference, therefore, he had been approached before (Clarke, op. cit. II, p. 489).

[2] Ibid. pp. 489–90.

do otherwise, yet this seem'd rather a contrivance, to rais his fortune which way soever the ballance inclined.'[1] As a result of this attitude, the author continues, 'the King...endeavour'd to have matters so order'd as not to depend upon so dubious a foundation, especially the faint assurances of...himself'; and a later hand, imbued with the Jacobite tradition, inserted in the vacant space the words 'Admiral Russel'.[2]

The only other occasion on which Russell is mentioned in 1692 occurs in Macpherson, in what purports to be a projected letter from Floyd (one of the Jacobite agents) to the Admiral.[3] After referring to a former letter from himself on 1 August, and to a reply from Russell on the 9th, Floyd is reported to have written: 'We are still of the same mynd hear, as to the purchas of the bayle No. 668 [Russell, by code]; and, therefore, we doubt not but, as soon as it can be come at, you will let us kno the terms we can hav it upon.' He goes on in a strain which leads one to think that he was not in fact writing *to* Russell, but *about* him: 'and, because it is so tender ware, you will take all imagineable care it be gently and carefully handled, that, if after all it should not answer expectations, you should not be to blame, who are the factors.' If this letter is genuine, it confirms the report sent earlier in the year upon Russell's attitude; if not, it shows the way in which subsequent Jacobites believed him to have acted. In either case, it suggests strongly that only a few weeks after he was supposed to have been treacherously engaged in obstructing an invasion upon the enemy's coast, he was in fact still avoiding any direct participation in the Jacobite conspiracy. On the only evidence which is avowedly concerned to prove that he was implicated in James's cause in 1692, he appears not to have promised anything to James at that time.

This evidence, therefore, does not suggest that Russell was at all deeply involved in a Jacobite conspiracy. It does not, on the other hand, mean to say that he was not. There is little actual proof either

---

[1] Ibid. p. 490.

[2] Ibid. p. 491, and note. I have ventured to assume that the later hand was imbued with the Jacobite tradition, on Mr Churchill's evidence that the *Life of James II* remained in such hands, or in those of later sympathizers with the cause, until its publication.

[3] *Original Papers*, I, p. 420. Floyd is presumably the Lloyd mentioned in p. 385, n. 2 above, and in p. 388, n. 1 below.

way in the Jacobite reports, and apart from them there is little trustworthy evidence of any kind.[1] It is, however, worth noting that Mary herself continued to rely upon the Admiral throughout this period. In 1690, as has been seen, he was recommended to her by William 'for sincerity',[2] and in the spring of 1692, according to Nottingham, she still depended 'entirely' upon him.[3] Nor was this a meaningless compliment, as was shown when his intercession alone kept Marlborough's brother, the naval captain Churchill, out of prison on suspicion of treachery during the nervous months before Barfleur.[4] Even in his subsequent quarrel that year with her ministers and indeed with her own commands, she never attributed his attitude to treachery, but only wondered and lamented at his 'strange letters'.[5]

It is in these 'strange letters', and in Russell's actions, that the most valuable evidence of his attitude is to be found. For in the particular circumstances of 1692 this indirect testimony, which does not specifically mention the problem of treachery, is yet of more value than the direct evidence which does so, even apart from the latter's prejudice. As Macaulay noted, the motive for Russell's treachery could lie only in his dissatisfaction with the régime which he was serving;[6] there could be no other reason why he, with a record of opposition to James, should join the Jacobite cause. The clue to his intentions, therefore, lies in the extent of this dissatisfaction; and to know its extent, we must know its cause. His own correspondence and actions alone can furnish this. The one, however, should not be taken without the other. The actions without the letters can easily be, and were, taken as evidence of deliberate and treasonable obstruction to the plans which he was nominally carrying out. The failure to find the enemy in 1691, and the failure to follow up the victory of 1692, could both be read in this way as well as in any other. The letters without the actions, too, show a man driven by opposition and disappointment to the pitch of deliberately ruining the designs of his colleagues. But each source modifies the impression left

---

[1] Nottingham suggested that Russell had something to do with the Jacobite agents, but could say nothing definite. He mentioned Lloyd, Fenwick and a certain Vassor as the Admiral's contacts. The passage was written after Nottingham had quarrelled bitterly with Russell (*Conduct*, p. 101).

[2] See p. 348 above. [3] Finch Transcr., Nottingham to Russell, 11/5.

[4] Ibid. [5] *Memoirs of Mary*, pp. 52–3. [6] *History*, IV, p. 2020.

by the other. In the letters, the dominant note is one of failure: it is this which gives rise to their bitterness and which turns them constantly to the theme of personal misfortune and unjustified opposition. But as one reads the correspondence, the failures appear emphatically as failures, not as successful and deliberate evasions of duty. At the same time, the attitude of self-pity and recrimination to which they gave rise never quite led to the consequences which the Admiral foretold; for after fighting tooth and nail against a project to which he was (often rightly) opposed, Russell ended in every case by obeying his orders. In 1691, despite his initial reluctance to detach ships to the Irish coast, and his strong objections later to sending the fleet to sea for a second cruise at the end of August, he confined himself to lamentation and prophecy while he set to work to carry out his instructions; and in 1692, when he attacked the plan for an invasion of France with such bitterness in the late summer that he was suspected on all sides of treachery, it was overlooked that he himself had been the first to propose it, and that he differed from the government solely on the grounds of practical experience gained in trying to carry it out. It must not be forgotten, also, that Russell behaved in the same way when he was successful as when he was not: he grumbled after a victory as he grumbled after a failure. His quarrels in 1694–5, when he was generally acknowledged to be doing well, were even more furious than in 1691–2, when he was not. His attitude, in fact, was the result of temperament as much as of design. Ambitious and vindictive though he could undoubtedly be, the occasions on which this ambition and vindictiveness were brought into play reflected temper as well as calculation. He did not behave like a traitor, if only because traitors are not always threatening to resign. His personal denunciations were too open and his strategic advice too sound for such a combination to be anything but what it seemed. It is unsatisfactory to generalize without specific examples, and also to cite as evidence events which must themselves be judged on evidence; but it can only be said that, granted the motive for Russell's disaffection to be resentment at his treatment, a review of his career and the impression left by reading such of his correspondence as is known to have survived, both suggest that this resentment was not such as to result in a sustained and coherent series of treacherous activities, but was rather the product of a self-interest, a ready suspicion and a ready temper which made the Admiral a good hater of his friends as well as of his foes.

With Russell's treachery there must be considered the problem of disaffection in the fleet. The two questions are closely connected, for the Admiral had considerable influence among both officers and men. This disaffection was one of the factors on which James particularly relied in his memorandum of February, and it would seem that there must have been some foundation for it. Certainly, rumours of it were prevalent in 1691. But many of the stories may well have been the result as much of Jacobite failure as of Jacobite success. For instance, the confessions of two Jacobites taken in the spring of that year implicated Dartmouth in charges which made it appear that the former Admiral had a well-organized and active party in the fleet;[1] but it soon became clear that he had declined to enter into any detailed conspiracy and that, although his connexions in the fleet were doubtless strong, he had not made use of them at all.[2] His arrest, however, was calculated to produce a crop of rumours, and it is now impossible to distinguish whether there was any truth in them. Treachery, moreover, was a convenient political label to pin upon a rival; and there was plenty of political animosity and personal rivalry in the navy. Two of the most notorious favourites of James, for instance, Delavall and Killigrew, were engaged in an intrigue in 1692 to be appointed respectively Commissioner at Portsmouth and a Rear Admiral in the fleet, and neither they nor their opponents on this particular issue scrupled to accuse each other, on the one side of Jacobitism and on the other of republicanism.[3] It was the faction among the officers that led contemporaries, as it has led later ages, to hear of their disaffection rather than of any among the men, and this in turn led to further accusations, as the moral was indefatigably pointed by the champions of the tarpaulin against the gentleman officer.[4]

---

[1] See Matthew Crone's confession in Finch Transcr. 1/5, and Lord Preston's statement, ibid. 13/6. The latter gives a fuller account of the whole affair than any that has yet appeared in print.

[2] *H.M.C.* 11, v, pp. 285–92.

[3] Finch Transcr., Delavall to Nottingham, 14/5, 24/5, 30/5, 14/6; Killigrew to Nottingham, 28/5; Nottingham to Delavall, 11/5.

[4] 'The State of Parties...' (1692), in *A Collection of State Tracts, Publish'd during the Reign of King William III*, vol. II (1706), pp. 215–16; 'A Descent from France...' (1692), in *Harleian Miscellany*, I (1808), pp. 597–8.

No doubt, however, the men were less interested in the question; in the spring of 1692, at any rate, it was the officers who attracted the attention of the government. By the second week in May, both William in Flanders and Mary at home were seriously concerned over the strong rumours that 'severall in the Fleet' were likely to desert. But Mary came to the conclusion that these were the work of the Jacobites, and despite the fact that the highest officers in the fleet were being mentioned in this way, she declined to take any steps against them. The government, indeed, seems to have handled the matter sensibly. There was little point in dismissing commanders and flag officers without definite proof, and thus fanning a suspicion which nothing could avert. Moreover, as the Secretary remarked for William's ear, '"Tho' I will answer for no man in this age, yet I may boldly say others who are not named are much more to be suspected"'; and he returned to the question of Captain Churchill.[1] At the same time, Nottingham wrote to Russell on the subject. There was proof, he said, that at least some of the rumours came from distinctly suspect sources, and he gave the Admiral Mary's personal assurance that she did not believe them, and her command that he should communicate this to all the officers in the fleet.[2] The officers, in reply, at once signed a declaration of their loyalty;[3] and in the event, whatever may have been the intentions of any Jacobite group within their ranks, no open sign of disaffection was reported during the battle which followed.[4] As the summer progressed Jacobite hopes began to sink. In September, Floyd wrote from St Germains: 'I am sorry that you should have so smal hopes of the boxes No. 215 [the fleet, in code] and No. 551 [Parliament]....We must endeavour to make the best we can of them; and, tho' they be much spoil'd, yet if great paynes and care be taken, and right ingredients applied, we hope they may yet turn to account.'[5] It was a poor end to a plan that had been intended to open the way to a kingdom.

It may be said, therefore, that there is not enough evidence of treachery on the part of the Admiral, or of disaffection on the part of

---

[1] Finch Transcr., Nottingham to Blathwayt, 10/5. [2] Ibid. 11/5.

[3] The text is given in Burchett, pp. 136–7.

[4] Finch Transcr., Nottingham to Russell, 6/6. [5] Macpherson, op. cit. I, p. 421.

the fleet, to treat the events or the arguments of 1692 as the results of either. Both must be taken on their own merits. In the spring the events began to move fast. The preparations on both sides were well under way, but those in France were more advanced than those in England. Curiously enough, they were also kept less secret. French intentions were normally difficult to discover, and one of the complaints voiced in Parliament and outside was that the enemy's security was so much better than that of the government. But the penalty of accepting James's offers of help was that Jacobites had to some extent to be given access to the plans. By the end of February there were strong rumours in England of an intended invasion, but for another month there was some doubt of their validity.[1] The troop movements towards the coast of Normandy were noted, but it was generally thought that these were defensive, to guard against an English descent;[2] and although it began to be suspected early in April that they were in fact offensive, until the 19th both William and the government in England thought that the design was against the Channel Islands.[3] A small squadron was accordingly ordered there on the 8th, and as the news of the gathering concentration in the bay of La Hougue grew more circumstantial, this was reinforced by the advance squadron of the main fleet which had originally been intended for the normal cruise in the Soundings, and a battalion of infantry was also ordered to embark to strengthen the defences of Guernsey.[4] But on the 19th some startling news came to hand. The day before, a small French vessel had run ashore on the Goodwin sands, and some letters had been found in her addressed to various Jacobites in England, from which it was clear that the objective

[1] Rumours had been circulating about an invasion since December (James, loc. cit., citing Bodl. Carte MSS., 16/12/91). In February they were stronger than usual (*Cal.S.P.Dom. 1691–2*, p. 197).

[2] *Cal.S.P.Dom. 1691–2*, pp. 207, 217.

[3] The first mention of the Channel Isles occurs on the 6th, on which day also the Admiralty was ordered to send scouts to watch the French at Havre de Grace (Finch Transcr., Nottingham to Lord Hatton, and Nottingham to Admiralty, 6/4). See also ibid., Nottingham to Blathwayt, 8/4 and 12/4, for the government's attitude; *Archives d'Orange-Nassau*, 3rd series, I, p. 276, for William's attitude on the 14th; and B.M.Addnl. 17677, MM, f. 168*v* for that of the Admiralty at the same time.

[4] Finch Transcr., Nottingham to Blathwayt, 8/4, 9/4, 16/4; heads of instructions for Carter, 13/4.

was not the Channel Islands but England herself.[1] William's intelligence in Flanders still suggested that the islands were the main target, and for the next three days letters crossed from Nottingham to the King, informing him of the change in plan, and from the King to London, stressing the need for speed in sending help to Guernsey and Jersey.[2] But on the 20th, while William was still urging Nottingham to take the threat to the islands more seriously, Mary countermanded the orders to the battalion of foot which was about to embark for Guernsey, and the next day the militia was called out along the coast.[3] On the 22nd, orders were prepared for Delavall to put to sea with a second squadron of the fleet composed, like Carter's squadron now cruising off Guernsey, of third and fourth rates, to cruise down the French coast from Calais to Le Havre and to report any movement of the enemy fleet.[4] The same day, the rest of the fleet under Russell[5] was ordered to sail for the Flats of the Foreland and to stay there until further orders.[6] The troop movements and the collection of stores for the descent upon France had by now been stopped, as all efforts were turned towards preparing against the threatened invasion.[7]

The first stage in the race had thus been won by the French. Their own preparations went ahead while the English movements were adapted to meet them. But from the beginning of May the balance began to shift. This was partly due to chance. The main French fleet in Brest consisted at the beginning of the year of only 44 ships, for a strong squadron of 35 sail had gone to the Mediterranean for the winter; and although this had sailed in March to join the fleet for the summer campaign, it was held off the west coast by head winds which prevented

---

[1] Ibid., Nottingham to Blathwayt, 19/4. The incriminating letters themselves can no longer be found. According to Ranke (op. cit. v, p. 47, n.) they were preserved in Sir Thomas Phillipps's library at Cheltenham. This has now been dispersed.

[2] Finch Transcr., Nottingham to Blathwayt, 19/4, 21/4, 22/4; B.M.Addnl. 37991, ff. 43, 52 (Blathwayt to Nottingham, 21/4, 26/4).

[3] Finch Transcr., Nottingham to Carter, 20/4.

[4] Ibid., Nottingham to Blathwayt, 22/4. See also ibid., Queen's orders to Delavall, 23/4.

[5] He had been sworn in as Admiral of the fleet on 11 January (P.R.O.Adm. 3/6: 11/1).

[6] P.R.O.Adm. 1/4080, f. 123.

[7] Finch Transcr., Nottingham to Blathwayt, 19/4.

the squadrons from joining. But on 2 May the ships at Brest put to sea on their own under the command of Tourville, with the intention of catching one of the detached English squadrons which by now were hovering off the Cherbourg peninsula, if not of getting well into the Channel to break up the concentration of the main English fleet before it could be completed. Given the westerly winds which might have been expected at this time of the year, they stood a good chance of success. But the wind held in the east, and while Tourville hung off the coast near Brest the English under Russell, who had put to sea from the Thames on the 3rd, were able to gather off the Isle of Wight. Real as this disadvantage was, however, it played only a limited part in swinging the balance towards the English; for the test of such fortune is how it is used by those whom it affects, and on this occasion the English used it better than their opponents. With the wind as it was, Tourville's obvious action was to draw his enemy towards the Toulon squadron in the west, and to face him only when numbers were equal. But on 16 March he had received explicit orders from Louis, whose concern lay in diverting the enemy fleet from his troop transports, and who was not prepared to risk the argument of a fleet in being on this occasion, to sail with or without reinforcements as soon as he was ready and to engage the English under any circumstances. On 2 May, on the day on which the Admiral sailed, his King signed fresh orders for him to wait until he had at least seventy ships of the line. But by then it was too late. The revised instructions, sent after the fleet by advice boat, failed to find it until the battle had been fought; and when he sighted the English on the 19th, Tourville was as handicapped in his choice of action as his opponent had been two years before.[1]

Russell, on the other hand, was singularly free. He had himself been allowed to draw up his instructions with the advice of some of his flag officers,[2] and the successive orders which he received during May left him with considerable freedom of action.[3] In contrast to the French,

---

[1] Roncière, op. cit. VI, pp. 99–104; P.R.O.Adm. 3/7: 3/5.

[2] B.M.Addnl. 37991, f. 18*v*.

[3] They are contained in Finch Transcr., Queen's orders to Russell, 3/5, 11/5, 17/5. See also ibid., Nottingham to Blathwayt, 10/5: 'The Queen has not thought fitt to give any particular orders to Mr. Russell on this occasion for his conduct, but left him to act with the fleet as shall be judged most expedient at a council of warr.'

moreover, the English government made every effort to concentrate the squadrons already at sea upon the rest of the fleet, and recommended the Admiral to avoid an action until they had joined. As soon as the news was received in London that the enemy was out,[1] Delavall and Carter were ordered to return to St Helens, and the Dutch, who had begun to arrive in the Downs towards the end of April, were similarly directed to this rendezvous.[2] In consequence, an allied fleet of 61 sail of the line was concentrated there on the 13th.[3] Four days later it received reliable news of the French fleet and at once set sail to intercept. On the morning of the 19th, after 24 hours at sea, the leading ships sighted the enemy off Barfleur.[4]

The numbers on each side were as follows:[5]

	Allies	French
English	63	44
Dutch	36	—
Fireships	38	13
Total Line	99	44
Guns	6756	3240

The allies, however, were unable to take advantage of their superiority in the first stages of the battle, for Tourville, committed as he was to

1 The first rumour of this seems to have come from Delavall on the 4th (Finch Transcr., Delavall to Nottingham, 4/5). By the 6th, the Queen was able to tell him that the French had left Brest on the 2nd, but it was mistakenly supposed that they were on their way into the Channel (ibid., Queen to Delavall, 6/5).

2 Ibid., Queen to Delavall, 6/5; Nottingham to Carter, 9/5; Queen to Dutch commanders, 28/4; Nottingham to Russell, 14/5.

3 Ibid., Nottingham to Blathwayt, 17/5.

4 The best account of this campaign, and of the battle that followed, is given by Sir J. K. Laughton (anonymously) in 'The Battle of La Hougue and Maritime War', in *Quarterly Review*, vol. CLXXVI, pp. 461–89. It should, however, be supplemented by Roncière, op. cit. VI, pp. 95–132; de Jonge, op. cit. III, pp. 287–321; and a valuable article, 'M. de Bonrepaus et le désastre de la Hougue', in *Annuaire Bulletin de la Société de l'Histoire de France* (1877). Various contemporary accounts of the battle exist. Russell's report was published a few weeks after the action, as *Admiral Russell's Letter to the Earl of Nottingham: Containing an exact and particular Relation of the late happy Victory and Success against the French Fleet* (1692). Other accounts are contained in *The Life of Sir John Leake*, I, pp. 46–54; 'Battle of La Hougue, A.D. 1692', ed. S. Andrews, in *The British Archivist*, I, pp. 9–12; and 'The Battle of La Hougue', ed. W. C. Boulter, in *E.H.R.* VII, pp. 111–13. Two unpublished descriptions are contained in Finch Transcr. under the date 27 May 1692.

5 Laird Clowes, op. cit. II, pp. 348–9; Roncière, op. cit. VI, pp. 108–11.

an engagement, resolved to make the best of it, and formed his line before Russell, who had approached in loose order, managed to re-dispose his rather scattered force. For some time, indeed, assisted by the westerly wind which had now at last sprung up, the effective French force was superior to that of the allies; but as Russell's own squadron came into action the balance tilted heavily in his favour. Towards the end of the day Tourville disengaged to the north. No ship on either side had been sunk, and it looked once more as though the usual indecisive action was drawing to its unsatisfactory close. But this was prevented by a remarkable combination of circumstances. After a calm and foggy night, in which both sides became scattered about the area, the wind again shifted the next morning to the east, and before the French could draw clear, Russell—whether on his own initiative or on that of his old tutor David Mitchell, at that time his first captain—gave the order for a general chase.[1] Some of the enemy got away to the north and reached Brest after a difficult passage, in the case of four of them around the north coast of Scotland; but the rest found themselves by the evening still pursued off Cape la Hague. In desperation, they decided to risk the dangerous passage through the race of Alderney into St Malo, and 22 succeeded in getting through.[2] The others were caught by the floodtide and, after an unsuccessful attempt to anchor, were swept back to the east to find refuge in the open bays of Cherbourg and La Hougue. On the morning of the 21st, three of their largest ships were found by Delavall off Cherbourg, where they were boarded and set on fire. The rest were penned in the bay of La Hougue by a squadron under Rooke, and of these twelve were similarly boarded and burnt on the 23rd under the eyes of the invading troops and of James himself on the cliffs above. At the close of the five days fifteen French ships had been destroyed, including the pride of their navy, the great *Soleil Royal*.[3] The English, on the other hand, had lost none.

---

[1] Laughton, who had a poor opinion of Russell's tactical ability, seems inclined to give either Mitchell or Benbow (then master of the fleet) the credit for this (*Quarterly Review*, vol. CLXXVI, p. 464).

[2] This was the incident commemorated by Robert Browning in 'Hervé Riel'.

[3] Two of 104 guns, one of 90, two of 80, four of 76, four of 60 and two of 56 (Burchett, p. 146).

The course of the campaign and battle of Barfleur[1] have been given in some detail, because they emphasized two important lessons, both of which had been taught before and both of which had their importance for administration and policy. First, the action itself suggested once again that the sea battle, even with the odds so heavily weighted on one side, was likely to be an inconclusive affair. For the destruction took place entirely after the battle had finished,[2] and thanks only to an unusual combination of circumstances. Moreover, the agent of destruction was not the gun but the boarding party and the fireship. Secondly, the campaign which preceded the battle proved once more how dangerous it was for a government to intervene directly in strategy beyond a certain point. The inflexibility of Tourville's first set of orders was alone responsible for the inferiority in numbers which the French enjoyed; for on the 19th, the first day of the engagement, the Toulon squadron reached Brest. To add to this initial gamble of sending a weaker fleet to sea, a positive order to fight its stronger opponent under any circumstances, so as to allow the invading transports time in which to slip past the enemy fleet, was to subordinate naval to military operations in a manner that could only endanger both. To the victor, Barfleur was a lesson not to expect too much from the instrument of victory; to the loser, it was a lesson to respect the limitations of that instrument, by allowing it to operate on its own terms and not subordinated to a hypothetical alternative which could in fact benefit only from its success.

Despite the inconsiderable losses which it inflicted upon the French—for after all, some seventy ships of the line still remained intact—the battle proved to be a turning point in the war at sea. It had indeed this quality of a great victory, that it gave dramatic form to a process the results of which were already becoming apparent. The French never

---

[1] I have called the whole action by this name for convenience. There were, in fact, the two distinct engagements, off Barfleur (or off Cape La Hague) and in the bay of La Hougue; and that is the system which obtains for battle honours to-day. The action is often, however, called La Hogue, and has recently been perpetuated as such in the naming of a new destroyer. There is in fact no such place.

[2] And the damage, as distinct from the destruction, was slight. Only one English ship, the *St Andrews*, needed more than a week's repair (P.R.O.Adm. 3/7: 7/6).

again sought a fleet action, and after one more campaign they abandoned the use of a fleet altogether. Command of the sea had passed in one blow to the allies, and in particular to the English. For here again, Barfleur reflected the new balance of power. It was peculiarly an English victory. The Dutch had played their part, but it was the English who burnt the ships at anchor, who supplied the most illustrious of the dead, and to whose Admiral the credit was given for the result.[1] It was English pride, moreover, that was particularly solaced by a victory which redeemed so dramatically the disgrace of Beachy Head. The burning of the French ships in full view of their own troops was a peculiarly satisfactory example of sea power in relation to land power, well calculated to strengthen the national belief in a navy and the opposition to a large army. Barfleur remained for at least sixty years the greatest triumph of the British fleet, surpassed at length only by the events of *annus mirabilis* in 1759. The song which was made to commemorate it was sung on the messdecks of the fleet well into the eighteenth century, and survived into the Napoleonic wars.[2] Even fifty-five years later, in 1747, Anson wrote of his own victory off Cape Finisterre that 'this is the best stroke that has been made upon the French since La Hogue'.[3] And although the fame of the battle has been dimmed for us by Nelson's achievements, in his own day it was still a vivid tradition; when his commander at Cape St Vincent, Sir John Jervis, was offered an earldom, his first choice of a title lay between Yarmouth, where he was born, and Orford, which had been conferred in 1697 upon Russell, the victor of Barfleur.[4]

Something of the importance of the victory was realized in England at the time. The immediate acclamation was, of course, tremendous. The freedom from fear of an invasion, and the decisive nature of the result, particularly coming on top of the forebodings of the spring,[5]

---

[1] This is well put by Macaulay, op. cit. v, p. 2192. The only allied flag officer and the only captain of an allied man-of-war to be killed were respectively Carter and Hastings.

[2] Firth, *Naval Songs and Ballads*, p. xlvii. The song itself is given in full, ibid. pp. 128–9.

[3] Quoted in *Quarterly Review*, vol. CLXXVI, p. 461.

[4] J. S. Tucker, *Memoirs of Admiral the Rt Hon. the Earl of St Vincent*, I (2 vols., 1844), p. 421.

[5] Mary, for instance, had expected little from Russell that year (*Memoirs of Mary*, p. 46).

made Russell a popular hero. By 26 May, when he officially reported his victory, both Nottingham and the Admiralty were already congratulating him upon it.[1] On the same day, a new third rate, which was about to be launched at Portsmouth and had already been called the *Sussex*, was renamed the *Russell*,[2] and verses, pamphlets and engravings in his honour at once began to appear in large numbers.[3] Medals were struck to commemorate the battle, and the officers and men who had taken part in it were rewarded, the former with medallions, the latter with a month's pay.[4] But the noblest monument to the occasion was the foundation of Greenwich Hospital in its final form, which sprang partly from the fate of the casualties suffered in the battle.[5] Russell's own adherents, of course, were particularly jubilant, and his relations, according to an unfriendly witness, tried without success to put up a statue to him in London.[6] He himself always regarded the action as the climax of his career at sea, and in later years gave to the home farm on his estate at Chippenham the name of 'La Hogue', and planted a grove of trees, some of which still survive, to represent his tactical formation on that day.[7]

Behind these demonstrations of immediate joy lay a more substantial appreciation of its implications. So far from being threatened by a French invasion, it was appreciated at once that there was now little to stop an English invasion of France.[8] On the day on which the news of the victory reached London, Mary ordered three of her Council—

---

[1] Finch Transcr., Russell to Nottingham, and Nottingham to Russell, 26/5; P.R.O.Adm. 3/7: 26/5.

[2] P.R.O.Adm. 3/7: 26/5.

[3] Finch Transcr., Nottingham to Russell, 1/6. Many of the engravings, dating from this year, may be seen at the British Museum. Among the verses and pamphlets, 'Admiral Russell scouring the seas', and 'The Royal Triumph' (Firth, *Naval Songs and Ballads*, pp. 117–20), and the *Relation of the Late Happy Victory and Success against the French Fleet* (1692) are conspicuous.

[4] P.R.O.Adm. 3/7: 1/6. As had been the case with the gratuity for Bantry Bay, many of the men had not received this bounty a year later (P.R.O.Adm. 3/9: 4/7).

[5] See pp. 443–4 below.

[6] *Camden Miscellany*, VIII, p. 185.

[7] I am indebted for this information to the late Mrs Gerard Tharp, owner of Chippenham Park. Whether the farm was called 'La Hogue' or 'La Hougue' originally, I do not know.

[8] Finch Transcr., Nottingham to Russell, 26/5.

Rochester, Portland and Sydney—and Galway, the commander of the troops in Ireland, to meet the fleet at Portsmouth on its return and to hold a council of war with Russell on how best to follow up its advantage.[1] This reached no definite conclusion, for it was not certain exactly where the French fleet now was; but in the early days of June, all the authorities were agreed upon the desirability of some sudden stroke to complete the victory. William was certain that the French would not put to sea again that year, but left it to the ministers to decide exactly how to take advantage of the position;[2] Mary and the Council were inclined to favour a direct attack upon the ships in St Malo;[3] while Russell himself favoured invasion, provided that the troops could be got ready in time.[4] By the middle of the month, the project had narrowed to an attack on St Malo; and as Russell remarked on the 13th, its success would be worth the possession of two provinces in France.[5]

---

[1] Finch Transcr., Nottingham to Russell, 26/5 (mentioning only Portland and Galway); Nottingham to Blathwayt, 27/5. [2] B.M.Addnl. 37991, f. 87.

[3] Finch Transcr., Queen to Russell, 3/6.

[4] *H.C.J.* x, p. 717 (Russell to Nottingham, 27/5).

[5] Ibid. (to Nottingham, 13/6). There are five distinct sources for the events and arguments of 1692 relating to the descent on France:

(1) *H.C.J.* x, pp. 714–23, which contains documents submitted to the House of Commons by the Admiralty, the Transport Commissioners, the Duke of Leinster (the commander of the troops) and Russell, for its debate upon the campaign in November. The papers of naval interest reproduced there are mainly extracts from the early orders of the Admiralty for transports, the resolutions of the more important councils of war, the Queen's orders to Russell, and Russell's correspondence with Nottingham.

(2) Ibid. pp. 749–59, which contains Nottingham's papers submitted to the House of Lords, and listed in *H.L.J.* xv, pp. 153–7.

(3) *H.M.C.* 14th Report, appendix, pt VI, pp. 198–245, which contains in full the papers submitted to the House of Lords for their debate upon the summer campaign. Some of these duplicate the material in (1) and (2), and the rest, consisting of the correspondence of Russell and his subordinates with the Admiralty, are contained in the Admiralty papers at the Public Record Office.

(4) *A Naval Miscellany*, II, pp. 168–205, which reproduces Nottingham's own précis of his correspondence with Russell. According to Mr James, there is another copy of this in the library at Lambeth Palace (Tenison MS. 684(5)).

(5) Finch Transcr. for 1692.

This last authority contains, in a fuller and more accurate form, all the material for its own level which is reproduced elsewhere. The orders from the Queen, and Nottingham's letters to the commanders at sea, particularly to Russell, and to Blath-

But the plan was soon seen to need troops as well as ships, for the entrance was too difficult for the fleet to force its way in without a diversion.[1] It was therefore decided to send 12,000 men on the expedition, and throughout June the preparations went forward for victualling and embarking them, while the fleet sailed to the vicinity of St Malo to have a look at the coast and to gain some idea of the navigational problems involved.[2] After a preliminary investigation, however, Russell began to doubt whether an attack on St Malo was practicable. On the 21st, he reported that the coast was a dangerous one for a big fleet, that the channel was intricate and narrow, and that he was not sure either that he could get in or that he could stop the French from getting out. The navigational hazards looked too great for him to force an entrance, while a southerly wind, which would enable the enemy to come out, would drive him into the Soundings unless he could anchor the fleet in the approaches to St Malo itself. On that point he awaited the pilots' report.[3] Nine days later, after some bad weather which confirmed his fears that the coast was a difficult one for big ships, he announced that he could see no possibility of carrying out the plan. The Dutch were strongly against it, and he himself disliked leaving his ships of the line with only six hours' clear sailing north or south before they were on a lee shore according to the direction of the wind. The

wayt, are given in full, as are many of Russell's letters in reply. There are only three letters from the latter in sources (1), (2) and (3)—those of 27 May and 13 June already referred to in this and the preceding note, and one of 22 July (on p. 720)—which are not contained in source (5); and indeed the only additional information of any importance for this level which source (5) does not contain, appears in Blathwayt's reverse correspondence in B.M.Addnl. 37991. The contents of source (4), which affect the same level of authority, are reproduced entirely in source (2)—itself contained in source (5)—despite the editor's assertion that it forms 'a correspondence which seems to be unknown except so far as it was abstracted by Burchett' (loc. cit. p. 142). For the discussions at Cabinet level, therefore, source (5) supersedes all others.

Sources (1) and (3), however, contain valuable information on the detailed preparations and orders at lower levels, which also exists in the Admiralty papers at the P.R.O. For decisions at departmental level, they may be taken as satisfactory authorities, which are not supplemented to any great extent by such MS. material as they do not include.

1 Finch Transcr., Nottingham to Portland, 22/6.

2 Ibid., Nottingham to Russell, 14/6.

3 Finch Transcr., Russell to Nottingham, 21/6.

pilots could not agree on the quality of the ground, but he himself doubted whether a fleet could anchor off the port. He announced his intention, accordingly, of returning to Torbay.[1]

The government was now confronted plainly with a difficult issue, in which the commander at sea differed, on professional grounds, both from his initial opinion and from its own requirements. The scene was set for the disputes which occupied the rest of the campaign, and to which no satisfactory solution was found. It is not necessary to describe in great detail the arguments used by both sides, for unlike the events of the previous year and of the spring, which provided the setting for the dispute, their interest for us is not intrinsic but indirect: not, as for the strategist, in their content, but rather in the stimulus which they gave to the participants and in the impact of their consequences upon administration. For if the problems which were posed were technical, they were not answered only on technical grounds.

The dispute itself was conducted by Nottingham and Russell. Neither William at the highest, nor the Admiralty at the intervening level entered into it. The King was in Flanders throughout, but that alone, as later events were to show, was not a sufficient reason for his abstention. He was of course kept fully informed of the situation, but once his permission had been obtained to continue the preparations for a descent, he seems to have been curiously apathetic about it. His chief, indeed almost his only, concern for sea affairs at this time lay in a quite different direction,[2] and his questions on the plans for the campaign in the Channel were perfunctory.[3] It was, indeed, only after Nottingham had remonstrated strongly that he was induced to cancel his initial orders for some reinforcements for Flanders to take priority over the descent, in the transports provided for it.[4] It was not until the first week in June that he bothered to ask the exact plan of attack, and where it was to be developed; and it was not until 18 August, almost three weeks after the idea of a descent had been finally

[1] Finch Transcr., Russell to Nottingham, 30/6. [2] See pp. 490–512 below.

[3] For instance, he interested himself only once, on 27 June, in the delays in the preparations for the invasion of France (B.M.Addnl. 37991, f. 103). And this was not because they were perfect.

[4] Ibid. ff. 95, 103; Finch Transcr., Nottingham to Blathwayt, 22/6.

abandoned, that this attracted his comment.[1] This is so unlike the concern which the King showed over anything in which he was interested, and which he was at that time showing in other directions, that it can only be assumed that his habitual indifference to sea affairs had by now been reinforced by the belief that he had found a capable minister for them in Nottingham. For two years the latter had been managing the navy conscientiously, if not with entire success; and so long as he remained in office with a sufficient modicum of support in Parliament, there was every opportunity for William to avoid the details of naval policy. Throughout the entire controversy, no letter seems to have survived from himself or from his secretary Blathwayt—whose correspondence remains largely intact—which gives any lead, or indeed any opinion, on the issues which were being so hotly debated in England.[2]

Nottingham's position in naval affairs had a complementary result at the lower level, where the Admiralty was virtually excluded not only from any participation in but also from any knowledge of naval policy. The Board above whose heads the storm raged had been changed slightly in the past year. On 16 November, 1691 the expected appointment had been made to replace Lee, when the vacant seat went to Sir Robert Rich. He was to remain a Commissioner until his death in 1699. A member of the famous family whose elder branch was headed by the Earl of Warwick, he lived near Dunwich in Suffolk, which he represented from 1689 to 1699 in Parliament.[3] A grandson, through his mother, of the great John Hampden, he was connected with the Whigs, was one of the Commissioners for the public accounts,[4] and was an active member of many of the Commons' committees on naval matters.[5] He had dealt, mainly in cattle, with the naval victuallers at

---

[1] B.M.Addnl. 37991, ff. 93, 146.

[2] My authorities for this statement are B.M.Addnl. 37991 and Finch Transcr., neither of which contains any reference to such an opinion. It is true that allusions in both sources make it clear that some letters from Blathwayt are not included in the former, and it is also fairly clear that many of William's personal letters to his ministers have since disappeared. But the correspondence in Finch Transcr. is so full that it seems unlikely that an important—indeed a decisive—event of this nature could have occurred without some reference to it being made.

[3] *D.N.B.*

[4] Luttrell, op. cit. II, p. 187; see p. 467 below.

[5] *H.C.J.* x, *passim.*

the beginning of the war,[1] and had canvassed for a post on that Commission in the victualling crisis at the end of 1689;[2] and to judge from later attacks, he did not relinquish his connexion with the trade after becoming a member of the Admiralty.[3] But whether or not he was corrupt, he was quite efficient and conscientious, and took an active part in the business of the Board. This Commission lasted until 10 March 1692, when Pembroke, who four days before had been appointed Lord Privy Seal, was succeeded at the head of the Board by Lord Cornwallis, a colourless personality with no strong politics, whose only claims to distinction were that as a young man he had been tried for manslaughter by his peers and that he had later married Monmouth's widow, the Duchess of Buccleuch, as his second wife.[4] This new Board lasted out the year.

It was, however, in no better position to intervene in the dispute than its predecessors had been to intervene in similar discussions earlier in the war. In one sense it had the advantage of them, for it was now summoned regularly to attend Mary in Cabinet.[5] From March to the end of July it attended the ministers almost every week at Whitehall, generally on Thursdays, and there seems to have been a regular system of consultation.[6] But this regularity of attendance does not point to any increase in the Board's importance, but implies on the contrary that it had become by now a subordinate body. It was not because the

---

[1] P.R.O.Adm. 29/48. [2] *Cal.Treas.Bks. 1689–92*, p. 65.

[3] *H.M.C. Portland*, III, p. 506, and VIII, p. 58; *The Present Condition of the English Navy set forth in a Dialogue betwixt Young Fudge of the Admiralty and Captain Steerwell, an Oliverian Commander* (1702), pp. 6–7, 13.

[4] G.E.C., *Complete Peerage*, III (1913), p. 454.

[5] The phrase in the Board Minutes is almost always 'the Cabinett'; occasionally 'the Cabinet Councill'. On 16 September, when neither King nor Queen was present, the same body was called 'the Committee'.

[6] This seems to have been the case not only from the entries in P.R.O.Adm. 3/6 and 3/7, which refer directly to these meetings and often reproduce the minutes of them, but from the fact that the Board seldom met on Thursday whether or not such minutes are included in its books. In the summer of 1692, for instance, there are references to Board meetings with the Cabinet at Whitehall on Thursday 4, 18 and 25 June, and on Thursday 9 July, while there was no Board meeting on Thursday 11 June and 2 July. The Board, however, also attended at Whitehall from time to time on other days—e.g. 6 and 15 June, and 7 July.

Commissioners were now admitted to decisions of policy that they went to Whitehall more often than in the past, but because any prospect of this kind was out of the question. Their ignorance of events was shown even more clearly during the summer than it had been shown before. On 8 June they wrote to Russell to inquire whether he planned to do anything against St Malo, as they heard only the gossip of the town, and a week later they complained that he told them nothing of his intentions or even of his movements, and that they knew only what they were told by the Cabinet.[1] On the 29th, they made a note 'to enquire of the Cabinett where the Ships ordd. to joyne the Fleet shall find the Fleete', and again on 4 July they had to ask Nottingham where it was, as they had expected to find it in Torbay and it did not seem to be there.[2] On the 18th, they requested him in future to give them an account 'from time to time' of its whereabouts, so that they knew where to send their letters to Russell;[3] and in fact throughout the campaign they used the Secretary's messengers and dispatch boats whenever they wished to make sure of their communications reaching the Admiral.[4]

The issue, therefore, lay between the Cabinet and Russell, and the conduct of it between himself and Nottingham. Their personal relations grew worse as the gap widened between the Admiral and the government. It was impossible to argue strategy with Russell without entering into personalities, and Nottingham, though long-suffering, had his own pride and stubbornness, particularly on naval matters. After the Admiral's announcement of his return to Torbay at the end of June, the tone of the correspondence grew increasingly acrimonious. The news came as a shock to ministers,[5] and Mary at once ordered Nottingham to inform Russell of her anxiety over his decision, and to ask him not to give up thoughts of attacking St Malo.[6] Russell at first admitted that a success there was most desirable, although he could no longer agree that the attempt was practical;[7] but on 10 July, after a further

---

[1] P.R.O.Adm. 3/7: 15/6. [2] Ibid. 29/6, 4/7. [3] Ibid. 18/7.

[4] They had received permission to do this regularly in the previous August (P.R.O.Adm. 3/6: 25/8).

[5] Finch Transcr., Nottingham to Blathwayt, 5/7; *Conduct*, p. 103.

[6] Finch Transcr., Nottingham to Russell, 4/7.

[7] Ibid., Russell to Nottingham, 8/7.

note from the Secretary begging him not to give up his original idea, he lost his temper and wrote the latter a bitter memorandum on the situation. In this, he shifted his ground from the technical difficulties of the task to the wider questions of the government's attitude towards the war and the failure of its preparations for the descent.[1] In the tone of its general remarks and in its personal attack upon Nottingham's attitude, the paper struck a new note in the argument, and began the deep estrangement between the two men which was to last for the rest of their lives. The Secretary sent a formal acknowledgement of the communication, and replied more fully to it a few days later in still friendly but noticeably less cordial terms. The Queen, after reading it, ordered Russell to call a council of war to decide what was to be done.[2] At the same time, she directed the 14,000 troops who were now ready at Portsmouth to stand by to embark aboard the transports in the harbour.[3]

The completion of the preparations for invasion now found the fleet, the army and the government equally at a loss what to do, and all in a thoroughly angry mood. With Russell refusing, in ever more vehement terms, to make any attempt upon St Malo, with the generals at Portsmouth insisting that St Malo was the best place to attack, and with the available time growing uncomfortably short in which to do anything, the Cabinet virtually washed its hands of the whole business. Russell was ordered to sail to meet the transports in the Channel, and there to hold a joint council of war with the generals to decide on the immediate plans.[4] At the same time Nottingham, in a private letter to Russell, added fuel to the fire by inquiring about the possibility of attacking Brest or Rochefort after the forthcoming descent had been accomplished.[5]

Russell's reply to both communications was vitriolic. Words, he wrote in a three-page letter to Nottingham, were not enough to express his feelings about orders which ordered nothing and suggestions which so entirely ignored the facts. He enclosed the resolutions of his own

---

[1] Finch Transcr., Russell to Nottingham, 10/7.
[2] Ibid., Nottingham to Russell, 11/7, 13/7; Queen to Russell, 14/7.
[3] Ibid. Queen to Leinster, 14/7.
[4] Ibid., Queen to Russell, 22/7.
[5] Ibid., Nottingham to Russell, 17/7.

council of war in the fleet, which recommended that the fleet should cruise off the coast of Normandy to prevent the French in St Malo from slipping round to Brest, and that the big ships should come in to be laid up at the end of August and the rest a month later.[1] In these circumstances, the joint council of war was not likely to reach any satisfactory conclusions, and in fact it spent the time largely in recrimination. The navy proposed a landing near Cherbourg, to destroy the coastal fortifications: the army stuck to the original plan of St Malo.[2] As a result, the Cabinet was forced to decide between them. On 30th July, Mary instructed Russell to land the troops as near to St Malo as possible, and to bombard the town with the fleet after forcing an entrance through the channel.[3] This suggested nothing that had not already been rejected; after a day's thought, the orders were cancelled, and the Admiral once more directed to do what he thought best with the main fleet, while a squadron was sent to the westward to stop the French from sailing for Brest.[4] Shortly afterwards, the whole armada, with the exception of this squadron, was ordered back to St Helens.[5]

A last effort was then made to save the campaign from a futility which would certainly expose some of the ministers to a Parliamentary attack in the winter. On 1 August, the Queen sent Carmarthen, Devonshire, Dorset, Rochester, Sydney, Cornwallis and Nottingham to Portsmouth, to hold a council of war with the council of war of the fleet.[6] This, however, failed either to persuade Russell to attempt anything more that year, or to reconcile him to the Secretary of State.[7] In the end it agreed that for the rest of the season the fleet should cruise in the western approaches, to support the squadron off the Normandy coast; and after a short stay in these waters the great ships were dispersed

---

1 Ibid., Russell to Nottingham, 23/7.

2 Ibid., resolutions of the joint council of war, 28/7. There is an extract of this in *H.C.J.* x, p. 721, and a further one in Burchett, pp. 162–6.

3 Ibid., Queen to Russell, 29/7.

4 Ibid., Queen to Russell, 30/7.

5 Ibid., Nottingham to Blathwayt, 1/8.

6 Ibid.

7 *Conduct*, p. 104. In contrast to the cordial references to their meetings with which Nottingham had formerly laced his letters to the Admiral, his only mention of the Portsmouth meeting was, 'I thank you for your civilitys to me when I waited on you' (Finch Transcr. 5/8).

to their ports.[1] The campaign, with all its high hopes, came to a fitting end on 30 August, when Nottingham, in a last letter to Russell at sea, remarked that the Cabinet hoped to be able to keep the winter squadron upon the French coast, to alarm the inhabitants and to lock up the St Malo ships until the following spring.[2] It was a sad decline from the plans of June, and on 7 September even this final hope was disappointed, when the St Malo squadron sailed successfully for Brest.[3]

By the time that Russell came ashore, the quarrel between himself and Nottingham had become too open for a reconciliation to be possible.[4] In all his later letters, the Admiral had taken his stand, as he had first done on 10 July, on the twin arguments of insuperable technical obstacles and the government's delay in providing the troops. It was useless for Nottingham to point out that if the first were correct, the second was irrelevant, for Russell, appreciating that the failure to follow up the victory was bound to lead to some strong debates in the House, was engaged in laying hold of every argument that offered. He was, moreover, on strong ground in his attacks on the inefficiency of the arrangements for troops and transports; for the troops had been ready to embark only six weeks after the date originally agreed upon, while the transports had taken three and a half months to reach Portsmouth from the time that they were hired in Bristol and the Thames.[5] Even then many of them had not arrived, and Russell had had to send some of his own auxiliaries to assist in the embarkation.[6] The arrangements had gone wrong at every stage. The main concentration of the vessels was supposed to take place at Minehead on the west coast, which was thoroughly unsuitable for the purpose,[7] and in the confusion and delay which resulted the navy pressed a large number

---

[1] Finch Transcr., Queen to Russell, 10/8; Nottingham to Blathwayt, 23/8; Nottingham to Russell, 25/8.

[2] Ibid., Nottingham to Russell, 30/8.

[3] Burchett, pp. 167–8.

[4] Nottingham ceased to write to Russell after the Portsmouth meeting, except to enclose the Queen's orders and to comment briefly upon them.

[5] *H.M.C.* 14th Report, appendix, pt VI, p. 198.

[6] Finch Transcr., Nottingham to Leinster, 16/7.

[7] For the condition of Minehead at this time, see the preamble to 12 and 13 Will. III, c. 9, for recovering and restoring the harbour.

of their men.[1] Meanwhile the concentration in the Thames had broken down completely; the transports were denuded of their men, and as they continued to lie in the river their owners insisted on the demurrage being paid before they were allowed to sail.[2] Early in July, when the vessels from the west reached Portsmouth, most of the Thames vessels were still in the river. Finally, some of the troops mutinied when ordered to embark, and more deserted at the last moment.[3] There was plenty of opportunity for the Admiral to carry the argument to his opponents, and every reason for him to do so before Parliament met.

When the winter session began on 4 November, the temper of the Commons was quickly shown. They immediately demanded papers from Russell, Leinster (who had commanded the troops), the Transport Commissioners and the Admiralty,[4] and these were soon forthcoming.[5] But before the debate upon them opened, the House, in which the Whig groups were predominant, passed a resolution to the effect that Russell had behaved with 'fidelity, courage and conduct',[6] and followed this up by debating whether to demand 'all papers whatsoever', which in effect meant Nottingham's correspondence. In the meantime, however, the Lords had themselves made this demand,[7] and on 6 December his papers were handed over.[8] A fortnight later they were sent down to the Commons, where they were read immediately,[9] and the next day the lower House returned them with a request that the Lords would concur with its resolution approving Russell's conduct.[10] This the upper House refused to do, but the Commons refused to withdraw, and an argument developed over the question which lasted for the rest of the session.[11]

Meanwhile, the main debate on the progress of the campaign had opened in the Commons, and Russell had made his defence, basing himself on the resolutions of his council of war and the arguments

---

[1] P.R.O.Adm. 3/7: 14/4. [2] Ibid. 15/5, 17/6.

[3] Finch Transcr., Nottingham to Treasury, 31/7; Nottingham to Blathwayt, 22/7.

[4] *H.C.J.* x, p. 698. [5] Ibid. pp. 699–701, 715; see p. 400, n. 5 above.

[6] *H.C.J.* x, p. 698. [7] *H.L.J.* xv, p. 129. [8] Ibid. p. 135.

[9] Ibid. pp. 153–7; *H.C.J.* x, pp. 749–59.

[10] *H.C.J.* x, p. 760.

[11] Ibid. pp. 765, 767–9; *H.L.J.* xv, pp. 158, 160, 162, 165–7.

which he had already put forward in private to the Cabinet.[1] The Admiralty Commissioners, who were concerned to avoid the limelight as much as possible, contented themselves with briefly supporting him. The majority in the House, however, was not content merely to approve this defence, but carried the argument a stage further in a resolution, aimed implicitly at Nottingham,[2] recommending that 'all orders for the future management of the fleet should pass through the hands of the Commissioners for executing the office of Lord High Admiral'.[3] Thus implicated in the debate, the Commissioners from an early stage had to endure a detailed discussion of their conduct and of the general progress of the war at sea.[4] The debates were soon given their direction by the merchant interest, which complained of heavy losses over the past two years due to inordinate and illegal pressing, to a paucity and maldistribution of 'convoys and cruisers',[5] and in some cases—particularly that of Henry Priestman[6]—to a lack of interest in, or a positive hostility to, their complaints. These arguments were taken up by Clarges and other familiar figures to prove that the trouble lay as much in the Admiralty's lack of control as in its inefficiency. The Commissioners, particularly now that they were invested with statutory authority,[7] should be given more power, while to ensure that this was used correctly the composition of the Board should be modified to allow for a greater number of 'gentlemen bred at sea'. To this end, Clarges urged that any resolution on the Admiralty should submit to the King 'that the Commissioners...may have an equal number mixed'.[8] Another member showed that the existing arrangements were well known, when he remarked that 'orders are sent to the Fleet from time to time and they have no knowledge of them; they give commissions to the Admiral and he is to have instructions elsewhere'.[9] The crux of the matter lay, as all speakers recognized, in the quality of the Commissioners appointed. Without more powerful men on the Board, they could not expect any transfer

[1] Grey, op. cit. x, p. 244. [2] See *Conduct*, p. 108. [3] Grey, loc. cit. p. 246.

[4] These debates are to be found ibid. pp. 247–8, 266–74, 294–7.

[5] I have given the contemporary phrase here. We would say 'cruisers and escorts'.

[6] They were particularly infuriated, not without reason, at Priestman's remark that even if they lost two ships out of every three, they would still make a profit.

[7] Grey, loc. cit. pp. 247–8. [8] Ibid. p. 266. [9] Ibid. pp. 268–9.

of power to the Office.[1] Against such arguments, a defence of the Admiralty's conduct was largely irrelevant, and whereas in former years the debates had centred on permission to inspect the books of the department, it was now appreciated that these were unimportant, and that the point at issue was not what the Admiralty had done but to what extent it had been kept in ignorance of events. Despite a series of speeches on its behalf, notably one by Russell, the main issue remained the same,[2] with the unexpected result that by the end of the winter the Admiralty had changed from being regarded as the representative of the executive to being treated as the representative of the House of Commons in its attack upon the executive. It was a curious step in the development of Parliamentary government.

In the course of the debates, the question had also been raised, in general terms, of the command of the fleet. Clarges had declared that the 'charge of so great a Fleet is too great for one man',[3] and had recommended that a commission should again be tried similar to that of 1690. It was an ironic comment upon the progress of the war at the time, that such a suggestion should have to be raised alike after the navy's greatest defeat and after its greatest victory. Whether or not the fact that it had first been aired in Parliament had any effect, the suggestion met the case. Russell's behaviour had alienated the Queen and disturbed the King, and William decided, since it was obvious that Admiral and Secretary could no longer work together, that the Admiral should be the one to go. In view of the support which he had recently enjoyed in the Commons, this might seem to have been a bold decision. But in fact this support was not a constant political factor. The opposition to Nottingham had been as much an expression of the antagonism felt by the mercantile and Whiggish interests to the High Church and Tory elements, as of any widespread discontent on purely administrative grounds; as the issues changed, so did the membership of the opposition, and several of those who were supporting the Admiral at the beginning of the session, when Nottingham and the Tories were the target, were debating with him at the end, when the target was the Board of Admiralty. It was, moreover, one of the most prominent of the Whigs who had first raised the question of a

---

[1] Ibid. pp. 269–70. [2] *H.C.J.* x, p. 775. [3] Grey, loc. cit. p. 272.

commission; and it is even possible that Russell himself, worn out, exasperated and frightened by the events of the past few months, did not object to this solution.[1] In December 1692, the Admiralty was ordered to submit a list of suitable names,[2] and by a warrant of 24 January Admirals Killigrew, Delavall, and Shovell were appointed as joint Admirals for the coming season.[3] In view of the recent debates, the first two were also appointed to the Board of Admiralty in April, with permission not to sign orders or letters unless they had the opportunity to do so, and Shovell was made an extra Commissioner of the Navy Board.[4] Possibly as compensation, Russell was given the household post of treasurer of the chamber.[5]

But despite Russell's immediate removal from the fleet, Nottingham was unable much longer to keep control of naval affairs. Determined though William was not to part with the Secretary from the Cabinet, in the new year he was forced to appease the Whigs by appointing one of their number to the vacant Secretaryship of State, and by transferring naval business to his department. Nottingham moved to the southern department, and on 29 March the King issued orders to prepare the necessary warrant for the northern department in the name of Sir John Trenchard, an extreme Whig of the old Exclusionist party who had been exiled for a time by James II. By the end of the month he was in office,[6] and in the middle of April Nottingham wrote his last letter on naval matters, except for those which continued to fall directly within the supervision of his new province.[7] Although he continued to act as Secretary for the southern department for another six months, the correspondence with the Admiralty and the fleet passed completely into Trenchard's hands.[8] By the beginning of the next

[1] The Dutch ambassador thought that he might have suggested a commission of joint Admirals himself (B.M.Addnl. 17677, NN, f. 39, cited by James); and cf. Nottingham: 'After this, Admiral Russell desired to be excused from the command of the fleet the next year; and His Majesty put it into commission' (*Conduct*, p. 116).

[2] P.R.O.Adm. 7/693, f. 1. [3] See Appendix X below.

[4] P.R.O.Adm. 3/7: 18/4; *Cal.S.P.Dom. 1693*, p. 82; see Appendixes VI and VIII below.

[5] *Cal.S.P.Dom. 1693*, p. 82. [6] Ibid. pp. 86–7. [7] Finch Transcr. for 1693.

[8] Nottingham himself ascribed the transfer of duties to the fact that, as he had handled naval affairs while 'second Secretary' (i.e. the most recently appointed) with Shrewsbury, so Trenchard handled them on becoming 'second Secretary' with

campaign, therefore, the two great figures of the past two years had disappeared from the naval scene. Where the defeat of the fleet in 1690 had resulted in the dismissal of its commander, the strategic vacuum left by its success in 1692 resulted in the removal of the commander and of the naval minister who had been the architects of the victory.

II

Throughout these two years, as in the two preceding them, the main fleet had operated for the most part in the west; and although the defeat of 1690 had again thrown the most important repair work of the summer on the traditional facilities of the Thames and Medway, the campaigns in the following years emphasized what the campaign in 1689 had first suggested, that the main naval bases were badly placed for the needs of a French war. In 1691 and 1692 most of the ships had still to be fitted out on the east coast, so that compared with the enemy they had a long and often difficult passage to make before they reached their station, particularly in the early summer when the prevalent winds were from the west; and on reaching the western Channel or the Soundings they were several days' sailing from the nearest base at Portsmouth, while the French could put in with less delay to the greatly superior dockyard of Brest.

The only advanced base for stores and minor repairs in earlier years had been Kinsale, and after its recapture in 1690 efforts were soon made to re-establish it. In December of that year the first stores were sent there from Portsmouth, and a master shipwright appointed.[1] By the following March, after more stores had been shipped from the Thames yards, the yard was ready to clean some of the lesser men-of-war,[2] and during the summer the old buildings were repaired and refitted.[3] From June, too, it acted as a victualling port, with provisions for two months in store;[4] and in the winter, after the experience of the campaign, the Navy Board was asked to report on its

himself (*Conduct*, pp. 116–17). This practice, however, did not obtain when Shrewsbury became 'second Secretary' on Nottingham's dismissal in November 1693. I prefer, therefore, to attribute the transfer to political and not administrative causes.

[1] P.R.O.Adm. 3/5: 8/12. [2] Ibid. 18/3.

[3] P.R.O.Adm. 3/6: 12/5, 3/7. [4] Ibid. 17/6.

potentialities as a repair base for the duration of the war.[1] Little more, however, was done during 1692. At the end of that year stores were still not provided on any establishment, but were sent there as occasion arose.[2] But as year after year the fleet continued to cruise in the west, and as incoming merchantmen continued to be taken by privateers in the Soundings, the need became increasingly obvious for a well-equipped advanced base, where stores might be regularly obtained and cruisers regularly cleaned, and where homebound convoys might call for supplies and orders before proceeding up Channel. In November 1693 the Navy Board was again ordered to report on all harbours on the south-east coast of Ireland,[3] and its answer was received the same month.[4] The only possibilities, in its opinion, were Cork and Kinsale. Cork, though a spacious harbour, was undefended and had not the equipment to clean and refit men-of-war of any size. It could not therefore be used immediately as a base. Kinsale, on the other hand, was already partly equipped, and was in any case nearer the scene of action. It was also well sheltered and quite well fortified. Its drawback lay in the bar that stretched across the mouth of the harbour, which had barely sixteen feet of water over it at low water and which the big ships could therefore not clear at all states of the tide; but if wanted at once, it could undertake to refit the smaller rates. After a further delay of several months, the Admiralty acted on this report. In August 1694 Kinsale was at last officially established as a yard for the cleaning and fitting of men-of-war, and the Admiralty set about selecting its officers.[5] Russell had already proposed that the yard should be given its own Commissioner,[6] and in September the most junior of the resident Commissioners of the Navy was duly appointed.[7] The officers' salaries, and their allowance of clerks, were fixed at the same rate as those of their counterparts at Plymouth;[8] and in the estimates for 1695, Kinsale appeared for the first time in the war as a properly constituted yard, with a Commissioner, clerks of the cheque and the survey, master

[1] P.R.O.Adm. 3/6: 11/1/92. [2] E.g. P.R.O.Adm. 3/8: 30/11.
[3] P.R.O.Adm. 3/9: 15/11. [4] P.R.O.Adm. 1/3570, ff. 852–3.
[5] P.R.O.Adm. 3/10: 16/8, 24/8; 1/3572, f. 897; 2/174, f. 438.
[6] P.R.O.Adm. 3/10: 18/5.
[7] Ibid. 3/9; see Appendix VIII below.
[8] P.R.O.Adm. 3/10: 4/10, 26/11; 2/174, f. 542.

attendant, master shipwright, storekeeper and master caulker.[1] In December of that year, workmen were mustered for the yard as for the other royal dockyards, and a total of 28 was returned.[2] By the end of the war this had risen to 66.[3]

One of the reasons for the delay in establishing Kinsale as a yard was the Admiralty's simultaneous attempt to provide an advanced base in the west of England. A base in Ireland, indeed, had some obvious disadvantages compared with one on the mainland. Orders took considerably longer to reach the ships than in England, and for the same reason an Irish yard was less amenable to control. It was also more exposed to attack. Throughout these years, therefore, the Admiralty made spasmodic attempts to set up a similar type of base in Devon or Cornwall. The first proposal of the sort had been made in August 1689, when a survey was ordered of all the harbours between Dartmouth and Falmouth;[4] but nothing happened after that until 1691, when it was suggested without success that Bristol should be made into a regular store base.[5] In the winter of 1692–3, the southern harbours again came under review, and the choice soon narrowed to Falmouth.[6] In March 1693 the Navy Board was ordered to survey the port, and Trinity House was called in to help in May.[7] The Navy Board made two detailed reports on completion. Both were much the same.[8] The harbour itself was large and safe, but the entrance was undefended and difficult in a north-westerly wind; there was no road outside the harbour where ships could easily ride; and the lie of the land was unsuitable for building more than a very few cleaning slips. The hinterland also was unsatisfactory; for there was no local market where the right provisions or stores could be obtained, and the roads to the east were bad. The Board therefore

---

1 P.R.O.Adm. 7/169, estimate of ordinary of navy for 1695.

2 Serg.MS. A 123. The only difference was that at Kinsale they were mustered quarterly until June 1697, while at the other yards they were mustered each month.

3 Ibid. November 1697; see Appendix V (*b*) below.

4 P.R.O.Adm. 3/1: 21/8. It was made during October (B.M.Lansdowne 847, f. 4).

5 P.R.O.Adm. 2/381, 28/5/91. The suggestion appears to have been made again in 1693 (P.R.O.Adm. 2/384, 11/10/93).

6 P.R.O.Adm. 3/8: 18/1.

7 Ibid. 27/3, 25/5.

8 P.R.O.Adm. 1/3568, ff. 216–20; 1/3569, ff. 328–32.

concluded that at a time when money was extremely short, the project should be abandoned. Later in the year, after another inquiry by the Admiralty,[1] it reported that if a base were to be set up in the area, Milford Haven, with an excellent harbour and with sufficient water at all states of the tide for the biggest ships, was preferable to Falmouth,[2] despite the fact that it faced into the prevailing westerly winds and that it was too remote to be really satisfactory. But in the event, neither Milford Haven nor Falmouth was developed as a naval base during the war.[3]

One of the most telling arguments put forward by the Navy Board in 1693 against the establishment of a base at Falmouth was its proximity to Plymouth.[4] For by that time, the new dockyard there was well under way and was already being used. Plymouth Sound, with its offshoots of Hamoaze and Cattewater, had been one of the harbours surveyed in the autumn of 1689 by Edmund Dummer, then assistant master shipwright at Chatham.[5] It had already been considered as an advanced store base in June, and before the end of that month a storekeeper had been appointed, with instructions—to muster the ships there, as well as to serve stores, 'untill the yard shall be settled, and a Clerk of the Cheque established'—which showed that something more was intended.[6] In August that intention became clear, when for the first time the Admiralty mentioned the possibility of building a dry dock somewhere within the Sound.[7] Two months later it received Dummer's report suggesting Point Froward, at the entrance to the Hamoaze river, as the most suitable site for the purpose.[8]

The proposal to build a dock at Plymouth set quite a different problem from that of Falmouth or the other advanced bases proposed for the west. It did not do away with the necessity for such a base, but itself met a different need. As has been seen,[9] a dry dock was the dividing line between a major and a minor yard; and in 1689 there were no docking facilities west of Portsmouth. Even there, the old double

---

1 P.R.O.Adm. 3/9: 15/11.
2 P.R.O.Adm. 1/3570, ff. 852–3.
3 The Cabinet Council eventually turned down the Admiralty's proposals for Falmouth (P.R.O.Adm. 3/9: 21/7).
4 P.R.O.Adm. 1/3568, f. 216.
5 B.M.Lansdowne 847, ff. 3–4.
6 P.R.O.Adm. 3/1: 22/6, 25/6.
7 P.R.O.Adm. 1/3559, f. 871.
8 B.M.Lansdowne 847, f. 4.
9 P. 80 above.

dry dock, which alone could take the largest men-of-war, was fast becoming useless through moisture and decay. By the end of 1690 it was in a very bad state, and throughout 1691 it was frequently out of action for repairs.[1] For days, occasionally for weeks at a time, there was therefore no dock on the south coast to which a first or second rate could be sent. It was obvious that, as well as finding a harbour for storing and refitting the cruisers of the fleet, the navy must set up a major base in the west with proper docking facilities as soon as possible.

But although the demand was recognized, it was not met for some time. Dummer's choice of Point Froward was soon approved, and the Admiralty ordered the Navy Board to put the arrangements in hand for building a single dry dock there capable of taking a third rate.[2] Towards the end of March 1690, the Board found a local contractor, Robert Waters or Walters, who put in a tender of £10,900 for the work and guaranteed to finish it in fifteen months.[3] But nothing more was heard of the project until the autumn, and this time it was in a proposal that the dock should be built, not at Froward Point, but in 'The Slate Quarry at the Ferry over against Saltash'.[4] This was turned down, and on 3 December the contract with Waters was signed, for a single dry dock to be built on the original site for £8909.[5]

Even now the plan allowed only for the docking of ships of medium size; and immediately after the contract had been signed a more ambitious design was put forward, once more by Edmund Dummer, who might be allowed the title of founder of the dockyard. Instead of building a dock which could take only third rates and below,[6] he suggested instead a large dry dock supplemented by a wet dock or

---

[1] P.R.O.Adm. 3/5: 9/1; 3/6: 28/9, 2/10. [2] P.R.O.Adm. 1/3559, f. 871.

[3] P.R.O.Adm. 1/3560, f. 1019. The contractor's name is given impartially as Waters and Walters in the many references to him over the next six years.

[4] B.M.Lansdowne 847, f. 4*v*. I have placed this proposal in the autumn because it came from Greenhill, whose connexion with Plymouth began only in September (P.R.O.Adm. 3/4: 15/9). See also P.R.O.Adm. 3/4: 7/11, 8/11, 10/11.

[5] B.M.Addnl. 33061, f. 127.

[6] 'Cruisers' was his own word (B.M.Lansdowne 847, f. 4). Dummer's claim to have been the author of the revised plan is confirmed by the Navy Board (P.R.O.Adm. 1/3559, ff. 871–3).

basin, from which the ships could be sent into dry dock more easily than from an anchorage, where they could be refitted with less trouble, and which would moreover protect the inner dock from the full effects of the westerly winds to which it lay exposed on the river bank. The draft of this plan was shown to the inner Council, where it was approved, and William himself directed that the dry dock should be large enough to hold a first rate.[1] The work was again undertaken by Waters, and the cost of the dry dock itself was now estimated at £11,008.[2] By the spring of 1691 the work was under way, and in the meantime a hulk was sent to the Sound to act as a base and repair ship.[3]

Staff	Annual salary		
	£	*s.*	*d.*
Agent	400	0	0
Two clerks, one at £50, one at £30	80	0	0
Storekeeper or muster-master	120	0	0
Two clerks, one at £30, one at £24	54	0	0
Master attendant	100	0	0
One clerk	24	0	0
Master shipwright	100	0	0
Clerk of the survey	60	0	0
One clerk	30	0	0
Master boatmaker or mastmaker	32	12	1
Master caulker	60	0	0
Total	£1060	12	1

While the foundations of the yard were thus being laid, its organization was taking shape. There is no record of how the workmen were supplied, but the appointments of the various officers can be traced, and are of some interest as an example of the sequence in which it was considered that the different branches of the yard should be filled. The first to join the storekeeper were the master attendant and master caulker, who were appointed by the end of 1689.[4] Aboard the hulk in the Sound were a boatswain and a carpenter, who also served for the yard.[5] Early in 1690, a clerk of the survey and a master shipwright

[1] B.M.Lansdowne 847, f. 5; P.R.O.Adm. 3/5: 15/12, 22/12.

[2] P.R.O.Adm. 7/169, no. 9.

[3] P.R.O.Adm. 3/5: 13/2.

[4] The proposed instructions for the storekeeper and master attendant are given in P.R.O.Adm. 1/3559, ff. 421–33. See also ibid. f. 695; 1/3558, f. 642. Two clerks may have been appointed at the same time: they were certainly there in February 1690 (P.R.O.Adm. 1/3560, f. 623).

[5] P.R.O.Adm. 1/3558, f. 641.

were appointed;[1] and on 15 September, the decisive step was taken of applying to the King for a Commissioner, and on the 24th Henry Greenhill, formerly an agent of the Navy Board in the embarkation of the troops for Ireland,[2] was given a commission as 'agent' for the yard.[3] At the end of the year the establishment stood as shown above on p. 418.[4] The only officers who received less salary than their most senior counterparts, the officers at Chatham, were the clerk of the survey and the master caulker. The agent was also paid £100 less than a full-fledged Commissioner of the Navy.[5] The establishment at Plymouth, in fact, was now on the same footing as those of the other yards. With the addition of £70 annual rent for a storehouse, the total estimated cost of its ordinary came to £1131; at the same time, that of Chatham came to £2312, that of Deptford to £1870, that of Portsmouth to £1788, that of Woolwich to £1345, and that of Sheerness to £840.[6] In January 1691, workmen were mustered for the first time at Plymouth yard, and a total of 74 was returned. In February this rose to 82, and in March to 83. It stayed at about that figure for the rest of the year.[7]

There is thus no one date on which it can be said that the new dockyard began. Once begun, however, it was developed by recognizable stages. The details of this development are of considerable interest, for Plymouth was the only dockyard to be founded in the later seventeenth century specifically to meet the needs of its time. It was, indeed, the only dockyard in this country to be built as a deliberate enterprise from a single plan between the first half of the sixteenth and the first

[1] P.R.O.Adm. 1/3560, ff. 135, 623. According to V. L. F. Millard, 'Plymouth and its Ships', in *M.M.* XXXII, no. 2, p. 106, the first master shipwright was appointed on 18 January 1690.

[2] See P.R.O.Adm. 1/3557–8, *passim*. He should not be confused with Captain William Greenhill, who was his brother.

[3] P.R.O.Adm. 3/4: 15/9, 24/9. There are at least two copies of his instructions, in P.R.O.Adm. 2/1728, ff. 31–3, and 7/639, ff. 131–6. He was given his warrant as a Commissioner of the Navy only on 1 February 1692 (P.R.O.Adm. 3/6: 1/2), so that until that date he continued to be addressed as 'agent' (e.g. P.R.O.Adm. 3/5: 27/12/90, 10/4/91; 3/6: 1/7/91, 20/1/92).

[4] P.R.O.Adm. 7/175, no. 1. This list, which comes in the annual estimates of the ordinary of the navy for 1691, is itself dated 15 August 1691; but all the salaries are calculated on the basis of a whole year, like those of the officers in the other yards.

[5] Ibid. [6] Ibid. [7] Serg.MS. A 123.

quarter of the twentieth century. Its progress will therefore be followed, beyond the chronological limits of this chapter, until the end of the war.

The yard on Froward Point was not only the first sign of naval building there: it was the first sign of building at all. It was over two miles away from the victualling stores which had been in the area for some years,[1] and it was entirely separate from the town of Plymouth itself.[2] Geographically at least, the navy had a free hand. But from the beginning it was faced with one great difficulty. The land on Froward Point, and the neighbouring barton of Mountwise, belonged to a certain Sir Nicholas Morris, who in 1690 was a boy of thirteen. The Admiralty had signed the contract with Waters before bothering to find out about the owner, and when the trustees were informed they immediately replied that an Act of Parliament would probably be required to empower them to sell the property,[3] and that in the meantime they had no intention of allowing any building to take place. The boy's guardian, a Hamburg merchant of obstinate and, as it was to be proved, litigious temper, was particularly awkward, and after first avoiding an interview altogether, stated his intention of removing any stores that the navy might send to the site.[4] In the event no Act was passed, but the dispute was finally settled only in May 1694 by the Admiralty agreeing to pay Morris £139 for the damage done to his property,[5] and in the next month a lease was signed by which the navy rented the land on Froward Point for seven years at £100 per annum.[6] The delay in settling this matter, which seems to have been mainly the fault of the owner's trustees,[7] gave both the contractors and the officials on the spot a great deal of trouble. By the middle of 1691, Morris's steward was obstructing Waters to such an extent that the Admiralty

---

[1] P.R.O.Adm. 1/3570, f. 890.

[2] Even in 1762, Dr Johnson, in his conservative way, could take the side of the town against the 'upstarts and aliens' of the dockyard (James Boswell, *Life of Dr Johnson*, I, ed. G. Birkbeck Hill (1934) p. 379).

[3] P.R.O.Adm. 1/3562, ff. 863–4.

[4] P.R.O.Adm. 1/3563, ff. 29–35, 113; P.R.O.Adm. 3/5: 3/1; P.R.O.Adm. 2/171, f. 151.

[5] P.R.O.Adm. 3/10: 15/5, 30/5.

[6] P.R.O.Adm. 2/174, f. 164.

[7] The Admiralty had been trying to get the lease signed since the beginning of 1691, but the lawyers and the trustees had delayed the negotiations (P.R.O.Adm. 3/5: 3/1, 18/2/91; 3/7: 14/11, 16/11/91; 3/8: 23/12/92, 30/5/93; 3/9: 9/2, 12/2/94).

was threatening to take the whole business to the Queen,[1] but that did not stop him from continuing intermittently to harass the contractor and his men. Early in 1693 he was causing more trouble,[2] and in 1694 he so terrified the local contractors and their workmen with threats of legal proceedings that for some time none of them would proceed with the work.[3] He also brought along some men to remove the piles of bricks which Waters had assembled on the site.[4] After the navy had come to an agreement with the trustees, nothing more was heard of his activities and the work went ahead more smoothly, despite occasional trouble as when a churchwarden in the town put the master shipwright of the yard into the bishop's spiritual court for working on a fast-day in Lent.[5] But real trouble, of the familiar kind, arose again when the Admiralty decided to expand the yard in 1697 by building workmens' lodgings on Mountwise. Morris's trustees on this occasion successfully blocked the necessary Act of Parliament, and at the end of the war the navy had still not managed to gain permission to start on the work.[6]

The site of the yard was good, but not ideal. The entrance to the Hamoaze was narrow and crooked, with strong eddies and rapid spring tides. The passage was not entirely free from rocks, and a westerly wind was needed before it could be navigated with any ease.[7] But these were not necessarily disadvantages for the nearest dockyard to France, particularly in the years before the battle of Barfleur put an end to the idea of a large-scale invasion; and the advantages of the site, with its concentration of facilities upon a naturally protected yet reasonably ample harbour, with room for all the ships which the yard was likely to have to deal with, but without the drawback of their being dispersed over a wide area, more than outweighed its shortcomings. Like many western harbours, moreover, it had deep water right up to the shore, on the western and southern sides of the point; and taken all round, no other port between Portsmouth and Land's End could offer the same facilities.[8]

---

1 P.R.O.Adm. 2/381, 9/7/91.
2 P.R.O.Adm. 2/174, f. 188.
3 P.R.O.Adm. 1/3571, ff. 188, 545.
4 P.R.O.Adm. 3/10: 23/4.
5 P.R.O.Adm. 2/173, f. 418.
6 B.M.Addnl. 9329, ff. 167–9.
7 See chart in Grenville Collin's *Great Britain's Coasting Pilot*. The arguments are set out in B.M.Addnl. 9329, f. 166.
8 Ibid. ff. 156–7, 165*v*.

The first parts of the dockyard to be finished were the two docks themselves. By the end of 1692 these were ready for inspection, and they were put into use the next year.[1] Between them, they represented a great advance on anything previously built in this country both in layout and material, and could indeed be compared with the docks at Toulon, which were always regarded as a model.[2] The basin, some 452 feet long and 23 feet deep, could take two large ships, and the dry dock one. Both were controlled by sluice gates, so that both could be flooded, both emptied, or one flooded and the other emptied. When a ship came in, she was usually put into the flooded basin for repairs above her waterline, was then examined if necessary below the water-line in an emptied basin, and if she needed under-water repair, passed without any difficulty into the dry dock while the wet dock was flooded once more. Ships could thus be properly examined, and the dry dock properly employed, instead of the former being delayed while the latter was wasted on examinations which should have been carried out elsewhere. When the basin was available for the purpose, ships could also be refitted there more efficiently than in the stream. Men and material did not have to be taken out to them from the shore; more difficult work, such as careening, could be carried on when a hulk in the river would have to desist; and a ship that needed repairs could store at the same time. The machinery of the docks also set a new standard in efficiency. The basin was connected with the dry dock by a second pair of sluice gates, which operated on a central hinge, and could be opened or shut quite easily in about two minutes by six men. Nor did they need to be caulked or shored to withstand water pressure like the gates of the older docks, which required eighty to ninety men in all to work and maintain them. The dock itself was built of Portland stone with steps cut in its sides, so that a ship could be supported more easily

---

[1] B.M.Addnl. 9329, f. 160*v*; Millard, loc. cit. p. 106. It had been hoped that they would be ready by midsummer (P.R.O.Adm. 3/6: 8/1).

[2] B.M.Addnl. 9329, f. 159*v*. The following account of the yard is based on this source, ff. 156–69, which contains a printed version of Dummer's MS. account in B.M. Lansdowne 847 together with later information, and on the detailed scale plans in B.M. King's 43. Apart from the latter, the best picture of the yard is the frontispiece to Dummer's pamphlet in B.M.Addnl. 9329, which, according to *B.M. Catalogue of MS. Maps, Charts and Plans*, I, p. 63, is by Kip.

than in the earlier docks with their smooth wooden slopes. The water was raised and lowered by sluices which worked on a screw, and an average height of seventeen feet could be controlled without any difficulty.

The building of these docks was not a simple affair. As may be seen from the plans of the yard shown overleaf, both docks had to be built on artificial ground, for it was impossible to excavate the rock. The basin was protected from the river by some 3000 feet of wharfing, between 22 and 23 feet deep to the westward and 14 feet deep to the south; and in all, over four acres of new ground were made into the river to the south and west, while the rest was levelled with a good deal of labour. The first buildings were begun with the docks, with the construction of a large central storehouse, or 'great square Magazine' as Dummer called it.[1] This square store, 60 feet on each side, was the pride of the yard, and excited the admiration of contemporaries. Two storeys high, with two large cellars and a loft, it could hold the gear for forty men-of-war, and in its courtyard could lie all their spars, grapnels and the like, which would not deteriorate from the weather. Standing on the point itself, at the confluence of the two channels, it could be approached at any state of the tide on two of its four sides, so that if the wind came from east or west it provided a lee under which ships could lie in safety and carry on the business of storing. For four years this remained the only store. At the same time, a range of offices and officers' houses was being built more slowly at the head of the dry dock, and on the southern shore a workhouse for white and tarred yarn. Two cranes were also fitted in the early years.[2] By the end of 1692 the foundations of the yard had been laid, and the first stage was almost complete.

In December of that year the next stage was inaugurated, when the Commons included in their vote for the navy for 1693 a sum of £23,406 for 'the finishing their Majesties' Naval Yard at *Hamoze* near Plymouth', including 'Dwelling-houses for the Officers, Storehouses, Workhouses, and inclosing the said Yard with a Wall';[3] and between

---

[1] B.M. Lansdowne 847, f. 6*v*. The layout of the buildings can be followed most easily from the plans shown overleaf, which are reproduced from B.M. King's 43.

[2] Ibid. ff. 6*v*–7.

[3] *H.C.J.* x, pp. 730–1.

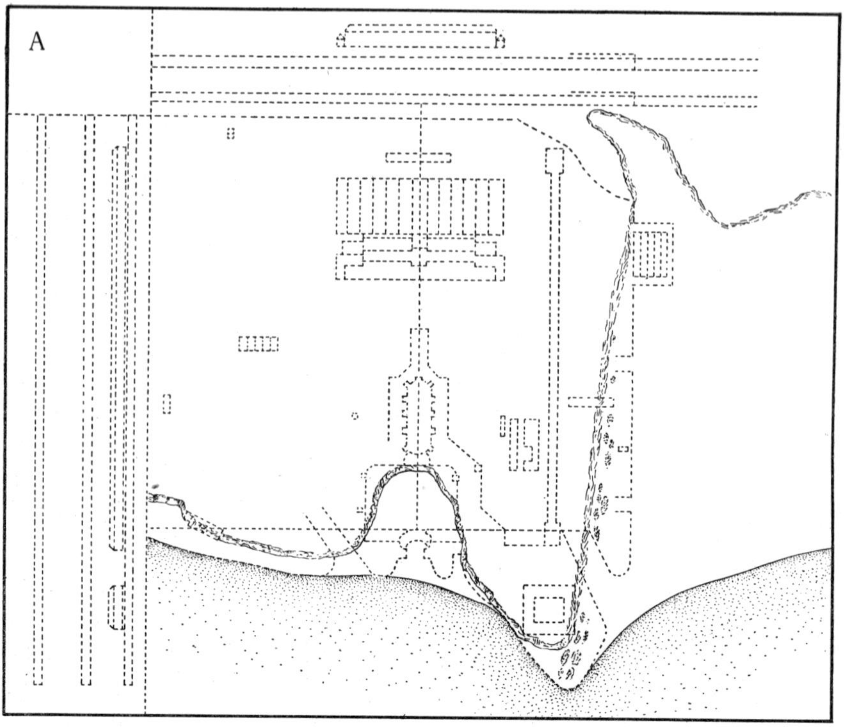
A

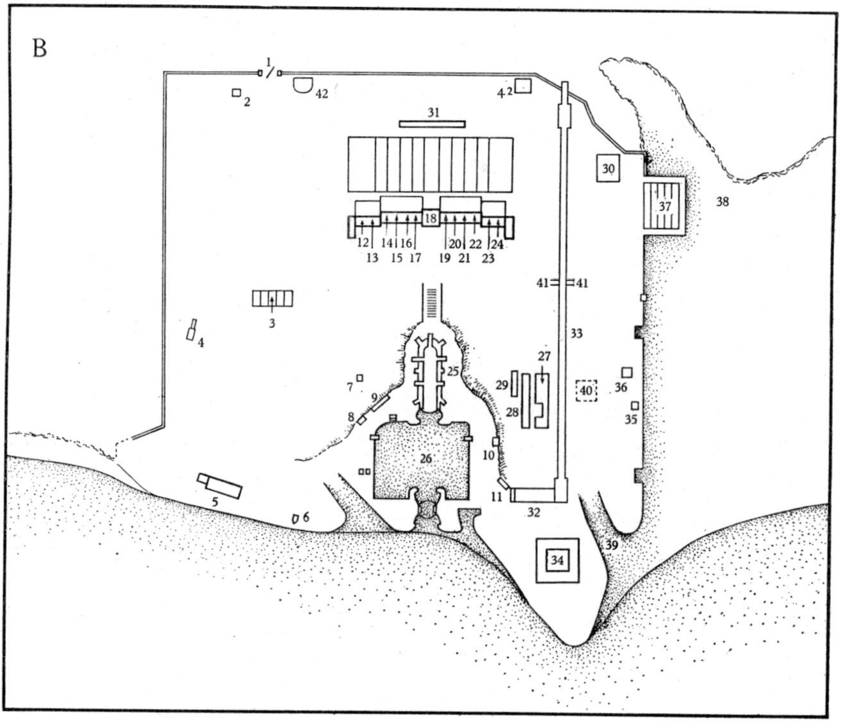
B
1
2
42
42
31
30
37
38
18
12
13
14
15
16
17
19
20
21
22
23
24
41
41
3
33
4
27
25
29
28
40
36
7
9
8
35
10
26
5
11
32
6
34
39

PLATE XI

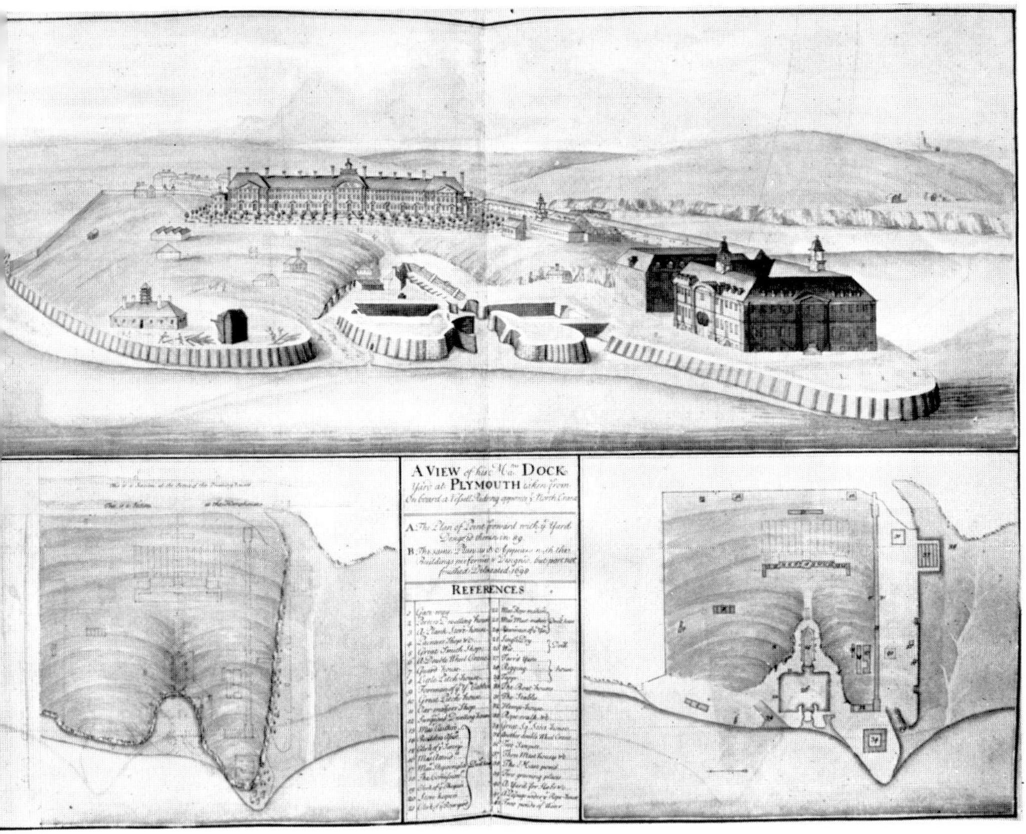

THE DOCKYARD AT PLYMOUTH

View and Plans

A. The plan of the Point facing inland in 1689, with a design of the Yard outlined upon it.
B. The same plan as it appears with the buildings erected as designed, but with a part still unfinished; drawn in 1698.

REFERENCES

1. Gateway
2. Porter's house
3. A plank store-house
4. Painter's shop, etc.
5. Great smith's shop
6. A double wheel crane
7. Guard-house
8. Little pitch-house
9. Foreman of the yard's cabin
10. Great pitch-house
11. Oar-maker's shop
12. Surgeon's house
13. Master caulker's house
14. Builder's assistant's house
15. Clerk of the survey's house
16. Master attendant's house
17. Master ship-wright's house
18. The commissioner's house
19. Clerk of the cheque's house
20. Storekeeper's house
21. Clerk of the rope-yard's house
22. Master rope-maker's house
23. Master mast-maker's house
24. Boatswain of the yard's house
25. Single dry dock
26. Wet dock
27. Tarred yarn house
28. Rigging house
29. Tap-house
30. The boat-houses
31. The stables
32. Hemp-house
33. Rope-walk, etc.
34. Great square store-house
35. Another double wheel crane
36. Two sawpits
37. Three mast-houses, etc.
38. The mast pond
39. Two graving places
40. A yard for slabs, etc.
41. A passage under the rope-house
42. Two ponds of water

the end of 1694 and the end of 1697 the work went ahead. It was carried out mainly by a new contractor. Waters was by now clamouring for the money owing to him for the initial work,[1] and there had been advertisements for some months in the *Gazette* inviting tenders for the other buildings. In September 1693 one Fitch, who had already undertaken construction elsewhere for the navy,[2] was named as the 'undertaker for ye docks at Plymo.'.[3] By the beginning of 1698 he had almost completed the original programme for a hemphouse and a rope-house, sawhouses and sawpits, pitchhouses and forge, and an encircling wall of a mile and a quarter. Their arrangement was well thought out. The hemp- and ropehouses stood together near the central store, as complementary store and workhouses for cordage. The ropehouse employed four spinners, which was sufficient for the needs of the yard. Next to them was a sailroom, separated from the other buildings so that the sails had plenty of space to dry outside in good weather, free from the dust and tar of the workshops—a convenience seldom possible in the other yards. Then came the yarn- and spinners' houses, in which the hemp was manufactured. These were subdivided in each case into rooms for the different stages of the process, partly because the basic material was liable to deteriorate if brought into contact with the other elements in its manufacture, partly because it was easy to steal and to carry out of the yard. Both elements required for the successful and economical production of hemp, the supervision of the material and the separation of the processes in its manufacture, were thus provided. To the south of these buildings stood the rigging house. The storage and manufacture of ships' gear were thus catered for in a logical order and compressed into a small area, all on the south side of the yard. Beneath the buildings lay a timber wharf over 1000 feet long and 200 feet wide, fitted with two double-wheeled cranes and ending in the east with three masthouses, and with a boathouse including workshops for carpenters and joiners on the second floor. The masthouses were conveniently placed near a shelving shore around the point, where the timbers could lie in the mud. At the western end of the wharf were two graving places, with a single slip for building.

---

[1] B.M.Addnl. 33061, f. 127.
[2] See p. 428 below.
[3] P.R.O.Adm. 3/9: 28/9/93.

These works covered about four acres. The yard itself, within its wall, occupied some 24 acres.[1] Most of the space was empty, with only some sawpits and small worksheds dotted here and there. The only considerable group of buildings apart from those along the southern wall was provided by the offices and dwelling-houses, facing west from the head of the dry dock. Built apparently on the plan of those at Chatham,[2] this range housed thirteen officers, centring on the Commissioner's house with its flight of steps down to the dock. There were gardens and stables at the back. The porter had his own house by the single entrance gate on the eastern wall.

Plymouth yard was thus a homogeneous, well-planned entity, representing the minimum required of a dockyard at that time. Its value was soon to be seen in the number of ships which it accommodated. At the end of 1691 there were no ships refitting there, but by the end of the next year there were one fourth rate and one fifth, by the end of 1694 three fourths, one fifth and one fireship, and at the end of 1696 five fourths, three fifths and two sixths. In the demobilization of 1697–8, ten men-of-war were laid up in the Hamoaze.[3] In 1694, also, the yard began itself to build ships. It launched two advice boats of 73 tons each in that year, and the 48-gun *Anglesea* of 620 tons; in 1695, it followed with the 384-ton *Lyme*, in 1696 with the 406-ton *Looe*, and in 1698 with the *Carlisle* of 720 tons.[4] Its organization responded accordingly. In December 1691, naturally a busy month, the yard was employing 75 workmen; in December 1692, 144; in December 1694, 139; in December 1696, when the new works were well under way, 311, and in the last month of the war, 319.[5] It was by then employing more than double the men employed at Sheerness, and half the number employed at Woolwich.[6] The establishment, on the other hand, did not

---

[1] B.M. King's 43.

[2] Compare the plans for them in the two yards, in B.M. King's 43.

[3] P.R.O.Adm. 8/2, 16/12/91; 8/3, 8/12/92, 15/12/94; 8/5, 16/12/96; 8/6, 1/8/98.

[4] Millard, loc. cit. p. 111. How far the King's yard was responsible for the *Anglesea* and the *Looe* is doubtful: they were both certainly built in a yard belonging to a Mr Fint (annual estimates for 1694 and 1696, in P.R.O.Adm. 7/169 and 7/175 respectively); but the dockyard may have supplied the labour, and almost certainly supplied the stores. [5] Serg.MS. A 123, under months concerned.

[6] Ibid.; and see Appendix V(B) below.

increase much after 1691. The only additional officers by 1696 were a surgeon, who had been on the establishment since 1692, a master sail-maker and a porter.[1] Some more clerks had been allowed in the interval, and following the general reform of 1695,[2] the officers' salaries were increased and made uniform with those of their counterparts in other yards. The final establishment of officers proposed when the yard had been completed was as follows: Commissioner, master attendant, clerk of the cheque, clerk of the stores, clerk of the ropeyard, clerk of the survey, master shipwright with either one or two assistants, surgeon, master caulker, master mast- and boatmaker, master rope-maker, and boatswain of the yard.

Although Plymouth dockyard was a well-balanced organization by the end of the war, with room for expansion inside its walls, in two respects it was not complete. First, the victualling arrangements had not been brought into line with the growth of the yard, and ships had still to fetch their provisions by river from a storeyard over two miles away. Proposals were made in 1693 to bring the brewhouse, and if possible the victuallers' storehouses, nearer to the docks, but nothing was done. Secondly, the workmen had to travel several miles every day between their homes and the yard. In 1695 the Commissioner accordingly proposed that a range of lodgings should be erected outside the walls, on the neighbouring land of Mountwise.[3] Nothing was done immediately, but by 1697 the Admiralty had approached Morris's trustees to lease or buy the ground. The chief trustee, however, threatened to oppose such action if necessary by law, and in the event managed to stop the navy from building by blocking the private bill which the Administration introduced for the purpose into Parliament.[4] In 1698, therefore, the first phase in the development of the yard was not quite complete; but enough had been done by then to make its completion only a matter of time.

Apart from the new yard at Plymouth, one other major work was begun after 1690. With the outbreak of war, Portsmouth had become

[1] P.R.O.Adm. 3/6: 30/3/92; 7/169, 7/175: annual estimates for the ordinary of the navy. [2] See p. 598 below.

[3] B.M.Addnl. 9329, ff. 161–2. The inconvenience had been noted as early as December 1691 (P.R.O.Adm. 3/6: 30/12).

[4] B.M.Addnl. 9329, f. 168*v*.

the obvious main base for the fleet to use in the summer, and the lessons of the first two campaigns had shown that it was also the most desirable base in the winter. In August 1689, the Admiralty raised the question, which had been originally considered in 1688, of the construction of a new dry dock in the yard to supplement the inadequate and decaying facilities then available, and in December William ordered that any dock built there should be capable of taking a first rate man-of-war.[1] For most of the following year, as in the case of Plymouth, nothing further was done; but in August 1690 the original scheme was enlarged, possibly following the model provided by the latter,[2] to include two basins as well as the original dry dock. In September the Navy Board sent in an estimate for the whole work, with an enthusiastic report on the advantages which would result from refitting a greater proportion of the fleet on the south coast.[3] In December it was ordered to put the scheme in hand.[4] But for almost a year it was unable to find a contractor owing to the bad state of naval credit, and it was only after 'much persuasion' that James Fitch agreed to undertake the work, on condition that he was given £2500 in tallies on the Excise as an advance and the rest according to the course of the navy.[5] The Navy Board promised that these terms would be honoured, and in October 1691 a contract was signed for the three docks, to cost £15,890 and to be completed in eighteen months.[6] In the event, after a protracted and bitter argument with the contractor, they were not ready for use until 1698.

Apart from this, there were constant but minor additions to the other yards. Some storesheds were added at Portsmouth, and a gunwharf was built on Blockhouse Point; some new ground, formerly occupied by the house of the Surveyor of the Navy, was added to the dockyard at Deptford; and workhouses, storesheds and cranes were erected there,

---

[1] P.R.O.Adm. 3/4: 27/8; 3/5: 15/12. See Vice Admiral Sir Henry Kitson, 'The Early History of Portsmouth Dockyard, 1496–1800, II', in *M.M.* XXXIV, no. 1, pp. 3–11.

[2] Dummer was concerned in the works at Portsmouth as well as Plymouth (see P.R.O.Adm. 1/3563, f. 627).

[3] P.R.O.Adm. 1/3562, ff. 405–6.

[4] P.R.O.Adm. 1/3564, f. 459.

[5] Ibid. ff. 459–60.

[6] P.R.O.Adm. 3/6: 7/10.

as well as at Chatham and Woolwich.[1] At Chatham, also, the apron and gates of the older of the two single dry docks were repaired.[2] The development of Sheerness, which was being used to capacity during these years, was more seriously considered; after the campaign of 1692, the Admiralty debated whether to build a dry dock there, and later it discussed plans to increase workmens' accommodation and to bring fresh water to the Isle of Sheppey.[3] But nothing came of these designs. The only other important extension to the base facilities during this period was the provision of a regular supply of ships' stores at Deal early in 1693, for the convenience of units lying in the Downs.[4] It was a small but definite link in the chain which now stretched, at least on paper, from the Thames to Ireland, with the traditional nucleus of the eastern dockyards now balanced, following the change in the direction of the war at sea, by the string of yards and bases along the south coast. By the beginning of 1695, the facilities which had served the Dutch wars of the seventeenth century had been extended to form the facilities which were to serve the French wars of the eighteenth century.

While the problem of adequately basing the fleet was thus being tackled, the fleet itself was enlarged. The first two years of the war had seen little major construction. Although 36 ships were added to the navy in that time, three had been rebuilt from earlier vessels, and sixteen either bought or captured. None of the prizes or bought ships, moreover, was larger than a fifth rate, and most of them were sixths and fireships. Of the seventeen ships built, one was launched in 1689 and the rest in 1690; but twelve of the latter were fireships, three of them fifth rates and one a fourth, while the solitary launching of the previous year was of a fifth rate.[5] The line itself, therefore, was almost exactly the same at the beginning of 1691 as it had been at the beginning of the war. In the same period, the Dutch, apart from hiring a few small ships, launched two 90-gun ships, two 72's, three 64's, three 50's, one 44, three 30–40's, three 20–30's, and three 10–20's: a total of twenty ships,

---

1 P.R.O.Adm. 3/4: 15/8, 14/11/90; 3/5: 27/3/91; 3/6: 19/8/91, 27/1, 28/3/92; 3/7: 27/5, 19/9/92; 3/8: 15/3, 6/7/93; 3/10: 2/5/94.

2 P.R.O.Adm. 2/173, f. 83.

3 P.R.O.Adm. 1/3567, f. 227; 2/172, ff. 443–4; 3/7: 24/8/92; 3/9: 27/3/94.

4 P.R.O.Adm. 1/3567, ff. 1155–6.

5 See Appendix II below.

of which eleven were of the line;[1] while the French fleet was increased by two first rates, five seconds, four thirds and one fourth—a total of twelve of the line—as well as by five fifths, eleven light frigates of 10–30 guns, nineteen light sloops of 10 guns and under, 22 galleys (of which ten were rebuilt) and eight storeships (all of which were built), and 25 fireships (all either bought or captured).[2] The allies, therefore, were falling behind the French in the race for superior numbers, and the English were falling behind their ally as well as their enemy.

At the end of 1690, it was realized that something should be done. On 15 December, a motion was raised in the House of Commons for an appropriation for building ten men-of-war,[3] and five days later the King's speech to Parliament referred to the desirability of such a supply to enable a programme of construction to be put in hand.[4] Without such a move on Parliament's part there was indeed little prospect of anything being done, for normally the cost of construction was included in wear and tear, and at a time of rising prices, when the estimates were more than usually overburdened, there was no money to spare for a large-scale shipbuilding programme. On Christmas Eve, however, the Commons resolved to act on the King's speech and to provide £570,000 for building 27 men-of-war.[5]

This supply was not the first Parliamentary grant of the war for such a purpose. In October 1690, when the annual supply for the navy had been debated, the naval estimates had included money specifically for building three new third rates, eight fireships and eight ketches, and this had been accepted as a supplement to the money vested for wear and tear.[6] In later years, also, similar estimates for individual ships were likewise agreed to in Parliament, and included as separate items in the annual supply.[7] But the grant of 1691 differed from these grants in that it was made by a separate Act[8] on a separate fund, and with its own terms. These terms were based on those of the Act's only predecessor,

---

1 *Soc. Naut. Research, Occas. Publns*, no. 5, pt IV, nos. 887–914.

2 Op. cit. pt II, nos. 110–11, 177–81, 252–5, 328, 395–9, 474–84, 578–602, 708–15, 789–806, 942–63.

3 *H.C.J.* x, p. 506. 4 Ibid. p. 515. 5 Ibid. p. 529.

6 P.R.O.Adm. 7/169, estimate of 8 October 1690; *H.C.J.* x, p. 492.

7 See the estimates in P.R.O.Adm. 7/169, and the grants in *H. of L. N.S.* I, pp. 12–13.

8 2 Will. and Mary sess. 2, c. 10.

the 'Act for the speedy building of thirty men-of-war' of 1677.[1] In both cases the money was supplied in the first instance for shipbuilding: in 1677 by a land tax, in 1691 by additional Excise duties on beer and other liquors. In both cases, too, the same stipulations were made for its handling and distribution: separate accounts on the fund were to be kept, all bills and tallies upon it registered in order, and no payments made upon it for any purpose other than that laid down in the Act. But in 1677 the supply, which amounted to £584,978, had been granted for two years, while in 1691 the smaller sum of £570,000 was to be raised within a space of four years from the passing of the Act. It might be expected, therefore, to form only a part of the total raised by the additional duties imposed for that period, and provision was made accordingly for purposes other than the shipbuilding programme itself. That programme, indeed, although specified as the reason for the Act, was not given the first claim upon it. The money that came in first on the fund was ear-marked for the last instalment of the debt of £600,000, part of which was still owing to the Dutch for the expenses of their invasion in 1688; and when that and the shipbuilding programme had been satisfied, the rest of the money, except for £50,000 which the Treasury could use as it pleased, was ear-marked for the normal naval grant of the year.[2]

In addition to laying down the conditions of payment, each Act defined the limitations of the shipbuilding programme itself. In 1677, it had been stipulated that the thirty ships were to be completed within the time in which the money was supplied, and thus within two years of 24 June of that year; in 1691, the 27 ships had likewise to be completed within four years of 25 March 1691.[3] In the later Act, moreover, the details of the programme were laid down. Of the 27 ships, seventeen were to be third rates, with a burthen of 1100 tons and 80 guns each; the other ten were to be fourth rates of 900 tons and 60 guns each.[4] It was significant that the first example of a Naval Defence Act in its later sense, in which the object of the supply as well as the supply itself was detailed, should have occurred by means of an appropriation.

The 80-gun third rates which were thus provided for in the grant,

---

[1] 29 Car. II, c. 1. [2] Articles v, xix, xxi of the Act.

[3] 29 Car. II, c. 1, art. xxxvi; 2 Will. and Mary sess. 2, c. 10, art. vi.

[4] Article v.

were the English reply to the French superiority in fighting power and general performance which had been demonstrated over the previous two years. With fewer guns to each deck, the latter held the advantage over their opponents at each rate throughout the fleet, since they always had the larger ship when gun-power was equal on either side. The 80-gun ship was an attempt to achieve the badly needed superiority of armament for size, at the stage where it would prove most useful: in the gap between the existing third rate, the largest class to be used for general purposes, and the second rate, which ranked with the leviathans of the line. She was meant to provide what naval architects have always tried to provide: a combination of fire-power and general utility, the armament of the class above her and the performance of the class below. In practice, she was a complete failure. In the attempt to retain the advantages of a two-decker, the eighty guns were mounted as the seventy had formerly been, so that the class was more overgunned than ever for its size and the defects which it was intended to offset were instead increased. The ships were even clumsier and more unstable than their predecessors, without the overwhelming addition in gun-power which to some extent justified a loss of manœuvrability.[1] Instead of dominating the classes below them they were drawn into the orbit of those above, as is the way with the unsuccessful hybrid. From the first it was obvious that they were a mistake, and after a long discussion of their demerits the last four of the class were built as three-deckers, thus definitely entering the ranks of the big ship. They had failed signally to meet the demand for which they were built, and all in all they represented the most expensive experiment of the war.

The administrative consequences were interesting. It was obvious that the royal dockyards, already working at full pressure, would be unable to tackle such a programme alone. Of the first batch of ships one was undertaken at Deptford and one at Portsmouth, but the rest were open to tender.[2] Phineas Pett, the contemporary representative of that apparently inexhaustible shipbuilding family, offered to build three of them on commission;[3] but his proposal was refused and the

---

[1] As Sir Henry Shere put it from his retreat in the Tower, they were 'great ungovernable Two-Decked Ships' (Bodl. Rawl. D 147, f. 34*v*).

[2] See Appendix III below.

[3] P.R.O.Adm. 3/6: 24/7/91.

normal practice retained of building by contract. Four shipbuilders were given five contracts between them in 1691; but of these only one had a yard in existence when his contract was signed, and he alone came from the traditional area for shipbuilding of the Thames.

This man was Edward Snellgrove of Redhouse, whose yard had been turning out men-of-war for some years;[1] and his contract was for the only fourth rate to be built in 1691. The other four ships were all thirds, and their builders all provincial men working on new sites where no yards existed at the time. The Winter brothers contracted for two ships to be constructed at Southampton, William Wyatt for one at Bursledon on the Hamble river off Southampton Water, and John Frame for one on the Humber.[2] The rest of the thirds which followed in the next three years were likewise built either in the royal dockyards or in the same three provincial shipyards. The eventual distribution of work was as follows:

Dockyards	Ships built	Shipyards	Ships built
Deptford	4	Southampton	3
Chatham	3	Bursledon	3
Portsmouth	2	Humber	2

In comparison, two of the ten fourth rates were built in dockyards, one each at Portsmouth and Sheerness; and the other eight in shipyards, four at Redhouse (Thames) and one each at Southampton, Bursledon, Humber and Bristol.[3]

This patronage of a limited number of new provincial yards was partly due to the fact that most of the existing Thames yards were already busy in 1691, and possibly also in part to the fact that the provincial builders from the start offered cheaper terms than the Thames builders, and could be kept under closer control.[4] But it was due mainly to the demands which the large thirds made upon the facilities of the private yard. According to their respective establishments, of 1677 and 1691, the old thirds of 70 guns had a burthen of 1013 tons, and the new 80-gun ships one of 1100 tons.[5] But in practice, the former varied between 950 and 1060 tons, and the latter between

[1] See *Soc. Naut. Research*, op. cit. pt I. [2] See Appendix III below.
[3] Ibid. [4] P.R.O.Adm. 106/411, John Winter to Navy Board, 15/1/91.
[5] Derrick, *Rise and Progress of the Royal Navy*, appendix XXIII.

1150 and 1200 tons.[1] Although they were still two-deckers, the new ships moreover were not only larger but more complicated than their predecessors. The subdivision of their internal space was more like that of a three-decker, and the class, as has been seen, finally became three-deckers in 1693. It marked the difference, which the class above had marked before, between the big ship and the medium rate; and no Thames yard had built a big ship for the navy since 1660.[2] The new yards, in this respect, were better placed to deal with the problem, for all were placed near deep water and with ready access to the sea. In comparison, the new fourth rates presented no difficulties of construction. Their 60 guns and 900 tons by establishment compared with a traditional maximum of 50 guns and 704 tons, and in practice these figures were not greatly exceeded.[3] They were well within the capacity of any of the regular Thames yards to build, and it was not for material but financial reasons that they were handled by only one yard in the river. In the event, like the third rates, they proved unstable and disappointing, although not to the same degree.[4] The Act for the 27 ships had also stipulated that, out of the money applied to the navy after the initial appropriations had been met, three 70-gun third rates should be laid down of approximately 1050 tons, to be completed within a year of 25 March 1691.[5] Two of these were built at Harwich, and one in the royal yard at Woolwich.[6]

The fact that the 27 ships were being built not only upon one programme, but largely in a group of yards founded under identical conditions, gave a certain uniformity to the terms of their construction. In the negotiations which took place between the Navy Board and the three shipbuilders the former had the advantage, acting as it did as patron to the new ventures. As a result the provincial rates were cheap

---

1 See *Soc. Naut. Research*, op. cit. pt I.

2 Ibid.

3 Derrick, loc. cit.; *Soc. Naut. Research*, loc. cit.

4 Robinson, loc. cit. p. 134.

5 Articles xix, xx. It is for this reason that the programme of 1691 is sometimes stated to have been one of thirty ships. But these three third rates were on a different fund and a different programme from the 27 which were mentioned in separate clauses of the same statute. On the other hand, the material for their construction was contracted for with that of the other ships.

6 They were the *Bredah*, *Ipswich* and *Yarmouth* (Serg.Misc. IV, f. 141).

compared with those of the Thames. The thirds contracted for in the Southampton district were all built at £11. 2*s*. 6*d*. per ton, and those on the Humber at £11. 5*s*. per ton,[1] and the builders bore the cost of transporting any gear and stores that had to be shipped to the site by the navy.[2] In turn, they were to be paid in seven instalments, each made at a different stage in the construction of the ship, with the first falling due on the signing of the contract, the second when the ship had been framed, the third on the completion of the gun deck and the planking to that level, the fourth when the planking had been carried to the upper deck and its beams had been laid, the fifth when that deck had been laid and the upperworks planked, the sixth when the half- and quarter-decks and forecastle had been laid, and the final instalment when the ship had been launched and dispatched on her way to the dockyard with the stores for the passage aboard. The individual amounts to be paid varied according to the financial conditions of the time rather than according to the total price. For each of the first batch of ships, the first payment was £1500, the next four £2000, and the last two £1000 each. Any money which was still due after this was to be paid within six weeks of the seventh issue. Later, the amounts fluctuated slightly but the order remained much the same, rising from a minimum of £1500 for the first payment to a maximum of £2000 in the middle instalments, and then falling to £1000 at the end. This represented roughly the proportion of expenditure at the different stages of construction, so that on paper it was a satisfactory arrangement; and in the event of an instalment not having been paid within three months of the date on which it was due, and later within six months of that date, the builder moreover received interest on it at six per cent. The terms for the fourth rates were similar, the provincial prices being noticeably lower than Snellgrove's—£10. 2*s*. 6*d*. in the Southampton area and on the Humber, £9. 15*s*. at Bristol, but £11 at Redhouse—and the instalments being usually, in order of payment, two lots of £1500, then one of £1000, and then alternately £1500 and £1000 for the rest of the seven payments. The terms for interest were the same as for the thirds at the same date.

[1] See Appendix III below.

[2] Some of the individual contracts may be found in the bundles in P.R.O.Adm. 106/3069–3071. The following details are taken from these contracts, and from the authorities cited in Appendix III below.

It is almost unnecessary to say that these arrangements to a great extent existed only on paper, and that the practice fell far short of the theory. A programme which was so largely in the hands of contractors who depended heavily on naval support, was bound to suffer in a period of financial stringency. How far Winter and Wyatt built merchant ships as well as their few men-of-war is not known. Wyatt probably did so later, for his yard continued well into the eighteenth century, and it could hardly have done so on naval custom alone.[1] But in the early 1690's, both firms relied largely, if not exclusively, on the navy. In both cases, the yards were founded when the contracts had been obtained, on sites chosen to suit the construction of the new thirds.[2] Frame's project on the Humber depended, if anything, even more directly upon naval support. He himself was a London shipbuilder,[3] who assembled his yard in the north only after his tender for a third rate had been accepted;[4] and peculiarly placed as the site was, with its great distance from any centre of supply for naval stores, and the long and dangerous voyage through the privateer-infested North Sea before the newly-launched and unarmed vessel could be delivered to the nearest dockyard, it can have been chosen only on the expectation of some regular official custom. In all three cases, therefore, large ships were being built in small *ad hoc* yards relying on naval assistance. Whenever that assistance was not forthcoming, the contractors suffered severely and at once.

It was not long before their payments fell into arrears. By the autumn, Winter and Wyatt were in sad need of money; their men were deserting, they could not buy materials, and they began to doubt whether they could comply with their contracts.[5] According to their agreements the ships were to be launched in fifteen months,[6] and in the event both builders succeeded in fulfilling their promises.[7] But Wyatt

---

[1] Henry Adams, who started a shipyard at Bucklers Hard in the 1720's (see p. 72 above), came straight from Wyatt's yard at Bursledon (Montagu, *Bucklers Hard and Its Ships*).

[2] P.R.O.Adm. 106/411, John Winter to Navy Board, 15/1, 12/2/91: Wyatt to John Winter, 12/3/91; Serg:Mins. XXII, 20/2, 27/2/91.

[3] B.M.Addnl. 9324, f. 6.

[4] Serg:Mins. XXIII, 2/3/91.

[5] P.R.O.Adm. 106/425: John Winter's letter of 30/8, Wyatt's letter of 8/10/91.

[6] Serg:Mins. XXII, 20/2/91.

[7] See Appendix III below.

did so only by sending his third rate to Portsmouth in an unfinished state, and he was promptly informed by the navy that one-tenth of his bill would be deducted.[1] Frame was at once in trouble on the Humber. The local justices of the peace refused to let him cart timber in the area, and the local landowners—doubtless in some cases the same men—frightened many of the workmen away who might otherwise have come.[2] Frame himself was not finding it easy to supervise the work, for he continued to live for most of the time in London and paid only flying visits to the north.[3] Money soon ran short in his case as with the southern ventures, and while the contract stipulated that his third rate should be launched in twelve months from the laying of the keel,[4] it was actually a few days over two years before she finally took to the water.[5] These results were repeated with the later batch of thirds, laid down in the spring and summer of 1693: Wyatt turned his out in thirteen months, the Winters theirs in eighteen months, and Frame his in 25 months.[6] In each case, the builder was pleading desperately for money throughout the period of construction.[7]

It was much the same with the fourth rates. Snellgrove launched his four vessels at the rate of one in fifteen months, two in ten months, and the last in twelve months, whereas his contracts stipulated for eight months in each case.[8] Wyatt turned out his fourth in fifteen months, the Winters theirs in eleven months, the Bristol builder, Clemence, took 23 months over his, and Frame took 31 months on the Humber.[9] In the event, of the eighteen contract-built ships, all of which should by statute have been completed by 25 March 1695, fourteen had been

---

[1] Ibid.; P.R.O.Adm. 106/425, Wyatt's letter of 6/10/92.

[2] P.R.O.Adm. 106/404, Frame to Navy Board, 7/9, 6/10, 7/12/91; 106/417, 17/1/92; 106/431, 30/1, 6/2/93.

[3] P.R.O.Adm. 106/417, Frame's letters of 6/3, 15/5/92; 106/431, 10/4/93.

[4] P.R.O.Adm. 3069, contract for the *Humber*.

[5] See Appendix III below. [6] Ibid.

[7] P.R.O.Adm. 106/425, Wyatt's letter of 26/7/92, John Winter's of 9/9/92; 106/441, Mrs Wyatt's of 2/7/93; 106/431, Frame's of 20/3, 24/10/93; Serg:Mins. XXVIII, 29/11, 11/12/94.

[8] See Appendix III below; P.R.O.Adm. 106/3070, 3071, contracts of the *Canterbury* and *Pembroke*; Serg:Mins. XXIX, 8/1/94.

[9] See Appendix III below.

launched by then and two thirds and two fourths remained in the yards. The last of these appeared only six months before the war came to an end.[1]

The royal dockyards, on the other hand, did not do much better. Although in one way they were better placed than the contractors, in that they could, and often did call on material in store[2] when money on the fund itself was running short, the shortage affected them too. They were also subject to other interruptions, when labour had to be put on to other and more urgent tasks, from which the private yards were largely free. Of the eleven ships for which they were responsible in the programme, four—three third rates and one fourth—had not been launched by 25 March 1695, and indeed three of these had probably not been laid down by that date; while of the other seven, three had been launched only within six weeks of that date.[3] The complaints from the royal yards were naturally included in complaints on more general grounds, which the private builders did not have occasion to make, and for the same reason the effects of the financial stringency on one particular fund were in this case less obvious. Nevertheless, although details are harder to ascertain, it is clear that the dockyards received no greater stimulus to complete the programme than did the shipyards, and the results in both cases were much the same.

The delay in the payments which led to this delay in construction, and to the interval between the completion of the first group of ships and the beginning of the second group, was due as usual to the difference between the Commons' estimate of the yield on the additional Excise and the rate at which it actually came in. As early as December 1691, the Admiralty was informing the Treasury that the programme was falling behind owing to lack of money,[4] and a year later, when the specified time was almost half completed and only four ships had been launched,[5] it began to send serious warnings of a breakdown unless the supplies came in more quickly.[6] These seem to have had an effect, for whereas only £47,936 had been paid to the Treasurer of the Navy on the Excise up to the end of March 1692, in the following year £112,200 was issued, mostly in the first three months of 1693. After that the

---

[1] See Appendix III below.
[2] P.R.O.Adm. 20/57.
[3] See Appendix III below.
[4] P.R.O.Adm. 3/6: 14/12.
[5] See Appendix III below.
[6] P.R.O.Adm. 3/8: 17/12/92, 27/3, 12/5/93.

issues, while still inadequate, were more regular: £77,700 from Lady Day 1693 to Lady Day 1694, £80,400 from 1694 to 1695, £71,154 in 1695–6, £31,660 from Lady Day to Christmas Day 1696, and £61,410 from 26 December 1696 to 25 December 1697.[1] By Lady Day 1695, in fact, when the last payment should have been made, only £318,236 had been issued from the Exchequer. In this period the navy should theoretically have received £485,744 out of the £570,000, the other £84,256 going to the Ordnance.[2]

The effect of this slow rate of payment was the more marked in that the cost of the programme, thanks to the low prices imposed by the navy upon most of the contractors, was kept almost to the figure first laid down. The separate accounts for the 27 ships, when finally submitted at the end of the century, showed a total expenditure by the navy of £485,897, or only £153 more than its original allowance.[3] How closely the Ordnance kept to its limits, I do not know.[4] The main shipbuilding programme of the war was in fact a good example, without the complicating factor of excessive expenditure to be considered, of the deficiencies of a Parliamentary fund applied to a specific purpose, operating upon private concerns and a government department alike, and relying upon anticipated revenue without the benefit of an accepted and negotiable means of credit.

The strategic emphasis on the great fleet in 1691–2, and the physical expansion of naval resources from 1691 to 1694, each led during this period to new developments in naval organization. At sea, a new stage was reached in the formulation of fleet tactics, which were brought by the summer of 1691 to the pitch at which they stayed almost unchanged until the War of American Independence.[5] Based upon the Duke of

---

[1] P.R.O.Adm. 20/57. [2] *Cal.Treas.Bks. 1689–92*, pp. 1269–70.

[3] P.R.O.Adm. 20/57. £3438 of this was paid in interest, after the deductions had been made from the shipbuilders' bills for defective workmanship and stores delivered short. These deductions came to almost £2000.

[4] I have been unable, on a cursory investigation, to find the ordnance accounts on this fund, which should have been kept on their own. But I have not looked thoroughly for them, and they doubtless exist in the War Office papers at the P.R.O.

[5] Corbett, *Fighting Instructions*, p. 175. The following account is based on Corbett's introduction to Russell's Instructions and to others of the same period (pp. 175–87), on

York's Instructions of 1673, the new orders emphasized the formal element of the line to the almost total exclusion of the squadronal tactics which had been appearing in those of the third Dutch war, and represented in its final form the reliance upon massed gunpower as opposed to manœuvrability. The line was never to be broken in an attempt to break the enemy's line, and the superiority which was thus denied through squadronal initiative was sought in the elaboration of line tactics themselves, particularly in the manœuvre of doubling upon the enemy in an unbroken succession of squadrons and subdivisions. These refinements appeared explicitly for the first time in Russell's Instructions of 1691, which Corbett has characterized as 'sagacious', and 'dominating' in the history of sailing-ship tactics.[1] They were not, however, necessarily his own work. Between 1689, when the instructions issued to the fleet were much the same as those of 1673, and 1691 when the new orders appeared, a set of instructions had been issued of which a copy has become available in recent years, and which anticipated the contents of the later orders in almost every respect. It would seem probable that these instructions were the work of Torrington, designed for the campaign of 1690, and that the possible author of the remarks upon the orders of 1673[2] had thus assembled his conclusions when called upon to put his theories into practice.[3] This similarity between the two separate sets of orders illustrated the contemporary position: the tactical instructions to the fleet did not yet form a permanent code which was added to or modified on experience by the Admiralty itself, but still represented simply the individual orders of the Commander in Chief for the year, according to his own tactical conceptions;[4] but the stage had now been reached when the size of the

---

the text of the Instructions themselves (pp. 188–94), and on R. C. Anderson, 'Two new sets of Fighting Instructions', in *M.M.* VI, no. 5, pp. 130–5.

[1] Loc. cit. pp. 176, 187. [2] See p. 276, n. 6 above.

[3] Ibid. Corbett, who did not know of the existence of these Instructions, remarked with his usual prescience that 'in all probability they [Russell's Instructions] followed more or less closely those used by Lord Torrington in the previous year' (loc. cit. p. 187).

[4] The Instructions were always the work of the individual commander in chief, to judge from the differences between Dartmouth's orders of 1688 (*Fighting Instructions*, pp. 168–72), those of 1689, those probably issued in 1690 (Anderson, loc. cit.) and those of 1691.

fleet forced all commanders to adopt virtually the same tactics, and made it necessary for them to issue a standard set of signals and orders which, even if theoretically their own responsibility, were coming to be regarded as the permanent property of the fleet.[1]

Ashore, the developments in organization were of two main kinds: those affecting the personnel of the navy, both officers and men; and those affecting its system of accountancy and financial management. The first group of developments may in turn be assembled under three heads: the changes in the organization of medical welfare, those in the conditions of service for the seamen, and those in the conditions of service for the officers.

The continual loss of men from sickness in the fleet, and the inadequacy of the administrative and medical facilities ashore, began to worry the navy in 1690. In October of that year the Navy Board was ordered to consider what steps could be taken to improve the men's health afloat,[2] and early in December a certain Dr Lower was asked to report on the organization of the department for Sick and Wounded. His answer was extremely discouraging, revealing as it did the unsatisfactory state both of the provincial sick quarters and of the London hospitals which, owing to the fact that they were required to bear the expense of the quota of naval seamen allotted to them,[3] were inclined to turn them out on the streets after a distinctly perfunctory treatment. Tower Hill, for example, which was a particularly well-known rendezvous for seamen, was always full of cripples and wounded men 'lying there till there were Maggotts in their wounds'.[4] A month after Lower had reported, he was accordingly asked to investigate the possibility of setting up a new hospital for naval seamen;[5] and as a result he suggested that six such hospitals should be established, at Carisbrooke Castle in the Isle of Wight, Dover Castle, Liverpool, Plymouth, Chatham and

---

[1] Russell's signals in the Instructions of 1691 were repeated in subsequent sets of orders (Perrin, *British Flags*, p. 163). For the continuity of flag signals after that date, the signal book belonging to Captain Graydon in 1693 (Bodl. Rawl. C 512) may be compared with the first printed signal book of 1714. The French also issued their first comprehensive signal manual at this period, in 1693.

[2] P.R.O.Adm. 3/4: 31/10.

[3] See p. 126 above.

[4] P.R.O.Adm. 3/5: 5/12.

[5] Ibid. 7/1/91.

Greenwich.[1] The Admiralty decided to inspect two places, Carisbrooke Castle and 'the King's house at Greenwich'.[2] By June 1691, a survey had been made of the latter; and on 1 June, the Commissioners for Sick and Wounded were ordered to attend the Treasury to report on the expense of converting 'the house'[3] into a naval hospital.[4] In the next few weeks the arrangements must have gone ahead, for on 10 July the Lords of the Treasury were requested to ask the Queen for a warrant to employ 'the House at Greenwich and Carisbrooke Castle for Hospitalls for the Seamen'.[5] On the same day they were able to reply that she had given her permission for Greenwich to be so used and had suggested that, since 'the house and ground must be settled on some corporation or trustees capable to take a grant of the inheritance', the corporation of Trinity House at Deptford should occupy this position.[6] This was soon agreed,[7] and the Commissioners for Sick and Wounded were directed to put an agent into the house to look after it for the time being.[8] The navy, however, had not been placed in sole or permanent charge of the buildings. Almost immediately after these arrangements had been made, the Ordnance was allowed to store its powder there, and it continued to do so for the rest of the year.[9] For almost a year, indeed, little seems to have been done other than to complete the new block of buildings begun by Charles II;[10] but in March 1692, with the advent of a new campaigning season and the prospect of an invasion of France, the plan was again brought to the fore.[11] Nothing, however, had been

---

[1] B.M.Addnl. 11602, f. 5.

[2] P.R.O.Adm. 3/5: 9/1. Richard Gibson afterwards claimed that it was he who first suggested the use of Greenwich to Lower, 'as is well known to my Lord Orford [then Russell]; Doctor Hutton; Mr. Baker of the Treasury-Chamber; Mr. Pawlin late of the Stamp-Office; and others' (B.M.Addnl. 11602, f. 1).

[3] Whether this referred to the whole of the palace I do not know. From the comparable size of Carisbrooke, and from the fact that the palace seemed usually to be referred to in this way (*Cal.Treas.Bks. 1689–92*, pp. 601, 1064), I presume that it did.

[4] P.R.O.Adm. 3/6: 1/6.

[5] Ibid. 10/7.

[6] *Cal.Treas.Bks. 1689–92*, p. 1226.

[7] P.R.O.Adm. 3/6: 17/7.

[8] P.R.O.Adm. 2/381, 21/7.

[9] *Cal.Treas.Bks. 1689–92*, p. 1279; P.R.O.Adm. 3/6: 31/7; P.R.O.Adm. 1/4080, f. 83.

[10] P.R.O.Adm. 3/6: 8/2, 10/2/92; *Cal.Treas.Bks. 1689–92*, pp. 1731, 1756.

[11] P.R.O.Adm. 3/6: 23/3.

done by the end of May, when Barfleur was fought, and the casualties had once more to be set ashore in the same unsatisfactory quarters as before.[1] But in October, Mary, who took a personal interest in the fate of the wounded, decided to transform the limited project of the previous year into a naval hospital which had sole rights over and an uninterrupted use of the palace. On the 18th, the Admiralty learned of her decision, and was informed that 'an adjacent piece of ground which is convenient for that service' was to be attached to the hospital.[2]

In the winter the navy got to work to convert the buildings to their new service. Drafts were made of the plans, and these were considered exhaustively by the three bodies concerned, the Admiralty, the Navy Board and the Commissioners for Sick and Wounded.[3] At the turn of the year, a joint expedition was planned by all three, accompanied by representatives of the College of Physicians, the Admiralty Surveyor and the Surveyor General of the Works, Sir Christopher Wren, 'to sett out the ground of the intended hospitall'.[4] But the visit was somehow never made, and after a series of postponements[5] the whole idea once more faded into the background. No mention of it was made again until July 1693, and then only when the plan of the ground was once more examined at the Admiralty.[6] There seems indeed to have been some legal difficulty over the extent of the property, for the Admiralty Solicitor was called in during December to submit a report on this question to the Queen, while the Admiralty Board itself raised 'the matter of the Hospitall' at one of their meetings with the King during the same month.[7] Nothing more was heard of Greenwich for almost a year, and there is no evidence that any seamen were accommodated there during this time. In the autumn of 1694 however, the project was raised again, and now at last with success. By patents of

---

[1] The number of casualties after the battle is usually given as the cause for Mary's foundation of Greenwich Hospital; in view of the evidence given above, it would seem to have been the final incentive to a development that had been under way for some time.

[2] *Cal.Treas.Bks. 1689–92*, p. 1870; A. G. L'Estrange, *The Palace and the Hospital*, II (2 vols., 1886), p. 84.

[3] P.R.O.Adm. 3/7: 7/11, 22/11.

[4] P.R.O.Adm. 3/8: 30/12.

[5] Ibid. 2/1, 6/1, 9/1, 11/1, 18/1.

[6] Ibid. 5/7.

[7] P.R.O.Adm. 3/9: 20/12.

10 September and 25 October, the extent of the hospital's ground was defined as some eight acres, and the property was placed in the hands of independent trustees;[1] and in the following February, to commemorate the death of Mary two months before, William transformed the whole plan into the magnificent monument which we know to-day, which he designed not only as a hospital for sick and wounded seamen but also as a home for pensioners and for the dependents of the disabled and the slain. To this end, Commissioners were appointed 'to consider how far the present buildings will be unfit for the Hospital hereby intended to be erected and how far to alter such as shall be thought fit to stand'; the foundation was endowed with £2000 from the King's purse; and an appeal was launched for voluntary contributions, with John Evelyn as its treasurer.[2] The next year the first of the new buildings started to rise from the plans of Sir Christopher Wren, and the long process had begun which, after Vanbrugh, James Stuart, and Hawksmoor had added their contributions to the original design, was by 1752 to stand, 'the apotheosis of secular glory',[3] as an unequalled monument to English sea power. It was not inappropriate that its uncertain preliminaries and its eventual foundation should have taken place during the decisive years in the first of the decisive wars for maritime supremacy.

With the foundation of Greenwich, absorbing as it did all available energy and finance, the plans for other hospitals were dropped; and indeed, from this point of view, it was not an unmixed blessing. The conversion of Carisbrooke Castle, which had been part of the original scheme, had been lost sight of by 1694,[4] and a proposal in 1692 to establish a supplementary hospital in London, in the Savoy, came to nothing.[5] The old sick quarters continued to be used; the authorities continued to worry, as they had worried at the start of the investigations

---

[1] Admty:Corbett, xx, f. 1; for the details of the warrant, see *Cal.Treas.Bks. 1693–6*, pp. 796–7.

[2] *Cal.Treas.Bks. 1693–6*, pp. 925–6.

[3] D. Mathew, *The Naval Heritage* (1945), p. 62.

[4] So long as Greenwich was connected with Trinity House, Carisbrooke was nominally considered as a hospital, for the Brethren were given powers over both (*Cal.Treas.Bks. 1689–92*, p. 1666). But with the appointment of trustees for Greenwich in 1694, Carisbrooke was separated from it and disappeared altogether.

[5] P.R.O.Adm. 3/7: 9/11, 3/10, 29/6, 23/8.

which led to the eventual establishment of Greenwich, over the loss of men who deserted after being discharged from them; and in times of crisis, the old alternatives were practised when the lodgings could not take the numbers set ashore, and the men put into taverns and at least on one occasion into tents.[1] In another direction, however, there was some improvement. The membership of the medical department itself was enlarged during this period. In 1691, surgeons were appointed to the three smaller yards, which hitherto had been without them, and paid, as were their colleagues in the other yards and afloat, partly by daily wage and partly by an allowance for the number of men treated.[2] In the same year, a physician was appointed to supervise the medical arrangements in all the yards, with a travelling allowance to enable him to visit each of them personally and a seat on the Commission for Sick and Wounded to give him the necessary authority.[3] In 1691, also, physicians were appointed to the fleet and to certain coastal bases and sick quarters.[4] On 27 March the Admiralty decided to send one each to the two main squadrons of the battle-fleet, at a wage of £1 per day, and some to various ports which were not yet specified, at £200 a year. At the same time it requested the College of Physicians in future to select the men for the posts.[5] In April the first batch was appointed, one physician going to the blue squadron, one to the red, and four to ports on the east and south coasts;[6] and this arrangement lasted until the end of the war. To these years also belongs the introduction of the regular hospital ship to accompany the fleet, with the hiring of the *Concord* and *Society* in 1690. In 1691 a further two vessels were hired for the purpose, making four hospital ships in all, and this was repeated in 1692. From 1693 to the end of the war there were never less than five. Before this period, there had been only eight years between 1608 and 1688 in which such ships had been put to sea at all, and then only one on each occasion.[7] Their equipment was improved

---

1 P.R.O.Adm. 3/9: 29/12.

2 P.R.O.Adm. 7/169, no. 9; Admty:Corbett, XIII, ff. 21, 111.

3 Admty:Corbett, XIII, f. 11; P.R.O. T. 38/615.

4 Russell had asked for them early in March (P.R.O.Adm. 3/5: 2/3, 4/3).

5 P.R.O.Adm. 2/171, f. 211; 3/5: 27/3.

6 P.R.O.Adm. 3/5: 13/4.

7 Sutherland Shaw, 'The Hospital Ship, 1608–1740' in *M.M.* XXII, no. 4, p. 426. The officers were paid as for a fifth rate; the freight was 8*s*. per ton; the owners found

in 1691, when the allowances for surgeons' chests were raised on the average by a quarter from those of the previous year.[1] But while these measures are evidence of an attempt on the part of the navy to alleviate the misery of the sick and wounded, they did little to remove the basic causes of their misery, which improved medical science and improved administration alone could mitigate. The inherent defects of the medical department were brought increasingly to light as the money available for it grew shorter at the end of the period now under review; and in 1694 a long and circumstantial report by two naval surgeons, William Lecky and William Barton, emphasized the necessity for its complete reorganization, and started a vigorous controversy which, conducted over the following years of financial stringency, exhibited but could not modify the shortcomings.[2]

Another group of administrative reforms, undertaken at the same time, was of far-reaching consequence. One of the drawbacks to the use of the great fleet was that it took so long to fit out in the winter. In the winter of 1690–1, and again in 1691–2, the dockyards were strained to their utmost; and although on each occasion they managed to put the ships to sea at much the same time as the main French fleet, and were indeed congratulated for their work in the spring of 1691 by the Commander in Chief,[3] it was only by pressing all the workmen that they could lay hands on and by employing as many Marines as could be quartered near the dockyard towns.[4] If the graph in Appendix V (A) is examined, it will be seen how steeply the numbers rose in those two winters. One of the aggravating causes of this pressure was that the seamen, who by custom were supposed to help refit their own ships so long as they were aboard, were often refusing

---

the ship's ordnance and ammunition and maintained her hull and fittings, while the navy found the medical supplies and the crew; and in the event of her being sunk or captured by the enemy, the owners received compensation (Admty:Corbett, XIII, f. 70). A hospital ship was also sent to the West Indies for the first time in 1691 (P.R.O.Adm. 3/7: 26/8, 13/9).

[1] Admty:Corbett, XIII, f. 107.

[2] The original of the report is contained in N.M.M., Bibl. Phill., VI, ff. 177–9.

[3] P.R.O.Adm. 3/5: 9/1.

[4] Ibid. 26/1.

to do so;[1] but even when they worked as required they were not all available, at least during the first of these winters, for in the autumn, when the first four rates of the fleet returned to harbour, the crews were paid off until the following spring and the whole burden of the refit fell upon the yards. If any men remained aboard, it was only because there was not enough money to get rid of them, so that thcy were hardly in the mood to work for wages that did not appear.

The Admiralty was well aware of the defects of this arrangement. Not only did the lack of seamen affect the dockyards in the winter; it also seriously affected the date at which the ships were able to sail in the spring. Time and again a vessel that was ready to clear the yard in March was held there, to the fury of the dockyard officers and of the Admiralty, until April or even May, while the countryside was scoured for the men who had failed to respond to the offer of the royal bounty. In September 1690, after the experience of the first winter of war, the Admiralty requested the King to allow a proportion of each crew to be kept aboard the ships then coming in to refit,[2] and ordered the Navy Board, when paying off the crews, to inquire of them whether a hundred men would be willing to stay aboard all winter on half pay, with leave of absence granted to fifty men at a time. But the reply was most discouraging, for the pressed men regarded any such service as an attempt to deprive them of their one chance of temporary freedom. The matter was therefore dropped for the year.[3] In the summer of 1691, Russell raised it again from sea,[4] and as a result the Admiralty set on foot another of the rather hopeless inquiries into the sources of naval manpower which were characteristic of the later seventeenth century, and once more inquired of the solicitor to the Board whether it did not possess the legal right to compile some sort of register of seamen.[5] Such queries never had any success; but they were followed in the winter by a significant measure, when the crews of the third rates refitting in harbour were directed to stay aboard their ships in full pay until the spring, taking their leave by turns.[6] The first two rates still paid off their

---

[1] P.R.O.Adm. 1/3567, ff. 709–12.
[2] P.R.O.Adm. 3/4: 19/9.
[3] P.R.O.Adm. 2/170, f. 399; 3/4: 3/11.
[4] P.R.O.Adm. 3/5: 1/6.
[5] Ibid. 22/6; Serg.Misc. v, f. 457; Admty:Corbett, x, f. 89.
[6] P.R.O.Adm. 1/3566, f. 832.

men, and were manned between February and May with the usual inefficiency.[1]

The battle-fleet of 1692 was so large, and much of its manning had proved so difficult, that as soon as it was at sea a discussion began over the measures to be taken for the next year. At first this turned, as in the previous summer, on the sources of manpower. The possibility of a register, the numbers to be extracted from Scotland, and the chances of pressing in Ireland were all raised, as usual with no success.[2] The excitement of the summer campaign relegated the more distant problems to the background, but in August the question of manning again became prominent, and this time with some results. On the 19th, the Admiralty debated the possibility of keeping the first two rates in sea pay for the whole of the year, and the Navy Board was ordered to report on all aspects of the question.[3] By the 30th the senior Board had decided to carry out the reform, and on 1 September it reported its intention to the Cabinet.[4] During the next three weeks the Navy Board was busy working out the consequences, and the Admiralty was discussing them with the Cabinet.[5] By 13 October, all was ready for Nottingham to move the Queen to issue the necessary proclamation,[6] and the next day it appeared, setting out the causes for the change in procedure and dividing the crews into two watches for leave, the first being sent away until 20 December and the second from then until 1 February.[7]

The decision to keep the men aboard the great ships raised its own problems. Allowing them as it did some freedom of movement by sending them on leave, its success depended upon the extent to which they were willing to return to conditions of employment which for the most part they detested. To induce them to do so, the usual financial pressure was applied, and the men were informed that if they stayed away they would lose all the wages still owing to them and furthermore

---

[1] P.R.O.Adm. 3/5: 20/1, 20/4. See the figures for the first and second rates from 7 January to 30 April, in P.R.O.Adm. 1/3567, f. 123.

[2] P.R.O.Adm. 3/7: 27/4, 29/4; Serg.Misc. v, f. 457.

[3] P.R.O.Adm. 3/7: 19/8; 2/172, ff. 359–60.

[4] P.R.O.Adm. 3/7: 30/8, 1/9.

[5] P.R.O.Adm. 1/3566, ff. 968–74; 1/3567, ff. 122–3; 2/172, ff. 406, 416; 2/382, Admiralty to Navy Board, 10/9; 3/7: 13/9, 16/9, 19/9.

[6] P.R.O.Adm. 3/7: 13/10.

[7] *London Gazette*, no. 2811.

would be treated as deserters.[1] Even so there was a strong possibility that many would not come back. As the Navy Board informed the Admiralty, the general opinion on winter service had been clear enough in 1690, and it had been borne out by the experience of the following year, when the third rates had lost so many men on leave that during the next spring their manning proved hardly less expensive than before.[2] The consequences in administration alone, moreover—the extra book-keeping that would have to be done to deduct the wages and victuals, and the complications that would arise in disposing of the latter—would largely offset the advantages to be expected in other ways; while the additional cost for the winter of 1692–3 was estimated at £41,171.[3] On the other hand, the Navy Board recognized that, however many men deserted, it should be possible to count on a nucleus of the crew being available in the early spring, so that whatever the expense of providing the rest the ship herself could get clear of the yard; and besides relieving the workmen of some of their duties aboard, the presence of even this nucleus would enable much of the standing rigging and tackle to be left up which formerly was taken down for the winter.[4] Balancing the advantages with the disadvantages, however, the Commissioners were not hopeful of the issue.

The immediate results were all that and more than the Navy Board had feared. When the Commissioner at Chatham read the proclamation of 14 October to the assembled crews, they left the yard in a body, and, after giving vent to their feelings by looting the neighbourhood, returned very drunk and tore down the copies which had been posted in various places.[5] The riot grew so dangerous, and the men continued so recalcitrant, that after two days another proclamation had to be issued to indemnify them against any damage caused to the surrounding buildings.[6] The crews of the big ships in Delavall's squadron at Spithead also mutinied promptly,[7] and in November, so far from the workmen being assisted by the seamen, at Chatham at least not only did the ships' companies refuse to help, but in many cases they prevented the yard

[1] Ibid.; P.R.O.Adm. 1/3566, f. 853.

[2] Ibid. ff. 852–3.

[3] P.R.O.Adm. 1/3567, f. 123. This does not allow for any deductions that might be made from wages becoming forfeit on desertion.

[4] P.R.O.Adm. 1/3566, ff. 968–9.

[5] P.R.O.Adm. 1/3567, ff. 447–8.

[6] Ibid. f. 511.

[7] P.R.O.Adm. 3/7: 27/10.

from going ahead with the work.[1] Throughout that month, the desertions rose at an alarming rate, and on the 23rd the Admiralty was forced to apply to the Privy Council for power to modify the terms of the proclamation, so as to defer the punishments which by its clauses were already falling due upon the seamen of the first and second rates. The memorandum on this occasion touched on the weak point of the measure: that as the delays in the refits—which might follow from the disobedience of their crews—increased, the ships' companies demanded and had to be given longer leave, and thus the incentive to postpone the punishment of deserters grew as the chances of their return were theoretically multiplied.[2] The date on which the wages of the first batch for leave became forfeit was pushed back from 20 December to 20 January, from 20 January to 1 February, and from 1 February to 20 February.[3] Meanwhile, many seamen were returning late from leave with excuses of varying probability, and the problem of deciding when to punish them by the traditional 'mulcts' (which formed a sliding scale by which a man forfeited part of his pay to Chatham Chest) and when not to do so, was proving too complicated for it always to be referred, as the orders for the 'mulcts' stipulated, to the Navy Office.[4] Similarly, the problem of when to postpone the date for the forfeiture of wages, which depended on how long there was a chance of the men returning to the ship, was one which only the officials on the spot could decide, and varied from case to case. In March 1693, therefore, the flag officers at Chatham submitted that they should be given the right to decide and to promulgate the orders on these points, and for the rest of the spring a long and wordy argument took place between them and the Navy Board, the former basing their claims upon expediency and the latter, in the end successfully, upon its legal rights.[5] At the same time, the bounty had to be offered and the press put into operation to man the great ships, on almost the same scale as before.[6]

---

[1] P.R.O.Adm. 1/3567, ff. 709–22. [2] P.R.O.Adm. 2/173, f. 23.

[3] P.R.O.Adm. 3/8: 4/1, 3/2, 8/2/93.

[4] P.R.O.Adm. 1/3568, ff. 608–9. The mulcts and the conditions of imposing them were laid down by orders of 29 April 1667 and 22 January 1668 (see P.R.O.Adm. 49/132).

[5] Ibid. ff. 608–12; 3/8: 16/3; 1/577, 3/4/93.

[6] P.R.O.Adm. 3/8: 6/2, 29/3.

The same process occurred in the next two years. The proclamation was issued, the men duly and promptly mutinied, deserted and misbehaved themselves ashore,[1] the dockyards found that they could expect no help from the ships' companies,[2] the Admiralty postponed the date of punishment throughout the winter, and in the spring the bounty and the press were put into effect at the same time as the additional wages for winter service, the savings on which should have gone to help pay for the other methods of manning the ships, were distributed to men who had done little to deserve them.[3] As a later Secretary of the Admiralty remarked, looking back on the experiment in its first three years, 'the number of runaways upon the great ships was more than double in one year, and treble in the others, to what it was in the two preceding years of 1690 and 1691. No money or vessels for pressing were saved and the Fleet was not manned more quickly in the spring than it had been before.'[4] Perhaps the most melancholy comment on the failure of the reform lay in the resolution of the Board of Admiralty in August 1694, as it faced once more the prospect of a turbulent and disappointing winter, to keep a new ledger in the office with the names and details of all the deserters from the ships refitting in harbour.[5] The inducement of continuous employment had failed, thanks to the conditions of that employment; and when it had become clear that the men could not be held by threats or concessions, it remained in the closing years of the war to consider the more difficult alternative, which had hitherto been evaded, of regulating their conscription by compiling a register of the seafaring population of the country.

The continued use of a great fleet each summer, and the decision to keep the men aboard its ships each winter, combined to develop and define the status of the sea officer. As the fleet became larger, and was

---

[1] E.g. St Lo's remarks on the men's behaviour when paid, in P.R.O.Adm. 1/3573, f. 467; 106/455, 21/11/94.

[2] P.R.O.Adm. 1/3573, ff. 683–4; 3/9: 29/12/93; 3/10: 27/7/94. This is reflected in the graph in Appendix V (A) below.

[3] P.R.O.Adm. 1/3571, ff. 577–84 gives the details of the money spent in this way in the winter of 1692–3.

[4] Admty:Corbett, x, f. 159. I have no figures to support this statement.

[5] P.R.O.Adm. 3/10: 17/8.

regularly employed as a fleet, a dual problem of seniority arose, affecting the mutual relations of the officers within it and their relations with those serving in other commands. At the beginning of the war seniority was ill defined, and represented only one element in the considerations governing an appointment. Among the junior officers its importance was diminished by the uncertain nature of their employment, and among the senior officers by the rival factors of favour and appointment by function. The latter was particularly noticeable on foreign stations, where the local commanders often made their own appointments according to the requirements of the moment. There were thus many officers who had held captains' commands abroad and were entered as lieutenants at home, or whose seniority under one Admiral differed from their seniority under another. There was no central record, either at the Navy Office or the Admiralty, to adjust these discrepancies, for the conception of permanent service still decided only an officer's eligibility for a pension on superannuation, and not his claims to command or even to promotion. With the rapid growth of the fleet campaign, a system based on such different foundations and comprising so many local discrepancies was unlikely to survive for long without modification; and in the middle years of the war, an effort was made to bring it under a logical and central control.

This effort took two forms: first, an increasing regulation of the system of promotion among the ships' officers; and secondly, a stricter control over the mutual relations of officers in command of formations both within and outside the fleet. In December 1690, it was decided that appointments to individual commands, which had not hitherto been made on any recognized system, should be subject to regular and comprehensive reports on their subordinates by the flag officers under whom they were serving.[1] This did not necessarily affect the question of seniority, but that was raised shortly afterwards, when in February 1691 the Admiralty suggested that Russell should consult a council of war of those flag officers and captains who were then with their ships at Chatham, on the best way to ensure that length of service should be adequately represented in considering all forms of promotion.[2] In

[1] P.R.O.Adm. 3/5: 1/12. [2] P.R.O.Adm. 2/371, f. 135.

reply, the officers recommended that as a first step a record of their careers should be kept in the Admiralty office, which, coupled with a system of regular reports from senior officers upon their juniors, should ensure that the Board had the information to make appointments on a combination of merit and length of service. But no suggestion was made—as indeed it could hardly have been made from such a source—that promotion should be controlled by any guarantee that would limit the Admiralty's right to appoint any man whom it favoured.[1] Nothing more was done that year, but the next summer the Navy Board, when asked to report on the same lines, also suggested that the Admiralty should compile a comprehensive seniority list to be kept up to date at the office.[2] This was put in hand in the autumn, and by the middle of November the Board, to its own satisfaction, had at its disposal for the first time a single table of seniority for all the captains, lieutenants, warrant officers and masters on the books of the navy.[3] At the same time, a separate investigation was begun into the warrant officers' records of service.[4] The compilation of the list produced many discrepancies and brought to light some curious irregularities, and in 1693 the Admiralty sent a series of questionnaires to commanders of squadrons on the conditions under which local appointments were made. The joint Admirals of the fleet were required to submit a report on the best methods of reconciling the seniorities of appointments which had lapsed at different times and for varying periods,[5] and at the end of the year sufficient data had been collected for the Board to take the unusual step of sending a seniority list of officers to the commander of a squadron just about to set out for the West Indies, with an order to him to report on any subsequent deviations from it which he had to make locally.[6] By the beginning of 1694, this prolonged activity had produced a body of sufficiently accurate information for some action to be taken upon it; and in March the first result was seen, when the Admiralty decided that in future the first lieutenants of the three highest rates should be appointed strictly on seniority, and that exceptions to

1 P.R.O.Adm. 3/5: 1/4.

2 P.R.O.Adm. 3/7: 20/7/92.

3 Ibid. 14/11.

4 P.R.O.Adm. 2/383, Secretary of Admiralty to clerks of the cheque at the ports, 18/11.

5 P.R.O.Adm. 3/8: 1/2/93.

6 P.R.O.Adm. 3/9: 1/12.

this rule should be made only with the consent of a full Board of Admiralty.[1] This was followed in the autumn by a discussion on the manner of appointing all other commissioned and warrant officers.[2] Four years after the question had first been raised, therefore, length of service had come to be accepted, for at least one stage in the career of the ship's officer, as the most important factor in making an appointment. Conditions of promotion are always the most accurate reflection of other terms of employment in the navy; and with this acknowledgement, in one particular, of the claims of permanent service, an important step had been taken in determining the status of the naval officer.

This determination of seniority, so far as it went, still applied chiefly to the ships' officers, whose contingent conditions of employment could be regulated on purely administrative grounds. Among the higher ranks, length of service was, by the nature of their duties, of only minor importance, and a combination of other factors—ability, political allegiance and personal favour—decided the choice of commander. But at this level too a certain consciousness of seniority was coming to be felt. A typical case occurred in October 1693, when a commander was required for a squadron going to the Mediterranean. Several names were submitted by the Admiralty, but the nomination was left to William, who took a strong personal interest in the list. His first choice fell upon Shovell, at that time the junior full Admiral in the fleet, but with the qualification that if 'there be an objection because of his Rank in the Fleet which may not be equal or agreeable to such a Command', Delavall—a senior full Admiral at the time—should be appointed.[3] Again, a month beforehand in a dispute over promotion to the only vacant Rear Admiral's flag, the King had ordered the senior candidate to be nominated to it, specifically because of his seniority.[4] While the final decision lay outside the Admiralty, and depended in the last resort upon political and personal factors, all else being equal the claims of seniority were allowed.

But these overriding factors themselves upset seniority. It was

---

[1] P.R.O. Adm. 3/9: 13/3/94. [2] P.R.O. Adm. 3/10: 25/9.

[3] N.M.M., Bibl. Phill., VI, f. 48*v*. See Appendix X below.

[4] Ibid. f. 46.

possible on political grounds, or as politics affected favour, for flag officers to go up and down in the scale in a manner bewildering to any seniority list. In 1693, for instance, Berkeley fell from Admiral of the Blue to Vice-Admiral of the Red, and Mitchell from Vice-Admiral of the Blue to Rear Admiral of the Red.[1] To nominate on seniority when seniority was thus confused was no simple task; and the reconciliation of the claims of the various flag officers was effected, therefore, by defining the precedence due to their rank when once that had been decided rather than by regulating the appointments themselves, which were still largely beyond any administrative control. Within the fleet this precedence was easy enough to determine. The flags to be worn by each rank, the extra stores and retinue allowed, and its rights and duties at sea were all clearly laid down when the squadrons were in company. But outside the fleet, when detached squadrons had to be considered, precedence was affected directly by the discrepancies of status. Commanders of detached squadrons might be classed as one of three kinds: on Channel service, they might rank and be paid as 'extra' Vice-Admirals or Rear Admirals; alternatively, they might be appointed as commanders of squadrons for special services; or thirdly, they might be placed in command of squadrons for overseas service, in which case they might or might not receive the additional appointment of Commander in Chief on the station.[1] Most of the commanders in the third category held flag rank, but others—such as Aylmer in the Mediterranean in the winter of 1690–1, Norris in Newfoundland in 1696–7, or Benbow and Beaumont in the Channel in 1695 and 1697 respectively—held the rank of captain,[2] and the peculiarity of their status was reflected in the emergence of the term 'Commodore' or 'Commadore', which was first taken from the Dutch in 1689 and was applied intermittently, but on no regular rule, to such posts throughout the war.[3] The conflict of function and seniority was thus posed in its clearest form when detached squadrons met at sea, or when one of them

---

[1] See Appendix X below.

[2] Ibid. In March 1691, it was even proposed that a pool of unemployed flag officers and captains should be formed, from which to provide commanders of squadrons when required (P.R.O.Adm. 3/5: 7/3/91).

[3] Sir R. Massie Blomfield, 'Naval Executive Titles: Commadore or Commodore?', in *M.M.* IV, no. 3, pp. 73–4.

encountered a squadron from the fleet. The disputes over precedence were indicated by the flags which their commanders wore, and a series of individual orders was promulgated, usually by the Admiralty but occasionally, when the quarrels grew intense, by the King, laying down the flags and pendants which might be hoisted in the different circumstances likely to arise.[1] On some occasions, commanders who were allowed to wear one flag when not in company had to haul it down when they met a superior officer with a right to the same flag;[2] on others, they were given flags or pendants not in use elsewhere at the time, or to be worn only in certain well-defined waters.

The disputes over precedence were also vigorously pursued at a slightly lower level, when there was a concentration of ships but no recognizable squadron. On these occasions, the argument was apt to turn entirely upon seniority, for no difference of rank was involved; and the rivalries of the different captains, although not so politically important to the authorities ashore as the rivalries of the flag officers, were just as virulent. One such concentration was recognized by the Admiralty, and the senior captain in the Downs at any time was given the right to wear a distinctive pendant which signified his temporary command.[3] But as the activities of the fleet and the winter squadrons grew, and possibly as more ships came to be kept in sea pay throughout the year, a system had to be found parallel to the normal chain of naval command when ships collected at the different rendezvous around the coast. Disciplinary powers had to be maintained, and the responsibilities of command assumed, while units were on their way to and from their bases as well as while they were operational. In the middle years of the war, therefore, a new rank emerged: that of Commander in Chief on a station.[4] It is difficult to trace its growth, or even to say when the post

---

1 For a discussion of the theoretical rights of the different commanders, see Perrin, *British Flags*, ch. IV. For the details of the orders promulgated, see Admty:Corbett, IX, ff. 9–21; P.R.O.Adm. 3/5: 6/11; 3/7: 26/8, 5/10; 3/9: 22/11.

2 For a good example of the complexities of such an order, see P.R.O.Adm. 3/10: 9/8/94.

3 Admty:Corbett, IX, f. 85.

4 Although the title is much the same, the modern Commander-in-Chief of a port or Home station is not descended from those of the late seventeenth century, but from the resident Commissioners of the dockyards.

was first recognized. The duties of its occupant were to exercise a general disciplinary supervision over any ships that might be in company on the station, to see that their orders reached them from London, and to hold courts martial when necessary; his rights were to wear a distinctive pendant,[1] and sometimes—but as yet only occasionally—to receive extra pay on the basis of a captain commanding a squadron. The stations were limited to the Downs, the Nore, and the Thames and Medway, and at first the local Commander in Chief seems to have been simply the senior captain to find himself in such an area. But as court martial duties became more frequent, commissions for the purpose had to be given by the Admiralty to specified men.[2] The command was still short-lived and intermittent, but by the end of 1692 its existence was recognized, and in January 1693 the Navy Board was asked to define its duties in relation to those of the captains of other ships on the station.[3] The following year, for what would seem to be the first time, the Commander in Chief at the Nore received additional pay for the five weeks of his command, and this was followed in the last two years of the war by his counterpart in the Thames and Medway also being paid, on two separate occasions and for an equally short period, for his special duties.[4] In their different ways, the Commodore and the Commander in Chief on the station illustrated the effect of the expanding material upon the hierarchy of the officers who had to control it.

The increasing control over naval rank did not result in a printed 'navy list', as they were later called, during the war. The first of these appeared in 1700, and it is significant that it was produced in connexion with a change in the rates of officers' pay.[5] For one of the reasons for the emphasis on seniority was the necessity to determine it for financial purposes. For the first four years of the war, there was little mention of the rates of officers' pay. Wages of any description were seldom

---

[1] P.R.O.Adm. 3/8: 5/12.

[2] E.g. to Delavall as 'commander-in-chief of the ships in the Thames and Medway' to act as president of the court at Torrington's trial (see p. 365 above). Although political reasons entered into this case, the membership of the court was conventional, comprised as it was entirely of captains of ships in the two rivers.

[3] P.R.O.Adm. 1/3567, ff. 1167–8.

[4] See Appendix X below.

[5] W. G. Perrin, 'The Navy List, I', in *M.M.* I, no. 10, p. 260.

touched in the seventeenth century, and there had in any case been a recent modification to captain's pay—at any rate in theory[1]—with James II's regulations for plate money in 1686.[2] At the end of 1690, the Admiralty rather tentatively raised the question of flag officers' pay, but although an increase in the rates was suggested to the King nothing more was heard of it.[3] The first modification to the current rates came early in 1692, when the fleet needed to be manned and officered as early in the season as possible. Officers of all ranks were then granted full pay from the time that they joined their ships in the yards, in place of the lower scale to which they had been accustomed in the winter.[4] A further encouragement was granted to the senior officers at the end of that year, after Rear Admiral Carter had been killed at Barfleur, by the extension of the pension scheme for flag officers to the widows of those killed at sea.[5] But the basic rates remained the same until the end of 1693. By then the practice of keeping the fleet in sea pay for the whole year had put the service of officers as well as of men upon a new, though not a similar footing; for whereas to the men it appeared as a further infringement of their liberty, to the officers it represented a further development in the establishment of a permanent employment to which all features of their service were tending. Although not all the officers were required throughout the winter, the measure greatly extended the number that were. With other means of employment disappearing, therefore, the question of their pay became more important to them; and in November the Admiralty, anxious to narrow the differences that existed for some ranks between the naval rates and those allowed in other seafaring occupations, and also to reduce the number of irregularities which were occasioned by the low pay,[6] proposed to the Privy Council that the wages of all flag officers, captains, lieutenants, masters[7] and surgeons should be doubled, and that at the same time—partly to offset the additional expense which this

---

[1] According to Corbett (Admty: Corbett, XI, f. 4), in the event the money was never paid. The fact that I have come across no mention of the allowance to support or disprove this statement possibly indicates that it is correct.

[2] See p. 142 above.

[3] P.R.O.Adm. 3/5: 5/12, 6/12/90.

[4] P.R.O.Adm. 3/6: 18/1/92.

[5] P.R.O.Adm. 3/8: 30/11.

[6] Admty:Corbett, XI, f. 4.

[7] But not pilots, by a later decision (P.R.O.Adm. 3/10: 10/10/94).

would incur, and partly as a disciplinary measure to curb the abuses to which it was known to be subject—the allowance of personal servants to the captains should be reduced from one to every twenty of the crew, to a maximum of ten for full Admirals, eight for other flags, six in first and second rates, five in thirds and fourths, and four in fifths and sixths. In addition, the Board proposed that all captains of first to fifth rates inclusive should be granted half pay while ashore, and similarly masters and first lieutenants of first to third rates who had served one year in such capacities, or had taken part in 'a general engagement'.[1] These proposals were accepted in principle by the King in Council,[2] and the details were worked out during the next few months.[3] On 12 March 1694 the new establishment was promulgated, to act retrospectively from 1 January.[4] Working on the basis of the ships in pay in 1693, it was estimated that it would raise the annual expenditure on wages by £60,938.[5]

The measure was immediately popular. Only three months after it had been announced, the Navy Board reported that none of the captains or masters in active service would take the post of master attendant at Chatham, one of the plums of the dockyard service, because they considered that they were better off if they remained where they were;[6] and while some captains, who had kept up to the maximum number of servants allowed and suffered financially from the restriction now placed upon them, lost by the new rates of pay,[7] most observers, both at the time and later, agreed that the other ranks undoubtedly benefited from them. In 1700, however, they were replaced by a lower scale of wages supposed to be more in keeping with a peacetime expenditure, and for the first half of Anne's war the officers were less well paid than they had been in the last half of the war of William III.

An earlier result of the growth of the navy than the increase in the sea officers' pay was the increase in their numbers. In January 1691, as the result of a recommendation by the same council of war at Chatham that proposed the compilation of a seniority list, the Admiralty

---

1 P.R.O.Adm. 3/9: 24/11.
2 Ibid. 28/11.
3 Serg.Misc. II, ff. 431–2.
4 P.R.O.Adm. 3/9: 12/3.
5 Serg.Misc. II, f. 432.
6 P.R.O.Adm. 1/3572, f. 6.
7 *The Case of the Captains of his Majesty's Fleet humbly offer'd to the Honourable House of Commons* (n.d., but probably 1698), in *B.M. Printed 816. m. 7.*

submitted to the Council a memorandum on the desirability of allowing more junior commissioned and warrant officers to the first five rates.[1] This was discussed early in the next month,[2] and on the 16th the Queen ordered the original recommendations to be put into effect.[3] The establishment affected the lower ranks and higher ratings only, and was as follows:[4]

	First rates	Second rates	Third rates	Fourth rates	Fifth rates
Lieutenants	5	5	3	2	1
Gunners' mates	4	4	2	1	1
Boatswains' mates	4	4	2	2	1
Carpenters' mates	2	2	1	1	1
Quartermasters	8	8	6	4	3
Quarter muster-masters	6	6	4	4	3
Surgeons' mates	5	4	2	2	1
Boatswains' yeomen	4	4	4	2	2
Midshipmen	24	24	16	10	6
Yeomen of the powder room	2	2	2	1	1
Quarter gunners	One to every four guns in each rate				

This establishment, which endured for the rest of the war, was supplemented once, in 1692, when the complement of officers for sixth rates was modified to include a qualified master as well as a captain.[5]

Certain developments also took place in discipline during this period. Besides the new rates of pay, which were partly intended to stop captains from taking convoy money and indulging in other forms of peculation,[6] there were several direct attempts to regulate the behaviour of the ships' officers. In 1692, a new edition of the printed captains' Instructions was issued, in which a revised form of the muster list was included and various supplementary orders of the previous decade inserted in the text.[7] In the following year, the growing cohesion of the national fleet was emphasized by the stipulation that only natural-born Englishmen should in future be appointed in command.[8] The Instructions for junior officers were left as they were, but it was laid down in 1694 that they should be read by the captain on deck, in the presence of the ship's company, on the first Monday in each month, after the manner of the articles of war.[9] After the increase in pay had

[1] P.R.O.Adm. 3/5: 16/1/91.
[2] Ibid. 11/2.
[3] P.R.O.Adm. 1/4080, f. 61.
[4] S.P.Dom. 44/204, f. 47.
[5] P.R.O.Adm. 3/7: 29/6/92.
[6] See the preamble to the announcement of the new rates of pay.
[7] P.R.O.Adm. 3/6: 6/1, 20/1, 18/3/92.
[8] P.R.O.Adm. 3/8: 3/1/93.
[9] P.R.O.Adm. 3/10: 5/12/94.

come into effect, ships' officers and flag officers were required to attend their ships and commands more regularly, the junior officers by watches like the men, and their seniors in such a manner as to supervise the work at reasonable intervals. A vigorous attempt was made to enforce the new orders;[1] but like all disciplinary measures in that age, they indicated what was required of the service rather than the standard of conduct that resulted. The way in which the officers might be expected to behave was conditioned not by any disciplinary regulations, but by the conditions of their employment; and while these were slowly changing under the impact of an expanding fleet, they had not changed sufficiently to make any difference as yet to the type of officer recruited or to his conduct when once appointed to his post.[2]

III

Inseparable from all these varied activities, and affecting them at every turn, were the problems of financial control. The dominating factor in departmental finance during the middle years of the war was the rapid growth of Parliamentary responsibility for both the distribution and the expenditure of the national revenue. This was achieved in two ways, by appropriations and by the emergence of the Parliamentary system of audit. Theoretically, they were not complementary: it is possible to imagine either in operation without the other. But in fact, although sums were appropriated without their expenditure being audited by Parliament, no Parliamentary audit was carried out without sums

---

[1] P.R.O.Adm. 3/9: 4/11, 5/11.

[2] Possibly the first sign of change came about fifty years later. In the middle of the eighteenth century, Commodore Edward Thompson, who was a good judge, remarked that whereas in the earlier wars 'a chaw of tobacco, a rattan, and a rope of oaths were sufficient qualifications to constitute a lieutenant...now, education and good manners are the study of all; and so far from effeminacy, that I am of opinion the present race of officers will as much eclipse the veterans of 1692 as the polite the vulgar' (cited in Laird Clowes, op. cit. III, p. 22). For the first time, 'politeness' and efficiency are not automatically contrasted. Cf. also the changes which the same officer made in the script of Shadwell's *The Fair Quaker of Deal* at about this time, to bring the characters of the naval officers up to date by modifying the contrast between the gentleman captain and the tarpaulin admiral (for the different editions of this play, see C. N. Robinson, *The British Tar in Fact and Fiction* (1911), ch. x).

having first been appropriated. The one device led to the other, and each made its independent contribution to the joint result.

The first stages in the development of appropriations have already been seen. With the vastly increased cost of the war over peacetime expenditure, and the lag between theoretical and actual supply, the gap had to be filled by other means. Between 2 November 1688 and Michaelmas 1691, the revenue to the Exchequer amounted to £8,693,331, while the Exchequer's total expenditure on government reached the sum of £11,681,335, of which £8,957,299 was spent on the three armed forces.[1] Discounting for the moment the fact that Exchequer payments to the departments did not fully cover departmental expenditure, these figures show the inadequacy of the normal sources of estimated revenue, even if promptly collected, to meet the demands of the war. The balance was supplied by loans.[2] Within the period already specified, these amounted to no less than £7,832,080.[3]

The loans came in neither at an even rate nor, at the beginning, all upon the same terms. But after June 1690 the earlier variety of conditions disappeared, and only one type of loan remained, raised upon a Parliamentary guarantee of repayment.[4] For the inadequacy of the revenue, which led the executive to borrow money, led the lenders of that money to demand something more than the unassisted credit of the executive. Financially, the first impact of the war upon Parliament

---

[1] There are two sources for assessing the national income and expenditure throughout the war, and annually after 1691: (1) *Cal.Treas.Bks. 1689–92*, pp. cciv–ccxvii, and Shaw's introduction to ibid. vols. XI–XVII; and (2) *House of Commons Accounts and Papers*, 'Income and Expenditure' (*H.C.* XXXV, 1868–9), pp. 4–19. Both are based on the same material (*Cal.Treas.Bks. 1689–92*, p. civ; *H.C.* XXXV, 1868–9, p. 327), but they do not give the figures in the same way. *H.C.* XXXV, 1868–9 includes money loaned to the government as income and repayments of loan money as expenditure, which Shaw condemns (*Cal.Treas.Bks. 1689–92*, p. clxiv). But it may be taken as a check on Shaw's figures, which are sometimes added up incorrectly (e.g. ibid. p. ccv), or are omitted in error without affecting the total (e.g. ibid. p. ccxvi). The figures in this section are taken from either source, as required.

[2] It was not, of course, a balance solely of income against expenditure on government. Once the first loan had been received, subsequent loans had to be applied, either wholly or in part, to repay the capital of, and later also the interest upon, their predecessors, as well as to pay for current expenditure.

[3] *Cal.Treas.Bks. 1689–92*, pp. clxxx–clxxxi.

[4] Ibid.

was to make it assume responsibility for money which it had not voted as well as for money which it had, and thus to relate one source of income to the other in its provisions for the treatment of the latter alone.

By the end of 1689, however, the increasing debt of the armed forces was leading the Commons to apply the system of appropriation not only to the distribution but to the expenditure of income. In the first place, the fact that their general supplies did not meet expenditure made them anxious to discover the causes for the unfavourable balance, and to check possible extravagance by limiting the supply; and secondly, the consequent decline in the credit of the armed forces which arose from this adverse balance, led the contractors to demand terms on the lines of the loans already being made with the sanction of Parliament. Thus appropriations for specific services, by tallies of assignment carrying the same sort of guarantee as was carried by tallies of loan, began to be inserted indirectly into the general provisions for supply, in the legislation upon ways and means.[1]

There were thus two incentives for Parliament to develop the system of appropriations, the one internal and arising from its own desire to secure the effects which were intended from its supplies, the other external and forced upon it by the requirements of the executive, thanks to the demands of the merchants. The two factors did not affect the development in the same way. The demands of the merchants gave rise to a purely technical process whereby tallies on the credit of the Exchequer gave way gradually to tallies on the credit of the funds, whereas the desire to control the expenditure of the supplies posed a question of responsibility which became directly involved in the political struggle already existing between the Commons and the executive. Financial control sprang from technical causes; but the direction which it took was not governed only by technical considerations, nor even calculated at all directly to satisfy technical requirements.

The development of this control was uneven, and indeed was never clearly defined. It is no accident that the best accounts of the Parliamentary grants were given later, when in retrospect the intentions of their authors could be related more conveniently to events. In the

[1] See pp. 336–7 above.

brief description of them which follows, only the outlines of a confused situation have been drawn, and it must be remembered that not all the members of the Commons who brought about the development of Parliamentary finance in these years thought in the same way about it, or appreciated what in fact they were doing. While it may seem obvious now that the appropriation was the weapon of Parliamentary control, and that where money was not appropriated only confusion could result, they themselves at times enlarged their control consciously by this means, while at other times restricted it unconsciously by refusing to vote a supply for the peacetime expenses of the executive, which they continued to place on the King's standing revenue. In one year they would take responsibility for all naval expenditure: in another year they would not. The whole process is attended by contradictory symptoms: by the traditional financial attitudes which had been used to oppose the executive under the Stuarts, and by revised conceptions which in fact largely superseded the necessity for opposition, but which naturally were used as before for that purpose.

In 1690, the Commons made no appropriation at all for the navy, for the initial appropriation of £400,000 which had been made in November 1689 was not supplemented in the second vote of supply which was made for the same year in the following April. On 1 April, a supply of £1,200,000 was added to the £2,000,000 already voted for the general purposes of the war, without any specific allocation being made to any service.[1] This benefited neither the service departments nor Parliament itself. The former had no guarantee of payment, other than the ability of the Exchequer to answer their requirements, and the latter no direct means of controlling departmental expenditure. The position was well illustrated when an inquiry was held in 1693 into naval expenditure since 1688 as compared with the Parliamentary grants and Exchequer payments for that purpose over the same period. When it came to 1690, no satisfactory answer could be obtained to the question of how much had been granted by Parliament to the navy for that year. As it happened, the navy in 1690 had received from the Exchequer less money than it had asked for, and no authority was anxious to accept the responsibility for the ensuing debt. The

[1] *H.C.J.* x, p. 327.

arguments seemed all equally convincing. The Navy Office, concerned to show that its expenditure had been approved but not in fact met by Parliament or Treasury, claimed that since no specific allocation had been made which was intended to meet its annual estimate, but no specific objection had been raised to it, Parliament could be inferred as having intended to meet the expenditure out of the general supply for the war, which had been granted only after the service estimates had been consulted. The Commons, anxious to justify their liberality in contrast to the defalcations of the Exchequer, likewise assumed that such a grant had in fact been made out of the £3,200,000 which they had voted for the general purposes of the war in that year. The Treasury, on the other hand, eager to prove that it had acted liberally towards the navy, relied on the fact that only £400,000 had been specifically allocated by Parliament to the service, and claimed that all payments made to the navy from other funds and above that amount were made on the responsibility of the executive, with only the general approval of Parliament.[1] There was, in fact, no one answer to the dilemma. The Treasury would have been within its rights if it had allowed the navy only the £400,000 laid down in November 1689, and a token sum from the £1,200,000 provided in April 1690, so long as the rest of the £3,200,000 had been applied to the army and the Ordnance; but the Commons could claim that these sums had been settled after debating the service estimates themselves, and that, provided both the services and the Exchequer managed their business correctly, the grants had been adequate to the occasion. This point of view, however, did not take account of the fact that the varying demands of the war often made the estimates inadequate, and that, under contemporary conditions of credit, it was only on a specific guarantee for one purpose that money could be raised for others. A general provision for all ended in an adequate provision for none.

In the autumn of 1690, however, the Commons once more resorted to the system of appropriations. On 8 October, they began to debate the supply for 1691.[2] Their first move, as usual, was to ask the King to provide them with a state of the war for the following year, and on the next day the service estimates were duly laid before them. For the

[1] *H. of L. N.S.* I, pp. 12–13, 16, 21. [2] *H.C.J.* x, pp. 430–1.

first time, these were given in detail. In the case of the navy, instead of the usual brief exposition of the executive's demands, giving only the total of men required by the department, they set out the exact number of men required for the different services and included details of the construction under way at the time. It was the first example of the practice that held good for the remainder of William's reign, and throughout that of Anne, but which then lapsed again until 1781, of submitting an estimate of material as well as of the money required to satisfy it.[1] In all, the estimate came to £1,791,695.[2] Taking it section by section, the House resolved that it was reasonable and voted that the separate sums which it demanded should be supplied, and each allocated to the purpose for which it had been specified.[3] The House followed this up, in the debate on ways and means, by appropriating £1,000,000 on the land tax for the year to the navy and naval ordnance, on the usual terms.[4] When, shortly afterwards, the construction of the 27 ships was proposed, a further appropriation was made on the Excise and, in return, the date of completion for the programme was laid down.[5] The system of appropriations, now covering both the purposes for which and the funds upon which they were granted, was leading the Commons to a more detailed knowledge of naval affairs.

At this stage, the interest shifts from the development of the machinery of appropriation to the way in which its effects were intended to be secured. For when the time came to vote the supply for 1692, the estimates were treated in a new way. On 6 November 1691 the House requested the state of the war for the following year, and on the 9th Onslow submitted the naval estimates.[6] From the 14th to the 18th the Commons examined them stage by stage, and on this occasion, instead of accepting them as it had done in 1690, it shifted its ground, and besides debating the financial details themselves, questioned the numbers of men and ships upon which such details depended.[7] The House, in fact, was now using the machinery of appropriation directly to approach

[1] *H.C.* xxxv, 1868–9, p. 326.

[2] Ibid. pp. 431–2. Further details may be found in P.R.O.Adm. 7/169, estimates of 8 October and 9 October 1690.

[3] *H.C.J.* x, p. 433.

[4] 2 Will. and Mary, sess. 2, c. 1, arts. xxxiv–xxxv.

[5] See pp. 430–1 above.

[6] *H.C.J.* x, pp. 546, 549.

[7] Ibid. pp. 553–5.

the policy of the executive. In the end, where the Navy Office had estimated that the total expenditure would amount to £1,855,054, including ordnance, the Commons voted a supply of £1,575,890.[1] For the first time on a full knowledge of the facts before them, they had granted less than had been asked.

In examining these estimates, the Commons made use of their own auditors, the Parliamentary Commissioners for auditing the public accounts. It has already been seen that an abortive attempt was made to create such a body in 1690, a few months after the first appropriation had been made to the navy.[2] This was followed up as soon as the House met again in October of that year. On the 9th, while the armed forces were preparing their annual estimates for the next year, a bill was ordered to be brought in 'for the examining and taking the public accounts'.[3] On 26 December it passed the Commons, and by 5 January 1691 it was law.[4] On 24 December the House balloted for the names of the nine Commissioners whom it was proposed should act on its behalf. Those chosen were Sir Robert Rich, Sir Thomas Clarges, Paul Foley, Robert Austen, Sir Matthew Andrewes, Sir Benjamin Newland, Sir Samuel Barnardiston, Sir Peter Colleton and Robert Harley.[5] In January, Parliament was adjourned until October, but on 10 November 1691 the Commons ordered their Commissioners to lay before the House a state of the public revenue from 5 November 1688 to Michaelmas of that year, with their observations.[6]

The shadow of the Commissioners soon fell upon the Navy Office. They examined its ledgers, summoned some of its members and those of the Admiralty to their headquarters at York House,[7] and made so many demands upon them that the Treasurer of the Navy was given three extra clerks to provide the figures which they required.[8] Their audit, and their remarks upon it, were products of their attitude. As

---

[1] P.R.O.Adm. 7/169, estimate of 31 October; *H.C.J.* x, p. 555. Nevertheless, it was not clear about the implications of what it was doing. For at the same time that it was using the weapon of the appropriation to question policy, it put the ordinary back on the standing revenue (*H. of L. N.S.* I, p. 12).

[2] See p. 340 above.

[3] *H.C.J.* x, p. 432.

[4] Ibid. p. 536; *H.M.C.* 13, v, p. 401.

[5] *H.C.J.* x, pp. 523, 525, 528.

[6] Ibid. p. 549.

[7] P.R.O.Adm. 3/6: 23/10, 9/11, 16/11/91, 14/1/92.

[8] Ibid. 3/4/92.

the executive, with memories of their predecessors in 1679, regarded them as its traditional enemies,[1] so they viewed its accounts and explanations with equal suspicion. They looked upon themselves, as their opponents looked upon them, as created to scrutinize the Treasury and the Exchequer, rather than to make use of them.[2] In the debate which arose upon their report, Clarges complained that the Commissioners had not had power to imprison those departmental Treasurers who did not comply with their demands, while the head of the Treasury Commission in return accused them of making frivolous accusations based upon malice and ignorance.[3] The report itself was misleading in several important details, including in its credit columns as income all loan money and all departmental remains from the previous year, and also various forms of revenue which were in fact not revenue at all, such as tallies of anticipation and deductions from army pay. In all it arrived at a total national income for the period of £18,108,586,[4] and to the Commons it naturally seemed amazing that such a sum could have been spent while the forces complained continually of inadequate payments. The Commissioners' observations on their figures were similarly misleading, and could often have been avoided by consulting the departmental officials whom they maligned. As has been truly remarked, the report, while based on all the factors which have survived as part of Parliamentary finance to-day—appropriation of supply, authorized borrowing powers, and (fairly) reliable estimates—failed to co-ordinate them because there was no co-ordination between Parliament itself and the executive.[5] What have since become guarantees of Parliamentary government were at the time facilities for effective Parliamentary opposition to the government.

The opposition of the House to the executive was stressed even more clearly when a bill was introduced, in January 1692, to replace the Act of 1691, by adding more members to the Commission of auditors.

[1] See, e.g., Pepys's remarks upon them from his retirement, in *Naval Minutes*, pp. 152, 291, 333–4.

[2] I have followed Shaw, in *Cal.Treas.Bks. 1689–92*, pp. cliii–clxvii, in this account of their attitude and their report of 1691.

[3] Speeches quoted ibid. pp. clvii, clx.

[4] See *H.M.C.* 13, v, pp. 356–434.

[5] *Cal.Treas.Bks. 1689–92*, p. clxv.

This contained a significant clause, prohibiting any Commissioner from holding a place or office under the Crown.[1] But the bill was lost, for the Lords insisted that the auditors should not be members of the Commons, while the Commons in turn insisted that they alone had the power to select their servants;[2] and while its main provisions were passed in the end as a tacking clause to a poll bill, this clause itself was not among them.[3] The subsequent report of the auditors in 1692, undertaken on the same terms as that of the previous year, was a milder affair and largely free from the other's mistakes. But as before, it did not make use of the Treasury, and the improvements in it were negative rather than positive, an avoidance of controversial technicalities rather than a positive advance upon earlier practice.[4] The Commissioners had taken their position in the struggle for power, and although their opposition to the executive may have been the only possible attitude at the time, and so in the long run proved to be the guarantee of a workable system of financial control, at the time it was undoubtedly a handicap to the latter's immediate development. While the system of appropriations had provided a temporary solution to the technical problem of credit, and was thus bringing the Commons into a new relation with the executive, its management was being mishandled thanks to the nature of these relations. While Parliamentary government rose upon the foundation

---

[1] *H.C.J.* x, p. 596.

[2] Ibid.; *H.M.C.* 14, VI, pp. 50–1.

[3] Ibid. pp. 653–4.

[4] I have ventured to disagree with Shaw here, as I can see no example in the report (which is contained in *H.M.C.* 14, VI, pp. 130–78) of 'The Commissioners [having] put themselves to school under the Treasury officials and...coming to a better understanding of the national accounts and of their own business as an auditing or traversing body, assistant to, rather than antagonistic to, the executive' (*Cal. Treas. Bks. 1689–92*, p. clxix). Admittedly, their second report is 'disfigured by none of the innuendoes and observations which had rendered their first report useless' (ibid.); but this is probably a sign of caution, after the damaging debate upon that report, rather than of any sudden wisdom. Their next report, of 1693, involved them once more in technical arguments with the Treasury which, while not of the same kind as those of 1691, were equally virulent (see *H. of L. N.S.* I, pp. 12–29). Moreover, some of the men who were on the Commission in 1692 were taking a prominent part in the vicious debates of the autumn, in which the executive and the Treasury were being attacked on the same inadequate grounds as before.

of Parliamentary finance, Parliamentary finance, in its early stages, suffered from the emergence of Parliamentary government.

But estimates and grants alike must be checked against the actual payments to the departments from the Exchequer.[1] In 1690 £956,669 was issued to the navy,[2] and there were also issues to the Ordnance for

---

[1] It should be noted that all payments, unless otherwise stated, are for the financial year, i.e. from Michaelmas to Michaelmas.

The problem of how much was paid to the navy during these years is a difficult one. Four main accounts exist, two contemporary and two given later. (i) A contemporary account is contained in P.R.O.Adm. 49/173, where the sums *received by the Treasurer of the Navy* are given, together with the funds or sources from which they were supplied, for all years from 1691.

(ii) In *H. of L. N.S.* VII, p. 225, the *receipts of the Treasurer of the Navy* are given, simply as totals from Michaelmas to Michaelmas, from an account dated 1697–8. They do not correspond to those in P.R.O.Adm. 49/173, possibly because payments on tallies issued in one year, which were themselves received in another, are transferred to the year in which they were originally intended to be redeemed. I can think of no other reason, but in this case have preferred to take, where possible, the contemporary rather than the later account.

(iii) In *H. of L. N.S.* VII, pp. 176–8, is given a list of totals of the sums *issued to the navy*. These again do not correspond either to the amounts ibid. on p. 225, or to those in P.R.O.Adm. 49/173. In this case, however, they include issues to all departments and individuals concerned with the navy, including the Board of Ordnance and the Commissioners for Sick and Wounded, and those for all services, including the 27 ships and the yard at Plymouth. This is probably the most reliable of the four accounts.

(iv) In *H. of L. N.S.* I, pp. 12–29, is given another, and Parliamentary account, dated 1693, of *issues to the navy*, in this case affected by all the uncertainties which are removed in the account just cited. It is, therefore, of use principally as a very good example of the confusion over the accounts which existed in the middle of the war. It is dangerous by itself because, with no accurate idea either of the amounts really issued or of those intended to be granted, it purports to give the deficiencies upon the Parliamentary grants.

In addition, the receipts given in P.R.O.Adm. 49/173 may be split up into the amounts received by the various services *paid by the Treasurer of the Navy*. His receipts and payments for the victualling may be checked in another contemporary account, given in P.R.O. T. 38/615.

[2] This is the Treasury account. The Parliamentary auditors reached a sum of £959,154 (*H. of L. N.S.* I, pp. 12, 16). In the later account, drawn up from the certificates of the Treasurer of the Navy, a sum of £910,344 is reached for the same period; but various sums were paid direct to the Victuallers and the naval contractors, which are presumably not included there (*H. of L. N.S.* VII, p. 225).

sea service. How much the latter amounted to it is difficult to say: between 30 June 1689 and 30 June 1690 they came to £139,150, and in the following twelve months to £104,424.[1] If three-quarters of the first sum and one-quarter of the second are taken as a reasonable average, the result comes to approximately £130,468; and the payments to the Ordnance are unlikely to have been more than this, and may well have been less. At the most therefore, £1,087,137 in all was paid for the navy in 1690, as compared with an estimate, excluding ordnance, of £1,224,000. In 1691, £1,660,287 was paid to the navy, and from 30 June 1691 to 30 June 1692 £69,783 to the Ordnance for sea service.[2] Taking the same average, therefore, as before on the payments to the latter, these may have come to about £110,297, and the total issues for the navy to about £1,770,584, as against an estimate and grant of £1,791,695 plus a proportion of the grant of £570,000 for the 27 ships.[3] In 1692, £1,375,446 was paid in all to the navy and naval ordnance,[4] compared with an estimate of £1,855,054, and a grant of £1,575,890 was made excluding the £100,000 supposed to be supplied from the standing revenue, and the proportion of the £570,000 due for the year on the 27 ships. The latter was said by the Parliamentary auditors to be £127,136.[5] So far as can be ascertained, therefore, the position stood for the three years as shown on p. 472.

---

1 *H. of L. N.S.* I, p. 17.

2 The difference between the size of this and of the earlier payments to the Ordnance was due to the fact that between November 1688 and June 1691 £98,333 worth of saltpetre was bought for naval gunpowder (ibid.).

3 The Treasury stated that £16,739 of the £570,000 was paid before Michaelmas 1691, including £1939 for guns (ibid. pp. 16–17, 26).

4 A good deal of confusion exists over this figure. I have taken it from *H. of L. N.S.* VII, p. 176, so that it includes all the payments made. Of these, £1,239,209 went to the navy, excluding the ordnance (see also *H. of L. N.S.* I, p. 17). On the other hand, according to *H.M.C.* 14, VI, p. 135, the payments from the Exchequer amounted to £1,232,424. Possibly the latter does not include all the issues on the fund for the 27 ships. According to *H. of L. N.S.* VII, p. 225, the Treasurer of the Navy received £1,254,226; but according to P.R.O.Adm. 49/173, he received only £1,153,598. Finally, according to *H. of L. N.S.* I, p. 12, the issues to the navy, exclusive of ordnance, came to £1,495,358. When examined, however, this last sum is found to include issues from Michaelmas 1691 to 31 December 1692, and need not therefore be considered (ibid. p. 26).

5 *H. of L. N.S.* I, p. 12.

In comparison with these deficits, as reached here, the Parliamentary auditors reported deficits as follows: for 1690, £638,222; for 1691, £146,208; for 1692, £307,667; total £1,092,097.[1]

	Naval estimates	Parliamentary supply	Exchequer issues	Deficiencies of issues on supply
1690	£1,224,000, excluding ordnance for sea service (unknown)	Minimum of £400,000. Maximum of £1,597,376	Approximately £1,087,137	Maximum of £510,239. Minimum (on estimate) of £136,863
1691	£1,791,695 (excluding 27 ships)	£1,808,434 (including 27 ships)	Approximately £1,770,584	Approximately £37,850
1692	£1,855,054	£1,803,026	£1,375,446	£427,580
Total (approximate):				
Maximum				£975,669
Minimum				£602,293

Until Lady Day 1692, however, the credit on which the defective issues were made was better than before. Between Michaelmas 1689 and Lady Day 1690, £190,904 had been paid to the Treasurer of the Navy in tallies on unappropriated money, and £62,290 between that Lady Day and the following Michaelmas. But between Michaelmas 1690 and Lady Day 1691 only £2000 was so issued, between that Lady Day and the following Michaelmas £100, and from then until Lady Day 1692 £500. Between Lady Day and Michaelmas 1692 about £47,000 was paid on these terms.[2] Most of the payments between Michaelmas 1690 and Lady Day 1692 were made on the credit of specific funds, chiefly the successive land and poll taxes and the loans on the various Excise Acts. Loans on the general credit of the Exchequer totalled £76,000 in this period, but these—together with other expedients, such as William's personal dividend from the East India Company—were all made in the last six financial months of 1692.[3]

The inadequacy of the issues on the one hand, and on the other the good credit which they enjoyed, largely explain both the difficulties and the success of the Navy Office between the autumn of 1690 and the spring of 1692. For while the period was one of acute financial strain, it was also one of considerable material achievement. In both 1691 and

---

[1] *H. of L. N.S.* I, p. 12.

[2] Taken to the nearest pound in each case, from the issues given individually in *Cal. Treas. Bks. 1689–92, passim.*

[3] Ibid.

1692 a large fleet was fitted out with dispatch, and it was in these years, when money was growing increasingly short, that the balance of earlier springs was redressed and that the English were at sea as soon as the French. At first sight it is remarkable that this should have been so. Throughout the summer of 1690, despite regular weekly payments,[1] the issues were failing to meet the expenditure, and the naval debt, which had stood at £867,203 on Lady Day,[2] was steadily increasing. In the autumn the position became worse. From August to the end of the year, the payments from the Exchequer amounted in all to £274,786, compared with £232,449 in the three previous months; but of this £150,000 was paid in the one month of November.[3] In January and February the issues showed a slightly worse average,[4] and on 21 March the Navy Board summed up the situation as follows:

> It is no small pleasure to Us that after the many difficultys Wee have struggled with all this Winter in Fitting out so great a Fleet and Building so many Fireships & Ketches, occasion'd mostly by the uncertaine and scanty supply's of Money for the said Services, Wee can at least presume to say Wee have timely performed our parts in those Affaires. But at the same time reflecting upon the condition of their Mat^{s} Magazines, how empty this Worke has left them, and considering the many other Workes which by yor. Hon^{rs}. directions Wee are now either in hand with, or going upon... And the vast Quantity of Stores that will be necessary to be provided...for Equipping [and] for Building...Ships, and for Maintaining this Fleet at Sea, and Re-fitting it again when it returnes...Wee say, when Wee reflect on these things and do not find any Tenders made us as yet of any sort of Navall Commodities, notwithstanding the Invitation Weekly published in ye Gazett...Wee cannot imagine how the Services shall be answered.[5]

The financial demands which confronted the navy as a result of this situation were now of two types. First, its own personnel—the workmen in the dockyards and the sailors in the ships—needed ready money with which to be paid, or else tickets which could be met on presentation by ready money itself raised on negotiable tallies. Secondly, its

---

1 Ibid. vol. II, *passim*.

2 P.R.O. Adm. 49/173, abstract of total debts 31 March 1690.

3 *Cal.Treas.Bks. 1689–92*, pp. 761–965.

4 £74,000 and £78,139 respectively (ibid. pp. 964–1039).

5 P.R.O.Adm. 1/3563, ff. 367–8.

contractors demanded payment by tallies on funds which could be redeemed in the near future, and not on those which fell due at a distant date. In the latter case, the emphasis thus shifted from a fight for priority on the general credit of the Exchequer to a fight for the best tallies on the specified funds. As usual, the East Country merchants were first in the field. In the spring of 1691 they refused to tender for Baltic stores unless they were given security for their debts in negotiable[1] tallies upon a Parliamentary fund. On 1 April, they attended the Navy Office in a body to state their views,[2] and they continued to stand firm throughout the negotiations over the following ten days. On the 10th they put forward a concrete suggestion, that they should be assigned tallies for £40,000 on the land tax to pay off some of the debt. William Gore, who led the attack, went further and asked for £100,000.[3] As the days passed, the traders, who were just as anxious to do business as the Navy Board, continued to press for a guarantee that their debts would be met, and Taylor even tendered for some masts during the discussions.[4] The Admiralty did its best,[5] but was able to get tallies assigned only on the additional Excise, which held only a remote promise of repayment.[6] Despite their dissatisfaction, however, and on the promise that their bills would be placed at the head of this fund, the Baltic merchants then agreed to tender. The bargaining accordingly began on the 27th. By 8 May the Navy Board was able to announce that it had secured the year's contracts for hemp and masts.[7] The other stores had still to be agreed, but on the 11th the Navy Board was at last granted its request, and given tallies upon the land tax to the extent of £80,000.[8] On the next day, in consequence, it was able to report progress.[9] By the 22nd several more contracts had been signed;[10] but on the 25th it seemed that all the work had been in vain. Under pressure from other claimants the Treasury withdrew the allocation from the land tax, and required

[1] 'Negotiable' in the sense that they could get rid of them if they wished to, not in the sense that the tallies carried a negotiable power like a banknote.

[2] Serg:Mins. XXIII, 1/4.

[3] Ibid. 3/4, 8/4, 10/4.

[4] Ibid. 17/4.

[5] P.R.O.Adm. 3/5: 17/4, 20/4.

[6] Serg:Mins. XXIII, 17/4.

[7] Ibid. 27/4, 1/5, 4/5, 6/5; P.R.O.Adm. 1/3563, f. 641.

[8] P.R.O.Adm. 3/6: 11/5.

[9] P.R.O.Adm. 1/3563, f. 673.

[10] Serg:Mins. XXIII, 13/5, 15/5, 22/5.

the Admiralty to wait for the redemption of the merchants' bills until after the first £100,000 of the additional Excise had been paid. In consequence, the traders refused to honour their contracts.[1] It was only after they had met the Navy Board on 3 June and had listened to its entreaties that they consented, unwillingly, to do so;[2] and the Board was busy during the next few days trying to persuade the Admiralty to find an escort for the Baltic convoy, so as to ensure that it left before they again changed their minds.[3]

While these negotiations were going on, a no less urgent, though less vocal demand was arising from the yards and the ships. Early in April an estimate was made of the money which would be required to pay the summer's wages to the first and second rates in commission and to twenty of the largest third rates. It amounted to £319,061.[4] There was little chance of this being supplied, however, until the back wages had been paid, and it was estimated that £472,672 on this account was still owed to Christmas 1690 alone.[5] At the end of April, when the ships began to come into commission, Haddock and Wilshaw of the Navy Board were sent down to begin paying this off; but the shortage of money pursued them throughout their task, and although more than half the amount was issued to the men by the middle of May,[6] it did not satisfy their demands, and moreover was achieved only at the expense of the yards, which themselves were badly in need of cash. By the third week in May, with six months' pay owing to Chatham and a quarter's pay to all the other yards, and with some of the old debts from three and four years back still unpaid, the workmen were beginning to 'clamour' for their money.[7] On the 23rd Gregory at Chatham stressed the urgency of their demands: 'I must begg leave to use my wonted Plainess, and to tell You, that if six months pay come not to this place between this and Midsummer, it will not be in my power to keep our People within any Compass.' 'No reasonings', he added, 'nor Arguments will Still a hungry Belly.'[8] On 4 June he repeated his warning; on the 14th he wrote that the lack of credit

---

[1] P.R.O.Adm. 1/3563, f. 743.
[2] Serg:Mins. XXIII, 3/6.
[3] P.R.O.Adm. 1/3563, ff. 761–2, 827–8, 853–4.
[4] Ibid. f. 431.
[5] P.R.O.Adm. 1/3564, f. 263.
[6] P.R.O.Adm. 1/3563, ff. 597–8, 649.
[7] The word is Edward Gregory's (ibid. f. 733).
[8] Ibid. f. 735.

had now made it impossible not only to satisfy the workmen but to deal any longer with the local contractors. After considerable trouble, he had induced '2 honest fellows' to deliver a hundred loads of oak and sixty loads of elm, at a very high price; otherwise he could get no stores at all. 'We must', he concluded, 'pay off the old debts, or we'll never get credit.'[1]

The existence of these old debts was one of the limitations to the procedure by which the Navy Board hoped to tackle the shortage of money. Faced with the various demands upon the appropriated funds, throughout the summer of 1691 the Admiralty juggled with the allocations between the two chief groups of creditors. As each sum was received from the Treasury, it attempted to allot one part to the seamen and the yards, and the other to the merchants for their back bills. The distribution of this money was the responsibility of the Treasurer of the Navy on the advice of the Navy Board, and the latter solved the problem of precedence among the contractors by adhering firmly to the course of the navy. Where only one fund was involved, this was simple: the bills were filed in order of payment, as the money came in the tallies were redeemed, and when either the time or the money allowed to the fund came to an end, the outstanding debts were transferred to its successor.[2] But when more than one fund was devoted to the same purpose in the same year, the course was less easy to determine, and the struggle to get bills assigned to the most popular appropriation became intense. But despite these difficulties, the course was the only possible way to allot the inadequate supplies, and as the Navy Board rightly recognized, it was through it alone that the fleet was able to put to sea.[3]

The course, however, was subject to four serious limitations, two internal and two external. The first of these lay in the fact, already noted, that the oldest debts for stores, those from the previous reign, were still unpaid. They were, as it happened, inconsiderable—in May 1691 only £14,000 remained unpaid for stores from before 1689[4]—but nevertheless they were proving impossible to pay off, and were thus

---

[1] P.R.O.Adm. 1/3563, ff. 795–6, 875–6.

[2] E.g. 2 Will. and Mary, sess. 2, c. 10, art. v; 3 Will. and Mary, c. 6.

[3] P.R.O.Adm. 1/3563, ff. 367–8. [4] Ibid. f. 695.

assuming an importance to their creditors which in many cases their size alone did not warrant. By the system of the course, they should have been the first debts to be redeemed; but by the system of appropriations, which alone could implement the course, they did not come within the terms of redemption. The issue was raised in February 1691, when the Navy Board decided, at a meeting of the whole Board, that they could after all be included in the meaning of the word 'debts' as laid down in the latest appropriation,[1] and proceeded on its own authority to inform its standing contractors—who, like the rest, were threatening to stop supplies—that £5000 of the first £50,000 received on the appropriated fund would be assigned to the repayment of their old bills. According to the Navy Board, this had an immediate effect both on the standing contractors and on other merchants who were not immediately affected by the news. Men who had been refusing to tender for contracts, or who had been threatening to default on those formerly made, now tendered afresh, and prices came down on all types of naval stores. But a few weeks later the Treasury stopped payment on the old debts, on the ground that they were not in fact covered by the fund for the appropriation. Prices again rose, and contractors again withdrew their tenders, while the workmen in the yards, already dissatisfied with their condition but hitherto sustained by the hope that their old wages would be the next in order to be paid, began to clamour for their pay.[2] The redemption of the old debts had become a matter of confidence, almost a test case; and it was one which apparently could not be solved by the only system which offered any hope of general satisfaction. The course was handicapped by its failure to meet its own terms.

Another difficulty in the terms of the course lay in its treatment of merchants who had defaulted on their contracts. This arose as a question of principle early in 1692.[3] At that time, only £81,000 remained in the hands of the Treasurer of the Navy in tallies on the additional Excise (then the main fund for the navy) with which to pay the contractors. The course by then had been satisfied (mostly from other funds) to the end of June 1691, and those whose bills remained to be paid since that date were not anxious to be assigned tallies on that specific fund, which,

[1] Ibid. [2] Ibid. ff. 695–8. [3] P.R.O.Adm. 1/3565, ff. 57–60.

owing to its terms and to the nature of the commodities from which it received its yield was unlikely to satisfy their claims for some years, particularly since other services had already been granted payment on its earlier revenues. Among these contractors were some who had originally agreed to supply goods in the previous year, but had later refused to do so and had only recently been persuaded to comply with their contracts. In such cases, their bills had been put in course under the later date; but faced with payment only in the remote future, they were now claiming the right to be paid on the more favourable terms in existence at the time of their original contracts.[1] The Navy Board, anxious to appease them but fully aware that such an action might appear to others to be a violation of the course, could only suggest that the Exchequer be persuaded to allow the bills to be inserted under the additional Excise, but before the other bills still waiting to be paid.

These defects, however, although they damaged the course, were not such as to imperil it. The most serious danger came from outside, from the competition of other interests which at times deprived it of the guarantees on which its credit depended. These interests were of two sorts. First, as has been seen, there were the workmen and the seamen whose demands for ready money required the allocation of large sections of the funded credit. On occasion, particularly in the spring and autumn, these became so urgent that the original allocations were not enough to meet them, and raids were made on the allocations to the course, so that the satisfaction of the merchants' tallies, the precise terms of which had often been guaranteed when the contracts were signed, was further delayed.[2] Secondly, and far more serious, there were the claims of the victualling.

The Victuallers were in a particularly awkward position in 1691. The previous year, as they acknowledged,[3] had been a year of low prices. The harvest had been good, and the supply of cattle plentiful. But it was followed by a cycle of bad harvests and high prices, which

[1] Although the poll tax on which they would then have been paid had in the meantime come to an end, outstanding debts upon it could be met by its successor, under the usual terms of the appropriated funds.

[2] E.g. P.R.O.Adm. 1/3563, ff. 673–9; 1/3564, ff. 261–5, 979–81; 1/3565, f. 571.

[3] 'Wee consider that all Sorts of Provisions are as Cheape at this time, as they have been knowne to bee for many yeares' (P.R.O.Adm. 106/2349, f. 89).

began in the spring of 1691. The following figures for naval victualling illustrate the rapidity of the process:[1]

	Price in shillings			
	1689	1690	1691	1692
Barley (per 12 lb.)	3	3	3	3·25
Rice (per 12 lb.)	3	3	3	3·25
Currants (per 12 lb.)	5·25	5·5	5·5	6·5
Sugar, white (per 12 lb.)	6·5	7	7	6·75
Sugar, brown (per 12 lb.)	4·5	5	5	5
Mace (per lb.)	16·67	17·33	17·33	19·56
Wheat (per quarter)*	29·2	25·04	33·15	48·3
Peas (per quarter)*	20·67	16	24·25	35·46†
Hops (per cwt.)*	30	36	39·67	—
Malt (per quarter)*	15·73	14·77	17·93	24·36
Oatmeal (per quarter)*	27·97	26·36	35·28	38·25
Biscuit (per cwt.)	9·8	8·29	12·42	15·6
Butter (per 12 lb.)	3·75	4	4	4·5
Cheese (per 12 lb.)	2·16	2·89	—	2·25
White salt (per bushell)	1·74	1·33	1·68	—
Beef and oxen (per cwt.)*	19·85	20	18·67	19·25
Hogs (per cwt.)*	24·4	24·45	24·34	26·3‡

* The figures for these species are the average of their prices either for each month or for each quarter of each year, which are themselves given ibid. In the case of wheat, Beveridge's 'average B' (see ibid. p. 536) had been taken.

† In East Anglia, the Victuallers could get peas only at 40–42*s.* in the autumn of 1692 (P.R.O.Adm. 106/2349, f. 130).

‡ Figures available for the first six months only.

It will be seen that wheat, the staple index to agricultural prices, rose sharply, while of the important elements in the naval diet only the basic price of flesh showed a general decrease. Biscuit, and the ingredients for beer—two of the most important types of provision—both increased greatly. On the whole, too, it was the more expensive commodities which now became more expensive.

In this period of rising prices, the Victuallers continued to employ the methods of payment which had served them so badly when prices were lower. Their inadequate supplies, unlike those received by the Navy Office, were devoted to meeting the sudden demands made upon them as the different species of provisions fell due to be bought, or the ships complained of short supply. The deficiencies on the grants were substantial, and as usual the issues themselves were uneven. In November 1689 it had been estimated that, at the traditional rate of 20*s.* per

[1] They are taken from Sir William Beveridge (and others), *Prices and Wages in England*, I (1939), pp. 565–77. The prices are those for London only. The species have been selected on the basis of their importance in the naval diet.

man per month, the Victuallers would need £315,000 over the next year.[1] Between the 25th of that month and Michaelmas 1690, they actually received £226,248.[2] Although by May their debts had been largely cleared by the energetic action of the Treasury,[3] by the end of the year they had again risen to £150,000,[4] and in the spring of 1691 the Exchequer payments were quite inadequate to meet the demands. By 26 March, the Victuallers had received only £21,000 since the beginning of the year, and were having great difficulty in supplying the fleet.[5] In April, therefore, the familiar crisis arose. £60,000 had to be set aside for them to enable the ships to put to sea,[6] and in May, when the Navy Board as well as themselves were clamouring for assistance, their creditors were given priority in the allocations on the land tax, with the results which we have already seen for naval stores. Even so there was no money to spare, and early in the summer the fleet was warned that it must not expect to be revictualled to any extent later in the season. Russell accordingly placed the ships on short allowance, until in August they had to put back to Torbay through the shortage of meat and dry provisions.[7]

This return threw the Victuallers into a panic. They had not been given adequate warning of it and, as they justly remarked, they could not buy provisions in advance to meet this type of emergency.[8] They found it difficult to raise any credit, and once more the appropriations had to be diverted to help them do so. On this occasion, to the indignation of the Navy Board, they were allowed to impress money immediately upon their fund, and to disregard the course of payments.[9] This enabled them to meet the fleet's demands, but by the end of the year their debt stood at over £205,000, and the prospect for 1692 was

[1] P.R.O.Adm. 7/169, estimate of 22 November.
[2] *H.C.J.* x, p. 438.
[3] See pp. 327, 329, 331 above.
[4] P.R.O.Adm. 1/3563, f. 399.
[5] Ibid. ff. 399–400.
[6] P.R.O. T. 38/615, no. 2.
[7] See p. 379 above. The Victuallers had recommended in March that the fleet should be put to short allowance as soon as it sailed, with the disingenuous comment that many captains considered the men 'would be farr better pleased in this way than with their full allowance of Victualls which is generally more than they eat' (P.R.O. Adm. 1/3563, f. 400).
[8] P.R.O.Adm. 1/3564, f. 101.
[9] P.R.O.Adm. 1/3565, ff. 189, 571–2.

discouraging.[1] Whereas for the past year the Victualling Commission had been granted £391,071, on the basis—which it had accepted at the time—of 20*s.* per man per month,[2] for 1692, with prices far higher than before, it received a grant of only £370,500. This fell short of the standard rate by £19,500, and moreover only £235,105 of the grant was appropriated on the land tax, the rest being left 'at large'.[3] The victualling contractors were by now taking advantage of the scarcity and the high cost of provisions to insist on stricter terms than before, and were refusing to deliver without an assurance that they would be paid within a given time; there were only enough provisions of most sorts in store to last for a few weeks; and altogether the Victuallers doubted whether, on the Parliamentary allowance alone, they could carry on beyond the following September.[4]

The report in which they announced this news, the climax of many similar memoranda, provoked the Navy Board to review the claims of both Boards and to sum up the differences between them.[5] In its view, the preference given to the Victuallers, when both bodies needed equal assistance, was unjustified. Its chief grievance lay in the fact that the Victuallers did not pay their bills in course, but distributed their money according to their immediate needs, and it suggested that a course should henceforth be instituted for them. The Victuallers, however, insisted that this was impracticable. Relying as they did largely upon local men, who could not afford to wait for eventual payment on a distant fund, they were forced to reserve their best sources of credit for the redemption of the immediate bills, and to assign less urgent demands to the remoter supplies. At certain times of the year they could not, as they claimed, avoid heavy and immediate expenditure, which must necessarily take precedence of a system able to rely on a course of payment. Nor could they foretell how heavy these demands might be, partly because policy changed at short notice, but partly because their estimates for the year could not be based, as could those of the Navy

---

[1] Ibid. f. 1061.

[2] P.R.O.Adm. 7/169, estimate of 1 October 1690; *H.C.J.* x, p. 431; P.R.O.Adm. 106/2349, f. 87.

[3] P.R.O.Adm. 1/3565, f. 1061.

[4] Ibid. ff. 1061–4.

[5] P.R.O.Adm. 106/2349, ff. 111–17. The correspondence became distinctly heated on both sides before it finished (e.g. ibid. f. 117).

Office, on the accounts of the previous year. Such accounts had to take into consideration the quantities of victuals expended and remaining in store, and this was impossible until the pursers' accounts had been passed—the responsibility for which rested with the Navy Board—and until regular surveys could be taken at all the victualling ports of the goods in hand, which the size of the victualling staff made impossible. The problems of the two offices seemed to them to be distinct, and although appropriations were now the means of satisfying both, they could not see how both could have an equal claim on the appropriations. Each Board was right so far as it went. Credit could be sustained only by a course of payment, but no course could provide ready money; and in the financial conditions of the day, the short-term provision of cash, which was essential to the Victuallers, could not complement but could only endanger the long-term establishment of credit, without which the Navy Board could not carry on.

How was it, therefore, that this unstable system managed, under the circumstances of war, to finance the greatest and most concentrated expansion of the navy since the first Dutch war? In the last resort, it was because the machinery of financial supply was accepted by those who had to work it. The contractors—who, as the Navy Board remarked, were 'the foundacon and rise of all that can be expected from our Fleet'[1]—often refused to deliver their goods; but they did so because they hoped thereby to get a better security for repayment, not because they believed that repayment was impossible. They resented being given low priority on the funds, not being registered on the funds themselves. The Treasurer of the Navy relied on the course—itself a measure of faith—because it seemed the best means to control the payments which would be met eventually and which, if slow, seemed also to be sure. The Treasury, which distributed the allocations upon the funds, again relied on the funds to meet the demands eventually; while the Commons who guaranteed payment were concerned to collect the yield from their impositions in sufficient time to satisfy the creditors, and did not deny their obligation or their capacity to pay. The heyday of the great fleet was also the heyday of short-term credit.

[1] P.R.O.Adm. 1/3564, f. 261.

In 1693 and 1694, this system of credit was on the decline. The process did not affect the constitutional responsibility for payment, which had settled on Parliament in the previous two years, but rather the method by which this responsibility was secured. The exercise of Parliamentary control remained much the same as for the financial year 1692. In both years the estimates of the service departments were submitted in detail to the Commons; those for 1693 were criticized clause by clause, those for 1694 with less care.[1] The grants were made accordingly as follows:[2]

	Estimates (including ordnance)	Supply
1693	£2,077,216	£2,112,116
1694	£2,346,132	£2,581,700

This excess of supply over estimates is not so clear an indication of generosity on the part of the Commons as it seems. The grants actually made to the navy for the current services of the two years were £1,926,516 and £2,500,000 respectively, and of the latter figure £552,777 was designed to help clear the naval debt at Michaelmas 1693. In addition, the detailed appropriations for 1693 made it clear that they did not include the ordinary, for which £100,000 must be added, and it has been assumed that this was included in the general supply granted for the next year. In each case, moreover, a proportion of the grant for the 27 ships must be added, although the supply itself had been voted earlier. In the financial year 1693, £85,600 was issued on this head, and in the next year £81,700. The true picture, therefore, looks like this:[3]

	1693 £	1694 £
Appropriations to navy for war	1,926,516	1,947,223
To redeem debts	—	552,777
Ordinary	100,000	—
27 ships	85,600	81,700
Total	2,112,116	2,581,700

[1] *H.C.J.* X, pp. 709, 711, 713, 729–33; XI, pp. 175–6, 180–2.

[2] P.R.O.Adm. 7/169, estimates of 24 November 1692, 18 November 1693; *H. of L. N.S.* VII, p. 174.

[3] *H. of L. N.S.* VII, pp. 174, 176; I, p. 13. A further complication arises, in that the receipts at the Exchequer on the appropriation from the Excise for the 27 ships did not balance its issues on that head, at any rate in 1693 (*H. of L. N.S.* I, p. 13). I have, however, disregarded this.

The issues to the navy, as usual, fell short of the theoretical supplies. It is simpler to calculate the discrepancies in these years, because the payments from the Exchequer to the Ordnance are related directly, in the accounts, to the payments to the navy. The results were as follows:[1]

	Parliamentary supply	Total Exchequer issues	Deficiencies of issues upon supply
1693	£2,112,116	£2,109,380	£2,736
1694	£2,581,700	£2,203,027	£378,673

The issues may also be related to the estimates. If the payments made on behalf of the 27 ships and the Ordnance are subtracted from the former, they amount to £1,839,728 and £2,149,994 respectively. The deficiencies of these issues on the estimates were accordingly £237,488 in 1693 and £196,138 in 1694; and in the latter case, it must be remembered, some of the issues may have been made to pay off old debts and not to meet current expenditure.[2]

But the estimates themselves were inadequate to meet the expenses of the war at this stage. The calculations of the cost of maintaining a man for a month in wages, wear and tear, victuals and ordnance varied slightly between 1691 and 1694, but not so as to reflect the actual variations in prices. The figures accepted were as follows:[3]

	1691			1692			1693			1694		
	£	*s.*	*d.*	£	*s.*	*d.*	£	*s.*	*d.*	£	*s.*	*d.*
Wages	1	10	0	1	8	6	1	10	0	1	10	0
Wear and tear	1	10	0	1	7	6	1	10	0	1	8	0
Victuals	1	0	0		19	0	1	0	0	1	0	0
Ordnance		5	0		5	0		5	0		7	0
Total	4	5	0	4	0	0	4	5	0	4	5	0

The anticipated rate of expenditure, therefore, had hardly risen since 1688–89;[4] the increased size of the annual estimates merely reflected the

[1] *H. of L. N.S.* VII, pp. 176–7; I, p. 67. The latter source checks the former for the issues in 1693. The parallel source for 1694 does not exist in print (see *Cal. Treas. Bks. 1689–92*, p. clxxiii), so that no check has been made for that year. *H. of L. N.S.* VII, p. 225, gives slightly different figures for the issues in each case. P.R.O.Adm. 49/173 gives the issues to the navy alone for 1694 as £2,063,693.

[2] *H. of L. N.S.* VII, pp. 176–7. It is naturally impossible, owing to the way in which naval offices kept their accounts, to tell either from the figures given here or from those in P.R.O.Adm. 49/173 when issues were designed to redeem debt.

[3] P.R.O.Adm. 7/169, *passim*; see also *H. of L. N.S.* VII, pp. 173–4.

[4] For 1688–9, see pp. 159–60 above; for 1690, P.R.O.Adm. 7/169, estimates of 22 November 1689.

increased size of the navy, not the increased cost of individual naval activities. Prices, on the other hand, in 1693 and 1694 continued to rise in many instances over those of 1692, and in every single instance remained higher than in earlier years. The figures for four of the more important kinds of naval stores, coming for the most part from different parts of the world, are interesting; although it must be remembered that extraneous factors entered into the cost of imported goods:[1]

	Tallow: *s.* per cwt.	Tar: *s.* per last	Rosin: *s.* per cwt.	Hemp: *s.* per cwt.
1692	38·00	194·75	37·10	24·81
1693	46·19	220·83	30·14	26·13
1694	51·50	221·56	22·40	27·13

The prices paid by the navy for victuals rose in almost every case between 1692 and 1693, although only in some cases again in 1694:[2]

	Price in shillings		
	1692	1693	1694
Rice (per 12 lb.)	3·25	3·75	4
Wheat (per quarter)	48·3	50·62	35·39
Peas (per quarter)	35·46	28·63	25·57
Oatmeal (per quarter)	38·25	43·5	36·42
Flour (per cwt.)	—	13	19
Biscuit (per cwt.)	15·6	16·79	11
Malt (per quarter)	24·36	28·1	21·07
Hops (per cwt.)	—	41·5	91·5
Oxen (per cwt.)	19·25	22·91*	23·33
Hogs (per cwt.)	26·3	—	32·83
Butter (per 12 lb.)	4·5	5·36	5·17
Cheese (per 12 lb.)	2·25	2·5	2·42

* Based on two sets of prices only for August and September.

In no case were prices at their level of 1689 or 1690, and mostly they were far above them. While the rates of expenditure had been raised by one-quarter on the heads of the estimates, in most cases the cost of feeding the navy had risen often by half.

How far this general rise in prices was due to the inability of the navy to pay for its material promptly it is impossible to say, but it was

---

[1] Particularly in 1693, when for the first time customs duties were levied on imported naval stores (4 Will. and Mary c. 5, particularly art. xxi; *H.C.J.* x, p. 820; P.R.O.Adm. 1/3571, ff. 431–2). The figures given above are taken from Beveridge, loc. cit. pp. 672–3, 676.

[2] Ibid. pp. 565–9, 571, 574, 576–7; cf. p. 479 above.

certainly affected by it. The naval debt both reflected and was partly responsible for the increasing costs with which the service was faced. The Commons' attempt in the winter of 1693 to reduce it by allotting £500,000 towards the arrears of seamens' wages and £52,777 towards clearing the other debts,[1] was only a partial answer to a deficit which at Michaelmas 1693 stood at £1,782,597, with the arrears of seamens' wages alone amounting to £1,036,415 and the victualling debt to £308,486.[2] A year later, the total debt had risen to £1,931,246, with arrears of wages—despite the £500,000—standing at £1,126,803, and the victualling debt now £339,977.[3] Each year was proving the inability of the existing system to reduce its indebtedness, and in a State which was unable, thanks to the cost of the war, to live within its means, but which regarded the resulting gap between income and expenditure as only temporary, debt remained a source of embarrassment to the debtor and might well ruin the creditor. The problem was to change it into a source of strength to debtor and creditor alike. The foundations for such a process existed, thanks to the recent transference of responsibility for the debt to Parliament; for the deficit was purely internal, and the difficulty was merely one of restoring a confidence which the existing system of credit was beginning to undermine. The significant measures of the years 1693–4, therefore, are not of the same kind as those of 1691–2. Whereas the earlier period was remarkable for the assumption by Parliament of a large measure of financial responsibility, the later period is distinguished by its efforts to shift the obligation to meet its responsibilities from the immediate to the distant future, and to produce sufficiently attractive terms and to identify itself sufficiently with its creditors, for them to prefer to remain unpaid. Where the initial result of the new type of expensive war was the short term loan, made upon a Parliamentary guarantee of redemp-

---

1 *H. of L. N.S.* VII, p. 174.

2 Serg.MS. A 133, statement of 15 November 1693. The Victuallers themselves worked out their debt rather differently for the same date, and made it come to £330,532. It is possible that this sum represents the correct amount, as the statement was compiled later than that cited above, and included various sums for which the bills had not been received in 1693 (P.R.O. T. 38/658, no. 2).

3 P.R.O.Adm. 49/173. The corresponding figure for the victualling debts in P.R.O. T. 38/658, no. 3, is £342,657.

tion, its next and final result was the negotiable bill arising from the negotiable tally, and the funded national debt supported by a Parliamentary guarantee of interest.

But to an executive department the decline of the existing credit was of more importance than the first signs of the emergence of its successor. So far as the navy was concerned, the crisis was more apparent than the solution. As the deficit became greater, so did the demands for its redemption and the difficulty of meeting them. The struggle for priority on the most advantageous funds, pronounced in 1692, became intense in the following two years. At the end of March 1693, the Navy Board began a long series of memoranda on the situation. The mainstay of naval finance at the time was provided by the additional duties on the Excise of 1691, usually known as the 'double ninepences', and owing to the low priority which the department had been given upon this fund no substantial yield was expected from it for another three years.[1] The Treasury, and the Cabinet itself, promised to place the appropriations on a more useful fund; but nothing was done during the spring, and no ready money at all had been received by the third week in May, at a time when it was needed particularly to pay the men in the fleet.[2] The necessity for cash was becoming urgent by midsummer, for the dockyard workmen were growing restive, and were refusing any longer to take tickets which could not be redeemed on presentation at the Navy Office.[3] In July, after a desperate appeal by the Admiralty, a large sum of ready money was advanced by the Exchequer to pay the yards and some of the ships in the fleet,[4] and in August £2000 a week was set aside by the Treasury in an attempt to meet the rest of the arrears as the ships came in. But as the Navy Board remarked, that was of little use when almost £400,000 was needed to clear the back pay to the previous spring, let alone the most recent arrears.[5] By the autumn, the position had been reached which the navy had tried always to avoid: the arrears of wages had become so great that they had to be given priority over the current service of wear and tear. In November the yards were owed £257,600

---

[1] P.R.O.Adm. 1/3568, f. 694.
[2] Ibid. f. 1104.
[3] P.R.O.Adm. 1/3569, ff. 324–6.
[4] Ibid. ff. 627–8.
[5] Ibid. ff. 820–2, 962–71.

and the seamen five times that amount.[1] This meant ready money. For the first half of 1694, therefore, the contractors were not paid at all, and their tallies were assigned to the most remote funds at the disposal of the navy.[2] When the time came to contract for the Baltic stores, to the consternation of the Navy Board no tenders were received.[3] It was not until the end of April that the merchants could be induced to attend the Navy Office, and then they refused to deal except for small quantities of timber and masts. At the beginning of June, the Board had still secured no contracts for hemp or canvas, and in the second week of the month it abandoned the negotiations and withdrew the entire hemp contract for 2000 tons. Soon afterwards, John Taylor agreed to buy the necessary material on commission.[4] This was the only occasion throughout the war when the contract system broke down completely. It was not inappropriate that the limitations of short-term credit should have been exposed so clearly by the demand for ready money.

For the rest of the year, Navy Board and Admiralty continued to complain of the funds on which their issues were being made, while the Treasury balanced the increasingly inadequate allocations as best it could.[5] As usual, the chief grievance of the Navy Board was the priority given to the Victuallers. In 1693, the latter had received over two-thirds of their payments in cash, as compared with wear and tear which had received only one-sixth of its total in this way;[6] and in 1694 they received five-sixths of their payments in cash, compared with the one-quarter supplied during the same period in ready money to wear and tear.[7] The familiar quarrel between the two Boards became more bitter as the money grew more scarce. The whole machine, indeed, seemed to be in real danger of breaking down by the autumn of 1694. The Victuallers, despite the priority they received throughout 1693 and 1694, had failed each year to supply the fleet, and the ships had

---

[1] P.R.O.Adm. 1/3570, ff. 732–3.

[2] P.R.O.Adm. 1/3571, f. 471. Even in 1693 they had received only one-fifth of the amount in money which had been paid to the seamen and workmen (P.R.O.Adm. 1/3570, f. 767).

[3] Ibid. ff. 257–8.

[4] Serg:Mins. xxx, 13/4–15/6.

[5] See *Cal.Treas.Bks. 1693–6*, pp. 133, 325.

[6] P.R.O.Adm. 1/3570, ff. 767–8; P.R.O. T. 38/615.

[7] P.R.O.Adm. 49/173; 1/3573, f. 679; P.R.O. T. 38/615.

been on short allowance for the greater part of each campaign;[1] the dockyard workmen were deserting and downing tools in protest at the arrears of wages;[1] and the contractors were refusing to deal with the navy except at exorbitant rates and for small amounts. The creditors had lost faith in the system of credit, and the task was now to restore confidence before the system of responsibility on which the credit was based was endangered.

The agent of credit was the tally, and it was upon the tally that the process must concentrate. By the end of 1694, there was a great deal of money locked up in the large bundles of wooden sticks which remained with their owners awaiting redemption. The problem was how to set it free. No change of emphasis from one type of short-term fund to another would suffice; the only solution lay in replacing, or at least in supplementing, the existing basis of credit by one which would enable the tally to circulate indefinitely, with a value of its own derived from its very longevity. Only when the creditor was satisfied to remain a creditor, could credit be sustained.

The first attempt to introduce long-term credit had been made in 1692 with the experiment of the Tontine,[2] which established life annuities with benefit of survivorship upon the security of additional duties on the Excise. Those who subscribed to a loan of £1,000,000 were to receive ten per cent from 1693 to 1700, and thereafter the sum of £70,000, brought in by the fund, was to be divided annually among the subscribers or their nominees. As each subscriber died, his annuity passed to the survivors until only seven remained. On their deaths the annuity ceased altogether. The Tontine, however, was a failure; only £108,100 was subscribed towards it,[3] and considerably more was advanced on an alternative provision made in the same Act,[4] whereby those who subscribed £100 towards a fund designed to make up the deficit that might result from such a failure, were to receive an annuity of £14 during their own lifetime or that of a nominee. This alternative proved immediately popular, and was repeated in 1693 in another Act[5]

---

[1] P.R.O.Adm. 3/8: 26/4; 3/10: 1/5.

[2] 4 Will. and Mary c. 3. This paragraph is based on Shaw's *Introduction to Cal. Treas.Bks. 1695–1702*, pp. clxxxvii–cxcviii.

[3] E. L. Hargreaves, *The National Debt* (1930), p. 6.

[4] Art. xxii.

[5] 5 and 6 Will. and Mary, c. 5.

designed to provide the remainder of the £1,000,000 still called for. On this occasion, also, the annuities were exempted from all duties and taxes. The public creditor was thus placed in an advantageous position, a fact which was soon appreciated and resented by the opponents of funded debts.[1] In 1694, two further Acts were passed involving the same principle of long-term credit. In the first of these,[2] the attraction of a lottery was introduced, on the result of which the size of the individual annuities was determined. In the second,[3] an advance was made towards funding the debts for a longer period by offering annuities for longer than one lifetime, and opportunities were introduced for holders of annuities for single lives to exchange them later for annuities for two or three lives. Tallies on these funds, therefore, assumed a negotiable character in practice which they had possessed before only in principle.[4] Although the permanent funded debt had not yet appeared, with the establishment of the long-term debts the machinery of government loans was ready, by the end of 1694, for more extended facilities for credit than those provided by the wooden tally. The time was ripe for the reintroduction to government finance of the negotiable paper bill which had been tried once, unsuccessfully, over twenty years before.[5] With the emergence of the Bank of England in that winter, and the circulation of the privately issued but powerful Bank of England notes, an answer was to be found to the apparently antithetical but closely connected problems of Parliamentary financial responsibility and departmental credit.

IV

The administrative developments which follow a strategic demand often fail to correspond to the position that has arisen by the time they have become effective; and the full force of the growth of organization and expense which marked the years 1693 and 1694 fell during a period when the employment of the great fleet was uncertain. The very completeness of the victory at Barfleur had set a problem which

---

[1] Hargreaves, loc. cit. pp. 8, 38.

[2] 5 Will. and Mary c. 7.

[3] 5 Will. and Mary c. 20.

[4] See A. E. Feaveryear, *The Pound Sterling* (1931), pp. 105, 107.

[5] For the history of the Treasury Order of 1667–1672, see W. A. Shaw, 'The Treasury Order Book', in *Economic Journal*, XVI, pp. 33–40.

seemed in the following years to be insoluble. After the fiasco of the summer and autumn of 1692, the success of large-scale combined operations by sea and land appeared improbable; but with the French fleet unlikely to seek an encounter in 1693 there was no alternative employment for the English fleet. Accordingly, before he left for Holland in the winter of 1692, William decided to resume where the previous campaign had left off, and to stage a combined land and sea attack on Brest.[1] By the middle of January 1693 the preparations were under way,[2] and towards the end of February the troops were selected for the service.[3] In April, William ordered them to be distributed in camps along the coast of Hampshire and Sussex, so as to waste no time in embarking.[4] By the end of that month, the Transport Commissioners had already spent £33,000 on the preparations, and the expenditure of a further £22,125 by midsummer was authorized.[5] But in the event the money was laid out to no purpose, for no attack, and indeed no embarkation, ever took place.

The reason for its abandonment lay in the diversion of the fleet to a project which had originally been intended to occupy a single squadron. In the summer of 1692 it had been agreed that some ships should at some time be sent into the Mediterranean, to escort the trade which had been denied the chance of sailing for the Levant for a year.[6] Lengthy negotiations had gone on between the English and the Dutch over the size of the squadron, the length of its stay in those waters and the date on which it should sail;[7] but the complications of supplying the main fleet left little opportunity to organize any subsidiary expedition, and although a squadron of two third rates, three fourths, one fifth and one fireship was assigned to a 'convoy for Turkey',[8] and the

---

1 B.M.Addnl. 37991, f. 26*v*. The minutes of the conferences where the matter was discussed, and which were held, mostly on Sundays, between the King, the inner Council and the Admiralty at Whitehall, are given in P.R.O.Adm. 1/5248. It is difficult to tell when exactly the decision was taken, but it was probably during December.

2 P.R.O.Adm. 1/5248, 8/1, 15/1.

3 Ibid. 29/2.

4 B.M.Addnl. 37991, f. 6*v*.

5 Ibid. f. 26*v*.

6 P.R.O.Adm. 3/6: 22/5, 24/8.

7 B.M.Addnl. 37991, ff. 11, 12*v*; *Correspondentie van Willem III en van Hans Willem Bentinck*, I, pp. 369–72.

8 P.R.O.Adm. 8/3, 1 August, 1 October.

arrangements reached the point where its sailing orders were drawn up with the assistance of the Turkey Company,[1] the winter arrived without any serious effort having been made to put it to sea. On his return to England, however, William insisted that it was to receive priority so as to sail early in 1693,[2] and in January Rooke was appointed in command.[3] In February the merchants were informed publicly, as their representatives had been told in private in December, that a convoy would definitely be leaving for the Straits in the spring,[4] and on the 20th of that month Rooke was given his sailing orders and directed to appoint a rendezvous for a squadron of three third rates, five fourths and seven fifths, with two fireships, a bombvessel, a brigantine and a storeship.[5] On 16 March he was ordered to leave at the first opportunity,[6] but—much to the disgust of the merchants[7]—various administrative delays held him at Spithead until 30 May. On that day, with almost 400 merchant vessels of both nations in company, he weighed anchor from St Helens.[8]

The news that a large convoy would be sailing for the Mediterranean was naturally soon known to the French, and at the end of April the Brest fleet under Tourville and the Toulon fleet under d'Estrées were ordered to concentrate in Lagos bay to intercept.[9] By the middle of May William in Flanders had wind of this move,[10] and was urging that the convoy should leave England immediately. The Cabinet in reply inquired whether the escort should not be strengthened; but, as the

---

[1] P.R.O.Adm. 3/7: 23/10.

[2] P.R.O.Adm. 1/5248, 4/12, 11/12.

[3] Ibid. 11/12, 8/1.

[4] P.R.O.Adm. 3/7: 11/1; 3/8: 18/12; 2/383, Secretary of Admiralty to Turkey Company, 1/2/93.

[5] P.R.O.Adm. 3/8: 20/2; *H. of L. N.S.* I, pp. 107–9.

[6] *H. of L. N.S.* I, p. 110.

[7] The Dutch calculated that they had lost seventy per cent of the capital invested in their ships for the voyage, on account of the demurrage which this delay cost them (B.M.Addnl. 37992, f. 4).

[8] *H. of L. N.S.* I, p. 129. The delays were caused mostly by weather and shortage of victuals.

[9] Roncière, op. cit. VI, pp. 140–1.

[10] There had been earlier rumours of it in England (*Cal.S.P.Dom. 1693*, pp. 32, 52), but the allied espionage service, centred at Rotterdam, could not confirm them (S.P.For. 84/22, ff. 175–80).

King informed it with some asperity, this would be unnecessary provided that the convoy sailed without further delay.[1] Rooke, however, still seemed unable to get away, and on the 19th the main fleet, which was now concentrated at St Helens ready to cruise in his support in the Soundings before making its attack upon Brest,[2] was ordered to escort him 'so far as you [the joint admirals] shall think requisite'.[3] Accordingly, when the squadron sailed eleven days later, it was with the allied fleet of 102 ships in company.[4]

It will have been noticed, in this brief account of the preparations for the Mediterranean convoy, that William himself took an active part in them; and indeed the winter of 1692–3 and the following spring are remarkable principally for the detailed interest which, for the first time, he displayed in naval affairs. There is little direct evidence of this before the end of April 1693, for until that time the King was in England, and no correspondence therefore exists in which his influence may be traced. But from the tenor of the letters which began on his arrival on the continent, it is clear that this had been direct and considerable for some months beforehand. This was partly due to the fact that no competent naval authority existed after the simultaneous disappearance from the naval scene of Russell and Nottingham. All three of his original confidants had now gone, and the emphasis which, thanks to Nottingham, had been placed upon the Secretary of State in naval affairs, produced a disappointing result when the Secretary was not qualified to control them. Trenchard, who had been put into office as the least offensive of the Whig candidates for a post that could not be refused them, had neither political stature nor experience of sea warfare. The ministry itself was a weak one, 'incompetent to decide one day what the House of Commons would do the next',[5] and the Board of Admiralty was no more qualified than usual to replace or assist its superiors. The inclusion of Killigrew and Delavall in the Commission of 1693 strengthened its right to speak with some authority on technical questions, but although they attended its meetings while the fleet was fitting out in the spring, they naturally were not present after the end

[1] B.M.Addnl. 37991, f. 27; 37992, ff. 8, 12*v*.
[2] B.M.Addnl. 37991, f. 29; *Cal.S.P.Dom. 1693*, pp. 102–5.
[3] *H. of L. N.S.* I, p. 129. [4] Burchett, p. 178.
[5] Dalrymple, op. cit. II, appendix to pt II, p. 50.

of April. The remaining five members were no more impressive than they had been the year before. Indeed, they were less impressive, for in the interval the Board had lost one important and one unimportant figure and had received in exchange only a new and unimportant leader. When the patent for the new Board was issued on 15 April, the names of Cornwallis and Onslow were omitted. The former had probably resigned in January[1] and the latter, if rumour may be believed, in March.[2] According to the order of the names on the patent of 1692, Lowther should have succeeded Cornwallis; but, possibly because of his age and indisposition, he did not. The next survivor by precedent was Priestman, but he was so unpopular with a large section of the Commons that, although he did much of the work of the Commission,[3] he could not be made first Commissioner. Accordingly Falkland, whose name came next on the patent, and who enjoyed the two advantages of a peerage and of having been personally excepted from the Commons' attacks on the Board during the previous winter,[4] was placed at its head. Such a Commission was of no account, and far from replacing Trenchard in questions of policy, it did not even —despite the resolution of the Commons a few months before—replace him in administrative business. Although two of the three joint Admirals were Commissioners of the Admiralty, and although Trenchard was not a particularly powerful figure, the same detailed correspondence was conducted between the Secretary and the fleet as Nottingham had conducted with Russell,[5] and the Admiralty was limited to

[1] *Camden Miscellany*, II, p. 188. The Dutch ambassador also placed his resignation at the end of that month (B.M.Addnl. 17677, NN, f. 38, cited by James).

[2] Luttrell, op. cit. III, p. 54. He ceased to attend Board meetings on 11 March.

[3] He was summoned as its representative by both Lords and Commons the following winter, when the Admiralty's papers for the summer were examined (*H.L.J.* XV, p. 330; *H.C.J.* XI, pp. 5, 21).

[4] Grey, op. cit. X, p. 296. It is possible that his being the only peer on the Board was the decisive factor, but there is no evidence to support this assumption. Whether he would have been appointed as head of the Commission if he had been unpopular in the Commons, I cannot say.

[5] It may be seen partly in *Catalogue of Naval Manuscripts in the Library of the United Service Institution* (compiled by H. Garbett, n.d.), pp. 67–74, and partly in *Cal.S.P.Dom. 1693*. The arrangement of the material in *H. of L. N.S.* I, pp. 107–87, makes it difficult to follow the correspondence included there.

sending formal orders which had been largely decided elsewhere, and information on supplies and victualling arrangements.[1] It is indeed difficult at this time to see what function the Commission served.[2] Its control of naval movements was removed by the Secretary of State, and the Navy Board could have informed the fleet of the rest of its work. With none of the recognized authorities, therefore, capable of handling naval affairs, William himself descended into the arena.

The reason, however, for his emphasis on the Mediterranean was not merely negative, but positive: not simply the result of the inadequacy of the naval authorities, but also of his own interest in the area. This may be seen in the contrast between the attention which he paid to events there and to those in home waters; for the latter, although greater in 1693 and 1694 than it had been in earlier years, was still slight compared with the former. The Mediterranean, indeed, to judge from the scanty evidence of his initial dispositions in January 1689 and from the terms of the naval convention with the Dutch of the same year, had been William's objective for the allied navies from the time he invaded England.[3] From 1689 to June 1692, however, little opportunity had offered for any effective action in the south. A small squadron had been sent to the Straits in March 1690, and had cruised for three months east of Gibraltar, with considerable effect upon the Barbary states;[4] and in December of that year a slightly larger force had gone out, which stayed to convoy the trade home in October 1691. In one sense the squadron proposed for 1692 was their successor, but the aftermath of Barfleur placed it in a new setting. It is significant that the first mention of the squadron was made by the King immediately after that victory; and if uninterrupted concentration on one objective is the mark of a policy, then William's conscious Mediterranean policy may be said to date from that time. The greatest authority on this subject has remarked

---

[1] Trenchard on occasion even interfered with the latter, to the open annoyance of the Admiralty (e.g. P.R.O.Adm. 3/8: 14/7).

[2] Haddock, the experienced Comptroller of the Navy, evidently had a low opinion of its importance in March 1693, when, on being sounded on the possibility of his joining the new Commission, he declined on the ground that 'I know well I am capable of doeing his Maj^{ty} far greater service as I am, then if I were at that bord' (B.M. Egerton 2521, f. 75).

[3] See pp. 249, 252 above.

[4] Burchett, pp. 36–44.

that 'it was not till the fifth year of the war that a radical change in Louis's strategy opened William's eyes to his real power. Then there was something Napoleonic in the rapidity and completeness with which he grasped the new idea and changed his front' to the Mediterranean; and he places the moment of the change in May 1694.[1] But this theory cannot stand on the evidence of the correspondence which William conducted, through his secretary Blathwayt, with his Secretaries of State in 1692 and 1693. On the very morrow of Barfleur, in his first letter to Nottingham after the news had reached the King, Blathwayt wrote that His Majesty wished the inner Council to consider the possibility of sending a squadron to the Mediterranean.[2] Nottingham was unable to see the point of the suggestion,[3] and reported to Blathwayt that the Council was against any such move, and that Russell was 'absolutely against it'.[4] William, however, persisted in the idea, and the rare letters that he sent to England referred hardly at all to the events which were taking place in the Channel at the time, and which were so agitating the ministers, but almost entirely to the advantage of having a force of allied ships in the Straits before the winter.[5] In his later letters, the reason for this was given as the protection of the convoy for the Levant, which had been proposed and agreed to late in June. But, as Nottingham remarked earlier, when William first suggested the plan no convoy for the Mediterranean was intended;[6] and it would seem possible, although no reason for his proposal was given at this stage, that the King had in mind the diplomatic and strategic advantages of the move as much as any support of trade. In one of his letters in July, indeed, Blathwayt gave some indication of his master's intentions, using the cover that William often employed when he wished to sound the ground: the Dutch, he wrote, were eager to send a strong squadron to the Mediterranean to help force the Turks make peace with the Emperor.[7] He stressed this again at the end of July, when it had become clear that the

---

[1] Julian S. Corbett, *England in the Mediterranean*, II (1904), pp. 145–6, 158.

[2] B.M.Addnl. 37991, f. 87.

[3] Finch Transcr., Nottingham to Russell, 11/6.

[4] Ibid. 14/6.

[5] B.M.Addnl. 37991, ff. 95, 103, 106. See also *Archives d'Orange-Nassau*, 3rd series, I, p. 284.

[6] Finch Transcr., Nottingham to Russell, 11/6.

[7] B.M.Addnl. 37991, f. 11; letter of 7 July.

authorities at home could not control two sets of arrangements at the same time, and that the Levant convoy was going to prove impossible that autumn. Even so, he asked, would it not be possible for the English to fall in with the Dutch plan and send a squadron on its own in November?[1] By the middle of August, when the Council at last, and without much hope of success, turned its attention to the Mediterranean, William was getting somewhat impatient. He was very anxious, wrote Blathwayt on the 14th, that a squadron should be sent, and requested 'that ships for the purpose be found by any means'.[2] A few days later, however, Nottingham reported that the Admiralty could promise a force of six third and fourth rates only, for the rest were engaged either in refitting or in convoying and cruising in home waters;[3] and on the 23rd he inquired privately of the King's secretary what exactly the squadron was to do when it reached the Mediterranean.[4] On 1 September, after a few more letters had been received from England stressing the inability of the navy to produce a larger force for the purpose,[5] William repeated to Nottingham that he was most anxious for the Admiralty to find the ships, and as soon as possible;[6] but in the end he had to give way as the complete muddle of the autumn was revealed. It was, therefore, with particular vigour that he superintended the preparations for Rooke's squadron early the next year.

Exactly what William had in mind for the Mediterranean in the late summer of 1692 cannot be said for certain. He revealed his preoccupation with interests other than trade only when trade had failed him, and then he gave no clue as to his real intentions. Once again we must infer these largely from his attitude a few months later, when the situation was still much the same but when he himself was more explicit. Undoubtedly one reason for his plan lay in the diplomatic pressure which he hoped to exert upon the Turks, for he referred to this again in 1693.[7] But it is probable that he also had in mind its effect upon the Spanish court, which he knew by experience responded to a show

[1] Ibid. f. 121*v*.
[2] Ibid. f. 140.
[3] Finch Transcr., 19/8.
[4] Ibid. 23/8.
[5] Ibid., Nottingham to Blathwayt, 27/8 (two letters), 30/8.
[6] B.M.Addnl. 37991, f. 153.
[7] B.M.Addnl. 37992, f. 33.

of naval force.[1] In the summer of 1692, it seemed high time to remind it of the existence of allied sea power, for it was beginning to maltreat the English merchant vessels which made the passage to Bilbao, removing some of their men for the galleys and refusing to supply the ships themselves with stores.[2] The trouble, wrote the ambassador at Madrid, lay in the uninterrupted cruises of the Toulon fleet, which were having a bad effect on the Spanish king and enabling the Francophiles at court and in the seaports to get their way. The consul at Cadiz confirmed and added detail to these reports.[3] At the same time, William may have been influenced by the idea of supporting the unreliable Victor Amadeus of Savoy, who had recently made an unsuccessful attempt to invade France from the south-east and who, without some tangible proof of allied power, was always liable either to stop fighting or to raise his terms.

The extent to which the King hoped to fulfil these intentions, and the degree to which he was attached to each of them, may not have been clear at this time even to himself; but he had every cause towards the end of the year to look in their direction. His was a European problem, and the balance of the war was shifting towards the southern flank in Europe. The year had gone badly in Flanders and, after the initial success, at sea; there seemed little hope, as he himself told his friends at the close of the campaign, of invading France with any success in the north, and he was even inclining towards the idea of a negotiated peace.[4] The strategy of direct attack was proving bankrupt, and its bankruptcy might soon affect the attitude of the allies in the south upon whom the burden of an alternative flanking attack would fall. From his vantage point at the head of the alliance, with his varied sources of information of which he alone knew the sum, and with his European interests which separated him from all his English ministers, and of which he alone had always been acknowledged to be the judge, William looked at the Mediterranean with a different eye from that of the authorities at home. To him, it was now the one point at which allied sea power impinged upon allied strategy. But to the Cabinet in

[1] S.P.For. 94/73, Stanhope to Nottingham, 17/1, 7/3/91.

[2] S.P.For. 94/73, Stanhope to Nottingham, 2/4, 25/5–4/6/92.

[3] Ibid., Howell Gwynne's report of 18 April 1692.

[4] Clark, *Later Stuarts*, p. 164.

England, which had not hitherto been concerned with allied strategy or with the diplomatic complications in which that was involved, a Mediterranean squadron represented no diplomatic agent designed to support a failing alliance, but simply an unavoidable commitment from time to time to protect one of the most powerful and lucrative of the national trades. At the end of 1692, therefore, William's European interests met English domestic interests for the first time on their own ground; and the divergence between his ministers and himself in the autumn of that year, unimportant as it seemed in its contemporary setting, was the prelude to a major struggle over the distribution of naval power, in which their different attitudes were complicated by the fact that William could not inform the ministers of all the purposes for which he required the Mediterranean force, and the ministers could not fully comprehend a policy which affected them in this one instance but which they were not normally called upon to debate. At this stage, only a squadron was involved, and not yet a fleet. But the squadron was now no longer, as it had been, an appendage to be considered on its own, but rather the prelude to a fleet. And the importance of the events of 1693 lay in the way in which they introduced the latter to a policy which until then had been only half-formed, and confronted William with consequences of which hitherto he had probably not been fully aware, so that by the spring of 1694 there existed the foundations for a Mediterranean policy.

During the winter of 1692–3, some idea could be gained of the role which the projected squadron was designed to play. According to its orders, besides escorting the convoy it was to pay a visit to the Barbary states to induce them, if possible, to abandon the activities in support of France in which they had been intermittently indulging over the past year, and then to join the Spanish fleet to protect the coast and cover the movements of the Spanish shipping from America.[1] To this end, a convention had been signed with Spain which laid down the relative strength of the squadrons and the precedence of their commanders. As Blathwayt put it later, on William's instructions, the orders for the squadron were intended 'for the countenancing our allies in the Mediterranean, the preserving the Spanish Fleet from being destroyed and their towns from

[1] *H. of L. N.S.* 1, pp. 107–9.

being attack'd by the French...the giving Occasion to the Turks to make peace with the Emperor, and the keeping those of Algier, Tunis and Tripoli in awe'.[1] There was, in fact, explicitly a diplomatic side to the expedition, which had been only hinted at the year before. Its most important purpose, however, was not mentioned in the orders, and was not known to the Admiralty or to most of the ministers themselves; for in May, in one of his letters to Nottingham, now Secretary for the southern department, Blathwayt referred to some papers that 'his Majesty would have Your Lordship show onely to my Lord President and such as your Lordship shall think fit to trust with the Secret—I mean the design of the Duke of Savoy to enter into France as soon as he shall have the Countenance of Our Squadron'.[2]

It was therefore with the keenest interest and annoyance that William from Flanders watched the weeks slip by without the convoy setting sail. When it finally did so, his annoyance was greater than ever and was further sharpened by fear. For on 31 May, the day after the armada had finally cleared the Isle of Wight, a copy reached him of the council of war which had been held aboard the fleet on the 22nd to decide how far it should accompany the escort to the south.[3] Its contents were indeed disturbing, and William was not alone in fearing their outcome: the Admiralty, which had only extracted the minutes of the meeting from the joint Admirals with great difficulty, also remarked on the inadequacy of the plan they proposed.[4] The council was of the opinion that the Toulon fleet had by this time left the Straits and had very probably put into Brest, and it therefore decided that the fleet should stay with the convoy until both reached a position thirty leagues south-west of Ushant. It would then return towards the north.[5] William, who by now knew for certain that, so far from being at Brest, d'Estrées was cruising off the eastern coast of Spain, informed the ministers at once of his strong disapproval of this plan;[6] but the Admirals were already out of reach. They sailed past Brest without making any serious attempt to find out what in fact was inside, and arrived at the original point of departure on 4 June, where they held another council of war and

[1] B.M.Addnl. 37992, f. 33.

[2] Ibid. f. 7; 15 May.

[3] Ibid. f. 30.

[4] P.R.O.Adm. 3/8: 22/5, 26/5.

[5] *Catalogue of...Manuscripts in...United Service Institution*, pp. 76–7.

[6] B.M.Addnl. 37992, f. 30.

decided, in view of their ignorance of the enemy's movements, to carry on for another twenty leagues. Nine days later, at the further position, they left the convoy and the escort.[1] This news reached William on the 19th, after a disquieting week in which he had been rereading the minutes of the two earlier councils, both of which had now reached him, and complaining to Trenchard of their inadequacy.[2] Its arrival, wrote Blathwayt, 'exceedingly encreased his Majesty's greif and unspeakable concern for the Mediterranean Squadron and Merchantmen'.[3] It was not surprising that it did so; for he had just learnt that the main French fleet from Brest had been seen standing off Cadiz.[4]

For the next few weeks, the Admiralty, the ministers and above all the King waited for the half-expected news of the destruction of the escort and the scattering of the convoy.[5] William was so worried that he neglected his other business, for, as Blathwayt informed Nottingham in excuse, 'he finds it not easy to think of anything but the danger to our Mediterranean Fleet'.[6] His concern was increased early in July when he learnt 'with great surprize' that the main fleet, which was already almost out of victuals, had returned to Torbay, so that there seemed little chance of avenging the probable catastrophe.[7] When on 15 July he learnt of the French attack off the Spanish coast, and of the scattering of the convoy with the immediate loss of twelve large ships, he was 'under the greatest Affliction imaginable, but not under any Surprize'.[8]

The damage to the convoy was more serious than the first figures showed. Fortunately, Rooke had been given a day's warning of the presence of the French, and, although his scouts were not certain whether it was only a squadron or indeed the battle-fleet which they had sighted, had ordered the merchantmen to run for the coast while he fought a skilful and obstinate defensive action on their tail.[9] But nevertheless

---

1 *Catalogue of...Manuscripts in...United Service Institution*, pp. 77–8.

2 B.M.Addnl. 37992, ff. 33, 34*v*, 35.

3 Ibid. f. 35.

4 Ibid.

5 *H.M.C. Rutland*, II, p. 140.

6 B.M.Addnl. 37992, f. 14*v*.

7 Ibid. f. 37.

8 Ibid. f. 37*v*.

9 The various accounts and reports of the action may be seen in *H. of L. N.S.* I, pp. 200–6, 215–27. An account from a merchant ship is given in *H.M.C. Portland*, III, pp. 529–34. This was possibly the last occasion on which an Admiral thought of taking merchantmen into his line of battle in an emergency.

92 merchant vessels, with cargoes estimated at over £1,000,000, were sunk, burnt or captured, while the rest lay in Cadiz, Gibraltar and Malaga, unable to move for the French men-of-war cruising up and down the coasts and waiting outside the harbours. The outcry in England was naturally tremendous.[1] After waiting for a convoy for almost two years, and incurring considerable expense while it hung for over two months on the south coast, the Levant and Turkey Companies, and the Italian merchants, had suffered the greatest single loss of their careers,[2] and those ships which had not been captured were faced with a hazardous and probably expensive wait in harbour. The disaster of the Smyrna fleet, as it was known, threatened to provide the material for the most dangerous political attack on the naval administration that there had yet been. The immediate concern of the authorities, therefore, was to bring the French to action as soon as possible. All thought of a descent on Brest was abandoned, and the fleet was immediately ordered to stay at sea off the north Atlantic ports, so as to force the enemy to battle on his return.[3]

Tourville, however, had no intention of returning for the time being, and instead, after pausing to attack the allied shipping in Malaga, he proceeded up the Mediterranean displaying his strength as William had intended to display the strength of the allies. D'Estrées, meanwhile, returned to the Catalonian coast, to support the French siege of Rosas which was then under way and which resulted in an early surrender after his arrival. It was some time before the news of these exploits reached England, and the ministers were meanwhile unaware that the French fleet did not mean to come north again immediately.[4] William, however, with his acute interest in a Mediterranean campaign and his appreciation of the diplomatic issues involved, guessed at once that his opponents would do what he would have liked to do, and that Tourville would remain in the south to take advantage of an unopposed show of force in that area rather than sail tamely back to Brest to face a possible engagement. As soon as he received confirmation from Trenchard that the fleet had been ordered to cruise off Ushant, and even

[1] *H.M.C. Portland*, III, pp. 534–5; *Hastings*, II, pp. 230–1.

[2] Wood, *History of Levant Company*, pp. 110–12.

[3] N.M.M., Bibl. Phill. VI, ff. 39–40. [4] Ibid. ff. 57–8.

before he had any definite information that the French were not returning, he replied that such a plan was not of the slightest use, and that it was essential for the main fleet to sail at once for the coast of Portugal to give close cover to the remainder of the convoy in its passage through the Straits.[1] This was the first time that the idea of sending the fleet itself out of home waters had been suggested, and it was most unwelcome to all the authorities in England. With only three weeks of the normal campaigning season left, a voyage of that nature was unheard of, and Trenchard wrote immediately that the great ships could not possibly make such a passage, or the medium rates either, without risking a winter in the Spanish ports, where they could not be refitted for the spring.[2] William in reply saw no reason to change his opinion, which had indeed been strengthened in the interval by two letters from his ambassador at Madrid: the first with the news of the Spaniards' alarm at the activities of the French fleet off Catalonia, and of their disgust with the English; and the second informing him that the Spanish *flota* was on its way over from America, with large cargoes in which the English merchants had an interest, and that the court expected some protection for it from England in view of the proximity of the French.[3] The King therefore repeated his demand that the Queen and the ministers should send the fleet to Spain without delay.[4]

Meanwhile, however, a meeting had been held at Whitehall on 18 August of the Queen, the Cabinet, the Boards of Admiralty and Navy, and a selected number of experienced captains and pilots, to discuss the practicability of this plan; and as a result Trenchard was able to report their unanimous agreement that the first and second rates could not stay out beyond the end of the month, that they could not be careened at Cadiz without hulks and stores being sent after them, and that there was no dock on the coast of Portugal or the western coast of Spain which was suitable for the biggest ships. Twelve days before, an allied council of war in the fleet had reached the same conclusions. The Queen, therefore, proposed ordering the first and second

---

1 B.M.Addnl. 37992, f. 38*v*; 7 August.
2 N.M.M., Bibl. Phill. VI, ff. 65–6.
3 S.P.For. 94/73, Stanhope to King, 25/7; B.M.Addnl. 37992, f. 41.
4 B.M.Addnl. 37992, f. 42*v*.

rates into harbour in the next few days unless news came that the French after all were on their way back to Brest, while the thirds and fourths would be revictualled and ordered to cruise in the Soundings. The fleet itself, added the Secretary as a final discouragement, had once more run out of food and was back in Torbay reprovisioning.[1] William still refused to give up his plan, and in a last attempt to enforce it used a cover he had used before: the Dutch, he wrote, were anxious to keep their big ships out all winter and were making their arrangements accordingly.[2] But the ministers, although they recognized only too well the concern of the already exasperated merchant interest in the Spanish *flota*, submitted that the plan was impossible. So far from embarking on a foreign voyage, Trenchard announced, it was time that the ships had a rest, for some of the thirds and fourths had not been overhauled for three or four years, and were becoming slower and more unseaworthy every month.[3] On receipt of this letter at the beginning of September, William at last yielded. He had in any event heard in the past few days that the Brest fleet was at last on its way out of the Straits, and was bound for the north. Apparently uninterested in any prospect of an engagement off the French coast, he approved the Queen's orders for the first two rates to be laid up, and directed the ministers to settle a squadron to proceed to Cadiz for the protection of the *flota*, adding that if a fleet could not go he thought it absolutely necessary that a force of some kind should be sent.[4] The inner Council readily agreed to this more modest and familiar demand. A squadron of sixteen English third rates, seven fourths, one fifth, six fireships, two bombvessels, a hospital ship and a storeship, with a small Dutch quota, was prepared,[5] and, after some delay, the King appointed Shovell in command.[6] For some reason, however, this appointment was changed in the next month, and Sir Francis Wheeler, whose experience as a flag officer had so far been entirely in the West Indies,[7] was chosen instead. The opportunity was taken to send a small convoy with him, to give the merchants a chance to recoup some of their losses, and on 29 November

---

1 N.M.M., Bibl. Phill. VI, ff. 69–70.
2 B.M.Addnl. 37992, f. 44.
3 N.M.M., Bibl. Phill. VI, ff. 77–80.
4 B.M.Addnl. 37992, f. 44*v*; and see Roncière, op. cit. VI, p. 148.
5 Burchett, p. 201.
6 B.M.Addnl. 37992, f. 48.
7 Burchett, p. 204.

it sailed. It was a disappointing coda to the theme of the summer; but the significance of the campaign had lain less in its disappointments, great though these had been, than in the way in which they had brought to light the obstacles to a Mediterranean policy, and had thus defined a policy for the following year which had to take them into consideration. They left the whole work to be done again, but with a clearer appreciation on William's part of what such work involved. The 'Napoleonic' decision of 1694 was no flash of strategic genius, but the result of the sad experience of 1693.

Before Wheeler's squadron sailed, Parliament had begun to investigate the events of the summer. On this occasion, however, the inevitable demand for papers had been preceded by a demand for an inquiry by William himself, in his speech from the throne of 7 November.[1] In this he promised to punish those held responsible for the disaster of the convoy; and four days later Killigrew and Delavall, both of whom, as strong Tories, were by now being accused of enjoying Jacobite sympathies if not something more definite,[2] were informed that the King wished them to cease acting as Commissioners of the Admiralty until further notice.[3] A month later, together with Shovell, they were dismissed from all their offices.[4] Meanwhile, Lords and Commons were conducting separate inquiries into the loss of the Smyrna fleet. Papers were submitted in full by all authorities concerned; every conceivable witness was examined; and the results were subjected to long and vigorous debate.[5] It was the fullest investigation into naval affairs of the war, the fruit of the unusual combination of Parliamentary financial control and royal acquiescence in its consequences. The weight of the attack fell upon the joint

---

1 *H.C.J.* XI, p. 1.

2 *A Dialogue betwixt Whig and Tory*... (1693), p. 39; 'The History of the Rook and Turkeys', and 'Remarks upon the London Gazette relating to the Streights Fleet...' in *Somers Tracts*, XI, pp. 90–4, 462–71; *H.M.C. Portland*, III, p. 535.

3 *Cal.S.P.Dom. 1693*, p. 395.

4 Ibid. pp. 426–7; Ranke, op. cit. VI, pp. 225–6.

5 *H.L.J.* XV, pp. 319, 330, 339; *H.C.J.* XI, pp. 1, 3–9, 21. The papers are given in full in *H. of L. N.S.* I, pp. 93–294; the Commons' debates in Grey, op. cit. X, pp. 311–17, 319–29, 333–8, 344–8.

Admirals. The Admiralty itself, which was now recognized to be a purely subordinate department, escaped all censure, and indeed its leader, Falkland, was particularly bitter in his strictures upon the commanders at sea.[1] The Victuallers had a rough passage in trying to prove that they had supplied the fleet adequately, but the peculiarities in the victualling figures defeated the Commons as they defeated all other authorities, and they escaped a vote of censure.[2] So, after some long and bitter debates, did the Admirals themselves, although this did not save them from dismissal. On 6 December, after a month's examination into the papers, the motion was put that 'by not gaining such Intelligence as they might have done, of the Brest Fleet, and not sending into Brest for Intelligence, before they left the Streights Squadron, [they] are guilty of a high Breach of the Trust that was put in them'.[3] But it was narrowly defeated by 185 votes to 175, and the Lords in turn concluded their investigations by voting that the joint Admirals did well in the execution of orders received, thus throwing the blame upon the Whig Secretary of State.[4] As Blathwayt remarked to a correspondent, the Admirals had been 'cut down after hanging';[5] but their discredit was none the less complete. The opportunity was also taken, in the Tory debacle, to attack Nottingham. On 6 November, the King judged it wisest for him to retire from office, and ordered him to give up his seals,[6] and in the course of the debates of the winter he was accused of almost every crime, from peculation to betraying the Smyrna fleet to the enemy.[7] As he was able to show conclusively, he was in no way responsible for the convoy, and at times had not even been kept informed of the progress of events;[8] and in the end he was allowed to retire in peace. At the same time, Falkland was also

---

[1] Grey, op. cit. x, pp. 323–5, 347. L'Hermitage also noted the rigour of his attacks in the House (B.M.Addnl. 17677, NN, f. 377, cited by James, loc. cit.). Falkland was on bad terms with the three Admirals, and particularly Killigrew, at the time, following an open quarrel with them on 19 October, in the presence of the inner Council, while the minutes of the councils of war for the summer were being examined (B.M.Addnl. 9764, ff. 78–80).

[2] *H.C.J.* xi, p. 13.

[3] Ibid. p. 21.

[4] *H.L.J.* xv, p. 339.

[5] Jacobsen, *William Blathwaite*, p. 290.

[6] *Conduct*, p. 123.

[7] Grey, op. cit. x, pp. 333–8.

[8] His speech is given in *Conduct*, pp. 124–32.

attacked, in this case for corruption, and after being severely reprimanded was committed to the Tower on 16 February.[1] He was released after three days, but did not act any more at the Admiralty, although his name was not removed from the Commission until his death three months later.[2] It was, therefore, a weakened Board which emerged from the one winter session in which it had not been directly attacked, with three of its seven members no longer acting, and one, Lowther, in poor health. For all practical purposes, Priestman, Austen and Rich made the Commission.

The result of all the debates and motions of censure was negligible, unless the Admirals and the Administration may, in their different ways, be counted as having lost more prestige in the winter than the summer had already lost them. Neither the administrative nor the strategic difficulties had been mitigated, and at the beginning of 1694 almost exactly the same set of problems faced the navy as had faced it a year before, with only the sad experience of an unsuccessful campaign to suggest a solution. In one respect alone the position was slightly different, and that affected the fleet only indirectly. When the main financial supply for 1694 was granted by a tax on land, an article was included in the Act stipulating the number of escorts and cruisers to be employed in home waters for the future protection of trade.[3] The terms were quite definite: 'for the better securing the Trade of this Kingdom', over and above the men-of-war for the line of battle and for convoys to remote parts, at least four third rates, sixteen fourths, thirteen fifths and ten sixths 'shall be from time to time directed and appointed by the Lord High Admiral of England or Commissioners for executing the said Office for the time being to such proper stations as they shall deem meet to cruize for secureing the Merchant Ships in their goeing out and returning home'. Only in

---

[1] Grey, op. cit. x, p. 356; *H.C.J.* xi, pp. 22, 98. The date is wrongly given as 17 January in G.E.C., *Complete Peerage*, v (2nd ed.), p. 241 n. He had been bribing members of Parliament out of the fund of the Perquisites of the Admiralty.

[2] See Appendix VI below. He did not appear at the Board after the middle of February (P.R.O.Adm. 3/9), but William seems to have contemplated using him again, possibly as envoy at The Hague (B.M.Addnl. 17677, OO, f. 28 *v*, cited by James, loc. cit.).

[3] 5 Will. and Mary c. 1., art. lxxi.

'great necessity' were these ships to be taken for the line of battle.[1] Through its financial control, even if not through its investigations into the conduct of the war itself, Parliament was thus able to express its concern for trade.

But the effect of the measure, novel though it was as an expression of extraneous legal control which the Admiralty could not evade, had little effect on the employment of the medium rates. Since 1691, the Administration had made its own dispositions for escorts and cruisers, and had reserved between forty and fifty third to fifth rates for the purpose.[2] In July 1692 their numbers and stations for the year had been fixed by Order in Council,[3] and a regular coastal convoy system was established between Swansea and the Downs which operated for the rest of the war.[4] At the end of that year, when the composition of the force for the next year's service came up for discussion, a significant innovation was made. The 'convoys and cruisers' were considered first, and only when they had been settled were the lesser rates chosen for the line.[5] In 1693 the numbers and stations for the protection of trade were much the same as for the previous year, occupying forty named ships with an unnamed quota from the ships in the Downs at any one time;[6] and the dispositions made in December of that year under the new Act scarcely differed from those already in existence.[7] The Admiralty, moreover, had not often departed from the provisions which the executive had made; and, much as the merchants complained of the inadequacy of the convoy arrangements, these were due more to administrative inefficiency and to the irregular behaviour of the captains of the escorts, with their frequent demands for money before they would sail, their illegal pressing of men from the merchant vessels, and sometimes their abandonment of their charge altogether after a short time in company, and to the actual shortage of ships, than to any diversion to other duties of units selected for these purposes.

1 Article lxxii.

2 See the lists in *Naval Miscellany*, II, p. 145, which are attributed, it would seem correctly, to that year (pp. 140–1).

3 P.R.O.Adm. 8/3, list of 13 July implementing the order of the 7th.

4 Admty:Corbett, XIX, f. 16.

5 P.R.O.Adm. 3/7: 2/11.

6 P.R.O.Adm. 3/8: 1/12.

7 P.R.O.Adm. 2/174, f. 61.

One of the reasons, for instance, for the delay over the Mediterranean squadron in 1692, had been that it deprived the escorts and cruisers of some badly needed ships. Although, therefore, the Parliamentary restriction on the number of smaller ships available might seem at first to have affected the composition of the fleet in 1694, it was in fact more important as an example of the consequences of financial responsibility than as a strategic innovation.

Tourville's return to Brest in the autumn of 1693 had been made solely to relieve the excessive pressure of a fleet of 93 sail, as he and d'Estrées amounted to, upon the facilities of Toulon dockyard, and it was not unlikely that the next year he would try to follow up the impression which he had made in the Mediterranean.[1] To prevent a repetition of the recent disaster, therefore, the French must not be allowed to leave Brest, and as large a convoy as possible must be sent south before the campaigning season began. The latter precaution was taken when Wheeler's squadron sailed for the Straits at the end of November 1693, with instructions to make straight for Cadiz, to wait there for a month to cover the return of the Spanish *flota* if that had not already arrived, and then to see the convoy into the Mediterranean while a detachment from the escort took charge of the homeward-bound trade. On his return to the Straits, the Admiral was to co-operate with the Spaniards for the defence of their coasts.[2] But the success at least of the last part of these instructions, and of any similar expeditions which might be called for later in the year, depended entirely upon French intentions; and accordingly, the Cabinet fell back during the winter on the plan of a year before, to attack Brest by land and sea in the spring before the French fleet could put to sea. From the end of the year, William supervised the arrangements himself. On 29 December, the size of the fleet was determined as 92 sail excluding fireships

[1] Roncière, op. cit. VI, p. 148. In the following account of policy in the last three months of 1693 and the first six months of 1694, I have followed Corbett, loc. cit. pp. 150–60. Although I cannot agree with his contention that William's attitude to the Mediterranean suffered a dramatic change during this time, owing to the evidence which exists for earlier periods, I have little to add to his exposition of the events during these months.

[2] Burchett, pp. 201–3.

and auxiliaries,[1] and two days later the King ordered a weekly state of its progress to be submitted to him every Sunday until he left for Holland.[2] The preparations went ahead as usual, although some additional work was involved on many of the third and fourth rates, which were feeling the effects of long and uninterrupted service.[3] The rendezvous for the 'ships of the line of battle'[4] was fixed for 1 March in the Downs,[5] but it was the third week of April before all had assembled for the passage to Spithead.[6] By that time, the original plans had been qualified to meet a confused situation in the Mediterranean.

For in December, on arrival at Cadiz, Wheeler had found that the western Mediterranean was alive with French privateers and cruisers. On reporting the fact, he had been ordered to stay in port until the Spanish fleet was ready to strengthen the escort; but the Spaniards were as dilatory as ever,[7] and after another month the convoy was instructed to return to England. Before these orders reached him, however, Wheeler had sailed for the Straits, with the intention of fighting his way up the Mediterranean. On 18 February he was caught in the narrows between the Spanish and African shores by one of the sudden and violent gales which affect that area, and in the course of the next two days six of his squadron were sunk or had grounded with the loss of over 800 lives, including his own. Six merchant vessels were also lost, the rest of the convoy and its escort was damaged in various degrees, and several ran ashore in Gibraltar bay[8] where most of them were held by easterly winds until the beginning of May, open to the attack of any French fleet that might approach from Toulon or Brest. Fortunately, they were able to leave Gibraltar soon after the main fleet set sail from Brest.

---

1 P.R.O.Adm. 1/5248, 29/12; 2/174, f. 61.

2 P.R.O.Adm. 1/5248, 31/12. The results may be seen in P.R.O.Adm. 8/3.

3 P.R.O.Adm. 3/9: 19/1. The details of the preparations may be seen in *H. of L. N.S.* I, pp. 458–74.

4 This expression occurs frequently at this time, in P.R.O.Adm. 1/5248.

5 Ibid. 11/2.

6 Burchett, p. 204.

7 S.P.For. 94/73, Stanhope to Shrewsbury, 24 January 1694.

8 Burchett, pp. 209–11.

For almost a month beforehand, rumours of this had been current, and on 24 April the English fleet had received instructions accordingly. The original idea of an attack upon the harbour was now modified to take into account the possibility of the enemy having left it. If they were still in port, the fleet was to stage a direct attack; if they had put to sea, it was to search for them as far south as Cape Finisterre, but no further; and if it had reliable information of their having gone to the Mediterranean, or south of Finisterre, it was to follow them and attack. 'The Admiral', ended the instructions, 'is not to wait for further orders but is to report from time to time to a Secretary of State and the Admiralty.'[1] The initiative, in fact, had passed entirely to the French, and the orders to their opponents for the campaign were in effect simply to follow their movements, and made no attempt to reconcile the implications of the alternatives which were suggested.

The Admiral to whom these orders were addressed was not the man to accept them without complaint. On 7 November 1693, the day after Nottingham's resignation, Russell was appointed Admiral of the fleet for the coming season.[2] His year of enforced leisure had advanced his fortunes considerably, giving him the opportunity to develop his political power without fear of an immediate interruption, and to take advantage of the progress of the Whig cause which came so markedly in the latter half of the year. By November, according to Sir Charles Hatton, 'Ld. Keeper, Admiral Russell, and ye Secretary are ye governing men',[3] and it was as a leader of the party that he was consulted by its members on the name of the new Secretary of State to replace his old rival.[4] From the middle of November he seems to have attended meetings of the Cabinet,[5] and on 24 April 1694 his return to power was

[1] *H. of L. N.S.* I, p. 459.

[2] P.R.O.Adm. 3/9: 7/11. The relation of Russell's appointment to Nottingham's resignation was well recognized (see Falkland's speech in Grey, op. cit. X, p. 319).

[3] *Camden Miscellany*, II, p. 198.

[4] Coxe, *Correspondence of...Shrewsbury*, p. 24. The emergence of the 'first Ministry' of 1693, and Russell's part in it, are discussed by Macaulay, *History*, V, pp. 2386–94. Russell took part in the important meeting of the Whig leaders at Althorp in August (Feiling, loc. cit. p. 295).

[5] P.R.O.Adm. 1/5248, 12/11 *et seq.* This authority is concerned only with naval affairs; but it has been generally accepted that Russell was a regular member of the Cabinet from about this time (Feiling, loc. cit. p. 289).

officially recognized by his appointment to the head of a new Commission of Admiralty.[1] When he went to sea in 1694, therefore, it was as senior Lord of the Admiralty and a member of the Cabinet, as well as a commander of reputation; and it is not surprising that he expressed himself with freedom and authority upon his orders as Commander in Chief.

By May 1694, moreover, the Admiralty and the Cabinet were filled with Russell's friends. Although the nominal head of the Admiralty Commission in his absence was the Tory Lowther, he was now of little account and was in any case a moderate party man. Most of the business was done by the same three members as had conducted it during the previous winter, and of these Priestman, originally appointed to the Board by Russell's influence and still devoted to his interest, was nominal and actual head. There were only two new members of the Commission, Sir John Houblon and Sir George Rooke. The former was certainly no Tory, and was soon to be connected with Russell by financial ties when he became Governor of the Bank of England, to which the Admiral was one of the most substantial of the original subscribers;[2] while the latter, although often described as a Tory, might perhaps be described rather as not a Whig. Unlike Killigrew and Delavall, he was not active or notorious in party warfare, but tried to keep aloof from politics and simply to do his job. His was, in fact, just the character to attract William, and it was as the King's personal choice that he entered the Commission. He had already received the mark of royal favour immediately after the loss of his convoy, when, to the resentment of the joint Admirals, he was promoted to Admiral of the Blue;[3] and he was on good terms with Russell, whose subordinate he had been in 1692.[4] During the latter's absence, therefore, the weight of influence on the Board was in his own interest, and he experienced no trouble from it. In the Cabinet, also, his political associates were well represented. Somers and Montagu had joined Trenchard in 1693, and in March 1694 Shrewsbury was persuaded, after considerable difficulty, to

[1] *Cal.S.P.Dom. 1694–5*, p. 114. The patent was dated 2 May.

[2] Sir John Clapham, *The Bank of England*, I (1944), pp. 273–4. The significance of Houblon's appointment is discussed on p. 570 below.

[3] *Cal.S.P.Dom. 1693*, p. 283.

[4] Finch Transcr., Russell to Nottingham, 29/7.

accept the seals as Secretary of State for the north.[1] By the summer, only Russell's old enemy Carmarthen (created Duke of Leeds in April) and Sir John Lowther of Lowther remained from the Tory phalanx of a year before, and the former was to all intents out of power after the scandal of the East India Company's accounts in the spring. For the first time, therefore, the Admiral found himself with a sympathetic and even complaisant Cabinet behind him, and—even more important—with a Secretary of State with whom he was on the best of terms. For, although Trenchard still dealt with naval affairs within the ministry and for all official purposes, as Bonnet remarked in January 1694, 'avait le département de la flotte',[2] Russell revealed his thoughts mainly to Shrewsbury, who had for some years been his closest political associate and whose appointment he had done his best to secure; and as the campaign became more complicated, and the Admiral's attitude more equivocal, William used this relationship increasingly to persuade Russell to carry out his orders, and Shrewsbury found himself acting on occasions without the intervention of his colleague, in an unofficial but decisive capacity as the Admiral's counsellor and friend.

This role was soon thrust upon him, for from the moment he received his orders of 24 April Russell had his misgivings about them. As intelligence was received towards the end of the month of French preparations in Brest, and as Tourville put out a strong screen of cruisers to discourage the inquisitive English scouts, he became increasingly certain that the enemy was bound for the Mediterranean, and in his view, which Shrewsbury shared, the project of a descent on Brest was incompatible with a chase to the south.[3] The preparations for the former were still far from complete: troops and stores had not yet arrived at

[1] Trenchard moved to the southern department on Nottingham's resignation.

[2] Ranke, op. cit. VI, p. 233. In the three main sources for Secretarial activity in naval affairs, Trenchard's signature alone appears on the letters for this period. All the letters of the spring and early summer of 1694 in P.R.O.Adm. 1/4080, ff. 1031–1183 (In-Letters, Secretaries of State) are signed by him, as are all those in S.P.Dom. 204/44, ff. 73–102, for letters from April 1693 to April 1695, and in S.P.Dom. 204/45, ff. 1–181, for those from 29 March 1693 to 9 December 1694 (both State Papers Domestic, Entry Books (naval)). Russell corresponded with Trenchard on every subject, but by no means always fully stated his mind. His letters are largely contained in S.P.Dom. 42/3, and Trenchard's replies in N.M.M., Bibl. Phill. I.

[3] Coxe, loc. cit. pp. 192–3; *H.M.C. Buccleuch* (*Montagu House*), II, pt I, pp. 65–6.

Portsmouth, many of the ships themselves were not paid, and Russell, who was genuinely concerned for his men, refused to leave until they had received some satisfaction.[1] No large-scale attempt was possible for some time, while the French were obviously getting ready to put to sea. In the first week of May, therefore, he made the best of a depressing situation, and sailed on a reconnaissance with such strength as he could spare from the pay table: a total of 35 English and Dutch. To his surprise and fury, he found Brest practically defenceless with only a few companies of regular troops and the local militia in the neighbourhood, an easy prey if only it could be quickly assaulted. But, as he wrote to Shrewsbury on his return on the 23rd, the chance had been thrown away, thanks to the procrastination of the Treasury and 'that driveller, the general of the ordnance'.[2] Inside the harbour, however, there was no sign of the French fleet; and it had indeed sailed on 27 April for the Straits.

This news reached William soon after Russell had left the English coast, and on 14 May he wrote that the fleet should lose no time in the pursuit. Knowing the Admiral's temper, however, and aware by experience of the consternation which any mention of the fleet in connexion with the Mediterranean aroused in the Cabinet, he supplemented his instructions to Trenchard[3] by asking Shrewsbury to use his influence to hasten Russell's departure;[4] and he repeated his request on the 22nd.[5] Shrewsbury himself, however, had already urged the same

[1] 'I could not bring myself to carry ships to sea, and the men unpaid, when hundred of poor women was waiting for their husbands' money, to support their children and families' (*H.M.C. Buccleuch*, II, pt I, p. 64).

[2] Coxe, loc. cit. p. 195.

[3] N.M.M., Bibl. Phill. VI, f. 221.

[4] Coxe, loc. cit. p. 33. This is the letter which Corbett (loc. cit. p. 158) calls 'one of the leading documents of British naval history'. The relevant passage reads: 'There can be no longer any doubt that the squadron which left Brest on the 7th of this month [i.e. N.S.] has sailed for the Mediterranean, after joining the ships from Rochfort, so that admiral Russell has no time to lose in following them; and although it is not in your department, I am well assured that you will use all your endeavours to hasten his departure, and persuade him to leave the squadron, which remains in these parts, the execution of the attempt on Brest....' I cannot see that this says anything that had not been said the year before, or anything that the ministers themselves were not saying independently (see p. 515, nn. 1, 2 below).

[5] Coxe, loc. cit. p. 39.

course at the inner Council before the receipt of the first letter,[1] and on its arrival wrote at once to Russell that both the King in Flanders 'and all that are concerned with the government here' expected him to lose no time in making for the Straits.[2] He sent William's second letter on to the Admiral on the 26th; but Russell, who was 'as impatient to be gone as the King can be to have me',[3] was already getting under way.[4] He took with him the whole fleet and the troop transports for Brest, with the intention of dropping off the latter as he passed, with a strong squadron under Lord Berkeley, to make the attack and subsequently to act as the Channel fleet until his return.[5] He finally sailed on 2 June, and on the 6th he parted company with the detachment for Brest. Almost a month later, on 1 July, the main allied fleet, with 63 men-of-war excluding auxiliaries, entered the Straits for the first time in English naval history.[6]

The attack on Brest was a disaster. The French had suspected it for some months[7] and had known all about it for some weeks, and Russell himself feared that the delay would give them ample opportunity to make the necessary preparations.[8] When the troops landed at Camaret Bay near the port, they were met by heavy fire and encountered a large force of infantry and cavalry.[9] With almost 2000 casualties out of a total of 7000 men, and with the general, Tollemache, dying of an infected wound, the ships put back to Portsmouth. For the rest of the season Berkeley's squadron, consisting of three first rates, four seconds, twelve thirds, a fourth and two fifths, with fireships and auxiliaries,[10] formed the nucleus of the Channel fleet, and cruised rather aimlessly up and down the French coast bombarding the seaports until in August the big ships were laid up.[11] The great fleet had at last, after

[1] On the 14th (*H.M.C. Buccleuch*, II, pt I, p. 66).

[2] Coxe, loc. cit. p. 194. He followed this up with a second letter a few days later in which he quoted the King verbatim (*H.M.C. Buccleuch*, II, pt I, pp. 69–70).

[3] Coxe, loc. cit. p. 196; see also *Cal.S.P.Dom. 1693–4*, pp. 147–8.

[4] *H.M.C. Buccleuch*, II, pt I, p. 70.

[5] *Cal.S.P.Dom. 1693–4*, p. 157.

[6] Burchett, pp. 235–7.

[7] A Jacobite agent had sounded Russell about it in the third week in April (Churchill, op. cit. I, pp. 422–3).

[8] *H.M.C. Buccleuch*, II, pt I, p. 71.

[9] For a naval account of the assault, see Marquess of Caermarthen, *Journal of the Brest Expedition* (1695); also Burchett, pp. 215–24.

[10] Burchett, p. 217.

[11] Ibid. pp. 224–9.

frequent diversions and disappointments, been used as the government had wished it to be used since the winter of 1691: in support of a landing on an enemy harbour. And with the fiasco that resulted, all such attempts came to an end, and there remained nothing for the fleet to do in home waters, despite its high cost and complex administration, but to follow the course which had been rejected in 1692, of bombarding the coastal towns and villages. Its usefulness seemed to be limited to the major engagement; and it was thus in the Mediterranean, to which the French fleet had resorted, that it found its justification in the interlude before it was forced to return to the now pointless cruises which constituted a Channel campaign.

CHAPTER XII

THE FLEET IN THE MEDITERRANEAN JULY 1694–OCTOBER 1695

I

While Russell was on his way south to the Straits, the French had been concentrating their two fleets on the north-east coast of Spain, where an army under Noailles was attempting to reduce the chain of fortresses between the frontier and Barcelona; and by 1 July, when he passed into the Mediterranean, the situation was critical. The Spanish forces opposing Noailles had been decisively beaten in May, and Palamos and Gerona had fallen; only the small fortress of Hostalrich still remained between the French and Barcelona, and in June Tourville was already blockading the city.[1] It was generally recognized that nothing could save it but the English fleet, and since the middle of June the Spanish court had been pestering Stanhope at Madrid for news of its progress.[2] They had good reason to do so, for the French themselves, favourably situated as they were so long as the English were outside the Straits, were prepared to abandon the blockade of Spain as soon as they appeared in the Mediterranean itself, and on the news of their approach Tourville left his station before Barcelona and retreated with the whole of both French fleets to Toulon, where he set about fortifying the approaches in the expectation of an English attack.[3] The army came to a halt along the coast, and for the next few weeks a curious calm fell upon the Mediterranean campaign, as its participants waited to see what Russell would do.

Throughout July there was little that he could do, for a long spell of north-easterly winds kept him from his objective of Barcelona, where

---

[1] Corbett, loc. cit. pp. 161–2. Much of the ground in this chapter has already been covered by Corbett, loc. cit. ch. XXVII, and my indebtedness to him will be obvious.

[2] S.P.For. 94/73, Stanhope to Shrewsbury, 6/6, 27/6; see also B.M.Addnl. 37992, f. 52.

[3] Corbett, loc. cit. p. 164.

he expected to find the French fleet.[1] It was not until the beginning of August that he arrived there, and by then both provisions and time were running short. Despite his command of the sea and the sudden shift in the balance of power which his presence occasioned in the western Mediterranean, he felt his position to be precarious. With only four weeks to go before his big ships should be taken into harbour, he was over 1600 miles from home and with a hard passage ahead of him. A shift of wind to the west for a week, and he was caught inside the Mediterranean with no major base and with the Atlantic and the autumn between himself and Portsmouth. Unsatisfactory as the French position was, his own was becoming dangerous. As early as 1 July, on the very day on which he passed the Straits, he had voiced his fears to Shrewsbury and Trenchard,[2] and a month later he stated the position more explicitly. He then wrote to Shrewsbury:[3]

> I wish I were able to give any hopes of success in these seas, as you desire; but the french will not let me see them, and I dare not venture to attack them at Toulon; by what I can inform myself, the place is too strong; and a mortification or repulse would be of very ill-consequence. With probable hopes of success, I would venture a great deal; but the time of the year obliges me not to spend much time: besides, the dutch have provision only for the month of September.

He therefore intended to leave Barcelona within a few days, and to retrace his steps towards the Straits. At the same time, after a council of war aboard the *Britannia*, he informed the Spanish viceroy of Catalonia that while he remained in the area his assistance must be limited to supporting the Spanish forces in the immediate neighbourhood. He could neither land any troops himself, for none had been brought, nor

---

[1] Burchett, pp. 239–41. We possess two authoritative and largely first-hand accounts of the operations of July–November 1694 in the Mediterranean, by Russell's secretary and by his first captain aboard the *Britannia*. The secretary was Burchett, whose account is incorporated in his *Transactions at sea*, pp. 239–63; the first captain was Byng, later Lord Torrington, whose narrative—possibly supplemented by a later hand—is in *Memoirs relating to the Lord Torrington*, pp. 67–71. A further account, which adds nothing to either of them, exists in the propagandist pamphlet *An Exact Journal of the Victorious Expedition of the Confederate Fleet, the last year, under the Command of Admiral Russell*... (1695). [2] Coxe, loc. cit. pp. 197–8; *Cal.S.P.Dom. 1694–5*, p. 207.

[3] Coxe, loc. cit. pp. 198–9.

pursue the French any further, 'the fleet having now no more provisions than are absolutely necessary for their passage hence to England'.[1]

Meanwhile, however, events were moving fast at home. Since the beginning of July, the Cabinet had been requesting William to inform it as soon as possible when the fleet was to return; but for most of the month he would give no definite answer.[2] On the 23rd, to the anxiety of the ministers, he still had no orders to give,[3] but four days later he came to a decision. In his letter to Trenchard of that day[4], Blathwayt wrote:

> His Majesty has now declared his Pleasure concerning Admiral Russell's return home and Commands me to lett you know that he is Inclined that the Fleet should remain in the Mediterranean as long as may consist with its safety, and that upon Admirall Russell's coming away, he leave as considerable a Squadron as may be convenient in those parts.

To this end, he wished the Cabinet to send:

> Such Orders in relation to the time of his stay in those parts and the Force he shall leave behind him during this Winter as well as the Station of such a Squadron, as shall be thought most advisable in England.[5]

These instructions were not in themselves very startling. They left the ministers free to decide how long the main fleet should stay abroad, and their only positive order was to provide for a winter squadron in the Mediterranean. That the Cabinet viewed the letter in this light was shown by Trenchard's reply.[6] The inner Council,[7] he reported, had met

---

1 *Cal.S.P.Dom. 1694–5*, pp. 249–50.

2 B.M.Addnl. 37992, ff. 55, 55*v*, 56, 57; Blathwayt to Trenchard, 2–19/7.

3 Ibid. f. 57. 4 Dated 6 August N.S. 5 Ibid. f. 58.

6 N.M.M., Bibl. Phill. 1, ff. 207–13, dated 2/8 (O.S.). According to Corbett, 'towards the end of July, the Cabinet was startled by receiving from him [William] a proposal that Russell should remain out all the winter' (loc. cit. p. 165). The first time such a course of action was mentioned by William was on 6 August (O.S.), *after* he had received Trenchard's reply which had fully considered the arguments for and against it, and which itself asked for his orders on this question (see text on p. 520 below). I have followed in the main Corbett's argument that William was primarily responsible for making Russell stay abroad all winter, but I cannot agree with him that he reached his decision without any assistance from the Cabinet.

7 In this case, it was called 'the Committee', probably indicating that the Queen had not been present.

several times to debate the King's letter, and was of the opinion that if he wanted Russell to come home at any time during the winter, he should order him to do so at once before the weather became too dangerous for the big ships. It also thought that the Admiral himself was the man best qualified to appoint the squadron to be left behind and the stations which it should occupy. On the other hand, in view of the French Mediterranean policy, it had considered the possibility of the fleet's wintering abroad, and for this purpose had consulted the Admiralty and the Navy Board on the practicability of re-storing it at a Spanish port. The Admiralty had replied that the stores would have to be sent from England, and the Navy Board had given an assurance that, provided the orders were given at once, they could be ready in two months' time, and the gear for careening in one month. Accordingly, in case the King decided to keep the fleet abroad, the Cabinet had already sent the necessary orders to the Admiralty to go ahead with these preparations. Trenchard then developed the arguments against wintering the main fleet in Spain, pointing out that such a course presupposed that the Spaniards would allow it the freedom of their ports and that the Dutch were willing to let their main strength remain abroad; that it meant most, if not all, of the material for a fleet refit being sent from England, for Spain was quite unable to provide it; and that the difficulties of supplying Russell on a large scale and at all regularly across the Bay of Biscay in midwinter were going to be enormous. All sorts of obstacles, diplomatic, material and possibly strategic, were likely to arise over the next few months, and only the man on the spot, particularly since he had himself sat in Cabinet and was head of the Admiralty Board, could satisfactorily decide what was best to be done. The ministers recommended, therefore:

> that if the King be inclined to have Mr Russell remain in the Straights his Orders should not be to [*sic*] positive, but that he may have liberty to return, if upon notice of what supplyes he may expect from England, or upon other consideration of the state of the fleet under his command, he shall judge it not practicable to refit it at Cadiz in due time.[1]

This report reached William on the 6th. In itself, it was perhaps as much as could be hoped for when the situation was so novel, the

[1] N.M.M., Bibl. Phill. 1, f. 212.

consequences—for the nation and for those responsible for the decision—so momentous, and the prospects of success so uncertain.[1] But it did not provide the unambiguous support which the King would have liked in embarking on such a venture, and moreover he received by the same post two private letters, one from the Queen and one from Shrewsbury, the second of which at least gave him some cause for anxiety.[2] According to Shrewsbury,[3] at the meetings of the inner Council Somers, Pembroke, Trenchard and Romney had, like himself,[4] been in favour of the fleet's wintering in Spain; but Devonshire and Dorset had stayed away, Normanby had changed his mind after the first meeting and had ended by violently opposing the idea, and Carmarthen refused to give an opinion. 'Everybody', however, 'agreed the decision ought to be left to Mr. Russell.'[5] William, who could not have expected very much, nevertheless was annoyed that the matter had not been settled more decisively. He had not, he wrote to Shrewsbury on the 6th,[6] liked to issue any positive orders until he learnt the opinions of the ministers, and particularly before he could judge of the prospects of refitting the ships abroad; but the terms of Trenchard's letter seemed to him ambiguous, as if 'the committee are of opinion, that admiral Russell should winter at Cadiz, but dare not declare that opinion, through fear of being responsible for the event'.

I do wish [he continued] that they had spoken more clearly on this occasion, and indeed they ought to have done so, to prevent my being exposed to the supposition of acting solely from my own opinion; but as

[1] Corbett's description of the ministers' opinion at this stage as 'pusillanimous trifling' (loc. cit. p. 169) seems to me unwarranted. In view of the attitude to less dangerous ventures the year before it was remarkably favourable to the plan, and a testimony to the significant effect of the events of 1693 and the first seven months of 1694. But Corbett, of course, was not aware of the arguments of the previous two years.

[2] Mary's letter seems to have disappeared. It is mentioned in Blathwayt's reply to Trenchard's letter, in B.M.Addnl. 37992, f. 56*v*. Judging by what Shrewsbury had to say about her attitude in his letter, it was probably in the same strain as his own.

[3] Coxe, loc. cit. pp. 65–8.

[4] He had expressed his hopes that the fleet could stay abroad at the end of July (ibid. pp. 63–4).

[5] Ibid. p. 66. The same letter is reproduced in *Cal.S.P.Dom. 1694–5*, pp. 250–1.

[6] Ibid. p. 68.

> there is no time to deliberate, I am reduced to the necessity of coming to some determination, and I have accordingly resolved to order admiral Russell to winter, with his whole squadron, at Cadiz.

On the same day, he ordered the ministers to meet

> and prepare such Orders to Admirall Russell as they shall think necessary for the signifying to him Their Majestys' Directions for the stay of the whole Fleet under his command in those parts this Winter, which are to be transmitted to him in the best Manner from England.[1]

Before this letter was sent, the Cabinet on the 4th had already made out provisional instructions for Russell, designed to meet the fleet if it was on its way home. These informed him that he would be required to winter in Spain, but left it to him to decide whether to return there if he had already covered a large part of the voyage by the time he received the orders.[2] Their tenor reflected the uncertainty which the ministers felt initially about restricting the Admiral's freedom of action too closely, and in these circumstances it seemed possible—although it could not yet be said for certain—that William's letter of the 6th, which left the task of framing the final orders to the Cabinet, might, despite its terms, be followed by just the sort of indefinite instructions which he wished to avoid. On the 7th, therefore, he proceeded to draft his own orders independently of his ministers, instructing Russell to 'continue in those seas with Our...Fleet and...pursue, and endeavour to annoy the Enemy for so long time as you may do it with safety during this season, whereupon you are to cause Our said Fleet to Winter in the Port of Cadiz', for which purpose the necessary orders had been given in England and would at once be given in Holland, and the final

---

[1] B.M.Addnl. 37992, f. 56*v*.

[2] Corbett gives the sequence of events here in reverse. In the first place, he ascribes William's letter to Shrewsbury of 6 August (O.S.) to the 2nd; and secondly, he ascribes the instructions to Russell of the 4th to the 6th, following a minute of the Privy Council for the latter day (loc. cit. p. 169). It is this which leads him to remark that 'even then [i.e. after receipt of William's letter to Shrewsbury] the nervous ministers could not harden their hearts to send the Admiral a positive order to remain'. In fact, when the Cabinet's provisional instructions were drafted, William had not yet written his letter of the 6th, nor indeed received Trenchard's letter of the 2nd; and when they were sent, on the 6th, his (William's) letter of that date had not yet been received in London.

directions for which would be sent him by the Queen and the committee. 'You are nevertheless', continued the orders, 'to use this caution, that if the French fleet or any of it now in the Mediterranean pass the Straights in Order to come into the Northern Seas, You do in that case send after them att least an equal Force to engage them or in default thereof to come to England for the Strengthning Our Fleet there.'[1] On the same night, apprehensive lest Russell might have already left for England, and unwilling to await the result of the Cabinet's deliberations, the King made his own arrangements to send these orders to the Mediterranean.[2] The utmost care was taken to see that they reached their destination. Two copies were sent off at midnight, one by special messenger to go by the packet to Spain, the other 'by Dr. Charree a Spanish Courier under cover to Mr. Kirk', the English consul at Genoa;[3] and three days later a duplicate was dispatched by special messenger, to go through Frankfurt, Berne, and Piedmont to Genoa, and thence by local tartan to the fleet, where the packet was to be delivered personally to Russell.[4]

As Blathwayt wrote to Trenchard, in enclosing the orders themselves, it would be observed that they left Russell with no latitude to return unless it were to follow the French, 'least it bring [him] under doubts and uncertaintys'. In the event of 'any very extraordinary and pressing reasons', the King did not doubt that the Admiral would behave as he thought best for the safety of the fleet, which was always an overriding consideration; but that was understood, and need not affect the rest of the instructions.[5] The ministers, however, although the main decision had already been taken for them, could not agree entirely with this restriction, and their own instructions, which followed on the 14th, contained the proviso 'that if it appear to you impracticable to refit our fleet in those parts, so as that it may be timely serviceable the next year, you do then return with the same to England; but you are not to make

---

[1] The original draft of these orders, with corrections in Blathwayt's hand, and dated from Mons 7/17 August, is contained in N.M.M. Bibl. Phill. 1, ff. 243–4.

[2] B.M.Addnl. 37992, f. 59.

[3] Endorsements on the orders, N.M.M., Bibl. Phill. 1, f. 246.

[4] Orders to Peter Tom, the messenger; ibid. ff. 283–4. For William's anxiety over the timely arrival of his orders, see Corbett, loc. cit. p. 170.

[5] B.M.Addnl. 37992, f. 59.

use of this liberty except in case of very great necessity'.[1] As Trenchard wrote to Blathwayt the same day, in their view this was a necessary precaution to save them from attack if the preparations broke down during the winter; but it was not designed to run counter to the King's instructions, and he would inform Russell privately that it meant what it said by the phrase 'except in case of very great necessity'.[2] On the next day, accordingly, he wrote to the Admiral, explaining that although he would receive two sets of orders from separate authorities, which would not be exactly the same, the difference between them was not intended to absolve him of his duty to stay abroad, which overrode all but the most pressing considerations.[3] On the same day, the Cabinet's instructions were sent to him in duplicate, one copy going by the packet to Corunna, and the second by the first of the supply convoys which was by that time assembling at Portsmouth.[4] The ministers were now committed, with whatever qualifications, to an experiment which a year before they had considered impossible.

The King's anxiety that the Cabinet might allow Russell too much latitude to return, arose not only from his mistrust of their attitude over the principle of a Mediterranean expedition, but also from his experience of Russell. The Admiral's reaction to the news was indeed much what might have been expected. Towards the end of July the idea of wintering in Spain had first been suggested to him, by 'a Noble Lord' who was probably Galway;[5] but he replied that not only was there no

---

1 Article 7 of the Queen's instructions to Russell (*Cal.S.P.Dom. 1694–5*, p. 264).

2 N.M.M., Bibl. Phill. 1, f. 279.

3 Ibid. ff. 287–8. The précis of this letter given in *Cal.S.P.Dom. 1694–5*, pp. 266–7, is unsatisfactory. Mary was not entirely satisfied that the Cabinet's orders were strict enough for the King's purpose, but, after a further meeting, the ministers decided that they could not modify them (ibid. p. 280).

4 N.M.M., Bibl. Phill. 1, f. 295.

5 The phrase is Burchett's (p. 243). Corbett calls him '"a noble lord" in the fleet' (loc. cit. p. 166), but Burchett does not say this, and in fact it seems more likely that he was not in the fleet. A copy of Russell's reply to him exists in N.M.M., Bibl. Phill. 1, ff. 199–202, endorsed 'copie de la lettre que l'amira[l] Russell m'a escrivé'. The first sentence begins, 'I wish I and the Fleet could come on the coast of Savoy so as to correspond with you more frequently'. This, with the endorsement in French, strongly suggests Galway, then commanding the troops in Savoy. On 3 August, also,

port, except Port Mahon, which could take his numbers, nor any local facilities for refitting or even re-storing, but that in any case he could see no strategic advantage in the move. ''Tis impossible', he wrote, 'for any assistance the Allyes can give them [i.e. the Spaniards] to prevent the Country's being in the French hands in September at farthest.' Spain, with no money, virtually no army, and suffering from an administrative chaos that astonished even a Commissioner of the Admiralty, could not help herself enough for her friends to help her. 'As to what you say in the last Paragraph of your Letter', he concluded, 'namely, the Fleet's wintering in these Seas, if the King pleases to command it, it must be obeyed, but I should be far from advising it.'[1] In August, he dilated to Shrewsbury on his weariness and misfortune in commanding such an unprofitable expedition,[2] and it was not surprising that on the receipt of his first orders to winter abroad he should have protested strongly.[3] William at once wrote to Shrewsbury to try to persuade the Admiral to stay where he was,[4] and indeed the Duke had already been doing his best. On 4 August, when he sent Russell the news of the Cabinet's provisional instructions, which he assured him were 'of the greatest moment to yourself and England, of any that perhaps ever came to your hand', he had urged him 'that... you will take care to lay aside all the partiality that is natural to a man's returning home, after being so long absent, and so full of the spleen, as your's of the first of July shows you to be'.[5] On the 14th and again on the 26th, he had repeated his advice, the more strongly in the latter case because, as he said, 'though by your letter of the 3rd[6] I find you are not in a very good humour, I doubt the orders you have received since will put you in a worse'. 'Dear Mr Russell', he wound up, 'let a man that truly loves and values you, prevail upon you to practise patience and submission; and if his majesty is in the wrong in his commands, do you represent what you please; but then obey them, with a prudence you can be master of, if you please.'[7] And in the event,

Russell wrote to Trenchard, 'I have had no letter from the King; from Lord Galway I have received one, but there is nothing in it, except a wish that I would come upon that coast' (*Cal.S.P.Dom. 1694–5*, p. 252).

[1] N.M.M., Bibl. Phill. 1, ff. 199–202. [2] Coxe, loc. cit. pp. 198–9.
[3] Ibid. p. 71. [4] Ibid. pp. 70–1. [5] Ibid. p. 200.
[6] See n. 2 above. [7] Coxe, loc. cit. pp. 200–2.

as always, Russell took his advice. Although he grumbled vehemently both to Shrewsbury and the Council, and forecast that by the spring 'there will be an end of an old story and an old admiral',[1] he in fact acted not merely on the letter but the spirit of his orders. On their receipt he was at Malaga on his way out of the Straits, and he immediately called a council of war at which, despite the protests of the Dutch Rear Admiral, who was for carrying on to Cadiz, it was decided to remain in the western Mediterranean for the time being. Russell indeed himself announced his intention of not going to Cadiz until October, unless the French definitely disarmed their ships before then. The fleet accordingly stayed off the south-east coast of Spain during September, for most of the time under the command of Vice-Admiral Aylmer, since Russell had gone down with dysentery. When he recovered at the end of the month, information was coming in that the French were laying up at Toulon. As soon as he received reliable confirmation of this, he turned the fleet towards Cadiz, and on 8 October came to anchor in the bay and immediately set about making arrangements to refit his ships.

II

The refit of the main fleet at Cadiz in the following months is the most interesting administrative event of the war. In the summer and autumn of 1694 few stores had been sent out, and after the refit was over those which followed were less complicated to supply and to manage, designed as they were for the replenishment rather than the repair of the ships. But in the winter, all types and large quantities of material were used and, as had been anticipated, most of these had to be sent from England. So, too, did most of the victuals, and skilled officers and workmen had likewise to be provided to superintend the refit and to organize and handle the material. The nucleus of an English dockyard had in fact to be set up, at short notice, 1100 miles from England and in a foreign state. The administrative arrangements had financial and diplomatic consequences. Facilities for credit had to be established at Madrid and Cadiz, to enable the fleet to buy such stores and food as

---

[1] Coxe, loc. cit. p. 203. For his letter to the secretary of the Council, see Corbett, loc. cit. pp. 172–3.

it could on the spot, while its personnel had to be protected against all the mischances that were liable to befall seamen in a foreign country in the seventeenth century. To the authorities in England, the fleet at Cadiz involved an extension of the main administrative facilities to an unfamiliar sphere; to the English representatives in Spain—to the ambassador at Madrid, and to the consuls and merchants at the ports, particularly at Cadiz—it represented an extension of the existing facilities for credit and diplomatic protection to an unfamiliar level. The refit was, indeed, a microcosm of the whole task of administration, in which all the normal factors were represented, but removed from their normal context and in consequence given an unusual form and clarity. It was a concise and yet for that reason not altogether faithful example of the whole, usually ill-defined range of administrative activity. The surprising thing about it is that although the problems were more difficult than those of naval administration in England, which by the autumn of 1694 seemed to be on the point of breaking down altogether, the results, while not satisfactory in every respect, taken as a whole represent the most successful administrative achievement of the war.

In one way, their very difficulty made the problems simpler than usual. For given a modicum of efficiency, the unfamiliar challenge of a foreign commitment was stimulating. The obligation to send a definite quantity of stores within a given time, and with no possibility of a makeshift alternative, could not be evaded, and if necessary was met at the expense of other commitments. This had already been the case in July, before the Admiralty received any order to refit the fleet in Spain. The department had decided in the middle of June, on receipt of Russell's letters, to send a further two months' victuals to the Mediterranean to supplement the nominal supply of four months' dry provisions and eight months' wet, at whole allowance, with which he had sailed;[1] and early in the next month it determined to send with the victuals a reinforcement of naval stores.[2] These stores, which were purely for replenishment and minor repairs,[3] were not contracted for separately but, as might be expected at short notice, were taken

[1] P.R.O.Adm. 2/174, f. 320. [2] P.R.O.Adm. 3/10: 6/7.

[3] See the list in P.R.O.Adm. 1/3572, f. 575.

from the dockyards, mostly from Deptford and Chatham.[1] The chief difficulty lay in hiring a ship to take them, for the ideal kind of vessel for the purpose was one of 400–800 tons, with large holds adapted if possible for the mast trade, and only one such ship, the *Suffolk* hagboat, could be found for hire at the time. Her owners were reluctant to let her be freighted for a foreign voyage, so the Navy Board very sensibly bought her outright.[2] When the orders to refit the fleet were received, therefore, a suitable storeship and a nucleus of stores already existed.

These orders, following the Cabinet discussions at the end of July, were sent on 1 August[3]—although, as the Admiralty complained, no indication was given of their exact purpose. It was not indeed until November that any of the naval authorities was informed officially that the fleet was to winter abroad.[4] But this did not greatly handicap them in practice, for they all concluded that some such plan had been reached, and borrowed from their reserves accordingly.[5] By 4 August the Navy Board was composing the list of stores required,[6] and a few days later the Victuallers were instructed to collect provisions for a further three months.[7] Throughout August the preparations went ahead, accompanied by constant inquiries and admonitions from the Admiralty, which was anxious to redeem its assurances to the Cabinet that the stores would be ready in eight weeks' time and the careening gear in less. It was 10 September, however, before the first storeship was loaded; and two days later, with an escort of two third rates which

[1] P.R.O.Adm. 1/3572, f. 417. [2] Ibid. ff. 385–6. [3] P.R.O.Adm. 1/4081, f. 577.

[4] 'The Board have no knowledge of any Orders to Adm[ll] Russell for his staying in the Mediterranean this Winter, yet they have rec[d] direct[ns] to provide severall stores to be sent to him and Convoys for their security' (P.R.O.Adm. 3/10: 31/8). The first official indication that the fleet was wintering at Cadiz seems to have reached the Admiralty by the indirect means of a letter from Russell alluding to the fact (P.R.O.Adm. 2/175, f. 34).

[5] 'The Board is not aware that Admirall Rusell or any ships are to stay in the Straits all winter, but they have provided stores for the whole Fleet as if it were to stay there' (P.R.O.Adm. 3/10: 5/9). 'You are to get ready such stores as are necessary to refit Adm[ll] Russell in Cadiz Bay, that in case her Ma[ty] shall...direct that Fleet to remain this next Winter in those seas, you may be in a readiness to supply them Timely with all Materialls' (Admiralty to Navy Board; P.R.O.Adm. 2/174, f. 408).

[6] P.R.O.Adm. 3/10: 2/8; 1/3572, ff. 649–50. [7] P.R.O.Adm. 2/174, f. 423.

were going out to strengthen Russell's fleet, she sailed for Cadiz[1] with a welcome cargo consisting of fifty loads of oak timber, three sets of careening gear with six pumps, eight spare capstans, 48 masts of between 6 and 21 hands (that is to say, topmasts and spars), over 4000 deals, 10,000 trennels, 700 pairs of oars, 1500 bolts of canvas, thirty lasts of tar and ten of tallow, and blocks, hawsers and cables.[2] This well-proportioned supply would be enough to keep the ships busy until the rest of the stores arrived.

These stores were almost ready by the third week in September, but in the meantime Russell had been writing that he badly needed slop clothes for his seamen and Marines,[3] and accordingly on the 24th the Admiralty was ordered to send a supply with the two storeships which by now were about to go.[4] This held them up for another fortnight, and by that time their sailing orders had been cancelled, and they were forced to wait indefinitely at Spithead.[5] The blame for this lay with the Dutch, whose storeships had originally been supposed to accompany the English vessels to Cadiz, but who announced at the beginning of October that they would not be ready in time.[6] The Cabinet therefore ordered the Admiralty to send the two ships *Burton* and *Hopewell*, with the third and larger storeship *Josiah* which had recently been acquired, to the rendezvous at Spithead, and to keep them there until further notice.[7] During this delay, two more ships, the *Benjamin* and the *Mary*, were hired, and two of the existing hospital ships converted into storeships, in the hope that all the stores on the Navy Board's original list could be sent in one large convoy which need not then be repeated for the rest of the winter.[8] In the event, there was plenty of time to proceed with these preparations; for although the Dutch on 19 October were talking of sailing for the Downs with the first fair wind,[9] and the English thought of sailing on their own early in November,[10] it was 25 November before

[1] P.R.O.Adm. 1/3574, f. 209.
[2] P.R.O.Adm. 1/3572, ff. 821–3.
[3] P.R.O.Adm. 2/363, f. 34.
[4] P.R.O.Adm. 1/4081, f. 935.
[5] P.R.O.Adm. 1/3573, f. 289.
[6] B.M.Addnl. 37992, f. 87.
[7] *H.M.C. Buccleuch*, II, pt I, pp. 147–8; P.R.O.Adm. 1/3573, ff. 319–20.
[8] P.R.O.Adm. 1/3573, f. 715; 1/3574, f. 209; Sutherland Shaw, 'The Hospital Ship, 1608–1740', in *M.M.* XXII, no. 4, p. 426.
[9] B.M.Addnl. 37992, f. 89.
[10] The Admiralty strongly recommended this to Trenchard on the 5th (P.R.O.Adm. 2/175, f. 32).

the combined convoy left Spithead for Cadiz.[1] When at last it sailed, the English part consisted of the three original vessels and the two converted hospital ships; the *Benjamin* and the *Mary* were left behind.[2] Almost four-fifths of the naval stores, however, were in the first five ships;[3] and the rest followed in February.

The cargo taken altogether by the eight ships was considerable, and it is interesting to compare it with Russell's demands. In February 1695, the Navy Board drew up a debit and credit account of stores demanded and stores sent. If the most important commodities alone are taken, they show the following result:[4]

	Demanded altogether	Supplied short	Supplied in excess
Canvas, 12 types (in yards)	6,055	3,085‡	2,321§
Sails, all sorts*	341	—	67
Cables, 3½–22 in.	82	—	90
Buoy ropes (in fathoms)	326	326	—
Hawsers and shrouds	649	—	749
Spunyarn, thread and twine (in fathoms)	1,005	—	1,136
Nails, all sorts	15,157	—	23,744
Bolts, plates and rings, all sorts	571	69	—
Grindstones	51	23	—
Anchors, 2–56 lb.	17	13	—
Masts and yards, topmasts and below	8	—	93
Plank, 1½–4 in.† (in ft.)	3,673	—	1,345
Trennels	518	—	8,982
Wedges	581	—	4,319
Blocks, all sorts	1,838	1,048	—
Oil (in gallons)	134	134	—
Rosin (in lb.)	23	23	—
Tallow (in cwt.)	85	—	162
Tar (in barrels)	161	—	228

* There were deficiencies in topsails and topgallant sails, but mainsails and foresails were supplied sufficiently in excess of demand for there to be a total excess of sails. The sailmaker to the navy took over an extra workshop specifically for this additional order (P.R.O.Adm. 1/3572, f. 417).

† There are no records here of timber or deals. ‡ Eight types. § Two types.

With the three sets of careening gear, these supplies on the whole met the demands of the fleet more than adequately;[5] and despite the long delay in the first convoy, which was owing principally to the Dutch, most of them arrived by the end of the year.

But stores were only one item in the fleet's requirements. The ships' companies could not be expected to refit the ships without assistance,

1 P.R.O.Adm. 1/3574, f. 209.
2 Ibid.
3 P.R.O.Adm. 95/14, f. 63.
4 Ibid. ff. 51–63.
5 The Navy Board's conclusion, after comparing Russell's demands with its supplies, was that 'the Latter appear to exceed the Former in all things Material' (P.R.O. Adm. 1/3574, f. 278).

and this again had to be supplied from England. Such quantities of material, moreover, representing so large a proportion of the total dockyard stores, needed a dockyard staff to supervise their maintenance and distribution. The Navy Board was alive to the necessity for both workmen and officers, but its ignorance of the Cabinet's intentions for the fleet prevented it from making detailed arrangements. Towards the end of August it suggested that some caulkers and smiths should be sent, and this was approved early the next month.[1] By the end of September, when the storeships were supposed to be sailing, the number and types of workmen had been increased; and when the convoy finally left in November, it took with it twenty shipwrights and a foreman shipwright, nineteen caulkers and a master caulker, three smiths and a foreman smith, two bricklayers and four oakum boys.[2] By then, provision had also been made for officers to superintend the work and the storage of material. On 23 September, the Cabinet ordered the Admiralty to send with the first convoy a master attendant and a Commissioner of Victualling;[3] but the Board decided that these were not enough for the purpose, and within the next few days it added a master shipwright, a storekeeper and a clerk of the survey with some clerks, and decided to send a Commissioner of the Navy in charge.[4] For this last duty the Board selected Thomas Wilshaw, the Comptroller of Stores,[5] with instructions to establish a repair yard at Cadiz, run on English lines, and to distribute the gear and organize the refit in company with the Admiral, according to the rules of the navy.[6] It proved more difficult to find a Victualling Commissioner; but at length Mr Ayles, one of the Commission, was persuaded to take on the duties,[7] and an assistant—none other than the ubiquitous

---

[1] P.R.O.Adm. 1/3572, f. 929; 3/10: 4/9.

[2] P.R.O.Adm. 106/2974. Another list of these men, in Serg.Misc. v, f. 272, gives seventeen ordinary shipwrights. Some coopers were also sent for the provisions (P.R.O.Adm. 3/10: 18/10).

[3] P.R.O.Adm. 1/4081, f. 935.

[4] P.R.O.Adm. 3/10: 24/9, 27/9.

[5] Ibid. 24/9; see Appendix VIII below.

[6] Wilshaw's instructions are given in P.R.O.Adm. 1/3573, ff. 561–71. The Navy Board had not thought it necessary to give him any, but he insisted that it should (Serg.Misc. II, f. 627).

[7] P.R.O.Adm. 2/175, f. 5; 3/10: 7/11; 1/3573, f. 463.

Phineas Bowles, once victualling agent at Lisbon and Tangier and now a former Secretary of the Admiralty—was soon appointed for him.[1] The other officers were selected without much difficulty,[2] and when the convoy sailed the nucleus of a dockyard establishment went with it.

The victualling proved less easy to arrange. The original two months' supply was sent successfully in August;[3] but the delays to the convoy which was to have taken the provisions for a further three months in September, prevented it from taking them when it finally sailed in November. For while naval stores could be kept aboard the ships without any trouble until they were ready to sail, most of the victuals could not; and when the orders were cancelled early in October, the Victuallers distributed most of the food to the ports and awaited further instructions.[4] In the middle of November they began to collect it again, and they were then ordered to provide a further three months' supply at the same time.[5] The arrangements for both lots went on simultaneously, but the provisions for the first three months, after being successfully loaded in the Thames, were held up in the Downs towards the end of the month by head winds; and of the thirteen vessels with victuals aboard, only seven reached the convoy in time for their contents to be transferred. The other six were still making their way to the storeships when they sailed for Cadiz.[6] William, therefore, ordered that the proportion left behind should be sent, with the supply for the next three months, by the beginning of January.[7] The Victuallers were finding it difficult to raise the money for this additional service, and throughout December the Admiralty was inquiring anxiously over their progress.[8] January 1695 and most of February passed with complaints of shortage of cash from the lower Board and with exhortations to do better from the higher, until on 23 February the Victuallers were able to report that all the provisions had been acquired and loaded in the river.[9] But it was not until

[1] P.R.O.Adm. 3/10: 14/11. [2] P.R.O.Adm. 1/3573, ff. 315, 319–21.

[3] In fourteen small ships (P.R.O.Adm. 2/174, f. 420).

[4] P.R.O.Adm. 106/2349, f. 263. [5] P.R.O.Adm. 1/3573, f. 875.

[6] Ibid. ff. 1023, 1051; 3/10: 29/11. [7] P.R.O.Adm. 3/10: 3/12.

[8] P.R.O.Adm. 1/3573, ff. 875, 1051, 1101, 1233–4; 3/11: 12/12, 28/12.

[9] P.R.O.Adm. 1/3574, ff. 185, 333, 429; 3/11: 23/1, 1/2, 14/2.

24 March that the small convoy finally left for Cadiz[1], and that the Victuallers could report, in answer to a query by the Admiralty, that Russell now had sufficient provisions to last him until the beginning of July at whole allowance, or to the beginning of September at short allowance.[2]

The conception in England of how the fleet should be supplied had thus been adequate, and its results not inadequate. Despite the delays in both stores and victuals, Russell was never entirely without either, or entirely unable to carry on with his work during the winter and spring. The organization of the refit at Cadiz itself was efficient. It did not begin until the middle of November, for shortly after Russell put in to Cadiz on 8 October, the king of Spain requested him to sail again to Barcelona, on receipt of the news—which, as Russell suspected, was incorrect[3]—that the French fleet had reappeared at Palamos on the eastern coast. He accordingly put to sea once more, but remained near the Straits in case the enemy should attempt to slip past him to the north. After a month of uneventful cruising, and with winter coming on, he returned to Cadiz, and on 8 November issued the necessary orders to begin the refit.[4]

Its course was not made any the easier by the physical and diplomatic circumstances. Cadiz bay is not an ideal place in which to repair a large number of ships in a limited time. It lies open and undefended to the north-west for about four miles, until its eastern shore curves to the north-east to form an inner bay, protected from the west by a long spit of land at the end of which stands the town of Cadiz itself. Within this spit, and just inside the inner bay, lies an area called the Puntalls, and it was here that the units of the fleet were taken in hand, while the rest lay outside. In view of the exposed nature of the bay, the latter were always kept ready to sail at short notice, the first and second rates with water for a month aboard and the lesser rates with enough for six weeks.[5] Not more than two or three ships could be refitted at once, and

---

[1] P.R.O.Adm. 2/386, Secretary of Admiralty to Bowles, 26/3.

[2] P.R.O.Adm. 1/3574, f. 277; 2/175, f. 232.

[3] Coxe, loc. cit. pp. 206–7. Russell's own comment was not uncalled for: 'I am like to have a fine time all this winter, by reason of the foolish fears of the spaniards.'

[4] Burchett, pp. 260–3.

[5] Ibid. p. 263.

even in the Puntalls they were affected by the weather, which was uniformly bad throughout the winter.[1] The stores themselves were not free from the dangers which a high wind could bring to the harbour, for they were either aboard the storeships or distributed in piles and sheds along the foreshore. In January, the programme was severely interrupted by a week of gales. All the masts, and 'several hundred' barrels of pitch and tar, many of them purchased locally, floated about the bay, and had to be rescued by parties of sailors searching the marshes;[2] and shortly afterwards, the *Josiah* storeship and two of the big ships under refit blew ashore.[3]

Throughout February and March, the prevailing Atlantic winds delayed the preparations in the Puntalls, and often made the long anchor watches aboard the vessels in the outer bay an anxious time for their captains and for the Admiral. The latter's worries were increased by the attitude of the governor of Cadiz, who throughout the war had been a strong Francophil and for some years had been maltreating the English whenever he got the chance.[4] Russell soon had occasion to echo his predecessors' complaints.[5] To the authorities at home, however, the most significant aspect of the governor's activities was that they were obviously tolerated at Madrid, where although the idea of an English fleet in the south during the winter had been warmly welcomed, little enthusiasm had been shown, much to Stanhope's surprise, over the prospect of its refitting at Cadiz. Carnero, the Foreign Minister, had at first even declined to put a house at Russell's disposal, and had submitted a long memorandum to the English ambassador to show that Port Mahon, inside the Straits, closer to Catalonia and the French, and with a prosperous agricultural hinterland, would be more suitable for a base. He even offered, if Russell would winter there, to provide workmen from Barcelona and the island of Majorca itself, to help careen his ships; if the fleet chose to use Cadiz, however, he could not guarantee this support.[6] This astonishing communication, which

[1] *H.M.C. Buccleuch*, II, pt I, pp. 172–3, 174–6.

[2] P.R.O.Adm. 106/478, Wilshaw to Navy Board, 13/1/95. [3] Ibid. 23/1.

[4] S.P.For. 94/73, Stanhope to Nottingham, 30/12/91, 30/8, 9/9/93; 104/196, ff. 29–30.

[5] *H.M.C. Buccleuch*, II, pt I, p. 140.

[6] S.P.For. 94/73, Stanhope to Shrewsbury, 19/9/94, in which Carnero's memorandum is enclosed.

seems to have been a *ballon d'essai*, was modified a fortnight later by a letter from the king to Russell, assuring him that if he wished to use Cadiz he would be given all facilities; but once again the arguments for Port Mahon were put forward, and the same inducements offered for its use.[1] When the English continued to favour the west coast, the Admiral was met by a complete lack of co-operation, which increased the normal procrastination and inefficiency of a Spanish naval base. With intrigue at Madrid[2] and a hostile governor at Cadiz, he was forced back largely on his own resources.

In these adverse circumstances, however, officers and men set to work methodically and with some vigour, with that consciousness of their superiority to their surroundings which distinguishes the Royal Navy in the ports of southern Europe. The dockyard officers and workmen were on the whole treated well.[3] The latter were all given equal pay, whatever their jobs, at 40*s*. a month, the boys getting 19*s*. a month, and in addition they were victualled aboard the storeships, where they lived. With no expenses for lodgings or food, even the shipwrights, who were getting 8*s*. a month less than at home, were probably no worse off, while most of the other trades undoubtedly gained by the terms. The skilled members of the ships' companies, after an initial refusal on the part of the Admiralty,[4] were given a daily allowance for helping to refit their ships, ranging from 4*d*. a day to the master carpenters to 2*d*. a day for their crews and 1*d*. a day to the boys. The dockyard officers were treated generously. Wilshaw received £1000 a year so long as he remained abroad; his master attendant, master shipwright and storekeeper £400 a year each, and the latter an extra £200 a year for two clerks; and his clerk of the survey £300 a year. In most cases, this was double their pay in the most highly-paid yards at home at the same time, but it was designed to cover all their expenses. They received no

[1] A copy of this letter is contained in N.M.M., Bibl. Phill. 1, ff. 345–8.

[2] See Russell's mock comedy in which he cast the principal figures of Spanish politics for Shrewsbury's benefit, in *H.M.C. Buccleuch*, II, pt 1, p. 174.

[3] The following financial details are taken from P.R.O.Adm. 106/2974, and Serg. Misc. v, ff. 272–6.

[4] P.R.O.Adm. 106/479, Wilshaw to Navy Board, 5/2/95. He was forbidden to offer extra pay to members of ships' companies refitting their ships, by article 8 of his instructions.

house rent, no perquisites and no allowances for travelling, paper or heating. The junior officers, for whom there was no question of living ashore, were paid at more familiar rates but, unlike the normal practice, by the month. The foreman of shipwrights, the master caulker and the master smith got £6 a month each, and the former was allowed one servant, as were all the senior officers, at 19*s*. a month. On the whole, they were paid less than their most senior counterparts in England, and they also received no perquisites; but on the other hand, their expenses, while they were hard at work in the Puntalls, were probably few.

The refit went ahead quite well. By the end of January 1695 all the second rates and a few of the firsts and thirds had been careened,[1] and by 25 February Russell was able to report that the whole fleet would be ready, if the weather got no worse, in fourteen or fifteen days.[2] By 11 March, all the three-deckers except two were ready, and all the third rates that stood most in need of repair.[3] During the next week, the flagship herself was careened, 'amidst a great No. of boats...of all nations as Spectators'; and the English factory in the town was given a holiday to watch the event.[4] On the 25th, the Admiral reported to Shrewsbury 'that the ships here with me are all ready for sea, but', he added, 'we want the main ingredients, men and provisions'.[5] The provisions reached him in time before he sailed early in May, although only when he was reduced to one month's supply for the whole fleet;[6] but the men were to prove the main difficulty throughout the next campaign.

In the event, the fleet was ready to sail as soon as the French with their greatly superior, although overloaded, facilities at Toulon.[7] But despite all that Russell had done, it was in poor shape. It is no reflection on the work done at Cadiz, that according to his report at the end of February only 16 out of the 41 ships of the line then in the bay were in a condition to remain abroad beyond the coming summer.[8] In December, he had written to the Admiralty that many of the third rates stood badly in need of repair, particularly the contract-built ships, which he singled

[1] P.R.O.Adm. 106/479, Wilshaw to Navy Board, 5/2/95.

[2] *H.M.C. Buccleuch*, II, pt I, p. 175.

[3] Ibid. p. 176. I have been unable to find exact figures during the stages of the refit.

[4] P.R.O.Adm. 106/479, Wilshaw to Navy Board, 20/3.

[5] *H.M.C. Buccleuch*, II, pt I, p. 178.

[6] Ibid. p. 180.

[7] Roncière, op. cit. VI, pp. 154–5.

[8] *H.M.C. Buccleuch*, II, pt I, p. 175.

out for particularly poor performance and endurance; and before the end of that month he discovered, to his dismay, that some of them were badly wormed.[1] Wilshaw removed a few strakes from one of the ships affected and sent them to England for the Navy Board to see,[2] and the symptoms worried the authorities a great deal. For while a state of disrepair, and the sluggishness and discomfort that resulted, could often be, and had often been, accepted as an inevitable feature of war, the activities of the Mediterranean *teredo navalis* was a different matter, for which there was no known remedy. But while the reports of worm produced an alarm that the reports of disrepair did not, the administrative implications were the same in each case: if the fleet were to be kept abroad for two successive campaigns, it required not only a refit but a partial replacement of its units. While the authorities in England had catered not inadequately for the refit, it was only in the course of it that they had been led to think seriously about replacements; and it was this factor, together with the paucity of men, which was responsible for the troubles of the subsequent campaign.

But before we examine their effect upon it, we must look at one more aspect of the refit itself: that of finance. In his description of the Mediterranean venture, Macaulay remarked that 'the crews had better food and drink than they had ever had before; comforts which Spain did not afford were supplied from home; and yet the charge was not greater than when, in Torrington's time, the sailor was poisoned by mouldy biscuit and nauseous beer'.[3] If we

[1] P.R.O.Adm. 2/363, ff. 5, 20. [2] P.R.O.Adm. 106/479, 11/2.

[3] *History*, v, p. 2454. It is perhaps not irrelevant to note that the whole passage from which this quotation is taken is a good example of that curious combination of inaccurate detail leading to a perfectly correct effect which so often marks Macaulay's treatment of sea affairs. In this instance, quite apart from the question of whether the men were *better* fed than before, the remarks would seem to apply to the summer of 1694 rather than the winter; but during the summer not a single supply ship reached the fleet from England. The good effects of administration in that year, also, are related to the fact that Russell was now 'First Lord of the Admiralty'; but the administrative preparations for his fleet had been made before he rejoined the Admiralty Commission in May, and the subsequent arrangements were affected by him only in so far as his demands carried a greater influence than those of most Admirals of the fleet. The material for both these judgements existed, at least in part, in the sources which Macaulay is known, from

place the emphasis upon stores rather than victuals, and upon the ease rather than the quantity of financial supply, this passage sums up correctly the most significant feature of the winter preparations. The money for the fleet during the autumn and winter of 1694 had to be supplied in Spain as well as in England; for although most of the important stores, and most of the victuals, came from home, the ships were forced to rely to some extent on Spanish assistance, however grudgingly given. In the summer of 1694, they had watered and to some extent provisioned in Altea bay, and had revictualled as best they could at Barcelona.[1] At Cadiz, they were continually buying odd quantities of food,[2] and they also purchased in quite large quantities a few of the stores which had not been sent from England. Oil and tar were acquired in this way,[3] and although no evidence has been found to prove it, it would seem likely that the reason for so few anchors being dispatched from home was because Spanish iron was considered the best material for the purpose.[4] Russell, Wilshaw and Ayles each made his own purchases at Cadiz, and Wilshaw's alone were considerable. By the end of January, he estimated that he had spent £7000 to £8000, and in March he announced on one occasion that he had just spent 7400 dollars.[5] 'The exchange', he reported then, 'runs very high', and local stores were expensive. Ayles's expenditure during the winter has not been traced; but by May 1695 he had spent £22,399 since an unknown date, which at the furthest could be only the previous January, and it rose steadily during the summer.[6] Russell had his own account, which was separate from those of the two Commissioners; but how much it

his journal, to have used; although he cites Burchett alone in support, from whom no judgement of any sort on these points could have been gained. His antithesis between naval administration in Russell's day and in Torrington's, with the emphasis on personality, calls for no comment, since in this case the evidence—which is to be found only in the Admiralty records, then partly stored in a shed at Deptford, and partly in a disorderly heap in the Tower—was not readily available to him.

1 Burchett, p. 240; S.P.For. 74/93, Stanhope to Shrewsbury, 21/7.

2 Foreign ambassadors at Madrid were under the impression that the Spaniards had promised to supply the fleet with provisions in return for its remaining in the Mediterranean. Stanhope's comment on this was that he wished it were true (S.P.For. 74/93, 1/8).

3 P.R.O.Adm. 106/478; Wilshaw to Navy Board, 13/1/95.

4 See p. 65 above.

5 P.R.O.Adm. 106/478, 27/1; 106/479, 25/3.

6 P.R.O. T. 38/615, no. 6.

amounted to is not known. But it is worth noting that while he claimed to have spent his own money in his efforts to supply the ships,[1] one of the heads of his impeachment seven years later was 'for applying to his own use, a summ of Money, and great quantities of Wine, Ale, etc. given by the King of Spain, for the use of the English Fleet, when they were in the Streights'.[2]

Some of the money for these transactions was supplied by the Spaniards themselves,[3] and some by imprests made to Russell from time to time by the Admiralty. The latter was the usual method for supplying a Mediterranean squadron: Killigrew, Aylmer and Wheeler had all received imprests of between £1000 and £2000 before they sailed, and the precedent was followed in March 1694 when Russell was given £2000 in cash, with which he sailed in June.[4] In the following April he received another £1103. But the latter was paid to him, on Treasury instructions, by a firm of merchants in Cadiz, William Hodges and Company;[5] and it was on the credit provided by this and other English firms in Spain that most of the local purchases were made. On 13 June it was arranged that credits for £20,000 should be placed at the fleet's disposal at Cadiz, Alicante and Leghorn, and that payments should be made on it by Hodges and Company at Cadiz, by Watts and Company at Alicante, and by Western, Burdett and Company at Leghorn. A week later, the total was raised to £50,000.[6] When Wilshaw sailed for Spain, arrangements were made for more credit with Hodges;[7] and it was on that firm accordingly that he drew his bills, 'in the name of John Corfield, one of my clerks, who receives and pays all the moneys here,

---

[1] 'What you are pleased to say of the King's being possessed with an opinion I should make great profits here, I do not wonder at, these voyages having proved very beneficial to the chief commanders; but I cannot bring myself to make the profits formerly practised.... Upon the whole, I do assure you, I have not, since I came into the Straits, made to myself the advantage of a pistole, and many a thousand it has cost me' (Russell to Shrewsbury, 10/2/95; Coxe, loc. cit. pp. 222–3).

[2] Article 3 of *The Chief Heads of the Articles of Impeachment against the Earl of Orford...* (1701) (in *B.M. Printed 1851*, c. 19). See also the investigation of this accusation in P.R.O. T. 38/614, ff. 24–5.

[3] How much I do not know. There was certainly no official agreement for Spain to bear any of the expenses of the fleet (S.P.For. 74/93, Stanhope to Shrewsbury, 1/8; 104/196, ff. 126–7).

[4] P.R.O. T. 38/608, ff. 3–4, 6–7.

[5] Ibid.

[6] P.R.O.Adm. 3/10: 13/6, 15/6, 20/6.

[7] Ibid. 10/10, 11/10.

for the use of the Fleet'.[1] A small group of large creditors on the navy was thus formed abroad by the end of the year, able to exercise considerable pressure upon it to secure the repayment of their bills.

But the main expense, like the main task of supplying the fleet, occurred in England. It did not fall equally on all of the naval departments. The stores came mostly from the dockyard reserves, so that the financial commitment in that case was their replacement rather than their purchase; but the victuals had mostly to be bought for the occasion, and when reinforcements of ships and men were sent out, as they were mainly in the new year, they were paid before they left. Thus, although it is impossible to separate the total cost of supplying the fleet in Spain from the general naval expenditure at the same time, its demands upon ready money may be seen in the demands of the Victuallers, and in the amounts required to make up the pay of the ships and the drafts before they left England. Both interrupted the course of naval credit at a time when such credit was low, and when recent interruptions had almost led to disaster. Yet in the late autumn and winter of 1694–5, the commitments were met without undue strain. The reason lay entirely in the foundation of the Bank of England. The Bank had been incorporated in May 1694 by the Tonnage Act,[2] for the purpose of lending £1,200,000 to the government at 8% interest. The sum was to be subscribed by 1 August, and to be wholly paid into the Exchequer by 1 January 1695. In the event, it was subscribed to the full in twelve days from the time that the books were opened on 21 June; the first loan of £112,000 was paid into the Exchequer on 1 August; and the whole sum was paid up before the end of the year, and allocated to the different departments.

These payments financed the navy almost single-handed between 1 August and 31 December. If the issues from the Exchequer to the navy over this period are set side by side with the allocations to the navy from the Bank loan—which were sometimes, but not always, made directly through the Exchequer—the extent to which they did so may be clearly seen. The details are as shown on p. 541.[3]

---

[1] P.R.O.Adm. 106/479, 25/3/95. [2] 5 and 6 Will. and Mary c. 20.

[3] *Cal.Treas.Bks. 1693–6*, pp. 725, 744–5, 752, 754–5, 760, 765, 768, 772–4, 776, 782–3, 788–9, 794–5, 806, 812–13, 824, 833, 843, 848, 858.

	Exchequer issues to the navy			Allocations to the navy from Bank of England loans		
	£	s.	d.	£	s.	d.
1 August	—			24,000	0	0
7 August	—			19,000	0	0
14 August	—			19,000	0	0
22 August	23,859	0	0	23,859	0	0
30 August	11,000	0	0	11,000	0	0
5 September	48,179	0	0	48,179	0	0
12 September	20,000	0	0	20,000	0	0
19–20 September	18,738	4	7	27,030	0	0
25 September	32,472	9	7½	32,472	9	7½
28 September	630	0	0	—		
5 October	5,000	0	0	5,000	0	0
12 October	20,000	0	0	20,000	0	0
17 October	28,663	10	5	23,663	10	5
24 October	25,000	0	0	25,000	0	0
31 October	23,399	10	0	18,399	10	0
15 November	—			10,000	0	0
6 December	—			20,000	0	0
12 December	10,000	0	0	250,000	0	0
21 December	12,000	0	0	44,335	18	8¾

Thus, out of the £1,200,000 lent by the Bank in this time, £640,939. 8*s*. 9¼*d*. was allotted to the use of the navy; while, of the Exchequer issues made to the Treasurer of the Navy, only £32,630 was provided from sources other than the Bank loan. On 28 September, he was supplied with £630 from money paid into the Exchequer by the executors of the late collector of Customs at Bristol, who had died before all his returns had been made; on 17 and again on 31 October, £5000 was issued on loans on the temporary and hereditary Excise, in both cases for victualling Russell's fleet; and on 12 and 21 December, two issues of £10,000 and £12,000 were made from loans on the general credit of the Exchequer, the whole of the first and £10,000 of the second again being devoted to the victualling of the ships at Cadiz. The other £2630 was designed for purposes not connected with the Mediterranean.[1] Thus, except for £30,000 for victualling, £10,000 of which was spent before the first convoy left, and £20,000 before the departure of the second convoy, all immediate payments for the maintenance of Russell's fleet were made with the support of the Bank.

Not all of the Bank's loan of £1,200,000 was paid into the Exchequer in ready money. Only sixty per cent of the subscriptions were called up immediately, so that only £720,000 could be supplied to the government in cash. The remaining £480,000 was supplied in notes

[1] Ibid. pp. 776, 795, 813, 848, 858.

under the seal of the Bank, known as 'sealed Bank bills'.[1] What proportion of the £640,939 allocated to the navy was in cash, and what proportion in notes, has not been discovered. Certainly the Victuallers received a far higher proportion of their annual payments in ready money between Lady Day 1694 and Lady Day 1695 than usual—£518,289. 15*s.* 8*d.* out of a total of £608,863. 3*s.* 7*d.*[2]—and much of this may have come in the Michaelmas quarter. But the great difference for the Exchequer between receiving loans from the Bank and from other sources, lay precisely in the fact that those payments from the Bank which were not in cash could be disposed of immediately and at par, and bought commodities at the same rate as ready money. Guaranteeing as they did repayment by an institution which was known to command the support of a large and important part of the City of London, and whose foundation, despite the opposition, seemed to have been crowned by success, they were readily accepted by the contractors. The contrast between the forms of supply, which had hitherto characterized all payments to the Exchequer, was in this case of only minor importance. As the first Deputy Governor of the Bank remarked, while the Directors had 'called in but £720,000...they have paid into the Exchequer the whole of the £1,200,000 before the time....The rest is left to circulate in trade.'[3]

The same margin of sealed bills which itself circulated so successfully, also affected the circulation of the tallies which for the moment the bills were replacing.[4] For with £480,000 still to be issued, the Bank looked around for some investments for its reserve. The loan to the government was not repayable before 1706,[5] and it needed some short-term securities to bring in immediate assets. Under the Tonnage Act, the Bank had the right to discount tallies or bills of exchange; and the former offered the greater advantages. Thanks to the appalling state of the government's short-term credit at the end of the summer, many of them were to be had very cheap. The Bank, therefore, proceeded to buy them up. Its own credit was good, the tallies were plentiful, and soon the market found itself relieved of a high proportion of the wooden sticks

[1] See Feaveryear, *The Pound Sterling*, p. 116. [2] P.R.O. T. 38/615, no. 5.
[3] Quoted in Feaveryear, loc. cit. p. 117.
[4] I have followed ibid. pp. 117–18 in this paragraph.
[5] Clapham, loc. cit. p. 18.

in which so much trade was locked up. In the autumn and winter of 1694, for the first time since the beginning of the war, the navy was able to buy its material promptly and without too much difficulty. For the first time, an agent of long-term credit had re-established confidence in short-term credit, and the Administration was given a breathing space just when it needed it most. Without the Bank of England, there is no reason to suppose that the fleet could have stayed in the Mediterranean for another campaign.

The influence of the Bank was to be seen more directly in Spain itself. For one of the earliest of its commitments was the remittance of money abroad, to Flanders and the Mediterranean, for the conduct of the war. In October 1694, a committee of Directors of the Bank was established 'for the remises', or remittances, and a separate ledger was started for this type of business.[1] Early in 1695, eight English firms abroad, outside Holland, were selected to act as the Bank's agents, and of these three bore names familiar to the navy. In Cadiz, Hodges and Company acted as the chief Spanish agent; in Alicante, Watts and Company; and in Leghorn Western, Burdett and Company. In addition, the firm of Ballard and Stone at Madrid was brought into the business.[2] Unfortunately, very little is recorded of the precise nature of the Bank's activities with these companies at this time: the chief authority on its history alludes to its remittances for the fleet, but gives no details as to their number or size, and earlier histories are equally unhelpful in this respect.[3] To the navy, their importance lay in the relief which they afforded to its course of payment, removing its responsibility for meeting the substantial bills incurred by subordinates abroad, and ensuring that they could count on the facilities of the English merchants to make local purchases so long as the credit of the

---

[1] Ibid. p. 26. [2] Ibid. p. 28 and n. 2.

[3] Ibid. p. 27. There is a detailed account of the machinery of remittances to the army in Flanders in R. D. Richards, *The Early History of Banking in England* (1929), ch. VII; but little is said about the remittances to Spain (see, however, p. 179 and n. 2). The same author's *The First Fifty Years of the Bank of England* (1934), J. E. Thorold Rogers, *The First Nine Years of the Bank of England* (1887), A. Andréadès, *History of the Bank of England* (1909), and W. M. Acres, *The Bank of England from Within* (1931) are also silent on the subject. I have not, however, consulted the original records of the Bank, which may well contain the answer.

Bank itself was sustained. At Cadiz, as at home, the naval authorities were not crippled by lack of money, and the degree of success which the refit enjoyed was for once an accurate measure of the degree of success which the Administration itself could command, when freed from the distractions of financial anxiety.

III

In 1695, the favourable financial conditions disappeared which the Bank of England had created. But this did not affect the issue in the Mediterranean, where the difficulties of the summer were administrative. Russell's limitations in his second campaign lay in the decay of his ships and in the shortage of men. Few ships had been sent home during the winter. In November, four third rates were exchanged for a fresh four from England,[1] which escorted the first convoy out to Cadiz, and a further exchange took place in January when the second convoy sailed.[2] In all, Russell sent home eighteen ships suffering from worm or in a state of bad disrepair, and received eight fresh ships in return. The balance was made up in bombvessels, which he had asked for early in November, and which he hoped to use against the French Mediterranean ports during the next campaign.[3] With them, at the end of January, came his first reinforcements of men. By then they were badly needed. On 2 November the Admiral had estimated that by the following March he would need 2900 to 3000 fresh men, and it is interesting that, apparently from fear of sickness breaking out in the fleet, he preferred that some of these should be old soldiers rather than young seamen who would fall a prey more easily to disease. The Admiralty agreed to send him mostly Marines and land soldiers, partly to enable him to support the Spaniards with a landing force if necessary, and partly because seamen of any quality seemed to be impossible to get. Towards the end of the month one regiment of Marines was reserved for the Mediterranean;[4] three regiments of infantry were added soon afterwards; and the whole force of some 3500

[1] P.R.O.Adm. 3/10: 12/11.

[2] P.R.O.Adm. 2/175, f. 5.

[3] P.R.O.Adm. 3/10: 7/12; 3/11: 25/1; Coxe, loc. cit. p. 211; *H.M.C. Buccleuch*, II, pt I, pp. 158, 162.

[4] P.R.O.Adm. 3/10: 26/11.

men sailed—some in the escorting warships, and the rest in transports—with the second convoy.[1] A number of seamen accompanied them. Meanwhile Russell had been complaining steadily of the increasing shortage of men, as his crews were gradually cut down by illness.[2] No epidemic broke out, but there was a continual drain of men while the ships lay in Cadiz bay, partly owing to the shortage of slop clothes; and the refusal of the Spaniards to allow more than a small quota ashore at any one time did not help to keep down the sick rate.[3] The Admiralty was sympathetic, but pointed out in February that the Admiral had sent no muster lists for the whole time that he had been abroad, so that the Board found it difficult to meet his exact requirements.[4] A muster-master existed in the fleet; but, as he complained to the Navy Board, Russell disliked him, and the captains of the ships in consequence usually refused to allow him aboard to take the musters. He was given no vessel or boats of his own, and if he managed to get aboard one of the ships of the fleet he was liable to find that he could not get off again. During the winter, he had gone on two enforced cruises in smaller rates in this way, and by the end of May 1695 he had altogether been absent from Cadiz for 69 days since the previous October.[5] In the end, the wretched official found himself aboard a third rate leaving Cadiz for home, and one day the Navy Board was surprised to receive a letter from him from Chatham.[6] Thus, as the summer wore on and the numbers continued to decline, no reliable information of the rate at which they were decreasing was available either to the Admiralty or to the Admiral himself, although both realized that his ships were not up to their proper strength. When the fleet put to sea after its refit, not all of its units were therefore in equally good shape. Dry rot and disease between them had materially reduced the efficiency of the force that had entered the Straits nine months before.

---

1 P.R.O.Adm. 3/11: 28/12, 28/1; *H.M.C. Buccleuch*, II, pt I, p. 168.

2 Coxe, loc. cit. pp. 217, 226; *H.M.C. Buccleuch*, II, pt I, pp. 171, 178.

3 No figures were given for seamen, but of the 51 workmen sent out in November, ten were dead in February 1695 (P.R.O.Adm. 106/2974).

4 P.R.O.Adm. 2/363, f. 19.

5 Serg.Misc. IV, ff. 85–6; R. Wilkins to Navy Board.

6 Ibid. f. 87.

The discrepancy between the situation as Russell knew it to be in April, and as it was seen by the rest of the world, accounted to some extent for his moroseness and impatience, which increased the more popular he became at home and the more powerful abroad. By the spring of 1695, his fortunes appeared to be higher than ever before. The retreat of the French to Toulon on his arrival, and the consequent relief of Barcelona, had greatly raised hopes at home, where the Lords had passed a vote of thanks to him;[1] while the continuance of the fleet abroad had at last given proof of the reality of allied sea power.[2] The commander of this fleet had become a figure of European importance, and, as Shrewsbury wrote to Russell in October, 'I cannot think but that you are in much the considerablest station of any subject in Europe, and in a circumstance extreme safe and happy for your reputation'.[3] He had already suggested that the Admiral might like a peerage,[4] and later he mentioned that the King was ready to offer him the office of Vice-Admiral of England as a mark of his favour, provided that he himself was ready to accept it.[5] In the Mediterranean itself, Russell was a great figure, and the flagship in Cadiz bay became a centre of diplomatic as well as naval activity. Stanhope at Madrid, and the consuls along the Spanish and Italian coasts, sent him the news of the courts and the markets;[6] Galway kept him informed of the position on the Italian front;[7] and the governors of the Spanish coastal towns and provinces bombarded him with news and petitions.[8] 'I may say', wrote the Admiral himself, 'without appearing vain, I have settled...myself as much in the spaniards' esteem, as I could do with all the titles that have been given me. I hope they speak well of me behind my back; they make great compliments to my face, and in their letters.'[9] He took care to foster their respect for his position by persuading William to grant him the title of Captain-General as well as Admiral, which had sometimes been held by commanders of Mediterranean squadrons before and which in Spanish eyes lent grandeur to the

---

[1] *H.L.J.* xv, p. 511. See also Coxe, loc. cit. p. 213: 'The court, the parliament, the people, are in better humour than you can imagine' (Shrewsbury to Russell, 4/12/94).

[2] See Corbett, loc. cit. p. 176.

[3] Coxe, loc. cit. p. 209.

[4] Ibid. p. 206.

[5] Ibid. p. 225.

[6] S.P.For. 94/73, 25/7, 4/8, 7/8, 8/9.

[7] Ibid. 11/8, 13/10.

[8] P.R.O.Adm. 2/363, ff. 20, 23, 31.

[9] Coxe, loc. cit. p. 222.

office—'for admiral in Spain, is squire in England, so insignificant a name it is in these parts'.[1] The commission was readily granted, and Russell's prestige remained as high as he had hoped.[2] On the other shore of the Mediterranean, the influence of the English fleet was also obvious: the Dey of Algiers wrote in flattering terms, and sent the Admiral a piece of jewellery; and the corsairs reduced their activities, and even saluted the English ships when they met. Even on the far shores of the Levant, where trade had been at a standstill and the English merchants in despair after the loss of the Smyrna fleet in 1693, trade was now brisk; although French privateers continued to harass shipping, a regular convoy system was restarted, and in 1695 a substantial merchant fleet, with over 12,000 cloths on board, successfully negotiated the voyage from Turkey to England.[3] The English fleet was, for the moment, the arbiter of the Mediterranean; and the English Admiral, for a year, enjoyed the semi-ambassadorial position which was to distinguish his successors in that sea.

Nevertheless, Russell was as usual disgruntled and anxious: disgruntled, because his difficulties in Cadiz and the hardships of his exile were not sufficiently appreciated at home; anxious, because he foresaw that much was expected of him in the coming summer, while the efficiency of the fleet was bound steadily to decline. His letters to Shrewsbury, in which he poured out his fears and grievances, contained the familiar and curious mixture of strategic common sense and personal idiosyncrasies, and their recipient was kept busy in calming the Admiral's sudden apprehensions and in giving him good advice. But despite all that the Duke could do, Russell declined both the peerage and the office of Vice-Admiral of England that were offered him,[4] and continued to write that he had rather be at home in England than plagued with a command abroad.[5] By the time that the fleet put to sea, he was

---

1 Ibid. p. 209. 2 Ibid. pp. 214, 222.

3 Wood, *History of the Levant Company*, pp. 112–13.

4 Coxe, loc. cit. pp. 215, 223.

5 A typical example was the following: 'My ship...is a dwelling much worse than a country gaol, but, as the Irishman says, it is nothing. I suppose, when all the difficult work is over, the officers of the navy from England, will arrive to assist me. I am admiral, commissioner of the navy, victualler, store-keeper, in short every thing but a happy man' (ibid. p. 216).

writing that he could not stay out for another year; apart from his private affairs, which needed attention, his health was bad, and he feared that he would die in Spain, 'where you know they will not give us heretics christian burial'.[1] He asked Shrewsbury, therefore, to propose to the King that he should be relieved before the autumn.

At the same time, he warned the authorities in England that if his ships were not back there before August, most of them would fall to pieces. 'Whatever can be done upon the enemy', therefore, 'must be over by the last of June, or the middle of July.'[2] He suggested that if the King wished to keep a fleet in the Mediterranean over the following winter—and he now agreed that this offered great advantages—its entire composition should be changed by degrees during the course of the summer, so that the quality of the force during the campaign could be kept at a reasonable level, and a fresh concentration could be assembled by the time that he himself was ready to leave.[3] Such a plan commended itself at first to William, and at the end of May he informed ministers from The Hague that he would send orders accordingly.[4] Those orders, however, never came.

At the beginning of May, Russell sailed from Cadiz with the intention of attacking the French at either Toulon or Marseilles.[5] Before doing so, he detached a squadron to transport a Spanish force from Finale near Genoa to the Catalonian coast, so as to secure that province against Noailles, while he cruised in support. At the same time, he wrote to Galway to inquire whether the Duke of Savoy would co-operate in a combined operation upon Toulon. While waiting for a reply, he himself took a closer look at the port. All seemed quiet; and at the beginning of June, with six weeks to go before (by his own reckoning) he would have to leave the area, the prospects seemed quite good. A few days later, however, they suddenly changed. A strong summer gale sprang up, which drove the fleet to the south for three days and nights; and by the time it had regained station it was running short of

[1] Coxe, loc. cit. pp. 226–7.

[2] Ibid. p. 227.

[3] Ibid. p. 217.

[4] Ibid. pp. 83, 227–8; B.M.Addnl. 37992, f. 93 *v*.

[5] The accounts of this campaign are contained in Burchett, pp. 266–90; *Memoirs relating to the Lord Torrington*, pp. 72–7; and *Journal of the Victorious Expedition of the Confederate Fleet under Admiral Russell*.... They are summarized in Corbett, loc. cit. pp. 177–9, 181–2.

water, and the homeward-bound Levant convoy, which had been preparing since the winter, had reached the central Mediterranean and needed protection. Russell accordingly sailed for Sardinia to water, and it was not until the end of June that he was once more at sea. He then saw the convoy to Alicante and afterwards made for Barcelona, still confident in the hope of making his combined attack with Savoy upon Toulon. But in the meantime, the Duke had taken the French fortress of Casale, and—although Russell did not recognize the fact—his interest in any venture against a French port had slackened. The time was now running short; but after picking up the English mail, which he expected any day from Madrid,[1] the Admiral was determined to sail once more for France. When the letters arrived, however, they upset all his plans.

For in May the argument of the previous summer had begun again between the King and the Cabinet.[2] When William had agreed that Russell's weakest ships should be replaced by others from home in the course of the campaign, he had added that in return the Admiral should be sent 'specific orders' to stay in the Mediterranean until the end of September or the beginning of October.[3] This greatly perturbed the Lords Justices, and they consulted Rooke, as the man whose opinion was most likely to influence the King, on the practicability of this plan. All agreed that it was dangerous. It would be better, wrote Shrewsbury to William in reply, to keep the fleet abroad for another winter rather than to risk such a voyage, and he urged the King to order Russell to return in August.[4] William's only reply to this, at the beginning of June, was that the thought of the fleet's leaving the Mediterranean at any time in the next three months 'excites my astonishment, as it may be attended by the most fatal consequences'.[5] He refused to

[1] Letters for Russell were sent normally by packet from Falmouth to Corunna, whence they were dispatched, with the rest of the diplomatic mail, to Madrid. Stanhope then acknowledged receipt, and sent them on to the Admiral (S.P.For. 74/93; Stanhope to Shrewsbury, 11/7, 18/8/94).

[2] When he left for Holland in 1695, William appointed Lords Justices to govern in his absence, for Mary had died in December 1694. They were equivalent to the Committee of the previous year.

[3] Coxe, loc. cit. p. 83.

[4] Ibid. p. 84

[5] Ibid. p. 85.

shift from his position in the correspondence that immediately followed.[1]

His refusal to do so may seem unreasonable, in view of the facts. But to himself, the arguments used by the Admiral and the Lords Justices were the familiar obstructions which had been placed in his way in 1693 and again in 1694, and which he had now proved could be overcome. Impatient as he was of technical detail, and concerned only with the diplomatic results of a Mediterranean fleet, the difference between wintering ships abroad and bringing them across the Atlantic on a winter voyage had to be pointed out to him, and the fact brought home that while in the former case he was dealing with administrative difficulties, in the latter he was faced with the limitations of the material of administration and policy itself. Until that could be done, he continued to regard the arguments as merely one more example of the timidity of his advisers, which had already been demonstrably exaggerated in similar circumstances. The Lords Justices, accordingly, were forced to convey his wishes to Russell not to leave the Mediterranean before the end of September. But on 21 June they addressed a memorandum to William, which was signed by them all, protesting against the plan, and Shrewsbury wrote a long and detailed comment upon it for the King's private eye:[2]

> Ever since we received your majesty's last instructions [he remarked] and in obedience to them, ordered Mr Russell not to return till September or October, several of us have more exactly informed ourselves of the danger of such a voyage; and not one, but every seaman that any of us have discoursed with, do not only say, the hazard is very great, but almost certain... sir George Rooke's expression to me was, 'It is a thousand to one several of them miscarry'. This concurrence of all persons here, skilful in sea affairs, has frightened us into the representations we have made to-day.

He proposed that Russell should leave behind twenty English and a proportionate number of Dutch, and should come home with the rest as he designed. In their place, a squadron of big ships could go out to Cadiz with a convoy of provisions which was intended to be sent in July. On 27 June, impressed at last by the weight of opinion expressed

---

[1] Coxe, loc. cit. pp. 86–8; B.M.Addnl. 37992, f. 95*v*. [2] Coxe, loc. cit. pp. 88–9.

in the memorandum, William gave Russell leave to come home if he thought fit before the end of September;[1] and a week later Shrewsbury informed the Admiral accordingly, adding that he hoped he was pleased with the latitude now allowed him.[2]

This last letter, however, had not reached Russell by the middle of July, when he received the original instructions to stay until the end of September. The news, coming on top of his other disappointments, threw him into an ungovernable fury, and he at once sat down to write to Shrewsbury. He represented once more the arguments against the King's plan, emphasizing that not only was the voyage dangerous in itself, but that it was doubly so when the ships were so short of experienced seamen and when so many were in bad condition. He attributed its adoption to the Dutch, on whose influence over William he dilated with considerable freedom, and he ended with the comment that the King was not only obstinate over the plans for the fleet, but had been mean in providing personally for its commander.[3] With a resentful carelessness which was not far from treachery, he then included this letter in a covering note to Blathwayt in Flanders, which made it likely that it would be seen by William himself, and sent it off by the overland route through France, where it stood every chance of being intercepted and read. The King, who duly opened it as intended, was furious, particularly as he suspected that the Admiral had chosen the overland route on purpose that the French might know of the disagreement. 'Even if that was not his intention', as he said, 'it was inconceivably imprudent.'[4] Shrewsbury hastened to apologize on Russell's behalf and to answer for his fidelity, and wrote at once to the Admiral that he had been entirely in the wrong to send any such letter through enemy territory.[5] But after his display of spleen, Russell was as usual preparing to carry out his unwelcome orders. With the prospect of a stormy passage ahead of him, he sent his most defective ships off to England at once with the homeward-bound Levant convoy, and then

---

1 B.M.Addnl. 37992, f. 98. The letter is dated 7 July, but this is obviously N.S.

2 Coxe, loc. cit. p. 231. Corbett (loc. cit. pp. 179–81) in his account of this controversy does not mention William's modification of his original instructions.

3 Coxe, loc. cit. pp. 234–6.

4 Ibid. pp. 103–4.

5 Ibid. pp. 105, 236–7.

once more set about considering his attack upon Toulon. Weakened as he now was by the loss of several units, and with Savoy showing no sign of co-operating in a joint attack, he turned to the Spaniards with a request for a squadron of galleys. The Viceroy of Catalonia, however, to whom he applied, was prepared to lend him such a force only on condition that he would first help retake the fortress of Palamos. Russell could not refuse, and early in August the siege began. With the help of the English soldiers from the fleet, it went well; and the Admiral was already thinking of leaving the scene, when his scouts reported that the French fleet of sixty sail was at last getting ready for sea at Toulon. On receipt of this news Russell sailed from the Spanish coast, but on arriving off the French port it was only to find that the enemy did not design to come out after all. With the force at his disposal, he could do nothing against the harbour; and after hanging off the coast for a few days he returned disconsolately to Spain.

It was now early in September, and the Dutch squadron announced its intention of making for home before the North Sea ports became icebound. Russell himself was still hoping to stay until later in the month; for although he had now received his modified instructions, he had also heard that a squadron was coming out under Rooke to relieve him before the winter,[1] and he wanted to see its commander before he left. But the Dutch decision forced his hand; and not altogether unwillingly, he set sail for England with one first rate, seven seconds, one third, three fourths, one fifth and three fireships, besides the Dutch, leaving a squadron of third and fourth rates, with the bombvessels, some fireships and seven Dutch men-of-war under the command of Sir David Mitchell at Cadiz.[2] Rooke was already on his way, and early in October the two forces passed each other in the Bay. On 16 October the new ships reached Cadiz. The combined squadron then amounted to thirty sail of the line: a force not strong enough to deal with the Toulon fleet, but large enough to patrol the Mediterranean in support of trade and to hold the Spaniards to the alliance. With it had gone a new set of stores and some more workmen—a further 29 shipwrights, twelve caulkers, five smiths, three bricklayers, six sawyers and one oakum boy, together with a master boatbuilder and a master mast

[1] Coxe, loc. cit. p. 233; B.M.Addnl. 37992, f. 99. [2] Burchett, pp. 285–6.

maker[1]—to repeat, on a minor scale, the refit of the previous year. But with a force of less than half that of the fleet in November 1694 and involving much less than half the work, and with the legacy of its stores and organization, the task set no new administrative problems. With Russell's departure, the interest both at home and in Europe shifted once more from the Mediterranean to the northern front.

[1] P.R.O.Adm. 106/2974.

CHAPTER XIII

THE ADMIRALTY OFFICE, 1690–1697

The expansion of the navy after 1689 naturally led to an increase in the amount of naval business. Some idea may be gained of its extent from the amount of clerical work for which the Admiralty and the Navy Board between them were responsible during the war:[1]

	(Both Boards) Letters written*	(Navy Board) Bills examined	(Navy Board) Muster books examined	(Admiralty) Petitions examined
1689	6,624	5,606	552	—
1690	7,546	6,329	649	—
1691	9,036	8,342	1,248	—
1692	9,929	10,561	1,290	—
1693	9,818	9,047	2,371	—
1694	11,687	10,401	2,230	3,305
1695	11,460	11,739	2,619	7,250
1696	11,121	9,791	2,794	10,049
1697	9,455	10,729	2,716	7,971

* These figures include letters signed by the Secretary of the Admiralty, as well as by the Commissioners. In each column, the year is taken as 1 January to 31 December.

These figures illustrate not only the development of business, but also the fact that an organization existed which was capable of recording it. The development of this organization was partly the result of the political context in which it worked. The increase of departmental business made it necessary; but the way in which that business was controlled was determined by the relations of the department with other organs of government.

The constitutional position of the Board of Admiralty was reflected in the regularity of its procedure. After 1689, the arrangements for tackling business were those to be expected of a purely administrative and subordinate department. They suffered from none of the irregularities which affected, as they always affect, the composition and procedure of the higher organs of government, concerned with making policy. The quorum settled at three members, and in practice business was conducted by an inner group of three or four who usually remained

[1] B.M.Addnl. 9303, f. 142.

the same throughout any one Commission. Lee, Chicheley and Lowther in 1689 and 1690 were followed by Lowther, Onslow, Priestman and Austen in 1691, with the addition of Rich in 1692 and 1693, and by Priestman, Austen, Rich and Houblon in the later years of the war. After the first year, however, there were no absentees comparable with Sacheverell and Sir Michael Wharton; all members transacted business from time to time, even if they did so irregularly.[1]

There seems to have been no allocation of individual duties to individual Commissioners, although the 'merchant members'—Onslow, and later Houblon and James Kendall[2]—usually attended when questions affecting trade were to be debated. There was, indeed, no differentiation between the members of the Board by custom, law or salary. The patent gave no more authority to one than to another; all were paid £1000 a year throughout the war;[3] and all received their allowances of coal and lighting, and possibly of house rent as well.[4] In one respect the conditions for payment of salaries altered in the course of the war; for whereas in 1689, as in earlier years when Commissions of Admiralty had existed, salaries were paid to and from the quarter in which the Commissioners had ceased to act and had been appointed, by 1692 it had become the practice for payment to be made for the actual tenure of office, if necessary involving a 'broken quarter'.[5] With one exception, this held good until the end of the century.[6]

Eighteen months after the war ended, in May 1699, a modification was suggested to the principle of equal salaries, by raising the salary of the first Commissioner above that of his colleagues. But the Treasury was able to find a valid legal excuse for its refusal of this proposal, in that it was 'perfectly unacquainted with any extraordinary trust

---

[1] P.R.O.Adm. 3/2–14, *passim*. [2] See pp. 570, 604 below.

[3] P.R.O.Adm. 7/169, 175, *passim*.

[4] P.R.O.Adm. 2/378, f. 18; 3/9: 28/4. There is no entry referring to house rent in the naval accounts, but it seems probable that this was paid out of the contingency fund of the office, which rose steeply after 1689 (P.R.O.Adm. 7/169; 2/179, ff. 45, 78, 97).

[5] P.R.O.Adm. 3/378, f. 169; P.R.O.Adm., Signet Dockets Index; *Cal.Treas.Bks. 1689–92*, pp. 168, 1646–7.

[6] *Cal.Treas.Bks. 1699–1700*, pp. 201–2. The exception was in the case of James Kendall, appointed by patent on 24 February 1696, who was paid from the previous Christmas (*Cal.Treas.Bks. 1693–6*, p. 1334).

or charge in the first commissioner of the Admiralty more than in the rest'.[1] Any superiority on his part was in fact (as it remained until the Letters Patent were supplemented by Orders in Council in the second half of the nineteenth century) purely conventional.[2] In theory at least, he remained merely chairman of the meetings of the Board. His influence in practice varied according to his political or personal eminence. Torrington and Russell, the two seamen whose professional position in each case was linked with their personal importance to William, were the two most influential leaders of the Board during the war; but their effect on administration in every case was negligible, for the more influential they were in the department the less they worked through it. They did not derive importance from their official position, but rather conferred importance upon it. Often—when Torrington was head of the Commission in 1689, and during Russell's tenure of the post in 1694 and 1695—they were absent from the office. But whether they were absent or not, it was not they who were responsible for the development of its organization but their colleagues, whose work, although interrupted and deflected by higher authority, was not itself concerned with such authority, and thus sustained the growth of an office organization unaffected by the vagaries of policy.

As the war progressed, the Board meetings were put into some sort of order.[3] Meetings of a full Board were rare, and were concerned mainly with the drafting of orders to commanders at sea, or with the provision of the more important convoys; but ordinary meetings continued on most days of the week, including Sundays, for most weeks of the war, and the only two days on which no business took place were Christmas day and Good Friday. After a time, particular days of the week were set aside for particular business. At the end of 1692, Tuesday afternoons (Tuesday mornings after September 1694) were reserved for hearing petitions, while Tuesday evening from six till eight was devoted to the consideration of applications for employment.[4] Thursdays and Sundays tended to be 'Cabinet days'

[1] *Cal.Treas.Bks. 1698–9*, pp. 400–1. See also *H.M.C.* 14th Report, appendix, pt II, p. 605.

[2] Murray, 'The Admiralty, I', in *M.M.* XXIII, no. 1, pp. 30–1.

[3] The rest of this and the following paragraph are based upon P.R.O.Adm. 3/1–14.

[4] P.R.O.Adm. 3/7: 13/11/92; 3/10: 25/9/94.

from early in 1692, and regular business settled on Mondays, Wednesdays and Fridays, when the Board met at ten o'clock in the morning until an indefinite time in the afternoon, and again 'two hours after the house riseth' at night.[1] In 1694, Friday morning was reserved for private business,[2] and all people wishing to speak to the Board without appointment, who did not bring petitions, were directed to attend either that evening or on Monday at seven o'clock, or alternatively on Wednesday evening at six o'clock.[3] Meanwhile the Navy Board continued to attend once a week, apart from the many occasions on which it was summoned for particular business, between November 1692 and March 1693 on Wednesdays (instead of on Fridays as before) and after that on Tuesday mornings.[4]

The procedure of business was also clarified in some respects in the course of the war. In the autumn of 1693, a series of office rules was drawn up. All papers for the Board's signature were to be read through first by one of the chief clerks; copies of all memoranda or letters for the Cabinet Council were to be distributed to all members of the Board; and letters from Secretaries of State were to be kept separate and unopened from the rest of the documents placed before it, and were to be dealt with before other business.[5] In 1694, two other domestic arrangements were made. The Board was to decide before it adjourned whether any matters were to be placed on the agenda for the next day, and if so all relevant material was to be collected and presented with the subject for debate; and from time to time, normally once a fortnight, it was to devote one day to 'clearing the table of papers', or settling outstanding business.[6] Such routine, which might seem to be unimportant and not particularly comprehensive, had not existed in the early years of the war, and was a real sign of the growth of an organized department.

For each subdivision of business made a fresh demand upon the clerical staff and the classification of the records. At first the organization

---

[1] This was laid down as a resolution in December 1692 (P.R.O.Adm. 3/8: 2/12). It did not, of course, bind the successors of the Board which made the resolution; but they seem to have abided by it on the whole.

[2] P.R.O.Adm. 3/10: 16/5.

[3] Ibid. 25/9.

[4] P.R.O.Adm. 3/7: 13/11; 3/8: 15/3.

[5] P.R.O.Adm. 3/9: 4/8, 20/9/93.

[6] P.R.O.Adm. 3/10: 21/8, 16/11/94.

of the office simply responded to the pressure of business, but later in the war it was able itself to modify this pressure, thanks to improvements in its technique. Most of these came in 1693 and 1694, when the work of the department was growing rapidly; but the response which was made by the office at that time was not occasioned by this demand alone, but also by a separate development affected but not occasioned by it: the definite but subtle change which took place in the status of the Secretary of the Admiralty.

The position of Bowles as Secretary of the Admiralty depended, as has been seen, on favour. He came in with Torrington in March 1689, and left soon after Torrington in January 1690. His successor, James Sotherne, entered by another door, coming straight from the subordinate post of Clerk of the Acts, which he had held since 1680.[1] An old associate of Pepys, he had something of his capacity for organization; and the Admiralty records of his period of office leave the impression of a painstaking official, whose minutes and correspondence are entered with an attention to detail not always apparent under his predecessor. Little of note, however, occurred during his Secretaryship. In the summer of 1694 he resigned at his own request, probably on account of ill-health,[2] and returned to the Navy Board as an extra Commissioner.[3] He was succeeded by William Bridgeman,[4] whose appointment illustrated a third method of entry into the post. Bridgeman came in neither from favour, like Bowles, nor from a junior position in the naval hierarchy, like Sotherne, but from a comparable post in another government department. Since 1693 he had been

---

[1] See Appendix VIII below. He had been joint Clerk of the Acts with Hayter from 1677 to 1680 (Jackson, *Naval Commissioners...from 1660 to 1760*).

[2] Luttrell, op. cit. III, p. 341. According to James Vernon, then under-secretary in Shrewsbury's office, he 'at last broke his mind to the Commissioners' in May, 'and declared that he desired to bee discharged from that Employment as finding it too heavy a burden for him, now hee grows in years and his Infirmitys encrease upon him' (B.M. Egerton 920, f. 117). His last letter, however, was dated 4 August (P.R.O.Adm. 2/385, 4/8).

[3] See Appendix VIII below.

[4] His appointment was approved by William on 12 July (B.M.Addnl. 37992, f. 56), and he was in office by the middle of the following month (*Cal.S.P.Dom. 1694–5*, p. 230; P.R.O.Adm. 2/385, 6/8). See also Appendix VII below.

a clerk of the Privy Council,[1] and in the past few months an under-secretary to Trenchard.[2] An administrator pure and simple, with no known aptitude for naval affairs when he joined the Admiralty, his tenure of office saw the greatest advance in its organization since Pepys's first Secretaryship. Between 1694 and the end of the war, the classification of and departmental control over the office records were developed, an establishment was promulgated for the office staff, and the move was made to an Admiralty office in which records and staff could be properly housed. Bridgeman himself seems to have been energetic and capable. He had collections made of naval documents for his private reference, although not on a scale comparable to that of Pepys, and the rate at which the organization of the department developed in the last half of 1694 strongly suggests the impact of his personal influence. He also passed perhaps the best test which could be applied to an administrator at this time: William respected his ability.[3]

He was not, however, left sole Secretary for long. The steady increase in the work of the office had for some time made the duties of the post extremely heavy for one man. Bowles's memorandum of 1690 had stated the position in his own day, and since then it had become worse. By the autumn of 1694 it was clear that two Secretaries were required, and on 25 September Josiah Burchett was named as Bridgeman's colleague.[4] The choice was obviously made on favour, for at the time Burchett was secretary to Russell in the Mediterranean. His earlier career, indeed, had been remarkably similar to that of Phineas Bowles.[5] He had begun as one of Pepys's clerks, but had been dismissed for some reason in 1687[6] and had then, like Bowles but in a humbler capacity, joined Dartmouth's retinue in 1688.[7] It was probably at that time that he came to know the Admiral's secretary, and when Bowles became

---

[1] P.R.O. Privy Seal Warrants, February 1693. See also Luttrell, op. cit. III, p. 3.

[2] Luttrell, op. cit. III, p. 61. [3] B.M.Addnl. 37992, f. 56.

[4] P.R.O.Adm. 2/174, f. 496.

[5] For his antecedents see G. F. James, 'Josiah Burchett', in *M.M.* XXIII, no. 4, pp. 477–9. His career is outlined ibid. pp. 480–97, and in *Bulletin of the Institute of Historical Research*, XIV, pp. 53–4.

[6] Burchett's letters to Pepys on this occasion may be seen in Bodl. Rawl. A 189, ff. 1, 7, 9, 11; A 179, ff. 16, 20, 22.

[7] *M.M.* XXIII, no. 4, p. 481.

Secretary of the Admiralty Burchett joined him as an Admiralty clerk. In the course of the next two years he made Russell's acquaintance, and in January 1691 joined the latter's flagship as his secretary.[1] He continued in this post until the autumn of 1692; but during the summer of 1693, while Russell was unemployed at sea, he returned to the Admiralty from 18 July to 28 August, acting as temporary Secretary to relieve Sotherne.[2] In April 1694, he was again taken by the Admiral as his secretary, and was with the fleet off Barcelona when the news of the appointment reached his patron.

Burchett's position as Russell's nominee was recognized both by himself and by others. 'Russell's Birket' one observer called him,[3] and he himself acknowledged his debt to the Admiral when writing of his appointment to Bridgeman.[4] Russell, indeed, had already found that he was not receiving enough information in the Mediterranean of what was happening at the Board, and in September was making overtures to Bridgeman through one of his captains, Matthew Aylmer, to supply him regularly with news. He was concerned, explained Aylmer, 'that no friend of countenance at home gives him the least account of affairs there...all standing upon their guard as if they feared the bar of the House of Commons....Now what I was thinking was that since you are in a post of which he is the head, whether among the common business of the office you might not now and then mix affairs worth his knowing'.[5] Bridgeman seems to have complied with this request;[6] but his background did not put him in the same intimate relation to the Admiral as Burchett's, and it is indicative of the contemporary solution that the Secretary who ended by holding the post uninterruptedly for 49 years,[7] and whose account of naval transactions during his period of office has always been taken as a (somewhat exasperating) model of official reticence, should have been appointed to it as a creature of a member of the Board, with a commission to send private information to him on the activities of his colleagues.

---

[1] *M.M.* XXIII, no. 4, pp. 481–2.

[2] P.R.O.Adm. 2/384, under these and intervening dates.

[3] *H.M.C.* 14th Report, appendix, pt II, p. 551. The spelling is interesting as a possible indication of the contemporary pronunciation of the name.

[4] B.M. Lansdowne 1152B, f. 206.

[5] Ibid. f. 273. [6] Ibid. ff. 283–4. [7] See Appendix VII below.

Burchett left for England in November, when the fleet returned to Cadiz, and arrived home in January 1695.[1] From then until June 1698 he and Bridgeman acted as joint Secretaries.[2] The latter was the senior of the two, and had additional responsibilities in transacting business with the Dutch, for which he was appointed by name in June 1695.[3] Apart from that, however, there was no division of duties between them: they attended the Board, and conducted its correspondence, on equal terms; exercised the same degree of supervision over the office staff; and received the same salary. It was in the course of these years that the position of the Secretary assumed the form that it was henceforward to retain. The loss of status which followed the resignation of Pepys now came to be replaced by a new status, subordinate to the Board but independent of its fortunes. Whereas Bowles had fallen with Torrington, Burchett did not fall with Russell, but continued in his post for over forty years. The Secretary's strength was now drawn, not, as with Pepys, from his own powers of decision, but—and this was more telling in the end—from the continuity of administration which he represented. He stood for the department as distinct from the Commission, where such a distinction had formerly been blurred. When, later in the war, the Admiralty moved to a new office, and acquired some land to go with it, it was in the names of the two Secretaries that the latter was held in trust for the Lord Admiral;[4] and by that time their position was fast becoming as it was described by a hostile observer in 1700: 'Whoever conns the Ship of the Admiralty, the Secretary is always at the Helm....He is the Spring that moves the Clock-work of the whole Board, the Oracle that is to be consulted on all Occasions.'[5] In the settlement of his status, indeed, may be seen the justification of the Admiralty at a time when its purpose is often hard to see in the activities of the Board itself, for in him it produced an administrative figure who met a genuine administrative demand, and

---

[1] B.M. Lansdowne 1152B, f. 297; P.R.O.Adm. 3/11: 25/1.

[2] See Appendix VII below.

[3] B.M.Addnl. 37992, unfoliated, Blathwayt to Lords Justices, 7/6/95.

[4] G. F. James, 'The Admiralty Buildings, 1695–1723', in *M.M.* XXVI, no. 4, p. 364.

[5] *Remarks on the Present Condition of the Navy, And particularly the Victualling....In a Letter from a Sailor to a Member of the House of Commons* (1700), p. 7.

who, unlike the Commissioners, derived a genuine importance from the fact. In the event, the activities of Bridgeman and Burchett were of more lasting significance than the activities of the Board which they served, for it was through them that a distinctive type of administration survived.

The consolidation of the Secretary's position was reflected in the change in his salary in 1694. Since the Revolution, the Secretary had been paid £500 a year, together with certain fees.[1] The most profitable of these were levied on warrants and commissions of appointment. According to an anonymous contemporary, the Secretary received the following sums when issuing commissions:

	First and second rates			Third, fourth and fifth rates			Sixth rate		
	£	*s.*	*d.*	£	*s.*	*d.*	£	*s.*	*d.*
Captains	3	0	0	2	0	0	1	10	0
Lieutenants	1	0	0	1	0	0		—	
Boatswains	1	10	0	1	0	0		15	0
Carpenters	1	10	0	1	0	0		15	0
Cooks	1	0	0		10	0		10	0
Pursers	3	0	0	2	0	0		—	
Midshipmen extra	1	0	0	1	0	0		—	
Volunteers		10	0		10	0		—	
Chaplains		10	0		10	0		—	

and £6. 5*s.* for each warrant issued to a Commissioner of the Navy.[2] When Bridgeman and Burchett were appointed, their salaries were raised to £800 each, and fees were abolished.

This measure was part of a more general reform of the office establishment. Until 1694, the Admiralty clerks were also paid by fee, in their case without any supplementary salary and entirely by private arrangement with the Secretary. If the fees proved inadequate, the deficiency was met either by the latter or out of the contingency fund of the office. In August 1694, the Admiralty Commissioners declared that this system led to abuses, and that to put an end to 'the clamour and reflections' which it had aroused they intended to prohibit all such perquisites and to inaugurate a system of payment by salary, and salary alone, throughout the office.[3] When Treasury approval had been gained, the new establish-

[1] P.R.O.Adm. 7/169. [2] B.M.Addnl. 9316, f. 341.
[3] P.R.O.Adm. 2/174, ff. 452–3; memorandum to Trenchard.

ment came into force as from midsummer, involving an estimated total additional cost of £2060.[1]

Once the members of the Admiralty Office became salaried officials, their number and status could be ascertained; and it is from the establishment of 1694 that we obtain the first reliable list of the permanent staff of the department.[2] It amounted at that time, besides the two Secretaries, to two chief clerks, six clerks, a messenger with two subordinates, a porter, a watchman and a woman to look after the office.[3] When the amount of business is considered, these numbers are not impressive; and while the increase in the number of Secretaries was due largely to the particular need for trained officials at a higher level, it was also partly because they were doing work which a larger subordinate staff could have done for them. These fifteen men and one woman formed the first permanent Admiralty staff, borne for the first time as its responsibility on the books of the Treasurer of the Navy, and included in his annual declared accounts.[4] When extra clerks were temporarily added at times of extra work, as they were at the end of the war, they continued to be paid, as all the office employees had formerly been paid, out of its contingency fund.[5]

The chief clerks soon came to have a recognizable status. When either Secretary was away one of them acted in his place, and they enjoyed the prospect of promotion to a Secretaryship on the retirement of their superiors. The two chief clerks appointed in 1694 were John Fawler and Edward Burt; and while Burchett's long tenure of office was fatal to their hopes, Fawler eventually became under-secretary of the Admiralty in 1705,[6] while Thomas Corbett, who succeeded Burt as chief clerk in 1719, joined Burchett as joint Secretary in 1741 and succeeded him in the following year.[7] From 1694, too, they were given definite duties.[8] The junior clerks could also look forward to promotion,

[1] S.P.Dom. 44/204, f. 896; see Appendix XIV below.

[2] Before this, references to its members are few and scattered.

[3] See Appendix XIV below.

[4] P.R.O. Audit Office, 1/1721, et seq.

[5] P.R.O.Adm. 3/14: 14/7/98.

[6] Admty:Corbett, 1, f. 23.

[7] See Appendix VII below.

[8] P.R.O.Adm. 2/179, ff. 45, 78, 97; 3/12: 27/1, 31/7/95; B.M.Addnl. 25198, ff. 403, 465, 526 (the latter source cited by James, loc. cit.)

either within the office itself or within the naval hierarchy. Most of those who did not become chief clerks in the Admiralty went to dockyards and out-ports, or to other naval offices; and in turn clerks from the subordinate departments, particularly the Navy Office, were brought into the Admiralty.[1] When, after the end of the war, severe cuts were imposed on naval expenditure, the department opposed, more than any other economy, the retrenchments in the clerical staff; not only on the grounds of efficiency, but also because a return to earlier conditions would destroy much of the work that had been done over the past four years in building up a regular and permanent clerical hierarchy.

The junior clerks soon found their duties laid down for them, including the supervision of the records; and in this way the organization of the staff was brought into line with an organization of documents which had been proceeding for two years. One of the drawbacks to the intervention of the Secretaries of State in naval affairs was that many naval records remained in their hands; and by the summer of 1692 the loss of influence by the Admiralty had become so pronounced that, paradoxically enough, it was demanding complete control over papers relating to naval affairs. Otherwise, with external authorities liable to take over its business at any stage, it could not answer the demands which they were liable to make upon it. In June 1692, an order was issued to Sir Joseph Williamson, the head of the State Paper Office where the documents were supposed to be deposited, to deliver to Sir Charles Hedges, the Judge of the Admiralty Court, all papers (judicial and otherwise) relating to Admiralty affairs; and Hedges in turn handed over the relevant documents to the Admiralty office.[2] Later in that month, Cornwallis, then first Commissioner, employed two copyists at his own expense to transcribe many of the papers for his use; but it was made clear that this was in his capacity as leading Commissioner, and not for his private purposes, and two more copyists were added, on the responsibility of the Board, one in July and one in November.[3] In 1695, the Board decided to form two new classes of documents: all letters from Secretaries of State were to be bound

---

[1] P.R.O.Adm. 1/3573, f. 255; 3/10: 19/7/94; 3/12: 1/8/95.

[2] S.P.Dom. 44/341, f. 344; P.R.O.Adm. 3/7: 1/6/92.

[3] P.R.O.Adm. 3/7: 24/6, 4/7, 2/11.

together and kept separate from other correspondence,[1] and all depositions made before the Board were likewise to form a series of their own.[2] But the great advance, as in other directions, came with Bridgeman; and it was in the first five months of his Secretaryship that the arrangements were made to which we owe the filing and binding of the Admiralty records as they exist to-day. In July 1694, he began the long task of a marginal index to the Board letters, by which their contents were briefly noted and relevant references given to other papers.[3] In September he took the minutes, as the first class of records, for rebinding in a more permanent and more convenient form,[4] and collected all Orders in Council on naval matters into a single class. He also rearranged and rebound the in-letters from the Secretaries of State.[5] A month later, he started a book for petitions;[6] and it is possible that at the end of the year a new class of Commission and Warrant books was begun.[7] In January 1695 a separate series of out-letters to Secretaries of State was inaugurated;[8] and in the same month Peter Pett, whose name had occurred in that connexion six years before, was officially allocated the task of keeping the records.[9] In February he was recognized as the 'Clerk of the Papers', with a salary of £60 a year.[10] No further development took place after this before the end of the war; but the arrangements made between 1692 and 1695 did for the new department of state what Pepys had done for the old, completing and expanding his work in the changed conditions that had arisen since his resignation.

The expansion of business over these years was raising awkward physical problems. The department was fast outgrowing the limited facilities of a private house, while the frequency of the Board meetings involved the Commissioners in constant journeys between the office

[1] P.R.O.Adm. 3/8: 20/9/93. This, however, had probably already been the practice beforehand. [2] Ibid. 25/9. [3] P.R.O.Adm. 3/10: 21/7/94.

[4] Ibid. 3/9. The next occasion on which they were rebound seems to have been in 1926 (note inside covers of P.R.O.Adm. 3/1–14), and several volumes of the out-letters still retain the bindings which Bridgeman gave them (P.R.O.Adm. 2/169 *et seq.*, 2/377 *et seq.*). [5] Ibid. 5/9. [6] Ibid. 2/10.

[7] The series as it stands begins in January 1695, but earlier volumes may have been lost. There is a hint that they may have been started in November 1692 (P.R.O.Adm. 3/8: 29/11).

[8] Now P.R.O.Adm. 2/363. [9] P.R.O.Adm. 3/11: 28/1; see p. 285 above.

[10] Ibid. 15/2.

and their homes. The Admiralty could no longer be considered simply as the place where the Admiral's office was kept at the time.[1] The scope of its work and the establishment of a recognized permanent staff made it increasingly necessary for it to be permanently housed in a departmental building, if possible with private dwellings for at least some of its members such as were provided at the Navy Office. Several alterations had been made to the house in Duke Street,[2] but in the spring of 1694 the Board was on the look-out for a more suitable building, or for a site on which one could be erected.[3] In the summer, Wallingford House in Spring Gardens, the former residence of the Duke of Buckingham where Admiralty business had been transacted 75 years before,[4] fell vacant. It was bought by one John Evans, a speculative builder, who demolished the house; and on 1 September the Board signed a contract with him for the erection of a block of buildings designed specifically to meet its requirements.[5] The new block was to be ready by midsummer 1695, and in December 1694 the Commissioners informed the landlord of the house in Duke Street that they would be moving before that date.[6] On 20 January 1695 they met in the new office for the first time.[7]

The new building stood on the site of the present Admiralty Old Building, facing Whitehall. It was a rectangular structure, without wings, standing on a plot of land—as originally leased from Evans—of 45 foot in depth, and separated from the street by a courtyard 78 feet long, on the further side of which the contractor had the right to erect a range of single-storey buildings.[8] By November 1695, part of Old Spring Gardens at the back of the office had also been leased for a

---

[1] This, according to the *N.E.D.*, was one definition of it earlier in the same century.

[2] P.R.O.Adm. 3/9: 30/1/94; 3/10: 19/4, 24/8/94.

[3] Ibid. 23/4.

[4] D. Bonner Smith, 'The Admiralty Building', in *M.M.* IX, no. 9, p. 272.

[5] The text of the contract is given in G. F. James, 'The Admiralty Buildings, 1695–1723', in *M.M.* XXVI, no. 4, pp. 360–3. This article is the best single account of the building of the office in Spring Gardens. It may be supplemented by *London County Council Survey of London*, XVIII.

[6] P.R.O.Adm. 3/10: 10/12.

[7] James, loc. cit. p. 363.

[8] The best-known view of the office is by Kip in 1720, 'The Prospect of Whitehall from the Park of St. James'. This, however, does not represent the building as originally erected. In a rarer print, attributed to Knyff and dated *c.* 1696, it is seen from Whitehall.

PLATE XII

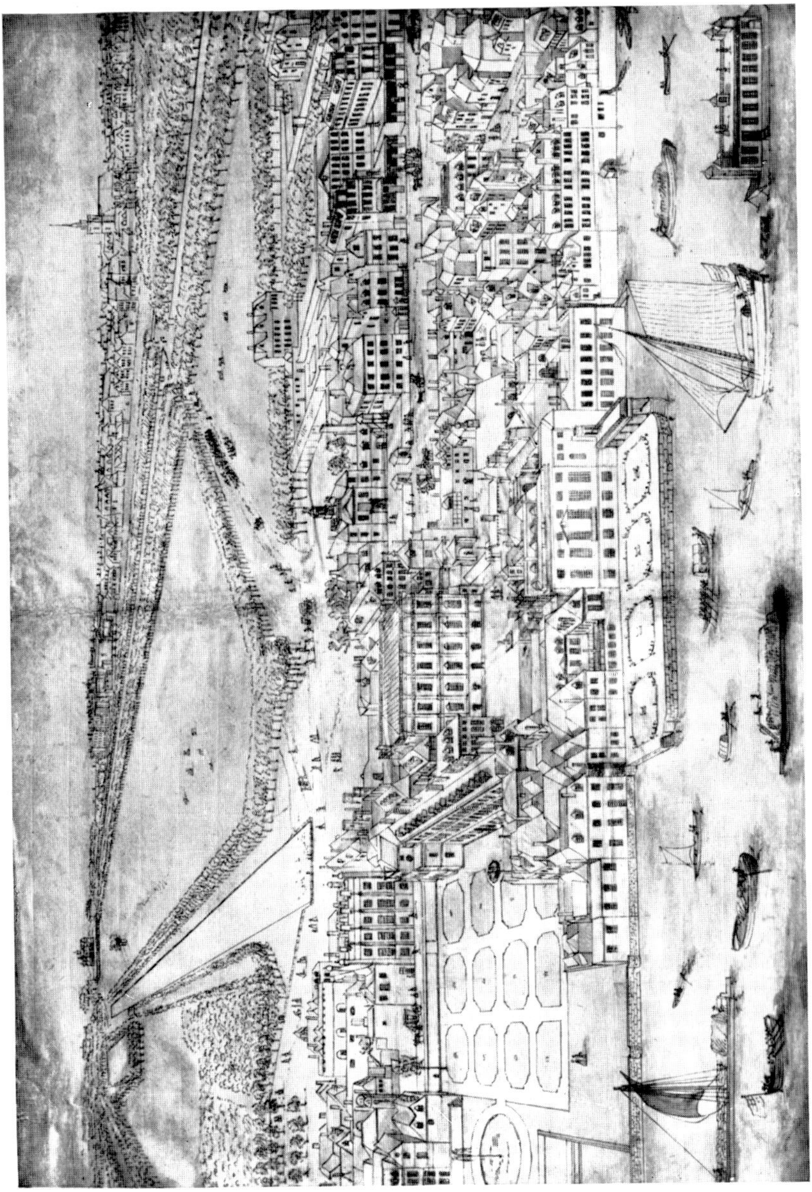

THE ADMIRALTY AND WHITEHALL, *c.* 1696

The Admiralty may be seen at the extreme right, on the northern side of Whitehall

[LEONARD KNYFF]

garden, and more was added in the following February.[1] In July a gardener was appointed, and a small house built for him at the end of the garden, in which in later years some of the departmental records were stored. The Commissioners were so pleased with their new office that in March 1696 they agreed with Evans to buy it outright, and the buildings facing the street were included in the purchase. One of these was already inhabited by a Commissioner, Sir Robert Rich, and another was referred to later in the year as the 'Secretary's House'. In 1697 two vaults were acquired under the courtyard, and in April 1698, by which time the money for the original purchase had been paid, the Board tried to buy from Evans the site of the courtyard itself. The negotiations were long and intricate, and were complicated by the fact that Parliament intervened to veto the price demanded, and to inquire into the curious appointment (which had recently taken place) of Evans as purveyor of the navy at Portsmouth. But by the spring of 1699, the price had finally been fixed at £2100, and the frontage of the office was secured. Further purchases at the back were made over the next fifteen years, and it was in odd houses there, rather than around the yard itself, that various Commissioners and officials seem to have lived.

On the Whitehall side, the buildings remained mostly shops, dealing largely with the Admiralty. But in 1723, the original structure had to be pulled down, for its foundations were discovered to be insecure and the unembanked river, occasionally overflowing into the lower streets of Westminster, made the office excessively damp. The opportunity was taken to pull down the buildings in front of the office, and the courtyard was redesigned on its present lines, with the present Old Building surrounding it on three sides. But inadequate as the first office proved to be, it met, at least temporarily, the requirements of a department whose organization had already expanded well beyond the limits of a decade before, and indeed by the end of the war compared favourably with that of any department of state.

---

[1] The rest of this paragraph follows James, loc. cit. pp. 364–74.

CHAPTER XIV

THE LAST PHASE AND DEMOBILIZATION, 1695–1698

I

The last years of the war, from the spring of 1695 to the winter of 1697, were years of disappointment and decline. At sea, little of importance occurred, while administration ashore gradually deteriorated until in the last few months before peace was declared the whole naval organization was almost completely passive. Those who have written on the war at sea have therefore dismissed this period briefly, as one in which there was no strategic or tactical innovation, and in which the machinery of naval government simply ran down. But in a survey of administration decline has its own significance; and while there may be little to say of the work of the navy, both ashore and afloat, in these years, the reasons for its unimportance may not themselves be unimportant.

When we speak of decline, moreover, it is as well to be sure what we mean. It was not the case that the scale of naval activity became less in this period. On the contrary, it was in many ways greater than before. Both the fleet and the dockyard organization continued to expand, more stores were bought than before, and more money continued to be spent and voted. The new ships which were launched in 1695, and whose numbers were the largest of any year of the war, were the result of earlier policy; but in the three years 1696–8, the last of which witnessed the launching of much of the construction laid down in the war, 47 ships were built and four rebuilt; and although these were mostly fourth and fifth rates, there were launched in the last year of the war the only three new second rates which appeared in the course of it.[1] The numbers of dockyard workmen rose from some 3200 in the first months of 1695 to some 4200 in the autumn of 1697, and at

[1] See Appendix II below.

no time in the interval did they fall below the first figure.[1] The quantities of naval stores imported from the Baltic were greater in these years than ever before: hemp, the easiest to measure in bulk, rose from 1850 tons in 1692, 1820 tons in 1693 and 2000 tons by commission in 1694, to 2270 tons in 1695 and 2260 tons in 1696, while it amounted again to 2000 tons in 1697;[2] and the imports of other commodities were on a proportional scale. The estimates of naval expenditure, which stood at £2,077,216 for 1693 and at £2,346,032 for 1694, amounted for 1695 to £2,603,492, for 1696 to £2,765,149 and for 1697 to £2,523,954;[3] and the grants voted to meet these last three sums were respectively £2,382,712, £2,516,927 and £2,372,197.[4] Neither the resources of administration, nor the intention to use them, were lacking. Why, then, has the period always, and rightly, been considered as one of administrative decline?

The answer lies in the deterioration of the contingent factors of policy and finance. It was not that less was being done, but that what was done was done unsuccessfully. We have suggested earlier that the clear-cut superiority which the allied fleet now enjoyed over the French left it with only two strategic alternatives, to support an invasion and to pursue a Mediterranean policy on a large scale. The former had proved apparently impossible to carry out, and with the decision to bring the main fleet home in 1695 the latter came to an end. For the rest of the war the fleet was therefore engaged on tasks for which it was not suited, on bombarding the French coastal towns and occasionally on the close protection of trade. The second duty did not require big ships, and the first brought results incommensurate with the cost. The administrative efforts did not seem worth while, particularly in view of the difficulties imposed upon them by the financial problems of the time; and the futility of the war at sea reacted unfavourably upon the organization which served it.

The alternatives of fleet bombardment and the protection of trade were no more distinct than the earlier fleet cruises and ocean convoys.

---

[1] See Appendix V (A), (B) below. [2] Serg.Misc. v, ff. 409–11.

[3] P.R.O.Adm. 7/169, estimates of 25/11/94, 2/12/95 and 28/10/96.

[4] *H. of L. N.S.* VII, pp. 174–5.

The bombardments had their prototype in the blockades of Dunkirk, which in 1694 included for the first time an attempt to shell the town by the third and fourth rates, and which were intended to protect the North Sea commerce from the depredations of Du Bart. The diversion of big ships to this kind of work, which occurred in 1695, arose not only from the apparent absence of any strategic alternative, but also from the growing dissatisfaction of the merchant interest with the naval measures for guarding their ships, and its increasing control over naval policy. Debates in Parliament on the losses had, of course, been common since 1689; they became more frequent and, if the references to them in Grey's and Cobbett's compilations may be trusted, more bitter as the war progressed. In 1693, as the Commons became more used to interfering in detail with policy, a possible solution was suggested in the appointment of a committee of merchants, with powers similar to those of a committee of the Privy Council, which would handle all intelligence about trade and represent its needs to the Admiralty;[1] and in December of that year the formation of such a body was actively rumoured.[2] But no such direct action was taken, and the development of the merchants' control over naval measures took place, during 1694, by other means: by the appointment of Sir John Houblon, who shortly afterwards became the first Governor of the Bank of England and a year later Lord Mayor of London, and whose main interests lay in the Spanish and Portuguese trades,[3] to the new Admiralty Commission, and by the insertion of a clause for 'convoys and cruisers' in the vote of supply for that year.[4]

In the winter of 1693–4, the navy had presented a detailed list of the dispositions in defence of trade, and this was repeated in 1695.[5] But the next year the merchant interest, incensed at the continual and heavy losses, took the offensive in Parliament and made a proposal which, in

---

[1] James Whiston, *A Discourse of the Decay of Trade*... (1693).

[2] *Cal.S.P.Dom. 1693*, pp. 426–7.

[3] *D.N.B.*; Lady Alice Houblon, *The Houblon Family*, I (2 vols., 1907).

[4] A different example of the relations between the merchants and the executive was to be seen in the successive bills introduced into Parliament between 1690 and 1694 to regulate the privateers (see Clark, *The Dutch Alliance and the War against French Trade*, pp. 57–60).

[5] *H.C.J.* XI, pp. 10, 348–50.

the estimation of Edmund Burke in 1780, 'struck, not only at the administration, but at the very constitution of executive government'.[1] This was for a Council of Trade, the members of which were to be nominated by Parliament, with power to gather all necessary information on overseas trade and to represent its needs and forward complaints to the Admiralty. It was to keep a close watch on naval dispositions and convoy arrangements, and to have direct access to the Secretaries of State if its requirements were not met.[2] The exact terms of this proposal were debated outside Parliament as well as within it, in pamphlets and memoranda by Davenant and Whiston;[3] and in January 1696 a bill was framed which contained many, if not all, of their suggestions as well as those originally raised.[4] William, alarmed at its radical nature, was driven to forestall the merchants' Act by the formation of his own body, a Board of Trade on more familiar lines; and on 15 May 1696, Letters Patent were issued to the 'Lords Commissioners for promoting the trade of our plantations in America and elsewhere'.[5]

This Commission was, in effect, the old Privy Council Committee for Trade and Plantations, which had been used decreasingly over the past few years,[6] with a new reference and new financial resources. Like its predecessor, and unlike the Board proposed by Parliament, it derived its authority from the Privy Council, and was intended to advise rather than to administer.[7] Only eight of the fourteen members, however, were necessarily Privy Councillors, and the other six were salaried Commissioners charged with the ordinary work of the Board.[8] The Plantation Office, as their meeting place was known, stood next to the new Admiralty building in Whitehall, and there was soon a close

---

[1] In his speech on 'Economical Reform'. The passage is quoted in R. M. Lees, 'Parliament and the Proposal for a Council of Trade, 1695–6', in *E.H.R.*, LXIV, p. 41.

[2] Cobbett, *Parliamentary History*, V, p. 977.

[3] For details see *E.H.R.* LXIV, pp. 43–61.

[4] *H.C.J.* XI, p. 423.

[5] *Cal.S.P.Col. Am. and W.I., 1696–7*, p. 1.

[6] It averaged only forty sessions a year between 1689 and 1696, and less in the later than the earlier years (Winfred T. Root, 'The Lords of Trade and Plantations, 1675–1696', in *American Historical Review*, XXIII, p. 37).

[7] Its instructions are given in Sir Hubert Llewellyn Smith, *The Board of Trade* (1928), appendix III.

[8] Llewellyn Smith, loc. cit. p. 16.

connexion between the two departments. Merchants and shipowners regularly presented their memorials to the Admiralty through the Board of Trade,[1] and maintained through it a parallel correspondence with the Secretaries of State.[2] The annual allocation of men and shipping to the overseas trades, and the details of escorts for ocean and occasionally for coastal convoys were settled with its assistance, and it was kept informed by the navy of the whereabouts of all cruisers in home waters.[3] Although the new Board could not be said to control the Admiralty in matters affecting commerce, as the merchants had originally desired, it formed a standing and effective check on it which, with their support and with its independent access to the Secretaries of State and the Council, ensured that commercial interests were not neglected in the distribution of naval strength and the formulation of naval policy.

It was against this background of increasing mercantile discontent that the bombardments of 1695 took place, as the offensive counterpart to the defensive measures of escorts and cruisers. The first of them was staged in June, after a Dutch contingent had joined Berkeley's division, against St Malo, the main privateering centre in the west of France. It had little success, and the force then moved on to Granville to repeat the attack.[4] Some fires were started, and the ships withdrew to cruise off the Channel Islands until August, when another bombardment was staged, this time against Dunkirk. The attempt was expensive, for the port was well defended; and Berkeley found, as many naval commanders have found since, that this sort of action usually favours the shore batteries. Four English vessels and one Dutch were lost in return for some negligible damage to the harbour buildings. Soon afterwards, however, Calais was bombarded with better results. But by the time that the ships had revictualled in the Downs after this attack it was late in August, and no further operation was undertaken. Little comfort was to be gained from the results of the campaign, and perhaps the most

---

1 *Cal.S.P.Col. Am. and W.I. 1696–7, passim.*

2 P.R.O.Adm. 1/4082–6, *passim.*

3 B.M.Addnl. 9764, f. 85; P.R.O.Adm. 2/387–392, *passim.*

4 Burchett, pp. 293–304. A misprint on p. 303 gives the false impression that the later part of the account refers to 1696.

interesting feature of the bombardments was the introduction for the first time on a large scale of the 'machine vessel' into naval operations.[1] This was a small ship, of between 20 and 100 tons, which was filled with explosive 'machines' resembling to a remarkable degree the 'depth charge' of our own day,[2] and was then towed inshore before the bombardment and exploded by means of a pre-set firing mechanism. The detonation usually acted as the signal for the attack to begin. But the arrangements often went wrong, with a consequent loss of surprise; and when the vessels were given their big opportunity at Dunkirk, they proved a complete fiasco. After that, the ordinary ships and bomb-vessels were used without the assistance of the machines, and what had looked like a promising experiment in an unpromising type of operation came to an end.

The same sort of campaign seemed to be in prospect for 1696, but during February intelligence was received of unusual preparations in the French ports. Brest, St Malo and Rochefort were all said to be exceptionally busy, and there were conflicting reports of Louis's intentions.[3] At first it was thought that the activity was directed against a possible return of Rooke's squadron from Cadiz before it could join the main fleet;[4] but before the end of the month it became clear that its purpose was nothing less than an invasion of England. Louis, indeed, unable to defeat the allies decisively in the field, with the reverse of Namur just behind him and the evidence of French exhaustion now before his eyes, was making one more attempt to swing the war violently in his favour. The usual Jacobite support had been planned in England. William was to be assassinated as he passed through Turnham Green, on his way to Kensington from a hunt in Richmond Park, and James was then to set sail from Calais while the English ships still lay in harbour.[5] The usual assurances of disaffection in the fleet were relayed to the French court,[6] and by the third week in February all was ready.

---

[1] See E. W. H. Fryers, 'The Story of the Machine Vessels', in *M.M.* XI, no. 1, pp. 57–78.

[2] A specimen of one of the 'great machines', probably dating from 1692 when they were first designed, was preserved in the museum of Portsmouth dockyard, where it was photographed and reproduced in Fryers, loc. cit.

[3] P.R.O.Adm. 1/4083, f. 465. [4] Ibid. ff. 465, 473. [5] Ibid. f. 625.

[6] Ibid. f. 635; Roncière, op. cit. VI, p. 214.

But on 24 February, William startled the country by announcing the plans in Parliament. The news removed at one stroke the dissatisfaction which had been growing with his régime since Mary's death in December 1694. An association was immediately formed to defend the King's person, and Parliament suspended the Habeas Corpus Act. More effective steps, however, had already been taken against an invasion. Before his announcement, William on the 21st had ordered Russell, who had been back in England since November 1695, and who commanded the greatest confidence throughout the country since his Mediterranean expedition, to take all the ships he could find and to concentrate in the Downs; and on the 24th, when the news was made public, the Admiral was already there with one first rate, two thirds, six fourths, two fifths and three auxiliaries.[1] Within three days, Shovell arrived from the Thames with thirteen more English ships, and another 21 joined from Spithead and the west. The squadron then put to sea, and by the 28th was cruising off Gravelines with a strength of 62 men-of-war and a number of fireships. By 1 March, it had grown to a force of eighty men-of-war, as the English dockyards sent every available unit to sea. The fleet—for so it now was—took up its station off Dunkirk, where a large number of transports could be seen inside the harbour, and sent in a squadron to attack.[2] But the sands proved as difficult as ever to negotiate, and as it soon became obvious that the French plan had miscarried, and as the ships were in any case unable to stay out for long with only emergency stores aboard, Russell put back to the Downs, leaving Shovell to patrol the French coast.[3] Placed again momentarily on the defensive, with the prospect of a major action before it, the English fleet had shown that it was as formidable as in earlier years; but once the immediate threat passed, and the offensive had to be renewed against an elusive enemy, its employment again became uncertain, and the campaign of 1696 promised to be as unrewarding as that of 1695.

---

[1] Burchett, p. 322. [2] Ibid. pp. 323–5.
[3] P.R.O.Adm. 3/13: 10/3.

II

It was, moreover, affected by financial difficulties unknown to its predecessor. The beginning of the campaigning season, in April 1696, coincided with the worst financial panic in London between the stop of the Exchequer in 1672, which it exceeded, and the suspension of payments by the Bank of England in 1797. To see how this crisis and its consequences affected the navy over the year, we must first consider the developments that preceded it.

When we last looked at government finance, it seemed for once to be in a good position. The armed services, which claimed over four-fifths of the annual national expenditure, were being supplied almost entirely by the loan from the Bank of England, which also liberated the tallies paid on other loans and contracts and thus stimulated trade. The loan, however, had been fully paid into the Exchequer by the beginning of 1695, and for its supplies in that year the government fell back upon its familiar alternatives for anticipating revenue. These resulted in more tallies, on various kinds of funds, being placed upon the market; and there seemed every likelihood of the return of the earlier state of affairs, when money remained locked up in inconvertible forms of credit. But in fact this did not happen to the extent that might have been expected, owing to the behaviour of the Bank. According to the terms of its foundation, its outstanding liabilities were limited to the £1,200,000 which it agreed to lend to the government. But during the winter of 1694, the Directors seem to have decided to go beyond these limits, in an effort to increase the short-term assets which they had so successfully acquired while awaiting the long-term redemption of the loan. They were not allowed to issue bills under the seal of the Bank for more than the £480,000 which had not been paid in cash during 1694; but they overcame this difficulty by issuing notes signed by the cashier of the Bank, and known, from his name, as 'Speed's notes'. Thanks to the confidence which the institution now enjoyed, these circulated with the same success as the original sealed bills, and with them the Bank continued to invest in tallies during the spring of 1695.[1] This increase in the amount of paper credit came, moreover,

[1] Feaveryear, loc. cit. pp. 118–19.

during a period when there was a considerable amount of floating capital in the country ready for investment and speculation. The shipping losses and the enforced reduction of overseas trade, which was particularly serious from 1693, had already led to money being put into domestic industry and to some extent into experimental ventures. With the unlocking of more money, and the establishment of confidence in the Bank bill, there was a boom in London which lasted through the summer of 1695. At the end of that year, when the boom was already on the decline, there were about 150 joint-stock companies in existence, 85 per cent of which had been incorporated since 1688, and most of those since 1692.[1] While it may not be accurate to say that in the spring and summer of 1695 'there was a fever of gambling in the stock market', on the lines although not on the scale of the South Sea Bubble,[2] it seems undoubtedly to have been the case that the favourable financial position had been directly reached by a considerable measure of credit inflation on the part of the Bank of England.[3]

The benefits of the increased circulation of trade were felt by the fighting services during the campaign of 1695; but the position was not really strong, and a loss of confidence would almost certainly have dramatic and possibly serious consequences. The uses to which credit was put, and the machinery by which it operated, were still largely experimental; and the excessive reliance on credit, which was being created by the over-issue of Bank bills, was likely to react unfavourably upon the government if its own financial position deteriorated. By April 1696 this had happened, and the combination of the government's embarrassment and inflation in the City led to the panic, the effects of which were felt for the rest of the year.

---

[1] W. R. Scott, *The Constitution and Finance of English, Scottish and Irish Joint-Stock Companies to 1720*, I (1912), pp. 327–8.

[2] Feaveryear, loc. cit. pp. 119–20. Scott, in his earlier work (loc. cit. p. 347) argues against this theory.

[3] Feaveryear, loc. cit. p. 119. I would emphasize the word 'seems' because Callender (*Bank of England*, I, p. 45) is cautious on this point, and confines himself to remarking that 'signs which normally suggest inflation were present in 1695'.

How much the Bank issued in bills by the end of 1695 I have failed to discover. Shaw, in his *Introduction to Cal.Treas.Bks.* XI–XVII, gives the total only for the end of the following year (pp. cxxxviii–cxl), Feaveryear gives no figures, and the historians of the Bank of England sum up the position only in 1696.

The immediate cause of this panic was the recoinage of the national currency which began in February. Throughout the previous year the state of the coin had been causing increasing alarm. Until the reign of Charles II, the standard currency of the realm, which was silver, was still coined inaccurately by hand and hammer as it had been in the thirteenth century, and the results lent themselves easily to clipping and shearing. The weight and value of the coin was thus steadily reduced the longer it remained in circulation. In 1662, a mechanical press was introduced into the Mint. This turned out a uniform coin with a milled edge that defeated the efforts of the clipper, and the remedy to the former abuses was thought to have been found. But this proved not to be the case, for instead of the good coin driving out the bad, the bad coin drove out the good. The old money was still treated as of equal value with the new, with the result that while abroad, where the measure of a coin's value was its weight and quality, the milled piece fetched a higher price than the clipped piece, in England both fetched the same price. The superior money, therefore, fled largely to the continent, while the inferior stayed at home. As Macaulay put it, 'nobody chose to pay twelve ounces of silver when ten would serve the turn'.[1] The export of bullion, against which the Treasury complained so regularly throughout James II's reign and the early years of the war, and which was conducted extensively by naval ships hoping to use their privilege to evade the Customs,[2] combined with the traditional practice of clipping to drive out the good money and to lower progressively the value of that which remained. Most of the currency of the realm at the time of the recoinage dated from before the Civil War;[3] and most of that was constantly being whittled down, until it was impossible for a man to tell the intrinsic value of the money which he carried in his pocket.

The King's speech to Parliament in November 1695 referred to the necessity for reforming the coinage,[4] and in December a proclamation was issued, stating that all clipped coins would be withdrawn from

[1] *History*, v, p. 2564.

[2] E.g. P.R.O.Adm. 3/2: 14/12; 3/5: 27/4; 3/10: 18/4, 25/6.

[3] See the remarkable figures given in Sir Charles Oman, *The Coinage of England* (1931), pp. 338–9.

[4] This and the following paragraph follow Feaveryear, loc. cit. pp. 125–8.

circulation and replaced by milled coins which were already being minted. It also gave the dates on which the various denominations of the old coin would cease to be legal tender. The last of these dates was 2 April, after which no clipped money could be used for any purpose. A mild panic ensued on receipt of this news, and a few riots occurred in the provinces among the poorer classes, who could not hope to get rid of their coin in that time. Parliament therefore extended the period for payment to 4 May, and furthermore stipulated that clipped money would continue to be taken until 24 June, in payment of loans to the government. A further Act enabled those who were assessed on the land and property tax of 4*s*. in the pound, to pay their contributions in clipped money, by the same date, for 1697 as well as for 1696. A third Act entitled those who already had annuities on government funds, to add to them or to pay for an extension in time on the same terms. When payment was made, all clipped coins were to be surrendered before milled coins were issued in return. Four provincial mints were set up to receive the old money and to help manufacture the new.

These measures promised quite well. But their effect was spoilt in March, before they were put into practice, when Parliament tried to use the issue of milled coin to force down the rate of the most highly priced denomination of the existing currency, the guinea. It was stipulated that after Lady Day the guinea should not pass for more than 26*s*., instead of the 30*s*. at which it was then standing, and for more than 22*s*. after 10 April; and in support of this policy, the importation of gold was made illegal after 2 March, and the Mint was forbidden to coin any more. The immediate result was to upset the confidence which the measures of January had restored. Gold at once became impossible to sell, and this affected the rate of silver. With the standard currency once more fluctuating uncertainly, the approach of 4 May saw a rapid rise in the rate of discount. The price of money rose sharply; in the last week of April, the government therefore advanced the date for the withdrawal of clipped money by two days, to 2 May, and in its anxiety to end the confusion forbade the payment thereafter of any dues in clipped coin. So far from putting an end to the muddle, this merely intensified it and extended it beyond May. All those who could unload money on the Exchequer did so if possible, and the Office found itself in the unusual position of being besieged by people clamouring to pay their taxes. Although not all the depreciated money was brought in immediately, by the middle of June little was left in circulation among the tax-paying classes.

With such a large proportion of the national currency literally removed, it was essential that the Mint should issue new currency to the same value as soon as possible. Unfortunately, it found itself unable to do so. A few days after they had rushed to the Exchequer to get rid of their clipped coin in dues and taxes, the same people rushed to the Bank of England to exchange their bills for milled coins. On 6 May there was a run on the Bank, and owing to the fact that the Mint had not supplied it with enough coin, and also because the value of the bills then in circulation exceeded the reserves of cash to which it was entitled, the Directors partly suspended payment. The bills were cashed for a small amount, and the balance noted on the back with a promise of repayment with interest. Their value at once fell heavily; and since the provision made for interest turned them from a medium of credit into a security, their circulation further decreased. The principal medium of credit thus virtually disappeared at the very time when it was needed to cover the decrease in the quantity of coin available. There was, in fact, a serious deflation, in which the confidence of the previous inflation collapsed like a pricked bubble, and which lasted for the rest of the campaigning season.

This process has been described in some detail, because the provisions under which it was carried out affected different social classes in different ways, and thus determined the attitudes of those among them who dealt with government departments. But before we examine their consequences, so far as they are concerned with the navy, we must look at the other side of the picture, and see how the government departments themselves were placed at this time, and how the deflation affected their financial position.

The situation in 1696 was made more serious by the fact that in that financial year the government finally became bankrupt. Since 1690, when the three armed forces were already substantially in debt, Parliament had been postponing payment by placing the unredeemed deficits which were intended to be met from one fund, on the books of the fund which succeeded it. As revenue constantly failed to meet expenditure in time, and as the volume of loans grew, the effect of these constant postponements of payment was, as Shaw put it, like a snowball—ever increasing;[1] and although the various devices of long-term credit, which had been initiated since 1692, had so far postponed actual bankruptcy, they could not themselves reconcile the difference between income and expenditure, or prevent the day from coming when the size of the government's deficit would equal the size of its annual revenue. So long as the Administration was responsible for meeting its creditors within a given time, however delayed, its receipts had to be devoted to paying them as well as to paying for its immediate requirements; and when the volume of their claims swallowed up one year's income, then theoretically the government was bankrupt, and there could be no current expenditure. This was the state of affairs in 1696.

The full gravity of the position was not appreciated for most of the year, for it was only in the autumn that a balance was drawn which showed it in its true light. But some idea of its nature could be gained the year before. At Michaelmas 1695, the naval debt amounted to £839,774, and the total debt for the war to £2,469,835. The deficit on civil government at the same time was £441,505, so that the government's debt came to £2,911,340.[2] For the financial year 1694–5, the anticipated revenue, excluding loans, amounted to £5,139,008;[3] but probably not much more than £3,000,000 of this was actually received within the year.[4] The effects could be seen in the winter of 1695–6, in the provisions made for supplying the armed forces for the new financial year. On 6 December, the Commons voted a supply for the navy of £2,500,000 and one of £16,972 for the Marines, who were borne on the books of the navy; and they followed this up with a grant of £2,524,854 for the army,[5] thus making themselves responsible for a total credit of slightly over £5,000,000. To meet this, they imposed the

[1] *Introduction to Cal.Treas.Bks.* XI–XVII, p. lxxx.

[2] *Cal.Treas.Bks. 1689–92*, p. cxcvii.

[3] *Return of Public Income and Expenditure*, pt I. In *Cal.Treas.Bks. 1689–92*, p. cxcvi, the revenue is given as £6,816,343; but that includes the net balance of unrepaid loans, which should not be considered for the present purpose.

[4] At Michaelmas 1696 there was still a deficiency amounting to approximately £1,560,000 on three of the main Acts of supply for that year (*Introduction to Cal. Treas.Bks.* XI–XVII, p. lxxxiv).

[5] *H.C.J.* XI, pp. 255–6.

usual land tax of 4*s*. in the pound, and extended the duration of certain other Acts, by which they were already laying duties upon various goods.[1] But it was estimated that altogether these measures would bring in only £3,682,469,[2] and each was moreover saddled with the repayment of the loans made on its predecessor before the yield could be applied to current expenditure. The Commons, therefore, had still to find new ways to raise the rest of their grants for the fighting services, and the government had still to raise sufficient money to meet the purposes for which they were intended. The solution was thought to have been provided by the statute 7 and 8 Will. III, c. 31, normally called the Salt Act. By this, certain duties were levied on salt, the tonnage of ships, glassware, earthenware, coals and culm, the yield of which was to be devoted to the repayment of a loan of £2,000,000: it was to be paid into the Exchequer within the year, to carry 7% interest, and to be raised by a group of subscribers who in return would be incorporated as a Land Bank, in the same way that the promoters of the subscription to the Tonnage Act had been incorporated as the Bank of England. Despite the strong opposition of the latter body, the Tory interest, which the new bank represented, carried the day; and at the end of April the experiment began. It proved a complete fiasco. The books of the bank were open for subscription in the first week of June, but apart from £5000 which was subscribed by the Treasury itself, only £1600 came in during the first five days and a further £500 in the next ten.[3] The trouble lay with the form of security offered. The money market at the end of the seventeenth century was unable to use the long-dated paper bonds which alone could be issued against land, and the promoters were further handicapped by the recoinage, which prevented them from paying their first instalment to the Exchequer in clipped coin as they wished to do. As a result, the scheme collapsed by the end of July, and the Treasury was left with the unwelcome prospect of finding a substitute through which to raise the money to pay for the current campaign.

---

[1] Ibid. pp. 372–3, 377, 383, 450, 497; 7 Will. III, c. 2, 7 and 8 Will. III, c. 5, 7 and 8 Will. III, c. 10.

[2] *Introduction to Cal.Treas.Bks.* XI–XVII, p. xliv.

[3] Ibid. p. lii.

A little of this money came in from the salt tax itself, now free from the lien to the Land Bank. But this amounted to only £68,835, and the problem remained of turning the eventual proceeds of the fund into sufficiently attractive credit to produce a large loan at a time of financial chaos. Two methods were tried: first, tallies were charged on the Act in the familiar way; and secondly, a new type of credit was issued, redeemable on the same Act, in the form of Exchequer bills. These bills were much the same as the Treasury Orders of Charles II's reign. They were a paper issue, limited by the terms of the Salt Act, in which they had figured as an alternative means of raising a loan if the Land Bank did not succeed, to a total of £1,500,000, and made negotiable between any two persons at face value.[1] On presentation, they would be cashed at the Exchequer. In other words, they paralleled the Bank of England's sealed bills, substituting the government for the Bank as the guarantor of repayment. Had they succeeded, it is indeed not improbable that the former would have replaced the latter as the authority for issuing paper money. However, they did not succeed. The wording of the clauses which provided for their operation was vague, and considerable doubt existed over their position as legal tender. Such bills as were put on the market, moreover, carried interest at 3%, so that they acted as an investment rather than as a medium of exchange.[2] By the end of September 1696, only £133,709 worth of the bills had been issued, of the £1,500,000 authorized, and only £24,880 worth were disposed of in the following twelve months.[3] The other alternative, that of loans on tallies, produced even less by Michaelmas 1696—a sum of only £126,465. In the event, therefore, the total receipts within the financial year upon the salt tax came to £329,009, or £1,670,991 less than had been anticipated from the Land Bank on the same fund. Thus by the middle of the summer of 1696, little of the national revenue

---

[1] *Introduction to Cal.Treas.Bks.* XI–XVII, p. cxl–cxli.

[2] Shaw (loc. cit. pp. cxlii–cxliii) attaches more importance to the second than to the first consideration as a cause for the failure of the bills. But the fact that they were treated as a security and not as a means of exchange does not itself explain why so few were accepted at all. I have therefore attached more weight to the fact that their legal status was ill defined.

[3] Ibid. p. cxliii. This total amounts to £158,509. E. L. Hargreaves, in *The National Debt*, p. 11, gives a different total of £159,169 for the same issue.

itself could be spent on the war, while of the alternative means of raising money, the Bank of England was fighting for survival and was in no state to contemplate a further loan, the Land Bank had failed, and the promotion of a new form of government credit as a last resort had proved completely ineffective. It was in this setting that the navy faced the agents of administration, many of whom were already hamstrung by the shortage of coin or ruined by the conditions of its withdrawal and reissue.

The social effects of the unreformed currency have been described by Macaulay, in a passage which in this context demands quotation:[1]

> When the great instrument of exchange became thoroughly deranged, all trade, all industry, were smitten as with a palsy. The evil was felt daily and hourly in almost every place and by almost every class.... The workman and his employer had a quarrel as regularly as the Saturday came round.... No merchant would contract to deliver goods without making some stipulation about the quality of the coin in which he was to be paid. Even men of business were often bewildered by the confusion into which all pecuniary transactions were thrown.... The labourer found that the bit of metal, which, when he received it, was called a shilling, would hardly, when he wanted to purchase a pot of beer or a loaf of rye bread, go as far as sixpence.

To this may be added the conclusions on the recoinage of this currency by a later economist:[2]

> The landowners with land and property tax to pay, the merchants with customs and excise duties to pay, the tax-collectors, the bankers, the stock-jobbers, and the well-to-do middle-class people of the towns who could subscribe to loans and annuities...had not only been able to unload upon the Exchequer any stock of bad money they possessed, but in many cases, no doubt, had made a nice profit by purchasing clipped money at a discount from less fortunate persons. The people who were left with it were the wage-earning and poorer classes...who found no chance of getting it into the Exchequer before the time.

These two quotations have been made at length, because so little has been said upon the precise social effects of the bad currency and of the recoinage that it is best to cite the exact words of those who, with

---

[1] *History*, v, p. 2567. [2] Feaveryear, loc. cit. pp. 128–9.

a claim to do so, have drawn conclusions upon them. If, with no detailed study of the subject available, these conclusions are examined from the point of view of a government department which came into contact with the classes affected, they are found to illuminate and to be illuminated by its experiences. In each case, it will be noted, the emphasis is upon the poorer classes: Macaulay mentions the merchants and business men, but only with a qualification, and it is upon the labourers and the countrymen that the weight of his description falls; while Mr Feaveryear draws a sharper contrast between the classes in describing the effects of the recoinage, with a similar emphasis upon the wage-earner as the chief sufferer. If, with this in mind, we look at the agents through whom the navy was supplied, we would therefore expect to find that the naval departments most affected by the state of the currency late in 1695 and throughout 1696, were those concerned with wages and victualling; and this is precisely what we do find. A contrast, indeed, may be drawn between the fortunes of the Victuallers, and the Treasurer of the Navy in paying the fleet, on the one hand, and those of the Navy Board in dealing with the contractors for naval stores on the other. The former were continuously in difficulties: the latter were still able largely to carry on as before.

The trouble over pay had been growing since the autumn of 1695. In the winter both seamen and dockyard workmen staged demonstrations against being paid with clipped coin, and the former presented a petition to Parliament on the subject.[1] The clerks who went down to pay the ships at Chatham at the end of the year received rough treatment from the men and the junior officers; and in January 1696, the paymaster of the navy wrote that although he had taken down £10,000 in small denominations to pay the ships of the fleet, he could not induce the men to take the shillings and sixpences. 'The trouble', he remarked, 'is of the nation, thro the prospect of a reformed coinage... ye silver Money is rejected by ye lower Order of people.'[2] The Admiralty

[1] P.R.O.Adm. 1/3576, f. 1237; Macaulay, *History*, v, p. 2568; *An Humble Representation of the Seamens Misery in... their Payment, and the Misery of some Officers and Masters Represented to His Majesty, and the Two most Honourable Houses, the Lords and Commons of England in Parliament Assembled...* (1696).

[2] P.R.O.Adm. 1/3577, ff. 179–80.

thereupon instructed him to apply for milled coin to the Treasury, but by the beginning of March he had to confess that he had been unsuccessful. There was no alternative, he then wrote,[1] but to try as before to induce the men to take the clipped money; the Treasury refused to give him enough milled coin for him even to begin paying the £40,000 which the fleet required, and with so few coins in circulation he could not buy them on the Exchange. There was little prospect, moreover, of the situation easing; for just as in individual cases the new coin was issued in proportion to the old coin received, so for the purposes of government the policy was to allocate new coin in proportion to the money received in loans upon the allocated funds. In this way the embarrassment of the government came into direct contact with the shortage of coin. The funds still outstanding for wages in March, from the Parliamentary appropriations of December, amounted to £151,340, and there was another £173,566 in deposit at the Exchequer for the purpose, in Bank of England notes and clipped money. But the second sum was soon to become virtually worthless, while the first was distributed among funds on which, as has been seen, very little came in for current expenditure, or which were supposed to be met by the loan from the Land Bank. Few milled coins, therefore, found their way to the ships during 1696.

The result was a year of continuous trouble. Complaints of desertion came incessantly, and on a new scale.[2] For the first time since 1689, mutiny over wages played a part in the court martial records;[3] while the dockyard workmen were also unruly, and demanded to be paid in the new money. By the end of July, the navy was faced not only with serious trouble among the men, but with a rapidly increasing debt for wages which, in the circumstances, could only delay payment further. Whereas at Michaelmas 1695 this had amounted to £321,612, at midsummer the next year it came to £1,219,277, and by Michaelmas it promised to be £1,427,229.[4] By then, only one department was

---

1 Ibid. f. 539.

2 Ibid. f. 967; 1/3578, ff. 671–3, 975.

3 P.R.O.Adm. 1/5257, courts martial of the carpenter and men of the *Portsmouth*, of some men of the *Dolphin*, and of some men of the *Vanguard*.

4 *Cal.S.P.Dom. 1696*, p. 280.

proportionately more deeply in debt; it need hardly be said that it was the victualling.

Always the most sensitive element in naval finance, and dealing as they did with contractors who were obliged largely to pay cash for their goods, the Victuallers were particularly badly hit by the terms of the recoinage. Their payments from the Exchequer had been utterly inadequate since the autumn of 1695. In August, they had received two payments amounting to £24,000; two more, on 2 and 7 September, totalling £18,995; and two in October, totalling £150,000, of which £130,000 was for the ships at Cadiz. They then received nothing until 13 January 1696, when they were paid £20,000. There was one issue in the next month, of £60,000, and two more in March, on the 10th and 11th, amounting to £151,239. After that they were given nothing until 8 August.[1] Only a proportion of these payments was in money, and all of that was in clipped coin.[2] This was bad enough; but the same state of the currency which kept the Victuallers short of cash, sent up the cost of victuals. The harvests of 1694 and 1695 were both disappointing, and the impact upon them of the financial crisis resulted in the steepest total rise in prices of the war. The following figures for naval victualling illustrate the position:[3]

	Price in shillings		
	1694	1695	1696
Rice (per 12 lb.)	4	5·75	5·75
Currants (per 12 lb.)	7·67	9	9
Wheat (per quarter)	35·39	49·68	49·74
Peas (per quarter)	25·57	33·19	33·61
Biscuit (per cwt.)	11	14·17	16·62
Flour (per cwt.)	19	19	21·83
Butter (per lb.)	5·17	4·88	4·88
Cheese (per 12 lb.)	2·42	2·13	2·13
Hops (per cwt.)	91·5	130·71	167·22
Malt (per quarter)	21·07	25·94	26·3
Beef (per cwt.)	23·33	22·62*	23·33
Hogs (per cwt.)	32·83	—	30·38

* Based on prices for five months only.

The Victuallers were thus being asked to spend far more than before, when they had far less money at their disposal. There was a further

1 P.R.O. T. 38/615, nos. 6, 7.

2 P.R.O.Adm. 106/2349, ff. 274–7.

3 Beveridge, loc. cit. pp. 565, 567–9, 571, 574, 576–7; cf. pp. 479, 485 above.

difficulty. In 1694 and again in 1695, the department had issued more provisions than had been declared for those years, thanks mainly to its habitual inability to reconcile the quantities which it claimed to have delivered to the ships with the quantities which the ships claimed to have consumed. The deficit for the two years amounted to victuals for 20,400 men, and in money to £265,200.[1] This had to come out of the declaration for 1696, which was for 40,000 men; and thus at the beginning of that year, the Victuallers could demand less than six months' provisions in money from the Exchequer, while the first claim on the funds allotted for the purpose went to the creditors who remained unpaid for the previous two years' supplies.[2] None of the new coinage, therefore, found its way to the department at a time when, from the nature of the business, it was needed more urgently there than anywhere else in the navy. The victualling, as usual, provided the most accurate reflection of the current financial difficulties.

The results were to be seen from the beginning of the campaign in 1696. By the middle of April, the Victuallers were complaining that the Treasury would not listen to their demands for milled coin,[3] and by June the yards were reporting that their victualling stores were almost empty.[4] At the end of that month, Plymouth had only 7 tons of beer, 115 pieces of pork (of 2 lb. each), 2 bushels of peas, 7½ bushels of oatmeal, 4¼ lb. of butter and 5½ lb. of cheese, while it had exhausted its stocks of biscuit. Portsmouth also had no biscuit or beer, and under 500 pieces of beef (of 2 lb. each); otherwise it had stocks of most commodities for another three to four weeks. At London itself—to take some of the more important articles—there were only 13 lb. of butter and 8¾ lb. of cheese, 15 tons of beer and 2166 pieces of beef. Kinsale was destitute of all provisions whatsoever.[5] When asked to explain these figures, the Victuallers replied that it was simple: they had received no money of any sort since March, and were therefore living entirely on stocks. No fresh provisions had been bought since the winter.[6] As a result, ships were constantly coming in to be

[1] B.M.Addnl. 9323, f. 42; P.R.O.Adm. 106/2349, ff. 292–4.
[2] P.R.O.Adm. 1/3578, f. 813.
[3] P.R.O.Adm. 1/3577, f. 1014. [4] Ibid. ff. 417–18.
[5] P.R.O.Adm. 112/68; returns for 30 June 1696.
[6] P.R.O.Adm. 106/2349, ff. 304–5.

revictualled, and then staying in port indefinitely while they waited for fresh provisions, and while the men deserted or fell ill from the stale food which was all they had. The health of the fleet, according to the physician of the Blue squadron at the end of the year, had never been worse than it was that summer.[1] Meanwhile, the prospect of further supplies grew worse. By August, the cheesemongers refused to deal any longer with a department which did not pay its bills, and the bakers and brewers were threatening to follow suit. Appeals for patience, and attempts to register the debts in course, were useless when dealing with contractors who needed cash;[2] and it was fortunate that the campaigning season was virtually over. The winter guard, however, had still to be catered for; and early in October, in reply to frequent exhortations from the Admiralty to hasten their supply, the wretched Victuallers could only remark: 'Wee assure you it is very greivous to us, wee may say almost heart breaking, to receive Orders to pres upon us to do that wch we are in no capacity enabled to.'[3] At that time, despite a welcome though meagre resumption of payments from the Exchequer —£20,000 in August, and £10,800 in September[4]—they had stores for only ten ships, and were finding it very difficult to buy any meat for the following year.[5] Although money was now coming in regularly, after a series of meetings with the Treasury,[6] it had to be devoted exclusively to satisfying the old debts, which by this time amounted to £478,435;[7] and there seemed no possibility of meeting the demands of the declaration for 40,000 men in 1697.[8] In the first week of November, the Victualling Office came 'to a full stand for want of money', and the

---

[1] W. C[ockburn], *Account of the Nature...of the Distempers that are incident to Seafaring People: With Observations on the Diet of the Sea-men In His Majesty's Navy...Illustrated with some Remarkable Instances of the Sickness of the Fleet during the Last Summer* (1696), introduction. *The Term Catalogues, 1668–1709 and 1711*, vol. II (ed. E. Arber, 1903), does not mention the work; but from internal evidence, 'the Last Summer' of which Cockburn speaks refers to 1696.

[2] P.R.O.Adm. 1/3577, ff. 921–2.

[3] P.R.O.Adm. 1/3578, f. 537.

[4] P.R.O. T. 38/615, no. 7.

[5] P.R.O.Adm. 1/3578, ff. 538, 629.

[6] *Cal.Treas.Bks. April 1696–March 1697*, pp. 238, 256, 270. £27,589 was issued from the Exchequer in October, and £20,000 in November.

[7] P.R.O. T. 38/658, no. 5. This did not include debts for current service, or all old debts incurred overseas.

[8] P.R.O.Adm. 1/3578, f. 630.

Commissioners disclaimed responsibility for supplying any ports in the west for the following year.[1] At the end of 1696, it seemed that the department had at last reached the position which it had approached in earlier years, of a complete breakdown of administration.

Naval stores were not bought on the same terms as provisions, and the Navy Board did not experience the same difficulties with the contractors as the Victuallers. There is, indeed, a curious change in 1696 in the relative positions of the different types of merchant with whom it dealt. Hitherto, the strongest and best-organized opposition had come from the Baltic traders, and the smaller men of the domestic market had followed suit; but now it was the domestic merchants who proved most recalcitrant, while the Baltic merchants did not cause undue trouble. The negotiations for the annual contracts for imported stores began as usual in the spring, and at first the merchants were extremely reluctant to deal. They complained, as the Navy Board had expected,[2] of the remoteness of the funds allocated to their payment,[3] and for five weeks refused to tender. But on 5 May, after a series of fruitless meetings at the Navy Office, the Board 'advised them'—and it is a measure of its control in this field at a time when the department had lost financial control elsewhere—'to contract as formerly, otherwise some other Methods should speedily be taken to serve his Ma^{ty} with ye goods wanting'.[4] The tenders began to arrive on the next day; and, after the customary bargaining, the Board was able to report to the Admiralty by the end of the month that almost all the contracts had been signed without a rise in price from the previous year.[5] At the moment when money was shortest, the navy thus successfully threatened its most difficult creditors, and purchased its goods with less trouble than in some of the earlier and less unfavourable years of the war.

At first sight this is surprising. The answer may lie partly in the fact that at a time when trade was suffering from the recent panic, and when the outlook was most discouraging, the naval contracts offered the

---

1 Ibid. f. 861. 2 P.R.O.Adm. 1/3577, f. 1099.

3 Ibid. ff. 1117, 1131, 1133–4; Serg:Mins. XXXIV, 11/3 *et seq.*

4 Serg:Mins. XXXIV, 5/5.

5 Ibid., May *passim*; P.R.O.Adm. 1/3578, f. 199; Serg.Misc. IV, f. 142.

Baltic merchants one of the few reliable, or even available, opportunities for business. How far that is true depends upon the extent to which the naval contractors for imported stores dealt outside the navy, which I am unable to say. But a more important reason for their attitude was their dependence upon these contracts under any circumstances. Their refusal to tender two years before had been the result of the exhaustion of short-term credit, when there seemed to be no chance that they would be paid. Now, with the establishment of long-term credit, they were theoretically assured of repayment eventually so long as the government remained solvent; and in the spring it was not yet clear that in fact it was bankrupt. The navy was their biggest customer and their biggest debtor; and while they could drive a hard bargain with their customer, in the last resort, provided that it could pay at all, their debtor held the whip hand. It was this fact which enabled a government department to achieve its greatest success with its most powerful creditors, just before it became insolvent.

The smaller merchants at home set a different problem, and one which on this occasion was not solved so easily. Standing, as it were, midway between the contractors for victualling and the Baltic merchants, their demands, while less compelling than those of the former, were more awkward than those of the latter. With no information on their status or wealth, beyond the indirect evidence of the naval contracts, it is difficult to do more than suggest the reason for this. But it may be argued that the domestic merchants were largely, and in the timber trade, very largely, small, local men; and as such were unlikely to have lent money to the government, or in many cases to be taxable on land or property. Many of them, therefore, must have been unable to get rid of their clipped coin, as wealthier men could do; and this was doubtless why some of them insisted in the summer of 1696 on being paid in cash, and in milled coin.[1] When their terms could not be satisfied, they ceased to deal with the navy.[2] The Sussex timber merchants, in particular, refused to deliver wood, and the Admiralty was forced to raise with a new urgency the old question of felling timber in the New Forest,[3] and to build one of its fourth rates there.[4]

---

[1] P.R.O.Adm. 1/3578, f. 418.

[2] Ibid. ff. 672, 793–4.

[3] P.R.O.Adm. 3/12: 14/6, 24/8.

[4] See pp. 71–2 above.

By July, the Navy Board was complaining that local contractors were failing to deliver the goods which they had promised;[1] and one of the reasons for the extension at this time of the system of standing contracts at Portsmouth and Plymouth was the absence of any other means of supply.[2] Where normally the domestic market could be relied upon if the Baltic merchants were satisfied, it now raised its own problems which, in the circumstances of the time, seemed unlikely to be solved.

By the time that the campaign of 1697 began, the national finances had been set straight in many respects; and the calamities of 1696 were not repeated. The navy itself was not intended to operate in 1697 upon the scale which had been intended the year before. The emphasis was on the squadron rather than any longer upon the fleet, and the annual estimates fell by some £240,000.[3] But they still amounted to over £2,500,000, and the reasons for the improvement in the financial position lay less in any reduction of expenditure than in the restoration of confidence in the system of national credit. This was brought about in two ways: first, by the issue, as the five mints began to go into production, of more new coin; and secondly, and more important, by the reappearance of the Bank of England on the market as a large-scale investor in government tallies, and on a firmer basis than before.

In the late autumn of 1696, Parliament set to work to draw up a national balance sheet of income and liabilities, and in November the Treasury presented its findings. This placed the total deficit at £5,558,816. A month later, the committee of the Commons which was investigating the same question independently, submitted a report which estimated the debt at about £125,000 less.[4] Since the estimated revenue for the financial year 1695–6, excluding loans, was £5,645,961,[5] and since the deficit was owed entirely to the government's creditors, some new financial device was obviously required to save the government from bankruptcy. The solution was found in the Bank of England. On

[1] P.R.O.Adm. 1/3578, f. 921. [2] P.R.O.Adm. 1/3579, f. 1049.

[3] See p. 569 above.

[4] *Introduction to Cal.Treas.Bks.* XI–XVII, p. lxxxiv. The final deficit, adopted early in 1697, amounted to £5,160,459. 14*s.* 9¼*d.*

[5] *Public Income and Expenditure*, p. 17.

29 December, the Commons called upon the Directors to raise enough money both to meet the expenses of the next year, and to guarantee that the debts themselves would be paid. After some negotiation, a single device was found to cater for both requirements. It was agreed, and embodied in a statute,[1] that the Bank should open its books to an unlimited subscription for new capital, from which a loan would be made immediately to the government. To secure their assets to cover this loan, the Directors were persuaded to add to their stock, or to 'ingraft' upon it, those government tallies which were not provided for on any of the existing funds. Additional duties on leather and other goods were levied to pay off the net balance of the rest. In return, the Bank was to be paid interest upon the tallies at 8% for an unspecified period, with no date mentioned for the repayment of the capital, and was granted a monopoly of joint-stock banking at least until 1711.[2] Thus accorded the favour of the government, the new subscription went well, and the Bank was able to assure the Treasury of a loan for the coming campaign. A similar position to that of 1694–5 was in fact created, in which the Bank of England financed the immediate cost of the war, its bills commanded confidence as negotiable tender, and the tallies, instead of standing at a discount of up to 40%, as at the end of 1696,[3] could be sold at par. But in two respects the position was better than at the earlier date: in the first place, the Bank was operating upon surer foundations after the experience of 1696; and secondly, the funding of the government's debt to it as a permanent debt, at last removed from national finance the nightmare which had disturbed it hitherto, of a day of ultimate reckoning. As the long-term credit, introduced two years earlier, had first helped to identify the wealth of the country with the war, so the permanent national debt now carried this identification a stage further, by removing the onus of repayment altogether and thus turning a loan to the government into a government security. Although only a small proportion of the total deficit at the end of William's war was in the form of permanent debt,[4] in the next war it formed the basis of the national credit, soon outweighing the long and short-term debts which still encumbered the balance sheet at the turn of the century.

---

[1] 8 and 9 Will. III, c. 20. [2] Clapham, op. cit. I, pp. 46–50. [3] Ibid. p. 47.
[4] See *Introduction to Cal. Treas. Bks.* XI–XVII, p. CCXIX.

This re-establishment of credit took place before the complementary process, the return of coin, had taken effect. The recoinage was slow, and it was two to three years before the currency was fully restored. In 1697, therefore, the well-to-do were again able to operate at their level more easily than the poor at theirs. Those who worked on credit had credit once more: those who needed cash were still short of cash. The effect on naval administration was much what might have been expected. The Baltic merchants made no difficulty about importing stores, for they were given credit on the salt tax, on which the Bank of England was largely proposing to make its loan. The domestic merchants remained more awkward, and many continued to refuse to deal until the end of the war. But in general it may be said that the stores came in more easily than in 1696, as the course of the navy stood firmer on the renewed credit of the Bank.

Victualling was not so successful. The issues to the Victuallers in 1697 were the largest of any year of the war, accounting indeed, to the disgust of the Navy Board,[1] for over a third of the issues to the navy for the year. Out of a total of £2,821,931 received by the Treasurer of the Navy, no less than £1,270,066 went towards provisions.[2] Of this sum, however, only £23,481 was in cash.[3] Far the largest single source was the loan on the salt tax, the proceeds of which for this purpose were £732,227. Thus victualling credit was good, but cash for victualling was scarce. In terms of administration, this meant that the larger creditors could be satisfied but that many of the smaller men could not. The current service therefore, as in 1696, was almost at a stand. In the last year of the war, indeed, the Victuallers gave up trying to supply the ships from England. Their stores were consistently low,[4] and in May they arranged for the main supply to come from Ireland. The victualling agent in Dublin was instructed to buy enough provisions to store 40 men-of-war for four months, and shortly afterwards this was raised to 45 men-of-war.[5] The experiment was not a success. Not only were Irish victuals more expensive than English, but according to the ships their

[1] P.R.O.Adm. 1/3579, f. 981.

[2] *H. of L. N.S.* VII, p. 178. The first sum accounts for the issues to the Treasurer of the Navy, and not for all those made for the navy during the financial year. These amounted to £3,097,947.

[3] P.R.O. T. 38/615, no. 8.

[4] P.R.O.Adm. 112/69.

[5] P.R.O.Adm. 1/3988, ff. 15, 28.

quality was worse.[1] This may well have been thanks to the conditions in which the food was packed, which even the agent acknowledged were not all that they might have been.[2] It soon became apparent, moreover, that delays in getting provisions were not confined to England; the meat particularly came in very slowly,[3] and in the event only enough food was provided for twenty men-of-war for four months, and some of that was rejected by the ships.[4] There seemed, indeed, no hope that the navy would be satisfactorily victualled again so long as the war lasted, and it was with open eagerness that the Victuallers asked in August 1697 whether it were true that peace was in sight.[5]

The payment to the men also went ahead slowly in 1697. Less was issued under the head of wages than in the previous year—£743,175 compared with £927,460[6]—and with ready money still scarce not much could be done. Fewer ships were in commission in this last year than there had been in 1696, so that the strain was slightly eased; but at the end of 1697, the arrears of seamen's wages amounted to the appalling total of £1,862,849.[7] The authorities were thus faced with an awkward problem, when in 1698 the demobilization gave many of the men the opportunity to claim their back pay in person.

The navy was thus able to avoid a complete breakdown of administration at the end of the war, such as had seemed only too likely a year before; but on the other hand, it had neither catered satisfactorily for the current service of 1697, nor had been able to pay off its debts. Where these could be converted into long-term securities, this did not greatly matter; but the bulk of the deficit remained enormous. A week after the peace treaty had been signed, the Navy Board estimated that the total naval debt was as follows:[8]

	£
Bills of before 25 March 1686	40,000
Wear and tear	376,051
Wages	1,862,849
Victuals	227,234
Various (no details given)	16,389
Total	£2,522,523

[1] P.R.O.Adm. 1/3580, ff. 12, 713.
[2] P.R.O.Adm. 1/3988, ff. 32, 45–6.
[3] Ibid. ff. 28–9.
[4] Ibid. f. 57.
[5] P.R.O.Adm. 106/2349, f. 378.
[6] *H. of L. N.S.* VII, pp. 177–8.
[7] Serg.MS. A 133, estimate of 9 November 1697.
[8] Ibid. This does not include the debt of the ordnance for naval supplies.

This was roughly £150,000 more than the Parliamentary grant for the service of the year, and almost thirteen times the size of the debt which had so worried the naval authorities nine years before. Perhaps, more clearly than any figures of ships or stores or men, these figures of debt show the difference between the problems which faced the administration of Charles II and James II, and those which confronted the administration of William III.

III

The financial circumstances of the last three years of the war were not propitious for administrative development; and in fact the period was marked principally by attacks upon administration. These may be seen in the pamphlet warfare which reached its height in 1695 and 1696. Tracts and pamphlets on naval affairs had been appearing plentifully enough since 1689; but it was in the second half of the war that a group of persistent and effective pamphleteers emerged who, for the first time, seriously worried the object of their attacks. This development was perhaps not unaffected by the end of the licensing system in 1695, which was the signal for a considerable increase in the quantity and vigour of political literature;[1] but, while external circumstances may account for the rise of the named pamphleteer,[2] they cannot account for the change of target in the pamphlets. If the dividing line is taken as 1694–5, the titles themselves reveal the shift of interest. Before that, the emphasis is upon events at sea, or on politics; after it, upon administration. In the first five years of the war, so far as I have been able to discover, there was only one publication which referred to the problems of man-power,[3] and only two which dealt at all with abuses in the Navy Office and the dockyards.[4] In the last four years, such tracts were not only numerous, but largely displaced the earlier type of pamphlet.[5]

The attacks on dockyard abuses centred on a pamphlet by one

[1] Laurence Hanson, *Government and the Press, 1695–1763* (1936), introduction.

[2] See Bibliography, pp. 683–4 below.

[3] George St Lo, *England's Safety, or a Bridle to the French King* (1693).

[4] Henry Maydman, *Naval Speculations, and Maritime Politicks* (1691), and Robert Crosfeild, *England's Glory Reviv'd...* (1693).

[5] The pamphlets may be compared by date in the Bibliography, pp. 683–6 below.

George Everett,[1] a Thames boatbuilder who had carried out some contracts for the navy earlier in the war,[2] but who then abandoned his business almost entirely for the unprofitable task of routing out irregularities and fraud in the naval service. He seems to have started with a grudge against the officials at Chatham;[3] but, as he travelled along the tortuous byways of departmental corruption, he succumbed to a disinterested passion for reform. The naval authorities, who had begun by accusing him of malice, ended by concluding that he was mad, as indeed his unrestrained and largely ill-directed zeal gave them reasonable cause.[4] His memoranda, petitions and personal appearances before the Council and Admiralty, which continued from 1694 to 1700,[5] attracted some attention, and a literature sprang up around his case before it finally died down.[6] There is little point in detailing the abuses which Everett specified, for they were of the familiar kind. The importance of the case lay rather in the attention which it drew publicly to the corruption existing throughout the service, and in its illustrations of the way in which the average naval official regarded his illegal behaviour as perfectly normal.

At the same time, a group of tracts and pamphlets was concentrating upon the shortcomings of the manning. They were of two sorts. First, there were the petitions of the naval officers and men to Parliament,[7] which concentrated upon abuses of the existing regulations of pay and service, particularly the 'Q's and 'R's; and the pamphlets whose object was the same, such as William Hodges's *Dialogue concerning the Art of Ticket-Buying* of 1695, his *Great Britain's Groans* and *Misery to Misery* of the same year, and part of his *Ruin to Ruin, after Misery to Misery* of 1699. Secondly, and for our purpose more significant, there were the

---

1 *The Pathway to Peace and Profit*... (1694).

2 P.R.O.Adm. 49/29.

3 Serg.Misc. III, ff. 116, 118.

4 Ibid. ff. 120–2, 124–5.

5 His own pamphlets on the subject were *Loyalty and Fidelity, Rejected and Oppressed*... (1698–9), and *A Word in Season*... (1699). An abstract of the documents of the case exists in B.M.Harl. 7471.

6 Robert Crosfeild, *Justice Perverted, and Innocence and Loyalty Oppressed*... (1695), and *Justice the Best Support of Government* (1697); William Hodges, *Ruin to Ruin, after Misery to Misery*... (1699).

7 The best single collection of these is in *B.M.Printed 86 m. 7*; see Bibliography, p. 685 below.

pamphlets which suggested new regulations for service and, in particular, for the recruitment of men. These came again mostly from the naval officers, such as St Lo with his two books *England's Safety* in 1693[1] and *England's Interest, Or, a Discipline for Seamen* in the following year; John Perry, whose *Regulation for Seamen* was written in 1695 while he awaited in prison a court martial for alleged cowardice; William Hodges's *Humble Proposals for the Relief, Encouragement, Security and Happiness of the Seamen of England* of 1695; and the *Proposal for the Incouragement of Seamen* produced in the last year of the war by Thomas Mozin and Nicholas Jennings. But the professional pamphleteer Robert Crosfeild also turned his attention to the subject in 1694 in his *Truth Brought to Light*; and there were some anonymous tracts, such as the *Encouragement for Seamen and Manning* of 1695,[2] and the *Discourse upon Raising Men* of 1696.[3] The proposals made by this second group of pamphlets, although their details varied considerably, all amounted to the same. They asked that a register should be compiled of the seafaring population, and that a levy of some sort—it was usually suggested that it should fall upon those merchants and shipowners who were granted protections from the press[4]—should be imposed to pay for the cost of the work, and for an improved system of medical attention and pensions. It was generally accepted that before the navy could be properly and reliably manned, the conditions both of recruitment and of employment must be improved; and the only differences between the pamphlets lay in their different suggestions on how best to bring about the necessary reforms.

Both series of pamphlets, those arising from Everett's investigations into the dockyards, and those on the manning, reflected official opinion to some extent even while many of them attacked official practice. While Everett was accusing the Navy Board of countenancing the frauds in the yards, the Board itself was suggesting to the Admiralty that

---

[1] Republished in 1695 with the title of *Gloria Britannica*.

[2] *Harleian Miscellany*, IV (1811), pp. 392–400.

[3] *A Collection of State Tracts, Published during the Reign of King William III*, vol. II (1706), pp. 539–50.

[4] But Mozin and Jennings proposed that the navy should benefit from the proceeds of a national lottery.

such frauds might be reduced by raising the pay of the officers concerned, so that the temptation to embezzle or to connive at embezzlement would be at least partly removed.[1] In March 1695, the Admiralty responded by requesting the yards to report on the allowances and perquisites enjoyed by their officers, with a view to equalizing their salaries.[2] The replies came in over the next three months, and revealed a considerable variation in the extras, in money or kind, allowed in the different establishments. Although most of these extras were supposed to have been removed by successive Yard Orders since 1685,[3] it was clear that in practice the traditional perquisites remained, according to the custom of the individual yard.[4] In some yards, the officers were allowed fuel, candles and stationery for their offices: in others, they were not. Sometimes, but not always, they were allowed house rent; sometimes, but again not always, allowances for travelling on business; and sometimes, certain old stores which had been officially condemned. When these extras were added to the already unequal salaries and wages of the officials at the different dockyards, no real comparison between wages could be drawn. The Admiralty, therefore, decided to raise and level the inclusive salaries of all grades of dockyard officer from 1 January 1696, 'to prevent', as it was stated in the minutes, 'the recurrence of the many Imbezlements and Frauds that now are practised'.[5] After the necessary permission had been obtained from the Treasury and the Council,[6] the new rates of pay came into effect in the new year, as shown on p. 599 for the six major yards.[7] By the end of the war, therefore, the dockyard service had been brought into line with the sea service, with higher and more equal rates of pay, suitable at last to the growing complexity of its material and to the increase of organization which that involved.

The pamphlets which appeared on the manning problem reflected the official attitude more closely than those upon the dockyard abuses. One of them, the anonymous *Encouragement for Seamen and Manning* of 1695, was even able to declare that its proposals were made with 'the

[1] P.R.O.Adm. 1/3577, ff. 1013–15; 1/3578, ff. 209–10.
[2] P.R.O.Adm. 3/11: 11/3. [3] Admty:Corbett, XVIII, f. 17.
[4] The details are given in Serg.Misc. III, ff. 139–66.
[5] P.R.O.Adm. 3/12: 14/8. [6] P.R.O.Adm. 1/5249, 20/10.
[7] P.R.O.Adm. 7/175, estimate of the ordinary for 1696.

	Salary per annum					
	Chatham, Deptford, Portsmouth			Woolwich, Plymouth, Sheerness		
	£	*s.*	*d.*	£	*s.*	*d.*
Clerks of the cheque and survey, storekeeper, master shipwright, master attendant	200	0	0	150	0	0
Master shipwright's assistants, master caulker, master ropemaker, clerk of the ropeyard	100	0	0 (Where borne)	80	0	0 (Woolwich only)
Boatswain of the yard	80	0	0	70	0	0 (Woolwich and Sheerness only)
Purveyor	50	0	0 (Chatham and Portsmouth only)	—		
Master mastmaker, boatbuilder, sailmaker, joiner	46	19	0	46	19	0 (Woolwich and Plymouth only)
Master bricklayer, house carpenter	39	2	6	39	2	6 (Woolwich only)
Porter	30	0	0	25	0	0
Surgeon	40	0	0	40	0	0

special approbation of the honourable Admiral Russell'.[1] The attempt to improve the system of recruitment, which was made in that and the following years, was indeed Russell's main contribution to administration, and he seems to have imbued his personal associates with his own sense of the urgency of the problem. It is significant that Burchett, who had served as his secretary since 1691, mentioned manning alone of the administrative factors affecting the navy, in the introduction to his narrative of the war at sea.[2] The shortage of men in the Mediterranean in 1694–5, and its serious effects, had turned the Admiral's attention to the problem as early as April 1695, and he then urged that Parliament should be moved to legislate in some way for a more efficient method of conscription than was provided by impressment.[3] The Admiralty debated the point during the summer,[4] but it was not until the fleet's return that anything was done. Early in December, the Navy Board was ordered to submit a detailed report on the possibility of compiling a register of the regular seamen inhabiting the coastal areas,[5] and on its receipt the Admiralty forwarded it to the Council.[6] Later in the month, however, Russell's original hope was satisfied. On 31 December, leave was granted for a bill to be brought into the Commons 'for the increase and encouragement' of seamen, Onslow

1 *Harleian Miscellany*, x, p. 221.
2 Burchett, pp. xi–xii.
3 B.M. Lansdowne 1152B, f. 272.
4 P.R.O.Adm. 3/10: 14/7, 20/7, 18/8.
5 P.R.O.Adm. 3/11: 4/12.
6 P.R.O.Adm. 2/363, ff. 120–6.

being one of the members ordered to prepare its clauses.[1] On 6 January, it was read for the first time; and, after some debate on detail, became law on 10 April 1696.[2]

The Act[3] enshrined in the main the proposals of the Admiralty and Navy Board. All seamen who would enrol voluntarily on the register, giving their names and domiciles, would receive £2 a year in return. If called upon to serve in the navy, they would be granted certain substantial benefits: they would be given double their existing shares of prize money, and would be admitted to the privileges of Greenwich Hospital; they alone would be eligible for the rank of warrant officer; and in the event of their being killed in action, their widows would be provided for and their children educated at the navy's expense. In return for these advantages over their fellows, they were to report for duty within thirty days of a summons, with a forfeiture of six months' pay and all the other privileges of the registry if they failed to do so; and they were to notify the registering officers of their whereabouts once a year, and whenever they changed their permanent address. The provisions of the Act applied also to watermen and fishermen.[4] Landsmen were to be encouraged to train for the sea by serving for two years in merchant ships with the same benefits, and with full protection from the press.

The task of organizing the register was first entrusted to the Navy Board, which rented a house on Tower Hill to serve as a head office.[5] On 5 May, Commissioners were appointed, of whom two, Matthew Aylmer and John Hill, were extra Commissioners of the Navy,[6] and two, George Byng and Thomas Baker, were naval officers.[7] The head office acted locally through the Customs officers, who sent in their lists from time to time from the principal ports;[8] and in July 1696 a second office was set up at Dover, to deal with the lists submitted from the Cinque Ports and the surrounding countryside.[9] The Commissioners

[1] *H.C.J.* XI, p. 373. [2] Ibid. pp. 380, 488. [3] 7 and 8 Will. III, c. 21.

[4] The Watermen's and Fishermen's Companies petitioned unsuccessfully for permission to control their own registers (*H.C.J.* XI, pp. 387, 392).

[5] P.R.O.Adm. 105/41, unfoliated. Among the staff of the office, as receiver general, was Russell's steward.

[6] See Appendix VIII below. [7] P.R.O.Adm. 105/41.

[8] Ibid. [9] P.R.O.Adm. 1/3997, unfoliated.

were responsible to the Admiralty, which reserved the right to discharge men from the register.

During the summer of 1696, while the organization was slowly settling down, few lists seem to have been compiled. But by September, the registry office was ready to begin submitting weekly returns to its superiors. These soon revealed the disappointing results. By the 26th, after nine months in existence, it was able to report only 426 names for the whole of England; and in November, after an intensive drive to get more men to enter the scheme, the lists amounted to only 3801 names.[1] Captains reported that none of their men would register, while the Customs officers complained that the local seamen were being continually snatched away by the press, or turned over from ship to ship, before the registering officials could lay hold of them.[2] Soon, also, the press began to molest the few seamen who were registered, and many of them promptly gave their £2 back and took their names off the lists.[3] At the Nore, there was utter confusion by the end of the year, and probably that station was not untypical of the rest.[4] The Watermen's and Fishermen's Companies, seeing that the project was a failure, took no steps to encourage their members to register, and by the spring of 1697 not a single waterman or fisherman was on the books of the head office.[5] By that time, another difficulty had arisen. No system in the seventeenth century was without its abuses, and the registering tickets were soon being used in an attempt to cheat the press, and were passing at a high rate from hand to hand.[6] By October 1697, a few weeks before the war ended, the Commissioners had to report that 'we have hitherto registered not a single seafaring man but as was at the time of his registering in actual service on board his Majesty's ships'.[7] Although the register survived the war and the short peace that followed, it failed utterly to touch the problem of manning the fleet, and served merely to illustrate its recalcitrance in the conditions of the late seventeenth century. With the administrative machinery available, only a voluntary system of recruitment could be introduced to relieve the chaos of the existing system of compulsion; and the principle of

---

[1] P.R.O.Adm. 105/41. [2] P.R.O.Adm. 1/3997. [3] Ibid. [4] Ibid.
[5] P.R.O.Adm. 105/41; *Cal.S.P.Dom. 1697*, p. 46. [6] P.R.O.Adm. 105/41.
[7] Ibid.

voluntary service stood little chance when its own provisions were disregarded by the complementary methods of recruitment, and when the contingent conditions of employment remained as unattractive as they were in 1696. With wages in arrears, with food and drink scarce and bad, and with the press and the turn-overs in force, the voluntary register was doomed from the start; but with a powerful trading interest in the Commons, with the new Board of Trade suspicious of the naval control over men and shipping, and with the Admiralty and the Navy Board already fully occupied by the existing chaotic administration, only a voluntary register could be started at all. The conditions which led to its inauguration were as likely to ensure its failure.

IV

Weakly manned[1] and short of provisions, the fleet during 1696 had a thoroughly unsatisfactory campaign.[2] After Russell returned from Dunkirk, the by now familiar expedient was tried of bombarding Calais with the squadron which had been left at sea under Shovell, while the rest of the ships completed their refits and storing before concentrating with the Dutch in the Downs. By the third week of April, a line of battle of 81 ships had been assembled, and Rooke took over the command. But he found himself almost immediately reduced to a line of 55 ships, for in the absence of any plan for their employment on the part of the Lords Justices, the Admiralty's demands for more escorts and cruisers, to protect the trade which was being badly mauled in the west by the French privateers, were satisfied at the expense of the fleet. There seemed little reason, indeed, for keeping a strong force of big ships at sea, for the enemy had now laid up most of his three-deckers, and was using their men to fit out more small vessels to attack commerce.[3] Complaints of losses soon poured in from the merchants, and before even he received his sailing orders,

---

[1] At the beginning of May, the third rates of the fleet alone were short of over 3300 men out of their intended 19,500 (Burchett, p. 333; see also ibid. p. 330).

[2] The following account of the campaign is taken from Burchett, pp. 325–54. Some of the minutes of the Lords Justices are in *H.M.C. Buccleuch*, II, pt I, pp. 308–76.

[3] Roncière, op. cit. VI, pp. 217–18.

Rooke had been robbed of thirteen third rates and three fourths, together with a number of smaller units.

When the orders came, they directed the fleet to cruise in the Soundings to prevent the Toulon squadron, which was thought to be heading out of the Mediterranean, from reaching Brest. The French, however, managed to slip past in May, and by June the Lords Justices were completely at a loss to know what to do with this cumbrous and expensive instrument, whose useless cruise was causing such administrative difficulties. William, who was keeping a watchful eye upon events from Flanders, could also suggest nothing;[1] and on 13 June, as a last resort and for the first time since 1689, the Admiralty was asked to state its opinion as to how the fleet should be employed.[2] But the Commissioners could only reply that they 'cannot propose any particular undertaking...and have no opinion what is practicable'.[3] It was, indeed, a hopeless situation. Apart from the continuous drain upon the fleet of individual units for the close protection of trade, which went on steadily throughout the summer, the acute shortage of victuals was continually sending ships into harbour and keeping them there indefinitely before they returned to sea. As the Admiralty acknowledged the next year, 'it was the Victualling which brought our Efforts to nought' in 1696.[4] Under these circumstances, any attempt to take the offensive stood little chance of success, and Berkeley's plan in June to attack the French fleet in Camaret bay, where many of the ships were lying, was soon seen in London to be impossible. After another month's cruising, the line of battle—or what was left of it[5]—by now almost completely out of food and extremely short of men, returned to Spithead, while a squadron, itself only partially provisioned, was left in the Soundings until October. The fleet in effect had given up the campaign by August, and for the rest of the year only scattered cruisers and odd escorts kept the sea. Throughout August the big ships of England and France lay at anchor, an illustration of the administrative exhaustion which by now seemed to have overtaken all the contestants.

---

1 B.M.Addnl. 37992, f. 139.
2 P.R.O.Adm. 3/13: 13/6.
3 P.R.O.Adm. 1/4083, f. 1165.
4 P.R.O.Adm. 3/13: 12/7.
5 By the end of July there were only sixteen English and eleven Dutch men-of-war left in company with four fireships (Burchett, p. 347).

When the Lords Justices referred to the Admiralty in their search for a naval policy, it was a gesture of despair rather than any recognition of the Board's importance. Nevertheless, the department improved its position during the last two years of the war. This was not due to any increase in strength in the composition of the working Board. The Commission of 1694 lasted until February 1696, but for its last three months it had to do without the services of Lowther, who retired to Cumberland in the winter of 1695.[1] On 24 February, a new patent was issued, which named James Kendall as the junior Commissioner.[2] The appointment was made, as all appointments now seemed to be made to the Board, to conciliate the merchants; for Kendall was a well-known and wealthy West Indies trader,[3] with a certain amount of administrative experience as Governor of Barbados earlier in the war. In Parliament he was a placeman, as one of the members for Looe, and an associate of Godolphin and Ranelagh. He was thus acceptable to the government as well as to the merchants, and, with his knowledge of colonial affairs, proved a useful member of the Board. He could not, however, be considered as adding to its political stature. Nor most certainly could the other appointment which was made before the end of the war. In June 1697, only a few months before peace was signed, the Commission was renewed once more to appoint a substitute for Robert Austen, who had died the previous August. The vacant seat went to Goodwin Wharton.[4] Member of Parliament for East Grinstead since 1679, when he had taken some part in the Exclusion debates, and a close political associate of Sir John Lowther of the Treasury, his record, if taken alone, might suggest that he was one of that group of experienced moderates on whom William always liked to draw for administrative position. But his character scarcely fitted him for executive office. His unpublished diary shows him to have been of an original but eccentric turn of mind, liable to strong bouts of depression which robbed him of any capacity for decision, and which perhaps were

---

[1] He attended the Board for the last time on 10 November (P.R.O.Adm. 3/12: 10/11).

[2] See Appendix VI below.

[3] The following details have been kindly supplied by Dr J. H. Plumb.

[4] See Appendix VI below.

the result of constant ill health.[1] Possibly because of this, he took little part in business, and certainly was of no political importance to the Board. He remained a nominal member, however, for two years; for the Commission of June 1697 lasted throughout the rest of the war and the period of demobilization, until the end of May 1699.

The Board's importance in 1696 and 1697, such as it was, came purely from its head, Edward Russell. These years saw the Admiral at the height of his influence and power. The influence came from the public esteem which he now enjoyed. A popular hero since his stay in the Mediterranean, he was the more firmly established thanks to the marked absence of any rival in either service. The dearth of English generals, when the English command on land was subordinate to the Dutch and the commanders themselves mostly not English, had been shown in the rather unsuccessful attempt to represent the unfortunate Tollemache as a hero after his death in 1694; while at sea, where the public was always more willing to applaud success, with the exception of Barfleur and the Mediterranean campaigns there had been nothing to applaud. All the other Admirals had failed conspicuously, except Shovell in an individual capacity; but he and Rooke, the other successful flag officer of the war, had achieved fame as subordinates, and mostly under Russell. As the only victor of the war at sea, therefore, and fresh from his defensive expedition against the projected French invasion, as yet untouched by the public scandal of his financial dealings, which later provided the main excuse for his impeachment,[2] Russell's position seemed secure; and in April 1697 he was created Baron Shingay, Viscount Barfleur and Earl of Orford.[3]

His political power matched his public influence. The Whig junto was in office, and he was one of its acknowledged leaders. Except for the brief expedition at the beginning of 1696, he did not go to sea again during the war after his return from the Mediterranean, and was therefore able to devote all his time to politics. The one serious attack

[1] I am indebted to Dr J. H. Plumb for this information; see also *H.M.C.* 12th Report, appendix, pt VII, pp. 226, 265; E. R. Wharton, *The Whartons of Wharton Hall* (1898).

[2] The investigation at this stage was still confined to government circles. It had been started by the Treasury at the end of 1695, and continued throughout 1696 (*Cal.Treas.Bks.* XI, *passim*).

[3] *Cal.S.P.Dom. 1697*, p. 125.

upon him, when the Jacobite conspirator Fenwick tried to implicate him with Shrewsbury in the assassination plot, ended by strengthening his position;[1] and for the first time, the navy was represented continuously at the highest level by a figure who himself belonged to the inner group where decisions were taken, and who could use his power to confer importance upon the Board of which he was a member.

This importance was bound to be administrative, for the Commission was not designed to intervene in policy; and at the level of administration, a complementary process was taking place which increased the Admiralty's chances of consolidating its position. From 1695 to the end of the war, the Secretaries of State temporarily lost their control over naval affairs. In May of that year Trenchard, who had not been well for some time, was succeeded by Sir William Trumbull, a governor of the Turkey Company, a former ambassador at Constantinople, and at the time of his appointment a Lord of the Treasury.[2] Trumbull was an unsympathetic and unimportant figure; as the aged Ailesbury said, he was 'but your obedient servant to all', and when he resigned from office in December 1697 it was with the complaint, which could not be denied, that he had been treated by the Lords Justices 'more like a footman than a secretary'.[3] Although officially he conducted naval affairs as his predecessor had done,[4] he was without experience in them, and his supervision of administration was not that of Trenchard, let alone of Nottingham. His successor, James Vernon, was of even less importance. An experienced under-secretary in Shrewsbury's office, he was not of the stuff from which responsible ministers are made;[5] and after the war he took no share in the supervision of the demobilization, which from the nature of the work did not in any case favour

[1] For a glimpse of his political activities at this time, see *Letters Illustrative of the Reign of William III, from 1696 to 1708...by James Vernon*, I (ed. G. P. R. James, 3 vols., 1841), pp. 21, 23–5, 31, 33, 35, 37, 47.

[2] *D.N.B.*; *H.M.C. Downshire*, I, pt I, *passim*.

[3] Quoted in *D.N.B.*

[4] I say 'his predecessor', because Trumbull succeeded Trenchard, and moreover took on his naval business. Nevertheless Trenchard had been secretary for the south, while Trumbull was made secretary for the north. Shrewsbury took the southern department in 1695.

[5] His first reaction on hearing of his appointment was to exclaim, 'the thing I have so long dreaded is fallen upon me' (*Letters...of the Reign of William III...*, I, p. 432).

Secretarial intervention. Shrewsbury himself remained in office until 1698; but his interest in the navy ceased with Russell's return, and he played no part in the direction of administration as a Secretary, and only a minor part in the direction of policy as one of the Lords Justices.

The Lords Justices themselves took over some of the functions which hitherto had been exercised by the Secretaries. This was not strictly their province, for they had been formed to govern the country in the absence of the King abroad; but as the Secretaries, with their administrative powers, lost importance at the higher level of policy, the Lords Justices, who were responsible for policy, encroached upon administration. The line between the two functions was too vague for the authority which exercised the one not to exercise the other in some degree. The letter books of the Admiralty over these years, and particularly over 1696 and 1697, accordingly show an increasingly detailed correspondence with the Lords Justices as the quantity and the importance of its correspondence with Trumbull decreases.[1] Nevertheless, the exchange of capable for weak Secretaries was not entirely balanced by the intervention of their superiors; and thus, at the time when the department was benefiting from the status of its head, it found itself to some extent in a position to act upon its advantage. In 1696, it began to submit memoranda and to initiate correspondence on administrative reforms without waiting to be asked, and on several occasions even requested audiences with the Lords Justices,[2] much to their annoyance. 'It were better', wrote one of them, 'if the Admiralty went back to the former ways'; and another, correctly enough, saw the increased activity of the Board as merely a reflection of Russell's importance.[3] Little enough came of these moves; but, at least in retrospect, the Admiralty seems to some extent to have justified its existence in the last two years of the war, as it had not done over the previous three years.

At the higher level of policy, these years were marked by William's personal supervision of naval strategy. He had by now become accustomed to the detail of naval affairs, and, thanks to the

---

[1] See P.R.O.Adm. 1/4084–6, *passim*.

[2] E.g. P.R.O.Adm. 3/12: 12/4, 25/5, 18/7; 3/13: 14/11, 27/2, 14/4.

[3] P.R.O.Adm. 1/4084, ff. 17, 158.

correspondence over the middle years of the war on the Mediterranean ventures, the authorities in London had become accustomed to refer such affairs regularly to him. Whereas from 1689 to 1692 there is no sign of his interest in the fleet, and from 1692 to 1695 his interest is concentrated entirely on the Mediterranean, in 1696 and 1697 there is abundant evidence of his concern over the progress of all naval operations.[1] In the last year of the war, indeed, scarcely a decision was taken without his consent, and although policy was debated and sometimes initiated by the Lords Justices, action awaited approval from Holland or Flanders. The explanation for this would seem to lie partly in the fact that in the closing years of the war the King, increasingly contemptuous of his ministers in England, took upon himself the conduct of affairs in every sphere, and found himself, almost by habit, saddled increasingly with detail; and partly in the growing gap between his determination to retain the offensive and the administrative ability of the government to support his plans. He had every incentive to inquire into detail, at a time when he was becoming accustomed to such inquiry.

In 1696, William's naval correspondence centred upon his desire for combined land and sea operations against the French coast.[2] In June, when Berkeley suggested his attack upon Camaret Bay, the King urged the Lords Justices to turn this into a joint attack on Brest; and when the Admiralty's inconclusive report upon policy was sent him, he expressed the strongest dissatisfaction with it.[3] For the first time, he began seriously to consider the administrative implications of a frontal assault upon France, which in earlier years he had left to his advisers;[4] and when in August it became clear that nothing was to be expected from the campaign, he wrote to the Lords Justices to lay plans for a descent in 1697.[5] But before the time came for such an attempt, his attention had been diverted further afield.

For in 1697 the emphasis on the protection of commerce, which had largely deprived the fleet of its strength in the previous year, was

---

1 P.R.O.Adm. 1/4084–6, *passim*; B.M.Addnl. 37992, ff. 180–97.

2 B.M.Addnl. 37992, ff. 140*v*, 141–2, 163.

3 Ibid. ff. 164, 166; P.R.O.Adm. 1/4083, f. 1166.

4 B.M.Addnl. 37992, ff. 145*v*, 169–170*v*.

5 Ibid. ff. 176–7.

increased at the expense of any fleet action whatsoever. But the form which it took was not that of 1695 and 1696, when the western Channel was the main scene of interest. In the last year of the war, and for the first time, attention was fixed primarily upon America.

Nothing has been said in this work of the operations in the colonies, for until this time they had no direct bearing upon administration, and their course did not impinge seriously upon the course of naval policy. Both sides, however, had been sending contingents of varying strengths to America and the West Indies since 1689.[1] The English expeditions were characterized by a number of well-defined, recurring and distressing symptoms: by a lack of co-operation between army and navy, an intense antagonism between them and the local officials, a heavy death-roll and a decay in the hulls of the ships. All four were to be seen in the first venture under Captain Lawrence Wright, which was set on foot in May 1689, was finally ready only in March 1690, and, after undertaking some combined operations against the French possessions in the West Indies, the most successful of which resulted in the recapture of St Kitts, came to a dismal end later that year, when the ships returned to England sadly short of men and in some cases riddled with worm. No squadron left for the West Indies or America after that until, in the autumn of 1692, Wheeler was sent to attack the French islands with a larger force of eight ships of the line, four smaller men-of-war, three fireships and three auxiliaries, and with 1500 troops aboard. Great hopes were entertained of his success. But these were brought to nothing by a series of quarrels with the local authorities and the army; and in June 1693, when the rains made operations impossible in the West Indies, the ships sailed for New England, whence Wheeler hoped to stage a combined land and sea attack upon the French in Canada. Here again, however, the local preparations proved unequal to the task, and early the next year the squadron returned home, once more with a heavy list of sick and dead and with no achievement to its credit. Another, smaller expedition to the West Indies in 1695

[1] The following details are taken from Burchett, pp. 110–27, 168–75, 305–21, 350, 354–85, 397; W. T. Morgan, 'The British West Indies during King William's War', in *Journal of Modern History*, II, no. 3 (University of Chicago), pp. 378–409; and G. H. Guttridge, *The Colonial Policy of William III in America and the West Indies* (1922), pp. 47–84.

reproduced the main features of 1693, and the next year the only step taken to guard the colonies was to send a few ships under Captain Norris to Newfoundland, which the French had occupied earlier in the war. This expedition was successful, and indeed represented the one concrete achievement by the English in the sporadic naval warfare across the Atlantic. But in the autumn of 1697 the French recaptured the forts and overran the colony, so that even here little had been gained.

All these expeditions, however important to the colonies themselves, had been incidental to the main campaigns. In the winter of 1696, however, news was received of a different kind of French expedition to the area. Early in December it was learnt that de Pointis, one of the more energetic of the French commanders, was being sent, with the financial backing of the French West Indies merchants, to interrupt and if possible destroy the Spanish West Indian trade.[1] This closely affected English interests, for English merchants had a substantial connexion with the *flota*, and it was therefore decided to concentrate the main effort in the spring upon preventing Pointis from achieving his object. Rear Admiral Neville, who had sailed for the Mediterranean with fifteen allied men-of-war and a convoy bound for the Levant, was ordered to rendezvous with a strong squadron sent out to Madeira under Captain Meese, and then to sail in pursuit of the French. In the middle of April 1697 the English forces met, and early in May they reached Antigua. Soon, however, they heard that Pointis was besieging the rich city of Cartagena, and they sailed accordingly in that direction. But before they arrived, the city with its plunder had fallen to the French, and after a long chase, in which he sighted but did not catch the enemy, Neville returned to the Spanish possessions, which were now being plundered by buccaneers. The squadron then cruised unsuccessfully about the West Indies. Meese died of the fever, and the death-roll rose and supplies fell with the usual rapidity while Neville waited for

---

[1] De Pointis's description of the preparations for and the course of the expedition is contained in his *Account of the Expedition to Cartagena in the Year 1697*, which was soon translated into English. The financial arrangements for his expedition form an interesting illustration of the relations between the import traders and the government in France.

the disorganized *flota*, which he proposed to escort across the Atlantic. But even here he was disappointed, for its commander, with the suspicion which the Spaniards always displayed towards their allies, refused to accompany him. The English therefore retired in June to Virginia, to re-store in preparation for the voyage home. Before they left Neville himself died, and it was a dispirited and fever-stricken squadron that returned to England in the autumn.

Meanwhile, only small squadrons had been cruising in home waters. With the main French fleet laid up, Russell in the previous winter had urged that the English should follow suit;[1] and only a few of the three-deckers put to sea in the summer.[2] Throughout June and July nothing of note occurred; but towards the end of that month the news of Pointis's departure from the West Indies reached England, and hopes ran high that he, with his booty and his prizes, would be intercepted before he reached France. Dispositions were made accordingly, and in mid-August a small squadron of cruisers managed to sight the French in the western approaches; but after a three days' chase the enemy safely reached Brest, and the summer came to a depressing and inconclusive end.

This last failure was not only annoying but serious, in view of the diplomatic position at the time. Since the winter of 1696, Dykvelt had been in touch, on behalf of William, with the French envoy de Callières; and in December the Earl of Pembroke, Viscount Villiers and Sir Joseph Williamson had been appointed as English plenipotentiaries in the peace negotiations.[3] In May 1697, the prospects of a treaty were advanced by secret talks between Portland and Marshal Boufflers, which continued until July; and by the end of that month, the remaining differences had narrowed to matters affecting the New World. The French successes since 1689 in Hudson Bay and Newfoundland had alarmed the commercial interests in England, and on their behalf Pembroke and his colleagues, through the intelligent medium of Matthew Prior, drafted two articles (the fourth and seventh) to the treaty, by which injuries were to be redressed and territorial captures restored. These, however, bedevilled the negotiations throughout the autumn of

[1] P.R.O.Adm. 3/13: 7/11, 28/12, 14/1. [2] P.R.O.Adm. 8/5, 1 June, 1 July.
[3] Davenport, *European Treaties*..., II, p. 355.

1697.[1] In such a situation, as always, the arguments were affected by the progress of events; and it was therefore with dismay that William learned of the failure to injure Pointis on the voyage home. His position was further threatened by the news, in the same month, that the French had finally taken Barcelona, after an urgent but fruitless appeal by the king of Spain for an English squadron. In these circumstances, William was determined to conclude a treaty before worse befell. He conceded the forts of Hudson Bay to the French, and on 21 September 1697 England, Holland, Spain and France signed the treaty at Ryswick. On 2 November, the Emperor added his signature, and Europe was again at peace.

The terms of the treaty made no mention of the naval or military relations between the powers concerned. Its intention, as befitted an instrument which proclaimed a truce between equals, was to restore the *status quo ante bellum*, and a definition of armed power was inappropriate—even if it had not been abnormal—under the circumstances. Navigation and commerce were declared free,[2] and possessions, with the exception of the Hudson Bay forts and the Newfoundland forts apart from Albany, were returned to their original owners of 1688.[3] As a reflection of an unsettled dispute, the treaty indeed promised little but another war.

The demobilization at the end of the war was a very different affair from the mobilization of almost ten years before. Where a considerable effort was needed to raise the navy from a state of peace to one of war, little effort was required to restore it to its original state. To contemporaries, the transition in 1698 seemed desirable and indeed necessary owing to the large scale and high expenditure of the war; and since both the government and the country were anxious to return to the small cost of a peacetime department, and were confronted by few technical difficulties, within a few months of the end of the war the navy was completely at peace.

The desire to cut down expenditure was shown as soon as Parliament assembled in the winter. By the middle of December 1697, the scale of the

[1] Davenport, *European Treaties*..., II, pp. 355–7; L. G. Wickham Legg, *Matthew Prior* (1921), ch. III.

[2] See article 4.

[3] See articles 7 and 8.

fleet had been settled for the next year at 10,000 men, with the old rate of expenditure of £4 per man per month.[1] The naval debt had already been met to the Commons' satisfaction, with the provision of £1,100,117 as a particular supply,[2] and when the occasion arose in March 1698 to vote on the annual estimates members were in parsimonious mood. The first object of attack, as was to be expected, was the register; but its continuation was finally assured by a good majority,[3] and the debate turned upon the Admiralty's programme for repairing and augmenting the fleet. The Administration had asked that £150,000 be set aside specifically for this purpose; but the Commons, after prolonged discussion, decided to include such expenditure in the normal provision for the ordinary,[4] and followed this up by flagrantly disregarding the problem with a vote of £15,000 for shipyards and dockyards and £5000 for the 'ordinary repair of ships'.[5] The details of the supply, indeed, are of interest as an example of the way in which the difficulties of demobilization were ignored by a system which still, despite the lessons of the war, preferred to distinguish between the 'ordinary' and 'extraordinary' activities of the navy:[6]

	£
Salaries	24,000
Half pay to commanders	28,000
Payment of officers and men aboard ships in harbour	43,000
Victuals for same	19,000
Pensions	9,000
Register and Greenwich Hospital	37,000
Yards, docks, etc.	15,000
Ordinary repair of ships	5,000
Moorings	5,000
Expenses of musters	1,300
Two Marine Regiments	55,000
Ordnance Office	60,000*

* A sum of £99,000 had been proposed originally for the ordnance, but this was reduced to £60,000 (*Cal.S.P.Dom. 1698*, p. 134).

The lesson that retrenchment itself cost money had still to be learnt. As a result, the department had to meet the distinctive demands of the demobilization with funds designed to meet the debt of the war and the small-scale activities of a normal year of peace. Although in some

---

1 *H.C.J.* XII, pp. 13, 17.
2 *H.C.J.* XI, p. 573.
3 *Cal.S.P.Dom. 1698*, p. 129.
4 Ibid. p. 134.
5 *H.C.J.* XII, p. 152.
6 Ibid.

cases, as in the payment of back-wages before the men could be discharged, or in the payment of those who were retained to supervise the repair of the ships, the problem was covered by existing supplies, in most cases it was not; and it was moreover exacerbated, as usual, by the fact that the issues from the Exchequer did not equal the theoretical grants from the Commons. Of the £1,361,417 voted for the financial year 1698, only £922,991 was received by the Treasurer of the Navy.[1] It was not surprising that throughout the first six months of 1698 the Administration was constantly complaining of penury.

Both Admiralty and Navy Board were particularly annoyed by the reductions imposed upon their staffs. At a time when each office was faced with an increase in clerical work in order to reduce the rest of the naval organization, the allowance for salaries was cut by a third, from £36,000 to £24,000. The office staffs had naturally grown over the past nine years. The development of the Admiralty has already been observed. A similar, though less marked growth had taken place in the Navy Office, the Victualling Office and the office of the Commissioners for Sick and Wounded. The first of these had eight more clerks than in 1689, including those in the office of the Treasurer of the Navy; and the third, which had been refounded at the beginning of the war, now had a chief clerk and four subordinates.[2] The question arose, therefore, of how best to distribute the inevitable cuts.

The problem seems to have been shelved for some time, for it was not until July 1698 that the Admiralty issued its first instructions.[3] They provided for a return in each case to the establishment of 1691—a significant illustration of the dividing line between the early and the middle stages of the war. Some exceptions were made for the Admiralty office itself, which required more clerks, watchmen and messengers in its new building in Whitehall than had been necessary in the house in Duke Street. The subordinate offices, however, suffered severely; and they were not slow to complain that the cuts affected them unfairly.[4] The

[1] Compared with £2,789,157 received by him during the financial year 1697 (*H.C.J.* XII, p. 381).

[2] Admty:Corbett, XIV, ff. 73–5; XVII, f. 111; P.R.O. T. 38/615, payments for sick and wounded.

[3] P.R.O.Adm. 3/14: 14/7.

[4] P.R.O.Adm. 1/3584, ff. 17, 35; 106/2349, f. 781.

Admiralty in reply pointed out that it had reduced the staff of the Provost Marshal and had dismissed three of its clerks,[1] and that Bridgeman's retirement in June was a severe retrenchment. But it could not convince the Navy Board that the burden of the cuts had been equally distributed, and by the end of the month the two bodies were busily engaged in recrimination.[2] The Navy Board, indeed, went so far as to ask the Admiralty why, in its anxiety for retrenchment, the Commissioners' salaries had not been reduced; and at this point relations became so strained that the junior Board was forbidden to attend the senior until it thought fit to apologize.[3] It was not until December 1698 that the two bodies met again;[4] but in the meantime each had made its cuts along the original lines, and by the end of the year they had between them saved some £7867.[5]

The Commission for Sick and Wounded had come to an end on 30 June 1698, and such of its work as remained was handed over to the Commissioners of the register.[6] At the same time, the latter were ordered to reduce their staff from nine clerks to six.[7] This order fell hard upon them, for the medical branch was one of the few naval activities which was not severely retrenched at the end of the war. Greenwich Hospital was already growing, and the work on the new buildings was not checked by the change from war to peace; while the hospital at Plymouth, which had been founded in 1689, was established on a permanent footing in 1698.[8] The register itself, moreover, after the favourable debate in the Commons, was confirmed as an integral part of the naval administration, and in April its Commissioners were authorized to prosecute those who failed to subscribe their sixpences in return for receiving its privileges.[9] With the extra work, therefore, it seemed impossible for them to reduce their staff. Until September they

---

1 P.R.O.Adm. 2/179, ff. 4–5; 3/14: 28/3.

2 P.R.O.Adm. 1/3584, ff. 40–2; 2/395, f. 92.

3 P.R.O.Adm. 2/395, f. 123; 3/14: 3/8.

4 P.R.O.Adm. 3/14, *passim*.

5 P.R.O.Adm. 1/3584, f. 1101.

6 Ibid. f. 167. In May, there had been a proposal that the office of Chirurgeon General should be restored; but nothing came of this plan (P.R.O.Adm. 3/14: 17/5).

7 P.R.O.Adm. 2/179, f. 56.

8 I am indebted to Commander Merriman for this information.

9 P.R.O.Adm. 3/14: 18/4.

were able to procrastinate, but in the middle of that month the Admiralty ordered them to dismiss three of their clerks forthwith.[1] The order was duly carried out, but only to the accompaniment of a series of petitions which were strongly backed by a not altogether disinterested Navy Board, and in the event the Commissioners were allowed to engage three more clerks at the end of the year.[2]

The remainder of the £12,000, amounting to some £4000, had thus to be saved by the Victuallers, and as early as 12 November 1697 they were ordered by the Treasury to discharge their unnecessary workmen to the tune of £3000.[3] A fortnight later, their commitments were defined for the coming year by a declaration for 10,000 men.[4] But in the event this proved insufficient to meet the case,[5] and although their responsibilities were reduced by half, the Commissioners still found that they could not operate satisfactorily on the money allowed them. Their difficulties, of course, were exacerbated by their indebtedness; and although they did their best to meet their numerous and importunate creditors,[6] by February 1698 the combination of a heavy deficit and a disorderly demobilization had brought them to their familiar state. At the beginning of that month they began a series of demands for cash which continued until the middle of the year,[7] and which were only partly satisfied by issues from the Exchequer. The trouble, as usual, lay in the nature of the funds on which payment was made, for although a total of £732,227 was issued, it was mostly upon the credit of an unreliable salt tax,[8] and their requests for a better fund were ignored. By starving the current service, the Commissioners succeeded by mid-summer in reducing the debts; but the effort exhausted them to such an extent that the Mediterranean squadron which had been designed to leave England in the summer, was still in port in August without the twelve months' victuals with which it should have been supplied.[9] It

1 P.R.O.Adm. 2/179, f. 98.

2 P.R.O.Adm. 1/3585, f. 27.

3 *Cal.Treas.Bks. October 1697–August 1698*, p. 152.

4 P.R.O.Adm. 3/14: 27/11.

5 P.R.O.Adm. 3/14: 10/3.

6 See *Cal.Treas.Bks. October 1697–August 1698*, and P.R.O.Adm. 3/14, *passim*.

7 *Cal.Treas.Bks. October 1697–August 1698*, pp. 236, 296; P.R.O.Adm. 3/14: 10/3, 14/3, 14/4, 6/6; *Cal.S.P.Dom. 1698*, pp. 31–2.

8 *Cal.Treas.Bks. October 1697–August 1698*, p. 296.

9 *Cal.S.P.Dom. 1698*, p. 371.

was in such circumstances, when more and not less clerical control was required, that the office was ordered to reduce its staff. Unfortunately, in the absence of its records, it is impossible to say how far it did so.

It may be seen from this brief account of the Victuallers' difficulties that the demobilization did not affect all departments of the naval organization equally or in the same way. Ships, dockyards, stores, food and men, each presented their own problems. The men themselves, and their officers, were quickly reduced. In December 1697 there were 184 units of the fleet in sea pay with a complement of 35,395 men; three months later these had been reduced to 145 ships, with a complement of 19,734 men.[1] Even allowing for the fact that in many cases the returns were grossly inaccurate, and that many skilled men who had been reported as discharged, were retained by their captains to help lay up the ships,[2] this was a marked and rapid reduction. As was to be expected, it occurred rather than was planned. With a debt for wages amounting to some £1,863,000, of which the back pay to seamen probably consumed two-thirds, and with a grant of some £1,100,000 to cover the total debt of the navy, it was obvious that orderly payment, and therefore orderly demobilization, was going to prove almost impossible. As early as October 1697, the Admiralty was trying to collect a reserve of cash with which to satisfy the men when the time came,[3] but the contingent financial difficulties upset the scheme. Even at the beginning of 1699, only £1,346,323 had been paid of the total owed for wages before 1 January 1698,[4] and the correspondence and minutes of Admiralty and Navy Board bear ample witness to the resulting confusion.[5] Men were turned off the ships, where at least they were housed, fed and partly clothed, with only tickets of credit, which might be sold at a discount of some 40%, between them and starvation. It is not surprising that often they refused to go, or that some kind-hearted captains declined to turn them ashore. While many of the men were petitioning against the delay in their discharge, on the grounds

[1] B.M. Stowe, 478, f. 2.

[2] The Admiralty was so flooded by petitions from seamen retained in this way, that in April the Board refused to accept any more until it gave notice that it would do so (P.R.O.Adm. 3/14: 4/4).

[3] *Cal. Treas. Bks. October 1697–August 1698*, p. 117.

[4] *H.C.J.* XII, p. 381.

[5] See particularly P.R.O.Adm. 1/3584 and 3/14.

that they had been separated from their families or abducted from their business for some years, others, who had nowhere to go, clung to their one form of security.[1] Others again, who were glad enough to be free of the navy but who also wanted to be paid, formed bands and marched upon the Navy Office.[2] In February and March the situation looked quite ugly;[3] but the men lacked cohesion, and fortunately some found a billet in the overseas trades which expanded so rapidly during 1698. Nevertheless, the country was treated to the sight of some thousands of discharged seamen wandering from parish to parish in search of food and a job. The years between the wars of William and Anne are remembered largely for the increase of vagabondage which followed on the demobilization of the army; on a smaller scale, the navy was also responsible for contributing to the vagrant population of the country.

The officers were treated better than the men, possibly because the figures concerned were smaller. The provision of £28,000 for half pay in the grant for the ordinary was generous, and those officers who were continued aboard the ships in harbour were moreover confirmed in full sea pay for twelve months from the end of the war, and not placed at once on rigging wages.[4] Although the practice of allowing the full scale of payment, while vessels were laid up, had been established in the course of the war,[5] the Admiralty could well have made a case for returning to the reduced scale once hostilities had ceased, and under the circumstances it is of interest that they declined to do so.

In the dockyards, naturally, the effect of the demobilization was soon felt, but less violently than in the fleet. Within a fortnight of the treaty having been ratified, the numbers of workmen had fallen from some 4200 to some 3400.[6] But it was principally the shipwrights and the allied crafts who were discharged,[7] for the riggers and workmen of that type were still required to dismantle the masts and rigging before the ships were put into ordinary. Once the numbers had fallen to about 3300 they remained steady, and indeed in the course of the following year,

---

1 P.R.O. Adm. 3/14: 22/3, 25/3.

2 P.R.O. Adm. 1/3584, ff. 453, 621–3.

3 P.R.O. Adm. 3/14: 7/2, 4/3.

4 Ibid. 31/3.

5 See p. 458 above.

6 Serg.MS. A 123; see Appendix V (A), (B) below.

7 See Appendix V (C) below.

as the repairs to the fleet got under way, they began once more slightly to rise.[1] The dockyard organization, in fact, had now reached the stage where its efficient operation, even with a fleet in ordinary, demanded such numbers; and whereas in 1687 and 1688 the navy had employed some 1800 to 1900 men in the royal yards, after 1698 it seldom employed less than 3500, and never again less than 3000.[2] This scale of organization demanded continuous supervision, and the numbers of the dockyard officers, unlike those of the fleet, were accordingly not reduced. The dockyard service had gone a long way, during the nine years of William's reign, towards acquiring that permanent character which a decade before had still been in process of formation. There was, indeed, plenty of work for the yards. The signing of the peace did not stop building which had already begun, and at first the numbers of ships continued to rise. Within six months of the peace treaty being signed, one second rate, one third, six fourths and two fifths were added to the fleet, and another six ships of the line were on the stocks.[3] Within the same time, however, the navy sold eight of the smaller rates, and a number of fireships, bombvessels and auxiliaries;[4] and as the last of the war construction appeared, the department made preparations to sell or to break up many of the smaller and older units. By the end of 1698 the size of the fleet had been well reduced. The final numbers were as shown on p. 620.[5] The reductions in the rated classes were wise, for they affected mostly the older ships, or those which had proved unsatisfactory over recent years. The force of 266 ships was a well-balanced fleet with which to face the possibility of another war; and it was with substantially those numbers that the navy began the war of Queen Anne.[6]

Besides continuing with the new ships, the navy was faced with the task of repairing the veterans of the war. The campaign of 1697 had

---

1 The totals were 3301 in January; 3329 in April; 3501 in September; and 3516 in December (Serg.MS. A 123). 2 Serg.MS. A 123, 1698–1702, *passim*; 1715–17, *passim*.

3 B.M. Stowe 478, f. 2*v*. The ships launched were the *Triumph, Somerset, Dartmouth, Hampshire, Winchester, Salisbury, Carlisle, Worcester, Hastings*, and *Bridgewater*.

4 Ibid. f. 3.

5 Derrick, *Memoirs of the Rise and Progress of the Royal Navy*, pp. 111–14.

6 In the interval, one first and two third rates were added, and two fourth rates, four fifths and three sixths were broken up or sold (ibid. p. 116).

	November 1697	November 1698
First rates	6	6
Second rates	13	14
Third rates	43	45
Fourth rates	56	64
Fifth rates	42	34
Sixth rates	40	18
	200	181
Fireships	17	10
Bombvessels	19	13
Ketches	2	2
Smacks	5	2
Yachts	18	13
Advice boats	5	4
Brigantines	9	7
Towboats	2	2
Machine vessels	14	—
Pinks	2	1
Storeships	5	4
Hoys	14	16
Hulks	11	11
Total	323	266

shown the necessity for thoroughly overhauling the fleet, some of whose units had not been refitted or repaired for three or even four years. In January 1698 the Admiralty began to consider a repair programme, to cover by well-defined stages the whole of the line; and in March it arrived at a figure of £150,000 for the cost of the work.[1] When the debate began in the Commons upon the ordinary for the year, the government spokesmen attempted to get a separate provision for this purpose, on the lines of the extraordinary grant for the 27 ships of 1691.[2] But the times were not right for such a proposal, and in the end, as has been seen, only £20,000 was allowed.[3] This was a bitter blow for the Administration, particularly as it had intended to divide the programme equally between the royal yards and the merchant shipyards, and had therefore hoped for a special fund with a credit which might prove satisfactory to the shipbuilding fraternity.[4] Throughout 1698, the Admiralty continued to solicit for the money, while the Navy Board distributed the work as best it could among the dockyards and those merchant yards which would accept a delay in payment.[5] The eventual course of the repairs has not been followed, for it covered

[1] P.R.O.Adm. 3/14: 7/1, 3/3. [2] *Cal.S.P.Dom. 1698*, p. 129.
[3] See p. 613 above. [4] P.R.O.Adm. 3/14: 17/3.
[5] P.R.O.Adm. 3/14, Serg.Mins. XXXIX, *passim*.

the years between the wars; but at least in its early stages the programme fell mainly upon the royal yards, the numbers of whose workmen were affected accordingly.

In the meantime, the Admiralty had to distribute the ships among the ports, and to issue instructions for their maintenance and safety. The second task was begun at the end of 1697, and in the following spring the orders went out to the local authorities.[1] For the most part they repeated the earlier orders which had been promulgated for the same purpose by James II in 1686, with suitable modifications of those which had been proved unsatisfactory in the interval. Thus, a greater emphasis was placed upon the necessity for ventilating both ships and stores, to avoid the effects of dry rot and mildew, and for supervising the conduct of ships' caretakers and guardboats, which in June were placed upon a regular dockyard establishment. The orders also dealt in some detail with the precautions to be taken against sabotage or attack; and in this they reflected an attitude which was also to be seen in the final disposition of the fleet.

This disposition was made by May 1698. A summer guard of thirty ships was retained for the Channel, two small squadrons were designed for the Mediterranean and the North Sea, and a few units, as usual, for the West Indies. Otherwise, the fleet was put into ordinary in the five major ports, with the ships of the line allotted as follows:[2]

	First rates	Second rates	Third rates	Fourth rates
Chatham	4	8	7	5
Woolwich	—	—	2	6
Deptford	—	—	1	4
Portsmouth	2	3	6	8
Plymouth	—		2	8

These figures were not decided without some consideration of future strategy.[3] The French threat was not over, and the Admiralty did not pretend to think that it was. It was with reluctance that it agreed to reduce the facilities at Kinsale;[4] and one indication of its views may be seen in the efforts which it made, at the height of the demobilization,

[1] They are contained in P.R.O.Adm. 49/137, no. 6; see also P.R.O.Adm. 106/2507, no. 47.

[2] P.R.O.Adm. 8/5, 1/11/97; 8/6, 1/8/98. These lists do not account for all the ships mentioned in Derrick, loc. cit.; but I have been unable to trace the rest.

[3] P.R.O.Adm. 3/14: 14/5.

[4] Ibid. 31/3, 9/5.

to establish a small naval base at Dover, on the basis of that set up during the war at Deal.[1] As early as February 1698, the government was worried by the reports of French naval preparations which continued throughout the spring,[2] and in May the Admiralty was once more sending scouts to lie off Brest and Dunkirk.[3] The navy and the country were faced with a truce rather than with peace; and when the orders were issued for a fresh mobilization in January 1701, the Administration was not entirely unprepared. The history of the intervening years is not our concern, for they may be regarded rather as a prologue to the war of Queen Anne than as an epilogue to the war of King William. But it is an interesting history, and one which remains to be written, if only to point the comparison between the conditions of 1688 and those of 1700. For in the ensuing mobilization, as in the conduct of the war itself, the lessons of the past emerged; and the naval Administration of Queen Anne found itself able to rely to a considerable extent upon the strength and the experience which had been provided for it, in the numbers and composition of the fleet, in the equipment and disposition of its bases, and in the relations established with the merchant and financial interests of the country, by its sorely tried predecessors during the first and more hazardous of the two great wars with France.

---

[1] P.R.O.Adm. 3/14: 25/4.

[2] *Cal.S.P.Dom. 1698*, pp. 78, 83, 139, 198, 241; see also P.R.O.Adm. 1/4086, *passim*.

[3] P.R.O.Adm. 3/14: 6/5.

APPENDICES

Material and finance

I The English fleet in December 1688

(A) Numbers and composition

(B) Dimensions of ships, with their guns and men

(C) Age of the fleet

(D) Length of life of ships (rated ships and fireships only)

(E) Where built

II Ships added to the navy, 1689–1698

III Details of the 27 ships built by order of Parliament, 1691–1698

IV Naval debt, 1688–1697

V Numbers of workmen in the royal dockyards, 1687–1698

(A) Total numbers

(B) Numbers in each dockyard

(C) Total numbers of shipwrights and riggers

Lists of office-holders and officers

VI Lords Commissioners of the Admiralty, 1689–1697

VII Secretaries of the Admiralty, 1689–1698

VIII Principal Officers and Commissioners of the Navy, 1686–1698

IX Commissioners of Victualling, 1688–1698

X Flag officers and commanders of squadrons and stations, 1688–1697

Documents and lists concerning the Admiralty

XI Letters Patent appointing the Lords Commissioners of the Admiralty, 8 March 1689

XII An Act concerning the Commissioners of the Admiralty, 2 Will. and Mary, sess. 2, c. 2

XIII The memorandum of Phineas Bowles on the duties of the Secretary of the Admiralty

XIV The Establishment of the Admiralty Office

APPENDIX I

THE ENGLISH FLEET IN DECEMBER 1688

A. *Numbers and composition*

There are different, and superficially contradictory lists of the English fleet at the time of the Revolution. Those of the primary and the most important secondary authorities are given below.

Authorities: (*a*) *Catal.* I, pp. 302–3
(*b*) Pepys, *Memoires*, pp. 178–207
(*c*) Serg.MS. A 115
(*d*) Charnock, *Marine Architecture*, II, p. 432
(*e*) Charnock, loc. cit. pp. 426–31
(*f*) Derrick, *Rise and Progress of the Royal Navy*, p. 106

	(*a*)	(*b*), (*d*), (*f*)	(*c*)	(*e*)
First rates	9	9	9	9
Second rates	11	11	11	11
Third rates	39	39	39	39
Fourth rates	41	41	41	36[3]
Fifth rates	2	2	2	8[4]
Sixth rates	6	6	6	7[5]
Bombvessels	3	3	3	3
Fireships	26	26	26	17[6]
Yachts	14	14	14	14
Ketches	3	3	3	3
Smacks	4	5	5	5
Pontoon	1	—	—	—
Towboat	1	—	—	—
Hoys	6	6	6	6
Hulks	7	8	9[2]	8
Total	173	173[1]	174	166

[1] The total printed in (*d*) is 174, but this is a misprint. The details are as in (*b*) and (*f*).

[2] The extra hulk given is the *Alphen*, actually sold in 1687 (*Soc. Naut. Research, Occas. Publns*, no. 5, pt I, no. 560).

[3] The *Tiger Prize*, *Sweepstakes*, *Reserve* and *Woolwich* are given on p. 431 as 'Names given by Secretary Pepys, but omitted in the preceding list'. The *Sedgemoor* is also not given, but in this case is not mentioned, presumably because she had not yet joined the fleet.

[4] Six of these ships are given as fireships by the other lists (*Dartmouth*, *Garland*, *Guernsey*, *Mermaid*, *Richmond*, *Swan*). Four of them were built and one bought as fifth rates, and later converted.

[5] One ship (*Sally Rose*) given as a fireship (*Rose*) in the other lists.

[6] These seventeen ships were all built, bought or captured for use as fireships, unlike those in note 4 above. Three fireships are not included which are given in the other lists (*Pearl*, which is included among the fourth rates, *Half Moon* and *Richard and John*). But, in view of the seven fireships given as fifth and sixth rates, the total differs by only one from the 26 given in the other lists. The discrepancy is that the *Swan* is given twice, once as a sixth rate and again as a fireship.

B. *Dimensions of ships, with their guns and men*[1]

Built as:	Length *a*, on gundeck *b*, of keel ft. in.	Beam[2] extreme ft. in.	Draught at deepest point ft. in.	Tonnage[3] (largest ship) (smallest ship)	Guns	Men	Average tonnage of rest of class
First rate	167 5 (*a*)	47 4	20 0	1708 (*Britannia*)	100	780	1392 (6)[4]
	162 6 (*a*)	42 6	21 0	1229 (*St George*)	96	710	
Second rate	163 11 (*a*)	45 0	21 0	1377 (*Neptune*)	90	660	1314 (9)
	153 1 (*a*)	39 8	20 0	1003 (*Royal Katherine*)	82	540	
Third rate	157 6 (*a*)	40 6	18 8	1107 (*Royal Oak*)	74	470	924 (36)
	141 5 (*a*)	33 4	17 0	662 (*Dunkirk*)	60	340	
Fourth rate	138 3 (*a*)	35 7	16 4	741 (*Woolwich*)	54	280	546 (35)
	90 0 (*b*)	28 2	12 8	379 (*Constant Warwick*)	42	180	
Fifth rate	89 0 (*b*)	27 0	13 2	346 (*Sapphire*)	32	135	Only two ships in rate
	75 0 (*b*)	24 0	12 6	229 (*Rose*)	28	125	
Sixth rate	74 0 (*b*)	22 6	9 0	199 (*Lark*)	18	85	Only two ships in rate
	85 0 (*b*)	18 0	9 0	146 (*Drake*)	16	75	
Bombvessel	85 9 (*a*)	27 0	11 6	279 (*Firedrake*)	12 (+2 mortars)	50	Only three ships in rate
	64 4 (*a*)	21 6	9 3	134 (*Salamander*)	10	35	
Fireship	Ranging from 370 to 79 tons (ten converted from fifth and sixth rates; thirteen bought)						

[1] The dimensions of the largest and smallest men-of-war are given. The numbers of guns and men are those settled by Establishment.

[2] The beam is measured to the outside of the planking.

[3] The formula of measurement used is: K×B×B/2÷94, the beam being taken to the outside of the planking. For the measurement of K (the keel) see *Soc. Naut. Research, Occas. Publns*, no. 5, pt I, p. 19.

[4] The figures in brackets show numbers of ships selected as representatives from each class.

Authority: Soc. Naut. Research, Occas. Publns, no. 5, pts I, V, *passim*

C. *Age of the fleet*[1]

Built in:[2]	1688	1687	1686–3	1682–79	1678–69	1668–59	1658–49	1648–39	1638–	Totals
First rates	—	—	1	1	6	1	—	—	—	9
Second rates	—	—	2	5	2	2	—	—	—	11
Third rates	—	—	—	15	9	7	8	—	—	39
Fourth rates	—	4	—	2	6[3]	5[6]	20	2	—	39
Fifth rates	—	—	—	—	1	—	—	—	—	1
Sixth rates	—	—	—	—	3[4]	1	1	—	—	5
Bombvessels	1	1	—	—	1[5]	—	—	—	—	3
Fireships	—	—	—	—	1	—	7	—	—	8
Yachts	—	—	1	2	8	3	—	—	—	14
Ketches	—	—	—	—	—	1	—	—	—	1
Smacks	—	—	—	—	3	—	—	—	—	3
Hoys	—	—	2	—	2	1	1	—	—	6
Hulks[7]	—	—	—	1	1	1[8]	—	—	1[9]	4
Bought	12 fireships	—	1 4th, 1 ketch	—	1 5th, 2 fireships 1 ketch	1 smack	—	—	—	19
Prizes	—	—	1 6th, 3 fireships 1 hulk	1 fireship	1 4th, 2 hulks	1 hulk	—	—	—	10
Total	13	5	13	27	50	24	37	2	1	172[10]

[1] Ships are given according to classification of December 1688. Where they were built under different rate or class, this is shown. Those built before 1659 were classed by gun-power alone, and have been given later rating.

[2] Charnock, *Marine Architecture*, II, is very inaccurate for dates. Pepys's list in *Catal.* I, p. 222, does not include rebuildings, which are taken here as the date of construction.

[3] One built as a fifth rate.

[4] One built as a fifth rate.

[5] Built as a yacht.

[6] Three built as fifth rates.

[7] A pontoon is included in the hulks.

[8] Built as a third rate, later made a second rate, wrecked in 1672 and then converted to a hulk.

[9] Converted to a hulk in 1687.

[10] One towboat was included in the fleet, whose age I have been unable to discover.

Authorities: *Catal.* I, pp. 222, 302–3, for names of ships and some dates
Charnock, *Marine Architecture*, II, pp. 426–31, as a check on and supplementing Soc. Naut. Research lists
Derrick, loc. cit. p. 105, for additions 1686–8
Soc. Naut. Research, *Occas. Publns*, no. 5, pt I (main authority)

D. *Length of life of ships (rated ships and fireships only)*

When built	First rates (9)	Second rates (11)	Third rates (38)[1]	Fourth rates (41)	Fifth rates (2)	Sixth rates (6)	Fireships (25)[2]	Totals (132)	Length of life (Years)
Before 1650	—	—	—	1S	—	—	—	1S	50+=7
1650–59	—	—	2R, 1W	1R, 1W, 1C	—	—	—	3R, 2W, 1C	(3R, 1S, 1C, 2W)
1660–69	—	—	—	—	—	—	—	—	—
1670–6	—	—	—	—	—	—	—	—	—
1677–84	—	—	—	—	—	—	—	—	—
1685–8	—	—	—	—	—	—	—	—	—
Before 1650	—	—	—	1R	—	—	—	1R	40–50=16
1650–59	—	—	2R, 1W	4R, 1S, 1A, 1C, 1W	—	1Co	2SHdel, 1S	6R, 2S, 1Co, 2SHdel, 1A, 1C, 2W	(7R, 2S, 1Co, 2SHdel, 1A, 1C, 2W)
1650–59	—	—	1L, 1W	2R, 2A, 3C, 2W	—	—	1R, 1S, 1Co, 1W	3R, 1S, 1Co, 1L, 3C, 4W, 2A	30–40=32
1660–69	2R	1R	5R	1R, 1S	—	—	—	9R, 1S	(19R, 2S, 1Co, 1L, 2A, 3C, 4W)
1670–6	2R	—	—	—	—	—	—	2R	—
1677–84	1R	3R	1R	—	—	—	—	5R	—
1660–9	—	1Co	1W	1SH, 3C	—	1 made pitchboat	—	1Co, 1SH, 1 pitch-boat, 3C, 1W	20–30=43
1670–6	3R	—	2R	3R, 1A	1S, 1B	2S, 1C	1S, ^{T}1SHdel	8R, 4S, 1SHdel, 1B, 1A, 1C	(25R, 4S, 1Co, 2SH, 1 pitch-boat, 1K, 1B, 1U, 1A, 5C, 1W)
1677–84	—	3R	12R, 1U, 1C	1R	—	—	—	16R, 1U, 1C	
1684–8	—	—	—	1R	—	—	^{P}1K	1R, 1K	—
1670–6	—	—	1R, 1W	1R, 1W	—	—	^{T}1W	2R, 3W	10–20=19
1677–84	—	1R, 1W	1R, 1U, 1A, 1C, 1W	1SHdel, 1W	—	—	1S, ^{T}1SHdel	2R, 1S, 2SH, 1U, 1A, 1C, 3W	(6R, 1S, 2SH, 1B, 1U, 1A, 1C, 6W)
1684–8	1B	—	—	1R	—	—	^{T}1R	2R, 1B	—
1684–8	—	1W	—	1W	—	^{P}1Co	^{T}1L, ^{T}2A, ^{T}1C	1Co, 1L, 2A, 1C, 2W	5–10=7
1684–8	—	—	—	1W	—	—	^{T}4SHdel, ^{T}2A, ^{T}1W	4SH, 2A, 2W	-5 =8

A. Lost in action
B. Burnt
C. Captured by enemy
Co. Condemned
del. Deliberately
K. Broken up
L. Lost
P. Originally prize
R. Rebuilt
S. Sold
SH. Sunk in harbour
T. Originally bought
U. Blown up
W. Wrecked

[1] One ship (the *Lion*) not traced after 1688.

[2] One ship (the *Supply*) not traced after 1688.

Authorities: *Catal.* I, pp. 302–3
Soc. Naut. Research, *Occas. Publns*, no. 5, pt 1

E. *Where built*

	First rates	Second rates	Third rates	Fourth rates[1]	Fifth rates	Sixth rates[1]	Bomb-vessels	Fireships[1]	Yachts[1]	Ketches	Smacks	Hoys[1]	Totals
Royal dockyards:													
Chatham	2	1	7	1	—	—	1	—	3	—	2	—	17
Deptford	2	3	5	8	—	2	1	—	—	1	1	—	23
Woolwich	2	3	5	5	—	—	1	—	2	—	—	—	18
Sheerness	—	—	—	—	—	—	—	—	—	—	—	1	1
Harwich	—	2	5	—	1	1	—	—	—	—	—	—	9
Portsmouth	3	2	5	4	—	1	—	2	3	—	—	2	22
Private yards:													
Thames *A*	—	—	1	—	—	—	—	—	—	—	—	—	1
Thames *B*	—	—	—	1	—	—	—	—	—	—	—	—	1
Thames *C*	—	—	2	—	—	—	—	—	—	—	—	—	2
Thames *D*	—	—	—	1	—	—	—	—	—	—	—	—	1
Thames *E*	—	—	—	1	—	—	—	—	—	—	—	—	1
Thames *F*	—	—	6	—	—	—	—	—	—	—	—	—	6
Thames *G*	—	—	—	1	—	—	—	—	—	—	—	—	1
Thames *H*	—	—	—	1	—	—	—	—	—	—	—	—	1
I	—	—	—	1	—	—	—	—	—	—	—	—	1
J	—	—	—	1	—	—	—	—	—	—	—	—	1
K	—	—	1	—	—	—	—	—	—	—	—	—	1
L	—	—	—	1	—	—	—	—	—	—	—	—	1
M	—	—	—	1	—	—	—	—	—	—	—	—	1
N	—	—	2	—	—	—	—	—	—	—	—	—	2
Totals	9	11	39	27	1	4	3	2	8	1	3	3	111

PRIVATE BUILDERS

A Taylor at Wapping
B Munday at Woolwich
C Castle at Deptford
D Castle at Rotherhithe
E Johnson at Deptford
F Johnson at Blackwall
G Deane (younger) at Blackwall
H Deane (younger) at Cuckold's Point
I Goddard at Chatham
J Sterling at Malden
K Bright at Horslydown
L Castle at Shoreham
M Eastwood at Portsmouth
N Bayly at Bristol

[1] I have been unable to discover where twelve of the fourth rates and one of the sixth rates, and where six of the fireships, six of the yachts, and three of the hoys were built.

Authorities: *Catal.* I, pp. 224, 302–3
Charnock, *Marine Architecture,* II, pp. 426–31
Soc. Naut. Research, Occas. Publns. no. 5, pt I

APPENDIX II

SHIPS ADDED TO THE NAVY, 1689–1698[1]

	First rate	Second rate	Third rate	Fourth rate	Fifth rate	Sixth rate	Fire-ship	Bomb-vessel	Yacht	Sloop	Ketch	Yacht	Hoy	Brig-antine	Advice boat	Pink	Store-ship	Hulk	Tow-boat, etc.	Totals
1689	—	—	—	—	1B	—	1T	—	—	—	—	—	—	—	—	—	—	—	—	1B
	—	—	—	—	1R	3P	1P	—	—	—	—	—	—	—	—	—	—	1T	—	1R
	—	—	—	—	2P	—	—	—	—	—	—	—	—	—	—	—	—	2P	—	2T
	—	—	—	—	—	—	—	—	—	—	—	—	—	—	—	—	—	—	—	8P=12
1690	—	1R	1B	—	3B	—	12B	—	—	—	—	—	—	—	—	—	—	—	—	16B
	—	—	—	1R	2P	2P	1T	—	—	—	—	—	—	—	—	—	—	—	—	2R
	—	—	—	—	—	—	1P	—	—	—	—	—	—	—	—	—	—	—	—	1T
	—	—	—	—	—	—	—	—	—	—	—	—	—	—	—	—	—	—	—	5P=24
1691	—	—	—	—	1B	—	—	—	—	—	8B	—	1B	1B	—	—	—	—	—	25B
	—	—	—	4B	1R	3P	8B	—	—	—	1P	—	—	—	—	—	—	—	2B	1R
	—	—	—	—	—	—	—	—	—	—	—	—	—	—	—	—	—	—	(towboat)	4P=30
1692	1R	—	5B	—	1T	1T	6P	1T	—	—	—	—	—	2B	1P	—	2T	1T	—	7B
	—	—	—	—	1P	4P	—	—	—	—	—	—	—	—	—	—	—	—	—	1R
	—	—	—	—	—	—	—	—	—	—	—	—	—	—	—	—	—	—	—	6T
	—	—	—	—	—	—	—	—	—	—	—	—	—	—	—	—	—	—	—	12P=26
1693	1R	—	4B	11B	1R	1B	1T	—	—	—	—	—	—	—	—	—	—	—	—	26B
	—	—	—	1R	1T	1T	2P	4B	—	—	—	1T	2B	2B	—	1B	1B	—	1P	6P
	—	—	—	—	—	3P	—	—	—	—	—	—	—	—	—	—	—	—	etc.	3R
	—	—	—	—	—	—	—	—	—	—	—	—	—	—	—	—	—	—	—	4T=39
1694	—	—	—	—	4B	9B	3B	—	—	—	—	—	—	—	—	—	—	—	1B	33B
	—	—	3B	5B	1T	3P	1T	8T	16T	—	1B	2B	—	—	5B	—	2T	—	2T	30T
	—	—	—	—	—	—	—	—	—	—	—	—	—	—	—	—	—	—	—	3P=66

1695	1R	—	6B	9B	4B	—	—	—	—	—	—	—	—	—	2B	—	—	—	—	38B
	—	—	1R	1R	1T	6B	—	9B	4T	—	—	—	—	1B	1P	—	—	—	—	3R
	—	—	1P	1P	1P	—	—	—	—	—	—	—	—	—	—	1B	—	—	—	5T
	—	—	—	—	—	—	—	—	—	—	—	—	—	—	—	—	—	—	—	4P=50
1696[2]	—	—	—	4B	9B	—	—	—	—	—	—	—	—	—	—	—	—	—	—	18B
	—	—	1R	1T	1P	—	—	1B	—	2P	—	—	—	3B	1B	—	—	—	—	1R
	—	—	—	—	—	—	—	—	—	—	—	—	—	—	—	—	—	—	—	1T
	—	—	—	—	—	—	—	—	—	—	—	—	—	—	—	—	—	—	—	3P=23
1697	—	—	—	2B	3B	—	—	—	—	—	—	—	—	—	—	—	—	—	—	14B
	—	3B	1B	1P	1T	4B	—	—	—	—	—	—	—	—	1B	—	—	—	—	1T
	—	—	—	—	2P	—	—	—	—	—	—	—	—	—	—	—	—	—	—	3P=18
[1698	—	1B	3B	7B	—	—	—	—	—	—	—	—	—	—	—	—	—	—	—	15B
	—	—	1R	2R	3B	—	—	—	—	—	—	—	—	—	—	—	—	—	1B (etc.)	3R=18]
Totals	3= 3R	4= 3B 1R (+1B)	23= 20B 2R 1P (+3B 1R)	41= 35B 3R 1T 2P (+7B 2R)	42= 25B 3R 5T 9P (+3B)	40= 20B 2T 18P	37= 23B 4T 10P	23= 14B 9T	20= 20T	2= 2P	10= 9B 1P	3= 2B 1T	3= 3B	9= 9B	11= 9B 2P	2= 2B	5= 1B 4T	4= 2T 2P	6= 3B 1P 2T (+1B)	178B 12R 50T 48P=288 (+15B 3R= 18) =306

B=*built*; R=*rebuilt*; T=*bought*; P=*prize*

[1] Ships are given the rates in which they were built and rebuilt; thus some of the ships in Appendix I(A) are under rates before rebuilding which occasionally (in two instances) differ from this list.
[2] Excludes one fifth and two sixth rates built in the Thames for Scotland and taken over in 1707 (*Soc. Naut. Research*, I, pp. 51–2).

Authorities: *Soc. Naut. Research*, *Occas. Publns*, no. 5, pt I, *passim*
Charnock, *Marine Architecture*, II, pp. 433–8
Derrick, *Rise and Progress of the Royal Navy*, p. 238

APPENDIX III

DETAILS OF THE TWENTY-SEVEN SHIPS BUILT BY ORDER OF PARLIAMENT, 1691–1698

Name	Builder	Place	Date of contract	Date of launching	Burthen (to nearest ton) By contract	Burthen (to nearest ton) On launching	Rate per ton by contract	Interest paid (6%)	Price by contract[1]	Value of work done in excess of contract	Value of work defaulted on contract
							£ s. d.		£ s. d.	£ s. d.	£ s. d.
Cornwall[2]	Winters	Southampton	12 Mar. 1691	28 April 1692	1147	1186	11 2 6	3[3]	12,757 10 8	1 5 0	16 14 6
Devonshire	Wyatt	Bursledon	12 Mar. 1691	5 April 1692	1138	1159	11 2 6	—	12,686 0 8	—	1,193 4 1
Humber	Frame	Humber	12 Mar. 1691	30 Mar. 1693	1160	1205	11 5 0	3	13,051 13 6	114 10 0	13 5 7
Boyne	R. dockyard	Deptford	—	21 May 1692	—	—	—	—	—	—	—
Russell	R. dockyard	Portsmouth	—	3 June 1692	—	—	—	—	—	—	—
Norfolk	Winters	Southampton	21 Dec. 1691	28 Mar. 1693	1154	1184	11 2 6	3	12,839 8 8	1 5 0	2 14 0
Sussex	R. dockyard	Chatham	—	11 April 1693	—	—	—	—	—	—	—
Torbay	R. dockyard	Deptford	—	16 Dec. 1693	—	—	—	—	—	—	—
Lancaster	Wyatt	Bursledon	3 Mar. 1693	3 April 1694	1151	1198	11 2 6	3	12,807 4 10	50 0 0	28 16 1
Shrewsbury	R. dockyard	Portsmouth	—	6 Feb. 1695	—	—	—	—	—	—	—
Chichester	R. dockyard	Chatham	—	6 Mar. 1695	—	—	—	—	—	—	—
Newark	Frame	Humber	17 May 1693	3 June 1695	1154	1216	11 5 0	6[3]	12,984 13 1	385 1 4	57 4 0
Dorsetshire	Winters	Southampton	1 June 1693	8 Dec. 1694	1127	1177	11 2 6	6	12,617 1 4	—	50 10 6
Cambridge	R. dockyard	Deptford	—	21 Feb. 1695	—	—	—	—	—	—	—
Cumberland	Wyatt	Bursledon	4 May 1694	12 Nov. 1695	1150	1220	11 2 6	6	12,798 19 1	1,033 10 6	36 16 0
Ranelagh	R. dockyard	Deptford	—	25 June 1697	—	—	—	—	—	—	—
Somerset	R. dockyard	Chatham	—	? 1698	—	—	—	—	—	—	—
Carlisle	Snellgrove	Redhouse	30 Dec. 1691	11 Feb. 1693	893	913	11 0 0	3	9,825 11 5	—	—
Winchester	Wyatt	Bursledon	20 Jan. 1692	11 April 1693	903	934	10 2 6	3	9,140 7 11	1 0 0	31 6 1
Medway	R. dockyard	Sheerness	—	20 Sept. 1693	—	—	—	—	—	—	—
Canterbury	Snellgrove	Redhouse	24 Feb. 1693	18 Dec. 1693	892	904	11 0 0	3	9,812 0 0	42 0 0	5 0 0
Gloucester	Clemence	Bristol	27 Mar. 1693	5 Feb. 1695	888	896	9 15 0	6	8,659 2 9	47 11 0	241 14 9
Sunderland	Winter	Southampton	20 April 1693	17 Mar. 1694	898	915	10 2 6	6	9,088 5 3	—	58 0 0
Pembroke	Snellgrove	Redhouse	8 Jan. 1694	22 Nov. 1694	879	908	11 0 0	3	9,871 10 0	—	8 3 6
Kingston	Frame	Humber	10 Aug. 1694	13 Mar. 1697	898	924	10 2 6	6	9,088 5 3	149 2 7	—
Windsor	Snellgrove	Redhouse	22 Oct. 1694	31 Oct. 1695	898	910	11 0 0	6	9,873 13 4	397 15 9	—
Exeter	R. dockyard	Portsmouth	—	26 May 1697	—	—	—	—	—	—	—

[1] These totals are taken from B.M.Addnl. 9324. Those in Serg.Misc. IV, f. 255, are slightly different.
[2] The first seventeen ships, from the *Cornwall* to the *Somerset*, were third rates of 80 guns, the last ten, from the *Carlisle* to the *Exeter*, were fourth rates of 60 guns.
[3] *I.e.* after three months or six months on each payment.

Authorities: B.M.Addnl. 9324, ff. 1–10
[illegible]

APPENDIX IV

NAVAL DEBT, 1688–1697

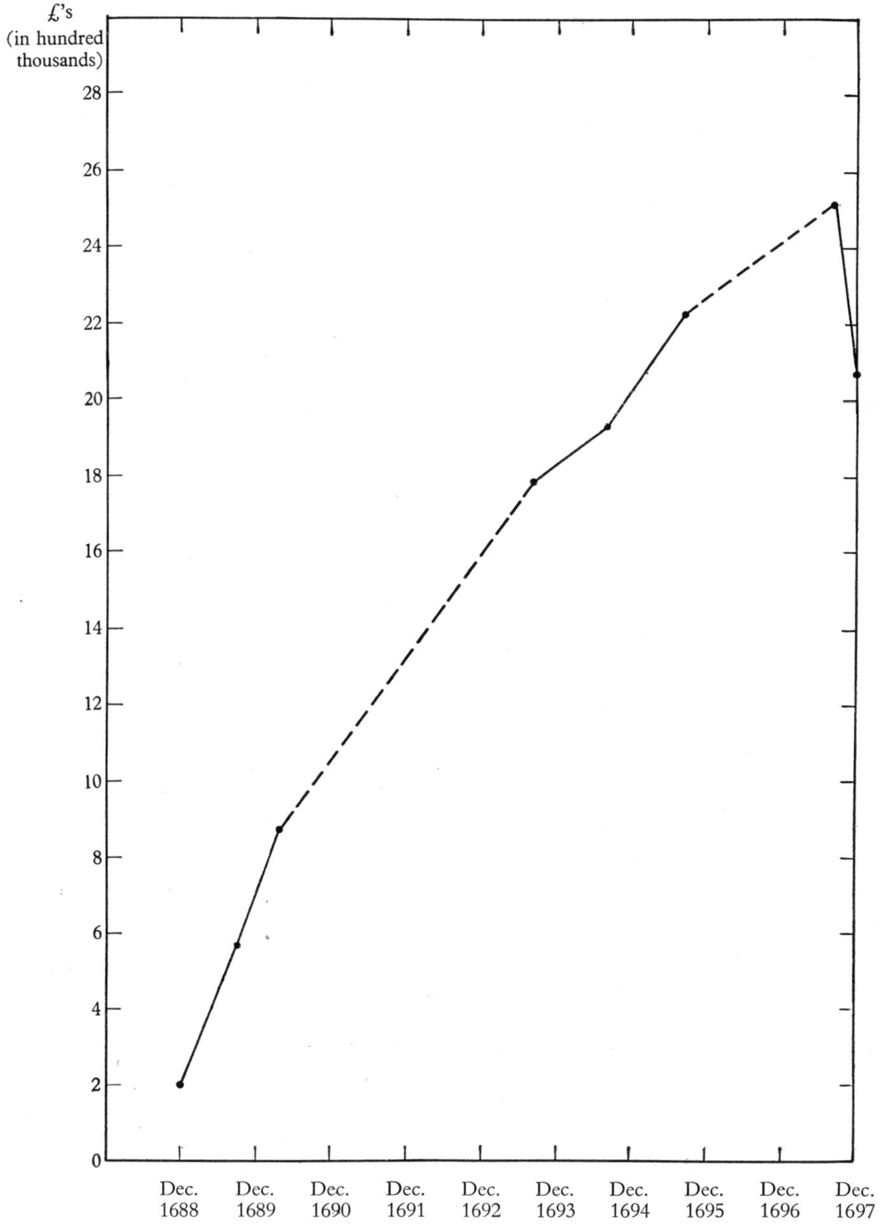

Authorities: The authorities for compiling the naval debts are various and scattered. They are indicated in the relevant notes to the text, as well as in the Bibliography below.

APPENDIX V

NUMBERS OF WORKMEN IN THE ROYAL DOCKYARDS, 1687–1698

A. *Total numbers*

B. *Numbers in each dockyard*

C. *Total numbers of shipwrights and riggers*

From July 1693 the figures are those for the 14th of each month. Before that date no day is given for them.

Authorities: Serg.MS. A 123
P.R.O.Adm. 49/157
B.M.Addnl. 9324, ff. 17–52

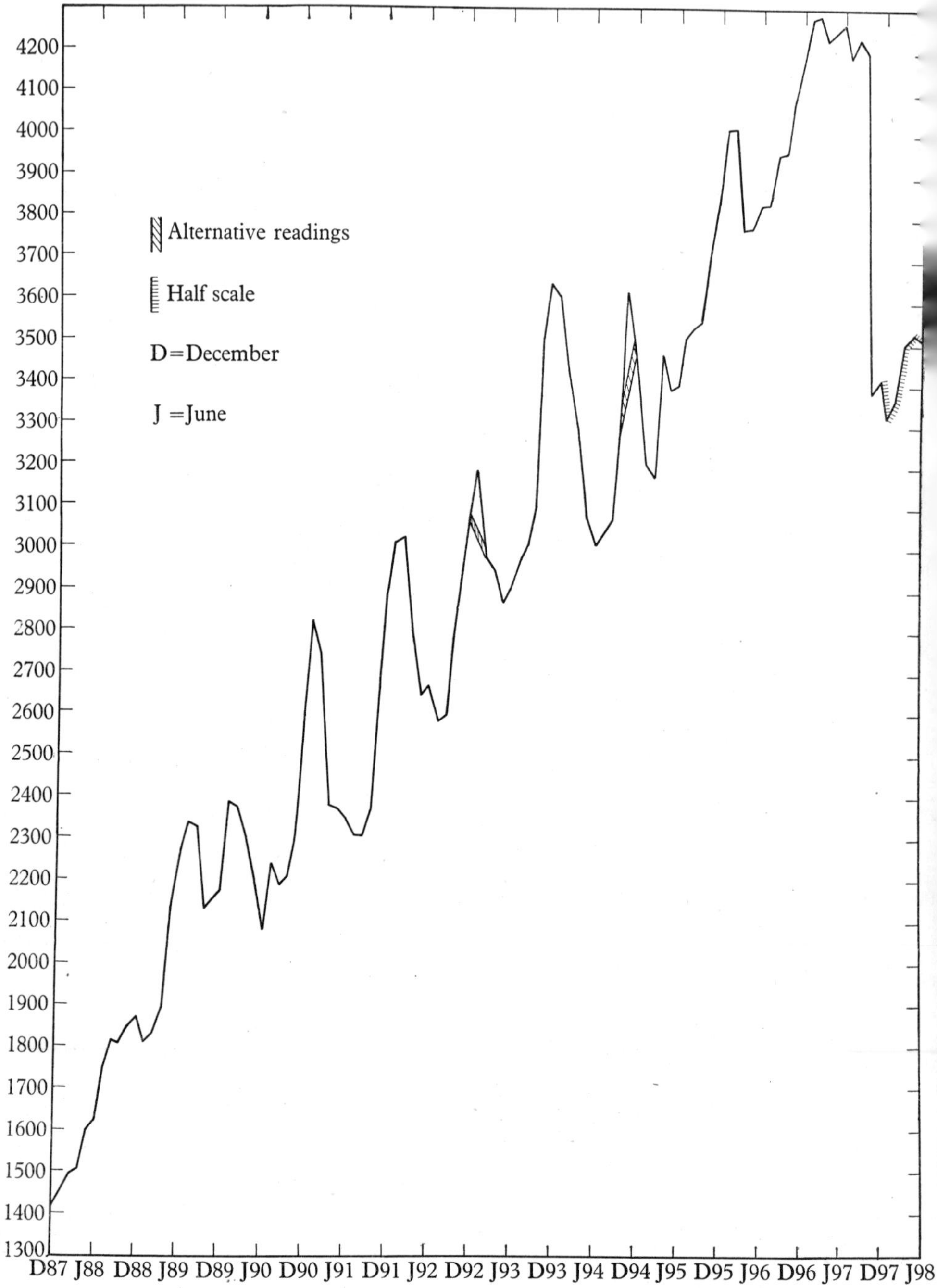
Alternative readings
Half scale
D=December
J =June
4200
4100
4000
3900
3800
3700
3600
3500
3400
3300
3200
3100
3000
2900
2800
2700
2600
2500
2400
2300
2200
2100
2000
1900
1800
1700
1600
1500
1400
1300
D87 J88 D88 J89 D89 J90 D90 J91 D91 J92 D92 J93 D93 J94 D94 J95 D95 J96 D96 J97 D97 J98

A

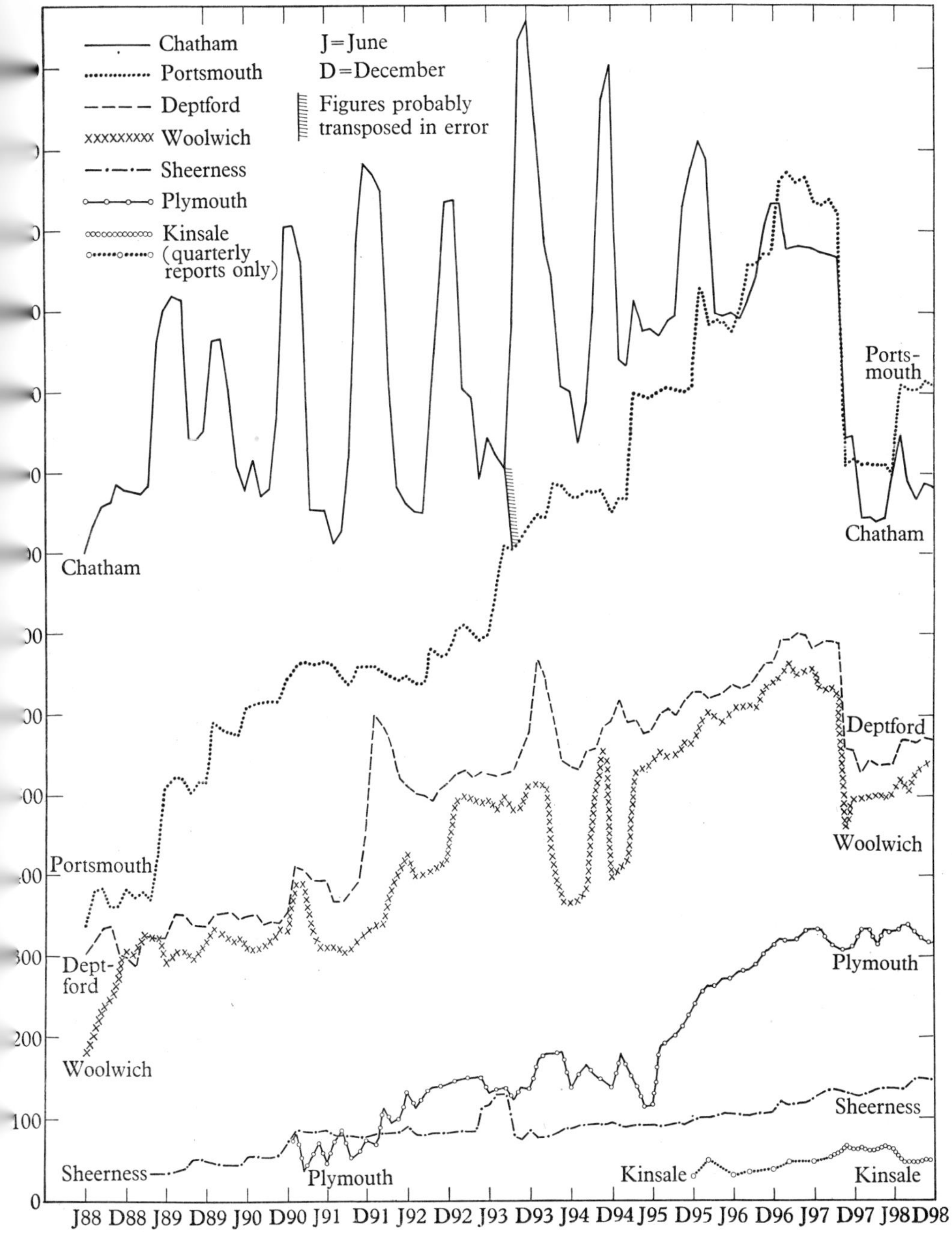
Chatham
Portsmouth
Deptford
Woolwich
Sheerness
Plymouth
Kinsale
(quarterly reports only)
J=June
D=December
Figures probably transposed in error
Chatham
Portsmouth
Dept-ford
Woolwich
Sheerness
Plymouth
Kinsale
Ports-mouth
Chatham
Deptford
Woolwich
Plymouth
Sheerness
Kinsale
0
100
200
J88 D88 J89 D89 J90 D90 J91 D91 J92 D92 J93 D93 J94 D94 J95 D95 J96 D96 J97 D97 J98 D98

B

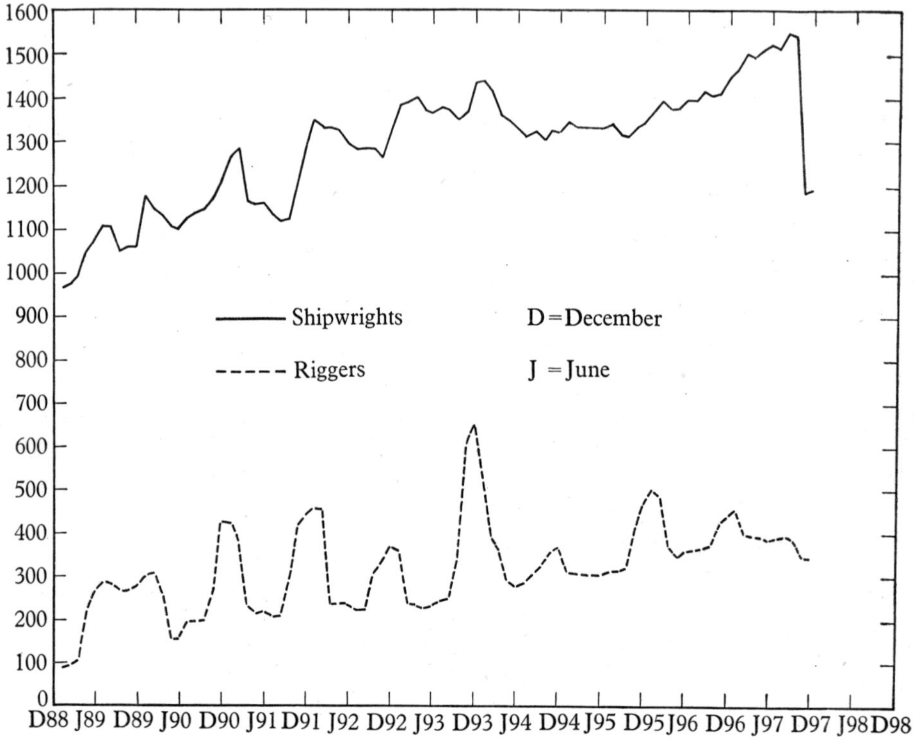
1600
1500
1400
1300
1200
1100
1000
900
800
700
600
500
400
300
200
100
0
Shipwrights
Riggers
D = December
J = June
D88 J89 D89 J90 D90 J91 D91 J92 D92 J93 D93 J94 D94 J95 D95 J96 D96 J97 D97 J98 D98

C

APPENDIX VI

LORDS COMMISSIONERS OF THE ADMIRALTY, 1689–1697

Date of Warrant	
28 February 1689	Arthur Herbert, temporarily acting for a Commission of Admiralty
Date of Patent	
8 March 1689	Arthur Herbert (resigned mid-December) John Vaughan, Earl of Carbery Sir Michael Wharton (paid until 25 March 1689) Sir Thomas Lee Sir John Chicheley Sir John Lowther, of Whitehaven William Sacheverell (never paid)
20 January 1690	Thomas Herbert, Earl of Pembroke John Vaughan, Earl of Carbery Sir Thomas Lee Sir John Lowther, of Whitehaven Sir John Chicheley (ceased acting 28 May 1690)
5 June 1690	Thomas Herbert, Earl of Pembroke John Vaughan, Earl of Carbery (resigned 16 December 1690) Sir Thomas Lee Sir John Lowther, of Whitehaven Edward Russell Sir Richard Onslow Henry Priestman
23 January 1691	Thomas Herbert, Earl of Pembroke Sir Thomas Lee (died February 1691) Sir John Lowther, of Whitehaven Sir Richard Onslow Henry Priestman Anthony Cary, Viscount Falkland Robert Austen

16 November 1691	Thomas Herbert, Earl of Pembroke Sir John Lowther, of Whitehaven Sir Richard Onslow Henry Priestman Anthony Cary, Viscount Falkland Robert Austen Sir Robert Rich
10 March 1692	Charles Cornwallis, Baron Eye (resigned *c.* 23 January 1693) Sir John Lowther, of Whitehaven Sir Richard Onslow Henry Priestman Anthony Cary, Viscount Falkland Robert Austen Sir Robert Rich
15 April 1693	Anthony Cary, Viscount Falkland (reprimanded by House of Commons for misdemeanour, January 1694; died May 1694) Sir John Lowther, of Whitehaven Henry Priestman Robert Austen Sir Robert Rich Henry Killigrew (suspended 11 November 1693) Sir Ralph Delavall (suspended 11 November 1693)
2 May 1694	Edward Russell Sir John Lowther, of Whitehaven Henry Priestman Robert Austen Sir Robert Rich Sir George Rooke Sir John Houblon
24 February 1696	Edward Russell Henry Priestman Robert Austen (died August 1696) Sir Robert Rich Sir George Rooke Sir John Houblon James Kendall

5 June 1697[1] Edward Russell, Earl of Orford
Henry Priestman
Sir Robert Rich
Sir George Rooke
Sir John Houblon
James Kendall
Goodwin Wharton

[1] This Commission lasted until 31 May 1699.

Authority: Patent Rolls

APPENDIX VII

SECRETARIES OF THE ADMIRALTY, 1689–1698

	From	To
Samuel Pepys	19 May 1684	20 February 1689
Phineas Bowles	28 February 1689	9 March 1689[1]
	9 March 1689	15 January 1690
James Sotherne	16 January 1690	1 August 1694
William Bridgeman	4 August 1694	10 January 1695
William Bridgeman, Josiah Burchett[2]	10 January 1695	24 June 1698

[1] While he was secretary to Arthur Herbert.

[2] Burchett was appointed 25 September 1694, while in the Mediterranean; but he only arrived in England in January 1695, and is not known to have acted before 10 January. From 24 June 1698 until 20 May 1702 he was sole Secretary, from that date until 25 October 1705 he was joint Secretary with George Clarke, from then until 23 April 1741 he was again sole Secretary, and finally he was joint Secretary with Thomas Corbett until his retirement on 14 October 1742.

Authorities: P.R.O.Adm. 3/1–14
G. F. James, 'Josiah Burchett', in *M.M.* XXIII, no. 4, pp. 477–97

APPENDIX VIII

PRINCIPAL OFFICERS AND COMMISSIONERS OF THE NAVY, 1686–1698

Commission of 1686–1688

	Paid			
	From	To	Date of Patent	Notes
COMMISSIONERS FOR CURRENT BUSINESS				
Sir Anthony Deane	6 March 1686	12 October 1688	1686	—
Sir John Narborough	6 March 1686	29 September 1687	1686	—
Sir John Berry	6 March 1686	12 October 1688	1686	—
Sir John Godwin	6 March 1686	25 December 1687	1686	—
William Hewer	6 March 1686	12 October 1688	1686	—
Sir William Booth	25 December 1687	12 October 1688	23 February 1688	—
RESIDENT COMMISSIONERS				
Sir Phineas Pett (Chatham)	25 December 1687	12 October 1688	1686	—
Sir Richard Beach (Portsmouth)	25 December 1687	12 October 1688	1686	—
Balthazar St Michel (Deptford)	25 December 1687	12 October 1688	1686	—
COMMISSIONERS FOR THE OLD ACCOUNTS				
Sir Richard Haddock (Comptroller)	25 December 1687	12 October 1688	1686	—
Sir John Tippetts (Surveyor)	25 December 1687	12 October 1688	1686	—
James Sotherne (Clerk of the Acts)	25 December 1687	12 October 1688	1686	—

Treasurer of the Navy

Anthony Cary, Viscount Falkland	24 June 1681	4 April 1689	13 June 1681	—
Edward Russell	4 April 1689	16 October 1699	4 April 1689	—

	Paid: From	Paid: To	Date of Patent	Notes
Comptroller				
Sir Richard Haddock	26 March 1682	29 January 1715	2 February 1682	Patent renewed, 28 October 1689; 28 August 1702; 6 October 1707; 15 November 1714
Surveyor				
Sir John Tippetts	30 September 1672	29 September 1692	5 September 1672	Patent renewed during 1689
Edmund Dummer	25 June 1692	10 August 1699	9 August 1692	—
Clerk of the Acts				
James Sotherne	26 March 1680	25 December 1689	1679	Patent renewed during 1689
Charles Sergison	26 December 1689	1 May 1719	6 February 1690	Patent renewed, 11 February 1702; 28 August 1702; 26 August 1706; 6 October 1707; 16 November 1714
Comptroller of the Treasurer's Accounts[1]				
Dennis Lyddell	25 March 1691	19 November 1717	1 May 1691	Patent renewed, 28 August 1702; 6 October 1707; 16 November 1714
Comptroller of the Victuallers' Accounts[2]				
Sir John Berry	13 October 1688	25 December 1689	1688	Patent renewed during 1689
Sir Richard Beach	25 March 1690	24 June 1692	—	—
Samuel Pett	25 December 1692	25 March 1699	4 March 1693	—
Comptroller of the Storekeeper's Accounts[3]				
Sir William Booth	13 October 1688	25 March 1689	—	—
Henry Priestman	26 March 1689	24 June 1690	28 October 1689	—
Sir John Ashby	24 June 1690	24 June 1693	11 July 1690	—
Thomas Wilshaw	26 March 1693	23 September 1702	26 June 1693	Patent renewed, 28 August 1702

[1] Office not occupied since 1679. [2] Office not occupied since 1686. [3] Office not occupied since 1686.

		Extra Commissioners		
George Rooke	25 December 1691	25 March 1694	22 January 1692	—
John Hill	25 December 1691	24 June 1702	27 January 1692	—
Sir Cloudesley Shovell	25 March 1693	25 March 1699	20 April 1693	—
George St Lo	24 June 1693	25 March 1695	28 September 1693	—
Matthew Aylmer	25 March 1694	16 July 1702	22 April 1694	—
James Sotherne	22 September 1694	10 September 1701	6 May 1695	—
Benjamin Tymewell	30 September 1696	25 December 1704	—	Patent renewed, 28 August 1702
		Resident Commissioners		
CHATHAM				
Sir Phineas Pett	6 March 1686	25 March 1689	—	Patent renewed during 1688
Sir Edward Gregory	25 March 1689	24 June 1703	8 October 1689	Patent renewed, 28 August 1702
DEPTFORD				
Balthazar St Michel	6 March 1686	29 April 1689	1685	Patent renewed during 1688. First Commissioner at Deptford and Woolwich Yards. The office subsequently lapsed again to Chatham
PORTSMOUTH				
Sir Richard Beach	22 October 1679	25 March 1690	—	Patent renewed in 1685, 1688, 8 October 1689
Thomas Wilshaw	14 March 1690	25 March 1693	15 April 1690	—
Benjamin Tymewell	25 March 1693	25 March 1695	4 March 1693	—
Henry Greenhill	25 March 1695	12 August 1702	—	—
PLYMOUTH				
Henry Greenhill	25 December 1691	25 March 1695	19 December 1691	First Commissioner at Plymouth Yard
George St Lo	26 March 1695	29 April 1703	25 April 1695	—
KINSALE				
Benjamin Tymewell	25 March 1695	29 September 1696	—	First Commissioner at Kinsale. The next Commissioner there was in 1702

Authorities: Patent Rolls
Sir George Jackson, *Naval Commissioners from 1660 to 1760* (it should be noted in using this work, that all dates are Old Style; this is not specifically mentioned in the text)

APPENDIX IX

COMMISSIONERS OF VICTUALLING, 1688–1698

	From	To
Sir Richard Haddock	25 December 1688	24 November 1689
Sir John Parsons	25 December 1688	24 November 1689
Anthony Sturt	25 December 1688	24 November 1689
Nicholas Few	25 December 1688	24 November 1689
Thomas Papillon[1]	25 November 1689	—
Simon Maine[1]	25 November 1689	—
Humphrey Ayles[1]	25 November 1689	—
John Agar	25 November 1689	15 July 1697
James How	25 November 1689	25 March 1693
John Fielding	24 June 1693	25 March 1694
John Burrington[1]	25 March 1695	—

[1] Still acting on 1 January 1698.

Authority: Serg.MS., 'Officers of the Navy'

APPENDIX X

FLAG OFFICERS AND COMMANDERS OF SQUADRONS AND STATIONS, 1688–1697

Admirals

RED

	From	To	Salary
Dartmouth[1]	24 Sept. 1688	14 Jan. 1689	£3 pay
Torrington[1]	15 Mar. 1689 28 April 1690	12 Mar. 1690 6 Aug. 1690	£4 pay and table money
Haddock, Killigrew, Ashby[1]	6 Aug. 1690	7 Dec. 1690	£3 each pay
Russell[1]	23 Dec. 1690	10 Jan. 1693	£4 pay and table money
Killigrew, Delavall, Shovell[1]	24 Jan. 1693	6 Nov. 1693	£4 pay and table money
Russell[1]	7 Nov. 1693	3 Dec. 1697	£4 (7 Nov. 1693 to 31 Dec. 1693), £7 (1 Jan. 1694 to 27 April 1696), £6 (28 April 1696 to 3 Dec. 1697) pay
Rooke	28 April 1696	1 June 1696	£7 pay and table money
Berkeley	2 June 1696	31 Dec. 1698	£7 pay and table money
Rooke	19 April 1697	2 Dec. 1697	£7 pay and table money

BLUE

	From	To	Salary
Russell	30 May 1689	14 May 1690	£3 pay + 20*d. per diem* extraordinary allowance
Killigrew	3 June 1690	5 Aug. 1690	£3 pay and table money
	7 Dec. 1690	3 Dec. 1691	£3 pay and table money
Ashby	20 Jan. 1692	19 Jan. 1693	£3 pay and table money
	26 Jan. 1693	12 June 1693	£3 pay and table money
Berkeley	4 July 1693	22 Aug. 1693	£3 pay and table money
Rooke	23 Aug. 1693	23 April 1694	£5 pay and table money
Berkeley	1 Jan. 1695	27 April 1696	£5 pay and table money
Shovell	1 Jan. 1695	3 Dec. 1697	£5 pay and table money
Rooke	25 April 1695	25 May 1695	£5 pay and table money

Vice-Admirals

RED

	From	To	Salary
Berry	13 Dec. 1688	27 Mar. 1689	£1. 10*s*. pay
Killigrew	17 Feb. 1690	10 Mar. 1690	£1. 10*s*. pay
Ashby	17 Feb. 1690	5 Aug. 1690	£1. 10*s*. pay
	23 Dec. 1690	19 Jan. 1692	£1. 10*s*. pay

[1] Commission as Admiral of the fleet.

	From	To	Salary
Delavall	20 Jan. 1692	23 Jan. 1693	£1. 10*s*. pay
Rooke	26 Jan. 1693	20 Feb. 1693	£1. 10*s*. pay
Aylmer	3 July 1693	22 Aug. 1693	£1. 10*s*. pay
Berkeley	23 Aug. 1693	31 Dec. 1693	£1. 10*s*. pay
Shovell	16 April 1694	1 Jan. 1695	£3 pay
Aylmer	1 Jan. 1696	3 Dec. 1697	£3 pay

BLUE

Killigrew	8 June 1689	16 Feb. 1690	£1. 10*s*. pay
Ashby	17 Feb. 1690 (one day)		£1. 10*s*. pay
Delavall	3 June 1690	23 Dec. 1690	£1. 10*s*. pay
	24 Dec. 1690	19 Jan. 1693	£1. 10*s*. pay
Rooke	20 Jan. 1693	25 Jan. 1693	£1. 10*s*. pay
Berkeley	30 Jan. 1693	4 July 1693	£1. 10*s*. pay
Mitchell	4 July 1693	22 Aug. 1693	£1. 10*s*. pay
Aylmer	22 Aug. 1693	31 Dec. 1695	£1. 10*s*. to end of 1693, then £3 pay
Mitchell	19 Aug. 1695	31 Dec. 1697	£3 pay

Rear Admirals

RED

Berry	5 Nov. 1688	12 Dec. 1688	£1 pay
Berkeley	1 May 1689	8 Feb. 1690	£1 pay
Delavall	13 Feb. 1690	3 June 1690	£1 pay
Rooke	6 May 1690	19 Jan. 1692	£1 pay
Shovell	20 Jan. 1692	23 Jan. 1693	£1 pay
Aylmer	6 Feb. 1693	3 July 1693	£1 pay
Mitchell	7 Feb. 1693	4 July 1693	£1 pay
Carmarthen	1 July 1693	6 Oct. 1693	£1 pay
Mitchell	22 Aug. 1693	26 Oct. 1693	£1 pay
	29 Dec. 1693	29 Sept. 1695	£1 until end of 1693, then £2 pay
Neville	30 Sept. 1695	31 Dec. 1696	£2 pay

BLUE

Ashby	8 June 1689	16 Dec. 1690	£1 pay
Shovell	3 June 1690	19 Jan. 1692	£1 pay
Carter	1 Jan. 1692	19 May 1692	£1 pay
Wheeler	6 Feb. 1693	27 Oct. 1693	£1 pay
Carmarthen	6 Oct. 1693	1 Jan. 1694	£1 pay
Mitchell	26 Oct. 1693	29 Dec. 1693	£1 pay
Carmarthen	8 Jan. 1694	30 April 1696	£2 pay
Benbow	1 May 1696	3 Dec. 1697	£2 pay

First captains to Admirals of the fleet

Mitchell[1]	28 Mar. 1689	24 Sept. 1689	10*s*. to complete pay to £1. To Torrington, in the *Elizabeth*
Neville[2]	28 April 1690	13 Sept. 1690	5*s*. to complete pay to £1. To joint Admirals, in the *Royal Sovereign*
Mitchell	24 Jan. 1691	7 Oct. 1691	£1 pay. To Russell, in the *Britannia*
	8 Feb. 1692	6 Feb. 1693	£1 pay. To Russell, in the *Britannia*

[1] Retrospectively granted by Order dated 4 November 1691.
[2] Retrospectively granted by Order dated 25 November 1691.

	From	To	Salary
Neville	27 Jan. 1693	6 July 1693	£1 pay. To joint Admirals, in the *Britannia*
Meese	12 July 1693	6 Nov. 1693	£1 pay. To joint Admirals, in the *Britannia*
Byng	27 Dec. 1693	2 Dec. 1695	£1 to end of 1693, then £2 pay. To Russell, in the *Britannia*
Bokenham	2 Sept. 1695	25 Dec. 1695	£2 pay. To Rooke, in the *Queen*
Byng	24 Dec. 1695	7 May 1696	£2 pay. To Russell, in the *Britannia*
Bokenham	26 Dec. 1695	27 April 1696	£1. 10*s*. (to abate overpayment in his former account). To Rooke, in the *Queen*
	28 April 1696	3 Dec. 1697	£2 pay

Commanders of squadrons

CHANNEL SERVICE

Ranking as extra Vice-Admirals

Berry	13 Dec. 1688	27 Mar. 1689	£1. 10*s*. pay
Davis	1 May 1689	8 Feb. 1690	£1. 10*s*. pay
Hopson	10 Nov. 1693	8 April 1694	£1. 10*s*. until end of 1693, then £3 pay
	13 June 1694	7 Oct. 1694	£3 pay

Ranking as extra Rear Admirals

Berry	24 Sept. 1688	12 Dec. 1688	£1 pay
Hopson	28 Feb. 1692	9 Nov. 1693	£1 pay
Neville	7 July 1693	29 Sept. 1695	£1 until end of 1693, then £2 pay
Hopson	13 Sept. 1695	1 Oct. 1695	£2 pay

OVERSEAS

Commanders and Commanders in Chief of squadrons in Mediterranean

Killigrew	11 Mar. 1690	3 June 1690	£1. 10*s*. above pay as Vice-Admiral of the Red
Aylmer[1]	17 Dec. 1690	19 Oct. 1691	10*s*. above captain's pay
Rooke[2]	20 Feb. 1693	22 Aug. 1693	£3 pay
Wheeler[2]	1 Nov. 1693	19 Feb. 1694	£3 until end of 1693, then £4 pay
Rooke[2]	1 Aug. 1695	27 April 1696	£5 pay and table money

Commanders of squadrons in West Indies

Lawrence Wright	14 Mar. 1690	9 July 1691	£1 pay
Wheeler	9 Sept. 1692	6 Feb. 1693	£1 pay
Neville	1 Jan. 1697	17 Aug. 1697	£3 paid as a Vice-Admiral
Meese	3 Feb. 1697	17 July 1697	£2 pay

[1] Captain's rank only.
[2] Commission as 'Commander in Chief'.

Commander in Chief of squadron in Newfoundland

	From	To	Salary
Norris[1]	12 Mar. 1697	26 Feb. 1698	10*s.* above captain's pay

Commanders of Stations

Graydon[1]	20 May 1694	27 June 1694	£1 Nore.
Munden[1]	26 Feb. 1696	3 April 1696	10*s.* Thames and Medway. 10*s.* above captain's pay
	16 Sept. 1696	8 May 1697	

Special Services

Benbow[1]	8 Mar. 1695	25 April 1695	£2 commanding squadron attending bombvessels before St Malo. Paid 'as a Rear Admiral'
Beaumont[1]	15 May 1697	26 July 1697	10*s.* Commander in Chief of squadrons before Dunkirk. Above captain's pay of his own ship, he having been sent aboard small ships of squadron

[1] Captain's rank only.

Rates of pay are those *per diem.* The first and last dates only are given for service in a rank or capacity. On several occasions, the Commissions were renewed during the period.

Authorities: B.M.Addnl. 9324, ff. 140–53
Serg.MS., 'Officers of the Navy'

APPENDIX XI

LETTERS PATENT APPOINTING THE LORDS COMMISSIONERS OF THE ADMIRALTY, 8 MARCH 1689

March 8th, 1689.

William and Mary by the Grace of God of England, France and Ireland, King and Queen, Defender of the Faith, etc., to our Trusty and Well-beloved Arthur Herbert Esq., our Right Trusty and Well-beloved Cousin John, Earle of Carbery, our Trusty and Well-beloved Sir Michael Wharton, Sir Thomas Lee, Bart., Sir John Chicheley, Knight, Sir John Lowther of Whitehaven in our County of Cumberland, Barronett, and William Sacheverell Esquire.

GREETING, Know ye, thatt Wee, Reposing especiall Trust and Confidence in the approved Wisdoms, Fidelities and Experiences of you the said Arthur Herbert, John, Earle of Carbery, Sir Michael Wharton, Sir Thomas Lee, Sir John Chicheley, Sir John Lowther and William Sacheverell, have nominated, ordained and appointed and by these presents doe nominate, ordaine and appoint you to be our Commissioners for Executing the Office of Lord High Admirall of England, Giving this by these presents,

Granting unto you or every three or more of you full Power and authority to doe, Execute, exercise and perform all and every act, matter and thing which to the office of Lord High Admirall of England appertaineth and belongeth, as well in and touching those things which Concerne our Navy and Shipping as those things which concern the Rights and Jurisdictions of or appeartaining to the Office or Place of High Admiral of England.

And Wee doe further by these presents Give and Grant unto you and every Three or more of you full power and authority to make such orders and issue such Warrants for the repayring and preserving of our shipps and vessels already built and to be built in Harbour With all things belonging to them and every of them according to your good directions and for the new building, Reparing, fitting, furnishing, Arming, victualling and setting forth such ships and fleets as you shall receive direction for from our Privy Council.

And also to establish and Direct such Entertainments, Wages and Rewards for and unto all and every such Person and Persons as are or shall be employed in those our services or anything appertaining thereunto and further to give such discharges for those services or any of them as to you or any three or more of you in your wisdom and good directions shall be thought fitt in as Ample a manner as any Lord Admirall of England might have done by vertue of his Office or place of Lord Admirall or by vertue of any Commission granted in that behalfe might doe or perform the same,

And our Will and Pleasure is and Wee doe hereby strictly charge and command all our officers and Ministers of or belonging to our Navy or Shipps and every of them now and for the time being, and all others in their severall places Whom it may in any Wise concerne, that they and every of them be from time to time attending upon our said Commissioners and doe carefully and dilligently observe, Execute and performe all such orders, Warrants and Commandments, as our said Commissioners or any three of them shall make, give or direct touching the Premises in such manner and sort as if the Lord Admirall of England had made, given or directed the same,

And to the intent you may be the better instructed how to perform these Great and Weighty Services to our Best Advantage, and Wee and our Privy Council may be the better informed What directions to give therein, our further Will and Pleasure is and Wee doe hereby give unto you or any three or more of you Power and Authority not merely by yourselves but also by any other fitt person or persons Whom you or any three or more of you shall to that purpose make choice of and appoint. With all convenient Speed to make a true and perfect survey and account of all our Shipps and Pinnaces and vessells of or belonging to our Navy and of all the munition, Tackle and furniture belonging to them and every of them and of all Stores, Munitions and furnitures prepared for them and every of them of all sorts, and also of all Courses now held in the managing, ordering and Governing of our Navy and to deliver the same soe made and taken to us in Writing, and to propound such Wages and meanes for the Establishing of such orders and Instructions for Regulating of the same as shall be found agreeable to our Service and may increase our Power and forces by sea and remove such Corruptions and abuses as may preindite the same and especially may reduce the mariners and seamen and Sea Services thereupon Wee may take such speedy and effectual courses for the supplying of all Defects and the Reforming of all Abuses as shall be necessary to make and continue our Navy serviceable for our Honour and for the honor and safety of our Realms and Dominions,

And whereas all Wrecks of the Sea, Goods and Shipps taken from Pirates and Enemies and divers Tenths and other Droits, Rights, duties and Privileges have been by express words or otherwise heretofore granted to the Lord Admirall and to former Admiralls to theyr owne use and benefitt, as Duties appertaining to that Office or place of Lord High Admirall of England, Now our will and pleasure is and Wee doe hereby charge and command that all those casuall Duties, Droits and profitts be taken, Collected and received in all places where they shall happen by the vice-admirals and other officers of or belonging to the Admiralty in such sort as they were formerly or ought or have been taken, collected and received by them and every of them respectively when there was a Lord High Admiral of England and the said vice-admiralls and others so taking, collecting or Receiving the same shall account for the same and every part thereof unto or before you our said Commissioners or any three or more of you or unto such other person or persons and in such manner or forms as you or any three or more of you shall to that purpose appoint but to our onely use and behoof and not otherwise.

And whereas Wee conceive it just and reasonable that those who have or shall truely and faithfully account for what they have received should have sufficient discharges for the same, according our Will and pleasure is and Wee doe therefore by the presence Give to you our said Commissioners or any three or more of you full power and authority to

Issue forth discharges, Releases and Quietus ests upon such accounts for tenths of Prizes and all other Duties and Droits and Profitts Whatsoever received or to be received by the aforesaid vice-admiralls and other collectors authorised by the Court of Admiralty to receive any Droits or profitts of Admiralty or any Register or Registers of his or theyr deputy or Deputies Exercising the Office of Register in the High Court of Admiralty itselfe or any other inferior Court of the Admiralty as you our said Commissioners or any three or more of you shall approve of the said Releases, Discharges or quietus Ests to be under the hand of you our said Commissioners or any three or more of you and the Seale commonly used by you for things appertaining to the said Commission which Wee will shall be and remaine of Record in the High Court of Admiralty under the custody of the Register there to the end that the parties Interested in such Accounts and Discharges may according to their occasions if they desire it Receive the same Exemplified under the Great Seale of the Admiralty and our Will and pleasure is and Wee doe hereby declare that the said Releases, Discharges or Quietus Este soe signed by you our said Commissioners or any three or more of you and sealed with your Seale aforesaid or the Duplicate thereof Recorded in the High Court of Admiralty shall be held and be a full, sufficient and lawfull discharge, release and Quietus Est to every such Accountant, his executors or Administrators,

And whereas divers offices, places and employments belonging to the Navy or Admiralty are properly in the Gift and disposing of the Lord Admirall of England for the time being, Now our Will and pleasure is and Wee doe declare the same by these presents that all such offices, places and employments as shall void dureing the vacancy of the place of Lord Admirall of England shall be given and disposed by you or any three or more of you and our Will and pleasure is that this our Commission shall continue in force untill wee shall Declare our pleasure to the contrary Notwithstanding the same be not continued by Adjournment.

In Witness whereof, Witness our Seales att Westminster the eighth day of March,

BY THE KING

Authority: Patent Rolls

APPENDIX XII

AN ACT CONCERNING THE COMMISSIONERS OF THE ADMIRALTY, 2 WILL. AND MARY, SESS. 2, C. 2

Whereas the Office of Lord High Admirall of England hath at sundry times and for severall yeares beene executed and all the Authorities to the same belonging exercised by diverse Commissioners for that purpose appointed by their Majestyes and the late Kings but of late some doubt hath risen whether certaine Authorities belonging to the said Office of Lord High Admirall did or doe of Right belong to and might may or ought to have beene or be exercised by such Commissioners for the time being Now for avoiding all such Doubts and Questions Bee it declared and enacted by the King and Queens most excellent Majestyes by and with the advice and consent of the Lords Spirituall and Temporall and Commons in this Present Parliament assembled and by the authorities of the same that all and singular Authorities Jurisdictions and Powers which by any Act of Parliament or otherwise have been and are lawfully vested setled and placed in the Lord High Admirall of England for the time being have alwayes appertained to and of right might have beene and may be and shall be enjoyed used exercised and executed by the Commissioners for executing the Office of High Admirall of England for the time being according to their Commissions to all intents and purposes as if the said Commissioners were Lord High Admirall of England.

II. Provided that nothing in this Act contained shall extend or be taken or construed to extend to give or allow to the Lord High Admirall or to the Commissioners for executing the Office of Lord High Admirall any other Authority Jurisdiction or Power then the Lord High Admirall lawfully had or might have had used and exercised if this Act had not beene made.

III. Provided alwayes and bee it enacted that upon all Tryalls of Offenders by Courts Martiall to be held by vertue of any Commission to be granted by the Lord High Admirall or the Commissioners for executing the Office of High Admirall every Officer present shall before any Proceeding to Tryall take an Oath before the Court (which Oath the Judge Advocate or his Deputy for the time being are hereby authorised to administer) in these words following

You shall well and truely try and determine the Matter now before you betweene our Sovereigne Lord and Lady the King and Queens Majestyes and the Prisoner to be tryed

Soe help you God.[1]

---

[1] These articles were annexed in separate schedules to the Act as originally brought in.

Authority: Statutes of the Realm, vol. VI (1819), p. 218

APPENDIX XIII

THE MEMORANDUM OF PHINEAS BOWLES ON THE DUTIES OF THE SECRETARY OF THE ADMIRALTY

The Humble Petition of Phineas Bowles Late Secretary to the Lords Commissioners for executing the office of Lord High Admiral of England

Sheweth that upon your Majesty's granting a Patent to the Rt. Honourable the Commissioners of the Admiralty in March last the said Commissioners chose your petitioner for their Secretary which having received your Majesty's gracious confirmation by your Majesty's Letters of Privy Seal dated the 18th of July last, entitling your petitioner to a salary of five hundred pounds per annum for officiating the said office and trust, which your petitioner hath faithfully discharged with diligence, integrity and utmost affection and devotion to your Majesty's service, notwithstanding which the said Commissioners of the Admiralty (to whose character and your Majesty's pleasure he humbly submits himself) have appointed Mr. Southerne (Clerk of the Acts of your Majesty's Navy) in your petitioner's place.

Wherefor in regard your petitioner hath spent above 20 years in the service of the Crown and hath great arrears due to him for employments of considerable trust which he hath well acquitted himself of, without obtaining such a competence as will give subsistence to his family, he most humbly submits his case and condition to your Majesty's princely consideration, imploring your Majesty will be graciously pleased to continue him in the said employment of Secretary to the Admiralty (as is humbly proposed in the paper herto annexed), or grant him such other for the support of him and his family as your Majesty in your great wisdom and clemency shall think fit.

And your petitioner and them will ever pray etc.

The proposals of Phineas Bowles, late Secretary to the Right Honourable the Commissioners for executing the office of Lord High Admiral of England,

Humbly submitted to consideration.

The performance of his Majesty's service in relation to the duty of Secretary to the Admiralty requiring at all times constant and diligent attendance and dispatch but more especially in this time of great action to which consideration that being added of his Majesty's joining to the Patent of Lord High Admiral of England the management of the affairs of the Admiralty in relation to the plantations and his Majesty's foreign dominions, the business and employment of Secretary to the Admiralty will become much more great and considerable, wherefore it is humbly proposed that it will be most of his Majesty's service as well in regard to dispatch as other respects, that this employment be vested in two persons (to be equally and jointly concerned) for and to whom his Majesty's gracious allowance of salary (as his Majesty shall be advised) and the fees and perquisites of that office will be a very sufficient compensation and reward.

Reasons and motives humbly alleged for the office of Secretary of the Admiralty being in two persons.

The attending his Majesty (as well in as out of town) frequently if not daily for his Majesty's information of all necessary advices, intelligences and other affairs concerning this office, and receiving his Majesty's commands, when the Rt. Honourable the Commissioners of the Admiralty shall not have leisure or judge it of consequence enough to do it themselves.

The attending the Council Lords of the Treasury, Secretaries of State etc. with memorials etc. on and informations of all such matters as by the command of the L.H.A. or Commissioners for executing that office is incumbent on the Secretary to lay before the Council etc. and receive their directions upon.

The sitting frequently with the Navy Board as hath been customary for the Secretary of the Admiralty (which will appear by many records) for the informing himself to lay before the Rt. Hon. the Commissioners of the Admiralty such accounts of affairs (as hath been usual) and may quicken the despatch of business and orders concerning the affairs of his Majesty's Navy and also if it shall be thought fit to sign warrants and contracts with the Commissioner of the Navy as Sir William Coventry did when he was Secretary.

Several officers employed in his Majesty's naval service and others on sundry occasions that have applications to make to the Admiralty Board do require frequent discourses with and answer from the Secretary to save time and trouble to the Commissioners and their being interrupted on many occasions.

Besides the aforesaid services which the Secretary must often be employed in, he must minutely attend the sitting of the Board (which since I have been in that office hath been day by day without intermission) and must constantly be at the office as well before as after for perusing and preparing what his Majesty's service requires to be laid before them and making the necessary answers, orders and despatches thereon.

That by two officiating this employment, one will be always at hand to despatch letters and countersign all orders and directions of the Board when his Majesty's service as aforesaid shall call the other from being personally at the office, as it may also happen by sickness and indisposition.

The well despatch of the service makes it more necessary than formerly that the office be in two persons (joint and equal) from the consideration of the great increase of the navy, which while one is employed in the common business of (when it is not so great as in this time of action) the other may apply himself to think of what may be for the welfare and better government of the navy in general and prepare drafts for the emending and altering several things in the economy of the Navy, as the changes of time and circumstances may make necessary for the King's service.

Instances.

In King Charles the first's time there were with the navy board two clerks of the acts, as there were also on King Charles the second's time, namely Mr. Hayter and Mr. Pepys and (after) Mr. Hayter and Mr. Southerne.

Clerks of the Council are four, which attend by months, but I humbly propose constant attendance of both, that according they may be always prepared to answer the urgency and pressure of the service.

Objections answered.

Mr. Southerne, late clerk of the acts, being called to succeed to the employment (for his long experience in the navy) if therefore (notwithstanding what is humbly proposed) it shall be objected on his behalf, that he may have the office alone, I humbly answer, that by our acting jointly, he will have as much ease and repose in this business as in his former employment, and his income I may modestly affirm will be twice as much, wherefore I hope these so reasonable proposals for his Majesty's service and the maintenance and support of myself and family will with my past diligence and integrity and the affection and duty I have for the King's service, move his Majesty and the Rt. Hon. the Commissioners of the Admiralty to continue me in the said employment on the terms herein humbly proposed.

Authority: P.R.O.Adm. 2/169, ff. 25–7

Further Correspondence on the Petition

AT THE COURT AT WHITEHALL
the 13th day of March, 1689/90

His Majesty having a gracious sense of the petitioner's long and faithful service to the Crown and of his good affection to his Majesty's service as the same is set forth in the petition and being thereupon disposed to gratify him in such manner as may conveniently be done, his Majesty is pleased to refer this petition and the proposals thereto annexed to the Rt. Hon., the Lords Commissioners of the Admiralty to consider thereof and to report to his Majesty whether the petitioner's proposals are such as may conduce to his Majesty's service and the petitioner be thereby provided for or else what their Lordships think may be fitting to be done for the gratification whereupon his Majesty will declare his further pleasure.

[sgd.] SHREWSBURY

ADMIRALTY OFFICE
25th May 1690

In obedience to your Majesty's order of reference on the petition of Mr. Phineas Bowles, late Secretary of the Admiralty, we do humbly report that the petitioner hath been several years employed in the service of the navy and we judge him a person deserving encouragement, and humbly recommend him to his Majesty's favour for further employment according as his Majesty shall think fitting. But as to his proposal that there may be two Secretaries of the Admiralty we do not think it will be for their Majesties' service to have that office executed by more than one person.

[sgd.] PEMBROKE, THOMAS LEE, JOHN LOWTHER, JOHN CHICHELEY

Authority: P.R.O.Adm. 2/169, ff. 27–8

APPENDIX XIV

THE ESTABLISHMENT OF THE ADMIRALTY OFFICE

Order for the New Establishment

By the Commissioners for executing the Office of Lord High Admiral of England and Ireland, etc.

Her Majesty having been pleased to appoint the following salaries to be established on the Secretaries, Clerks and other officers belonging to this Office, viz.,

			£	
To Two Secretaries,	...	each	800	per annum
Two chief clerks,	...	each	200	
Six other clerks,	...	each	80	
A Messenger,			50	
Two servants, to ditto	...	each	25	
A Porter,			30	
A Watchman,			20	
A Woman to look after the house,			20	

We do hereby require and direct you to cause the said establishment to be placed in the ordinary charge of their Majesties' Navy and inserted in the estimates thereof, and you are to sign bills quarterly on the Treasurer of the Navy, according to the course of your Office, for paying the said sallaries unto such persons as our secretaries or either of them shall give you notice thereof, the same to commence at Midsummer day last past.

And whereas Josiah Burchett, Esq., whom we have appointed one of our Secretaries is at present absent, being with Admiral Russell in the Straits you are to sign quarterly bills for the payment of his salary to commence from the quarterday immediately preceeding his return into England, and for so doing this shall be your warrant,

Dated at the Admiralty Office this 26th September 1694.

H. PRIESTMAN. G. ROOKE.
R. RICH. JN. HOUBLON.

To the Principal Officers and Commissioners of their Majesties' Navy.

By Command of the Commissioners,

WM. BRIDGEMAN.

Details of the Staff Appointed

ADMIRALTY OFFICE
27th Sept. 1694

Gentlemen,

In my Lords of the Admiralty's orders to you of yesterday's date, you are directed to pay several salaries to the secretaries, clerks and other officers belonging to this office. I do hereunder mentioned send you the names of the persons employed therein for your making out bills for them accordingly, viz.

John Fawler } chief
Edward Burt } clerks.
Thomas Gibbs, }
Edward Halford, }
Samuel Sanders, } clerks.
Thomas Parmiter, }
Thomas Warren, }
Richard Marratt, messenger.
Marmaduke Hartwell, late porter, to be paid to his widow, Anne Hartwell.
James Burrowes } messenger's
Thomas Claridge } servants.
Gregory Mason, watchman.
Elizabeth Buck, woman that looks after the office.

I am,
Gentlemen,
Your most humble servant,
WM. BRIDGEMAN.

To the Principal Officers and Commissioners of their Majesties' Navy.

Authority: Admty. MS. Salary and Pension Book, II, ff. 20, 21 *v*

BIBLIOGRAPHY

I. BIBLIOGRAPHIES

A. Manuscript Sources

Bodleian Library. Catalogi cod. MSS. Bibl. Bodl. partis quintae. Ricardi Rawlinson, codicum classes complectens. confecit W. D. Macray (5 vols., 1862–1900). (*A good introduction to MSS. of naval interest is by* C. H. Firth, 'Papers relating to the Navy in the Bodleian Library', in *M.M.* iii, no. 8, pp. 225–9.)

British Museum. Catalogues and Indexes of MSS.; King's (1 vol., 1921), Lansdowne (2 vols., 1812–19), Harleian (4 vols., 1808–12), Stowe (2 vols., 1895–6), Sloane (1 vol., 1904), Additional (A Catalogue of the Manuscripts Preserved in the British Museum, hitherto undescribed, ed. S. Ayscough, 1832; and Acquisitions 1783–1920 (14 vols.)).

Class Catalogue in the Manuscript Room at the B.M. (*Begun by Sir E. A. Bond. Not duplicated elsewhere.*)

Pepysian Library. Bibliotheca Pepysiana: A Descriptive Catalogue of the Library of Samuel Pepys. Part i, Sea Manuscripts, ed. J. R. Tanner (1914).

Public Record Office. Lists and Indexes, vols. ii (Pipe and Audit Offices, 1893), xviii (Admiralty Records, 1904), xix (State Papers, Foreign, 1904), xliii (State Papers relating to Great Britain and Ireland, 1914), xlvi (Records of the Treasury, 1921). (*These volumes should be consulted through the copies in the P.R.O. itself, which have been substantially corrected and added to by the staff.*)

No bibliographies exist for the MSS. in the Admiralty Library, *nor as yet for those in the library of the* National Maritime Museum, Greenwich. *A useful guide to naval MSS. in general is the* 'Catalogue of the Naval Manuscripts in the Library of the Royal United Service Institution' (compiled H. Garbett, n.d., but about 1930).

B. Printed Sources

Admiralty Library. Subject Catalogue of Printed Books, Part i (1912).

British Museum. Catalogue of Printed Books (1931–); Subject-Index (1902–).

Callender, G. A. R. Bibliography of Naval History, Part i (Historical Association Leaflet no. 58, 1924).

Catalogue of Pamphlets, Tracts, Proclamations, Speeches, Sermons, Trials, Petitions from 1506 to 1700, at Lincoln's Inn (1908).

Clark, G. N. Guide to English Commercial Statistics, 1696–1782 (1938).

Davis, Godfrey. Bibliography of British History, Stuart Period, 1603–1714 (1928).

Manwaring, G. E. Bibliography of British Naval History (1930). (*Incomplete, but useful for both manuscript and printed sources.*)

The Term Catalogues, 1668–1709 and 1711, ed. E. Arber, vol. ii (3 vols., 1903–6).

II. MANUSCRIPT SOURCES

The manuscript sources for this study are so various as to appear miscellaneous, and an introduction to the principle which has led to their selection therefore seems advisable. That principle has been to cover, so far as possible, the material for the three levels of authority in naval affairs during this period: the King and his Secretaries of State, the Admiralty, and the Navy Board.

The Admiralty is the central authority, connected by its correspondence with those above and below it; and its records have been taken as the basis for this work. They exist mainly in the Public Record Office, as P.R.O. Admiralty Papers; but they are supplemented by copies of certain documents no longer available there, which are among the miscellaneous collections in the British Museum. For 1688, the Pepysian manuscripts at Magdalene College, Cambridge, have been used, supplemented by those in the Bodleian Library.

The higher level of authority, itself diffuse and subdivided, is represented by no single collection. Some confidential papers kept by William himself exist in the State Papers, Domestic, at the Public Record Office, and are inadequately calendared in *Cal.S.P.Dom.* Much of his correspondence, and many of the Orders in Council and the letters from its members on naval affairs, are also in that publication or in the Admiralty Papers. The correspondence of the Secretaries of State on naval affairs is contained partly in the State Papers, Domestic, partly in the relevant Admiralty Papers, but largely in miscellaneous collections, some of them in private hands and already published by the Historical Manuscripts Commission, some in private hands and still unpublished, and some in the British Museum or the National Maritime Museum, Greenwich. The correspondence of commanders at sea with the Secretaries of State is contained mainly in the collections outside the Public Record Office.

The lower level of the Navy Board, with its subsidiary local officials, is represented partly by its correspondence in the Admiralty Papers at the Public Record Office, and partly by its Minutes and miscellanea among the Sergison Papers at Greenwich. Most of the records of the Victualling Commissioners have disappeared.

In addition to its own work, the work of different external authorities affected the naval administration at different times. For the fleet's stay in Cadiz during the winter of 1694–5, the State Papers, Foreign (Spanish) have been used; and for various financial questions throughout the period, the Treasury Papers and the Rolls of the Pipe and Audit Offices at the Public Record Office.

Finally, certain sea officers and naval officials made observations on and digests of naval affairs, both at the time and after the end of the war. Some of these are among the manuscripts at the British Museum and in the Bodleian and Admiralty Libraries.

The sources are given below in the normal way, under the collections in which they are now to be found. Their disposition varies according to the history of the departments and offices to which they initially belonged. Some of the collections have grown organically, and represent in their arrangement the organization which they describe. Others do not. In view of the changes that have affected the various classes of records in various degrees, and in view of the corollary that many of the documents in the miscellaneous collections are of unequal value—a fact which is necessarily irrelevant to the intention of their catalogues—a critical bibliography has been attempted, with particular emphasis on the manuscripts outside the main and largely self-explanatory body of papers in the Public Record Office. Where documents in this category are of particular importance, they are marked with an asterisk, thus *.

A. Public Record Office

I. Admiralty Papers

(*a*) *Secretary's Department*

In-Letters

1/577 Admiral's Despatches, unemployed: 1693–1742.

1/3557–3583 Letters from the Navy Board: 1688–March 1698. (*The principal authority for the working of the Navy Board. Have been read in detail.*)

1/3930 Intelligence: 1697–1705.

1/3988 Letters relating to Ireland: 1691–1701.

1/3997 Register Office Letters: 1696–1715.

1/4080–4086 Letters from Secretaries of State: 1689–July 1700. (*Important, if read with the complementary official letters in* Cal.S.P.Dom. *and with the private correspondence in other MS. collections. See* II, B; II, E (6) *and* (7); II, F (1) *below.*)

1/5114 Miscellaneous Letters and Reports: 1686–1730. (*Some letters relating to pressing.*)
1/5247–5249 Copies of Orders in Council: 1688–1705.
1/5253–5259 Reports of Courts Martial: 1680–July 1698. (*The account of Torrington's court martial is missing.*)

Out-Letters

2/3–25 Admiralty Orders and Instructions: March 1689–May 1699. (*Not read in detail.*)
2/169–178 Lords' Letters: March 1689–July 1698. (*Have been read in detail.*)
2/363 Lords' Letters to Secretaries of State: January 1695–May 1699. (*Have been read in detail.*)
2/377–393 Secretary's Letters: March 1689–January 1698. (*Have been read in detail.*)
2/1728 Promiscuous Admiralty Orders: 1690–1695.

Minutes

3/1–14 Minutes of the Board of Admiralty: March 1689–July 1698. (*The most valuable single source. Have been read in detail.*)

Miscellanea

7/169, 175 Estimates, 1st and 2nd series: 1684–1730. (*Useful, but must be supplemented by scattered estimates in Sergison and unnumbered MSS. at Greenwich.*)
7/633, 638, 639, 640, 641, 644 Instructions to Officers of Navy Board. (*Incomplete series of orders. Of occasional value only.*)
7/675, 678, 691 Collections relating to pay. (*Later collections of minor value.*)
7/676 Collection relating to schoolmasters and chaplains. (*Later collection of minor value.*)
7/677 Collection relating to ordnance. (*Later collection of minor value.*)
7/692 Admiral Russell's Order-Book, 1692. (*Useful specimen of several similar order-books.*)

List Books

8/1–7 List Books: 1673–1703. (*Disposition lists for most months of the war. Most important, but not always accurate.*)

(*b*) *Accountant General's Department*

Treasurer's Ledgers

20/48 Victualling Ledger: 1688–9.
20/50 Navy Ledger: 1689–1690. (*Both these are useful for contracts, and for structure of victualling and naval stores' business at beginning of war.*)
20/57 Shipbuilding Ledger: 1691–1697. (*Accounts of the 27 ships.*)

Registers, various

30/2 Arrears of Officers and Seamen, 1689 1700.

Various

49/29, 30 Abstracts of Contracts: 1688–1693. (*Supplement* P.R.O.Adm. 20/50 above. *Useful for prices and amount of business done by individual contractors.*)

49/119, 120 Prices of stores: 1660–1798. (*Many useful lists.*)

49/123 Statistics of stores: 1686–1721. (*Includes the establishments for ships of 1686.*)

49/132, 136, 137, 139 Orders to Yards: 1658–1765. (*One of three series of the Standing Orders to the yards which supplement each other.*)

49/157 Statistics of Yards: 1691–1709. (*See* Sergison MS. A 123 *below.*)

49/173 Naval Debts: 1686–1715. (*Includes details of Exchequer payments in 1689, and several statements of annual debts. See* Sergison MS. A 133 *below.*)

IND. 9310, 9315 Digest of Standing Orders to Yards: 1658–1765. (*The second series of these orders.*)

(*c*) *Controller of the Navy's Department—Miscellanea*

95/3 Estimates for building ships in dockyards: 1689–1699.

95/13–14 Orders as to stores: 1688–1698. (*Useful lists not contained in* P.R.O.Adm. 49/119, 120.)

(*d*) *Navy Board*

In-Letters

106/394, 402, 404, 411, 417, 425, 431, 434, 451, 455, 457–8, 470, 476, 478–9, 489–90, 496–8, 506, 513–14, 519 Miscellaneous Letters: 1689–1698. (*Arranged by letters. Letters* F, H–J, S–W *consulted, for correspondence with individual contractors and shipbuilders.*)

Out-Letters

106/2349 Letters to Victualling Department: 1674–1699.

106/2507 Standing Orders to Yards: 1658–1768. (*The third collection of this type.*)

106/2974 List of Artificers sent to the Mediterranean: 1694–1696.

Miscellanea

106/3069–3071 Contracts: 1676–1710. (*Mostly individual original contracts for ships. Important.*)

106/3249 Deal Yard Letter-Book: 1696–7. (*The only Yard letter book of the period in the P.R.O. Of occasional interest.*)

106/3551 Appendix of Warrants to Yards: 1695–1773. (*See* P.R.O.Adm. 106/2507 *above.*)

(e) *Victualling Department—Accounts*

112/67 Account of Provisions returned: 1685–1704.

112/68–69 Accounts of Issues and Remains: 1689–1702. (*Monthly accounts, in detail, of victuals at different ports.*)

(f) *Medical Department—Miscellanea*

105/41 Register Office Minutes: 1696–1699.

2. TREASURY PAPERS

(a) *Departmental Accounts, Navy*

38/608 Imprest Accounts: 1689–1697. (*Contains imprests to commanders at sea.*)

38/611 Abstract of Accounts: 1689–1702. (*Receipts and payments during Russell's Treasurership of the Navy.*)

38/614 Printed reports of the Commissioners of Public Accounts on Lord Orford's Treasurership, 1704. (*See* III, E, 2(*b*), *Russell, below.*)

38/615 Papers relating to the foregoing: 1689–1704. (*Includes details of Exchequer payments for victualling,* 1691–1697.)

38/658 Victualling Office, quarterly accounts of Debt: 1693–1697.

(b) *Miscellanea*

48/12 Lowndes Papers, Naval and Military: 1678–1713. (*Includes estimated annual distribution of funds,* 1693–1695.)

64/298 Lists of Mariners, Kent and Middlesex: 1691.

3. STATE PAPERS, DOMESTIC

King William's Chest. 8/5–18. (*Consulted for individual papers not fully reproduced in Dalrymple,* Memoirs of Great Britain, *vol.* II, *appendix, or in* Cal.S.P.Dom.)

William and Mary. 32/3, 14, 16–17. (*Occasional references from* Cal.S.P.Dom.)

Entry Books, Naval. 44/204–5. (*Occasional references from* Cal.S.P.Dom.)

The references in Cal.S.P.Dom. *to those State Papers, Domestic which are concerned with naval affairs, are confusing, for the system changes after the volume for 1694–5. It may be of use to give the references as they appear in the different volumes covering this period:*

MSS. referred to throughout, and so calendared after 1694–5	*References until end of 1694–5, unless otherwise stated*
S.P.Dom. King William's Chest. S.P. 8/5–18.	S.P.Dom. King William's Chest (until 1698).
S.P.Dom. William and Mary. S.P. 32/1–10.	S.P.Dom. William and Mary (until 1698).
S.P.Dom. Naval. S.P. 42/1–5.	H.O. Admiralty 1, 2, 4–7, 9–11.
S.P.Dom. Naval. S.P. 42/11.	H.O. Admiralty 8.

S.P.Dom. Entry Books:

Secretaries' Letter-Books, S.P. 44/97–9.	H.O. Letter-Books 1–3.
S.P. 44/100.	H.O. Letter-Book 5.
King Letters, S.P. 44/162–3.	S.P.Dom. King's Letters 1, 2.
Naval, S.P. 44/204.	H.O. Admiralty 3.
S.P. 44/205.	H.O. Entry Book 1.
Regencies, S.P. 44/273.	—
S.P. 44/274–5.	H.O. Regencies 71–2.

4. STATE PAPERS, FOREIGN

Spain

S.P. 94/73–74 Letters and Papers of Alexander Stanhope: 1689–1699. (*Useful letters from the English ambassador.*)

S.P. 75 Letters and Papers of William Aglionby and others: 1692–1705. (*Of minor interest.*)

Foreign Entry Books

S.P. 104/195–8 Secretaries of States' Letter Books: 1691–1706. (*Reverse correspondence to above. Sometimes useful on naval affairs, particularly in* 1694.)

S.P. 100/55, 101/92, 102/55, *all concerned with Spanish relations during the war, are of no interest for naval affairs.*

5. PIPE AND AUDIT OFFICES, DECLARED ACCOUNTS

Pipe Office, Rolls 2322–32 }
Audit Office, Bundles 1718–21 } Treasurer of the Navy's Declared Accounts, 1689–1698.

B. Transcripts of the Finch MSS., 1691–1693

**Transcripts of the Finch MSS. have been made by the staff of the Historical Manuscripts Commission for the projected volumes* III *and* IV *of* H.M.C. Finch, *which have not yet been published. They contain Nottingham's correspondence from* 1691 *to* 1693, *and are almost wholly concerned with naval affairs. They form the principal authority for the naval policy of* 1691 *and* 1692, *and are of particular value for Nottingham's relations with Russell, many of whose letters are included.*

C. Pepysian Library, Magdalene College, Cambridge

SEA MSS.

*2861, 2862 Samuel Pepys's Admiralty Letters, vols. XIV, XV. (*The principal authority for the work of the Admiralty during* 1688.)

2879 Samuel Pepys's Miscellanies, vol. XI.

2902 Samuel Pepys's Day Collection.

2827 Rules for Ordnance Office, 1684.

2997 Surveys of the Thames, 1684 and 1687.

977 'The Method of Building...Ships of War', by Edward Battine, 1684. (*One of many copies, with different dedications at different dates, of a useful work.*)

D. Bodleian Library

Rawlinson MSS.

A 170, 171, 179, 186 Papers of Samuel Pepys. (*Contain items not included in his papers at Magdalene, and private correspondence.*)

A 198 Account of charge of dockyards, 1687–1688.

C 512 Signal Book of 1693.

C 914 Tables of cordage and gunner's stores. (*An example of local compilation, from Portsmouth ropeyard.*)

D 147 'Naval Essays' by Sir Henry Shere.

D 794 Pepys's papers. (*Lists of those in his possession after* 1689.)

E. British Museum

1. King's MSS.

*43 Survey of Harbours and Dockyards, 1688 and 1698. (*Primary authority for appearance and equipment of royal yards. Scale plans and views.*)

53 Project for surprising Dunkirk Harbour, *c.* 1695.

70 Rules for Ordnance Office: 1683–1759.

2. Lansdowne MSS.

847 Progress of Plymouth Dockyard, 1694. (*By Edmund Dummer.*)

*1152B William Bridgeman's Letter Book, 1694–1697. (*Contains correspondence with Russell and Aylmer at Cadiz.*)

1153 Papers of Sir Paul Rycaut. (*For navy and shipbuilding at Hamburg.*)

3. Harleian MSS.

1324 Sundry Papers relating to Trade.

4318 Account of Portsmouth Docks, 1698.

6378 Health of Seamen in West Indies, 1696.

6843 Papers relating to Naval Affairs.

*7476 Proceedings of Commissioners of Navy in repair of Fleet, 1688–1692. By A. Deane and W. Hewer. (*Supplements Pepys's defence of the Commission of* 1686, *in his* Memoires.)

7479 Observations on Accounts of Treasurer of Navy, 1692.

7471 Everett's Case, and 7477, Letters relating to Victualling Office, 1690–1693 *are inferior collections of material available elsewhere.*

4. Sloane MSS.

3233 A Survey of the Ports on the South West Coast of England, 1698. (*The first joint coastal survey by Trinity House and the navy.*)

5. STOWE MSS.

143 ff. 90–7. (*For Torrington's court martial. The fullest account available.*)
305 ff. 184–5. (*For Torrington's court martial. Another copy of this is in* B.M.Addnl. MS. 38176.)
144 ff. 11*b*, 12. (*For ships built* 1677 *and* 1690. *Details of workmen.*)
478 Increase and decrease of Navy, 1692–1698.

6. EGERTON MSS.

670 Method of Building Ships of War. (*Additions to Battine's work. See* Pep:Sea MS. 977.)
*920 Correspondence of James Vernon, 1694–1701. (*For letters to Blathwayt. See* B.M.Addnl. MS. 34348.)
2521 Correspondence of Family of Haddock. (*Some letters published in* Camden Miscellany, *vol.* VIII.)
*2621 Correspondence and Papers of Admiral Herbert, 1680–1690. (*Useful for* 1688. *Some letters published in* E.H.R. *vol.* I.)

7. ADDITIONAL MSS.

There are collections relating both to the Admiralty and to the Secretaries of State. They have been listed separately below.

(*a*) *Collections relating to the Admiralty*

5439, 9303, 9316, 9320, 9322, 9324, 9331, 22617 Naval Papers. (*Each supplementing* P.R.O. Admiralty *papers in a few instances. Other volumes which do not do so are* 9312, 9313, 9315, 9317, 9318, 9325, 9327, 9328.)
9323, 36784 Victualling Papers. (*Occasionally of value.*)
9329 Description of Plymouth dockyard, 1698. (*By local officers. See* B.M. Lansdowne MS. 847.)
11602, 11684 Collections of Richard Gibson on the Navy. (*Remarks of an experienced minor official. Useful corrective on occasions to Pepys.*)
11643 Plan of Victualling Office, Chatham.
22183, 22184 Papers of Sir Henry Johnson. (*Of interest. Papers of the most prominent shipbuilder of the period.*)
33061 Newcastle Papers, vol. 377. (*Contains case of Robert Waters, contractor for the Plymouth dock.*)

(*b*) *Collections relating to Secretaries of State*

9734, 9735, 9764 Correspondence of William Blathwayt. (*A few items of naval interest.*)
*37991 Correspondence of William Blathwayt, 1692. (*Important letters to Nottingham, supplementing the latter's correspondence in* II, B *above.*)
*37992 Correspondence of William Blathwayt, 1693–1701. (*Important letters to different Secretaries of State. See* II, F (1) *below.*)
*34348 Correspondence of James Vernon, 1692–1705. (*Letters to Blathwayt. See* B.M. Egerton MS. 920.)

*21494 Southwell Papers, 1686–1740. (*Letters from Russell to Shrewsbury*, 1694.)

*38146 Entry Book of Sir Robert Southwell, 1690. (*Letters to Nottingham from Ireland, supplementing the latter's correspondence in* H.M.C. Finch, *vol.* II.)

15857, 28103 *For letters relating to Herbert and Russell.*

F. National Maritime Museum, Greenwich

MSS. were not catalogued when consulted. A few have been given temporary numbers, which are given below:

1. ACQUISITIONS FROM BIBLIOTHECA PHILLIPPICA

(*a*) Admiralty Papers, 8 volumes, especially vols. *I, *II, *IV, *VI: Blathwayt Correspondence, 1690–1697. (*Important. Most of the letters are originals and consist of letters from Trenchard which supplement Blathwayt's letters in* B.M.Addnl. 37992, *and from Sotherne and Bridgeman. Also rough drafts of William's orders to Russell in* 1694, *and letters to Southwell supplementing the Nottingham–Southwell correspondence. Vol.* IV *contains the only contemporary account of Torrington's defence of his conduct in the House of Commons.*) Vol. VIII: Naval Papers, 1635–1690. (*Miscellaneous interest.*)

(*b*) *Receipts signed by P. Bowles for official papers transferred by Pepys to Admiralty in 1689. (*Two lists, giving details of records which Pepys surrendered on retiring.*)

2. SERGISON PAPERS

*Navy Board Minutes, vols. XVII–XXXIX. (*Vols.* XVII *and* XVIII (*June* 1688–*February* 1689) *consulted in detail. The rest consulted for negotiations with east country merchants and with shipbuilders, and for miscellaneous information.*)

3. SERGISON MISCELLANY, 6 VOLUMES

Besides much duplication of correspondence in P.R.O. Admiralty Papers, contains rough drafts of letters, and office memoranda which are of interest. Many observations by Sergison. I have had the benefit of Commander R. D. Merriman's typed index to the 'Miscellany', which has greatly facilitated reference to its contents. See also III, A *below.*

4. SERGISON MSS. (MISCELLANEOUS)

A 115 Lists of Royal Navy, December 1688 and 1698. (*Differ slightly from similar lists in Pepysian Library and Charnock's* Marine Architecture.)

*A 123 Abstract of numbers of workmen weekly employed in H.M. Yards, 1686–1709. (*Important. Can be checked throughout by* B.M. Addnl. 9324, ff. 17–52, *and after* 1691 *by* P.R.O. Admiralty 49/157.)

A 131 Estimates of Navy, 1692–1698.

A 133 Estimates of Naval Debt, 1689–1698. (*Fill in gaps in P.R.O. Admiralty estimates and statements of debt.*)

A 135 Orders and Reports. (*Minor interest.*)

'Officers of the Navy.' (*List of all officers connected with Navy Office* 1688–1697, *presented to William. Useful.*)

5. UNNUMBERED MSS.

Tables of Wages and Estimates, 1692–1703. (*Some details, e.g. of allowances for surgeons, not shown elsewhere.*)

Upkeep of Navy, 1688–1705. (*Some details of naval accounts not given elsewhere. Book compiled for Lord North when Governor of Portsmouth,* 1711.)

G. Admiralty Library

CORBETT MSS.

Vols. I, IV–XI, XIII–XV, XVII–XXI. (*Collection of precedents and observations upon them, by the man who was first Burchett's colleague and then his successor as Secretary of the Admiralty, c.* 1740. *The observations are often valuable. Corbett greatly admired Pepys, and this is an obvious and largely successful attempt to do for the early eighteenth century what the latter had done for his own age. Thanks to its orderly arrangement and subject index, it is easy to trace in it the results of much of the work begun by the Admiralties of William's reign, and the relative success of their different measures; and thus, with Corbett's remarks, to see the first French war in retrospect from the commentary provided by the experience of its successors.*)

III. PRINTED SOURCES

A. General

Aiken, W. A. (ed.): Conduct of the Earl of Nottingham (1941). (*Nottingham's private papers have appeared in different publications. This work itself is composed of various manuscripts in the form of memoirs, notes and speeches, mainly but not all by himself, which have been made into a consecutive narrative by the editor.*

His letters on naval affairs while Secretary of State, other than his official correspondence, have been published mainly in H.M.C. Finch, vol. II (*see* III, B *below*), *which supplies much of the material by which the judgements recorded in the* Conduct *may themselves be judged, and which is continued in the as yet unpublished Finch MSS.* (*see* II, B *above*). *Some, however, have also been published in* H.M.C. 15th Report, appendix, pt II (*see* III, B *below*). *Others of his naval letters, and most of the reverse correspondence to him, have not been published* (*see* II, E (7); II, F (1) *above*). *Both published and unpublished private correspondence duplicate to some extent his official papers in* II, A (1); II, A (3) *above, some of which have been published in* H.C.J. vol. X *and* H.M.C. 14th Report, appendix, pt VI. *See also Laughton below.*)

Ailesbury, Earl of: Memoirs (Roxburgh Society, 1891).

Archives de la Maison d'Orange-Nassau, 3rd series, 1689–1702 (ed. F. J. L. Krämer, 3 vols., 1907–9).

Bentinck, Mechthilde Comtesse (ed.): Lettres et Mémoires de Marie, reine d'Angleterre (1880). (*See also* Bathurst, A. B. (ed.), Letters of Two Queens (1924).)

Browning, Andrew: Life and Letters of Thomas Osborne, Earl of Danby, vol. II (1939). (*Letters of Danby.*)

Browning, Andrew (ed.): Memoirs of Sir John Reresby (1932).
Burnet, Gilbert: History of My Own Time (ed. M. J. Routh, 6 vols., 1833).
Calendar of State Papers, Colonial: America and West Indies.
Calendar of State Papers, Domestic. (*The précis given of the important papers in King William's Chest must be viewed with caution for the volumes down to and including 1694–5. Many of these papers are given* in extenso *in Dalrymple's* Memoirs, *below. It is generally wisest to consult the manuscript for the text of any important document calendared, particularly for the volumes mentioned above.*)
Calendar of Treasury Books, vols. VIII–XI. (*There is an additional volume of introduction to vols.* XI–XVII *by W. A. Shaw. This and his introductions in vols.* VIII *and* IX, *while important, must be read with care. His figures should, where possible, be checked by the* Return of Public Income and Expenditure, pt I, *of* 1869 (*see* IV, B *below*).)
Calendar of Treasury Papers, vol. I.
Camden, William: Britannia Newly Translated into English with Large Additions and Improvements, Published by Edward Gibson (1695).
Chamberlayne, Edward: Angliae Notitia, or the Present State of England. (*The editions affecting this period are the sixteenth to nineteenth* (1687, 1691, 1694, 1700). *Part* II *is particularly valuable; although bound with Part* I, *it has a separate series of editions.*)
Clarendon, Earl of: State Letters...and Diary (2 vols., 1763).
Clarke, J. S.: Life of James II (2 vols., 1816). (*For the value of the 'Memoirs' of James II contained in this work, see W. S. Churchill's* Marlborough, His Life and Times, vol. I (1933).)
Coxe, William (ed.): Correspondence of the Earl of Shrewsbury (1821). (*Some of the letters are duplicated in the much fuller* H.M.C. Buccleugh (Montagu House), vol. II, pts I *and* II (*see* III, B *below*). *The earlier publication, however, is not entirely superseded by the later.*)
Dalrymple, Sir James: Memoirs of Great Britain and Ireland (2 vols., 1771–3). (*Original documents, including several from King William's Chest relating to the events of* 1690, *are reproduced* in extenso *in the appendix to vol.* II. *The first edition of this work is better than the second.*)
Davenant, Charles: Political and Commercial Works. Collected and revised by Sir C. Whitworth (5 vols., 1771).
Davenport, F. M. G. (ed.): European Treaties bearing on the History of the United States and Its Dependencies, vol. II, 1650–1697 (1929).
Doebner, R. (ed.): Memoirs of Mary, Queen of England (1886).
Du Mont, J. (ed.): Corps universal diplomatique (8 vols., 1726–31). (*This does not include the Anglo-Dutch naval convention of* 1689, *for which see Davenport above.*)
Evelyn, John: Memoirs (ed. W. Bray, 2 vols., 1823).
Foxcroft, H. C.: Life and Letters of George Savile, Marquis of Halifax (2 vols., 1898). (*Vol.* II *contains the 'Spencer House Journals', and Halifax's 'Rough Draught of a New Model at Sea' of* 1694.)
Foxcroft, H. C. (ed.): Supplement to Burnet's 'History of My Own Time' (1902). (*Several comparisons on naval and other prominent figures and events may be drawn between the characters and accounts given here, and those given later in the* History.)

Grant, James (ed.): The Old Scots Navy, from 1689 to 1710 (*N.R.S.* 1914).
Grey, Anchitell: Debates of the House of Commons, from the year 1667 to the year 1694, vols. IX, X (1763). (*Supplemented by Cobbett's* Parliamentary History of England (*see* IV, B *below*).)
James, G. P. R. (ed.): Letters Illustrative of the Reign of William III...from 1696 to 1708, vol. I (3 vols., 1841). (*Correspondence of William Vernon, mainly to Shrewsbury. See also* II, E (6), (7) *above.*)
Japikse, N. (ed.): Correspondentie van Willem III en van Hans Willem Bentinck (3 vols., 1927–37).
Journals of the House of Commons, vols. X–XII.
Journals of the House of Lords, vols. XIV–XVI.
Kennett, White: Compleat History of England... (1706).
Kerr, R. J., and Duncan, I. C. (ed.): The Portledge Papers...from December 10th 1687 to August 7th 1697 (1928).
Laughton, Sir J. K. (ed.): 'A Commissioner's Note Book, Annis 1691–1694', in *The Naval Miscellany*, vol. II (*N.R.S.* 1912), pp. 137–205. (*This includes Nottingham's précis of his correspondence with Russell during the Barfleur campaign of* 1692. *Although the editor describes it as 'a correspondence which seems to be hitherto unknown except so far as it was abstracted by Burchett in his* Transactions at Sea', *the papers are all printed in* H.C.J., vol. X, pp. 749–59, *and* H.M.C. 14*th Report, appendix, pt.* VI, pp. 198–245.)
London Gazette.
Luttrell, Narcissus: Brief Historical Relation of State Affairs (6 vols., 1857).
Macky, John: Memoirs of the Secret Services of (Roxburghe Club, 1895).
Macpherson, James: Original Papers containing the Secret History of Great Britain from the Restoration to the Accession of the House of Hanover (2 vols., 1775). (*For the value of this work, which contains extracts from the 'Nairne Papers' relating to Russell's treachery, see W. S. Churchill's* Marlborough, His Life and Times, vol. I.)
Marsden, R. G. (ed.): Documents relating to Law and Custom of the Sea, vol. II (*N.R.S.*, 2 vols., 1915–16).
Medows, Sir Philip: Dominion and Sovereignty of the Seas (1689).
Merriman, R. D. (ed.): The Sergison Papers (*N.R.S.* 1950). (*Important. Selections from* II, F (3), (4) *above, with valuable introductory notes to each section.*)
Miege, Guy: The New State of England (1691–5).
Molesworth, Robert: Account of Denmark (1694).
Molloy, Charles: De Jure Maritimo et Navali (4th ed., 1688).
Morris, C. (ed.): The Journeys of Celia Fiennes (1947).
Oeconomy of H.M. Navy Office, the: Being the First Rules Established by the Duke of York (1717). (*See also York below.*)
Ordonnances de Louis XIV pour les Armées Navales et Arsenaux de Marine (1689).
Papillon, A. F. W. (ed.): Memoirs of Thomas Papillon of London, Merchant, 1623–1702 (1887).
Pepys, Samuel: Memoires of the Royal Navy of England (1690). (*Pepys's defence of his last term in office. See also* II, E (3) *above.*)

Petty, Sir William: Treatise of Naval Philosophy (1691).
Petty, Sir William: Economic Writings of, ed. H. C. Hull (2 vols., 1899).
Petty, Sir William: Petty Papers, ed. Marquess of Lansdowne (2 vols., 1927).
Ranke, L. von: History of England mainly in the Seventeenth Century, vols. IV–VI (English translation, 6 vols., 1875). (*Vol.* VI *contains some of Bonnet's dispatches from London.*)
Robinson, J.: Account of Sueden (1694).
Scott, W. R.: Constitution and Finance of English, Scottish and Irish Joint-Stock Companies to 1720, vol. III (3 vols., 1910–12). (*Pp.* 536–9, 542–3 *reproduce accounts of Exchequer income and expenditure not available elsewhere.*)
Statutes of the Realm (9 vols. and index, 1810–28).
Steele, R. and Crawford, Earl of (ed.): Tudor and Stuart Proclamations, 1485–1714 (2 vols., 1910).
Tanner, J. R. (ed.): Descriptive Catalogue of the Naval Manuscripts in the Pepysian Library at Magdalene College, Cambridge (*N.R.S.*, 4 vols., 1903–22). (*Important lists and papers, with a valuable general introduction by Tanner which synthesizes the many articles and papers by him on the same subject elsewhere. See also* IV, B *below.*)
Tanner, J. R. (ed.): Private Correspondence and Miscellaneous Papers of Samuel Pepys, 1679–1703 (2 vols., 1926).
Tanner, J. R. (ed.): Samuel Pepys's Naval Minutes (*N.R.S.* 1926). (*Interesting notes and reflections by Pepys after his retirement.*)
Thompson, E. Maunde (ed.): 'Correspondence of Admiral Herbert in 1688', in *E.H.R.* vol. I.
Thompson, E. Maunde (ed.): 'Correspondence of the Family of Haddock', in *Camden Miscellany*, vol. VIII (1893).
Thompson, E. Maunde (ed.): 'Correspondence of the Family of Hatton', in *Camden Miscellany*, vol. II (1878).
Thorold Rogers, J. E. (ed.): Complete Collection of the protests of the Lords with historical introductions, 1624–1874, vol. I (3 vols., 1875).
Warner, Rebecca (ed.): Epistolary Curiosities...Illustrative of the Herbert Family, series I (1818). (*A few letters of Torrington's after his dismissal.*)
York, James Duke of: Memoirs of English Affairs, 1660–73 (1729). (*Largely naval, and includes many of his administrative orders.*)

B. Publications of the Historical Manuscripts Commission

(*The more important volumes are marked with an asterisk*)

Ancaster.
Bath, vols. II, III. (*Vol.* III *contains the Prior papers, for the Treaty of Ryswick.*)
Beaufort.
*Buccleuch and Queensberry, vol. II, pts I and II. (*Important Shrewsbury correspondence, and minutes of inner Council meetings. See Coxe,* III, A *above.*)

★Dartmouth, vol. I (11th Report, appendix, pt V). (*Important letters to and from the fleet*, 1688.)
★Dartmouth, vol. III (15th Report, appendix, pt I). (*Grenville Collins's journal in the fleet*, 1688.)
Denbigh.
★Downshire, vol. I, pts I and II. (*Sir William Trumbull's papers.*)
Eliot Hodgkin (15th Report, appendix, pt II). (*Minor correspondence of Nottingham, and of William III.*)
★Finch, vol. II. (*The highly important Nottingham papers for* 1689–90, *which are continued in* II, B *above.*)
Fitzherbert (13th Report, appendix, pt VI).
Frankland-Russell-Astley.
Hastings, vol. II. (*Interesting news-letters.*)
Hope-Johnstone.
★House of Lords, 1689–90 (12th Report, appendix, pt VI); 1690–1 (13th Report, appendix, pt V); 1692–3 (14th Report, appendix, pt VI); continued in House of Lords MSS., New Series, vols. I–VIII, 1693–1710. (*All vols. covering the war years are highly important:* 1689–90 *contains orders concerning Ireland,* 1692–3 *orders for the Smyrna convoy, and these and other vols. include detailed reports from the Parliamentary Commissioners for auditing the public accounts. Vol.* VII *in the New Series has some accounts relating to the war, and miscellaneous information on the years* 1689–98 *may be found in general in the volumes for Anne's reign.*)
Kenyon (14th Report, appendix, pt IV).
Leeds (11th Report, appendix, pt VII).
Le Fleming (12th Report, appendix, pt VII). (*Interesting news-letters.*)
Leybourne-Popham.
Lindley Wood (Reports on Various Collections, vol. VIII).
Lindsey (14th Report, appendix, pt IX).
Lindsey, Supplementary Report. (*Sir William Warren's papers.*)
Lonsdale (13th Report, appendix, pt VII).
Lothian.
Muncaster (10th Report, appendix, pt IV).
Onslow (14th Report, appendix, pt IX).
Portland, vol. II (13th Report, appendix, pt II).
Portland, vol. III (14th Report, appendix, pt II). (*Correspondence of Robert Harley, with comments on public affairs.*)
Portland, vols. VIII, X. (*Interesting miscellaneous correspondence and naval information, as well as Harley's correspondence.*)
Rutland, vol. II (12th Report, appendix, pt V).
Stuart (Windsor Castle), vol. I.
Westmorland (10th Report, appendix, pt IV).

C. Events and Life at Sea

Allyn, Rev. Richard: A Narrative of the Victory Obtained near La Hogue (1744). (*The diary of the chaplain of the* Centurion; *also contains Delaval's and Shovell's reports.*)

Andrews, S. (ed.): 'Battle of La Houge, A.D. 1692', in *The British Archivist*, I, pp. 9–12. (*Contemporary description from the parish registers of Northwood, Isle of Wight.*)

Anon: An Exact Journal of the Victorious Expedition of the Confederate Fleet, the last year, under the Command of Admiral Russell... (1695).

An Account given by Sir John Ashby, Vice-Admiral and Reere-Admiral Rooke of the Engagement at Sea...June 30th, 1690...(1691).

Barlow's Journal of his Life at Sea in King's Ships, East and West Indiamen, and other merchantmen, from 1659 to 1703, ed. B. Lubbock (2 vols., 1934).

Boulter, Rev. W. C. (ed.): 'The Battle of La Hougue', in *E.H.R.* VII, pp. 11–13. (*Contemporary account.*)

Burchett, Josiah: Memoirs of Transactions at Sea during the War with France (1703). (*Much of this is reproduced in his* Complete History of the Most Remarkable Transactions at Sea *of* 1720 (*see* IV, B *below*) *which is more often cited. For William's war, the earlier work should normally be used. See also Lillingston, below.*)

Caermarthen, Peregrine Osborne, Marquess of: Journal of the Brest Expedition (1695).

Ingram, Bruce, S. (ed.): Three Sea Journals of Stuart Times (1936). (*Includes journal of Jeremy Roch.*)

Leake, Life of Sir John, ed. G. Callender (*N.R.S.*, 2 vols., 1920).

Leslie, R. C. (ed.): Life aboard a Privateer in the time of Queen Anne (1889). (*Contains extracts from the journal of Woodes Rogers.*)

Lillingston, Colonel Luke: Reflections on Mr Burchett's Memoirs...(1704). (*On West Indian affairs only.*)

Lists of Fleets:[1]

Gloria Britannica, or the Boast of the British Seas, containing a True and Full account of the Royal Navy of England...(1689). (*The first printed 'Navy List'.*)

A list of the French King's Fleet now at Sea...(1689) (in B.M. Printed 816 m. 7).

A True List of the French Fleet for the year 1692, commanded by the Count de Tourville...(1692) (printed in *Somers Tracts*, XI, pp. 456–8).

An Exact list of their Majesties and the Dutch Fleet, designed for the year 1692 (1692) (*Somers Tracts*, XI, pp. 459–61).

An Exact List of their Majesties and the Dutch Fleet designed for the Year 1693. For a Line of Battle (1693).

[1] This does not include MS. lists published later in *Cal.S.P.Dom.* or *H.M.C.* publications, and does not pretend to be a complete list of contemporary printed sheets. For example, the Admiralty initiated a search in May 1691 for an unauthorized list of the English fleet which had recently been published (P.R.O.Adm. 3/6: 8/5); possibly for that reason, I have been unable to find a copy of it.

The List of the English Royal Navy as it is ordered for the Line of Battle. St Heylins, May 19, 1694.

The Glory of the British Seas, Being a List of the Royal Navy (1697).

A Compleat List of the Royal Navy of England....This 31st of December, 1697 (1697/8).

Martin, Life of Captain Stephen: ed. C. Markham (*N.R.S.* 1895).

Pepys, Samuel: Tangier Papers, ed. Edwin Chappell (*N.R.S.* 1935).

de Pointis, M.: An Account of the Taking of Carthagena by the French in the Year 1697 (1698).

Admiral Russell's Letter to the Earl of Nottingham: Containing an exact and particular Relation of the late happy Victory and Success against the French Fleet (1692).

Shadwell, Charles: The Fair Quaker of Deal (1715). (*For the difference between the various editions of this play, see C. N. Robinson,* The British Tar in Fact and Fiction (1911), *ch.* x.)

Teonge, Henry: Diary, ed. G. E. Manwaring (1927). (*Although this covers the years* 1675–9, *it often applies to the conditions of William's reign. The author was chaplain in several men-of-war.*)

Tourville, Mémoires du Maréchal de...(1758).

Ward, Edward: The Wooden World Dissected (1706).

There are several accounts of life at sea in merchant ships and privateers under Queen Anne, particularly those published by the Hakluyt Society, all of which throw some light on conditions during the previous reign.

D. Technical Manuals

Some works cover more than one subject. They have been listed according to their main interest. Many of them were written or published before William's reign, but have been given where there is evidence that they were still in use or where their contents still apply.

I. Naval Architecture, Shipbuilding and Seamanship

Anderson, R. C. (ed.): 'A Treatise on Rigging' (approx. 1625) (*Soc. Naut. Research, Occas. Publns*, no. 1).

Bond, Henry: The Boate Swaine's Art or the Compleat Boat Swaine (1642; many later editions).

Boteler, Nathaniel: Six Dialogues about Sea Services, ed. W. G. Perrin (*N.R.S.* 1929). (*Published* 1685, *but written probably in* 1634.)

Bourne, William: The Safeguard of Sailors or a Sure Guide for Coasters (1677).

Bushnell, Edmund: The Compleat Ship-wright (3rd ed. 1679; many later editions).

Childe, L.: A short Compendium of the New and Much-Enlarged Sea-Book or Pilot's Sea Mirror (1663).

Collins, Greenville: Great Britain's Coasting Pilot (1693).

Dassié, F.: L'Architecture navale...(1677).

Fournier, Georges: Hydrographie (1643; 2nd ed. 1663, enlarged).

Hayward, Edward: The Sizes and Lengths of Riggings...(1655).

Hollond, John: Second Discourse of the Navy, ed. J. R. Tanner (*N.R.S.* 1896). (*Written in* 1659.)

Hoste, Paul: Théorie de la Construction des Vaisseaux (1697; *bound together with his* L'art des Armées navales, *for which see* III, D, 2 *below*).

Mainwaring, Sir Henry: The Seaman's Dictionary (1644; later editions). (*For the date of this work see G. E. Manwaring and W. G. Perrin,* The Life and Works of Sir Henry Mainwaring, II, pp. 69–74 (*N.R.S.* 1922).)

Miller, Thomas: The Compleat Modellist (1664).

Monson, Sir William: Naval Tracts, Book III, ed. M. Oppenheim (*N.R.S.*, vol. IV, 1913). (*Written about* 1635.)

Narborough, Sir John: The Mariner's Jewel...(1695). (*Later editions edited by James Love.*)

Norwood, Matthew: The Seaman's Companion...applied chiefly to Navigation (1671; later editions).

Pardie, Père: L'Architecture navale...(1677).

Renaud, Chevalier: De la Théorie de la Manœuvre des Vaisseaux...(1689).

Savery, Thomas: Navigation Improv'd...(1698).

Sellers, John: The Coasting Pilot...(1675).

Smith, John: The Seaman's Grammar...(1691). (*This is a reprint, with some new matter, of his* Accidence for Young Seamen *of* 1626, *reprinted under different titles in* 1627 *and* 1636, *and as* The Seaman's Grammar *in* 1653, 1691 *and* 1692.)

Sprat, Thomas: History of the Royal Society of London (1667).

Sutherland, William: The Ship Builder's Assistant...(1711).

Sutherland, William: Britain's Glory or Shipbuilding Unvail'd (1717).

Van Yk, Cornelius: De Nederlandsche Scheeps-Bouw-Konst open geselt (1697).

Wagenaer, Lucas Janszoon: De Spiegel der Zeevaert (1584; translated into English as *The Mariner's Mirror* by A. Ashley in 1588; 2nd ed. 1605). (*The basis of all subsequent pilots in the seventeenth century.*)

Witsen, Nicolaes: Aeloude en Hedendaegsche Scheeps-Bouw en Bestier (1671). (*The 2nd ed. of* 1690 *has the title* Architectura Navalis et Regimen Nauticum.)

Worcester, Edward Somerset, Marquess of: A Century of Inventions... (1663).

2. NAVAL TACTICS

Corbett, Julian S. (ed.): Fighting Instructions, 1530–1816 (*N.R.S.* 1905). (*Texts of the different sets of Instructions, with valuable introductions to each.*)

Hoste, Paul: L'Art des Armées navales ou Traité des Evolutions navales (1697). (*The only contemporary work devoted to naval tactics, and a classic for over a century.*)

3. GUNNERY

Anderson, Robert: The Genuine Use and Effect of the Gunne...(1672). (*Useful.*)

Anderson, Robert: To Cut the Rigging and Proposals for the Improvement of Great Artillery (1691).

Binning, Thomas: A Light to the Art of Gunnery...(1676; later editions).

Eldred, William: The Gunner's Glasse (1646).

Gaya, Sieur de: Traité des Armes, ed. C. Ffoulkes (1911). (*Published in* 1678.)
Harris, John: Lexicon Technicum or an Universal English Dictionary of Arts and Sciences (1704).
Moore, Sir Jonas: A Mathematical Compendium...(1681).
Moore, Sir Jonas: A General Treatise of Artillery or Great Ordnance. (*Translated from the work by Tomaso Moretii,* 1683.)
Moore, Sir Jonas: Artificial Fireworks useful both by Land and Sea. (*A reprint of the work by Sir Abraham Dager. Included with* A General Treatise of Artillery.)
Moore, Sir Jonas: Modern Fortification...(1689). (*Usually cited but, where it covers the same ground, largely reproducing the contents of a* General Treatise of Artillery.)
Norton, Robert: The Gunner shewing the whole Practice of Artillery (1628).
Nye, Nathaniel: The Art of Gunnery...(1674).

4. MEDICINE

(Cockburn, William): An Account of the Nature, Causes, Symptoms and Care of the Distempers That are incident to Seafaring People. With Observations on the Diet of the Sea-men In His Majesty's Navy. By W.C. (1696).
(Cockburn, William): A Continuation of An Account... (1697).
Molye, John: The Sea Chyrurgeon...(1702).

E. Pamphlets, Petitions and Poems[1]

I. PAMPHLETS BY KNOWN AUTHORS

Byrne, Gerald: Several Instances of the Wrongs and Oppressions Suffered by Sailors of the English Navy from the Beginning of the Late War...(n.d., but about 1700).
Crosfeild, Robert: England's Glory reviv'd...(1693).
Crosfeild, Robert: Truth Brought to Light (1694).
Crosfeild, Robert: Great Britain's Tears...(1695).
Crosfeild, Robert: Justice Perverted, and Innocence and Loyalty Oppressed...(1695).
Crosfeild, Robert: Justice the Best Support of Government...(1697).
(Dennis, John): An Essay on the Navy.... By the Author of the Seamen's Case (1702). (*See* III, E, 2 (*a*), *Pamphlets presented to Parliament, below.*)
Everett, George: The Pathway to Peace and Profit...(1694).
Everett, George: Encouragement for Seamen and Mariners...(1695).
Everett, George: Loyalty and Fidelity, Rejected and Oppressed; or the case of George Everett, Shipwright...(1698–9).
Everett, George: A Word in Season...with some Particulars relating to the imbezling of Prizes...(1699).
Hodges, William: Humble Proposals for the Relief, Encouragement, Security and Happiness of the...Seamen of England...To which is added A Dialogue concerning the Art of Ticket-Buying...(1695).
Hodges, William: Great Britain's Groans...(1695).

[1] Except where otherwise stated, the place of publication is London.

Hodges, William: Misery to Misery...(1695).

Hodges, William: Ruin to Ruin, after Misery to Misery...(1699).

(Littleton, Edward): A Project of a Descent upon France....By a Person of Quality (1691).

Maydman, Henry: Naval Speculations, and Maritime Politicks (1691).

Mozin, Thomas and Jennings, Nicholas: A Proposal for the Incouragement of Seamen (1697).

Perry, John: A Regulation for Seamen... (1695).

St Lo, George: England's Safety: Or, a Bridle to the French King (1693). (*A second edition, with a different title page entitled* Gloria Britannica, *appeared in* 1695.)

St Lo, George: England's Interest; Or, a Discipline for Seamen (1694).

Whiston, James: A discourse of the Decay of Trade...(1693). (*Suggestions for the control of convoys and cruisers.*)

Dr Williamson's Memoirs of a few Passages Transacted by Mr Joseph Allen, late Master-Builder at his Majesty's Ship-Yard, Deptford...(1717). (*See also* III, E, 2 (*b*), *Miscellaneous, below.*)

2. ANONYMOUS PAMPHLETS

(*a*) *Collections*

THE HARLEIAN MISCELLANY (1808–13)

Vol. I, An Inquiry into the Causes of the Naval Miscarriages...(2nd ed. 1707), pp. 562–9; A descent from France...(1692), pp. 596–8.

Vol. III, Political Remarks on the Life and Reign of King William III...(n.d.), pp. 354–66.

Vol. IV, Encouragement for Seamen and Manning...(1695), pp. 392–400.

Vol. V, The Parable of the Bear-Baiting (1691), pp. 181–93 (*on Torrington and Beachy Head*).

Vol. VI, A Letter to a new Member of the...House of Commons; touching the Rise of all the Embezzlements and Mismanagements of the Kingdom's Treasure... (Amsterdam, 1710), pp. 304–20 (*retrospective remarks on Orford's Treasurership of the Navy*).

Vol. VIII, Reasons for settling Admiralty Jurisdiction...(1690), pp. 371–82; A Letter to a Country Gentleman, Setting forth the Decay and Ruin of Trade...(1698), pp. 506–13.

SOMERS TRACTS (2ND ED. 1809–15)

Vol. X, The Dear Bargain...(1689?), pp. 349–77.

Vol. XI, The History of the Rook and Turkeys (probably 1693), pp. 90–4 (*relating to the Smyrna convoy*); Remarks upon the London Gazette relating to the Streights Fleet...(probably 1693), pp. 462–71 (*on the Smyrna convoy*).[1]

A COLLECTION OF STATE TRACTS, PUBLISHED DURING THE REIGN OF KING WILLIAM III, VOL. II (1706)

A Modest Inquiry into the Causes of the Present Disasters...(1690), pp. 95–104.

[1] Vol. XI also contains St Lo's 'England's safety' of 1693, on pp. 50–73 (see III, E, 1 above).

The State of Parties...(1692), pp. 208–17.
An Impartial Inquiry into the Causes of the Present Fears...(1692), pp. 218–33.
A Dialogue betwixt Whig and Tory...(*c.* November 1692), pp. 371–92.
A Discourse about Raising Men (1696), pp. 539–50.
A Letter to a Member of Parliament concerning the Four Regiments commonly call'd Marines (January 1698–9), pp. 680–4.
The Seaman's Opinion of a Standing Army[1]... (January 1698–9), pp. 684–92.

PAMPHLETS AND PETITIONS PRESENTED TO PARLIAMENT (contained in B.M. Printed 86 m. 7).[2]

Captain George St Lo his Proceedings against Me...whilst I was Store Keeper of His Majesty's Dock-Yard near Plymouth under him....
An Humble Representation of the Seamens Misery in the Loss and Abuse of them in their Payment....
The Case of the Registered Seamen....
The Case of the Captains of his Majesty's Fleet....
Some Reasons...to Hear the Petitioner John Dennis, when the Report of the Q's and R's shall be read.
Some farther Reasons...offered by the Sailors...for taking off the Q's and R's....
The Case of Many Inhabitants of the Town of Deptford....
The Case of Many Inhabitants of the Town of Chatham....
The Case of Divers Seamen, belonging to His Majesty's Royal Navy; and the Wives of Seamen...together with several of the Widows and others their Friends, who are Executors and Administrators of the said Seamen, with many other Persons, who are their Creditors.
The Humble Recital of Robert Ledgingham....
Some Considerations...Concerning the Lords of the Admiralty and the Commissioners of the Navy (possibly 1698).

(*b*) *Individual pamphlets*

TORRINGTON

A Plain Relation of the Late Action at Sea...from June 22 to July 5, last...by E.S. (1690). (*Probably by Edward Stephens.*)
Some Modest Reflections on Mr S's...book, entituled 'A Plain Relation...' by W.S. (1691). (*Possibly by Randall Taylor, an accountant in the office of the Treasurer of the Navy.*)
Reasons for the Tryal of the Earl of Torrington by Impeachment by the Commons in Parliament, Rather than any other Way (1690).
The Earl of Torrington's Speech to the House of Commons in November, 1690 (1710). (*See* II, F (1) *above.*)
An Impartial Account of Some Remarkable Passages in the Life of Arthur Earl of Torrington Together with some Modest Remarks on His Tryal and Acquitment (1691).

[1] The whole controversy on this subject is included in this volume.
[2] None of these is dated, but most are concerned with other pamphlets or events of the war. B.M. Printed 86. m. 7 also contains George Everett's *A Word in Season* (see III, E, 1 above).

RUSSELL

A New-Years-Gift to the Honourable Admiral Russell on his glorious victory over the French Fleet (1693).

The Chief Heads of the Articles of Impeachment against the Earl of Orford...(1701) (contained in B.M. Printed 1851 c. 19).

The Answers of the Earl of Orford...to the Observations made by the Honourable Commissioners of Accompts upon his Accompts of the Navy...(1704). (*This is also included in* P.R.O. Treas. 38/614.)

MISCELLANEOUS

A Sailor's Garland, ed. John Masefield (1906).

Naval Ballads, ed. C. H. Firth (*N.R.S.* 1908).

Poems on Affairs of State (1697).

The State of the Navy Consider'd in relation to the Victualling. Particularly in the Straits and the West Indies...by an English Sailor (1699).

Observations on a Late Scandalous Paper reflecting on the Admiralty etc....by one who is not a Sailer, tho' of long Service in the Navy (1699). (*Possibly by Randall Taylor. The B.M. copies of both these pamphlets are dated* 1700.)

Remarks on the Observations offer'd by a True Englishman, who is not a Sailor, tho' of Long Service in the Navy (1699).

Observations on the Case of the Paymaster of the Navy (n.d., but 1699 or 1700).

The Present Condition of the English Navy, set forth in a Dialogue betwixt Young Fudge of the Admiralty, and Capt. Steerwell, an Oliverian Commander (1702). (*Some remarks upon the position of the Secretary of the Admiralty.*)

An Historical and Political Treatise of the Navy...(1703). (*Many remarks on the late war, particularly on the victualling.*)

The Secret History of His Majesty's Ship-Yard at Deptford, giving an Account of Some Material Transactions, since its beginning until the Year 1716 (1717). (*See Williamson's* Memoirs, III, E, 1 *above.*)

IV. SECONDARY AUTHORITIES

A. Unpublished

James, G. F.: 'The Lords Commissioners of the Admiralty, 1689–1714.' *My obligation to these chapters of an unpublished work is considerable. The more obvious instances are recorded in the notes to the text. A copy of the work may be found in the library of Birmingham University.*

McLeod, Norman: 'Shipwrights Wages, 1496–1788.' *An unpublished paper, based on dockyard books at the Public Record Office which have since been destroyed.*

Richmond, Admiral Sir Herbert: notes on the war of 1689–97. *Admiral Richmond made a considerable number of notes and observations upon this period, which are of value for the relations between ministers and commanders at sea. They deal in many cases with subjects not touched upon in his* Statesmen and Sea Power (1946).

B. Printed

The authorities given below are confined to two classes: first, lists of ships, material or prices, and biographical collections; secondly, standard histories of the principal navies, and works directly related to primary sources. Other authorities used will be found in the notes to the text.

Beatson, R.: Political Index... (3 vols., 1806). (*Lists of office-holders and dignitaries.*)

Beveridge, Sir William: Prices and wages in England, vol. I (Price Tables, Mercantile Era) (Publications of the International Scientific Committee on Price History, 1939). (*Very useful tables of prices for naval stores and victuals.*)

Burchett, Josiah: Complete History of the Most Remarkable Transactions at Sea... (1720). (*See* III, C *above.*)

Campbell, John: Lives of thc Admirals (8 vols., 1812–17). (*For the different editions, see G. F. James,* 'Collected Naval Biography', in *Bulletin of the Institute of Historical Research,* XV, pp. 162–8.)

Charnock, John: Biographia Navalis (6 vols., 1794–8). (*See James, ibid. pp.* 168–70. *Important, but inaccurate.*)

Charnock, John: History of Marine Architecture... (3 vols., 1800–2). (*Valuable lists, which must however always be checked by other authorities, and much miscellaneous information, badly arranged. Inaccurate but indispensable.*)

Chevalier, E.: Histoire de la Marine française jusqu'au traité de paix de 1763 (1902). (*Supplements de la Roncière, below.*)

Clark, G. N.: The Dutch Alliance and The War against French Trade, 1689–1697 (1923). (*Useful for the Anglo-Dutch naval convention of* 1689, *and for the attitudes of the Baltic powers throughout the war.*)

Cobbett, William: Parliamentary History of England, vols. V–VI (1811–13). (*Supplements Grey's* Debates of the House of Commons. *See* III, A *above.*)

Colliber, Samuel: Columna Rostrata, a critical History of English Sea-Affairs (1727).

Corbett, Sir Julian: England in the Mediterranean 1603–1713 (2 vols., 1904). (*Valuable for William and the Mediterranean policy in* 1694–5.)

Derrick Charles: Memoirs of the Rise and Progress of the Royal Navy (1806). (*Useful appendices.*)

Dictionary of National Biography (1885–1900). (*Most of the biographies of sea officers are by Sir J. K. Laughton, and are easily the best available. Corrections to the* D.N.B. *are published regularly in the* Bulletin of the Institute of Historical Research.)

Entick, John: A new Naval History (1757).

G. E. C(okayne): Complete Peerage (8 vols., 1887–98). (*The new edition, ed. the Hon. Vicary Gibbs,* 1910– , *should be used where possible.*)

Guérin, Léon: Histoire maritime de France (6 vols., 1851–2). (*Must be read in the light of more recent research, but still not entirely superseded.*)

Hannay, David: Short History of the Royal Navy (2 vols., 1898–1909). (*A good summary, but necessarily little detail. The best general introduction to the subject.*)

Jackson, Sir George: Naval Commissioners...from 1660 to 1760 (ed. with biographical notices by Sir George F. Duckett, 1889). (*Important lists and biographical details. All dates are in Old Style, which is not specifically stated.*)

James, G. F. and Sutherland Shaw, J. J.: 'Admiralty Administration and Personnel, 1619–1714', in *Bulletin of the Institute of Historical Research*, XIV, pp. 10–24, 166–183; and James, G. F.: 'Some Further Aspects of Admiralty Administration, 1689–1714', in ibid. XVII, pp. 13–27. (*Important articles with full and careful lists of Lord High Admirals, Boards of Admiralty and Secretaries of the Admiralty.*)

de Jonge, J. C.: Geschiedenis van het Nederlansche Zeewezen (6 vols., 1858–62). (*The standard Dutch naval history. Valuable lists.*)

Kealy, A. G. (compiled by): Chaplains of the Royal Navy, 1626–1903 (1903).

Laird Clowes, Sir W.: The Royal Navy, a History...(7 vols., 1897–1903). *A co-operative work, the standard naval history of England. The distinction between 'major' and 'minor' campaigns, which decides the arrangement of the work, often makes reference difficult. Contains much valuable material and many lists.*)

Lediard, Thomas: Naval History of England, 1066–1734 (2 vols., 1735). (*The first naval history of England, other than the largely autobiographical account of Burchett, above. A useful work.*)

Macaulay, T. B.: History of England from the Accession of James II (ed. Sir Charles Firth, 6 vols., 1913–15). (*For naval affairs, on which the detail is often misleading, it should be read with Sir Charles Firth's* Commentary on Macaulay's History (1938).)

Macpherson, David: Annals of Commerce, Manufacture, Fisheries, and Navigation... (2 vols., 1805). (*An expanded edition of Adam Anderson's* An Historical and Chronological Deduction of the Origin of Commerce...(4 *vols.*, 1787), *which for this period relies on the original text. Useful lists and information.*)

Moreau, César: Chronological Records of the British Royal and Commercial Navy (1827).

Murray, Sir Oswyn A. R.: 'The Admiralty'. (*This important series of articles by an ex-Secretary of the Admiralty, which was designed as a volume on the history of the department, was unfinished at Murray's death, and was published without correction in ten parts in M.M.* vols. XXIII, nos. 1, 2, 3; XXIV nos. 1, 2, 3, 4; XXV, nos. 1, 2, 3. *It is the best available history of the Admiralty as a department of state, with an important introductory survey in parts* I *and* II; *but it is necessarily of unequal value, and the article on William III's reign is only a fragment.*)

Oppenheim, M.: History of the Administration of the Royal Navy...1509–1660 (1896). (*First class, with valuable lists. It is continued, for dockyards, in different volumes of the* Victoria County History.)

Parliamentary Papers: Report of the Select Committee on the Board of Admiralty, 1861 (*H.C.* 438). (*Contains text of, and information on, Admiralty Patents, and Sir James Graham's evidence on the origin and powers of the Office.*)

Parliamentary Papers: Return of Public Income and Expenditure, Part 1 (1869). (*Begins with* 1689. *An essential check on W. A. Shaw's figures in* Cal.Treas.Bks. *See* III, A *above.*)

Powley, E. B.: The English Navy in the Revolution of 1688 (1928). (*Contains excerpts from Dartmouth's papers for that year.*)

Raithby, John (ed.): Statutes relating to the Admiralty, Navy, Shipping and Navigation of the United Kingdom from 9 Henry III to 3 George IV inclusive (1823). (*The best of several similar compilations.*)

de la Roncière, Charles: Histoire de la Marine française (1899–). (*In course of publication. Has reached vol.* VI, *which covers this period. Important, with several lists.*)

Schomberg, Isaac: Naval Chronology... (1802). (*Scrappy for this period, but a standard compilation of lists of ships and officials.*)

Shaw, W. A.: Knights of England (2 vols., 1906). (*A list of dates of knighthoods.*)

Society for Nautical Research, Occasional Publications, No. 5: Lists of Men-of-War, 1650–1700 (5 parts, 1935–9). (*The primary authority for details of warships of all maritime European nations for this period. The English list is compiled by R. C. Anderson.*)

Sue, M. J. Eugène: Histoire de la Marine française au dix-septième siècle, 1653–1712 (5 vols., 1835–7). (*Occasional information not in later histories.*)

Tanner, J. R.: *In addition to his catalogue of Pepys's naval papers, Tanner wrote chapters on the Restoration navy in the* Cambridge Modern History, *vol.* V, *with C. T. Atkinson. His articles on the same subject in* E.H.R. XII, XIII, XIV *were published as part of the introduction to* Catal. *vol.* I, *for which see* III, A *above.*

Tedder, Arthur W.: The Navy of the Restoration (1916). (*Supplements Tanner's works. Good bibliography.*)

Thorold Rogers, J. E.: History of Agriculture and Prices in England (7 vols., 1866–1902). (*Has been superseded in some sections by Beveridge, above; but the latter does no cover all the same ground.*)

Vesey Hamilton, Admiral Sir R.: Naval Administration (1896). (*Useful. Apart from Murray's articles, above, this is the only work on the subject.*)

Warnsinck, J. C. M.: De Vloot van den Stadthouder Koningk, 1689–1690 (1935). (*Very useful.*)

INDEX